CHARI
SOUTH CAROLINA
CITY DIRECTORIES

FOR THE YEARS
1816, 1819, 1822, 1825, AND 1829

James W. Hagy

CLEARFIELD

Printed for
Clearfield Company, Inc. by
Genealogical Publishing Co., Inc.
Baltimore, Maryland
1996

Reprinted for
Clearfield Company, Inc. by
Genealogical Publishing Co., Inc.
Baltimore, Maryland
2002

International Standard Book Number: 0-8063-4665-5

Made in the United States of America

This book is dedicated to J. Belcourt.

CONTENTS

INTRODUCTION

This is the third volume of city directories for Charleston, South Carolina. It represents a continuing effort to republish the directories of the city prior to the Civil War The first volume contained the city directories for the years 1782, 1785, 1790, 1801, and 1802 as well as the census reports for 1790 and 1800. This appeared under the title of *People and Professions of Charleston, South Carolina, 1782-1802* (Baltimore: Clearfield, 1992*)*. The second volume was *City Directories for Charleston, South Carolina for the Years 1803, 1806, 1809 and 1813* (Baltimore: Clearfield, 1995).

These city directories have separate sections for those people living in the Charleston Neck. At the time the city limit ended at the southern side of Boundary St. (now Calhoun). The area above that was the Neck which continued up the peninsula to The Lines (now Line St.). The Neck was governed by commissioners who were elected by people who lived there and who were qualified to vote for state legislators. The area was more thinly settled than the city and most houses did not have numbers. For protection, the citizens of the Neck carried out patrol duty under the leadership of the commandant of the Charleston Neck Rangers.

Both the city and the Neck had a considerable number of Free People of Color and slaves. Slaves were never listed in the city directories and the Free People of Color appeared in some. After the Denmark Vesey threat of an insurrection in 1822, the directories did not list these people again until 1831.

Some of the city directories contain valuable information in addition to the usual listings. For example, the directory for 1825 lists: (1) streets, lanes, alleys and courts; (2) officers and tutors for Charleston College; (3) public buildings; (4) churches, chapels, meeting houses; (5) commercial establishments; (6) insurance offices; (7) banks; (8) benevolent and charitable institutions and societies; (9) public amusements; (10) literary institutions; (11) public offices; (12) newspapers; (13) police of the city of Charleston; (14) officers of the Vigilant Fire Company ; (15) officers of Charleston Neck; (16) officers of the Customs House; (17) the harbor pilots; (18) the commissioners of public schools in Charleston; (19) commissioners of the Cross Roads and Poor of Charleston Neck; (20) justices and notaries; (21) officers of military units; (22) officers of lodges; and (23) consuls.

Some abbreviations found herein are:

Al. = Alley
Cont'd. = Continued
St. = Street or Saint
op. = opposite
btw. = between
cr. = corner
E. = east
W. = west
N. = north
S.= south
S.C. = South Carolina
Whf. = Wharf

Copies of this book and those listed above may be ordered from:
    Clearfield Company
    220 East Eager St.
    Baltimore, Maryland 21202

The 1816 City Directory

This directory was published by Abraham Motte under the title of *Charleston Directory and Stranger's Guide, for the Year 1816; Including the Neck to the Six Mile House* (Charleston: Printed for the Publisher, 1816). It has 3181 entries

Abbott, B., Widow, 49 Society St.
Abbott, Samuel, Teacher, Smith's Court
Aberigg, J., Tobacconist, 22 Archdale St
Abernethie, John J., Mariner, 220 Meeting St.
Abernethie, Mary, Widow, 220 Meeting St
Abrahams, Judith, 126 Church St.
Abrahams, Levy T., Fruiterer, 66 Meeting St.
Abrams, Elias, Dry Goods Store, 151 King St.
Abrams, -----, Mrs., Shop, 34 King St.
Adams, David & Sons, Factor, 28 E. Bay St.
Adams, David, Factor, 50 Society St.
Adams, Robert, Carpenter, 74 Wentworth St.
Addison, John, Carpenter, 2 Bottle Al
Adger & Pringle, Merchants, E. Side King St Road
Adger, James, Merchant, E. Side King St. Road
Aiken, Ann, Widow of James, 6 Cumberland St.
Aiken, William, Merchant, E. Side King St. Road
Airs, George, Custom House Officer, 12 Archdale St.
Airs, Thomas, Boat Builder, 50 Anson St.
Akin, Thomas, M.D., 6 Cumberland St.
Albagnac, P., Merchant Tailor, 136 Queen St.
Albert, John, Musician, 63 Anson St.
Aldrich, Robert, Wharfinger, 2 Stoll's Al.
Alexander, Abraham, Dry Goods Store, 251 King St.
Alexander, David, President, Union Insurance Co , 10 Broad St.
Alexander, Rachael, Fruiterer, 272 King St.
Allan, William, Factor, House, 10 Liberty St., Counting House, Blake's Whf
Allen, John, Capt., Mariner, 124 King St.
Allen, Thomas, Shipwright, 36 Pinckney St.
Allen, William, Merchant, 128 Queen St.
Alston, William, Planter, 13 King St.
Amant, Louisa, 34 Wall St.
Andeal, M. T , 18 Tradd St.
Anderson, Abigail, 2 Philadelphia St.
Anderson, -----, Mrs., Widow, 7 Magazine St.
Anderson, Robert, Vendue Master, 237 Meeting St.
Anderson, T. W., Printer, 30 Wentworth St.
Anderson, William, Sexton, St. Michael's Church, 30 Meeting St
Andral, M., Musician, 4 Longitude Ln.
Andrews & Barnum, Comb Makers, cr Vanderhorst & St. Philip's Sts.
Andrews, E., Mrs, Boarding House, 104 Queen St.
Andrews, J. O., Rev., Methodist Church, 12 Pitt St.
Andrews, M , Block Maker, 13 Laurens St., Shop, 180 E. Bay St.
Angel, Justus, Planter, Islington
Anoteau, Theresa, Fruiterer, 40 Church St.
Anthony, J. C., Mary St , Hampstead
Anthony, John, Harness Maker, 158 King St.

Armstrong, S., 1 Clifford St.
Arquet, C., Widow, 65 Meeting St.
Art, A., Dry Goods Store, 81 Meeting St
Arthur, George, Planter, Wraggsborough
Artman, P., Coach Maker, 9 Archdale St
Ash, Eliza, Widow, 9 Lamboll St
Ash, Sam, Planter
Ashe, Bella, 7 Smith's Ln.
Ashe, John, Jr , 16 S. Bay St.
Ashe, John, Planter, 16 S. Bay St.
Assalit, Joshua, French Teacher, 11 Elliott St
Atkinson, -----, Mrs., Widow of Joshua, 24 Coming St
Aubin & Lewis, Dry Goods Store, 59 King St.
Auransan, B., Blacksmith, 18 Amen St.
Austen, C., Widow, Upstairs, 68 E Bay St.
Austen, John, Jeweller, 90 Broad St.
Austen, Sam, Tailor, W. Side King St. Road
Austin, Sam, Grocer, 69 Queen St.
Austin, William, Book Seller, 194 Meeting St
Averell, Henry, Shoestore, 284 King St.
Averell, J. D., Shoestore, 296 King St.
Avery & Lankaster, Grocers, 237 E. Bay St.
Axon, J., Dry Goods Store, 39 King St.
Axon, Jacob, 62 Tradd St
Axon, Sam E , House Carpenter, 2 Adams St
Aydelot, J., Boarding House, 51 Church St.
Ayrault, P., Merchant, 235 E. Bay St., House, 54 Church St.
Azevedo, B. D., Confectioner, 82 King St.
Bachman, John, Rev., Pastor, German Church, W. Side Cannon's Bridge Road
Bacot, Henry H., Attorney, 24 Tradd St.
Bacot, P., Officer, S. C. Bank, 71 Meeting St
Bacot, T. W., Postmaster, 84 Broad St.
Badger, James, Grain Store, 154 Meeting St.
Badger, James, Jr., & Co., 140 King St.
Bailey, David, Merchant, 6 Green St.
Bailey, Henry, Attorney, 3 Blackbird Al.
Bailey, W. E., Classical Teacher, 3 Blackbird Al., School, 3 Society St.
Baker & Fraser, Dry Goods Store, 187 King St.
Baker, Joseph, House Carpenter, 39 Boundary St.
Baker, Noah D., Beer House, 46 Market St
Baker, Noah, D., Dyer, 170 Meeting St.
Baker, Priscilla, 155 Church St.
Baker, Richard, Custom House Weigher, 12 Legare St.
Baker, Sam, Planter, 3 St. Philip's St.
Baker, Thomas, Merchant, Vanderhorst's Whf.
Baldwin & Reed, Shoestore, 213 King St
Baldwin, William, 4 Meeting St.
Ball, Ann, Widow, 21 Church St
Ball, Isaiah, Planter, 166 E. Bay St.
Ball, John, Jr., Planter, 11 Hasell St
Ball, John, Planter, 168 E. Bay St.
Ball, Sarah, Widow, 7 Church St.
Ballund, Alexander, Dry Goods Store, 63 King St.
Bampfield, Thomas, 37 George St.
Bant, Samuel, Tailor, 193 King St.
Barell, Torre & Co., Optical & Print Store, 35 Broad St
Barguet, J. P., Umbrella & Bellows Maker, 70 Meeting St

1

Barker &Tollman, Shop, 185 Meeting St
Barker, James, Truss Maker, 30 Pinckney St.
Barker, Joseph S., Merchant, 20 Anson St., Counting House, 220 E. Bay St.
Barksdale, -----, Mrs., 6 New St.
Baron, A., Jr , M D , 45 Meeting St.
Barreau, L., Small Shop, 82 Wentworth St.
Barrett, Isaiah, Dry Goods Store, 216 King St
Barreyre, P., Baker, 129 Queen St.
Barron, Alexander, M.D., 36 Broad St
Barron, John, Merchant, 41 Pinckney St.
Barry, P., Lastmaker, E Side State St.
Bartholomy, Rene, Cigar Maker, 7 Wentworth St.
Bartless & Nelson, Blacksmiths, S Side of Daniel's Whf.
Bartless, Henry, Blacksmith, 22 Middle St.
Barton, Ann, 7 Lowndes St.
Barton, John B & Co., Oil & Paint Store, 222 E. Bay St.
Barville, Michael, Cabinet Maker, 31 Society St.
Bascome, Benjamin, Vendue Master, 19 Elliott St.
Bass, J., Capt., Mariner, 51 Pinckney St.
Batker, J A., Grocer, 108 E Bay St.
Baunay, P., Dry Goods Store, 92 King St
Bay, Andrew, Attorney, 5 St. Michael's Al.
Bay, John, Merchant, 363 King St.
Bay, -----, Judge, Hon., 8 Meeting St.
Beale, P., 3 Philadelphia St.
Beard, Eliza, Widow, 35 Wentworth St.
Beard, Frederick, Teller, S. C. Bank
Beard, John, Baker, 160 Meeting St.
Beard, William, Porter, S. C. Bank, 49 Church St.
Beatson, James, Shipwright, 71 Anson St.
Beaury, John, Fruiterer, 108 Tradd St.
Becais, Mary, Widow, 4 Guignard St.
Beckman, Edward, Jr., Barber, 124 E. Bay St.
Beckman, Mary, Widow of Samuel, 175 Meeting St.
Bee, Eliza, Widow, 90 Church St
Bee, J. S., Accountant, 90 Church St.
Bee, Jacob, S., Vendue Master, 119 Broad St.
Bee, -----, Mrs., Widow, 96 Tradd St
Bee, P. S., 38 Coming St.
Bee, R M., Accountant, 71 Anson St.
Bee, Thomas, Attorney, 131 Church St.
Bee, William, Teacher, S. C. Society's School, 225 Meeting St.
Beekman, Adolf, Painter & Glazier, 73 Meeting St.
Beggs, James, Dry Goods Store, 167 King St.
Beile, -----, Mrs., Widow, 5 Clifford Al.
Beille, J C , Dry Goods Store, 320 King St.
Belanton, Filette, Widow, 128 E. Bay St.
Belcher, E., Capt , 87 Wentworth St.
Belcher, M., School, 1 Bull St.
Belin, -----, Mrs., Widow of Allard, 40 Boundary St
Beljie, Benjamin, E. Side King St Road
Bell, A , House Carpenter, 21 Anson St.
Bell, D., Clerk, 9 Society St.
Bell, -----, Miss, Children's School, 18 Magazine St.
Bell, William, Bricklayer, 29 Society St.
Bellange, C., Shoestore, 17 State St.
Belser, F., E. Side King St. Road
Benjamin, C., Mariner, 1 Lynch Ln.

Bennet, I. K., Attorney, 17 Bull St., Office, 44 Meeting St
Bennet, Thomas, Proprietor of the Mills, 5 Lynch St.
Bennett, H , Deputy Collector, Hampstead
Bennett, J S., Bank of the State
Benoist, D., Bricklayer, 42 Pinckney St.
Benoist, J. B., Confectioner, 159 Meeting St
Benoist, -----, Mrs., Boarding House, W. Side State St
Benoist, -----, Mrs., Fruiterer, 40 Church St.
Benson, J H., Merchant, 118 King St., Res. Merchants Hotel
Benson, James B., Tailor, 168 Meeting St.
Bentham & Parker, Attornies, 4 Court House Sq.
Bentham, James, Merchant, 116 Church St.
Bentham, -----, Mrs , Widow of James, 10 Logan St.
Bentham, R., Attorney, 10 Logan St.
Berney, Mary, Widow of John, 100 Meeting St
Berrie, P., Grain Store, 76 Church St.
Besier, C., 10 Anson, St.
Besnier, P., 13 Linguard St.
Bessiers, S., Seamstress & Laundress, 11 Anson St.
Beswick, John, Clerk, 30 St. Philip's St.
Betard, Anthony, Small Shop, E Side State St.
Bethune, Margaret, Widow of Angus, 75 Broad St.
Betterson, W., House Carpenter, 9 Coming St.
Bevens & Tillinghast, Merchant Tailors, 15 Queen St.
Bicais, Claude, Cabinet Maker, 156 Meeting St.
Bidgood, S., Merchant, 245 E. Bay St.
Bigelow, Eliza, 130 Meeting St
Biggs, Sarah, 21 Berresford St.
Billings, John, Livery Stables, 52 Church St. & 74 Queen St.
Billir, John, Boot Maker, 91 Broad St.
Bingley, Edward, Grocer, 95 E. Bay St.
Bingley, -----, Mrs., Widow, 4 Wall St.
Birnie, William, Merchant, 84 Tradd St.
Bishup, Eliza, 27 Bull St.
Bize, J. S., Grocer, Gadsden's Whf.
Bizuel, Julien, Shopkeeper, 105 Church St.
Black & Bernie, Ironmongers, 11 Broad St.
Black, John, Boot Maker, 101 Broad St
Black, John, Merchant, 11 Broad St.
Black, L C , Attorney, 31½ Meeting St
Blackwood, John, Merchant, Chisolm's N. Whf.
Blackwood, Thomas, President, Planters' & Mechanics' Bank, 14 Pitt St.
Blain, Andrew, Wheelwright, E. Side Meeting St Road
Blair, -----, Mrs., Widow of James, Boarding House, 25 Mazyck St.
Blake, Edward, 19 Archdale St.
Blake, Margaret, Widow of John, 19 Archdale St.
Blakely, S., Tailor, 15 Tradd St.
Blamyer, William, Factor, E Side Meeting St., Mazyckborough, Counting House, D'Oyley's Whf.
Boardman, Hardy, 2 Bull St.
Bobbs, John, Cooper, 5 Champney St.
Boisseau, Rose, 348 King St.
Bolles, Abiel, Master, Orphan House School
Bolough, Elias, Custom House Officer, 9 West St
Bome, C & Co., Confectioners, 82 King St.
Bome, John, Confectioner, 113 Queen St.

Bone, William, Mariner, 70 Anson St.
Boner, Ann, 376 King St
Bonneau, E., Widow, 44 George St.
Bonneau, J. E., Merchant, 4 New St., Counting House, 266 E Bay St.
Bonneau, Sims, 59 Broad St.
Bonneau, Thomas, Colored Childrens' School, 14 Beaufain St
Bonnell, J, Capt., Mariner, 14 Lynch's Ln.
Bonsall, Eliza, Widow of Sam, 48 Wentworth St
Bonthron, John, Grocer, 96 Queen St.
Boone, Susan M. H, Widow, N. Side Charlotte St., Mazyckborough
Borch, P., Grocer, 83 E. Bay St
Bordeaux, Joseph, Clerk, 30 Pinckney St.
Bouer, Eliza, E. Side King St. Road
Boulineau, Andrew, Grocer, E. Side King St. Road
Boundo, E, Hatter, 74 King St.
Bounetheau, Edward, House Carpenter, 23 Montague St.
Bounetheau, Eliza, Widow of P., 101 Wentworth St.
Bounetheau, G. M., Printer & Clerk of City Council, 13 St. Philip's St.
Bours & Bascome, Vendue Master, 12 Vendue Range
Bours, Luke, Vendue Master, 9 Wentworth St.
Bousquet, P., Dry Goods Store, 309 King St.
Boutan, P, 342 King St.
Bower, J. F., W. Side King St. Road
Bowman, -----, Miss, 29 Beaufain St.
Boyd, M., Boarding House, 38 Elliot St
Boyd, -----, Mrs., Widow of William, 151 E. Bay St
Bradley, Charles, Printer, 14 Maiden Ln.
Brailsford, E, M.D., 31 Hasell St.
Brailsford, Eliza, 250 Meeting St.
Brailsford, Eliza, Widow of John, 41 Hasell St.
Brailsford, Mary, 111 Tradd St.
Brandon, David, Dry Goods Store, 113 King St
Breding, A., Widow, 22 Wall St.
Breid, Matthew, 4 Savage St
Breman, Henry, Dentist, 6 Maiden Ln.
Brennan, R., Merchant, 20 Beaufain St.
Bressat, -----, Mrs., Laundress, 18 Anson St.
Brewer, Martha, Widow, Islington
Bride, Eliza, Umbrella Maker, 208 Meeting St.
Bridgy, John, Tavern, 4 Bedons Al.
Bridie, R., Clerk, 52 Beaufain St.
Brindley, C., Widow, 4 West St.
Brisbane, William, Planter, 15 Meeting St
Britton, Sam, Clerk at Lucas' Mill, Cannonborough
Broadfoot, William, Merchant, 265 E. Bay St
Brochard, Charlotte, 16 Ellery St.
Brodie, A., Mrs., Widow, 42 Anson St.
Brodie, Robert, 42 Anson St.
Brodie, Robert, House Carpenter, 90 Tradd St.
Broeski, Sarah, Widow, 157 E Bay St.
Brookings, Henry, Capt., 73 Church St.
Brooks & Potter, Merchants, Vanderhorst's Whf
Broughton, Ann, 19 Anson St.
Broun, John D., Assistant Clerk, Bank of the State, 33 Wall St.
Broun, Mary, Widow of Archibald, 33 Wall St.

Brown & Moses, Vendue Masters, 5 & 6 Vendue Range
Brown & Tunis, Factors, 278 E. Bay St.
Brown, Alexander, Merchant, W Side King St Road
Brown, Daniel, Boarding House, 153 Church St.
Brown, Harriet L., 59 Tradd St.
Brown, J. G., Secretary of State, Residence in the Country
Brown, James, Justice of the Peace & City Coroner, 49 Wentworth St.
Brown, James, Planter, E. Side Washington St., Mazyckborough
Brown, John, Capt., 82 Meeting St.
Brown, John, Grocer, 38 Broad St
Brown, Jonathan, Capt, Mariner, 7 St. Philip's St.
Brown, Joseph, Justice of the Peace, 6 Champney St
Brown, Joshua, Vendue Master, 12 New St., Counting House, 5 Vendue Range
Brown, L., Army, 59 Tradd St.
Brown, Magdalen, Widow of Capt William, 17 Parsonage Ln.
Brown, Moses, Barber, 1 Elliott St.
Brown, Moses, Shoemaker, 123 Wentworth St.
Brown, Robert, Factor, 10 New St.
Brown, Robert, Rev., Pastor, Roman Catholic Church, 90 Wentworth St
Brown, Sarah, School, Court House Yard
Brown, William, Grocer, 214 Meeting St.
Brown, William, Mariner, 56 Elliott St.
Browne, B., Writing Master, 25 Mazyck St.
Browne, -----, Mrs., Milliner, 232 King St.
Browne, Sam, Broker, 232 King St.
Brownlee, John, W Side Meeting St. Road
Bryan, John, Planter, 38 Hasell St.
Bryan, Lydia, Widow of John, 38 Hasell St.
Bryant & Wansley, Grocers, 39 Elliott St.
Bryant, Jane, Widow of John, W. Side King St.
Bryant, Joseph, 5 Parsonage Ln.
Bryce, Henry, Merchant, 259 E. Bay St.
Bryce, -----, Mrs., Widow of Nicolas, 107 Meeting St.
Buchan, -----, Rev. Dr., Pastor, St. Andrew's Church, 3 Lynch's Ln.
Buchanan, Archibald, Brass Founder, 71 Market St.
Buckanan, P., Merchant, 10 Orange St.
Buckanan, Wood & Co., Merchants, 253 E. Bay St.
Buckingham, Mary, 15 Elliott St.
Buckley, James, Ship Chandler, 102 E. Bay St.
Buckley, Jessup & Co., Merchants, 97 Broad St.
Buckley, ----, Merchant, at the Merchants Hotel
Buckley, Stephen, Merchant, 134 King St.,Counting House, 39 E. Bay St
Buckminister, I., Teacher, 70 Wentworth St
Buckmyer, Mary A., Widow, 76 Wentworth St.
Buckner, James G, Planter, 9 Rutledge St
Budd, Abigail, Boarding House, 54 Church St.
Budd, William, Accountant, 54 Church St.
Bueser, -----, Mrs., 54 King St.
Buford, Eliza, Milliner, 107 Queen St.
Buist, Mary, Widow of Dr., 3 Church St.
Bull, Eliza, 4 King St.

3

Bull, Eliza, Widow of William, 14 Lamboll St.
Bull, W A , Attorney, 90 Church St.
Bull, William, Planter, 14 Lamboll St.
Bullfinch, Jeremiah, Shop, E. Side King St. Road
Bulow, John & Charles, Merchants, 238 King St.
Bunch, James, Shoemaker, 34 Beaufain St
Burch, -----, Mrs., School, 4 Society St.
Burden, Kinsey, Planter, 3 Short St.
Burger, Samuel, Acting Secretary of State, 120 Broad St.
Burger, William & Alexander, Grocers, 120 Broad St.
Burger, William, 103 Queen St.
Burgour, John, Grocer, 197 King St.
Burgoyne, William, Druggist, 121 Broad St.
Burke, John, 10 Water St.
Burke, Walter, Capt., Mariner, 6 Anson St.
Burn, Harriet, 8 Whim Court
Burn, John, Washington St.
Burn, William, Cannonborough
Burney, William, 29 Wentworth St.
Burnham, J , Carpenter, 6 Lowndes St.
Burns, James, Pilot, 12 Stolls Al.
Burrage, -----, Capt., Mariner, E. Side Meeting St Road
Burrows, A. & Co., Merchants, Blake's Whf.
Bussacker, Charles, Dry Goods Store, 157 King St.
Bussacker, Charles, Grocery, E. Side State St.
Butler & Meer, Merchants, 25 Broad St.
Butler, Charles P., Jeweller, 65 King St.
Butler, Melvin & Co., Merchants, 98 Broad St., Res.
    Merchants Hotel
Butler, Robert, Inspector, Union Insurance Co., 1
    Laurens St.
Butman, E., Merchant, W Side King St. Road
Byland, Jacob, Toy Shop, 187 Meeting St.
Byrd, John, Accountant, 2 Church St
Byrd, Orran, Proprietor, Planter's Hotel, 62 Church St.
Byrne, Patrick, Sail Maker, 13 Pinckney St.
Bythewood, Ann H., 18 Philadelphia St.
B[?]ne & Morrison, Druggists, 3 Broad St.
Cabeuil, Lewis, Tailor, 2 Tradd St.
Cadieu, Hortance, Grocer, W. Side King St Road
Caffarelle, Theresa & Ann, Snall Shop, 98 King St.
Calder, James, Cabinet Maker, 48 Broad St.
Caldwell, John, House Carpenter, 1 College St.
Caldwell, -----, Mrs , 1 College St.
Caldwell, Robert, Merchant, W. Side King St. Road
Caldwell, Sarah, Widow, 179 Meeting St.
Caldwell, William A., Vendue Master, 58 Meeting St.,
    Counting House, S. Vendue Range
Calhoun, Florida, Mrs., 33 Guignard St.
Callaghan, -----, Mrs., Widow, 14 Magazine St
Caloff, Mary, Washington Village
Calvert, Eliza, Boarding House, 49 Meeting St.
Cambridge, Eliza, Widow of Tobias, 7 Orange St.
Cameron, A., Boarding House, 262 E Bay St., Upstairs
Cameron, Lewis, Accountant, 262 E Bay St.
Cameron, Mary, French Al.
Campbell, Alexander, Capt., Mariner, 8 Wentworth St.
Campbell, Ann, Boarding House, 111 Broad St
Campbell, Archibald, Merchant, 121 Church St.
Campbell, Commodore, 138 Church St

Campbell, Henrietta, Widow of M'Millan, 148 E. Bay St
Campbell, James, Tailor, 21 Broad St
Campbell, James, Tailor, 84 Queen St.
Campbell, Margaret, 138 Church St
Campbell, Peter, Farmer, Washington Village
Campbell, William, Barber, 240 King St.
Canady, H., Grocer, 109 King St.
Candlish, Alexander, Baker, 5 Bedons Al.
Cansler, -----, Mrs., 21 Tradd St.
Canter, John, Portrait Painter, 14 Queen St
Canter, Joshua, Drawing Teacher, 64 Broad St.
Cantor, Emanuel, 8 Savage St.
Cape, Bryan, 3 Bull St.
Caquet, John & Co., Grocer, 14 Queen St.
Cardozo, David, Teacher, 47 Tradd St.
Carew, Edward, Boat Builder, Shop, 206 E. Bay St.,
    House, 14 Laurens St.
Carles, P , Merchant, 122 Queen St.
Carmand, Francis, Merchant Tailor, 328 King St.
Carmile, John, Farmer, W. Side King St Road, 4 Miles
    from Town
Carnes, Thomas W., Merchant, 136 King St.
Carnochan, R., Merchant, Counting House, 1 Crafts' S.
    Whf., House, 264 E. Bay St.
Carpentier, Charles, French Teacher, 21 Coming St.
Carr, Ann, 13 Tradd St.
Carr, James, Butcher, 212 Meeting St.
Carr, -----, Mrs., Boarding House, 212 Meeting St
Carrendeffez, Alexander, M D, 133 E. Bay St.
Carrere, Charles, Music & French Teacher, 60 Broad St.
Carrol, Bartholomew, W. End Boundary St.
Carrol, James P , Planter, W. End Boundary St.
Carruth, -----, Capt., Mariner, 16 Maiden Ln.
Carson, James, Merchant, 86 Tradd St., Counting House,
    10 Broad St.
Carsten, John, Grocer, 22 Boundary St
Cart, John, Factor, 22 Bull St
Cart, John, Jr., 22 Bull St.
Cart, Sarah, Milk Seller, 20 Philadelphia St.
Carter, Eliza, Shop, 269 King St.
Carvalho, N. D., Jeweller, 165 King St.
Carvin, E., Milliner, 75 King St.
Casey, Benjamin, Coach Maker, 95 Broad St.
Cassin, Patrick, Vendue Master, 5 Vendue Range, House,
    50 Pinckney St.
Castagnon, Amelia, Confectioner, 41 Meeting St.
Catherwood, J. J., Watch Maker, 32 Broad St.
Catonnet, Peter, Grocer, 117 Queen St
Cattle, Fanny, Small Shop, 11 Laurens St.
Caught, Thomas, Dry Goods Store, 140 E. Bay St.
Causse, A., 10 St. Philip's St.
Cavan & M'Cormick, Grocers, 8 Queen St.
Cavarue, Francis, Umbrella Maker, 218 Meeting St.
Cave, Thomas, 258 King St.
Caye, Julia, 7 Maiden Ln
Chace, Eliza, Widow, 56 Market St.
Chadwick, S., Merchant, 8 Crafts' S. Whf., House, 22
    Tradd St.
Chalmers, H. James, E. Side King St. Road
Champlin, Jane, 13 Tradd St.

4

Champlin, -----, Major, at the Planter's Hotel
Champneys, John, Planter, 105 King St.
Chancognie, S J., Merchant, 16 Laurens St., Counting House, 5 Fitzsimmons' Whf.
Chandler, Catherine, Widow of Isaac, 43 St Philip's St.
Chandler, John W., 55 Broad St.
Chanet & Duquercron, Merchant, 203 King St.
Chapeau, J. B., 110 Queen St.
Chapman, Joseph S., Liquor Shop, 7 King St.
Chapman, Muirhead & Co, Merchants, 273 E. Bay St.
Charles, Margaret, Widow, 4 Friend St.
Charles, Nancy, Shop, 83 Church St.
Charles, Sylvia, 34 Tradd St.
Chartrand, P , Capt , Mariner, 38 Market St.
Chaters, H., Wheelwright, 6 Pitt St.
Cheny, Ebenezer, Jr , Merchant, 233 E. Bay St.
Cheves, L., Counsellor at Law, 28 Church St
Chevillion, Lewis, Merchant, 149 King St.
Chevrier, M , M.D., 13 Ellery St.
Chew, Sarah, Hampstead
Chiffelle, T. P., Planter, 68 Broad St.
Childs, Ann, Dry Goods Store, 348 King St.
Chion, Caty, 35 St. Philip's St.
Chisolm, George & Tailor, Factors, Chisolm's Whf.
Chisolm, George, Factor, 17 E. Bay St.
Chitty, Ann B., Widow, Court House Yard
Chitty, Charles, Charleston District Sheriff, Court House Yard
Chitty, J. W., Out Door Clerk, State Bank, E. Side St Philip's St. Cont'd.
Christie, Alexander, 118 Church St.
Christopher, G , Rev. of the Methodist Church, 12 Pitt St.
Chupein, Lewis, Hair Dresser & Mineral Water, 6 Broad St
Church, Margaret, Umbrella Maker, 40 St. Philip's St.
Churr, John, Grocer, Prioleau's South Whf.
Clancy, John, H., Carpenter, 6 Market St.
Clare, Maria, 8 King St.
Claret, Cecelia, 42 Church St.
Clark, Bartholomew, Dry Goods Store, 332 King St.
Clark, Druly, Washington Village
Clark, Joseph, 82 E. Bay St.
Clark, Mary, 7 Back St
Clark, Mary, Widow, 134 Meeting St.
Clark, William, Shopkeeper, 4 Linguard St.
Clarke & Wright, Tailors, 109 Queen St.
Clarke, -----, Capt , Mariner, 8 Orange St.
Clarke, Eliza, 118 Tradd St.
Clarke, James, Tailor, 12 Elliott St.
Clarke, Mary, 2 Zigzag Ln.
Clarke, R., 6 Lynch's Ln.
Clarkson, William, Factor, 145 E. Bay St., Counting House, 3 Champneys Whf.
Clarkson, William, Jr , Merchant, 135 King St.
Cleaper, Charles, Sail Maker, 24 Ellery St., Loft on Lothrop's Whf.
Cleary & Guieu, Vendue Masters, 13 Vendue Range
Cleary, John R., Sheriff & Collection Clerk, Bank of the State, 96 Wentworth St.
Cleary, N G , Deputy Sheriff, 96 Wentworth St.

Cleary, R. W., Capt., Mariner, 90 Church St.
Cleland, Gilbert, Hat Store, 260 King St.
Clement, -----, Mrs., Widow of John, 51 Queen St
Clement, William, Planter, W. End Boundary St
Clerk, Thomas, Ship Carpenter, 7 Minority St , Federal Court Office, 1st Floor of Court House
Clifford, H., Factor, 5 Hard Al., Counting House, Mey's Whf.
Clime, Henry, Porter, 24 Boundary St.
Clissey, L., Milliner, 86 King St
Clissey, R., Harness Maker, Shop, 103 Church St
Clough, T., at the Carolina Coffee House
Coates, C., Widow, Cannon's Bridge Road, W. Side
Coates, C , Widow of Capt, 19 Society St.
Coates, Joseph S , Merchant, Counting House, 6 Fitzsimmons' Whf , House, 19 Lamboll St.
Coates, W. A., 354 King St.
Cobia, C. E., Widow, 19 Montague St.
Cobia, Francis, Butcher, W. Side Meeting St. Road
Cobia, N., Planter, W. Side King St. Road, 4 Miles from Town
Cochran, C B., President, Union Bank, 71 Meeting St
Cochran, Margaret, 342 King St.
Cochran, Robert E., Old Ship Yard, Cooper River, 4 Miles from Town
Cochran, Robert, Planter, 99 Wentworth St.
Cochran, Sam, Tailor, 185 E. Bay St.
Cochran, Susan, Widow of Thomas, 132 E Bay St
Cochran, Thomas, Planter, W. Side Cannon's Bridge Road
Cochran, Tissee, 113 Wentworth St
Cocks, Eliza, E. Side King St. Road
Cocks, J S., Capt, Mariner, 130 E Bay St
Cogdell, J. S., Attorney, 2 St. Michael's Al.
Cogdell, -----, Mrs., Widow of John, 1 St Michael's Al.
Cogdell, R. W., Teller, Bank of the State
Cohen, Mordecai, Merchant, 58 Broad St
Cohen, Moses, Dry Goods Store, 288 King St.
Cohen, S I., Dry Goods Store, 221 King St.
Coit, Jonathan, Merchant, 32 Hasell St., Counting House, Vanderhorst's Whf
Colcock, M., School Mistress, 10 Lamboll St.
Cole, John, Capt., Mariner, 26 King St.
Cole, Joseph, Bootmaker, 22 Broad St
Cole, Richard, Ship Carpenter, E. Side St. Philip's St Cont'd.
Cole, Ruth, Widow, 8 Guignard St.
Cole, Sarah, 15 Berresford St.
Coles, M., Mrs., Boarding House, 117 E. Bay St.
Colley, Eliza, Widow, Shopkeeper, 18 State St
Collier, William, Grocer, 30 Bull St.
Collins, John, Clerk, 20 Hasell St
Collins, Mary, Widow, 20 Hasell St
Collins, Menassah, Tavern, 334 King St.
Colman, Benjamin, Grocer, W. Side King St Road
Colzy, C., Merchant Tailor, 43 Church St.
Condy & Raguet, Merchants, 242 E. Bay St
Condy, Jeremiah, Merchant, 199 Meeting St.
Condy, Thomas D., 199 Meeting St.
Connard, C., Widow, Small Shop, 115 E Bay St.
Connolly, R., Liquor Shop, 14 S. Bay St.

Connoly, -----, Capt., 17 Meeting St.
Connoly, Mary Ann, 17 Meeting St.
Connover, Eliza, School, 28 Society St
Conyers, -----, Mrs., Widow of William, 29 Pinckney St.
Conyers, William N., Clerk, 29 Pinckney St.
Cook, Samuel, 10 Tradd St.
Cooke, E., Mrs , Boarding House, 109 Tradd St.
Cooke, William, Merchant, 109 Tradd St
Cooper, James, Capt., Mariner, 160 E Bay St.
Cooper, Matthew, Merchant, 31 E. Bay St.
Cooper, William, Shoemaker, 46 King St.
Coquereau, Charles, Cabinet Maker, 196 King St
Coram, Ann, Widow of Thomas, 76 Queen St
Coram, -----, Mrs., Widow of Francis, 22 George St.
Corbett, Margaret, Widow of Thomas, 27 Cumberland St
Corbett, Thomas, Planter, W Side, Cannon's Bridge Road
Corby, J., Blacksmith, W. Side State St
Cordes, -----, Mrs , Widow, N. Side of Charlotte St ,
  Mazyckborough
Cordray & Tuttle, Grocers, 20 Elliott St.
Cordray, Thomas, Grocer, 20 Ellery St.
Corie, Sam, Wheelwright, E. Side King St Road
Corker, Thomas, Ship Carpenter, 35 Pinckney St
Cormick, Thomas & Co., Merchants, 236 E Bay St
Cormick, Thomas, Merchant, 88 Broad St.
Cornell & Capper, Bakers, Wall St.
Cornell, Benjamin, Grocer, 128 Church St.
Cornier, Francis, House Carpenter, 21 Wall St
Corr, Charles, Tailor, 13 Queen St.
Coslett, Charles, 25 Anson St
Coster, I. C., Tailor, 18 Society St.
Cotton, Ann, 1 Parsonage Ln
Courtnay, H., Wine Merchant, 33 Meeting St.
Courty, John, Rigger, 125 Meeting St.
Courty, Peter, Tallow Chandler, E. Side Meeting St. Road
Coutin, Martha, 25 Wentworth St
Coutrier, Eliza, Widow, 3 Court House Sq.
Coveney, Eliza, Widow of Thomas, 30 Pinckney St.
Coventry, Alexander, Dyer, 103 Tradd St.
Cowan, John, 43 Boundary St.
Cowan, John, Grocer, 17 Anson St.
Cowan, John, Grocer, 67 Meeting St.
Cowan, John, Rigger, 196 E. Bay St.
Cowing, Henry, & Co., Merchants, 224 E. Bay St.
Cox, Amelia, 156 Church St.
Cox, Ann, Small Shop, 101 King St
Cox, -----, Capt., U. S. Army, 7 Amen St.
Cox, Henry T , Merchant, 1 Broad St.
Cox, -----, Mrs., Widow of James, 59 Broad St
Cox, Thomas, Coach Maker, 26 Broad St.
Crafts, Thomas, Attorney, 12 Meeting St.
Crafts, William, Jr., Counsellor at Law, Office, 115 Church
  St., House, 12 Meeting St.
Crafts, William, Merchant, 12 Meeting St
Cramton & Johnson, Saddlers, 278 King St.
Cranston, James, 12 Mazyck St.
Crask, P., Painter & Glazier, 18 Pinckney St.
Crawford, John, Wharfinger, 23 Friend St
Crawford, -----, Mrs., Widow, 20 Church St.
Crawley, Francis., 3 Philadelphia St

Crawley, H., Widow, 86 Broad St.
Credier, Martin, Cigar Maker, 19 State St.
Cregier, C, Grocer, W. Side State St.
Creighton, George, Barber, 106 E Bay St
Creighton, James, Barber, 5 Elliott St.
Creighton, Pierce, Barber, 10 Wentworth St
Crendall, Ann, Boarding House, 85 Church St.
Crevier, P., Porter, 36 Chamber's Al
Cripps, John, Planter, 51 Meeting St.
Cripps, Octavius, Factor, 51 Meeting St., Counting House,
  Prioleau's Whf.
Crocker, D., Merchant, 11 Tradd St., Counting House,
  Crafts' N. Whf.
Croft, George, Mariner, 125 Church St
Croft, Peter, Factor, Hampstead
Cromar, George, Coach Maker, 16 Guignard St
Cromwell, Charles, Capt., Mariner, 11 Stoll's Al.
Cromwell, Samuel, Bricklayer, 4 Back St.
Cromwell, Sarah, Widow, 11 Stoll's Al.
Crone, Herman, 30 Market St.
Crosby, Josiah, Capt., Mariner, 48 Anson St.
Cross & Trezvant, Attornies, O 231 Meeting St.
Cross, George, Merchant, 231 Meeting St.
Cross, George W., Attornies, 231 Meeting St
Cross, Sarah, Widow of Mathew, 18 Philadelphia
Cross, William, 120 E. Bay St.
Crouch, Abraham, Notary Public, 247 Meeting St.
Cruckshanks, Amos, Porter, 12 Linguard St.
Cruckshanks, Daniel, Shoemaker, 127 Queen St.
Cruckshanks, William, Boot Maker, 56 Church St.
Cruger, Eliza M., Widow, 9 Guignard St.
Cruger, Eliza, Widow of David, 28 Meeting St.
Crusoe, John, Merchant, D'Oyley's Whf.
Cuccow, William, Pilot, 1 Hard Al.
Cuder, Thomas, 37 Wall St
Cudworth, Benjamin, Coach Maker, 6 Boundary St
Cudworth, Nataniel, 9 Bull St.
Cugly, John, House Carpenter, 17 Mazyck St
Cumming, -----, Mrs., 4 Zigzag Ln
Cunningham, R., N. Side of Charlotte St , Mazyckborough
Cunnington, -----, Mrs., Widow of Col , 2 Miles from
  Town, on the E. Side of the Main Road
Curling, George, Ship Carpenter, 131 Meeting St
Curtis, E., House Carpenter, 3 Montague St.
Curtis, F. S., Master of the Poor House, 4 Mazyck St.
D'Oyley, Charles, W., Attorney, 28 E Bay St.
D'Oyley, Daniel, Wharf Owner, 28 E. Bay St.
Dalcho, Frederick, Rev , 20 Meeting St.
Dalgliesh, George, Slater & Tiler, 3 Mazyck St.
Dalton, James, Druggist & Chemist, 32 Church St.
Daniell, Lewis, Merchant, 163 E. Bay St., Counting House,
  on his Wharf
Darby, J., Silver Plater, 183 Meeting St.
Darby, Robert A , Tailor, 94 E. Bay St
Dare, Ann, Widow, 5 Maiden Ln.
Darell, Ann, Widow of Edward, 8 Wall St
Darell, Nicholas, Capt., Mariner, 115 Church St., Upstairs
Darrah., R , Dentist, 259 King St.
Dart & Spears, Factors, 7 Crafts' S. Whf.
Dart, Benjamin S , Factor, 26 Tradd St.

Dart, Isaac, Factor, 11 Montague St.
Dastas, J., 74 Broad St.
Dastas, Matthew, 44 Chruch St.
Datty, Julia, School, 85 Wentworth St.
Daujou, Lewis & Co., Grocers, 31 Church St.
Davego, Isaac, Merchant, W. Side King St. Road
Davenport, S. & Co., Merchants, 8 Crafts' N. Whf.
Davidson, Gilbert, Planter, 9 New St.
Davis, Benjamin, 124 Queen St
Davis, Catharine, Widow, Drake St , Hampstead
Davis, David, Store, Forks of the Road
Davis, John M., Broker, 40 E. Bay St., Res. W. Side
   Cannon's Bridge Road
Davis, John, Merchant, King St. Road, W. Side
Davis, Matilda, 91 Wentworth St.
Davis, Peter, Sausage Maker, 93 Queen St.
Davis, William G , Blacksmith, 298 King St.
Daviss, Moses, 110 King St.
Dawes, H. P., Factor, 225 E. Bay St.
Dawson, Ann, Widow, 24 Montague St
Dawson, Joanna B., Widow of John, 119 E. Bay St.
Dawson, John, Cashier, State Bank, 19 Bull St.
Dawson, Laurence, Planter, 119 E Bay St.
Dawson, William, Merchant, 35 George St.
Deas, Charles, Factor, Counting House, 99 E. Bay St.,
   House, 100 Wentworth St.
Deas, David, Planter, 73 Tradd St.
Deas, Henry, Planter, 1 Friend St.
Deas, Robert, Planter, 65 Queen St
Deas, Thomas, Merchant & Russian Consul, 99 E Bay St.
Deas, W A., Attorney, 9 Logan St.
DeBesse, J. J , Merchant, 1 Raper Ln.
Debonville, M., Widow, 27 Wentworth St.
DeBow, Garrett, 104 E Bay St.
DeBow, John, Coach Maker, 181 Meeting St
DeBow, William, Druggist, 104 E. Bay St.
DeCloriviere, P , Rev., Pastor, Roman Catholic Church,
   342 King St
Decottes, V., Widow, 48 Society St.
Defour, John, Baker, 14 George St
DeGland, -----, City Guard, 40 Broad St.
Dehon, -----, Right Rev., Bishop, Cannonborough near
   Lucas' Mill
DeJongh, J., Merchant, Cannon's Bridge Road W Side
Delaham, C , Nurse, 34 Anson St.
Delaire, Ann, Widow of James, 19 Middle St.
DeLamotta, Sarah, 7 Savage St.
Delany, M., Pilot, 13 Stoll's Al.
Delavincendiere, P., W. Side King St. Road
Delcho, Celestina, Shop 381 King St
Deletre, A , Factor, 64 Anson St.
Deliesseline, G. F., Factor, 27 E. Bay St
Delisle, N , Widow, 17 Cumberland St
Demsey, Thomas, Grocer, 35 Wall St.
Dennis, William, Grocer, 1 Tradd St.
Dennison, J., Cooper, 48 Elliott St.
Denny, James, Constable, 2 Elliott St.
Denny, Thomas, M.D , 13 Champney St
Denoon, Margaret, Widow of David, 104 Wentworth St
Dent, H J., U S. Navy, 43 Boundary St

Depau, B., Merchant, 7 Cumberland St.
Depau, Deas & Co., Merchants, 216 E Bay St
Desaussure, Henry A , Counsellor at Law, 18 Meeting St.
Descourdres & Crovat, Merchants, 143 King St
Desel, Mary, 14 Archdale St.
Desgrave, Peter, Grocer, W. Side King St. Road
Desire, Joseph, Barber, 331 King St.
Detroil, Rose, Widow, 31 Archdale St.
Devan, M., Milliner, 134 King St
Deveneau, Abraham, Shop, 324 King St.
DeVillers, L., Music Store, 52 Broad St.
Devix, Dominique, 41 Church St.
Dewees, William, Factor, E. Side Middle St.,
   Mazyckborough, Counting House, Prioleau's Whf.
Dewey, S., Profile Room, 209 Meeting St.
Dey, Benjamin, Grocer, S. Bay St., S. Side
Diamond, John, Land Surveyor, 7 Wall St.
Dick, James & Co., Merchants, 106 Broad St
Dickenson, Samuel, Vendue Master, 17 Vendue Range
Dickinson, F J., Grocer, 128 Tradd St.
Dickinson, F., Notary Public, Office, 50 E Bay St., House,
   26 Cumberland St.
Dickson, John, Soap Boiler, W. Side King St. Road
Dickson, Samuel, Tavern, 172 King St
Dieckerts, J. A., Grocer, 4 Market St.
Dier, John, Cigar Maker, 108 E Bay St
Diron, D., Capt., Mariner, 19 Cumberland St.
Dobbins, Rosanna, 5 Pitt St.
Dodd & Ingersoll, Merchants, 12 Crafts' S. Whf
Dodsworth, Amey, 8 Berresford St
Don, Alexander, Carpenter, 33 Society St.
Donaldson, William, Carpenter, 36 Tradd St.
Dorill, Robert, Factor, W. Side State St., Counting House,
   Magwood's Whf.
Dors, Henry, Pilot, 19 Lynch's Ln
Doucin, M., Boatman, 7 Elliott St.
Dougal, William, Shoe Store, 151 King St
Doughty & Mazyck, M.D & Druggists, 226 E. Bay St
Doughty, James, M.D , 6 Smith St.
Doughty, Mary, Widow of Thomas, 32 Anson St
Doughty, William, Planter, 6 Smith St.
Douglas, Campbell, Grocer, 77 Meeting St.
Douglas, James, Cabinet Maker, 63 Meeting St.
Dove, William P., Ship Joiner, Pritchard's Whf.
Dowling, Archibald, Store, 3 King St.
Dowling, Edward, Mason, 6 Society St.
Dowling, Felix, Grocer, 7 King St.
Downie, Robert, Tinman, 29 Broad St.
Doyer, John, Shop, 16 Queen St.
Drayton, Charles, Jr , M.D., 10 Legare St.
Drayton, Henry, 4 Swinton's Ln.
Drayton, John, Hon Judge, U. S , 7 Short St.
Drayton, Rebecca, Widow, Hampstead
Drayton, Thomas, Planter, 93 Wentworth St.
Drege, Peter, Store, 1 Queen St.
Drennis, -----, Mrs., Widow of George, 297 King St.
Dressler, Hans, Grocer, 13 Archdale St.
Drewes, Henry, Grocer, 155 Meeting St
Drummond, James, Shoe & Boot Maker, 130 Queen St.
Dubert, Frederick, E. Side King St Road

7

Duboc, Francis, Store, 35 King St.
Dubois, John, Tailor, 6 St. Philip's St.
Dubois, Lewis, Paper Hanger, 98 Queen St.
Dubois, S., Seamstress, 8 Maiden Ln
Duboise, Peter, Carpenter, Cannonborough
Duboise, Robert, Grocer, W Side King St. Road
Dudd, George, Merchant, at the Merchants Hotel
Dueard, Joseph, Shoemaker, 68 Meeting St.
Duffus, John, Accountant, 4 Short St
Duffy, Francis, Grocer, 1 King St
Dufregne, Mary, Widow, 15 Cumberland St.
Duggan, Thomas, Mason, St Philip's St Cont'd, E. Side
Duhadway, C. B., Saddler, 31 Broad St.
Duiles, Amelia, 10 Friend St.
Dujordin, M., Widow, 13 Maiden Ln.
Duke, J. C , Printer, E. Side State St.
Dumayne, John, M.D., 10 Archdale St.
Dumont, A , Widow, 16 Wall St.
Dumoulal, Maria, Seamstress, 2 Amen St.
Dumoutett, J , Jeweller, 99 Broad St
Dunbar, Eliza, 4 Mile House Tavern.
Duncan, Alexander, Blacksmith, 25 Pinckney St.
Duncan, John, Merchant, 31 Bull St.
Duncan, Patrick, Candle & Soap Factory, Cannon's Bridge
    Road, E. Side
Dunham, Thomas, 17 Bottle Al.
Dunkin & D'Oyley, Attornies, 86 Broad St.
Dunkin, N. B., Merchant, 10 Crafts' S. Whf
Dunn, John, Grocer, 186 Meeting St.
Dupere, George, 35 Elliott St.
Dupland, Leon, Barber, 7 Market St.
Duplantis, L., 15 Philadelphia St.
Duplat, J. B., Jeweller, 64 E. Bay St.
Dupont, J. B , Shoe & Boot Maker, 219 Meeting St.
Dupont, John, Fruit Shop, E. Side State St.
Dupont, Joseph, Crockery Store, 205 Meeting St.
Dupont, M. C., Widow of John, 321 King St.
Dupont, -----, Mrs , Widow, W. Side St. Philip's St. Cont'd
Duport, Lousia, Fruit Shop, 169 Meeting St.
Duprat, H , Shop, 81 Church St.
Duprat, Raymond, 43 Elliott St.
Dupre, Cornelius, Factor, 24 E. Bay St.
Dupre, ---, Dry Goods Store, 138 King St.
Dupre, James, Carpenter, Wraggsborough
Dupuy, A., Widow, 39 Society St
Duquercron, Francis, Merchant, 2 Blackbird Al.
Durang, J. B., Walking Stick Factory, 50 Broad St.
Durban, A., Hatter, 294 King St.
Durbec, J. Grain Store, W. Side King St. Road
Duryea, Jacob, Grocer, W. Side State St.
Duvall, C., Widow, 134 Church St.
Duvall, Joseph, Shoemaker, 74 Anson St
Duvall, Peter, Gardener, Hampstead
Dyott, John, Dentist & Druggist, 56 E. Bay St.
Dyre, Kendall, 234 Meeting St.
Eager, George, Bricklayer, 18 Philadelphia St
Eager, Robert, Clerk, S. C. Bank
Earhardt, John, Butcher, W. Side King St. Road
Eason, James, Shipwright, 124 Wentworth St.
Eason, Robert, Shipwright, Wraggsborough

Eason, S., Widow, 12 Wall St.
Easterby, -----, Capt , Mariner, 3 Broad St.
Eccles & Nash, Northern Store, 249 E. Bay St.
Eckhard, George B., Organist, St Philip's Church &
    Attorney, Office, 2 St. Michael's Al , House, 46 Tradd
    St
Eckhard, Jacob, Jr., Organist, German Lutheran Church,
    30 Coming St
Eckhard, Jacob, Organist, St. Michael's Church, 46 Tradd
    St.
Edes, -----, Mrs., Widow, 61 Meeting St.
Edmondston, Charles, Merchant, 224 Meeting St.,
    Counting House, 2 Crafts' Whf.
Edward, -----, Mrs , Widow of Evan, 26 Society St.
Edwards, George, Planter, 6 New St.
Edwards, J. F , 88 Anson St.
Edwards, Mary, Widow of Alexander, 3 St. Michael's Al.
Edwards, Timothy, Merchant, 221 E. Bay St.
Egleston, John, Merchant, 207 E. Bay St
Ehney, -----, Mrs., Widow, 39 Coming St.
Ehney, William, Tailor, 310 King St.
Elfe, Benjamin, Hampstead
Elfe, William, Factor, Prioleau's Whf.
Elford, J., Navigation School & Store, 70 E Bay St.
Elizur, E., Notary Public, Office, 92 E. Bay St.
Elliott, Amarinthia, Miss, 13 Legare St.
Elliott, Benjamin, Register in Equity, 9 Legare St.
Elliott, Charles, Attorney, 88 Broad St.
Elliott, Eliza, Dry Goods Store, 115 King St.
Elliott, Juliet, Widow of Bernard, 30 George St.
Elliott, Mary, Widow of Thomas., Office, 11 Legare St.
Elliott, Stephen, President, Bank of State, 20 Montague St
Elliott, Thomas, Planter, 5 Gibbes St.
Ellis, Mary, 40 Anson St.
Ellis, Thomas, Shoemaker, 109 Wentworth St.
Elmore, D., Widow, 191 King St.
Elsinore, Alexander, Clerk, 95 E. Bay St.
Elsinore, James, Clerk to Commissioner of Weights &
    Measures
Elsworth, John T , Gauger, 10 Maiden Ln.
Elsworth, T., Gauger, 194½ Meeting St.
Elwig, Peter, Carpenter, 2 Smith St
Emanuel, Isaac, Vendue Master, 100 Meeting St.
Embere, Mary, Fruiterer, 301 King St
Emerson, Ann, Grocer, W Side State St.
England, Alexander, Baker, 105 Tradd St.
England, James, Grocer, Champney St.
England, Jane, Grocer, 123 E. Bay St
English, James, 7 Water St.
Enslow, Joseph, Cooper, 62 Anson St.
Etenaud, Rose, School, 47 King St
Evans, James, Stone Cutter, 37 Wentworth St
Evans, L., House Carpenter, 337 King St.
Evans, William, Dry Goods Store, 145 King St.
Evans, William, Watch Maker, 155 King St.
Everhard, William, Dyer, 30 Society St.
Everingham, John, Merchant, 195 E. Bay St.
Ewing & Miller, Merchants & Agents, London Phoenix
    Insurance Co , Chisolm's N. Whf.
Ewing, Alexander, Merchant, 5 Laurens St.

8

Faber, C H., Factor, 253 King St.
Faber, J C , Jr., Bookkeeper, S. C. Bank, 213 E Bay St.
Faber, J. C., President, State Bank, 213 E. Bay St.
Faber, P. A., Druggist, 255 King St
Faber, W G., Merchant, 28 George St.
Fair, John, Boot Maker, 156 King St.
Fair, Richard, 170 King St.
Fairchild, Aaron, Blacksmith, 13 George St
Fairchild, -----, Mrs., Widow of Aaron, 13 George St.
Fairley, Martha, Widow of Hance, 21 Hasell St.
Falconer, Robert & Co., Merchants, 20 E. Bay St., Res. 61 Tradd St
Farquarson, Sarah, 9 Amen St.
Farr, John T , Planter, 29 Bull St.
Fassoux, -----, Misses, 74 Tradd St.
Faust, Jeremiah, Dry Goods & Grocery, 210 King St.
Fayole, P., Rigger, 13 Boundary St.
Fayole, Peter, Dancing Master, 359 King St.
Fell, Thomas, Tinman, Shop, 109 Church St., House, 9 Stoll's Al.
Fenwick, Susan, 5 Middle St.
Feraud, Thomas, Tradd St.
Ferguson, Ann, Widow of Thomas, 3 Liberty St.
Ferguson, Edward, Carpenter, 12 Parsonage Ln
Ferguson, Eliza M., School, 10 Lamboll St.
Ferguson, James, U. S Army, 3 Liberty St.
Ferguson, John, Tailor, 61 Church St.
Ferguson, S. W., M.D , 3 Liberty St.
Fernald, D., Grocer, 24 Archdale St.
Ferrett, J., Widow, 33 George St.
Ferrett, Mary, Fruiterer, 274 King St.
Fick & DeLiesseline, Boat Builders, 191 E. Bay St.
Fick, Charles, Grocer, 20 Lynch's Ln.
Fife, Mary, Widow, 11 Pinckney St.
Figueres, Peter B., Painter & Glazier, 111 E. Bay St.
Filette & Pineau, Jewellery & Dry Goods, 40 Queen St.
Finlay, J. E. B., M.D., 19 King St.
Fisher, George A., Saddler, 282 King St.
Fisher, James, Merchant, 52 Meeting St.
Fitch, Thomas, Grocer, 259 King St.
Fitzpatrick, Peter, Tailor, 35 Church St.
Fitzsimons, Charles, Grocer, 3 State St.
Fitzsimons, Christopher, Merchant, 37 Hasell St.
Flagg, -----, Dr., Dentist, 349 King St.
Flagg, George, 126 E. Bay St.
Flagg, Rachel, Widow of H. C , 103 Wentworth St.
Fleming, James, Grocer, 39 Tradd St.
Fleming, John H., Carpenter, 59 Anson St.
Fleming, Robert, Merchant, W. Side King St. Road
Fleming, Thomas, Merchant, 161 Tradd St.
Flinn, -----, Rev Dr., Pastor, 2nd Presbyterian Church, 19 S Bay St.
Flinn, Thomas, Grocer, 56 Queen St.
Flint, Joseph, Grocer, 102 King St.
Floderer, John, Grocer, 29 Church St.
Florance, Eliza, Dry Goods Store, 141 King St.
Florence, Lewis, Dry Goods Store, 275 King St.
Florin, Henry, Merchant, 36 Guignard St.
Fludd, Daniel, Planter, 18 S. Bay St.
Fogartie, C , Widow, 13 Wall St.

Fogartie, James, Planter, Hampstead
Foissin, Esther, Widow, 112 Tradd St
Foissin, Martha, Widow of Peter, 74 Tradd St.
Foley, -----, Capt., Mariner, 22 Guignard St.
Folker, C. John, 53 Beaufain St.
Folker, John H., Clerk, Sheriff's Office
Folker, Joseph, Academy, 63 Queeen St
Folker, Thomas, Druggist, 114 Church St.
Follin, A. & F., Grocery & Snuff Store, 180 Meeting St.
Forbes, John, Tinman, 276 King St.
Forbes, John, Tinman, 5 Tradd St.
Forbes, William, Tinman & City Lamplighter, 83 Wentworth St.
Ford & Desausure, Counsellors at Law, 46 Broad St.
Ford, Jacob, Counsellor at Law, 46 Broad St.
Ford, Timothy, Counsellors at Law, 232 Meeting St.
Fordham & Gourlay, Blacksmiths, 2 Ellery St.
Fordham, Richard, Blacksmith, Gillon St.
Forest, Charity, 3 Hasell St.
Forester, Susan, Hampstead
Forney, Norris & Co., Merchants, King St. Road
Forrest, A , Cooper, 51 Boundary St.
Forrest, Thomas H., Cooperage, 275 E. Bay St., Res. 45 Tradd St.
Forster, -----, Rev. Mr., 82 Wentworthrth St.
Foster, Nathan, Grocer, 47 Elliott St.
Foster, W. B., Discount Clerk, Bank of the State, 33 Meeting St.
Foucard, Joseph W , Musician, 353 King St.
Fourcroy, -----, Chevalier, French Consul, W Side Middle St., Mazyckborough
Fourgeaud, A., Baker, 159 King St.
Fowler, Andrew, Rev , 147 Church St.
Fowler, John, Carpenter, 8 Coming St.
Francis, John, Carpenter, 5 Smith St.
Francis, L., Grain Store, 15 Anson St.
Francois, John, Sexton, Roman Catholic Church, 9 Minority St.
Franklin, James, 18 Chamber's Al.
Fraser, Charles, Attorney, Office, 23 Tradd St., House, 27 King St.
Fraser, Donald, Wheelwright, W Side King St Road
Fraser, J. & L., Merchants, 235 E. Bay St.
Fraser, James, Farmer, W. Side King St. Road
Fraser, -----, Miss, Ladies School, 1 St. Philip's St.
Fraser, T. L S., Lumber Yard, S. End Rutledge St , House, 1 St. Philip's St.
Fraser, Thomas, Planter, 1 St. Philip's St
Frazer, John, Factor, Counting House, D'Oyley's Whf., Res 20 E Bay St.
Frazer, John M., Carpenter, 41 Wentworth St
Frean, -----, Mrs., Grocer, 106 Meeting St
Frean, Thomas, Grocer, 48 Anson St.
Frean, William, Merchant, 295 King St.
Freeman, Eliza M., Widow, 99 Tradd St.
Freer, -----, Miss, 29 Bull St.
Freer, Pleasant, College St.
Frey, Jacob, Tanner, E. Side King St. Road
Friday, William, Butcher, Cannon St, Cannonborough
Frink, Rebecca, Widow of Thomas, 44 Pinckney St.

9

Frish, Charles, Store, 263 King St.
Fritz, John, City Guard, E Side Meeting St. Road
Frobus, Rebecca, 36 Wall St.
Fronty, Michael, M.D., 307 King St.
Frost, Eliza, Widow of Thomas, 10 West St.
Frost, Thomas D., Rev , Assistant Minister, St. Philip's Church, 10 West St.
Fuller, Christopher, M.D., Hampstead
Fuller, Oliver, Grocer, 56 Meeting St.
Fuller, William, Hat Store, 87 King St.
Fulmer, John, Coach Maker, 135 Meeting St.
Furman, Richard, M D , 26 Church St.
Furman, Wood, Academy, 136 Church St
Furr, Jacob, Farmer, Washington Village
Futerell, James, Teller, S. C. Bank, 49 Church St.
Gabeau, Anthony, Tailor, 145 King St
Gabeau, James, Cooper, Bailey's Whf.
Gadsden & Ogden, Attornies, 112 Church St
Gadsden, James W., Planter, 78 Queen St.
Gadsden, John, Counsellor at Law, Mazyckborough, Offfice, 112 Church St.
Gadsden, Philip, Factor, Charlotte St , Mazyckborough, Counting House, Gadsden's Whf.
Gadsden, -----, Rev. Dr , Rector, St. Philip's Church, Mazyckborough
Gadsden, Thomas, Farmer, Left of the Lines
Gaillard & Mazyck, Factors, Chisolm's Whf.
Gaillard, Theodore, Factor, 4 Lynch St.
Galbraith, Ann, Widow, 15 George St.
Gallagher, Frederick, Tavern & Grocery, 130 Tradd St.
Gallagher, -----, Rev. Dr., Pastor, Roman Catholic Church, 90 Wentworth St
Gallebeau, Francis, Shop, 33 Pinckney St.
Galloway, James, Tavern, 77 Meeting St
Galluchat, John, Master of Lancaster School, 29 George St.
Gamage & Sewell, Merchants, Lothrop's Whf.
Gamage, Edward & Co., Merchants, 234 E. Bay St.
Gandoin, John, Dry Goods & Hat Store, 65 E. Bay St.
Garden, Adam, Shoemaker, 14 Bottle Al.
Garden, Alexander, Planter, 55 Tradd St
Garden, Harriet H., Widow of Alexander, 132 E. Bay St.
Garden, John, Planter, E Side Cannon's Bridge Road
Gardner, John & Son, Blacksmith's Shop, 112 E. Bay St.
Gardner, John, Blacksmith, House, 46 Society St
Gardo & Livingston, Grocers, 168 King St.
Garner, -----, Miss, 40 Hasell St.
Garnier, Jospeh, Grocer, 77 Church St.
Gaspar, Francis, Mariner, 174 Meeting St.
Gassaway, Eliza, 63 Queen St.
Gates, Jane, Widow, E Side King St Road
Gaugan, T., 129 Meeting St.
Gaugth, Francis, Grocer, W Side Meeting St. Road
Gaugth, Peter, Bricklayer, N. Side Warren St.
Geddes, Ann, Widow of Robert, 222 King St.
Geddes, Henry, Merchant, W. Side King St. Road
Geddes, John, Attorney, 98 Broad St.
Gefkin, C , Widow, 8 Society St.
Gefkin, Henry, Carpenter, 19 Mazyck St
Gensell, John, Steward, Marine Hospital, 6 Back St
Gentel, A., Grain Store, 31 Anson St.

George, James, Shipwright, 118 E. Bay St.
George, John, Grocer, 82 E. Bay St.
George, Mary, Widow, Shop, 40 Market St.
Gereneau, -----, Mrs , 41 King St
Germain, Joseph, Band Box Maker, 10 Society St.
Gerry, Gran, Clerk, 12 Beaufain St
Gerry, Samuel, Dry Goods Store, 80 Broad St., cr. King St
Gervais, P. T., Rev., 6 New St.
Geyer, John, Planter, 13 Lynch's Ln., Counting House, Mey's Whf.
Geyer, John S., Factor, 13 Lynch's Ln.
Gibbon, Samuel, Merchant, 87 E Bay St
Gibbs, George & Sons, Bakers, 40 Elliott St.
Gibbs, M G., Clerk, Planters' & Mechanics' Bank
Gibbs, Robert R., Planter, 7 S. Bay St.
Gibbs, William Hasell, Master in Equity, 5 Orange St
Gibson, Alexander, Merchant, 15 Laurens St., Counting House, Chisolm's N. Whf.
Gibson, James, Farmer, near Forks of Road
Gibson, James, Tanner, 138 Meeting St
Gibson, John R., Grocer, 123 Tradd St.
Gibson, Robert, 76 Tradd St.
Gibson, Thomas, Accountant, D'Oyley's Whf.
Gibson, William, Accountant, Chisolm's Whf.
Gibson, William M., Attorney, 37 Church St., House, Planter's Hotel
Giediere, Margaret, Dry Goods Store, 220 King St.
Gilbert, S. H., Wharfinger, D'Oyley's Whf , House, 12 Water St.
Giles, John, Merchant, 81 Queen St.
Giles, Othniel J., City Marshal, 71 Queen St.
Gilfert, Charles, Music Master at the Theatre
Gill, Charlotte, 4 Swinton's Ln.
Gill, Isaac, Watch Maker, 215 Meeting St
Gillespie & Co., Merchants, 47 E. Bay St.
Gilliland & Ferres, Merchants, 176 King St.
Gilliland, William, Dry Goods Store, 190 King St.
Gillon, Alexander, Factor, 2 Wall St., Counting House, 225 E. Bay St.
Gillon, Ann, Widow of Alexander, 2 Wall St.
Girty, George, 2 Short St.
Gissendanner, Susan, 37 Beaufain, St.
Gleize, Henry, M.D., 75 Anson St.
Glemet, Lewis, 40 Coming St.
Glen, Frances, Widow, 12 S. Bay St.
Glen, John, Teller, Planters' & Mechanics' Bank, 80 Wentworth St.
Glen, Margaret, Widow, 53 Tradd St
Glover, Charles, Notary Public, Office, Exchange, House, 95 Tradd St.
Glover, Henry C., M.D., 13 Coming St.
Glover, John H., Planter, 2 Meeting St.
Glover, Joseph, M.D , 1 Rutledge St.
Glover, -----, Mrs., Widow of Sanders, W Side St Philip's St. Cont'd.
Glover, Wilson, Planter, 2 Meeeting St.
Godard, Rene, 61 King St
Godet, John, 31 Wentworth St.
Godet, -----, Overseer at 6 Mile House
Godfrey, C., Widow, 85 Tradd St

Goldsmith, I. M., Vendue Crier, 29 Hasell St.
Goldsmith, M., Deputy Federal Marshall, in the
  Synagogue Yard
Goldsmith, Richard, Cabinet Maker, 104 King St.
Good, Sarah, School, 45 King St.
Goodman, Duke, Factor, E. Side King St Road, Counting
  House, Bailey's Whf.
Gordon, James, Merchant, 43 E Bay St
Gordon, John, 8 Stoll's Al
Gordon, John, Bricklayer, 105 Queen St.
Gordon, John, City Scavenger, 2 Smith's Ln.
Gordon, William, Grain Store, 96 King St.
Gorrie, William, Jeweller, 192 E. Bay St.
Gospray, Francis, Carpenter, 206 King St
Goss, William, 114 Queen St.
Gough, John P., M.D., House, 244 Meeting St , Shop, 43
  Broad St.
Gough, Mary, 2 Pitt St.
Gould, Thomas, Painter & Glazier, 7 Coming St.
Gourlay, Ann, Widow, 235 Meeting St.
Gourlay, U., Blacksmith, 193 E. Bay St.
Gowdy, Margaret, Widow, 28 King St.
Graddock, Ann, 6 Philadelphia St.
Graddock, Richard, W. Side St Philip's St Cont'd.
Gradier, John, 199 E. Bay St.
Grady, -----, Mrs., Boarding House, 57 Church St.
Graeser, C. J., Accountant, 37 Church St
Graham, Michael, Grocer, 155 Meeting St.
Graham, Michael, Grocer, W. Side Meeting St. Road
Graham, T , Baker, 58 King St.
Grame, Fanny, 37 Beaufain St.
Gran, J , Tailor, 7 Queen St.
Grand, F , Tailor, 103 Church St.
Granger, James, Painter & Glazier, N Side Boundary St.
Grant & M'Guffy, Merchants, 111 Broad St.
Grant, James, Printer, 158 E. Bay St.
Graves, Anthony, Factor, 54 Tradd St.
Graves, Charles & Sons., Factors, Chisolm's N. Whf.
Graves, Charles, Factor, 54 Tradd St.
Graves, Massey, 11 Smith's Ln.
Gray & Corby, Blacksmiths, 5 Queen St.
Gray, Alexander, Dry Goods Store, 181 King St.
Gray, Henry, Justice of Peace, 27 Guignard, Office, 26
  Ellery St
Gray, James, Teacher, 9 Bull St.
Green, Christopher R., Merchant, 235 E. Bay St.
Green, Daniel, Carpenter, 29 Wentworth St.
Green, Thomas P., Druggist, 4 Boundary St
Greenhill, Hume, Carpenter, 5 Adams St.
Greenland, Benjamin, 29 Meeting St.
Greenland, George, 94 Tradd St.
Greenland, W. P., Factor, 5 Cumberland St., Counting
  House, Prioleau's Whf.
Greenleaf & Goodwin, Merchants, 5 Crafts' S. Whf
Greenwood, M., Constable, 53 Meeting St.
Greenwood, William, Planter, 28 Beaufain St.
Greffin, C., Mrs , Dry Goods Store, 91 Broad St.
Gregorie, James, Planter, 13 Friend St.
Gregorie, Mary, Widow of James, 26 Anson St.
Gregson, Thomas, Clerk, State Bank, 39 Coming St.

Grenneker, Richard, Grocery & Boarding House, 223 E.
  Bay St
Griggs, Isaac, Attorney, E. Side State St.
Grille, C & Co., Hat & Dry Goods Store, 75 E. Bay St
Grimball, P., Teacher, 11 Pitt St.
Grimes, William, Shoemaker, Wentworth St.
Grimke, Frederick, Attorney, Office, 37 Church, House,
  156 E. Bay St.
Grimke, -----, Hon., Judge, 153 E. Bay St.
Grimke, John, M.D , 153 E. Bay St
Grimke, Thomas, S., Counsellor at Law, Office, 227
  Meeting St , House, 147 E. Bay St.
Grinley, Samuel, Bricklayer, 7 Price's Al.
Grogan, William, Merchant, E. Side Cannon's Bridge Road
Groning, L. & R., Merchants, 25 E. Bay St.
Groning, Lewis, Merchant, 18 Montague St.
Gross, John, Cabinet Maker, 25 Hasell St.
Gruber, Charles, Capt., Magazine Guard & Powder
  Receiver, at the Magazine, 4 Miles from Town
Gruber, Jacob & George, Masons, 73 Wentworth St
Guary, Ellen, 2 Archdale St.
Guc, John F., Tinman, 152 King St.
Guerard, Mary Ann, 367 King St.
Guerin, Jane, Fruiterer, 154 King St.
Guerin, John S., Carpenter, 20 George St.
Guertin, John, M D., 166 Meeting St
Guieu, L. P., 52 E. Bay St.
Guilbert, E., Music Master, 1 Wall St.
Guilou, -----, Mrs., Widow, W. Side of St Philip's St.
  Cont'd.
Gunter, P., 370 King St.
Guy, John, 8 Pitt St.
Guy, Thomas D., Grocer, 123 E. Bay St.
Guyot, Rene, Dry Goods Store, 103 King St.
Guyton, Ann, Widow, 78 Wentworth St.
Hagan, R., Dry Goods Store, 223 King St.
Hagan, Richard, Grocer, W. Side King St. Road
Hagans, Hetty, Grocer, E. Side Middle St.,
  Mazyckborough
Hagood, John, Clerk, 4 Minority St.
Hahnbaum, G. E , Clerk, Planters' & Mechanics' Bank,
  George St.
Hahnbaum, -----, Mrs., School, 7 George St.
Haig, David, Cooper, Shop, Crafts' Whf , House, 150
  Meeting St.
Haig, Robert, Carpenter, 111 Wentworth St.
Haig, Winter, Shoemaker, 379 King St.
Hall, George & Co., 316 King St
Hall, James, Stone Cutter, 78 Church St.
Hall, -----, Mrs., Widow of William, 152 E. Bay St.
Hall, Susanna, Widow of Daniel, 2 Court House Sq.
Hall, William & George, Merchants, 104 Broad St.
Hall, William, Liquor Store, 7 Elliott St.
Hall, William, M D., 152 E. Bay St.
Halsal, William, Butcher, 20 Guignard St.
Ham, Thomas, Factor, Hampstead, Counting House,
  Gadsden's Whf.
Hamilton, James, Planter, 28 Bull St.
Hamilton, John, Ship Carpenter, 5 Anson St.
Hamilton, M., School, 47 Meeting St.

11

Hamilton, Quamino, Mazyckborough
Hamlin, John, Factor, Bennett's Mill
Hammett, Charlotte, Widow, 44 Pinckney St.
Hammett, Thomas, Money Collector, 115 Wentworth St.
Hampton, Wade, Planter, 16 Church St.
Hanley, John, Grocer, 35 Elliott St.
Hannah, Alexander, 120 Tradd St.
Hannahan, Thomas, Mariner, 10 Pitt St.
Hanscomb, Thomas, Planter, 64 Wentworth St.
Hanson, Jacob, Grocer, 6 Pitt St.
Happoldt, Christopher, Butcher, Cannonborough
Happoldt, John M , Butcher, Hampstead
Harby, Isaac & Co., Editors of Southern Patriot, Office, 246 E. Bay St.
Harby, Isaac, 103 Broad St.
Hard, B F., Merchant, 27 Society St.
Hare, Frances, Mrs., 16 State St.
Harleston, Edward, Planter, 41 Boundary St.
Harleston, William, Planter, 72 Broad St.
Harper, James, Baker, 42 Tradd St
Harper, Thomas, Hat Store, 68 E. Bay St.
Harris, Abigail, Widow, 14 Berresford St.
Harris, E., Hat Store, 212 Meeting St.
Harris, Eliza, Dry Goods Store, 266 King St.
Harris, Hyman, Dry Goods Store, 291 King St.
Harris, Martha, Widow, 56 Tradd St
Harris, Tucker, M.D., 76 King St.
Harrison, Ann, Merchant, 18 Queen St
Harrison, Daniel W., Stationer, 13 Broad St.
Harrison, Francis, Grocer, 41 Elliott St.
Harrison, Mary, Nurse, 12 Ellery St.
Hart, Bella, Dry Goods Store, 72 E. Bay St.
Hart, Eliza, Fruit Shop, 30 Queen St.
Hart, Nathan, Dry Goods Store, 139 King St.
Hart, S. M., 17 Society St.
Harth, John, Planter, 1 Gibbes St.
Harth, William, Lumber Merchant, 2 Gibbes St.
Harvey, Mary, Widow of Archibald, 36 Society St.
Hasell, Andrew, Planter, 17 S. Bay St.
Hashagen, D., Grocer, 8 Bedon's Al.
Haskell, E., Planter, 155 E. Bay St.
Haskett, J , Saddler, 274 King St.
Haskett, Samuel, Saddler, 166 King St.
Haskins, S , Widow, Washington St.
Haslett, John, Merchant, 31 E. Bay St.
Hatch, Mary, Widow, 15 Pinckney St.
Hatter, Eliza, Widow, 36 Queen St.
Hattier, Mary, Dry Goods Store, 230 King St.
Hauck, John, Grocer, 51 Anson St.
Hawes, Benjamin, Clerk, Bank of the State, 15 Beaufain St.
Hawes, Nathaniel, Grocer, 53 Broad St.
Hayda, D., Grocer, 32 Market St.
Hayden, Jane, Widow, Drake St., Hampstead
Hayne, R. Y., Attorney, 6 Church St.
Hayne, William A., Bookkeeper, Bank of the State
Hays, E , Widow, 42 Beaufain St.
Hazard, J., Ship Joiner, 3 Hard Al
Hazlehurst, Robert, Merchant, House, 8 Church St., Counting House, 33 E. Bay St

Heath, Ann, Widow, 8 Maiden Ln
Heath, J. D., Attorney, 36 Church St.
Hedderly, William, Bell Hanger, 91 Queen St
Hedley, -----, Rev Dr , Academy, 88 Tradd St
Heffernan, John, Jailor, 5 Magazine St.
Helfrid, John, Constable, 10 Champney St.
Henrey, A., Midwife, 108 King St.
Henrickson, B., Carpenter, W. Side Meeting St. Road
Henry, Alexander, Cashier, Bank of the State, E. Side King St. Road
Henwood, S., Merchant, 8 St. Philip's St., Counting House, Chisolm's N. Whf
Heriot, B., Merchant, 7 Society St.
Heriot, -----, Mrs., School, E. Side King St. Road
Heriot, R. & B., Factors, Chisolm's Upper Whf.
Heriot, Roger, E Side King St. Road
Herring, John, Tailor, 1 Bank Sq.
Herron, Charles, Tailor, 31 Wentworth St
Hertz, H. M., Dry Goods Store, 160 King St.
Hertz, Jacob, Merchant, 9 Beaufain St.
Hervey, Josiah, Planter, Islington
Hervey, Samuel, Capt , Mariner, 73 Anson St
Hervey, Susan, Widow of Benjamin, Islington
Hervey, William, Coach Maker, 7 Clifford St.
Herviant, P., Baker, W. Side King St. Road
Hesley, John, Grocer, 53 Elliott St.
Hesley, John, Tailor, 87 Meeting St.
Hewitt, Susan, 29 Anson St.
Hewitt, Thomas, Dry Goods Store, 209 King St.
Hext, Joseph, Carpenter, 79 Church St.
Heydenfeld, John, Grocer, 189 Meeting St.
Heynes, James, Grocer, 142 Church St.
Heyward, Charlotte, Widow, 45 Hasell St.
Heyward, John, Planter, 2 Meeting St.
Heyward, N., Planter, 143 E. Bay St.
Heyward, Samuel, Custom House, Store Keeper, 1 Mazyck St.
Heyward, William, Boarding House, 40 Chamber's Al.
Heyward, William, Planter, 8 Legare St.
Higham, Thomas, Merchant, 263 E Bay St.
Hill, Henry D., Capt., Mariner, 98 E Bay St.
Hill, J., Victualler, 3 Market St.
Hill, Martha, 12 St. Philip's St.
Hillard, N., Capt , Mariner, 5 Wall St
Hillegas, -----, Mrs., 13 Berresford St.
Hillman, Ann, Boarding House, 40 E. Bay St.
Hillman, William, 6 Mile House
Hilson, -----, Mr., Comedian, 46 Meeting St.
Hinson, Thomas, Carpenter, 4 Berresford St.
Hislop, Hannah, 8 Back St.
Hobrecker, John G., Blacksmith, 5 Market St.
Hodgkinson, Ann, 9 Magazine St.
Hodgson, W. F., Boot Maker, 392 King St.
Hoff, John, Bookseller & Stationer, 117 Broad St.
Hoff, John M., Clerk of Markets, 20 Middle St.
Hoffman, George, Grocer, 46 Church, House, 33 Elliott St
Holland, E. C., Attorney, Office, 57 Broad St., House, 7 Legare St.
Holland, John, Merchant, 46 Meeting St.
Holland, -----, Mrs , Boarding House, 46 Meeting St.

12

Holliday, Eleanor, 6 Champney St.
Hollinshead, -----, Rev Dr., Late Pastor, Independent Church, 9 Maiden Ln.
Holloway, Richard, Carpenter, 18 Beaufain St
Holman, -----, Mr., Manager of Theatre, at Theatre
Holman, Susan, 1 Lamboll St.
Holmes & Glover, Vendue Masters, 8 Exchange St.
Holmes, Charles, Butcher, Cannonborough
Holmes, James, Notary Public & Dutch Consul, 46 E. Bay St.
Holmes, John B., City Recorder, 6 Meeting St.
Holmes, John, Planter, 78 Tradd St.
Holmes, John V., Dry Goods Store, 219 King St.
Holmes, Joseph B., Accountant, 90 Church St.
Holmes, -----, Mrs., Widow of Isaac, 24 Coming St.
Holmes, Sandford, Clerk, 52 Queen St.
Holmes, William, M.D., 6 Meeting St.
Holmes, William, Vendue Master, 46 Boundary St.
Holton, Lisette, 9 Cumberland St.
Holwell, Thomas, Boatman, 1 Zigzag Ln.
Honour, John, Saddler, 37 Meeting St.
Hopkins, John, Merchant, Counting House, 288 E. Bay St , House, 32 Hasell St.
Hordon, Eliza, Shop, 4 Middle St.
Horlbeck, C., Widow, 14 Wall St.
Horlbeck, Henry, Mason, 14 Cumberland St.
Horlbeck, John, Mason, 308 King St.
Horry, E. Lynch, Planter, 65 Broad St.
Horry, Elias, Intendant, 249 Meeting St
Horry, Harriett, Widow of Daniel, 60 Tradd St.
Horry, -----, Mrs., Widow of Jonah, 43 Boundary St.
Horry, Thomas, Planter, 24 Meeting St.
Horsey, Thomas J., Farmer, Islington
Horwood, -----, Mrs., Widow, 2 Zigzag Ln.
Hough, Wade, Merchant, 99 Broad St., Upstairs
Housten, James, Carpenter, 14 Middle St.
Howard, Alexander, City Escheator, 49 Wentworth St.
Howard, Eliza, Shop, 55 Boundary St.
Howard, John, Bricklayer, 140 Meeting St.
Howard, Richard, Cooper, Gillon St., Res Washington St., Mazyckborough.
Howard, Robert, Collector of Excise, Office, 241 E. Bay St., House, 35 Hasell St.
Howard, William V., 34 Boundary St.
Howe & Fitch, Merchants, 232 E. Bay St.
Howe, C., Merchant, at Planter's Hotel
Howe, Michael, Liquor Shop, S. Side S. Bay St.
Howe, S. & J., Shoe Store, 99 King St.
Howie, William, Merchant, W. Side King St. Road
Hrabowski, Richard, City Inspector, Cannonborough, Office, Exchange
Huard, S., Druggist, 74 E. Bay St
Hubbard, Elisha, Grocer, 127 Curch St.
Hubbell, S , Capt , Mariner, 157 E. Bay St.
Hudson, John, Capt., Mariner, 2 Whim Court
Hudson, Joseph, Capt., Mariner, 2 Whim Court
Hudson, -----, Mrs , Mantua Maker, 66 Queen St.
Huff, Abigail, Widow, 4 Price's Al.
Huger, Alfred, Planter, 70 Broad St.
Huger, Ann, Widow of John, 70 Broad St.

Huger, Carlos, Tailor, Shop, 304 King St., House, 29 Coming St.
Huger, Charlotte, Miss, 9 St. Philip's St.
Huger, D. E., Counsellor at Law, 36 Meeting St.
Huger, Daniel, Planter, 86 Queen St.
Huger, John, Planter, 2 Meeting St.
Huger, -----, Miss, Hudson St., Mazyckborough
Hughes, Edward, School, 87 Tradd St
Hughes, John, Assistant Clerk of Markets, 6 Lamboll St
Hugonpellisir, M , Widow, 29 Wall St.
Huguet, Maria, Widow, 2 Wentworth St.
Hule, Ann, Seamstress & Laundress, French Al.
Hull, Latham, Dry Goods Store, 330 King St.
Humbert, Godfrey, Carpenter, 12 Water St.
Hume, John, Planter, 61 Wentworth St.
Humphrey, M. L., Merchant, 4 Crafts' N. Whf.
Humphreys, Joseph, Tailor, 47 Queen St
Hunt, F., Benjamin, Attorney, 44 Meeting St.
Hunt, Thomas, Commissioner in Equity, 41 Broad St.
Hunter & Smith, Cutlers, 69 Market St.
Hunter, John L., E. Side King St. Road
Hunter, John, Milliner Store, 149 King St.
Hurbers, John, Grocer, 57 Anson St.
Hurd, Sarah, Grocery, W Side State St.
Hurlbut, Martin L. Classical Teacher, 70 Wentworth St.
Hussey, Brian, Capt., Mariner, 6 Stoll's Al.
Huston, James, Merchant Tailor, 61 Church St.
Hutchins, Mary, Fruiterer, 10 George St.
Hutchins, S., 22 Hasell St.
Hutchinson, Anna N , Widow of Leger, 17 Pitt St
Hutchinson, Charlotte, Widow, 10 Price's Al.
Hutchinson, Eliza, Widow of Thomas, 47 Society St.
Hutton, James, 9 S. Bay St.
Huxham, -----, Miss, 50 Meeting St
Hu[?], Charles, Dry Goods Store, 138 Queen St.
Hyams, Hannah, Dry Goods Store, 111 King St.
Hyams, Henry, 112 King St.
Hyams, Mordecai, 148 King St
Hyams, Rebecca D., Fruiterer, 43 Queen St.
Hyams, S , Vendue Master, 13 Vendue Range
Hyams, Samuel, Crier of the Court, 76 Meeting St.
Hyams, Solomon, Dry Goods Store, 303 King St
Hyer, Henry, Drayman, W. End Boundary St.
Hyslop, C., Widow, 39 Elliott St.
Inglesby, Henry, Merchant Tailor, 107 Tradd St.
Inglis, Mary, Cannonborough
Inglis, Thomas, Barber, 40 Meeting St.
Ingraham, Henry, Merchant, 7 Smith St.
Ingraham, Nathaniel, Merchant, 396 King St.
Ions, Samuel, Shoemaker, 42 Hasell St.
Ireland, Benjamin, Grocer, 25 Bull St.
Irvin, Moses, Shoemaker, 314 King St.
Irvine, Matthew, M.D., 7 Meeting St.
Isaacs, Abraham, Merchant, 305 King St.
Ives, Jeremiah, Grocer, Bailey's Whf.
Izard, Eliza, Widow of Ralph, 79 Broad St.
Izard, Ralph, U. S. Navy, 95 Wentworth St.
Jacks, James, Jeweller, 105 Broad St.
Jackson, Charles, 4 Philadelphia St.
Jackson, Edward & Co , Tallow Chandler, St. Phillip's St

Cont'd.

Jackson, Montague, Dry Goods Store, 300 King St.
Jacobs, Cecilia, 76 E. Bay St.
Jacobs, Lucy, Grain Shop, 67 Anson St
Jacoby, George & Co., Grocer, 16 St. Philip's St.
Jacques, D , 8 Middle St.
Jahan, Joseph, Carpenter, 120 Meeting St.
James, John, Carpenter, 176 Meeting St.
James, Robert, Carpenter, 192 King St.
Jamieson, Rebecca, Widow, N. Side Charlotte St ,
    Mazyckborough
Jandrell, -----, Mrs., School, 129 E. Bay St.
Jandrell, Thomas, Carpenter, 129 E. Bay St
Javain, Peter, Grocer, 95 King St.
Jeffords, John, Tailor, 41 Tradd St.
Jeffords, -----, Mrs., Widow, Islingston
Jeffords, Samuel, Sailmaker, Chisolm's W. Whf.
Jenerett, Christopher, Planter, 27 Wall St.
Jenerett, John, Clerk, 133 Church St.
Jenkins, Christopher, Planter, 20 Bull St.
Jenkins, Elias, Mason, 11 Liberty St.
Jenkins, Micha, Planter, 3 Legare St.
Jenklins, Eliza, Laundress, 20 State St.
Jervey, James, Clerk, District Court, 223 Meeting St.
Jervey, T. H., Surveyor of the Customs, 223 Meeting St
Jessup, J , Grocer, 25 State St.
Johnson, Andrew, Grocer, 43 Tradd St.
Johnson, Charlotte, Miss, 8 S. Bay St.
Johnson, D. W., Saddler, 106 King St.
Johnson, Edward, Grocer, 23 State St
Johnson, Eve, Cannonborough
Johnson, George, Wheelwright, 1 Maiden Ln.
Johnson, Hans, Shop, W. Side Anson St., Mazyckborough
Johnson, J. & I. A., M.D. & Druggists, 5 Broad St
Johnson, Jabez W., Watch Maker, 201 King St.
Johnson, James, Blacksmith, Chalmers Al.
Johnson, John, Dry Goods Store, 226 King St.
Johnson, John, Grocer, 14 Mazyck St.
Johnson, John, Grocer, W End Boundary St.
Johnson, John, Jr., Res. & Furnace, E. Side, Washington
    St., Mazyckborough
Johnson, Joseph, M D., 12 Church St.
Johnson, Sarah, Seamstress, 11 St. Philip's St.
Johnson, William, Blacksmith, 72 Anson St , Shop, 183 E.
    Bay St.
Johnson, William, Hon., U. S. Judge, E. Side Cannon's
    Bridge Road
Johnston, Eliza, Widow, 43 King St.
Johnston, P., Printer, 3 Amen St.
Johnston, P. W., Printer, 41 Queen St.
Johnston, Thomas, Store & Wagon Yard, W. Side of King
    St Road
Jones, Abby, Pastry Cook, 36 & 37 Broad St.
Jones, Abraham, Cabinet Maker, 5 Beaufain St.
Jones, Butler, Grocer, 93 Tradd St.
Jones, Edward, M.D., W. Side St. Philip's St. Cont'd.
Jones, Henry I., 62 Tradd St.
Jones, Henry, Ship Carpenter, 20 Pinckney St.
Jones, Jehu, Boarding House, 36 & 37 Broad St.
Jones, Jehu, Jr , Tailor, 30 Broad St

Jones, John, Grocer, 79 Wentworth St.
Jones, John S., Wire Worker, 120 Tradd St.
Jones, Joseph, Boarding House, 12 Tradd St.
Jones, Margaret, Widow, 30 King St.
Jones, Mary, Widow of Samuel, 1 Guignard St.
Jones, Peter, Tailor, 51 Church St.
Jones, T., President, S C Bank, 2 Guignard St
Jones, William, Tinman, 29 King St.
Jordon, C., Coach Painter, 134 E. Bay St.
Joseph, J., Dry Goods Store, 222 King St
Jost, George, Grocer, 1 Market St.
Jujardin, J., Widow, 41 Anson St
Julian, Henry, Cabinet Maker, 168 Meeting St.
Julli, Richard, Fruit Shop, 44 Elliott St.
Just, George, Shipwright, 15 Pitt St.
Justrobe, John, Merchant, 55 Church St
Kanapauk, William, Shoemaker, 110 Wentworth St.
Kay, -----, Mrs., Nurse, 4 Anson St.
Kay, -----, Mrs., Widow, 3 Smith's Ln.
Kean, William, Shoemaker, 121 E. Bay St.
Keanan, George, Merchant, E. Side King St. Road
Keating, M., Grocer, 178 Meeting St.
Keckerley, George, Planter, E. Side King St. Road
Keckerley, Michael, Planter, 25 Coming St.
Keeley, John, 375 King St.
Keith, George, Carpenter, 35 Society St.
Keith, Irvine, U. S. Army, 7 Meeting St.
Keith, -----, Mrs., Widow of Rev Dr. Keith, 50 Meeting St
Keith, Susan, Widow of Alexander, 7 Meeting St
Keith, Sylvanus, Merchant, 137 King St.
Kelly, A., John, Dry Goods Store, 129 King St.
Kelly, Joseph, Grain Store, 205 King St.
Kelly, Margaret, Fruit Shop, 31 Queen St.
Kelly, Maria, 22 Pinckney St.
Kelly, Mary, Dry Goods Store, 129 King St.
Kelly, Mary, Shop, 35 Beaufain St.
Kelly, Michael, Ironmonger, 52 E. Bay St.
Kelner, John, 207 Meeting St.
Kemnitz, Catherine, Grocer, 105 Wentworth St.
Kennedy, Edward, Deputy Naval Officer, 21 Mazyck St.
Kennedy, J. B., Merchant, 16 Magazine St.
Kennedy, L. H., Attorney, 72 Tradd St., Office, 213
    Meeting St.
Kennedy, Peter, Grocer, 51 Tradd St.
Kennedy, ---, Store Keeper, 109 King St.
Kennerly, I., Planter, Back of 4 Mile House
Keough, Owen, Accountant, 57 Church St.
Ker, J. C , Merchant, 145 Meeting St.
Ker, John, 388 King St.
Ker, Joseph, 388 King St
Ker, William S., Discount Clerk, State Bank, House,
    388 King St.
Kerr & Perry, Dry Goods Store, 268 King St.
Kerr & Verree, Factors, Bailey's Whf.
Kerr, Andrew, Accountant, 111 Church St.
Kerr, Joseph, Forage Master, U S., 6 Magazine St.
Kerrison, Eliza, Children's School, 35 Coming St.
Kershaw & Lewis, Factors, 264 E. Bay St.
Kershaw, Charles, Factor, 238 Meeting St.
Kershaw, Newman, Merchant, Counting House, 263 E.

Bay St., House, 98 E. Bay St.
Kesch, John, Grocer, 115 Tradd St.
Kettleband, David, Carpenter, 14 Logan St.
Key, Robert I., Tailor, 110 Church St.
Kidd, George, 213 Meeting St.
Kiddell, Charles, Merchant, 17 Broad St.
King & Jones, Merchants, 3 Crafts' S. Whf.
King, Benjamin, Carpenter, cr. King & Warren St.
King, Leonard, Carpenter, 40 Beaufain St.
King, Mary, Grocer, 23 King St.
King, Mitchell, Counsellor at Law, Office, St. Michael's
   Al., House, 45 Church St.
Kingman, E., Steward, Orphan House
Kingman, John, Toll Receiver, Ashley Bridge Ferry
Kinloch, Francis, Planter, 15 Bull St.
Kippenberg, Andrew, Grocer, 37 Queen St.
Kirk, Alexander, Merchant, 4 Logan St., Counting House,
   47 E. Bay St.
Kirk, Jane, Grocer, 20 Friend St.
Kirk, John, Liquor House, 17 Chalmers Al.
Kirk, John, Merchant at the Union Bank House
Kirkland, Joseph, M.D. & Druggist, 107 Church St
Kirkpatrick, Douglas & Hall, Merchants, Bailey's Whf.
Kirkpatrick, John, Factor, 61 Tradd St.
Kirtz, Frederick, Grocer, Gadsden's Whf.
Knauff, John, Hampstead
Knox, John, Ship Carpenter, 34 Guignard St.
Knox, Walter, House Carpenter, 3 Green St.
Knust, Henry, Grocer, 63 Broad St.
Koedler, Jacob, Butcher, Hampstead
Koffskey, Ann C., Shop, 97 King St.
Kohler, Frederick, Tanner, E. Side King St. Road
Kohne, Frederick, Merchant, 67 Broad St.
Kuhnle, John, Cooper, 38 Boundary St.
Kunhardt, William, Wharfinger, Bailey's Whf., House,
   Charlotte St , Mazyckborough
Labarben, A., Shop, 67 King St.
Labat, Andrew, Merchant, 37 King St
Labat, Catharine, Dry Goods Store, 126 King St.
Labat, Jane, Piano Forte Teacher, 37 King St.
Labatut, J., Musician & Painter, 82 Meeting St.
Labaussay, P., Baker, W. Side King St. Road
Laborde, Harriett, 347 King St.
Lachicotte, P. H., Planter, 64 Anson St.
Lacombe, Stephen, M.D., 17 Maiden Ln.
Lacoste, Charles, Dry Goods Store, 72 King St.
Lacoste, John, Dry Goods Store, 246 King St.
Lacoste, -----, Mrs., Widow of Stephen, E. Side King St.
   Road, 5 Miles from Town
Lacy, John, Mariner, 104 Meeting St.
Ladeveze, Raymond, Dry Goods Store, 94 King St.
Ladeveze, Victor, Dry Goods Store, 76 King St.
Ladson, James, 13 Meeting St.
Ladson, Judith, Widow of James, 13 Meeting St.
Ladson, William, 13 Meeting St.
Lafar, David B., Cooper, Magwood's Whf.
Lafar, Joseph & John, Jewellers, 163 Meeting St.
Laffeteau, M., Widow of Francis, School 47 Wentworth St
Laffeteau, -----, Widow, 3 Middle St.
Lafon, Francis, 3 Whim Court

Lafon, John, Cooper, 212 E. Bay St.
Laidler, Alexander, Capt , Mariner, 6 Blackbird Al.
Lamb & O'Donavan's Classical Academy, 213 Meeting St.
Lamb, David, Merchant, 104 Tradd St., Counting House,
   Blake's Whf.
Lamb, James, Merchant, 104 Tradd St., Counting House,
   Blake's Whf.
Lambert, Francis, Grocer, 84 E. Bay St
Lamboll, Rebecca, 6 Smith's Ln.
Lanaeau, B., Tanner, 1 Pitt St.
Lanaeau, F., Capt., Mariner, 16 Elliott St.
Lance, -----, Mrs., Widow of Lambert, 86 Queen St.
Lance, -----, Rev. Mr., 86 Queen St.
Lance, William, Attorney, Office, 4 St. Michael's Al ,
   House, 26 Beaufain St.
Landersheim, J. C , Wraggsborough
Lange, Jacob H., Merchant, 1 Church St , Counting House,
   254 E Bay St.
Langford, Ann, Widow, 12 Liberty St.
Langley, William, Riding Master, 41 St Philip's St
Langlois, Maria, School, 385 King St.
Langstaff, John, Farmer, E. Side Meeting St. Road, 2 Miles
   from Town
Langton, John, Bookkeeper, Planters' & Mechanics' Bank,
   361 King St.
Langton, John, Tailor, 229 King St.
Lapenne & Carivenes, Dry Goods Store, 8 Queen St.
Larbe, J., Shoemaker, 98 Church St.
LaRousselier, Lewis, Druggist, 90 King St.
Larry, Peter, Bricklayer, 75 Church St.
Larry, Robert, Carpenter, 75 Church St.
Latham, Daniel, Distiller, 2 Hasell St.
Latham, Daniel, Jr., Merchant, 2 Hasell St.
Latts, James, M.D., 8 Archdale St.
Laurence, Jane, Boarding House, 8 Chalmers Al.
Laurens, Henry, Planter, 169 E. Bay St
Laurens, Peter, Merchant, Counting House, 3 Lothrop's
   Whf., House, 27 St. Philip's St.
Lauries, L., Widow, 12 Cumberland St.
Laval, J , Jr., 16 Pinckney St
Lavandin, P., Shop, 217 Meeting St.
Lawton & Mandeville, Dry Goods Store, 211 King St.
Lazarus, J., Jr., Merchant, 3 Fitzsimons' Whf.
Lazarus, M. L., Dry Goods Store, 211 King St.
Lazarus, Mark, Merchant, 114 King St.
Lazarus, Michael, 146 King St.
Leadbetter, Agnes, Widow, 9 Liberty St.
Leader, Mary, 4 Clifford St.
Leaumont, -----, Mrs., Widow of Robert, 8 Minority St.
Lebby, William, Shipwright, 17 Amen St.
Lebreton, F. B., Merchant, 20 Cumberland St.
Lecat, Francis, Musician, 26 Ellery St
Lechais, J. P., Widow, 49 King St.
Lechais, -----, Mrs., Widow, 6 Orange St
Lecol, J., 121 King St.
LeCoq, Francis, Sign Painter, 82 Meeting St.
Lee & Parson's, Merchants, 137 King St.
Lee, Dorothy, Widow of Stephen, 43 Broad St.
Lee, J. A., School, 104 Wentworth St.
Lee, -----, Mrs , Children's School, Cannonborough

15

Lee, -----, Mrs., Midwife, 13 Society St.
Lee, -----, States, Rev , 43 Broad St.
Lee, Thomas, Comptroller General, 44 Society St
Lee, William, Attorney, 14 St. Philip's St.
Lee, William, Clerk, Union Bank
Leese, Benjamin, Broker, 146 Church St., Office, 49 E
Bay St.
Lefevre, J. B., Grocer, 32 Guignard St
Legare, James, Planter, 3 New St.
Legare, Juliet, 156 Church St.
Legare, Mary, Widow, E End of Boundary St.
Legare, S., Friend St.
Legare, S., Widow, 23 Anson St.
Legare, Thomas, Planter, 1 S. Bay St.
Legge, Ann, Widow of Edward, 130 Wentworth St.
Legge, Joseph, Farmer, Washington Village
Legrange, Francis, M.D., 88 Church St.
Lehre, Ann, Widow of William, 32 E. Bay St.
Lehre, Thomas, Commissioner of Loans, 371 King St.
Leitch, D., Grocer 283 King St.
Lejeune, Thomas, Cabinet Maker, 95 Queen St.
Leland, Joseph, Merchant, 87 E. Bay St.
Leland, -----, Rev. Dr., Pastor, 1st Presbyterian Church,
Mount Pleasant, 82 Wentworth St. or 228 Meeting St.
Lemaitre, J. B., Dry Goods Store, 77 King St.
Leman, James, Merchant, Hampstead
Lemke, C., Grocer, 50 Beaufain St.
Leport, Rene, W Side Meeting St. Road
Leprince & Dumour, French Store, 108 Queen St.
Lequex, -----, Mrs , Widow of John, 8 Wall St.
Leray, S., Shop, 162 Meeting St.
Lesage, John, W. Side Meeting St. Road
Leseigneur, V., M.D., 360 King St.
Lesesne, Hannah, Widow of Isaac, 16 Society St.
Lesesne, Isaac, Capt., Mariner, 16 Society St.
Leslie, Henry, Capt., Mariner, 69 Anson St.
Leuder, Frances, Confectioner, 110 Queen St.
Levin, Lewis, Dry Goods Store, 225 King St.
Levins, James, Capt., Mariner, 53 Anson St.
Levy, Emanuel, Dry Goods Store, 63 E. Bay St.
Levy, Hart, Dry Goods Store, 265 King St.
Levy, J. C., 311 King St.
Levy, M. C., Dry Goods Store, 311 King St.
Levy, Moses, Dry Goods Store, 261 King St.
Levy, Reuben, Broker, 161 Meeting St
Levy, Sarah, Dry Goods Store, 277 King St.
Levy, Simon, Dry Goods Store, 150 King St
Levy, Solomon, Dry Goods Store, 80 Broad St.
Lewis, David, Joiner, 49 Broad St.
Lewis, David, Merchant, Bailey's Whf., House, 119 Broad
St.
Lewis, Isaac, Merchant, 322 King St., House, 22 Tradd St.
Lewis, John, Factor, 144 Church St.
Lewis, John, Grocer, 113 E. Bay St.
Lewis, Lydia, 6 King St.
Lewis, Mary, Widow, 172 Meeting St.
Lewis, Sarah, Columbus St., Hampstead
Liblong, Henry, Shoemaker, 6 Liberty St.
Lighthouse, Elizabeth, Widow of Edward, 244 Meeting St.
Limehouse, Robert, 64 Tradd St.

Lindsay, Mary, Boarding House, 96 Church St.
Ling, John, Clerk, 24 Church St.
Ling, Philip, Coachmaker, 11 Guignard St
Ling, Robert, Coachmaker, 41 Market St.
Lining, E. B., Attorney, House, 13 Pitt St., Office, 6 Legare
St.
Lining, -----, Mrs., Widow of Charles, 6 Legare St
Linser, John L , Butcher, Cannonborough
Liot, Francis & Co., Grocers, 107 E. Bay St.
Lipman, A , Watchmaker, 152 King St.
Listin, Henry, Cooper, 72 Market St.
Little, John, Cabinet Maker, 9 Pitt St.
Little, John, Carpenter, House, 47 Beaufain St., Shop, 29
Hasell St
Little, Robert, Lumber Merchant, Counting House,
Chisolm's Upper Whf., House, Charlotte St ,
Mazyckborough
Livingston, John, Tailor, 241 King St.
Livingston, M. E. M., 9 Whim Court
Livingston, R. Y., Clerk, Union Bank, 42 Society St.
Lloyd, J. P., Venetian Blind Maker, 111 Meeting St.
Lloyd, John, 18 Bull St.
Lloyd, Joseph & Son, Dry Goods Store, 55 King St.
Lloyd, Mary, Widow of John, 190 Meeting St.
Lockwood, J. R. & Co., Grocers, 18 Vendue Range
Lockwood, Joshua, Clerk, State Bank, 1 Smith's Ln.
Loga, John, Dentist, 40 Wentworth St.
Logan, C. M., Broker & Vendue Master, 16 Archdale St ,
Office, 61 E. Bay St.
Logan, George, Carpenter, 21 State St.
Logan, George, M.D. Physician to Poor & Orphan House,
83 Meeting St.
Logan, Honoria, Widow of George, 16 Archdale St.
Logan, J. M., Carpenter, 7 Montague St.
Logan, William, Librarian, Charleston Library Society, W.
Side Cannon's Bridge Road
Long, Robert, Capt., Mariner, 7 Wall St.
Lopez, John, Grocer, 75 Market St.
Lopez, Precilla, Dry Goods Store, 366 King St.
Lord, Archibald B., U. S. Navy, Hampstead
Lord, Jacob N., Bootmaker, 186 King St.
Lord, Samuel, Merchant, 12 Crafts' N. Whf.
Lorent & Steinmetz, Merchants, 45 E. Bay St.
Lorrimere, Ann, Widow, 3 Beaufain St.
Lothrop, -----, Mrs., Widow of Seth, 228 E. Bay St.,
Upstairs
Lothrop, S. H., Merchant, House, 228 E. Bay St.
Lott, Peter, Shopkeeper, 93 Church St.
Louis, Henry, 89 Church St.
Lovell, Joseph, Merchant, 399 King St ,Counting House,
Crafts' S. Whf.
Lowell, Michael, Wheelwright, 125 Wentworth St.
Lowndes, James, Planter
Lowndes, -----, Mrs., Widow of Charles, 44 Anson St.
Lowndes, Thomas, Planter, 71 Broad St.
Lowndes, William, Planter on Ashley River 2 Miles from
Town
Lowry, Charles, Merchant Tailor, 16 Tradd St.
Lubet, John B., 17 Berresford St.
Lucas, Jonathan, Jr., Proprietor of the Mills,

Cannonborough.

Ludlow, Robert, Merchant, 22 Tradd St.

Lukens, John, Cashier, Planters' & Mechanics' Bank, 6 Hasell St.

Lusher, George, 92 E. Bay St., Upstairs

Lynah, Edward, Planter, 21 Montague St.

Lynch, Esther, 29 Beaufain St.

Lynch, Jane, Fruit Shop, 47 Broad St

Lynn, John, Fodder Scales, E. End Boundary St.

Lyons, Isaac, Dry Goods Store, 177 King St.

Lyons, Isaac, Mineral Water Shop, 62 E Bay St.

Lyons, Mordecai, Dry Goods Store, 71 E. Bay St.

MacBeth, James, Merchant, 260 E Bay St , House, 5 Lamboll St

MacKey, John, Teacher & Vendue Master, 2 Bank Sq.

Mackie, James, Grocer & Liquor Store, 54 E. Bay St., House, 15 Society St.

MacLish, M., Mrs., School, 17 Elliott St.

MacNamara, John, Vendue Master, 227 E. Bay St., Upstairs

Madden, James, Attorney, 355 King St.

Madelmond, -----, Mrs., 124 Church St., Upstairs

Magnes, Emanuel, Grocer, 52 Tradd St.

Magrath, John, Merchant, 108 Meeting St.

Maguire, Hugh, Merchant Tailor, 93 E. Bay St.

Magwood & Patterson, Factors, Magwood's Whf.

Magwood, Robert, M.D., 235 Meeting St.

Magwood, S., Wharf Owner, 79 Queen St.

Maillard, John & Co., Grain Store, 6 Tradd St

Main, James, Grocer, 393 King St.

Mairs, Simon, Merchant, 252 King St.

Malcolm, Thomas, City Assessor, 2 Short St.

Malone, John S., Tinman, 252 E. Bay St.

Mandihoff, C., Widow, 61 Anson St.

Manigault, Henry, Planter, 46 Meeting St.

Manigault, Joseph, Planter, E. Side Meeting St. Road

Mann, John, Bricklayer, 38 King St.

Manson, Andrew & Co., Merchants, 321 Anson St.

Mansuy, Maria, Baker, 2 Wentworth St.

Manuel, Philip, Tailor, 66 King St

Marchant, P. T., Planter, 142 King St.

Marel, Mayol, 83 Queen St.

Margart, John H., U. S. Army, Washington Village, W. cr King St. Road

Margat, Louis, Guard Man, 355 King St.

Marineau, D. V., 97 Wentworth St.

Markley, Abraham, Merchant, 14 St. Philip's St

Markley, Benjamin A., Attorney, 110 Meeting St.

Marks, Deborah, Dry Goods Store, 133 King St

Marks, Humphrey, Merchant, E. Side King St. Road

Marks, Joseph, Grocer, 135 Queen St.

Marley, Peter, Deputy Sheriff, 141 E Bay St.

Marr, Ann, Widow, 165 Church St.

Marsden, Benjamin, Accountant, Hampstead

Marsh, James, Shipwright, 200 E. Bay St., Shop on His Whf.

Marshall, John, Cutler, 92 Broad St.

Marshall, John, Merchant, 161 E. Bay St., Counting House, 265 E. Bay St.

Marshall, Louisa, Widow, 11 Logan St.

Marshall, Mary S., Widow, 55 Broad St.

Marshall, William, Shipwright, S. Side Washington St.

Marshall, William, Vendue Master, 229 E. Bay St., House, 138 E. Bay St.

Marshburn, Nicholas, Carpenter, 6 Market St.

Marsorati & Co., Optical House, 20 Broad St.

Martin, Charles, Bricklayer, 43 Anson St.

Martin, Christopher, Grocer, 25 Wall St

Martin, James, Merchant, 2 Fitzsimons' Whf.

Martin, John, M D., 21 Pinckney St.

Martin, John N., Mason & City Scavenger, 31 Beaufain St

Martin, Louisa, Mazyckborough

Martin, M., Cooper, 6 Bedon's Al.

Martin, Rebecca, 197 Meeting St

Martin, Robert, Dry Goods Store, E Side King St. Road

Martin, Sarah F., 23 Anson St.

Martin, Thomas & Co., Martin's Whf.

Martin, Thomas, Merchant, 54 Broad St

Martindale, James, Merchant, E. Side King St. Road

Mason, George, Clerk, Union Bank, 10 Lynch's Ln.

Massot, H., Watchmaker, 134 Queen St.

Matheson, Alexander, Merchant, Bailey's Whf.

Mathews, James, Factor, House, 22 Anson St., Counting House, Martin's Whf

Mathews, Sarah, Widow of John, 12 Rutledge St.

Mathewsen, F., Dry Goods & Grocery, 17 Queen St.

Matthews, James, Shoemaker, 9 Water St.

Matthews, Mary, Widow of Benjamin, 6 West St.

Matthews, Mary, Widow of George, 17 Beaufain St.

Matthews, Peter, 29 Boundary St.

Matthews, William, Jr., Planter, Charlotte St., Mazyckborough

Matthews, William, Planter, 4 Rutledge St.

Mattineau, Lewis, Grocer, E. Side King St. Road

Mattivier, Francis., Fruiterer, 3 Elliott St.

Mattuce, John, Butcher, 35 Anson St.

Mauger, John, Ship Chandler, 41 E. Bay St.

Maull, David, Tailor, 38 Beaufain St.

Maxwell, Harriet, Widow, 48 Meeting St.

Maxwell, R., Merchant, House, 50 Meeting St., Counting House, 268 E. Bay St.

Maxwell, William R., Planter, 48 Meeting St.

May, John, Boarding House, 260 King St.

Mayberry, Thomas, Theatre Box Keeper, 47 Broad St.

Mayer, John G., Attorney, 13 Archdale St.

Maynard, Richard, E. Side King St. Road

Mazet, J., Puppet Show, 206 King St.

Mazett, John, Cabinet Maker, 10 Ellery St.

Mazyck, Mary, Widow, 18 Church St.

Mazyck, -----, Mrs., Widow, 102 Meeting St

Mazyck, N. B., Factor, 101 Meeting St.

Mazyck, Philip, M.D., 3 Archdale St.

Mazyck, William, Planter & Factor, 3 Archdale St.

M'Bride, James, Jr., M.D., 19 Tradd St.

M'Bride, James, M.D., 74 E. Bay St.

M'Bride, -----, Mrs., Widow, 74 E. Bay St., Above Stairs

M'Call & Hayne, Attornies, 115 Church St.

M'Call, Ann, Widow of John, 132 Church St.

M'Call, Beekman, Clerk, State Bank, 1 Hasell St.

M'Call, Eliza, Widow of Hext, 14 Meeting St.

M'Call, Hagar, 5 King St.
M'Call, Hext, Attorney, 5 Church St.
M'Call, James, W. Side King St. Road
M'Call, Joseph, Clerk, 14 Meeting St.
M'Calla, Sarah, Widow of Dr., 38 Anson St.
M'Cauley, George, Jr., Merchant, 107 Broad St., Upstairs
M'Cauley, George, Merchant, 119 Church St.
M'Cay, J. R., Classical School, 57 Queen St.
M'Cormick, Richard, Attorney, 83 Broad St.
M'Cormick, Timothy, Owner, 54 Church St., Counting House, Martin's Whf.
M'Cready, Mary A., Milliner, 184 King St.
M'Donald & Bonner, Piano Forte Makers, 49 Broad St.
M'Donald, Christopher, Grocer, 363 King St.
M'Donald, John, Factor, 18 Beaufain St., Counting House, Prioleau's Whf.
M'Donald, -----, Mrs., 368 King St.
M'Donald, S. E., Widow, 18 Beaufain St.
M'Donald, Sarah, Boarding House, 217 King St.
M'Dow, William, Academy, 4 Montague St.
M'Dowall, A., Mrs., Fruiterer, 242 King St.
M'Dowall, John, 70 King St.,174 King St
M'Dowall, William, Accountant, 174 King St
M'Dowell & Black, Merchants, 70 King St.
M'Eachren, John, Merchant Tailor, 130 Queen St.
M'Elmoyle, William, Grocer, 24 King St.
M'Even, William, Custom House Officer, 2 St. Philip's St.
M'Faith, Eliza, Shop, 51 Elliott St.
M'Farlan, J., Merchant, at Carolina Coffee House
M'Farlane, Catharine, Shop, 43 Hasell St.
M'Farlane, James, Carpenter, 243 Meeting St.
M'Farlane, Mary, 161 Church St.
M'Gann, Patrick, Watchmaker, 251 E. Bay St.
M'Gillivray, Alexander H., Vendue Master, 17 Lynch's Ln., Counting House, 2 Exchange Al.
M'Ginness, Patrick, Cooper, Fitzsimons' Whf.
M'Gowan, Thomas, 87 Queen St.
M'Grath & Jones, Merchants, Lothrop's Whf.
M'Grath, John, Carpenter, 154 E. Bay St.
M'Grath, Michael, Merchant, 156 E. Bay St
M'Gregor, Jane, Widow, Vanderhorst St.
M'Guffy, A., Merchant, House, 264 E. Bay St.
M'Intosh, John, Capt., Mariner, 56 Anson St.
M'Intosh, Milly, 5 Swinton's Ln.
M'Kay, George, 2 Parsonage Ln.
M'Kee, J., Bricklayer, 378 King St.
M'Kenley, John, Mariner, 164 Church St.
M'Kenzie, Ann, Widow, Nassau St., Hampstead
M'Kenzie, Eliza, Widow, 15 Guignard St.
M'Kenzie, Hannah, 61 Queen St.
M'Kernan, Ann, 106 Queen St.
M'Kimmey, Clara, 21 Anson St.
M'Kimmey, Clarissa, 122 Wentworth St.
M'Kimmey, Ludlow & Co., Merchants, Lothrop's Whf.
M'Kinney, Christopher, Factor, Blake's Whf.
M'Kinsey, Henrietta, 21 King St.
M'Lachlan, Archibald, Mariner, 4 Pinckney St.
M'Lachlin, P., Capt., Mariner, 2 Pinckney St.
M'Lachlin, Smith & Co., Merchants, 4 Tradd St.
M'Lane, Margaret, Grainshop, 204 King St

M'Lean, Andrew, 5 Friend St.
M'Lochlan, Thomas, Grocer, 7 Berresford St.
M'Millan, John, Tavern, 212 King St.
M'Millan, Richard, Wagon Yard, 214 King St.
M'Namara & Craig, Vendue Masters, 4 Vendue Range
M'Namee, James, Bootmaker, 47 Church St.
M'Neil, Neil, & Co., Grocers, 102 Broad St.
M'Neil, S., Merchant, 264 E. Bay St.
M'Neill, Daniel, Capt., Mariner, 22 Montague St., Merchant, 264 E. Bay St.
M'Nellage & Byrne, Sail Makers, Bailey's Whf.
M'Nellage, William, Coach Maker, 43 Wentworth St
M'Nish, Henry, Planter, 24 Friend St.
M'Owen & Trescot, Vendue Masters, 15 Vendue Range
M'Owen, Patrick, Vendue Master, 386 King St.
M'Pherson, Duncan, 79 King St.
M'Pherson, -----, Mrs., Widow of the Gen., 77 Broad St.
M'Pherson, Peter, Tallow Chandler, Cannonborough.
M'Vicar, Archibald, Butcher, Hampstead
Mead, James, Grocer, 5 Hasell St.
Mease, C. B., Merchant, 73 King St.
Meed & Wheeler, Proprietors, Merchants Hotel, 73 E. Bay St.
Meed, William, at the Merchants Hotel
Meetwarp, E. W., Grocer, 21 Boundary St.
Meetze, Jacob, Grocer, 13 Mazyck St.
Melhado, Benjamin, 17 King St
Menud, John, Planter, 133 E. Bay St.
Mercier, Mathew, Grocer, 40 Pinckney St.
Mercier, -----, Mrs., Widow of Capt., Mazyckborough
Merritt, James H., 120 Tradd St.
Merritt, William, 120 Tradd St.
Messervey, Philip, Capt., Mariner, 4 Longitude Ln.
Mey, C. & H., Merchants, Mey's Whf.
Mey, Charles, Merchant & Wharf Owner, 201 E. Bay St.
Mey, F. C , Merchant & Wharf Owner, 51 Pinckney St.
Michael, Henry, Horse Dealer, 15 Mazyck St.
Michel, John, Merchant, 8 Tradd St.
Michell, Mary, Widow, 16 Coming St.
Middleton, Arthur, Planter, 21 Meeting St.
Middleton, Henry, Planter, 1 Meeting St.
Middleton, John, Planter, 41 George St.
Middleton, Mary, Widow, 90 Queen St.
Middleton, Solomon, Tailor, 247 King St
Milbury, A., Boarding House, 108 Broad St., Above Stairs
Miles, Ann B., Widow, 1 Legare St.
Mill, John, Book & Stationery Store, 108 Broad St.
Millar, Andrew, Accountant, 102 E. Bay St.
Miller, Ann, Widow of John David, 11 Middle St.
Miller, Benjamin, Butcher, E Side King St. Rd.
Miller, Catharine, Widow, 23 Society St.
Miller, David, Tanner, W Side St. Philip's St Cont'd.
Miller, Eliza, 11 Society St.
Miller, Eliza, Pastry Cook, 5 Short St.
Miller, Ezra L., Merchant, 218 E. Bay St.
Miller, Frederick, Butcher, E. Side King St. Rd.
Miller, George, Boarding House, 58 Elliott St.
Miller, George, Merchant, E. Side King St Rd.
Miller, James A., Custom House Officer, 2 Clifford St.
Miller, James, Jr., Merchant, 59 Anson St., Counting

18

House, Chisolm's N. Whf.
Miller, James, Merchant, 52 Anson St., Counting House, Chisolm's Whf.
Miller, Jane, Baker, 78 Meeting St.
Miller, Job P., Bricklayer, 351 King St.
Miller, John, 11 Society St.
Miller, Lydia, 33 St. Philip's St.
Miller, M. & Co., Liquor Store, Bailey's Whf.
Miller, Mary, Grain Shop, 24 Archdale St.
Miller, Matthew, Jeweller, 326 King St.
Miller, P. & Co., Dry Goods Store, 135 King St.
Miller, William, Tailor, 108 Queen St.
Milligan, Lucia, 19 Philadelphia St.
Millikin & Primrose, Vendue Masters, Vendue Range
Mills, E., Rev. Mr., E. Side King St. Rd.
Mills, Mary, School Mistress, Orphan House
Mills, Rebecca, Widow of William, 202 E. Bay St.
Minott, William B., Planter, 4 Gibbes St.
Miott, Charles Henry, Carpenter, Vanderhorst St.
Mishaw, John, Grocer, 122 E. Bay St.
Misroon & Timmons, Vendue Masters, 8 Vendue Range
Missroon, James, Vendue Master, 279 E. Bay St.
Mitchell, Alexander, Saddler, 32 Wentworth St.
Mitchell, Andrew, Plasterer, 12 Bottle Al.
Mitchell, Ann, Widow of Thomas, 43 Society St.
Mitchell, Ann, Widow of John, 242 Meeting St.
Mitchell, James, Blockmaker, 119 Wentworth St.
Mitchell, James, Cooper, 49 E. Bay St., Shop, 57 Elliott St.
Mitchell, James D., Ordinary, Charleston District, 71 Wentworth St.
Mitchell, John, Fiddler, 111 Wentworth St.
Mitchell, John H., Quorum Unis & Notary Public, 17 Guignard St., Office, 250 E. Bay St.
Mitchell, John, Jeweller, 168 Meeting St.
Mitchell, John, Mariner, 3 Pitt St.
Mitchell, Peter, Hatter, 208 King St.
Mitchell ----, Printer, 14 Society St.
Mitchell, Sarah, Tavern, 12 Bedon's Al.
Moderen, James, Capt., Mariner, 120 Tradd St.
Moderen, -----, Mrs., Boarding House, 120 Tradd St.
Moffett & Spears, Dry Goods Store, 316 King St.
Moir, William, E. Side Meeting St. Rd.
Moise, Aaron, Dry Goods Store, 234 King St.
Moise, Cherry, Vendue Master, House, 25 Society St., Counting House, 5 Vendue Range
Moise, Rodrigues M., 6 St. Michael's Al.
Moise, Sarah, Widow, 89 Tradd St.
Moison, John, Gunsmith, W. Side State St.
Moles, James, 200 King St.
Moles, Margaret, Dry Goods Store, 218 King St
Moles, -----, Mrs., Milliner, 200 King St.
Moll, John, Grocer, W Side Washington St., Mazyckborough
Moncrieffe, A., Widow of John, 129 E Bay St.
Moncrieffe, John, Merchant, 9 Meeting St.
Monies, Hugh, Merchant, Counting House, 46 Elliott St., House, 264 E. Bay St.
Monnar, Lewis, Hair Dresser, Shop, 2 Queen St., House, 7 Queen St.
Monpoy, H , Grocer, 6 Rutledge St.

Montang, F., Tailor, W. Side King St. Rd.
Montesquieu, R., Tinman, 184 Meeting St
Monyfeldt, -----, Mrs., Shop, 42 Market St.
Mood, -----, Mrs., Ladies School, 133 Meeting St
Mood, Peter & Son, Goldsmith, 318 King St.
Moodie, Benjamin, British Consul, 6 Short St.
Mooney, Ann, Dry Goods Store, 132 King St.
Mooney, Patrick, 1 Orange St.
Moore, James, Carpetenter, W. Side Meeting St. Rd.
Moore, John, 10 Smith's Ln.
Moore, Mary, Dry Goods Store, 119 King St.
Moore, -----, Mrs., Widow of John E., 102 Wentworth St.
Moore, Philip, Lumber Sawyer, 10 Bull St.
Moore, Richard, Painter & Glazier, 54 Wentworth St.
Moore, Stephen W., Discount Clerk, Union Bank, 29 St. Philip's St.
Moorhead, Robert & Thomas, Grocers, 40 Tradd St.
Mordecai, David, 126 Church St.
More, J. P., Surgeon & Dentist & Man Midwife, 50 King St.
Morell, Nicolas, Goldsmith, 64 Church St.
Morensen, John, Tailor, 60 Queen St.
Morford, Edward, Book & Stationery Store, 3 Broad St.
Morgan, Benjamin, Mariner, 16 Middle St.
Morgan, Edward, Accountant, 351 King St.
Morgan, Henry, Cooper, Crafts' N. Whf.
Morgan, Isaac, Carpenter, 20 Coming St.
Morgan, Matilda, 4 Wentworth St.
Morgan, -----, Mrs., Widow, 4 Wentworth St.
Morgan, S., Constable & Tavern, 8 Champney St.
Morland, W. B., Shoemaker, Shop, 121 King St., House, 8 Pitt St.
Morrell, Samuel, Tavern, 8 Champney St.
Morris, C. G. & Co., Merchants, Store, 262 E. Bay St., House, 131 Wentworth St.
Morris, Lewis, Planter, 239 Meeting St.
Morris, Simpson, Merchant, 19 Beaufain St.
Morris, Thomas, Jr , Merchant, House, 131 Wentworth St., Counting House, Daniell's Whf.
Morris, Thomas, Notary Public, Office, 261 E. Bay St., House, 131 Wentworth St.
Morrison, James, Cooper, 14 Water St , Shop, 4 Exchange Al.
Morrison, John, Grocer, Elliott St., cr. Bedon's Al.
Morrisson, John, Capt., Mariner, 97 Tradd St.
Mortimer, Edward, Merchant, 24 Anson St.
Morton, Alexander & Co., Grocers, 329 King St.
Morton, Eliza, Widow, 7 Stoll's Al.
Morton, Martha, Shopkeeper, 9 Pitt St.
Mosea, Philip, M.D. & Druggist, 103 Broad St., Res 11 Logan St.
Moses, Eliza, Slopshop, 77 E. Bay St
Moses, Esther, Dry Goods Store, 264 King St.
Moses, I. C., Merchant, 372 King St , Store, 2 Vendue Range
Moses, Israel, Cooper, Gillon St.
Moses, J., Fruiterer, 43 Beaufain St.
Moses, Levy, Dry Goods Store, 261 King St
Moses, Lyon, Broker, 10 Swinton's Ln.
Moses, Myer, Vendue Master, 34 Meeting St., Store, 5

19

Vendue Range
Moses, Philip, Watchmaker, 248 King St
Moses, Solomon, Constable, 277 King St.
Mosiman, J., Watchmaker, 67 E. Bay St.
Motta, Jane, 14 Anson St.
Motte, Abraham, 97 E. Bay St.
Motte, Francis, Factor, House, 152 Church St., Counting
House, Chisolm's N. Whf.
Motte, Mary, Widow of Col , 241 Meeting St.
Mouat, Mary, Widow, 19 Middle St
Moulin, Peter, Dry Goods Store, 350 King St.
Moultrie, Alexander, Attorney, 25 Cumberland St.
Moultrie, James, Jr., M.D., 25 Cumberland St.
Moultrie, James, M.D., 25 Cumberland St.
Mowbray, Martha, Baker, W. Side King St. Rd.
Mowbray, William, W. Side King St. Rd.
Mowzon, Charles, Bootmaker, 59 Church St.
Muck, Philip, Musician, 52 Broad St.
Muckenfuss, Henry, Bricklayer, 75 Wentworth St.
Muckenfuss, -----, Miss, 14 Archdale St.
Muir, -----, Mrs., Widow of William, 96 E. Bay St.
Muir, William & Co., Vendue Masters, Vendue Range
Muirhead, -----, Merchant, 22 Tradd St.
Mulligan, Barnard, Dry Goods Store, 178 King St.
Mulligan, Francis, Farmer, W. Side King St. Rd.
Mulvey, Charles, Spanish Consul, 60 Broad St.
Munch, Dorothy, Grocer, 2 Champney St.
Munds, I., Rev., School, W. Side State St.
Munro, C., Midwife, 35 Society St.
Munro, -----, Mrs., Boarding House, 36 Church St.
Murden, Jeremiah, Merchant, 10 Stoll's Al., Counting
House, Blake's Whf.
Murley, Samuel, Merchant, Charlotte St., Mazyckborough,
Counting House, Martin's Whf.
Murphy, Peter, Grocer, 279 King St.
Murphy, Sarah, Grocer, 34 Church St.
Murray, -----, Mrs., School, 9 George St.
Murrell, John N., Goldsmith, 26 Guignard St
Murrell, Martha, Shop, 14 Boundary St.
Mushett, John, Blacksmith, House, 72 Meeting St., Shop,
14 Ellery St.
Mussault, M , Widow, 12 Middle St.
Myer, John, Grocer, 256 King St.
Myers, L , M.D , 83 Tradd St
Mynott, Baxter O., Shoe Shore, 45 Church St.
Myot, Alexander, Merchant, Wolf St., Hampstead
Myot, Edward, Boat Builder, 4 Hard Al.
Naested, Frederick, Store, 306 King St.
Napier, Thomas & Co., Vendue Masters, 10 Vendue
Range
Napier, Thomas, Vendue Master, 105 Broad St., Above
Stairs
Narche, Francis, Shoemaker, 198 E. Bay St.
Naser, Ann, Warren St., Ratcliffeborough
Nathan, Henry, Dry Goods Store, 188 King St.
Nathan, Moses, Grocer, 131 Tradd St.
Neaton, J., Dry Goods Store, 325 King St.
Neele, Joseph, French Al
Neilson, George, Grocer, 11 S. Bay St.
Neilson, James S., Attorney at the Prothonotary's Office

Nell, Jesse, Roper Maker, 21 Mazyck St
Nelson, Christopher, Grocer, W. Side State St.
Nelson, R., Grocer, 15 Chalmers Al.
Nesbett, Abbey, Widow of Alexander, 142 Meeting St.
Netsell, John, Confectioner, 126 King St.
Neufville, Ann, Widow of William, 7 Parsonage Ln.
Neufville, Isaac, 39 Anson St.
Nevill, John, Grocer, 3 Magazine St
Neville, Joshua, Cabinet Maker, 322 King St
Newman, Charles, Tavern, 222 Meeting St.
Newton, Anthony, Butcher, Cannon St., Cannonborough
Newton, C., Fruiterer, 148 Church St.
Newton, Mary, Cannon St., Cannonborough
Neyle, -----, Mrs., Nurse, 367 King St.
Nicholls, Eliza, Widow, W. Side Cannon's Bridge Rd.
Nicholls, Richard, Shoemaker, 41 St Philip's St.
Nicholson, James, Attorney, E. Side Cannon's Bridge Rd.
Noisette, J. Farmer, E. Side King St Rd.
Nobbs, Samuel, Justice of Peace, Office, 67 Market St.,
House, E. Side St. Philip's St. Cont'd.
Noble, John, M.D , 179 King St.
Nolen, James, Carpenter, 3 Back St
Norman & Jones, Grocers, 12 Tradd St.
Norroy, John, Tobacconist, 13 George St.
North & Webb, Factors, Chisolm's Whf.
North, Richard B., Factor, 6 Adams St.
Norton, Catharine, 5 Smith's Ln.
Norton, John, of New York, 28 Tradd St.
Nowell, John, Cashier, Union Bank, 2 Berresford St.
Nowell, Thomas, Discount Officer, S.C Bank, 8 Anson St
Nugent, Margaret, 11 King St.
O'Conner, John, School, 26 Ellery St.
O'Driscoll, Dennis, Attorney, 8 George St.
O'Driscoll, Mathew, M D , 8 George St.
O'Driscoll, -----, Mrs., Widow of Capt., 81 Tradd St.
O'Hara, Charles, Merchant, 9 Smith's Ln
O'Hara, Daniel, Merchant, 390 King St
O'Hear, James, Planter, 1 Smith St.
Oates, John, Grocer, 81 E. Bay St.
Oelands, John, Dry Goods Store, 231 King St
Ogden, G. W., Tailor, 69 E. Bay St.
Ogden, Robert, Attorney, 112 Church St., House, W. End
Boundary St.
Ogier, John M., Clerk, Union Bank, 75 Tradd St
Ogier, Lewis, Factor, House, Tradd St., Counting House,
Crafts' S. Whf.
Ogier, Thomas, Factor
Ogilvie, -----, Mr , 23 Mazyck St.
Ohlweiller, Michael, Grocer, 35 Market St.
Oleron, ----, 117 Church St.
Olevier, F., W. Side King St. Rd.
Oliphant, David, Painter, 149 Meeting St
Oliver, James, Mason, E. Side King St. Rd.
Orawe, John, Grocer, 74 Meeting St.
Oring, Magnus, Mariner, 1 Wentworth St.
Orr, Mary Ann, Seamstress, 1 Amen St.
Osborne & Waring, Factors, Counting House, Chisolm's
N. Whf.
Osborne, Catherine, Widow of Thomas, 5 S. Bay St.
Osborne, Richard, Factor, 5 S. Bay St.

Osborne, Samuel, Saddler, 217 King St.
O'Hara, Charles & Henry, Merchants, 23 E. Bay St.
O'Neal, James, Carpenter, 8 Magazine St.
O'Sullivan, Charles, Painter, 15 Broad St.
Page, J. W., Keeper, Carolina Coffee House, 122 Tradd St
Palmer, Edward, Master of Free School, 24 Cumberland St.
Palmer, Job, Clerk, Independent Church, 98 Wentworth St.
Palmer, -----, Mrs., School for Young Ladies, 10 Meeting St.
Palmer, -----, Rev. Dr., Pastor, Independent Church, 49 Tradd St.
Palmer, -----, Sergeant of City Guard, 27 Meeting St.
Paque, Francis G , 38 St. Philip's St.
Parker & Osgood, Grocers, 129 Tradd St.
Parker, Ann, Dry Goods Store, 285 King St
Parker, Eliza, Widow, 5 Back St.
Parker, Florida, 4 Blackbird Al.
Parker, Isaac, Planter, 7 Legare St.
Parker, John, Planter, 13 Pitt St.
Parker, Martha, Widow, Coming St. Cont'd.
Parker, Mary, Seamstress, 9 Parsonage Ln.
Parker, -----, Mrs., Widow of Dr. William, 57 Broad St.
Parker, Samuel, 43 George St.
Parker, Thomas, City Guard Man, 24 Berresford St.
Parker, Thomas, U. S. Attorney for S.C., 32 Meeting St.
Parkinson & Baker, Grocers, 177 Meeting St.
Parks & Duke, W. Side King St. Rd.
Parsons, J. D., Teacher, E. Side King St. Rd.
Passelaigue, L., Grocer, 7 Maiden Ln.
Patrick, Philip, Merchant, 182 King St.
Patterson, Hugh, Secretary, Union Insurance Co., 4 Laurens St.
Patterson, Samuel, Factor, 46 Hasell St.
Patton, -----, Mrs., Liquor House, 68 King St.
Patton, William, Merchant, 245 E. Bay St.
Paujaud, Augustus, Merchant, 8 Tradd St.
Paul, Isaac, 163 Church St.
Paxton, Henry, Factor, House, 70 Queen St., Counting House, W. End S. Bay St
Payenneville, E., Shopkeeper, 9 Wall St.
Payne & Son, Vendue Masters, 110 Broad St., Auction Office, N.E. cr. Exchange
Payne, Laetitia, Widow of Capt., Hampstead
Payne, -----, Lt., U. S. Navy, 12 Hasell St.
Payne, Thomas, Harbor Master, 12 Hasell St.
Payne, W R., Marble Mason, 41 St. Philip's St.
Peak, -----, Mrs., Widow of John, 24 George St.
Peake, John Samuel, Merchant, 230 Meeting St.
Pearce E., Accountant, 2 Stolls Al
Pearce, Richard, Shoe Store, 286 King St.
Pearson, Catharine, 21 Friend St.
Peigne, J. L., Grocer, 55 Market St.
Peigne, Lewis, 6 Berresford St.
Pelzer, Anthony, Classical Academy, 7 Archdale St.
Pemble, David, Merchant Tailor, 98 E. Bay St.
Pennall, James, Merchant, W. Side King St. Rd.
Pepoon, B. F , Attorney, 15 Queen St , Office, 36 Meeting St.
Pepoon, Benjamin, Grocery & Grain Store, 85 E Bay St.,

House, 15 Queen St.
Pepoon, Joseph, Grocer, 25 Chalmers Al.
Percy, William, Rev. Dr., 80 Tradd St.
Perdriau, Isabel B., School, 4 Maiden Ln.
Perdriau, Peter, Carpenter, 4 Maiden Ln.
Perman, George, Grocer, 36 E Bay St.
Peronneau, Catharine, 59 Wentworth St.
Peronneau, H William, Planter, 4 S Bay St
Peronneau, Henry, Attorney, 4 S. Bay St.
Perry, Isabella, Midwife, 102 Queen St.
Perry, James, 158 Church St.
Perry, -----, Mrs., Widow, 13 Bull St.
Perry, W. S., Tailor, 335 King St.
Petch, Julius, Bookbinder, 20 Magazine St.
Peter, George, School Master, 21 George St.
Peter, John, Mrs., 21 Pinckney St
Peter, Mary, Widow, 61 Broad St
Peter, V., Grocer, 23 Church St.
Peterson & Co., Grocers, 77 Tradd St.
Peterson, John E., Butcher, W. Side King St. Rd
Petit, Felicity, Widow, 13 Wentworth St.
Petray, L. A., Merchant, E. Side King St. Rd.
Petre, George, Money Collector, 20 Society St.
Petrowich, John, Grocer, 23 State St
Pezant, John L., Grocer, 3 Boundary St.
Pezant, Lewis, Grocer, 197 E. Bay St.
Pezant, P., 29 Wall St.
Phelon, E. M., Grocer, 206 Meeting St.
Philip, Dorothy, Widow, 75 Queen St.
Philipe, John, Grocer, 12 Chalmers Al.
Philips, Aaron, Dry Goods Store, 71 King St.
Philips, Benjamin, Shoemaker, 119 Tradd St.
Philips, John, Capt., Mariner, 12 Pinckney St.
Philips, John, Painter & Glazier, 9 Elliott St.
Phillips, Daniel, Tavern, 100 Church St.
Picault, Francis, Union Coffee House, 123 Queen St.
Pickenpack, John, Clerk, Union Bank
Piere, Peter & Co., Shop, 167 Meeting St.
Pilot, O., Grocer, 267 King St.
Pilott, O., Grocer, E. Side Meeting St. Rd.
Pilsbury, Rebecca, Shop, 118 Meeting St.
Pilsbury, Samuel, Custom House Officer, 9 Anson St.
Pinatt, Francis, Grocer, 12 Market St.
Pincell, William, Tinman, 43 Meeting St.
Pinckney, Betsey, 12 Berresford St.
Pinckney, C. C., Gen., Planter, 118 E. Bay St.
Pinckney, C. C., Jr., Attorney, 86 Wentworth St.
Pinckney, Charles, Planter, 246 Meeting or 2 West St.
Pinckney, -----, Miss, 30 Hasell St.
Pinckney, Roger, Planter, 11 Archdale St
Pinckney, Thomas, Gen., Planter, 14 Legare St.
Pionville, Phiott, 80 Church St.
Plant, Henry, Ship Carpenter, 187 E. Bay St.
Plant, Isabel, Dry Goods Store, 224 King St.
Plissoneau, John, Dry Goods Store, 44 King St.
Plumeau, J. F., Secretary to S.C Insurance Co , 22 Tradd St.
Plumer, -----, Mrs., Widow, Boarding House, Above 54 E Bay St.
Plumet, Anthony, Dry Goods Store, 48 King St

21

Plunkett, Peter, Billiard Table, E. Side of St. Philip's St. Cont'd
Pogson, Milward, Rev., 170 Church St.
Pohl, Elias, Dry Goods Store, 327 King St
Poincignon, P. A., Tinman, 12 Queen St
Pointsett, R. J , E. Side Cannon's Bridge
Pollock, Levy, Dry Goods Store, 163 King St.
Port, Andrew, Fruiterer, 33 Broad St.
Porter, Ben R., Cabinet Maker, 393 King St.
Porter, John, Saddler, 189 King St
Porter, Peter, Grocer, 10 Church St.
Porter, William, Office, Scrivener, 92 E. Bay St
Postell, William, Planter, E. Side Anson St., Mazyckborough
Potter, John, Merchant, Counting House, 19 Broad St., House, 33 Society St.
Potter, Washington, Merchant, 33 E. Bay St., Counting House, Vanderhorst's Whf.
Poulnot, N., Bootmaker, 120 Queen St.
Poulton, Edward, 130 Church St.
Powell, John, Butcher, W Side St. Philip's St. Cont'd.
Powell, John, Carpenter, 135 E. Bay St
Power, Edward, Ship Chandler, 217 E. Bay St.
Powers, J., House Painter, 130 King St
Poyas, E. John, Planter, 26 Meeting St.
Poyas, James, Shipwright, 26 Meeting St., Yard, W End S. Bay St.
Pranninger, E., Cannon St , Cannonborough
Pratt, John, Capt., Mariner, 3 Laurens St.
Prentice, & Parker, Merchants, Res. Planter's Hotel, Store 124 Tradd St.
Prescott, G. W., Merchant, 1 Martin's Whf.
Pressley, -----, Miss, Hampstead
Preyle, J F., Watchmaker, 192 Meeting St.
Pribble, Mary, Boarding House, 50 Church St.
Price, Charlotte, E Side Cannon's Bridge Rd
Price, Thomas W., Planter, 39 George St.
Price, William, Jr., Attorney, Office, 5 St Michael's Al., House, 39 George St.
Price, William, Planter, 2 Orange St
Prieur, V., Widow, 102 Church St.
Prieur, Vieuse, Confectioner
Primerose, Robert, Vendue Master, 167 E. Bay St.
Prince, Charles, Lamplighter & Tinman, 344 King St
Prince, John, Porter, Planters' and Mechanics' Bank, 12 Guignard St.
Prince, Joseph P., Cooper, E. Side King St. Rd.
Pringle, J. R., Planter, 77 Broad St.
Pringle, John J., Counsellor at Law, 101 Tradd St.
Pringle, -----, Miss, 98 Tradd St.
Prioleau & Pinckney, Counsellors at Law, 111 Church St
Prioleau, Elizabeth, Miss, 248 Meeting St.
Prioleau, Jane, Widow, School, 24 Ellery St.
Prioleau, John C., Planter, 226 Meeting St.
Prioleau, -----, Mrs., Widow of Philip, 88 Queen St.
Prioleau, -----, Mrs., Widow of Samuel, 141 Meeting St.
Prioleau, P G., M.D., 141 Meeting St.
Prioleau, Samuel, Counsellor at Law, 28 Bull St.
Prioleau, T. G , M.D., 88 Queen St.
Pritchard & Shrewsbury, Shipwrights

Pritchard, Joseph, Accountant, 62 King St.
Pritchard, -----, Mrs., Widow of Paul, W Side St. Philip's St Cont'd.
Pritchard, Paul, Shipwright, 44 Hasell St.
Pritchard, William, Jr., Shipwright, 2 Anson St.
Pritchard, William, Shipwright, 1 Pinckney St.
Probst, A. H., Tinman, 160 King St.
Procter, John, Horse Dealer, 132 Meeting St
Purcell, Ann, Widow of Joseph, 4 Queen St.
Purse, Thomas, Watchmaker, 7 Liberty St
Purse, William, Watchmaker, 96 Broad St.
Purvis, William, Merchant, Hampstead
Puyot, Charlotte L., 38 Tradd St.
Pyne, Honoria, Mrs., Widow, 27 Church St.
Quan, Robert, Accountant, 90 Church St.
Quash, Robert, Planter, 73 Broad St.
Querard, Henry, Accountant, 7 Hasell St.
Query, Thomas, Book Binder, Smith's Court
Quiggins, Mary, Widow, 39 St. Philip's St.
Quin, Thomas, Grocer, 121 Meeting St.
Quinby, Joseph, Grocer, 6 Pinckney St.
Quinlan, Michael, Dry Goods Store, 299 King St.
Rade, J. C., M.D. & Druggist, W. Side King St. Rd.
Raine, John, Merchant, E. Side Meeting St. Rd.
Rainey, Ann, 5 Meeting St.
Ramsay, David, Attorney, 87 Broad St
Ramsay, John, M.D., 1 Anson St.
Ramsay, -----, Miss, 87 Broad St.
Ranall, James, Factor, S. Cellar of Exchange
Randall, Ann, 1 West St.
Rantin, William, Baker, 199 King St.
Ranzier, John, 160 Church St.
Ratcliffe, J. W., Tailor, 92 Broad St.
Ratcliffe, John, Tailor, 10 Cumberland St.
Ratcliffe, L. C., Widow of Thomas, 38 George St.
Ravenel & Stevens, Factors, Vanderhorst's Whf
Ravenel, Daniel, Attorney, 94 Broad St.
Ravenel, John, 94 Broad St.
Ravey, L., 7 Philadelphia St.
Rawlinson, Thomas W , Merchant, 256 E. Bay St
Raworth, G. F., Harness Maker, 85 Meeting St.
Raworth, George, Saddler, 8 Liberty St.
Ray, P., Comb Maker, 125 King St.
Read & Horsey, Shoe Store, 256 King St.
Read, A., Watch Maker, 77 E. Bay St.
Read, Jacob, Planter, 10 Montague St.
Read, John H., Planter, 103 E. Bay St.
Read, William, Planter, 103 E. Bay St.
Rechon, L. & C., Sail Makers, Fitzsimons' Whf
Rechon, Lewis, Tailor, 124 King St
Reeves, Abraham, House Carpenter, Shop, 69 Church St.
Reeves, Aeneas, Master of Work House, 4 Magazine St
Reid, Ann, Widow of George, 29 E. Bay St.
Reid, George, Transfer Clerk, Bank of S. C., 29 E. Bay St
Reid, John, Shoe Store, 69 King St.
Reid, John, Wheelwright, 196 Meeting St.
Reid, -----, Miss, W. Side Meeting St. Rd.
Reid, Moultrie, Clerk, Post Office, 29 E. Bay St
Reigne, John, Baker & Grocer, 105 E. Bay St.
Reilly, George, Tavern, 216 Meeting St.

Reilly, James, Saddler, 97 Church St
Reilly, Robert, Clerk, 18 Mazyck St.
Remington, Sarah, Cannon St., Cannonborough
Remousins, -----, Messrs., Music Masters, 44 Beaufain St
Renauld, John, Grocer, 84 Church St.
Revell, Hannah, Widow, 48 Anson St.
Reynolds, George, Coach Maker, Shop, 193 Meeting St.,
  House, 64 Meeting St.
Rhind, E., Widow, 67 Wentworth St.
Rhodes, J., Factor, 30 E Bay St.
Rhodes, -----, Mrs , Widow, 19 Coming St.
Rhodus, John, Butcher, 8 Rutledge St.
Ricard, Francis, Grocer, 53 E. Bay St.
Richard, L., M.D , 2 Hasell St.
Richards, Frederick, Bricklayer, 14 Coming St.
Richards, Henry, Grocer, 60 Meeting St.
Richardson & Bennett, Counsellors at Law, 1 Court House
  Sq.
Richardson, J. S., State Attorney General, 1 Court House
  Sq.
Richardson, James, Mariner, 7 Bull St.
Riggs, Maria, Milliner, 120 King St.
Righton, Eliza, 3 Water St.
Righton, Joseph, Cooper, 2 Water St.
Righton, -----, Mrs., Widow of M., 46 E. Bay St., Upstairs
Rignier, P. J., 7 Cumberland St.
Rindell, Eli, Liquor House, 49 Queen St.
Ring, D A., Painter & Glazier Shop, 55 Elliott St., House,
  29 Meeting St.
Ritter, Daniel, Grocer, 57 Market St.
Rivers, Francis, 1 Stoll's Al.
Rivers, George, Planter, 1 Legare St.
Rivers, George W., 8 S. Bay St.
Rivers, John, Grocer, 22 Church St.
Rivers, Mary G., Widow, 19 Meeting St.
Rivers, Samuel, Boatbuilder, 6 Water St
Rivers, Thomas, 1 Whim Court
Rivers, Thomas, 118 Wentworth St
Riviere, John P., Fruit Shop, 204 Meeting St.
Roach, John, Grocer, 101 Church St
Roach, Nash, Teller, Planters' & Mechanics' Bank, End
  Boundary St.
Roach, William, City Treasurer, 3 Society St.
Roach, William, Jr , Clerk to Commissioners of Streets &
  Lamps, 3 Society St., Office, 2nd Floor of Exchange
Robbins, Elijah, Grocer, 68 Market St.
Roberts, Francis, Saddler, 131 King St.
Roberts, R., Mrs., 114 Wentworth St.
Robertson, Francis, Factor, 6 Champney St.
Robertson, John, Merchant, 16 Meeting St., Counting
  House, 8 Crafts' Whf.
Robertson, S , Merchant, 202 King St
Robertson, Sylvia, 16 Parsonage Ln.
Robinson & Patton, Merchants, 6 Crafts' S. Whf.
Robinson, Harriet, 8 Logan St.
Robinson, John, Merchant, Store, W. Side King St. Rd.,
  House, St. Philip's St. Cont'd.
Robinson, Philip, Merchant & Portuguse Consul, House,
  Tradd St., Office, 6 Crafts' S. Whf.
Robinson, William, Tavern, 11 Bedon's Al.

Robiou, Charles, Cotton Presses, Lothrop's Whf.
Robiou, Charles, Merchant, W. Side King St. Rd.
Robiou, Eliza, Widow, 16 Cumberland St.
Roddy, James, Merchant, 149 E. Bay St., Counting House,
  6 Exchange St.
Roderick, Anthony, Sergeant, City Guard
Rodthert, E. A. P., Grocer, 33 Archdale St.
Rogers, A., Shoemaker, 8 Water St.
Rogers, Christopher, 23 Tradd St.
Rogers, Eliza, Widow, 134 Meeting St
Rogers, Joe, Shoemaker, 14 Philadelphia St.
Rogers, John B., Clerk, 74 Wentworth St.
Rogers, John R., 145 Church St.
Rogers, Maria, 113 Tradd St.
Rogers, -----, Mrs. Boarding House, 74 Wentworth St.
Rogers, Sarah, Widow, 145 Church St.
Roh, Jacob, Blacksmith, 59 Meeting St.
Rohmer, John, Billiard Table, 70 Church St.
Romayne, M., 63 Church St.
Roper, T. W., M.D., 89 E Bay St.
Roper, Thomas, Planter, 89 E. Bay St.
Roper, William, 22 E. Bay St.
Rose & Rogers, Merchants, 60 E. Bay St.
Rose, Arthur G., 15 St Philip's St.
Rose, Christian, Grocer, 10 S. Bay St.
Rose, George, Merchant, 46 Meeting St.
Rose, H. A., 15 St. Philip's St.
Rose, Henry, Merchant, Counting House, Bailey's Whf.,
  House, 254 King St.
Rose, Hugh, Planter, 245 Meeting St.
Rose, John, Merchant, 264 E. Bay St
Rose, John S., Accountant, 16 George St.
Rose, P., Mrs., Milliner, 254 King St.
Ross, A. E. & Co , Merchants & Wagon Yard, E Side
  King St. Rd.
Ross, Ann, Widow of Capt., 2 Liberty St.
Ross, Daniel, 65 Tradd St.
Ross, John, Grocer, 38 E. Bay St.
Rostant, Stephen, Baker, 126 King St.
Rotureau, Charles, Barber, 121 King St.
Roulain, -----, Capt., Shop, 42 Queen St.
Roulain, Catharine, 22 Berresford St.
Roulain, Robert, Mason, 42 George St.
Rouse, William, Tanner, 37 Market St., Tan Yard,
  Mazyckborough
Rout, C., Widow, 19 Friend St.
Roux, Lewis, Notary Public, 58 E. Bay St
Rowand, Charles E., Planter, 2 Friend St.
Rowand, Robert, Planter, 48 Meeting St.
Ruberry, John, House Carpenter, 4 Anson St.
Ruberry, -----, Mrs., Widow, 70 Tradd St.
Ruddock, Samuel, Surveyor, 20 King St.
Rush, Joseph, M.D., 397 King St.
Russ, Ben, House Carpenter, 3 Maiden Ln
Russell, Daniel H., Carpenter, 4 Anson St.
Russell, John, Livery Stables, 2 Bank Sq.
Russell, John, Shop, Blacksmith, 179 E. Bay St., House,
  124 Wentworth St.
Russell, Margaret, Widow, 34 George St.
Russell, -----, Mrs., Widow of Benjamin, 35 Guignard St

23

Russell, Nathaniel, Merchant, 21 Meeting St.
Rutledge, Charles, M D., 12 Rutledge St.
Rutledge, Frederick, Planter, 60 Tradd St.
Rutledge, Jane, Widow of Edward, 109 Tradd St
Rutledge, John, Planter, 102 Meeting St
Rutledge, Sarah, 17 St. Philip's St
Rutledge, States, Planter, 155 E. Bay St.
Rutledge, William, 1 George St.
Ryan, John, Merchant, 90 E. Bay St.
Ryan, Lawrence, Attorney, 8 Bull St.
Ryan, P. T., Merchant, 90 E. Bay St.
Ryley, -----, Mrs., Boarding House, 226 E. Bay St.,
Upstairs
Safford, -----, Capt , Mariner, 45 Society St
Saltar, Thomas R., Shipjoiner, House, 38 Guignard St.
Salter, Thomas R., Shop, Pritchard's Whf.
Saltus & Son, Factors, Vanderhorst's Whf.
Saltus, Francis, 398 King St.
Samory, C. N., Mattress Store, 111 Queen St.
Sampson, S. & Co., Boarding House, 56 Elliott St
Sanders, Sarah, 229 Meeting St.
Sandford, John, Grocer, 110 E. Bay St.
Sandoz, John F., Watchmaker, 42 Meeting St.
Sarazin, ----, Miss, 56 Wentworth St.
Sargent, John H., Homme de Loi, 41 Queen St.
Sarzedas, David, Jr., Vendue Master, Vendue Range,
House, W. Side State St.
Sarzedas, David, M.D., W. Side State St.
Sasportas, Abraham, 64 Broad St., Counting House, 15
Queen St., Merchant
Sass & Gready, Northern Warehouse, 61 King St.
Sass, Jacob, Cabinet Maker, 39 Queen St.
Satorius, Thomas, Grocer, 384 King St.
Savage, Ann, Milliner, 88 King St., Seed Store, 315 King
St.
Savage, Martha, Widow, 2 Savage St.
Savage, Peter, Button Mould Maker, 369 King St
Savage, Samuel, Cannon St., Cannonborough
Sax, Henry, Grocer, 86 Church St.
Schenk & Turner, Stationers, 13 Broad St.
Schirer, John, Gunsmith, 188 Meeting St.
Schirmer, John E., Cooper, 100 Queen St., Shop, 6
Exchange St.
Schmidt, John, M D., 3 Bedon's Al.
Schnell, John J., Grocer, 74 Church St.
Schnierle, H., Carpenter, 6 Friend St
Schovel, George, 14 Montague St.
Schrively, George, Seed Store, 137 Meeting St.
Schrobell, John, Overseer of the Neck Roads, W. Side
King St. Rd.
Schroeder, John, Grocer, 39 Hasell St.
Schultz, Charles, Grocer, E Side State St.
Schulz, John, Factor, 169 Church St., Counting House,
Fitzsimons' Whf.
Schutt, Lewis H. C., 26 E. Bay St.
Schwartz, John, Grocer, 149 Church St.
Scott, James, Merchant, 107 Meeting St.
Scott, Thomas, 126 Tradd St., Upstairs
Scott, William, Jailor, Charleston District
Scott, William, Jr., Meeting St. Rd.

Scott, William M., Broker, 88 E. Bay St , House, 4
Pinckney St.
Screven, Amarintha, Widow, 137 Church St.
Screven, Thomas, Planter, W. Side Cannon's Bridge Rd
Scriven, Rebecca, 12 Lynch's Ln.
Scwarch, Frederick, Butcher, W. Side Cannon's Bridge Rd
Seabrook, Thomas B., Planter, 10 Rutledge St.
Seaver, Abraham, House Carpenter, 42 Pinckney St.
Seavey, Catherine, Wagon Yard & Grocery, W. Side King
St. Rd.
Secress, M., Capt. Mariner, 24 State St.
Secress, -----, Mrs., Boarding House, 24 State St.
Seixias, Abigail, Fruiterer, 346 King St
Seixias, Isaac, Fruiterer, 340 King St
Selby, C , Drayman, 12 Swinton's Ln.
Semontain, Charles S. & Co , Merchants, King St Rd.
Senet, John S., Blacksmith, E. Side State St
Senet, Joseph, Shop, Blacksmith, 132 Queen St.
Senter, Anthony, Rev. of the Methodist Church, 12 Pitt St.
Serjeant, P., Capt., Mariner, 10 Blackbird Al.
Seyle, S., Saddler, 289 King St.
Seyler, P., Fruiterer, 215 King St.
Seymour, S., Pastry Cook, 91 Tradd St.
Shaffer, Charles George, Printer, 186 E. Bay St.
Shand, Robert, Custom House Officer, 14 Pinckney St.
Sharp, John, Block Maker, 15 Maiden Ln., Shop, 73
Market St.
Shaw, William D., Merchant, 240 E. Bay St.
Shea, Richard, Tavern, 8 Elliott St.
Shecut, J. L. E. W., Druggist, 337 King St.
Sheirer, Mary, Boarding House, 1 Bedon's Al.
Shepherd, James, Harness Maker, 34 Coming St
Sheppard, James, Saddler, 313 King St.
Sheppard, Thomas R., Planter, W. Side King St Rd.
Shepperd, Matilda, Cannon St., Cannonborough
Shirer, John, House Carpenter, 26 Archdale St.
Shirving, Bethia, Widow of William, 2 Orange St.
Shoolbred, James, Planter, 12 Lamboll St.
Shorthouse, Thomas, Merchant, 6 Hasell St., Counting
House, 220 E. Bay St.
Shoulters, A., Blacksmith, E. Bay St., near Battery, House,
Lynch's Ln.
Shrewsbury, Jeremiah, Carpenter, 13 Guignard St.
Shubrick, -----, Mrs , Widow of Thomas, at Belvidere
Mills
Sibley, B. R., Grocer, 1 Boundary St.
Sibley, Joseph, Blockmaker, Gillon St.
Sibley, Joseph, Merchant, 189 E. Bay St., Store, Bailey's
Whf.
Sibley, Joseph N., Grocer, E End Boundary St.
Sifley & Mintzing, Lumber Yard, W. End Queen St.
Signe, John, Barber, 115 E. Bay St.
Sigwald, Thomas, Cabinet Maker, 20 Berresford St.
Simmons, Henry, U. S. Army, 73 Queen St.
Simmons, Joseph, Grocer, 61 E. Bay St.
Simmons, -----, Mrs., Widow of John, 7 New St
Simmons, Ruth, Widow of Francis, 58 Tradd St.
Simmons, William, M.D., 7 New St.
Simmons, William, Tailor, 11 Coming St.
Simons, Anthony, Factor, 45 Wentworth St., Counting

House, Blake's Whf.
Simons, Benjamin B., M.D., 55 Meeting St.
Simons, Edward, Planter, 40 Society St.
Simons, K. & Sons, Factors, Martin's Whf
Simons, K. L., Counsellor at Law, 45 Broad St
Simons, K , Planter, 4 Orange St.
Simons, Maurice, Factor, 1 Middle St.
Simons, -----, Mrs., Widow of Charles D., 6 New St.
Simpson, John, Planter, 66 Tradd St.
Simpson, Lydia, 16 Lynch's Ln.
Simpson, P., Dentist, 202 Meeting St.
Simpson, S., House Carpenter, 94 Church St.
Simpson, William, Planter, 1 Minority St
Sims, William, Planter, Hudson St.
Sims, William, W. Side King St. Rd
Sinclair, Alexander, Merchant, 260 E. Bay St , Res. Carolina Coffee House
Singleton, Benjamin, China Store, 16 Broad St.
Singleton, James, Shopkeeper, 244 King St.
Singleton, Sarah, Widow, 50 Boundary St.
Singleton, Tabitha, 24 Wentworth St.
Sisell, William, Confectioner, W. Side State St.
Sisk, Sarah, 16 Philadelphia St.
Skinner & Whilden, Editors, City Gazette, 244 E. Bay St.
Skinner, Samuel H , At the Planter's Hotel
Skrine & Duke, Editors, The Times, 1 Broad St.
Skrine, Tacitus G., 20 Tradd St.
Slade, Margaret, Widow, 66 Queen St.
Slater, Jocob, Shopkeeper, 280 King St.
Slawson, Nathaniel, Baker, 100 King St.
Slowick, John, 10 King St.
Smallwood, Richard, Custom House Officer, 67 Market St.
Smart, John T., Deputy Sheriff, 54 Meeting St.
Smerdon, -----, Mrs., Boarding House, 22 Tradd St.
Smiley, Susan, Widow, 5 Church St
Smith & Cowdry, Merchants, S. Vendue Range
Smith & M'Leod, Vendue Masters, 16 Vendue Range
Smith, A. L., Shopkeeper, 252 King St.
Smith, Agnes, Jr., 389 Tradd St.
Smith, Agnes, Widow, 7 Broad St., Upstairs
Smith, Ann & Naomi, Misses, 36 Coming St.
Smith, Ann, 46 Anson St.
Smith, Ann, Widow, 119 Meeting St.
Smith, Benjamin & Co., Paint & Varnish Store, 1 Exchange St.
Smith, Benjamin B., Counsellor at Law, 112 Meeting St., Office, 84 Broad St.
Smith, Charles, Planter, 2 S. Bay St.
Smith, Charlotte W , Widow of William Loughton, 100 E. Bay St.
Smith, Eliza, Dry Goods Store, 164 King St
Smith, Eliza, Widow, 5 Blackbird Al.
Smith, George, Cabinet Maker, Vanderhorst St.
Smith, George, House Carpenter, Hampstead
Smith, George, Planter, 49 Anson St.
Smith, Henry, Planter, Washington Village
Smith, Hugh, Merchant, 7 Broad St., House, 22 St. Philip's St.
Smith, James, Cutler, 4 Anson St.

Smith, James, Grocer, E Side Meeting St. Rd.
Smith, James, Hampstead
Smith, Jane, Widow, 8 Anson St.
Smith, John, Clerk & Sexton, St. Philip's Church, 17 Magazine St.
Smith, John, Farmer, E. Side King St. Rd.
Smith, Josiah, 49 Anson St.
Smith, M Press, Factor, 3 Pinckney St., Counting House, D'Oyley's Whf
Smith, Mary Ann, School for Colored Children, 66 Church St.
Smith, Mary, Tavern, 42 Elliott St.
Smith, Mary, Widow of Roger, 37 Coming St.
Smith, -----, Mrs., Widow of John R , 28 St Philip's St.
Smith, Paul, Grocer, 31 Coming St.
Smith, Paul, Grocer, 31 Coming St.
Smith, Peat & Co., Saddlers, 245 King St.
Smith, Peter, Intendant P. T. of City, 2 S. Bay St.
Smith, Peter, Planter, 22 King St.
Smith, Peter, Sr , Factor, 27 Mazyck St., Counting House, S. Bay St.
Smith, Reubin, Merchant, Martin's Whf., House, 22 Tradd St.
Smith, Richard, Joiner, 27 Broad St
Smith, Robert, Planter, 6 New St.
Smith, Samuel, Beer House, 14 Champney St.
Smith, Samuel, Boot Maker, 83 Tradd St.
Smith, Samuel, Factor, 12 Broad St.
Smith, Thomas L., Attorney, 100 E. Bay St.
Smith, Thomas R., Planter, Ladson's Court, Back N. Meeting St.
Smith, Thomas Y , Planter, W. End Boundary St., N Side
Smith, Whiteford, Jr., Grocery & Beer House, 68 Church St.
Smith, William, Grocer, 44 Elliott St.
Smith, William, Jr., Planter, W. Side Washington St , Mazyckborough
Smith, William M., Planter, 62 Meeting St.
Smith, William S., Prothonotary, 12 Bull St.
Smith, William, Ship Carpenter, E. Side Washington St., Mazyckborough
Smylie, Andrew, Merchant, Counting House, 117 Tradd St., House, 121 Church St.
Smyth, Charles, Barber, 99 Church St.
Smyth, John, 80 Queen St.
Smyth, Robert, House Carpenter, 6 Bull St.
Snetter, B., Rope Maker, 228 Meeting St.
Snipes, Eliza, Widow, 9 Orange St.
Snow & Bowers, Merchants, 43 E. Bay St.
Snow, Lydia, 22 Society St.
Snowden, Ann, Widow, 28 King St.
Snowden, William E. & Co., Ship Chandlers, 214 E. Bay St.
Snyder, Christian, Grocer, 142 E. Bay St
Sobet, John, City Guard Man, W. Side St. Philip's St. Cont'd.
Sobieski, -----, Capt., Army, W. Side St. Philip's Cont'd.
Sollee, Frederick, 39 Church St.
Sollee, John, 39 Church St.
Solomons, Alexander, Shopkeeper, 257 King St.

Solomons, Catharine, 380 King St.
Solomons, Sarah, Slop Shop, 80 E Bay St.
Solomons, Solomon, Broker & Dry Goods Store, 171 King St.
Somarsall, Thomas, 129 Church St.
Sommers, J. W., Factor, 3 Church St , Counting House, S End Lynch's Ln.
Sommers, James, Factor, 5 Bull St., Counting House, S End Lynch's Ln.
Sommers, Rose, Mantau Maker, 11 Lynch's Ln.
Sompayrac, M., Merchant, 40 Church St.
Souche, Alexander, Fruiterer, 39 Broad St.
Souty & Grain, Hair Workers, 271 King St.
Sparks, Rachel, 44 Queen St.
Sparrow, James, Butcher, Cannon St., Cannonborough
Speakman, John, Merchant, Chisolm's N. Whf.
Spears, George, Factor, 5 Society St.
Spears, Mary, Widow of James, 5 Society St.
Speissegger, John, Musical Instrument Maker, 4 Hasell St.
Spencer, Mary, Widow of Capt J. V., 16 Queen St
Spencer, S., Shoemaker, Hampstead
Spindle, John G., House Carpenter, 25 Archdale St.
St Amand, J. A., Coachmaker, 36 Meeting St.
St. Clair, -----, Capt., Mariner, 186 E. Bay St.
St Clair, William, Purser, U. S. Navy, 136 E. Bay St.
St. Martin, A., Bookkeeper, Planters' & Mechanics' Bank, 13 Cumberland St.
Stafford, James, Capt., Mariner, 3 Wall St.
Stagg, Jacob D & Co., Merchants, 215 E. Bay St.
Stagg, Jacob D., Merchant, 1 Washington St.
Stall, Thomas D., Shoe Store, 211 Meeting St.
Stanyarne, Ann, 373 King St.
Steedman, Charles J., E. Side Middle St., Mazyckborough
Steel, John A., Clerk, Planters' & Mechanics' Bank
Steel, William G., Saw Pit, S. End Pitt St.
Steinmetz, J. E. A., Merchant, 50 Tradd St.
Steinmyer, G. W., Baker, 37 Boundary St.
Stents, John, House Carpenter, Shop, 1 Back Al., House, 23 Mazyck St.
Stents, Robert, House Carpenter, 6 Mazyck St.
Stephens, Thomas, Teller, Union Bank
Stevens, Daniel, Planter, 31 George St.
Stevens, Eliza, Widow, 39 Market St.
Stevens, J. H , 72 Tradd St.
Stevens, Robert & Co., Merchants, Counting House, 9 Chisolm's Upper Whf , Res. Planter's Hotel
Stevens, William, Custom House Officer, 17 Middle St.
Stevens, William S., M.D., 15 King St.
Stewart, Charles, Attorney, 44 Wentworth St.
Stewart -----, Merchant, 22 Tradd St.
Stewart, ------, Miss, School, 110 Tradd St
Stewart, Rebecca, 8 Smith's Ln.
Stewart, Robert, 7 Friend St.
Sticher, C., Farmer, E. Side King St. Rd.
Stillman, James, Grocer, 79 E. Bay St.
Stock, -----, Mrs., Widow, 4 George St.
Stocker, Henry, Boat Builder, 25 Guinard St.
Stocker, Henry, Shop, Boat Builder, 205 E. Bay St.
Stoll, Catherine, 19 Magazine St.
Stoll, J., Bricklayer, 41 Beaufain St.

Stoll, S., 15 Tradd St.
Stone, Ann, Widow, 362 King St.
Stone, William, Teacher, 22 Archdale St
Stoney, John, Merchant, Chisolm's Upper Whf , House, 150 E. Bay St
Stoutt, Isabelle, 16 Tradd St.
Stowe, Eliza, Widow, 44 Society St.
Street & Keating, Grocers, 245 E Bay St.
Street, Thadeus, Grocer, 165 Meeting St.
Street, Timothy, Grocer, 165 Meeting St.
Strobel, Benjamin, Merchant, 147 Meeting St., Counting House, 257 E. Bay St.
Strobel, Jacob, Capt., City Guard, 117 King St.
Strobel, John, Discount Officer, Planters' & Merchanics' Bank, 33 Boundary St.
Strobel, Lewis, Lt., City Guard
Strobel, Martin, Attorney, 139 Meeting St.
Stroheker, John, Blacksmith, 23 Cumberland St., Shop, 89 Meeting St.
Sturgis & Lovell, Merchants, 4 Crafts' Whf.
Sturgis, Josiah, Merchant, 8 S. Bay St.
Suares, Jacob, Charleston Coffee House, 112 Queen St.
Suares, Peter, Merchant, 22 Mazyck St.
Suarez, ------, 53 Queen St.
Suau, Peter, Merchant, Lothrop's Whf.
Suder, Ann, 6 Wentworth St.
Sullivan, Timothy, Vendue Master, 47 Anson St.
Sumney, J. & P., Dry Goods Store, E. Side King St. Rd.
Sutcliff, Eliza, Widow, 28 King St.
Swain, Rebecca, 5 Stoll's Al.
Sweeny, Diana, Grain Store, 7 Anson St
Sweeny, Esther, 4 Smith's Ln.
Sweet, -----, Mrs., Dry Goods Store, 121 Queen St.
Sweetman, Samuel, Shipwright, 6 Cock Ln.
Swift, D., Dry Goods Store, 236 King St.
Swift, -----, Mrs., Milliner, 173 King St.
Swift, William, Dry Goods Store, 175 King St.
Swinton, Susan, 25 Meeting St.
Syphon, John, Butcher, W. Side Coming St., Cannonborough
Taggart, Mary, Widow, 17 Meeting St.
Talvande, Andrew, 82 Broad St.
Talvande, M., Ladies' School, 22 Broad St.
Talvande, Rose, 81 Tradd St.
Tarnbull, James, Factor, 251 Meeting St.
Tastet, -----, Mrs., Dry Goods Store, 339 King St.
Tastet, Peter, Dancing Master, 339 King St.
Tate, James, Capt., Mariner, 121 Queen St
Tatem, William, Accountant, 120 Tradd St.
Taurney, B., Milliner, 84 King St.
Tavel, Frederick, Wharfinger, Fitzsimmons' Whf
Taylor, James, Capt , Mariner, 12 Anson St.
Taylor, Joseph, Capt., Mariner, 3 Anson St.
Taylor, Joseph, Mason, Gadsden's Whf.
Taylor, Joseph, Ship Carpenter, 183 E. Bay St.
Taylor, Josiah, Factor, 13 Lamboll St.
Taylor, Margaret, Widow, 9 Blackbird Al.
Taylor, Mary, 12 Anson St.
Taylor, Thomas S., Block Maker, 10 Laurens St.
Teasdale, John, Jr , Merchant, 2 New St., Counting House,

Vanderhorst's Whf.
Teasdale, John, Merchant, 19 E. Bay St.
Teasdale, Richard, Merchant, Vanderhorst's Whf.
Telfer, Robert, Merchant, 322 King St.
Tennant, Moses, Shopkeeper, 7 Pitt St
Tennant, Robert, 37 Tradd St
Tennant, Thomas, Cabinet Maker, 45 Queen St
Tew, Charles, Free School, 92 Wentworth St.
Thackman, J., Widow, 123 Meeting St.
Thackman, Thomas, House Carpenter, 123 Meeting St.
Thayer, E., Jr., Accountant, 48 Tradd St.
Thayer, Ebenezer, Broker, Office, 9 Broad St , House, 48 Tradd St.
Theus, Betsy, Laundress, 15 Parsonage Ln.
Theus, Deborah, Seamstress, 3 Berresford St.
Theus, Simeon, Collector, 338 King St.
Theus, Simeon, Jr., Factor, 274 E. Bay St.
Thineman, Charles, Music Master, 230 E. Bay St.
Thomas & Bass, Merchants, 253 King St.
Thomas, Francis, Clerk, 30 Archdale St.
Thomas, James, Merchant, 6 George St.
Thomas, John, Grocer, 59 Market St.
Thomas, John, Shopkeeper, 202 Meeting St.
Thomas, L. S , 244 E. Bay St. & 12 Hasell St.
Thomas, Mary L., 12 King St.
Thomas, -----, Mrs., Widow of Dr., 44 Meeting St.
Thomas, Sarah, 19 Linguard St.
Thomas, Stephen, Tanner, 11 Mazyck St
Thomason, V., Widow, 10 Wall St.
Thompson, Mary C., 10 Hasell St.
Thompson, -----, Mrs., Milliner, 90 Broad St.
Thompson, Rebecca, Widow of John, W. End Boundary St.
Thompson, -----, Saddler, 90 Broad St.
Thomson, Alexander, Mason, 28 Mazyck St.
Thomson, Ann, Laundress, 13 Parsonage Ln.
Thomson, Daniel, Custom House Officer, 64 Meeting St.
Thomson, George, Mason, 11 Church St.
Thomson, James, Boarding Officer, Custom House, 10 Hasell St.
Thomson, James, House Carpenter, 30 Beaufain St.
Thomson, John, Mariner, 27 Ellery St.
Thomson, ------, Mrs., School, 13 George St.
Thomson, William, Ship Chandler, 227 E. Bay St., House, 218 E. Bay St.
Thorne, John G., Sail Maker, House, 5 Cumberland St., Sail Loft, 270 E. Bay St.
Thornhill, John, Engraver, 285 King St., Shop, 33 Broad St.
Thwing, David, Grocer, 374 King St.
Thwing, Edward, Merchant, House, 3 Minority St., Store, 17 Vendue Range
Tidyman, Esther, Widow of Philip, 22 Coming St.
Tidyman, Philip, Planter, 84 Wentworth St.
Tiebout, Alfred, Merchant, 128 E. Bay St.
Tiebout, -----, Miss, 21 Bull St.
Timmons, William, State Tax Collector, S Side Charlotte St.
Timothy, Ann, Widow of Benjamin F., 13 Water St.
Timothy, Peter, 13 Water St.

Timrod, W. H., Bookbinder, 345 King St.
Tims, Jacob, Blacksmith, W. Side King St Rd.
Tisson, F., 46 King St.
Tobias, Abraham, 292 King St.
Todd, John, Planter, 35 Coming St.
Todd, -----, Miss, 5 Savage St.
Todd, Ruth S., Widow, 16 Legare St.
Tomatis, J. G., 14 Guignard St.
Tommer, J. W., Counsellor at Law, 169 E. Bay St.
Tongue, Susan, Widow, 166 Church St.
Tookey, M., Milliner, 169 King St.
Toomer & Sass, Vendue Masters, 14 Vendue Range
Toomer, Ann, Widow of Anthony, 5 Legare St.
Torlay, Peter, Jeweller, 273 King St.
Torre, C. D., Print & Optical Store, 100 Broad St.
Torre, Ezekiel, Pump Maker, 3 Meeting St., Shop, 109 E. Bay St.
Torrey, -----, Mrs , Widow of Capt., 11 New St.
Tourrette, Thomas, Cigar & Fruit Store, 195 Meeting St.
Toussiger, Eliza, 5 Water St.
Tovey, Henry, Block Maker, 147 E. Bay St., Shop, 219 E. Bay St.
Trapier, P., at Belvidere Mill on Cooper River, 3 Miles from Town
Trenholm, William, Grain Store, 3 Vendue Range
Trescot, Edward, Planter, Hampstead
Trescot, John, M.D., 60 Broad St.
Trescot, William, Attorney, 64 Queen St., Office, 213 Meeting St.
Trezvant, John F., Attorney, 25 King St.
Trezvant, Peter, Drawback Clerk, Custom House, 4 Stoll's Al
Truchelut, John B., Grocer, 137 Queen St.
Tucker, Sarah, Widow, 135 Church St.
Tucker, William B., Register of Mesne Conveyances, 135 Church St.
Tunis, Charles, Factor, 130 Church St.
Tunno, Adam, Merchant, 44 E. Bay St.
Tunno, Sarah, 63 Tradd St.
Tunno, Thomas, Merchant, 79 Tradd St.
Tupper, Tristan, Merchant, 239 E. Bay St.
Ture, P., Grocer, 13 Elliott St.
Turnbull, Robert F., Planter, 1 Logan St.
Turner, -----, Capt., Mariner, 22 Montague St.
Turner, Sarah, 13 Liberty St.
Turner, William, 7 Middle St.
Turner, William, Lamplighter, 58 Anson St.
Turpin, William, Merchant, 180 King St.
Tyler & Hough, Merchants, 233 E. Bay St.
Tyler, Joseph, Merchant, 99 Broad St., Upstairs
Tyler, -----, Mr., Theatre, 26 Mazyck St.
Ulmo, Anthony, M.D & Druggist, 20 Queen St.
Unmensetter, John, Tanner, 22 Beaufain St.
Urquart, C., Merchant, N. Cellar of Exchange
Utt, John, Comedian, at the Theatre
Vale, Eliza, Widow of John D , Islington
Valentine, Ann T., 33 King St.
Valk, Francis, Upholsterer, 101 King St.
Valk, J. R., Merchant, 109 Broad St., Cotton Press, 9 Champney St., Counting House, Chisolm's Whf.

Vance, Oliver, Merchant, cr. Market & Meeting Sts.
Vanderbussche, C., Dry Goods Store, 77 King St.
Vanderhorst, Elias, Merchant, Counting House, His Whf.
Vanderhorst, Mary, 7 Logan St.
Vandervortt, Henry, Grocer, 57 Market St.
VanEver, E., Boot Maker, 93 Broad St.
Vanruyter, Simon, House Carpenter, 1 Magazine St.
Vanryn, A. E., Dry Goods Store, 113 Broad St
Vanvelsy, William, Coach Maker, 24 St. Philip's St.
Vaughan, Ann, Widow, 1 Blackbird Al.
Venning, A., Shoemaker, W. Side State St.
Venning, N., Planter, 139 E. Bay St.
Veray, John, Clerk, 4 Amen St.
Vernon, Nathaniel, Jeweller, 115 Broad St.
Verree, Joseph, 19 Church St.
Verree, Robert, Factor, 5 Water St., Counting House,
  Bailey's Whf.
Verree, Samuel, 19 Church St.
Very, N., Grocer, E. End Boundary St.
Vesey, Charles, W. Side Washington St., Mazyckborough
Vesey, Joseph, cr. Society & Meeting Sts.
Vidall, John, Dry Goods Store, 117 Church St.
Vieuse, B., Confectioner, 317 King St.
Ville, P., Grocer, 59 E. Bay St.
Vincent, Benjamin, Merchant, 87 E. Bay St.
Vincent, Eliza, Boarding House, 3 Tradd St
Vincent, L., Shoemaker, 16 State St.
Vincey, James, Shop, Blacksmith, 117 E. Bay St., House,
  28 Ellery St.
Vineyard, John, Merchant, E. Side King St.
Vion, Theresa, Dry Goods Store, 93 King St.
Vose, J. T., Grocer, 26 Pinckney St.
Wadsworth, William, Grocer, 15 Archdale St.
Wagner, -----, Mrs., Widow of G., 23 St. Philip's St.,
  Merchant, 61 King St.
Wagner, Paul, Grocer, 52 King St.
Wagner, S., House Carpenter, 17 Archdale St.
Wagner, Samuel J., Custom House Officer, 123 Tradd St.
Wailey, Edward, Cannonborough
Wainwright, Ann, Widow of Richard, 363 King St.
Wakefield, -----, Miss, Lynch St.
Walbridge, Levi, Teacher, 20 King St.
Waldrop, Eliza, Boarding House, 38 E. Bay St., Upstairs
Wale, Job, House Carpenter, 3 West St.
Walker, Caleb, House Carpenter, 12 Magazine St.
Walker, Mary A., Widow, 15 Church St.
Walker, -----, Mrs., Widow, 28 Anson St.
Walker, Robert, Cabinet Maker, 53 Church St.
Walker, Thomas, Stone Cutter, 38 Wentworth St.
Wall, Richard, Grocer, 48 Queen St.
Wallace, James, 12 Lowndes St.
Wallace, James, Brass Founder, 108 Meeting St.
Wallace, Thomas, Cabinet Maker, 95 Church St.
Wallace, W., Merchant, 4 Martin's Whf , House, 96 E. Bay
  St.
Wallbridge, Levi, School, 20 King St.
Waller, Charlotte, Widow, 13 Magazine St.
Waller, William, Saddler, 51 Broad St.
Walpole, H., Planter, 3 New St.
Walton, Andrew, Blacksmith, 11 Blackbird Al.

Walton, C., Pilot, 3 Zigzag Ln.
Walton, Eliza, 3 Zigzag Ln.
Walton, John, State Treasurer, 213 King St.
Walton, William, Planter, E. Side Coming St.,
  Cannonborough
Wando & Teneman, Grocers, 66 E. Bay St.
Wansley, Eliza, Grocer, 49 Elliott St.
Ward, F. S., Clerk, Inferior Court, 106 Tradd St.
Ward, Ichabod, Tavern, 1 Parsonage Ln.
Ward, James M., Attorney, House, Washington Village,
  Office, 129 Church St.
Ward, John, Capt., Mariner, 14 King St.
Ward, John, Planter, 233 Meeting St.
Ward, Mary, Mrs , Widow, 19 Friend St.
Ward, -----, Mrs., Widow of Daniel, 106 Tradd St.
Ward, Sarah, Widow of Joshua, 233 Meeting St.
Warham, Mary, Widow, 7 Tradd St.
Warham, William G., 7 Tradd St.
Waring, H., M.D., W. Side Cannon's Bridge Rd.
Waring, Mary, Widow of John, 94 Wentworth St.
Waring, Morton A., Federal Marshall, W. Side St. Philip's
  St. Cont'd.
Waring, Morton, Factor, Counting House, 269 E. Bay St.,
  House, 82 Tradd St.
Waring, -----, Mrs., Widow of John L., 25 Mazyck St.
Waring, Thomas, Naval Officer, 31 Meeting St.
Warley, John, Clerk, 120 Tradd St.
Warley, Mary & Eliza, 40 Beaufain St.
Warley, William, M.D., 154 Church St.
Warner, Penelope, Sausage Maker, 223 Meeting St
Warner, Samuel, Tailor, 31 Boundary St.
Warnock, J., Attorney, 27 George St.
Warren, John, Capt., Mariner, 37 Elliott St.
Wartenberg, P., Grocer, 11 Market St.
Washington, Jane, Widow of William, 20 S. Bay St
Washington, William, Planter, 20 S. Bay St.
Waters, Jerry, Fish Store, E. Side State St.
Watson, Alexander, 135 E. Bay St.
Watson, Alexander, Tailor, 14 Church St.
Watson, James, 44 Tradd St.
Watson, James, Boarding House, 16 Chalmers Al
Watson, Lydia, 8 Friend St.
Watson, Thomas, 103 Queen St.
Watson, William, Dry Goods Store, 127 King St.
Watt, James, Grocer, 151 Church St.
Watts, Bridget, Widow, 15 Friend St.
Waugh, A. B., Merchant, House, 41 Society St., Counting
  House, 258 E. Bay St.
Webb, Daniel C., Factor, W. Side Cannon's Bridge Rd.
Webb, William, Merchant, Blake's Whf.
Webber, Samuel, Capt., Mariner, 2 Hard Al.
Webley, Abigail, Widow, 59 King St.
Weissenger, Leonard, Tanner, E. Side King St. Rd.
Weissenger, Magdalen, Widow, E. Side King St. Rd
Welch, J., Superintendant, City Burial Ground,
  Cannonborough or in City Council Room
Wellington & Ballantine, Harness Makers, 65 Meeting St.
Wells, Moses, 32 Beaufain St.
Wells, P., Laundress, 34 Pinckney St.
Wells, Richard, Boat Builder, 190 E. Bay St

Wells, Thomas B., Clerk, 18 Archdale St.
Wellsman, James, Pilot, 15 Lynch's Ln.
Welsch, Richard, Grocer, 66 E. Bay St.
Welsh, Edward, Capt., Mariner, 3 Logan St.
Welsh, Nathaniel, Mason, 32 Coming St.
Welsh, Thomas, Carver, 105 Meeting St.
Wesner, Francis, House Carpenter, 77 Queen St.
Wesner, Henry P., Clerk, 32 Coming St
West, T., Capt., Mariner, 131 E. Bay St
Westendorff, C. P. L., Merchant, 230 E. Bay St., Res.
  Planter's Hotel
Weston, P., M.D , Hampstead
Weston, Plowden, Planter, 35 Queen St.
Weston, William, Shipwright, 8 Blackbird Al.
Weyman, C., Widow of Edward, W. Side King St. Rd.
Wharton, Samuel, Grocer, E. Side King St Rd.
Wheeler, Henry & Co., Merchants, 231 E. Bay Co.
Wheeler, John, at the Merchants Hotel
Wheeler, Josiah, Vendue Master, 146 Meeting St., Office,
  S. Vendue Range
Whightman, John, Turner, 151 Meeting St.
Whightman, William, Jeweller, 210 Meeting St.
Whightman, William, Painter & Glazier, 152 Meeting St.
Whilden, Joseph, 13 Magazine St.
White, Daniel, Butcher, Hampstead
White, G , Joiner, 120 Church St.
White, George K., Factor, E. Side Middle St.,
  Mazyckborough, Counting House, Prioleau's Whf.
White, James, at the Work House
White, James J. B., Attorney, 85 Broad St.
White, John & Co., Factors, Chisolm's N. Whf.
White, John B., Attorney, 85 Broad St.
White, John, Factor, 144 Meeting St.
White, John, Grocer, 97 King St.
White, John P., Attorney, 34 Meeting St.
White, Joseph, Grocer, 33 Chamber's Al
White, M. A., School, 349 King St.
White, Mary A., Boarding House, 14 Bedon's Al.
White, William, Mariner, 58 Market St.
Whitehart, Peter, 114 E. Bay St.
Whiting, John, Grocery & Turner, 103 Meeting St.
Whitney, Archibald, Baker, 297 King St.
Whitney, John, Grocer, 70 Church St.
Whitney, Thomas, Fruiterer, 6 Beaufain St.
Whitney, Thomas, Mariner, 3 Market St.
Whitridge, B. J., M.D., 46 Meeting St.
Whyte, James, Vendue Master, 9 Vendue Range
Wienges, C., Grocer, 89 Wentworth St.
Wienges, Jacob, Grocer, 394 King St.
Wienges, John H., Grocer, 17 Church St.
Wigfall, C., Widow, 45 George St.
Wigfall, Robert, Small Shop, 23 Guignard St.
Wigfall, Thomas, Planter, Mazyckborough
Wiggins, William, Grocer, 164 Meeting St.
Wilder, Peter, Capt., Mariner, 1 Mazyck St.
Wilhelmi, J. P., Merchant, Cannonborough
Wilkie, George, Cooper, Prioleau's Whf.
Wilkie, James, Accountant, 9 Broad St.
Wilkie, W. B., Bookkeeper, Union Bank, 18 Tradd St.
Will, R. W., Mason, 16 Pitt St.

Williams, Ann, 11 Wentworth St.
Williams, Ann, Milliner, 198 King St.
Williams, Isham, Planter, on his Wharf
Williams, John, Master Rigger, 34 Beaufain St.
Williams, William, Tailor, 2 Magazine St.
Williamson, Abraham B., Smith's Ln.
Williamson, Eliza, Milliner, 198 King St.
Williamson, Hannah, 39 Beaufain St.
Williamson, Jane, Milliner, 122 Church St.
Williamson, John, Merchant, Chislom's Upper Whf.
Williamson, Maria, Seamstress, 8 Parsonage Ln.
Williamson, Mary, Widow, Green St.
Williman, Eliza, W. End Boundary St.
Williman, Jacob, Planter, 2 Montague St.
Willington, A. S., City Printer & Editor of Courier, 9
  Broad St.
Willis, John H., Broker, 191 Meeting St.
Wilson & Pall, Grocers, 23 Broad St.
Wilson, C., 19 Ellery St.
Wilson, Isaac, M.D., 21 Magazine St.
Wilson, James, Grocer, 10 Mazyck St.
Wilson John, House Carpenter, 127 Meeting St.
Wilson, John, Planter, 25 Bull St.
Wilson, John, Surveyer, 9 Friend St
Wilson, Margaret, 366 King St.
Wilson, Mary, Widow of Daniel, 154 Church St.
Wilson, Robert, Capt., Mariner, 3 Hasell St.
Wilson, Robert, M.D., 35 Meeting St.
Wilson, Samuel, M.D., 4 Archdale St.
Wilson, William, Butcher, Nassau St., Hampstead
Winchester, John, Small Shop, W. Side, Coming St.,
  Cannonborough
Windsor, Thomas, Capt., Mariner, 5 Maiden Ln.
Winslow, B., Grocer, 67 King St.
Winstanley, Thomas, Attorney, Office, 104 E. Bay St.,
  House, Charlotte St., Mazyckborough
Winthrop, Joseph, Merchant, Danish Consul, 57 Tradd St.,
  Office, Chisolm's N. Whf.
Wish, Ann, Widow, 34 Elliott St.
Withers, Thomas, Boat Builder, 7 Cock Ln.
Witt, John, Grocer, 10 Coming St.
Wittencamp, Charles, 96 Tradd St.
Woldrop, John, President, S. C. Insurance Co., 26 E. Bay
  St
Wolley, Thomas, Merchant, 147 King St.
Wood, Alley., Widow, Grocer, W. Side King St. Rd.
Wood, James, Blacksmith, W. Side St. Philip's St. Cont'd.
Wood, John, Butcher, Hampstead
Wood, Mary, Warren St.
Woodman, Mary, Dry Goods Store, 287 King St.
Woodrouffe, Eliza, Boarding House, 264 E. Bay St.,
  Upstairs
Woodward, -----, Mrs., Boarding House, 259 King St.
Wragg, E. R., Factor, 23 Bay St
Wrainch, John, English School & Clerk to Fire Master,
  173 Meeting St.
Wright, Rebecca, Res 79 Broad St.
Wright, Robert, House Carpenter, 18 Coming St.
Wurdeman, J. G., Dry Goods & Grocery Store, 133 Queen
  St.

Wyatt, Eliza, Widow, 73 Church St.
Wyatt, Peter, Lumber Sawyer, 1 Lynch St.
Yancey, B. C., Attorney, 36 Meeting St.
Yates, Ann, 5 Zigzag Ln.
Yates, Deborah, 22 S. Bay St.
Yates, Jeremiah A., 21 S. Bay St.
Yates, Joseph, Cooper, 9 Church St., Shop, 54 Elliott St.
Yates, -----, Mrs., Widow of Seth, 6 Zigzag Ln.
Yates, Samuel, Ship Chandler, 48 E. Bay St.
Ybert, N., Widow, 36 George St.
Yeadon, Richard, Assistant Cashier, Bank of the State, 18 King St.
Yeadon, William, City Sheriff, 48 Beaufain St.
Yoer, C. A., Widow, Milliner, 80 King St.

You, Eliza, Widow of Thomas, Columbus St., Hampstead
You, John C., School Master, 32 Archdale St.
Yough, Joseph D., 10 Logan St.
Young, Cox William, 44 Broad St.
Young, Joseph, Capt., Mariner, 144 E. Bay St.
Young, -----, Mr., of the Theatre, 69 Queen St
Young, Philip, Merchant, 42 E. Bay St.
Young, William P , Printer, 2 Broad St., House & Book Store, 64 Broad St.
Young, William, Tallow Chandler & Merchant, E. Side Cannon Bridge Rd., Counting House, 4 Champney St.
Zealy, Joseph, 32 King St
Zystra, J. P., Oil & Color Store, 125 Tradd St.

1819 Directory.

This directory was published by Schenck & Turner under the title of *The Directory and Stranger's Guide for the City of Charleston; Also a Directory of Charleston Neck, Between Boundary-Street and the Lines for the Year 1819. To Which is Added an Almanac: The Tariff of Duties on All Goods Imported Into the United States; Rates of Wharfage, Weighing, Storage, Cartage and Drayage, &c. &c.* (Charleston: A. E. Miller, January, 1819). James R. Schenck published the 1822 directory for Charleston, but it is not clear who Turner was. This directory has 3,933 entries. Those living between Boundary (now Calhoun) St. and the Lines are listed separately at the end of the directory. Here they have been included with the residents of the city with the word "Neck" added at the end of each entry.

Aberagg, John, Manufacturer of Cigars, 20 Archdale St
Abott, Barbary, Widow, 49 Society St.
Abott, Samuel, Justice of Peace, 10 Elliott St.
Abrahams, Elias, Merchant, cr. King & Liberty Sts.
Abrahams, Judith, Widow, 21 Guignard St.
Abrahams, Levi I., Grocer, 2 Market St.
Abrahams, Samuel, cr. Charlotte & Washington Sts , Mazyckborough, Neck
Adams, Ann, Widow, 20 Pinckney
Adams, David & Co., D'Oyley's Whf.
Adams, David L , Factor, 19 Tradd St.
Adams, George, Ship Carpenter, 20 Pinckney St.
Adams, Robert, Carpenter, 6 Mazyck St.
Adams, William,. Planter, cr. Pinckney & Cannon Sts., Cannonborough, Neck
Adams, William B., House Carpenter, Liberty St.
Addison & Martin, Merchants, King St. Road, Neck
Addison, Robert, Capt., 5 & 6 Magazine St.
Adger & Flemming, Merchants, cr. Spring & King Sts., Neck
Adger, James, Merchants, 2 Brownlee's Row, King St., Res. King St. Road, Neck
Adkin, James, Grocer, 169 Meeting St.
Aiken, William, Merchant, King St. Road, Neck
Aikin, Ann, Widow, 6 Cumberland St.
Aikin, Thomas, M.D., Vice President of Medical Society, Cumberland St.
Aiman, Sebastian, Grocer, 108 E. Bay St.
Airs, George, Custom House Officer, 12 Archdale St.
Airs, James, Inspector in Custom House, 9 Coming St
Airs, Thomas, Boat Builder, Res. 36 Society St., Shop, E. Bay St.
Albanac, Peter, Tailor, 5 Queen St
Aldridge, Robert, Wharfinger, Chisolm's Whf.
Alexander, Abrahm, Dry Goods Store, King St. Road, Neck
Alexander, Alexander, Dry Goods Store, 257 King St.
Alexander, David, President, Union Insurance Company, 4 Logan St
Allan, Dolly, F.P C., Boundary St.
Allan, Mily, Coming St., Radcliffborough, Neck

Allan, Thomas, Planter, cr. Pinckney & Anson Sts.
Allan, William, Factor, 108 Tradd St.
Allen, William, Factor, Counting House, D'Oyley's Whf.
Alston, Dinah, F.P.C., 29 Amen St.
Alston, William, Col., Planter, Hudson St., Cannonborough, Neck
Ancrum & Chiffelle, Steam Saw & Grist Mill, E. Bay St., op. Wentworth St.
Ancrum, James H., Planter, 145 E. Bay St. Cont'd
Anderson, Abigail, F.P.C., 28 Pinckney St.
Anderson, Isabella, Widow, 16 Magazine St.
Anderson, Judah, F.P.C., Washer, 4 Wall St.
Anderson, Samuel, Grocer, cr. Coming & George Sts.
Anderson, Thomas, Painter, Chalmers Al.
Anderson, W., Merchant, 33 Meeting St.
Anderson, William, Stay Maker, 30 Meeting St.
Andrews, Moses, Mast, Pump & Block Maker, 179 E. Bay St.
Andrews, -----, Mrs., Boarding House, State St.
Andril, Francis, Teacher of Music, 4 Longitude Ln.
Angel, -----, Planter, Tradd St.
Anthony, J. C., Tallow Chandler, Mary St., Fresh Water Pond, Neck
Anthony, John, Ship Master, 192 E. Bay St.
Anthony, Joseph, Cooper, Chalmers Al.
Anthony, Mary, Widow, N.E. Side Pinckney St., Cannonborough, Neck
Arman, Peter, Coach Maker, 13 Archdale St.
Arms, William, Bricklayer, 58 Boundary St., Neck
Armstrong, Louisa, F.P.C., 34 Wall St.
Armstrong, Sarah, Seamstress, 45 Beaufain St.
Arnaud, Elliner, Widow, 13 Liberty St.
Arnet, Elizabeth, Boarding House, 39 Church St.
Arnold, Amos, 30 Pinckney St.
Arnold, Louisa, Ladies Boarding House, 49 Queen St.
Arrion, William, Boarding House, cr. Meeting & Linguard Sts.
Arthur, George, John St., Wraggsborbough, Neck
Ash, Bella, F.P.C., 6 Smith's Ln
Ash, Elizabeth, Widow, 9 Lamboll St.
Ash, John, Planter, S. Bay St.
Ashe, Andrew, Planter, 101 Tradd St.
Ashlstrom, John A., Grocer, Market St.
Ashman, James, Shoe Store, 88 Broad St.
Assalit, Andrew, Carpenter, Vanderhorst St., City Lands, Neck
Assatil, Francis, Teacher, 11 Elliott St.
Atkins, Sarah, Widow, Anson St.
Atwill, John D., Shoe Store, 238 King St.
Aubin, Joseph, Merchant, King St.
Aubinaud, Mary, Widow, Seamstress, Guignard St.
Auld, David & Co., Hardware Store, 11 Broad St.
Austen, Catharine, Widow, Seamstress, 68 E. Bay St.
Austen, James, House Carpenter, 68 E. Bay St.
Austen, Samuel W., House Carpenter, 68 E. Bay St.
Austin, Harriet, Widow, 22 George St.
Austin, Hester, F.P.C., Washer, Elizabeth St., Mazyckborough, Neck
Austin, Isaac, Butcher, Elizabeth St., Mazyckborough, Neck

31

Aveilhe, Louis, Shop Keeper, 113 King St.
Averell & Goudey, Shoe Store, 284 King St.
Averell, Henry, Shoe Store, cr. King & Market Sts.
Avery, Prentice, Merchant, 237 E Bay St.
Avis, Mary Ann, Widow, 22 Berresford St.
Axon, Elizabeth, Widow, 22 King St
Axon, Jacob, Jr., Attorney, Res. 22 King St., Office, 214 Meeting St.
Axson, Jacob, Lumber Measurer, 62 Tradd St.
Babcock, S & W. R., Booksellers, 244 King St
Babson, John, Mariner, 97 Tradd St.
Backer, Priscilla, 161 Church St.
Backman, John, Rev., Pastor, German Church, Res. cr. Pinckney & Hudson Sts.,Cannonborough., Neck
Bacot, Daniel D., Bookkeeper, S. C. Bank, 84 Broad St.
Bacot, Henry H., Attorney, 4 Tradd St.
Bacot, Peter, Cashier, Bank of Discount & Deposit
Bacot, Thomas W., Jr., Assistant Postmaster, 84 Broad St.
Bacot, Thomas W., Sr., Cashier of Bank of S. C., 84 Broad St.
Badger, Daniel, Painter, 29 & 30 Archdale St.
Badger, Elizabeth, Widow, 29 & 30 Archdale St.
Bagnal, M., Widow, 19 Linguard St.
Bagnal, Robert, Shoemaker, 19 Linguard St.
Bailey, David N., Queen St.
Bailey, Edward William, Attorney, Res Blackbird Al.
Bailey, Eliza, F.P.C., 126 Queen St.
Bailey, Henry, Merchant, Res. Blackbird Al
Bailey, Isaac S., Accountant, 38 King St.
Bailey, Mary, Widow, Blackbird Al.
Bailey, Sarah, F.P.C , 126 Queen St.
Bailey, William, Shoemaker, 127 Queen St.
Baker & Watson, Grocers, cr. Market & Meeting Sts.
Baker, C., Mariner, State St.
Baker, Elias, Dyer, 94 Meeting St.
Baker, Joseph, Carpenter, Res. 39 Boundary St.
Baker, Noah D., Dyer, 93 Meeting St.
Baker, William, Bricklayer, Res. 39 Boundary St
Baldwin, Daniel, Grocer, 84 E. Bay St.
Ball, Ann, Miss, Seamstress, 21 Church St.
Ball, Caroline, Widow, Plantress, 168 E. Bay St.
Ball, John, Jr., Planter, 11 Hasell St.
Ball, William, Carpenter, Boundary St.
Ballantine, Silvia, F.P.C., 10 Whim Court
Ballanton, Felletto, 128 E. Bay St.
Ballund & Sarzedaz, Auctioneers, 2 Vendue Range
Ballund, Alexander, Merchant, 61 King St.
Bamfield, George, F.P.C., Butcher, Alexander St., Mazyckborough, Neck
Bamfield, James, Custom House Officer, 37 George St.
Bamfield, Maria, 13 Maiden Ln.
Bamfield, Thomas, Accountant, 37 George St.
Banks, Charles, 68 Broad St.
Barfield, Milly, Widow, Seamstress, Boundary St., Mazyckborough, Neck
Barker, J Sandford, 220 E. Bay St , Res. 43 Society St
Barker, James, Truss Maker, 18 Pinckney St.
Barker, William, Merchant, Res 17 Parsonage Ln.
Barksdale, Rebecca B., Widow, 9 Maiden Ln.
Barksdale, Thomas, Capt., Planter, Washington St.

Barnes, William B., Custom House Officer, 193 Meeting St.
Barnes, William, Tailor, 32 Beaufain St.
Barnwell, Nancy, 382 King St.
Barquet, John, Umbrella Maker, 61 Meeting St.
Barre, -----, Brass Founder, 109 E Bay St.
Barreille & Torre, Merchants, 35 Broad St.
Barrett, Esther, Widow, Crockery Store, 163 Meeting St
Barrett, Isaac, Merchant, Res. 225 E. Bay St.
Barrett, Star, Widow, Aged 120 Years, Guignard St.
Barron, Alexander, Jr., Dr., 45 Meeting St.
Barron, Alexander, M.D., 56 Broad St.
Barron, John, Wine Merchant, cr. Champney & E. Bay Sts., Res Society St.
Barrow, Ele, Confectioner, 83 Wentworth St.
Barry, Peter, Grocer, State St.
Bartless, Henry, Blacksmith Shop, Daniell's Whf.
Bartlett, William, Grocer, 18 Tradd St.
Barttles, Henry, Blacksmith, Charlotte St., Wraggsborough, Neck
Basden, Elizabeth, Widow, 27 Ellery St.
Bason, W. P., Bookseller & Stationer, cr. King & George Sts.
Bass, Henry, Rev., Parsonage, Pitt St.
Bass, Job, Dry Goods Store, 325 King St.
Bass, Thomas E., Block & Pump Maker, Chisolm's Upper Whf., Res. Cumberland St.
Basset, John, Grocer, cr. Pitt & Bull Sts.
Bateman, Edward, F.P.C., Hairdresser, 124 E. Bay St
Battker, John Andrew, Fruit & Toy Store, 36 Market St.
Bauman & Burch, Grocers, 115 Tradd St.
Baumay, Peter, Merchant, 92 King St
Baxter, Elizabeth, Miss, Ladies Boarding House, 53 King St.
Bay, Andrew, Logan St.
Bay, E. H., Judge, Logan St.
Bay, John, Merchant, Res. cr. King & Tradd Sts.
Bayard, Robert A , Tailor, King St.
Beach, Mary L., 12 King St.
Bealmore, John, Rigger, 42 Anson St.
Beard, Frederick, Teller, Bank of S. C.
Beard, John, Bank of S C., 19 Wall St.
Beaudrot, Joseph, Bookkeeper, 29 Pinckney St.
Becais, Mary, Widow, 199 E. Bay St
Becais, Peter, Mariner, 199 E. Bay St.
Beck, James S., Factor, Res. 89 Church St.
Beckman, Adolph, Painter & Paper Hanger, 71 Meeting St.
Beckman, Ann, Widow, 55 Hasell St.
Bee, Eliza, Widow, 89 Church St.
Bee, Frances Caroline, 38 Coming St.
Bee, J. Simmons, Vendue Master, State St., Res. Tradd St
Bee, James, 131 Church St.
Bee, William, School Master, S C Society
Beers & Rowland, Merchants, 118 King St.
Beggs, James, Merchant, 145 King St
Beile, John C., Merchant, 320 King St.
Belcher, Elijah, Capt., Broad St.
Belcher, M., School Mistress, Bull St.
Bell, Alexander, Lamboll St.

32

Bell, Ann, Miss, Teacher, 18 Magazine St.
Bell, David, Accountant, 9 Society St.
Bell, William, Bricklayer, 29 Society st.
Bellamy, Adam, F P.C., Cartman, Henrietta St ,
   Wraggsborough, Neck
Belser, Frederick, Attorney, 213 Meeting St.
Belser, Mary, Widow, King St. Road, Neck
Belshaw, Merchant, King St., at the Lines, Neck
Belton, Jonathan, Millinery Store, 302 King St.
Bemar, John, Confectioner, 41 Meeting St.
Benbage, Stephan, Alexander St., Mazyckborough, Neck
Bennett, Henry, Deputy Collector, Wolf St., Hampstead,
   Neck
Bennett, I S. K., Attorney, 14 Bull St.
Bennett, John Adams, Smith, Market St.
Bennett, John, Mariner, 17 Amen St.
Bennett, Samuel, F.P.C., Carpenter, Neck
Bennett, Thomas, Bull & Lynch Sts.
Bennett, Thomas, Charleston Mills, Ashley River, btw.
   Bull & Boundary Sts. Cont'd., Neck
Benoist, Catharine, Widow, 42 Pinckney St.
Benson, John H , Merchant, cr. King & Broad Sts.
Bentham, J. P., Attorney, 4 State House Sq.
Bentham, James, Merchant, 116 Church St., Res 297 King
   St.
Bentham, Mary, Widow, 397 King St
Bentham, Robert, Attorney, 397 King St.
Bentham, William, Capt., 397 King St.
Berbant, Samuel, Tailor, 201 King St., Neck
Bereard, -----, Widow, 5 Maiden Ln.
Bergman, Tobias, Grocer, cr. Queen & State Sts.
Berney, William, Mariner, cr. Boundary & Lowndes Sts.,
   Neck
Berry, Alexander, 124 Wentworth St.
Berry, Hales, F.P.C., Tailor, 33 Boundary St.
Berry, -----, Mr., Painter, 15 Clifford's Al.
Berry, Peter, Confectioner, 128 King St.
Beswick, Sophia, School, Cannon & Borough Sts , Neck
Bevet, Catharine, F.P C., 16 Ellery St.
Bezaul, Julian, Grocer, E. Bay St.
Big, Sarah, Seamstress, 52 Wentworth St.
Bigelow, Elizabeth, Widow, 130 Meeting St., Neck
Billing, John, Public Stables, 52 Church St.
Bingley, David, Blacksmith, 56 Anson St., Shop, Market
   Whf.
Bingley, Mary, Widow, Guignard St.
Bingley, William, Painter, 2 Cumberland St.
Bird, Sarah, Widow, 9 Magazine St.
Bird, William, Ship Carpenter, 12 Society St.
Birney, William & George, Hardware Store, 10 Broad St.
Birney, William, Tradd St.
Bishop, Elizabeth, F.P.C., 28 Bull St
Bivens, Adam, 4 Pitt St.
Bize, Daniel, Carpenter, N. Whf., Gadsden St.
Black, Alexander, Merchant, Res. 315 King St.
Black, Christopher, Attorney, Office, 32 Meeting St., Res
   Guignard St.
Black, Hester, Miss, 168 Church St.
Black, James, Boot Maker, 106 Broad St.
Black, John, 10 Broad St.

Blackhall, David, Tradd St. near King St.
Blackly, Seth, 15 Elliott St.
Blackman, Joseph, Ship Master, 28 Guignard St.
Blackmer, R., Carpenter, 41 Elliott St
Blackwood, Thomas, President, Planters' & Mechanics'
   Bank, Pitt St.
Blain, Andrew, Wheelwright, Meeting St. Road,
   Wraggsborough, Neck
Blake, Edward, Factor, Res. 10 Orange St
Blake, Margaret, Widow, 19 Archdale St.
Blamyer, Caroline, Miss, St. Philip's St.
Blamyer, Harriet, Miss, St. Philip's St.
Blamyer, William, Factor, Alexander St., Mazyckborough,
   Neck
Blamyer, William, Office, D'Oyley's Whf.
Blanchard, Glanne, Baker, 18 Wall St.
Blank, John, Bookkeeper, 148 Church St.
Blayer, Susan, 2 Mazyck St.
Blewer, Elizabeth, Widow, cr. Spring & Meeting Sts.,
   Neck
Blewer, John George, Wagon Yard, Neck
Block, Sarah, Boarding House, Martin's Whf.
Blondeau, Stephen, Hat Store, 74 King
Blum, Frederick, Butcher, N. Side Cannon St.,
   Cannonborough, Neck
Blum, Mary, Widow, 5 Cannon St., Cannonborough, Neck
Blumoir, James, Carpenter, 42 Church St.
Bolles, A., Teacher, College Yard
Bollough, Elias, Custom House Officer, 17 Archdale St.
Bond, Hager, F.P.C., Boundary St
Bondo, Louis, Goldsmith, cr. Queen & Church Sts.
Bone, Charles, Mariner, 9 Back St
Bonneau, John E., 16 Church St.
Bonneau, Sims, Attorney, 16 Church St
Bonneau, Thomas, F.P.C., Coming St
Bonnell & Saltus, Ship Chandlers, 34 E. Bay St
Bonnell, Elizabeth, Widow, 48 Wentworth St
Bonnell, John, Ship Chandler, 14 Lynch's Ln.
Boone, Susan, Widow, Plantress, 33 Wall St.
Boothe, Ann, Widow, 70 Anson St
Bootrenock, Stephen, City Guard, Lowndes St., Neck
Bordenace, John, Hairdresser, Shop, 44 Wentworth St.
Borndon, Jane Sophia, Widow, Seamstress, 40 Wentworth
   St.
Bosquet, Peter, Dry Goods Store, 309 King St
Bostick, Lucretia, F.P.C., Washer, 36 Anson St
Bouderdeaux, Eleanor, Boundary St., Wraggsborough,
   Neck
Boulinean, Andrew, Shopkeeper, King St. Road, Neck
Bounetheau, Bambary, Bricklayer, 101 Wentworth St.
Bounetheau, Edward, House Carpenter, 80 Wentworth St.
Bounetheau, Elizabeth, Widow, 101 Wentworth
Bounetheau, Henry, Clerk, 101 Wentworth St.
Bounetheau, James, Printer, Times Office, Res. 101
   Wentworth St.
Bourg, Margaret, Widow, cr. Minority & Middle Sts
Bourress, Ann, Widow, 6 Blackbird Al.
Bours, Luke, 33 Elliott St
Boutan, P B. & Co., Baker, King St. Road, Neck
Boutan, P B , Merchant, 12 Fitzsimons' Whf

Boutan, P. M. & J , Merchants, King St. Road, near the Lines, Neck
Bow, Ann, Widow, Church St.
Bowen, Nathaniel, Bishop, 5 Legare St.
Bowers, Augustus, Butcher, 9 King St.
Bowers, Augustus, Butcher, Meeting St Road, Neck
Bowers, Sarah, Seamstress, 4 Pitt St.
Bowmans, -----, Miss, 195 E. Bay St.
Boyce & Johnson, Dry Goods Store, 213 King St., Neck
Boyce & Johnson, Factors, Kunhardt & Leavitt's Whf.
Boyce, Robert, House of Entertainment, 259 King St.
Boyd, Alexander, Watch Maker, 13 Broad St.
Boyd, Eliza, Grocer, 23 Chalmers Al.
Boyd, John, Mariner, 38 Elliott St
Boyer, Mary, Widow, Clifford St.
Bradley, C B., Grocer, 109 King St.
Bradley, Charles, Printer, Times Office, 14 Maiden Ln.
Braid, Matthew, Carpenter, 86 Tradd St.
Brailsford, Edward, M.D., 7 Society St.
Brailsford, Elizabeth, Miss, S. Bay St.
Brailsford, Elizabeth, Widow, 41 Hasell St.
Brailsford, Mary, Widow, 111 Tradd St.
Brailsford, William, Surveyor, 47 Hasell St.
Brandon, Aaron, Coach Maker, 7 Anson St.
Brandon, David, Distiller, 7 Anson St.
Braselman, Isabella, Mantua Maker, 29 & 30 Archdale St.
Brelett & Godefroy, House & Sign Painters, 81 Meeting St.
Bremar, Henry, Dentist, cr. Maiden Ln. & Guignard St.
Brett & Barley, Merchants, 137 King St
Bridge, Matthew, Merchant, 12 Crafts' S. Whf.
Bridie, Robert, Cooper, E. Bay St.
Brindlay, Catharine, Seamstress, 34 Coming St
Brisbane, John, Planter, 5 Bull St.
Brisbane, William, 15 Meeting St.
Brittan, Frances H , Seamstress, 3 Amen St
Brittan, Samuel, Clerk, 21 Bull St.
Broadfoot & M'Neel, Counting House, 256 E. Bay St.
Broadfoot, Frances, Widow, 3 Tradd St.
Broch, Peter, Grocer, State St.
Brockway, Mary M , Widow, Seamstress, 23 Wentworth St
Brodie, Robert, Baker, 78 Meeting St.
Brodie, Robert, Lumber Measurer, 90 Tradd St
Broer, Martha, Widow, Shop Keeper, King St. Road, Neck
Broeske, Sarah, Widow, 157 E. Bay St
Brookings, Priscilla, Henrietta St., Mazyckborough, Neck
Brooks, Jane, cr. Archdale & Queen Sts.
Brooks, Mary, Widow, 20 Market St.
Brooks, Rachel, Widow, Seamstress, College Yard
Broughton, Ann, Miss, 19 Anson St.
Broughton, Elizabeth, Mrs., 28 Coming St.
Brow, William, Capt., 34 Church St.
Brown & Moses, Auctioneers, 6 Vendue Range
Brown & Tunis, Factors, D'Oyley's Whf.
Brown, Alexander, Merchant, King St. Road, Neck
Brown, Betsey, Seamstress, 82 Wentworth St.
Brown, C. A., Mrs., Millinery Store, 214 King St., Neck
Brown, Charles, M.D., Planter, 49 George St.
Brown, Daniel, Capt , Boarding House, 154 Church St

Brown, Edward, Merchant, Res. 142 Meeting St.
Brown, James, Butcher, Hampstead, Neck
Brown, John, Grocer, cr. Berresford & Archdale Sts.
Brown, Joshua, 12 New St.
Brown, Joshua, Lumber Yard, Savage St.
Brown, Lavinia, Mrs, Widow, Plantress, Washington St , Mazyckborough, Neck
Brown, Magdalene, Widow, 17 Parsonage Ln
Brown, Mary, Smith's Court
Brown, Mary, Widow, 65 Queen St
Brown, Morris, Shoemaker, cr. Anson & Wentworth Sts
Brown, Moses, Hair Dresser, F.P.C., 52 Elliott St.
Brown, Nancy, F P.C., 36 Beaufain St.
Brown, Peter, Mariner, 2 Guignard St.
Brown, Pollard, State St.
Brown, -----, Rev. Mr , cr Montague & Pitt Sts
Brown, Robert C., Tailor, 23 Tradd St.
Brown, Robert, Factor, 55 Tradd St
Brown, Samuel, Mariner, cr. Maiden Ln. & Market St.
Brown, Samuel Scott, Surveyor, 166 Meeting St.
Brown, Sarah, Widow, Teacher, State House Sq.
Brown, William, Capt , Team Boat, Ashley River Ferry, Neck
Brown, William, Carpenter, 30 Anson St.
Brown, William, Grocer, cr. Maiden Ln. & Market St.
Brown, William H., Grocer, 57 Church St.
Brown, William, Shopkeeper, cr. Doughty & Pinckney Sts., Cannonborough, Neck
Browne, Adam J., 234 King St.
Browne, Anna, Widow, Milliner, 173 King St
Browne, Elizabeth, Boarding House, 58 Church St
Browne, Elizabeth, Widow, 42 Wentworth St
Browne, John, Fisherman, 109 Philadelphia St.
Browne, Samuel & Frederick, Merchants, 233 King St.
Browning, William, Butcher, Reed St., near Meeting St , Neck
Brownlee, John, cr. Meeting & Hudson Sts., Wraggsborough, Neck
Brunet, Alexander, Ellery St.
Brushet, Joseph, Ship Master, Anson St
Bryan, Jonathan, Merchant, Res. 2 Hasell St.
Bryan, Lydia, Widow, Plantress, cr Anson & Hasell Sts
Bryant, Jane, Widow, 37 King St
Bryce, Henry, Merchant, Martin's S. Whf.
Bryce, Mary Elizabeth, Widow, 16 Laurens St.
Bucham, James, Planter, Archdale St.
Buchan, John, Rev., Harleston's Green
Buchanan, Ann, Widow, Seamstress, 125 Meeting St., Neck
Buchanan, Wood & Co., 25 E. Bay St.
Buckingham, Mary, Mrs., 15 Elliott St.
Buckley, Elizabeth, Widow, 75 Church St.
Buckner, James R., Planter
Budd, Abigail, Widow, 18 Cumberland St.
Budd, William, Merchant, Res. 360 King St.
Buese, John, Shopkeeper, cr. Pinckney & Lucas Sts., Cannonborough, Neck
Buford, Eliza, Miss, Boarding House, 111 Broad St
Buist, Mary, Widow, 3 Church St.
Buleau, John, Merchant, 20 Montague St

34

Bulet, Peter, Mount Pleasant, Coffee House, cr. Mary & Meeting Sts., Neck
Bulkley, ----- & Co., Cabinet Makers, 254 King St.
Bulkley, Ashbel, Merchant, 119 King St.
Bulkley, Stephen, Res. 134 King St.
Bull, Harry, F.P C., Swinton's Ln
Bull, William, Grocer, 11 S. Bay St.
Bullard & Jackson, Merchants, 10 Champney St.
Bullock, James B., Merchant, 248 E. Bay St.
Bullock, Nathaniel, Capt., Mariner, 19 Clifford's Al.
Bulow, Charles W., Planter, 112 Meeting St.
Bunells, -----. Misses, Seamstresses, 4 Blackbird Al.
Bunting, Jane, Widow, Nurse, 25 Pinckney St.
Burch, Sarah, Widow, Boarding House, 11 Pinckney St.
Burdell, John E., Carpenter, 2 Maiden Ln.
Burger & Alexander, Grocers, 120 Broad St.
Burger, Charles, Merchant, Vanderhorst's Whf.
Burger, Samuel, Tax Collector, 120 Broad St.
Burgoyne, William, Druggist, cr. E. Bay & Broad Sts.
Burk, D. F. George, Carriage & Harness Maker, King St. Road, Neck
Burk, Walter, Ship Master, 4 Guignard St.
Burkmire, Ann, Widow, 76 Wentworth St.
Burkmire, John C., Clerk, 76 Wentworth St.
Burn, William, Carpenter, 8 Cannon St., Neck
Burnet, Foster, Grocer, Vendue Range
Burnham, Thomas, Carpenter, 4 Lowndes St., Neck
Burns, James, Pilot, 124 Church St.
Burns, John, Shoe Store, 112 Church St.
Burns, Nancy, Fruit Shop, F.P.C., 68 Meeting St.
Burrell, William, Boot Maker, Market St., near Meeting St.
Burrows, Jeremiah, Grocer, 44 Market St.
Burrows, Mary, Widow, 6 Wentworth St.
Bussaker, Charles, Merchant, 157 King St.
Butler, Mary, Widow, cr. E. Bay & Inspection Sts.
Butler, Mary, Widow, Nurse, 17 Wentworth St
Butler, R. & D. R., Merchants, 98 Broad St.
Butler, Rachael, F.P.C., 8 Pinckney St.
Butler, Robert, Inspector, Union Insurance Company, 1 Laurens St.
Butman, Ebenezar, Merchant, King St. Road, Neck
Cabuel, Lewis, Tailor, 38 Church St.
Cafrel, -----, Madame, Dry Goods Store, 101 King St.
Caine, John, Drayman, 160 Church St.
Calder, Alexander, Merchant, 286 King St.
Calder, James, Cabinet Maker, 193 Meeting St.
Calder, James, Merchant, Chisolm's S. Whf., Res. 116 Broad St.
Caldwell, Robert, Merchant, King St. Road, Neck
Caldwell, Sarah, Widow, 32 St. Philip's St.
Caldwell, William A. & Co., Auctioneers, Vendue Range
Caldwell, William A., Auctioneer, Res. 58 Meeting St.
Callender, Joseph, Capt., 26 King St.
Calvert, Elizabeth, Widow, Boarding House, 49 Meeting St.
Cambridge, Eliza, Widow, Seamstress, 63 Anson St.
Cambridge, Elizabeth, Widow, 7 Orange St.
Camel, Maria, F.P.C., 7 Smith's Ln.
Cameron, -----, Widow, cr. Crafts' S. Whf., & E. Bay St.
Caminde, Veronique, Widow, Fruit Shop, 88 King St.

Campbell & Co., Grocers, 136 Queen St.
Campbell, Alexander, Capt., Mariner, 116 King St.
Campbell, Ann, Widow, 19 Boundary St.
Campbell, Ann, Widow, Boarding House, State House Sq.
Campbell, Hugh G., Naval Commander of S. C. Station, 37 King St
Campbell, John, Commission Merchant, 270 E. Bay St.
Campbell, Mary, Seamstress, F.P.C., Queen St.
Campbell, William, Hairdresser, cr. George & King Sts.
Canady, Henry, Grocer, 14 S. Bay St.
Canady, John, Carpenter, Jones' Lot, King St.
Canady, Joseph, Shoemaker, 156 Meeting St.
Cannolly, Richard, Grocer, 14 S. Bay St.
Cannon, Mary, Seamstress, F.P.C., Coming St.
Cansler, Margaret, Widow, Dry Goods Store, 102 King St.
Canter, Emanuel, Merchant, 3 Vendue Range
Canter, Jacob, Translator of Languages, 95 King St.
Canter, John, Limner, 3 Berresford St.
Canter, Joshua, Limner, 57 Broad St.
Canter, Rebecca, 57 Broad St.
Cape, Brian, 3 Bull St.
Caquet, J., Merchant, 91 E. Bay St.
Carden, J. & Conte, Tallow Chandlers, Meeting St. Road, Neck
Cardozo, Isaac, Clerk, Patriot Office, Res. 305 King St.
Cardozo, Jacob, Editor, Southern Patriot, Res. 305 King St.
Carew, Edward, Pump & Block Maker, Shop cr. Market & E. Bay Sts., Res. cr. Wall & Laurens Sts.
Carivene, Anthony, Baker, 159 Meeting St.
Carles, Peter, Merchant, 12 Fitzsimons' Whf.
Carlile, John, Grocer, 24 King St.
Carlile, William, 24 King St.
Carmand, Francis, Merchant Tailor, 96 Queen St
Carmele, John, Butcher, Hampstead, near South St., Neck
Carnighan, John, Custom House Officer, Zigzag Court
Carnochan, Richard, Merchant, Crafts' S. Whf.
Carpenter, Charles, Professor of Languages, 21 Coming St
Carpenter, Joseph, Butcher, Cannon St., Cannonborough, Neck
Carr, Ann, Seamstress, 145 Church St.
Carr, James, Butcher, 122 Queen St.
Carravan, Polly, F.P.C., Seamstress, Alexander St., Mazyckborough, Neck
Carrere, Charles, Professor of Languages, 60 Broad St.
Carrie, Lewis, Merchant, 2 Martin's Row, Res. Wentworth St.
Carroll, Bartholomew, W. Boundary St., near Mill Pond, Neck
Carroll, James Parson, Planter, Boundary St. W. Side King St., Neck
Carroll, Thomas, Painter, State St.
Carson, Elizabeth, Mrs., 86 Tradd St.
Carson, William A., 86 Tradd St
Carson, William, Grocer, 390 E. Bay St.
Carsten, John, Shopkeeper, cr. Charlotte & Elizabeth Sts., Wraggsborough, Neck
Cart, Charles, F.P.C., Carter, Elizabeth St., Mazyckborough, Neck
Cart, John, Jr., Bookkeeper in Planters' & Mechanics'

Bank, 40 King St.
Cart, John, Lumber Measurer, 22 Bull St.
Cart, Sarah, Widow, Philadelphia St.
Carter, Elizabeth, Widow, Dry Goods Store, 264 King St.
Carter, Elizabeth, Widow, Fruit Shop, 21 Archdale St.
Carter, Thomas, Ship Carpenter, 70 Market St.
Carvado, Amelia, 7 Logan St.
Carvalho, D. N., Watch Maker & Jeweler, 129 King St.
Carver, James, Veterinary Surgeon, 101 Broad St.
Carvin, Elizabeth, Mrs., Milliner, 75 King St.
Casey, Benjamin, Coach Maker, 95 Broad St.
Casey, Elizabeth, Store 95 Broad St.
Caskin, John, Carpenter, Charlotte St., Wraggsborough, Neck
Cason & Carn, Grocers, 41 Market St.
Cason, James, Grocer, Res. Maiden Ln.
Cassin, C., Auctioneer, 3 Vendue Range
Cassin, Mary, Widow, W. Side Boundary St., Neck
Catburt, Judith, Widow, Seamstress, 2 Rutledge St.
Catherwood, J. J., Watchmaker, 33 Broad St.
Catonet, Peter, Grocer, cr. Queen & Church Sts.
Cattle, Catharine, F.P.C., Elizabeth St., Wraggsborough, Neck
Cattle, William, Capt., Planter, W. Side Boundary St., Cannon St., Islington, Neck
Cauchois, Courdier, Mrs., & Co., Dry Goods Store, 54 King St.
Caught, Mary, Mrs., Dry Goods Store, 140 E. Bay St.
Caught, Thomas, Ship Carpenter, 140 E. Bay St.
Caussy, -----, Mrs., 10 St. Philip's St.
Chadwick, Samuel, Counting House, Crafts' S. Whf., Res. 14 Water St.
Chalmers, James Henry, Planter, St. Philip's St. Cont'd. Neck
Champney, John, Planter, 105 King St.
Chancognie, S. J. & Co., Merchants, Fitzsimons' Whf.
Chanler, Catharine, Widow, 43 St. Philip's St.
Chapman, Jane, Widow, 7 King St.
Charles, Adeline, Seamstress, 9 Guignard St.
Charles, John, Fisherman, 75 Church St.
Charles, Mary, 8 Cumberland St.
Charles, Sarah, Widow, 16 Coming St.
Charles, Silvey, 34 Tradd St.
Charles, Susan, 127 Wentworth St.
Charlon, Francis, Boot Maker, 176 Meeting St.
Charnock, George, Turner, 16 Magazine St.
Charnock, Thomas, Cabinet Maker, 16 Magazine St.
Chase, Elizabeth, Widow, Seamstress, 11 Laurens St.
Chatburn, Frances, Widow, Boundary St.
Chateau, Charles Rene, M.D., 156 Meeting St.
Chatelin, M. A. & Co., Fancy Store, 71 King St.
Chauet, Anthony, Merchant, 9 Tradd St.
Chazal, John P., Capt., Mariner, cr. Minority & Middle Sts.
Cheney, Eben, Jr., Merchant, 22 E. Bay St., Res. 11 Broad St.
Chifelle, Thomas, Steam Mill, Res. 143 Meeting St.
Child & Wotherspoon, Merchants, Duncan's Whf.
Child, Loring, Res. 54 Church St.
Chioh, Caty, F.P.C., Fruit Shop, St. Philip's St.
Chioh, Sarah, F.P.C., Fruit Shop, St. Philip's St.

Chisolm & Taylor, Factors, Chisolm's S. Whf.
Chisolm, Alexander, Planter, Montague St.
Chisolm, George, Factor, Res. East Bay St., near the Promenade
Chisolm, William, M.D., 2 Coming St.
Chitty, Ann B., Widow, State House Sq.
Chitty, C. C., Quorum Unis, Office, State House
Chitty, William John, Sr., Porter & Collection Clerk, State Bank, St. Philip's St., Radcliffborough, Neck
Choate, Catharine, Widow, 36 Wentworth St.
Chreitzberg, Thomas, Grocer, 45 Market St.
Chreitzbert, George, Custom House Officer, 17 Pinckney St.
Christin, Mary, Widow, S. Bay St.
Christy, Alexander, 118 Church St.
Chupein, Lewis, Mineral Water House, 6 Broad St.
Chur, George, Grocer, cr. Hasell & Meeting Sts.
Church, Margaret, Mrs., Umbrella Maker, 40 St. Philip's St.
Church, Mary, Widow, Seamstress, 4 St. Philip's St.
Clancy, John, Shop Keeper, S.W. cr. Coming & Vanderhorst Sts., Neck
Clark & Singleton, Attorneys, 29 Meeting St.
Clark, Bartholomew, Merchant, cr. Queen & King Sts.
Clark, Elizabeth, Miss, Seamstress, 110 Church St.
Clark, H., Bricklayer, Charlotte St., Mazyckborough, Neck
Clark, James, Chair Maker, 4 Back St.
Clark, James, Tailor, 39 Church St.
Clark, Martha, Widow, Mantua Maker, 7 Coming St.
Clark, Mary Eddy, Seamstress, Zigzag Court
Clark, Mary, Widow, Teacher, 13 Middle St.
Clark, Richard, Capt., Zigzag Court
Clark, Samuel, Dry Goods Store, 16 Tradd St.
Clark, William, Alexander St., Mazyckborough, Neck
Clark, William, F.P.C., Grocer, 23 State St.
Clarke, William, Planter, Boundary St. Cont'd., Cannonborough, Neck
Clyde, Thomas, Currier, at Crookshank's, Hampstead, Neck
Coastas, Shatiere, F.P.C., Meeting St. Road, Neck
Coates, S. Joseph, Steam Saw Mill, Washington St., Mazyckborough, Neck
Coates, Thomas, Ship Master, Charlotte St., Mazyckborough, Neck
Cobia, Ann, Miss, Teacher, Meeting St. Road, Neck
Cobia, Francis, Butcher, near Meeting & Read Sts., Neck
Coburn, John, Planter, cr. Warren & St. Philip's Sts., Radcliffborough, Neck
Cochran, Emiline Seamstress, Meeting St. Road, Neck
Cochran, John, Grocer, 42 King St.
Cochran, Nancy, F.P.C., Alexander St., Mazyckborough, Neck
Cochran, Samuel, F.P.C., Tailor, Alexander St., Mazyckborough, Neck
Cochran, Thomas, Broker, W. Side Pinckney St., Cannonborough, Neck
Cohen, Burnet A., Planter, Res. 343 King St.
Cohen, Mordecai, 58 Tradd St.
Cohen, Moses, Merchant, 288 King St.
Cohen, Philip, Auctioneer, Res. 241 E. Bay St.

36

Cohen, Rebecca, Widow, 8 Motte's Ln.
Cohen, S I., Dry Goods Store, 215 King St., Neck
Coiles, Margaret, Widow, 19 Pinckney St.
Coit, Jonathan, Merchant, Vanderhorst's Whf.
Colberry, Christopher, Grocer, 93 Tradd St.
Colcock, Charles, Judge, 10 Lamboll St.
Colcock, M., Widow, 10 Lamboll St.
Cole, Eliza, Widow, 26 King St.
Cole, John, Butcher, near the Lines, Hampstead, Neck
Cole, Joseph, Shoemaker, 125 Tradd St.
Cole, Sarah, F.P.C., School Mistress, 8 Clifford St.
Cole, Thomas,F P.C., Carpenter, 13 Maiden Ln.
Colhoon, Isabella, Widow, 73 Queen St.
Collier, William, Custom House Officer, 125 Wentworth St.
Collins, John M., House of Entertainment, 45 Queen St.
Collins, Mary, Widow, Hasell St.
Collins, W. J., Bricklayer, 89 Queen St.
Colngin, -----, Gunsmith, 111 E. Bay St.
Colzy, Charlemagne, Tailor, 43 Church St.
Condy & Raguet, Merchants, 242 E. Bay St.
Condy, Jeremiah, Merchant, 242 E. Bay St., Res. 201 Meeting St.
Condy, Thomas D., Attorney, 201 Meeting St.
Connel, Shavy, F.P.C., 157 Boundary St., Neck
Conner, John, Saddler, 210 King St.
Connet, William, Candle Maker, Henrietta St., Wraggsborough, Neck
Connoly, Eliza, Widow, Teacher, Lynch's Ln.
Connoly, Jeremiah, Capt., 17 Meeting St.
Connor, Samuel, Corn Store, 7 Martin's Row
Conover, Eliza, Widow, 28 Society St.
Conyers, Eliza, F.P.C., Shopkeeper, 88 Meeting St.
Conyers, John, Ship Carpenter, 363 King St.
Conyers, W. A., Accountant, 29 Pinckney St.
Coogly, Jacob, Butcher, Hampstead, Neck
Cook, Samuel, Dry Goods Store, 16 Tradd St.
Cooke, William, Merchant, 16 State St.
Cooley, William,Cabinet Maker, King St. Road, Neck
Cooper, Matthew, 29 E. Bay St
Cooper, Nathan, Merchant, Res. 48 Anson St.
Cooper, William, Boot Maker, 46 King St.
Coquenlonge, John B., Shoemaker, 82 Meeting St.
Corbe, Peter, 5 West St.
Corbett, Margaret, Widow, Plantress, cr. Cumberland & Church Sts.
Corby, John, Blacksmith, Res. 21 Hasell St.
Cord, Amelia, Anson St.
Cord, Praxall, Seamstress, Anson St.
Cordes, R., Widow Plantress, Charlotte St., Mazyckborough, Neck
Corker, Thomas, Ship Carpenter, 34 Pinckney St.
Cormea, Francis, Ship Carpenter, 7 Minority St.
Cormick, Thomas, Factor, Vanderhorst's Whf., Res. 88 Broad St.
Cornell, Benjamin, Grocer, 128 Church St.
Cornell, Gardener T., Grocer, cr. Beaufain & St. Philip's Sts
Cornwell, Sarah, F.P.C., Seamstress, 12 Philadelphia St.
Corr, Charles, F P.C., Tailor, 10 Coming St., Shop 137 Queen St.
Corrie, Samuel, Wheelwright, cr. of King & John Sts , Neck
Corun, Ann, Widow, 76 Queen St.
Coste, John C., Factor, 1 Blackbird Al.
Coste, Louis, Crockery Store, 103 Queen St.
Coste, Lucy, F.P.C., Linguard St.
Coste, Phillis, F P C., Shopkeeper, 38 St. Philip's St.
Costmagna, Mary Frances, Mrs., 12 Wentworth St.
Cotton, Christianna, Widow, Cannon St., Cannonborough, Neck
Cotton, Nancy, 22 Archdale St
Course, Isaac, Factor, 1 Magwood's Whf., Res. E. Bay St.
Courtney, Humphrey, Wine Merchant, 33 Meeting St.
Courtwrier, Eliza Maria, Widow, State House Sq.
Courty, John, Keeper of the Piquet Guard House, Meeting St., Neck
Coventry, Alexander, Dyer, 108 Tradd St.
Cowan, John, Cabinet Maker, 67 Meeting St.
Cowan, John, Pilot, 196 E. Bay St.
Cowing, S. E. & E. Wagner, Merchants, 124 E. Bay St.
Cowing, Seth L., Res 18 Cumberland St.
Cowles & Merriman, Tinners, King St. Road, Neck
Cox & Blake, Merchants, 7 Kunhardt & Leavit's Whf
Cox, George, Seedman & Florist, 114 King St
Cox, Henrietta, F.P.C., Savage St.
Cox, John S. H., Shipmaster, 130 E. Bay St.
Cox, Juliet, F.P.C., 33 Boundary St.
Cox, Mary, F.P.C., Linguard St.
Cox, Peter, Saddler, Res King St.
Cox, Thomas, Coach Maker, 26 Broad St.
Crafts & Eckhard, Attorneys, 115 Church St.
Crafts, Thomas, City Coroner, 29 Beaufain St.
Crafts, William, Jr., Attorney, Res. 29 Beaufain St.
Crafts, William, Sr., Wharf Holder, Counting House, Crafts' S. Whf., Res. 29 Beaufain St.
Craig, Jesse, Shipmaster, 243 E. Bay St.
Cramer, George, Grocer, cr. Anson & Pinckney Sts.
Cramer, John, cr. Amen & Philadelphia Sts.
Crampton & Johnson, Saddlery Store, 187 King St , Neck
Cranston, James, Broker, 12 Mazyck St.
Crask, Philip, Painter, 18 Pinckney St.
Craton, Dinah, Seamstress, 6 Smith's Ln.
Crawford, G., Widow, 20 Church St
Crawford, John, Wharf Holder, Vanderhorst Whf.
Crawley, Francis, F.P.C., Carpenter, Linguard St.
Cregrier, Clinton, 42 Anson St.
Creighton, James, F.P.C., Barber, 5 Elliott St., Res. 68 Wentworth St.
Cripps, -----, Misses, 25 Meeting St.
Cripps, Octavius, Factor, Vanderhorst Whf., Res. 19 Beaufain St.
Crocker, Dodridge & Co., Merchants, cr. E. Bay St. & Kunhardt & Leavitt's Whf.
Crocker, Shaw, Merchant, Res. 11 Tradd St.
Croft, Andrew, Storekeeper, 167 King St.
Croft, George, Capt., 9 Water St.
Croft, Peter, Factor, Nassau St., Wraggsborough, Neck
Croft, Peter, Factor, Smith's S. Whf., Mazyckborough, Neck

Croft, Sarah, F.P.C., Meeting St., Wraggsborough, Neck
Crofts, Clarisa, F.P.C., 8 Friend St.
Croker, Dodridge, Merchant, Res. 11 Tradd St.
Cromwell, Charles, Capt., 11 Stoll's Al.
Cromwell, Samuel, Bricklayer, 12 Back St.
Cromwell, Sarah, Widow, 11 Stoll's Al.
Crone, Harman, Merchant, cr. Anson & Society Sts.
Crookshanks, Daniel, Tanyard, Hanover St., Hampstead, Neck
Crosby, Hannah, Widow, 48 Anson St
Cross & Trezvant, Attorneys, cr. Meeting & Tradd Sts.
Cross, George W., Attorney, cr. Meeting & Tradd Sts.
Cross, James, Carpenter, Whim Court
Cross, Margaret, Widow, 116 King St.
Crouch, Abraham, Notary Public, 247 Meeting St.
Crow, Edward, Printer, 3 Guignard St.
Crow, Margaret D., Widow, 14 Wall St.
Cruckshanks, Amos, F.P.C., Painter, Market St.
Cruckshanks, William, Shoemaker, 56 Church St.
Cruger, Elizabeth, Widow, Meeting St.
Cruse, Amy, Seamstress, 8 Back St.
Cubie, John, Grocer, 64 Tradd St.
Cuckow, William, Pilot, 38 Guignard St.
Cudworth, Nathaniel, Clerk, 9 Bull St.
Cummings, Elizabeth, Widow, 56 Tradd St.
Cunningham, Andrew, Carpenter, 12 Magazine St.
Cunningham, Richard, Planter, Charlotte St., Mazyckborough, Neck
Curtis, Ephraim, Carpenter, 3 Montague St.
Cutting, John, Soap Chandler, at Hodge's factory, St. Philip's St., Radcliffborough, Neck
D'Oyle, Daniel, Wharf Owner, 1 St. Philip's St.
D'Vaneau, -----, Storekeeper, 36 King St.
Dagnau, Michael, Grocer, cr. Elliott St. & Bedon's Al.
Dalcho, Frederick, Rev. Dr., 20 Meeting St.
Dale, Elizabeth, Mrs., 125 Wentworth St.
Dalglish, George, Slater, 3 Mazyck St.
Dalton, James, Dr., Druggist, cr Church & Tradd Sts.
Daly, Margaret, Mrs., Widow, 42 Hasell St.
Danford, Eliza, Miss, 14 Water St.
Daniel, Josiah, Merchant, Res. 167 E. Bay St.
Daniell, Lewis, Lumber Merchant, Res. 57 E. Bay St., cr. Inspection St., Counting House, Daniell's Whf.
Danjou & Co., cr. Tradd & Church Sts.
Darby, John, Silversmith, 12 Archdale St.
Darby, Robert A., Harleston's Green
Dare, Ann, Widow, Mantua Maker, Guignard St.
Darrell, Edward, Accountant, 144 Meeting St.
Darrell, G.Y., Commission Merchant, 124 Meeting St.
Darrell, John S., Custom House Storekeeper, 114 King St.
Darrell, Josiah J., Factor, Res. cr. Anson & George Sts.
Dart & Spears, Factors, 7 Crafts' S. Whf.
Dart, Isaac M., of Dart & Spears, Res. Montague St.
Dart, Benjamin, 26 Tradd St.
Dart, John S., 26 Tradd St.
Datty, Julia, Miss, School, Wentworth St.
Datty, Mark, 86 Wentworth St.
Daugure, -----, Storekeeper, Church St.
Davega, Isaac, Factor, 87 Meeting St.
Davenport, Samuel & Co., Merchants, 8 Crafts' N. Whf.

David, Peter Rene, Storekeeper, 356 King St.
Davidson, Gilbert, Planter, Wentworth St.
Davidson, James, Capt., 48 Elliott St.
Davis, Aaron, 53 Meeting St.
Davis, David, Carpenter, 28 Coming St.
Davis, Elizabeth, Seamstress, 8 Beaufain St.
Davis, George, Peddler, 109 Queen St.
Davis, J. M., Quorum Unis & Notary Public, W. Side Pinckney St., Cannonborough, Neck
Davis, Jacob, Painter, Oil & Color Store, 40 Queen St.
Davis, John M., Notary Public, 40 E. Bay St.
Davis, John, Mariner, 37 Anson St.
Davis, John, Merchant, King St., near the Lines, Neck
Davis, M., Dry Goods Store, 323 King St.
Davis, Martha, Mrs., Widow, Pinckney St.
Davis, Matilda, Widow, 91 Wentworth St.
Davis, Sarah, F.P.C., Mantua Maker, 6 Clifford St.
Davis, Sarah, Widow, 87 Queen St.
Davis, Thomas, Capt., 12 Stoll's Al.
Davis, Thomas, Provision Store, 4 Champney St.
Davis, Thomas R., Carpenter, Boundary St., Wraggsborough, Neck
Davis, William, Grocer, 1 Tradd St.
Dawes, Hugh P , Factor, Store 1 Lothrop's Whf.
Dawes, Hugh P., Warehouse for Naval Stores, 6 Wharf St.
Dawson, Ann, Widow, 24 Montague St.
Dawson, Joanna, Mrs., Widow, cr. Guignard & E. Bay Sts
Dawson, John, Cashier, State Bank, 19 Bull St.
Dawson, John, Clerk, 24 Montague St.
Dawson, John, Jr., Factor, Gadsden's N. Whf.
Dawson, John, Merchant, King St., near the Lines, Neck
Dawson, William, Planter, 5 New St.
Deas & Brown, Factors, Martin's Whf.
Deas, David, Planter, 73 Tradd St.
Deas, Henry, Planter, 1 Friend St.
Deas, Joseph, F.P.C., Cook, Broughton's Lot, Church St.
Deas, Thomas, Merchant, 396 King St.
Deas, Venus, F.P.C., Cook, Broughton's Lot, Church St.
Deaus, G., Widow, Seamstress, 4 Pitt St.
DeBarville, Langlois Peter, Teacher of French, 31 Society St.
DeBayt, Arnaud, Widow, Seamstress, 18 Wall St.
Deberniere, William, Washington St., Mazyckborough, Neck
DeBow, Garret, Merchant, State St.
DeBow, John, Coachmaker, 182 Meeting St.
DeBow, William & Co., Oil & Colormen, 102 E. Bay St.
DeBurke, Glud, Shipmaster, 21 Wentworth St.
DeCarrendeffer, Alexander, M.D., 133 E. Bay St.
DeChamp, -----, Monsieur, Broker, 187 Meeting St.
DeCottes, -----, Widow, 48 Society St.
DeFranc, Mary, Widow, Fruit Shop, 44 Market St.
Deglame, Mary, Widow, cr. Minority & Middle Sts.
Deguer, P. A., Merchant, 3 Lothrop's Whf.
Dehemot, Francis, Ellery St.
Dehon, Sarah, Widow, Alexander St., Mazyckborough, Neck
DeJongh, Joseph, Planter, Montague St.
DeLacllotte, Emanuel, Auctioneer, Res. 9 Orange St.
DeLain, A. M., Widow, 19 Middle St.

DeLaMotte, Eugene, Clerk, Post Office
Delaney, Ann, Widow, Seamstress, Rutledge St.
Delaney, Michael, Pilot, 12 Stoll's Al.
Delavincendriere, H., King St Road, Neck
Delcol, Celestine, F.P.C., Confectioner, 381 King St.
DeLeon, M. H., Factor, Res. 40 Broad St , Counting House, Vendue Range
DeLettre, A , Ship Master, 8 Guignard St.
DeLiesseline, F. A., Planter, 1 Vanderhorst's Whf., Res. 109 Tradd St
DeLiesseline, F. G., Factor, 1 Vanderhorst's Whf., Res. 109 Tradd St
DeLorme, E. & W., Upholsterers, 99 Queen St.
Demar, Caddet, Sign Maker, 384 King St.
Demolard, Mary, Widow, Mazyckborough, Neck
Demore, -----, Widow, 17 Wall St.
Denny, Mary, Widow, 44 St. Philip's St.
Denoon, Margaret, Widow, 104 Meeting St.
Depau, Deas & Co., Merchants, 1 Chisolm's Upper Whf
Depau, -----, Merchant, Res. 20 Cumberland St.
Depeat, Cesaire, Merchant, Res. Meeting St.
Depeste, Lemere, Washer, 33 Hasell St.
Dereef, Nancy, F.P.C., Charlotte St., Mazyckborough, Neck
Deromas, Francis, 83 Tradd St.
Deromas, Jane, 168 Meeting St
DeSaussure, Harriot, School Mistress, 6 St. Philip's St.
DeSaussure, Henry, Lawyer, 18 Meeting St.
DesCoudres & Crovat, Dry Goods & Grocery, 163 & 143 King St
Desel, Charles L., Archdale & Beaufain Sts.
Desel, Joseph, F.P.C., 16 Berresford St.
Desgraves, Peter, Grocer, 184 King St.
Detruel, -----, Madam, Friend St
Devaga, Moses, Cryer, 29 Guignard St.
Devaux, -----, 42 Church St.
Devene, Clarissa, F P.C., Mantua Maker, Guignard St.
Devenseau, Priscilla, F.P.C., 4 Coming St.
DeVerja, Andriose, F.P.C., Washer, 37 St Philip's St.
DeVillers, Lewis, Stationer, cr. King & Broad Sts.
Dewees, John, Wharfinger, Martin's Whf , Res. Mary St., Wraggsborough, Neck
Dewees, Mary Ann, 89 Church St.
Dewees, William & Sons, Gibbes & Harper's Whf.
Dewees, William, Factor, cr. Alexander & Charlotte Sts., Mazyckborough, Neck
Dewet, William, Carpenter, 5 Cannon St., Neck
DeWolfe, James, Grocer, 256 King St
Dexter, Samuel W., Grocer, cr. Berresford & King Sts.
Deyeus, Francis, Confectioner, 42 Church St.
Diamond, -----, Surveyor, Res. 7 Wall St.
Dick, James, Dry Goods Store, 20 Broad St.
Dickert, John A., 9 Market St.
Dickinson, Elizabeth, Widow, Doughty St., Cannonborough, Neck
Dickinson, Francis G., Grocer, 120 Broad St.
Dickinson, Francis, Lawyer, 8 George St
Dickinson, Samuel, Vendue Master, Res 22 E. Bay St
Dickson, John & Co., Soap & Tallow Chandlers, King St. Road, Neck

Dickson, Samuel, Boarding House, 172 King St.
Dill, Eliza, Miss, King St.
Dill, Jane Eliza, Widow
Dill, Joseph, M.D., 13 Lamboll St.
Dillie, Jane, Mrs., Dry Goods Store, 84 Meeting St.
Dillingham, Catharine, Miss, 34 Anson St
Dinier, Christiana, Widow, 12 Mazyck St.
Diron, Dominique, Capt , 19 Cumberland St
Disher, Mary, Widow, Seamstress, Nassau St., Wraggsborough, Neck
Dixon, Robert, Butcher, Hampstead, Neck
Dobbins, Rosey, Seamstress, 4 Pitt St.
Dodd & Ingersoll, Merchants, 232 E. Bay St.
Dodd, John, Shipmaster, Res. 120 Wentworth St.
Dogherty, Joseph, Clerk, 3 King St.
Dolfin, Eliza, Widow, 141 E. Bay St.
Dolton, Mary, F.P.C., Dry Nurse, Elizabeth St., Neck
Don, Alexander, Carpenter, 33 Society St
Donnelly, William, Shipmaster, Gillon St.
Dorrill, Robert, Factor, William's Whf., Res State St
Dorrin, Patrick, Grocer, 35 King St
Dorson, Alexander, Mariner, 8 Cock Ln.
Dorson, Samuel, Mariner, 29 Chalmers Al.
Dotteloud, N., Grocer, 35 King St.
Dougherty, John, Stucco Plasterer, Charlotte St., Mazyckborough, Neck
Doughty, Emma, Miss, Smith St.
Douglass, Alexander, Tailor, 15 King St
Douglass, C., Grocer, cr. Market & Meeting Sts.
Douglass, Margaret, 11 Magazine St
Dove, William P., Ship Joiner, Pritchard & Knox's Whf.
Dowling, Archibald, Grocer, 2 King St
Dowling, Edward, Bricklayer, 6 Society St.
Downie, Robert, Tin Man, 30 Broad St.
Doyer, Benjamin, Grocer, 3 S. Bay St.
Doyer, John, Grocer, 4 S Bay St.
Doyle, Mary, Seamstress, 85 Tradd St.
Doyles, Charles A., Attorney, 1 St. Philip's St
Drayton, Andrew, F.P.C., School, 4 Swinton's Ln.
Drayton, Charles, Planter, St. Philip's St., near the Lines, Neck
Drayton, Jane, F.P.C., Market St
Drayton, John, District Judge, 7 Short St.
Drayton, -----, Miss, 154 Church St.
Drayton, Rebecca, F.P.C., Charlotte St., Mazyckborough, Neck
Drayton, Rebecca, Widow, Hampstead, on the Green, Neck
Drayton, William, Attorney, 9 St. Michael's Al.
Drayton, William, F.P.C., 8 Linguard St
Drege, Mary, State St.
Drege, Peter, Clothier, cr E. Bay & Queen Sts
Drewes, George, Shipmaster, cr. Anson & Pinckney Sts
Drewes, Henry, Grocer, 155 Meeting St.
Drummond, James, Shoemaker, 105 Queen St.
Dubarry, Mary, Widow, Henrietta St., Wraggsborough, Neck
Dubert, Frederick, cr. Spring & King Sts., Neck
Duboc, Francis, Merchant, 314 King St.
Dubois, Francis, 76 Church St.

39

Dubois, John, Tailor, 91 Meeting St.
Dubois, Lewis, Upholsterer, 94 Queen St.
Dubois, Peter, Carpenter, 14 Cannon St.,
    Cannonborough, Neck
Duchine, Francis, 18 George St.
Duese, Nancy, F.P C., Charlotte St., Mazyckborough,
    Neck
Duffus, John, Accountant, 4 Short St.
Duggan, Thomas, Plasterer & Stucco Man, St. Philip's St.,
    Neck
Duhadway, C. B., Saddler, cr. Church & Broad Sts.
Duke, John C., Printer, Amen St
Dukes, William C., King St.
Dukes, William C., Merchant, King St. Road, Neck
Dumoutet, Julia, 99 Broad St.
Duncan, Catharine Ann, Widow, Seamstress, 8
    Lowndes St., Neck
Duncan, John, Merchant, 31 Bull St.
Duncan, Patrick, Factor, N.E. Side Pinckney St.,
    Cannonborough, Neck
Dunkin & D'Oyley, Attorneys, 86 Broad St.
Dunkin, Rebecca, F.P.C., Seamstress, Zigzag Ln.
Dunn, John, 34 Chalmers Al.
Duplan, Leon, Hairdresser, 7 Market St.
Duplat, J. B., Jeweller, 322 King St.
Dupont, J. B., Shoemaker, Market St.
Dupont, Joseph, Crockery, cr. Queen & Meeting Sts.
Duporte, J. Fillette, Vauxhall, 74 Broad St.
Duporte, Louisa, F.P.C., Beaufain St.
Duporte, Peter, cr. Wall & Laurence Sts.
Dupoy, Francis, Dry Goods Store, 122 King St.
Duprat, Hannah, F.P.C., 81 Church St.
Duprat, R., Merchant, 43 Elliott St.
Dupre & Furman, Factors, 24 E Bay St
Dupre, Elsey, F.P.C., 1 Beaufain St.
Dupre, James, Carpenter, cr. John St. & Meeting St.
    Road, Neck
Dupre, Josiah, 6 Parsonage Ln.
Dupre, -----, Lumber Yard, E. Bay St.
Duquercron, Francis, Grocer, 203 King St Road, Neck
Durac, Mary, F.P.C., Seamstress, 68 Church St.
Durant, Matilda, Seamstress
Durbeck, Joseph, Grocer, King St. Road, Neck
Durrse, L., Accountant, Gibbes & Harper's Whf.
Durvill, George, 8 Tradd St.
Duval, Alexandrine, Widow, 168 Meeting St.
Duval, Catharine, Widow, 134 Church St.
Duvall, Peter, Shopkeeper, 10 Cannon & Borough Sts.,
    Neck
Dwight, D. W., Merchant, 177 E. Bay St.
Dwight, Elija, F.P.C., Pastry Cook, Meeting St.
Dwight, Rebecca, F.P.C., Pastry Cook, 124 Tradd St.
Dyot, John, Druggist, 56 E. Bay St.
Dyre, William, Saddler, Res. 10 Guignard St.
D'Oyle, -----, Lumber Yard, E. Bay St
Eager, George, Bricklayer, Philadelphia St.
Eager, Robert, Merchants Clerk, cr. King & Boundary Sts,
    Neck
Eager, Sarah, Widow, House of Entertainment, William's
    Whf.

Eason, Anthony, Carpenter, 3 Savage St.
Eason, James, Ship Carpenter, 6 Boundary St
Eason, -----, Mrs., Boarding House, cr. Tradd & E. Bay
    Sts
Eason, Robert, Shipwright, Chapel St., Wraggsborough,
    Neck
Eason, Susan, Widow, House of Entertainment, 6 Middle
    St
Easterby, George, Shipmaster, 11 George St.
Eckhard, George B., Attorney, Res 46 Tradd St.
Eckhard, Jacob, Jr., Teacher of Music, Coming St.
Eckhard, Jacob, Sr., Organist, 46 Tradd St.
Eckhoff, George H., Grocer, cr. Meeting & Guignard Sts
Eden, Charlotte, F.P.C., Johnson's Lot, Market St
Eden, Mary, F.P.C., Seamstress, Meeting St.
Eden, Nancy, F.P.C., Baker, Church St.
Eden, William Turner, F.P.C., 70 Meeting St.
Edmondson, Charles, Merchant, Crafts' S. Whf, Res. 3
    Laurens St.
Edmonston, Samuel, Merchant, 109 Queen St.
Edwards & Haigh, Merchants, 221 E. Bay St.
Edwards, Edward, Attorney, Res. 9 Maiden Ln
Edwards, George, Planter, 14 Legare St.
Edwards, Hannah, Widow, 197 Meeting St.
Edwards, James G., Planter, 27 Wall St.
Edwards, Jane, Washer, 14 Wentworth St
Edwards, Sarah, F.P.C., Seamstress, Charlotte St.,
    Mazyckborough, Neck
Edwards, Timothy, Merchant, Res. 23 Anson St.
Efin, Benjamin D., Dr., 369 King St
Eggart, Jacob, Grocer, cr. George & St. Philip's Sts.
Eggleson, George W., Attorney, Office, St. Michael's Al
Egleson, John, Grocer & Exchange Office, cr. E. Bay &
    Market Sts.
Ehaney, George, Carpenter, Whim Court
Ehaney, William, Factor, 1 Mazyck St.
Eheney, Catharine, Widow, 39 Coming St.
Elders, Sarah, F.P.C., Seamstress, College St.
Elfe, Benjamin, Bricklayer, Washington St.
Elfe, Benjamin, cr Hanover & Nassau Sts., Hampstead,
    Neck
Elfe, John P., Accountant, 23 Wall St
Elfe, Thomas, Lumber Measurer, 23 Wall St.
Elfe, William, Factor, 3 Magwood's Whf
Elfe, William, Factor, Chapel St., Wraggsborough, Neck
Elford, James M., Mathematician, 71 E Bay St.
Ellard, Michael, Carpenter, 260 King St.
Ellery, Mary, Widow, 106 Queen St
Elliott & Sommers, Merchants
Elliott, Ann, Widow, Meeting St
Elliott, Benjamin, 9 Legare St.
Elliott, Benjamin, Register in Equity, Office, State House
Elliott, Charles P., Merchant, Res. 11 Legare St
Elliott, Elizabeth, near the Lines, Hampstead, Neck
Elliott, Elizabeth, Widow, 41 Tradd St.
Elliott, George, 22 George St.
Elliott, Hannah, 66 Tradd St.
Elliott, Hannah, F.P.C., 15 Beaufain St.
Elliott, Juliet Georgiana, Widow, Plantress, cr. St.
    Philip's & George Sts.

Elliott, Mary, Widow, Legare St.
Elliott, Stephen, President, Bank of the State of S. C.
Elliott, Thomas O., Attorney, 11 Legare St.
Elliott, Thomas, Planter, 5 Gibbes St.
Ellis, Ann, Widow, 40 Anson St.
Ellis, David, Carver, 40 Anson St
Ellison, Mary, F.P.C., Washer, cr. Reapers Al & Ellery St.
Elliss, Myer J., Merchant, 139 King St.
Elliss, Thomas, Tailor, Pinckney St.
Elsinore, Alexander, Clerk, 41 Elliott St.
Elsworth, Frederick, Gauger, 76 Wentworth St.
Elsworth, John, Gauger, 10 Maiden Ln.
Emanuel, Isaac, Merchant, 250 King St.
Ember, ------, Madam, Grocer, 17 State St.
Emily, Cate, F.P.C , Zigzag Court
Emmery, Jonathan, Capt., 50 Church St.
England, Alexander, Baker, 105 Tradd St.
England, James, Baker, 134 Queen St.
English, James, Ship Carpenter, 5 Pitt St
Enslow, Joseph L., Cooper, Res 62 Anson St
Enslow, Mary, Widow, 62 Anson St.
Ererne, Ann, 5 Guignard St.
Erga, Frances, F.P.C., Johnson's Lot, Market St.
Eufamy, Gara, Meeting St. Road, Neck
Evans, James, Marble Cutter, 37 Wentworth St.
Evans, John, Custom House Officer, Archdale St.
Evans, William, Watchmaker, 159 King St
Eveleth & Thayer, Merchants, 2 Gillon St
Everard, William, Dyer, Society St.
Everingham, Rebecca, Franklin Hotel, 78 E. Bay St.
Ewing, Eliza, Mantua Maker, 5 Minority St.
Faber, C. H., 253 King St.
Faber, C., Widow, 25 Montague St.
Faber, Mary M., Widow, 213 E. Bay St.
Faber, Philip A., Dr., 255 King St.
Fabian, Mary Ann, Widow, 19 Anson St.
Fable, John, Shopkeeper, St. Philip's St., Cannonborough, Neck
Fair, John, Shoemaker, 156 King St.
Fair, Pleasant, F.P.C , College St.
Fair, William, 2 West St
Fairbridge, Robert, Carpenter, Ellery St.
Fairchild & Jones, Porter House, 3 Queen St.
Fairchild, Aaron, Wood Measurer, 120 Meeting St. Cont'd., Neck
Fairchild, Alexander, Grocer, cr. Liberty & St. Philip's Sts.
Fairchild, Margaret, Widow, 19 Pinckney St
Faree, Felicity, Widow, Columbus St., Neck
Farley, John, Teacher of Free School No. 5, Wolf St., Hampstead, Neck
Farr, Jenar, F.P.C., Seamstress, Johnson's Lot, Market St.
Farrell, ------, Mrs., Grocer, 4 Elliott St.
Faures, ------, Miss, 3 Clifford St.
Fauste, Jeremiah, Grocery & Dry Goods Store, King St. Road, Neck
Fayole, Peter, Dancing Master, 359 King St.
Fayssoux, James H., Dr., Meeting St. Road, Neck
Fegan, Simon, Grocer, William's Whf.
Fell, Thomas, Tin Plate Worker, Shop, 109 Church St., Res. 29 Church St

Fellette, Francis, Jeweller, cr. Meeting & Queen Sts.
Fenwick, Bella, F.P.C., Washer, 5 Boundary St.
Fenwick, Rose, 44 Boundary St
Fenwick, Susan, F.P.C , 5 Middle St.
Feraud, Alexander, Merchant, 220 King St.
Feraud, Thomas, Grocer, cr Queen & State Sts.
Ferguson & Clark, Merchant Tailors, 108 Broad St.
Ferguson, Ann, Widow, Planter, 3 Liberty St.
Ferguson, Edmund, Carpenter, 12 Parsonage Ln.
Ferguson, James, Planter, 3 Liberty St.
Ferguson, John, Merchant Tailor, Res 108 Broad St.
Ferguson, Samuel W., Dr., 3 Liberty St
Fernald, Dennis, Constable, 11 Linguard St.
Fernet, K., Milliner & Mantua Maker, 95 Queen St
Ferrell, Francis Ann, Shopkeeper, State St.
Ferres, Phoebe, F.P C., Cake Baker, Boundary St
Ferret, Charles, F.P.C., Cake Baker, 12 George St
Ferret, John F , Fruit Shop, 66 Meeting St.
Fiche, Peter, Guilder, 331 King St.
Fick, Charles, Grocer, 20 Lynch's Ln
Fife, James, Bookkeeper, 133 Church St.
Fife, Mary, Widow, 133 Church St.
Figures, Peter B., Painter, 104 E. Bay St., Res. 8 Pritchard's Whf.
Findley, Jacob, Bricklayer, 159 E. Bay St.
Findley, James E. B., M.D., President, Medical Society, 10 Meeting St.
Finklea, Elizabeth, 17 Wentworth St.
Finklea, Thomas, Saddler, Res. 175 Meeting St.
Firmon, Anthony, Henrietta St., Wraggsborough, Neck
Fisher, George A., Saddlery Store, 288 King St.
Fiske, S. H., Merchant, 241 E. Bay St
Fitch, Joseph, Merchant, Res. 175 Meeting St.
Fitch, Thomas, Grocer, cr. Market & Meeting Sts.
Fitch, William, Boat Builder, Pritchard & Knox's Whf., E. Bay St.
Fitzpatrick, -----, 19 Amen St.
Fitzsimmon, -----, Wharf & Stores, near the Market
Fitzsimmons, Charles, Grocer, 34 Elliott St.
Fitzsimmons, Christopher, Planter, 37 Hasell St
Fitzsimmons, ------, Counting House, 6 Fitzsimmons' Whf.
Fitzsimmons, Dolly, 19 Magazine St
Fitzsimmons, Thomas, Carpenter, Cannon St., Cannonborough, Neck
Flachat, Ciprian, Merchant, 224 E. Bay St.
Flagg, Eliza, Widow, 17 Elliott St
Flemming & Ross, Merchants, Counting House, Duncan's Whf.
Flemming, James, Grocer, cr. Cumberland & King Sts.
Flemming, John H , Carpenter, 110 Wentworth St.
Flemming, Thomas & Co., Merchants, 161 King St.
Flemming, Thomas, Res. 76 George St.
Flinn, Andrew, Rev., D. D., 21 S. Bay St
Flint, ------, Mrs., Widow, Boarding House, 112 Church St.
Florence, Levy, Merchant, 276 King St.
Florence, Sarah, Mrs., Dry Goods Store, 219 King St.
Florin, Henry, 37 Guignard St.
Florin, Mary, Nurse, F.P.C., Charlotte St., Wraggsborough, Neck

41

Flornay, Francis, Mariner, Ellery St.
Flud, Daniel, Planter, 20 S. Bay St.
Flurney, May, Bricklayer, F.P.C., Alexander St ,
　Mazyckborough, Neck
Fogartie & Munson, Merchants, 106 King St.
Fogartie, Christiana, Miss, 13 Wall St.
Fogartie, James, Res. 297 King St.
Folker, James, 58 Beaufain St
Folker, John H., Accountant, 58 Beaufain St.
Folker, Joseph, Teacher, 56 Beaufain St.
Folker, Rebecca, Widow, 58 Beaufain St.
Folker, Thomas, Druggist, cr. Elliott & Church Sts.
Follin, A. & F , Merchants, 328 King St.
Follin, A. & F , Tobacconists, 288 Meeting St.
Follin, Augustus, Wax Candle Factory, Meeting St. Road,
　Neck
Foot & Meacle, Public Stables, Church St.
Footman, John W., Broker, 4 Wentworth St.
Forbes, John, Tin Plate Worker, 5 Tradd St.
Forbes, William, Tin Plate Worker, 158 King St., Res. 11
　Coming St.
Ford & Dessasure, Attorneys, Office 46 Broad St.
Ford, Jacob, Attorney, Res. 46 Broad St.
Ford, Mary, Miss, Seamstress, King St. Road, Neck
Ford, Timothy, Attorney, 232 Meeting St
Fordam, Ellinor, Mrs , Nurse, 28 Ellery St
Fordam, John G., Blacksmith, Res. 2 Ellery St.
Fordam, Richard, Blacksmith, Res. Gillon St.
Forest, Aberdeen, Cooper, F.P.C , 51 Boundary St., Neck
Forrist, Charity, Widow, 8 Hasell St
Forrist, Thomas H., Cooper, 25 Tradd St., Shop, D'Oyley's
　Whf
Forster, Anthony, Rev., 252 King St.
Foster, Henry, Boarding House, Martin's Whf.
Foster, Isaac, Merchant, 119 King St.
Foster, Nathan, Grocer, cr. Gadsden's Al. & Elliott St
Foster, William B., Discount Clerk, Bank of the State, W.
　Side Boundary St., Neck
Foucard, Celia, Widow, 353 King St.
Fourgeaud, Arnold, Baker, 20 Guignard St.
Fowler, Andrew, Rev., Teacher, 57 Queen St.
Fowler, John, Carpenter, 15 Pitt St.
Fowler, John James, Accountant, Anson St.
Fowler, Michael, Grocer, 10 S. Bay St.
Fox, Patrick, Capt., Merchant, Res. 139 E. Bay St.
Francis, John, F.P C , Upholsterer, 47 King St.
Francis, John V., F.P.C , Carpenter, 20 Coming St.
Francis, Mary N., Friend St.
Franklin, James, Boarding House, 25 Chalmers Al.
Fransway, Margaret, F P C , 20 Coming St
Fransway, Mary, Friend St.
Fraser & Son, Carpenters & Boat Builders, Daniell's Whf
Fraser, Charles, Office, Tradd St.
Fraser, Eliza, Miss, Teacher, 7 Magazine St.
Fraser, John & Co., Factors, D'Oyley's Whf.
Fraser, John, Carpenter & Boat Builder, 41 Wentworth St.
Fraser, John, Carpenter, Res. 19 E. Bay St.
Fraser, Luke H., Merchant, Chisolm's Whf.
Fraser, Thomas, Planter, 7 Magazine St.
Frazor, James, Soap & Candle Factory, King St. Road,

　Neck
Frean, Margaret, Grocer, cr. Meeting & Wentworth Sts
Frean, William, Merchant, cr. Market & King Sts.
Fredericks, Ellinor, Widow, Seamstress, 5 Parsonage Ln
Freeman, Elizabeth, F.P.C., 20 Coming St.
Freeman, Henry, F P C., Mariner, French Al
Freeman, Luther, Grocer, 247 E. Bay St.
Friday, William, Jr., F.P.C., Butcher, Cannon St ,
　Cannonborough, Neck
Friday, William, Sr , F.P.C , Butcher, Cannon St ,
　Cannonborough, Neck
Friedle, John A., Museum, cr. Market & King Sts.
Friend, Ann, Widow, Anson St.
Friezeman, James Edward, Painter, Henrietta St ,
　Wraggsborough, Neck
Frink, Thomas B., 44 Pinckney St.
Frish, Charles, Dry Goods Store, 263 King St.
Fritz, John, Deputy Marshall, 21 Wall St
Frobus, John, Bricklayer, 88 Wall St
Frobus, Rebecca, Widow, 38 Wall St
Frost, Elizabeth, Widow, 10 Archdale St.
Frost, Henry R., M.D., 10 Archdale St., Office, 34 Society
　St.
Frost, Thomas, Rev., 143 E Bay St.
Fuller, Oliver, Capt., Mariner, Meeting St.
Fuller, William, Hat Store, 87 King St.
Fulmor, John, Chair Maker, 135 Meeting St
Furguson, Sarah, F.P.C., Amen St.
Furman, Charles M., Attorney, 117 Church St.
Furman, Josiah B., Factor, Res. 117 Church St.
Furman, Richard, Jr., M.D., 117 Church St.
Furman, Richard, Rev , D. D., 117 Church St
Fursman, Nicholas, M.D., cr. Wall & Boundary Sts.
Gabeau & Smith, Coopers, Gibbes & Harper's Whf
Gabeau, Anthony, Tailor, 145 King St.
Gabeau, Daniel, Cooper, 39 Market St.
Gabeau, James, Cooperage, Mitchell's Al., Res. 54 Queen
　St.
Gabeau, Simon, Accountant, 145 King St.
Gadsden & Collins, Lumber Merchants, Gadsden's Whf
Gadsden, Christopher E., Rev., D. D., 132 E. Bay St
Gadsden, Cloey, F.P.C., Seamstress, Meeting St ,
　Wraggsborough, Neck
Gadsden, John, Attorney, Res. 9 Maiden Ln
Gadsden, Philip, Factor, 27 Wall St.
Gadsden, -----, Widow of J. W., Plantress, 87 Queen St.
Gaillard, Daphne, F.P.C., Washer, Alexander St ,
　Mazyckborough, Neck
Gaillard, Harriot, Widow, 40 Boundary St.
Gaillard, Samuel, F P C., Carpenter, 11 Archdale St
Gaillard, Theodore, Factor, Montague St.
Gaillard, Theodore, Judge, 15 Society St
Galbraith, James S., Blacksmith, 43 Anson St., Shop, 13 E
　Bay St.
Galhagen, William, Grocer, 6 Elliott St
Gallachat, Joseph, Bookkeeper, U. S. Bank, Res. College
　Yard
Gallagher, -----, Rev., D. D., cr. St. Philip's & Wentworth
　Sts.
Galloway, James, Masonic Hall, cr. of Market &

Meeting Sts.

Gamage, Edward, Merchant, Res. 2 Friend St

Gamage, Moore & Co., Merchants, 269 E. Bay St.

Gandoine, Isidore, Merchant, 65 E. Bay St.

Ganter, Phillis, Seamstress, 19 Coming St.

Gantt, Thomas, Attorney, 3 State House Sq

Gappen, William, Wheelwright, Lynch's Ln.

Gardeer, Taman, F P.C. Woman, Boundary St , Neck

Garden, Adam, Shoemaker, 396 King St.

Garden, John, Planter, N.E. Side Pinckney St., Cannonborough, Neck

Gardener, Betsey, F P.C., Elizabeth St , Mazyckborough, Neck

Gardner, Ann, Confectioner, F.P.C., 62 Broad St.

Gardner, Henry, Blacksmith, Res. 46 Society St.

Gardner, Jack, F.P.C., 6 Swinton's Ln.

Gardner, John & Son, Blacksmith's Shop, cr. Market & E. Bay Sts.

Gardner, John, Blacksmith, Res. 46 Society St.

Gardner, Rebecca, 11 Archdale St

Gardner, Sophia, F.P.C., Seamstress, 6 St. Philip's St.

Garfiu, John, Mariner, 14 Bedon's Al

Garner, Ann, Widow, 40 Hasell St.

Garnier, Joseph, 76 Church St.

Garth, Peter, Bricklayer, Warren St., op. St. Paul's Church, Radcliffborough, Neck

Gasway, Eliza, Miss, Philadelphia St.

Gates, Jane, Widow, King St. Road, Neck

Gates, -----, Rev. Mr., Charlotte St., Mazyckborough, Neck

Gaultier, Mary, Widow, Teacher, Blackbird Al.

Geddes, Henry, King St. Road, Neck

Geddes, John, His Excellency, Gov. of S. C., 98 Broad St.

Geddes, -----, Widow of Robert, Plantress, St. Philip's St., Neck

Gefkin, Christiana, Widow, 8 Society St.

Gefkin, H.C., Carpenter, 19 Magazine St.

Gennings, Mary, Teacher, 74 Queen St.

Gensell, John, Keeper of the Marine Hospital, 6 Back St.

George, James, Shipwright, 188 E. Bay St.

Gerald, Mary, Widow, 29 Pinckney St.

Gerard, Peter, Tailor, 47 Church St

Geraud, Francis & Co., Merchants, King St. Road, Neck

Gereno, Louisa, 11 King St.

Gest, State, Planter, 3 Meeting St.

Getty, Samuel, Grocer, cr. Meeting & Boundary Sts.

Geyer, John, Capt., 13 Lynch's Ln.

Geyer, John S., Factor, Mey's Whf., Res. 13 Lynch's Ln.

Gibbes, James L., Planter, cr. George & St. Philip's Sts.

Gibbes, Sarah, Mrs., Plantress, cr. George & St. Philip's Sts.

Gibbes, William H., Master in Equity, cr. Queen & Meeting Sts.

Gibbs & Harper, Counting House, End of Vendue Range

Gibbs, Elizabeth, Seamstress, 21 Church St.

Gibbs, G & J., Bakers, 40 Elliott St.

Gibbs, George, 7 State St.

Gibbs, Joseph, 12 Lamboll St.

Gibbs, Margaret, Seamstress, 9 Elliott St.

Gibbs, R. Robert, Meeting St., Wraggsborough, Neck

Gibbs, Robert, 7 Parsonage Ln.

Gibbs, Robert, Doughty St., Cannonborough, Neck

Gibbs, Robert, Jr., Planter, John's St., Wraggsborough, Neck

Gibbs, Susannah, Widow, Meeting St.

Gibson & O'Hara, Attornies, 25 Meeting St.

Gibson, Alexander, Merchant, 20 E. Bay St

Gibson, Calaghan Thomas, Accountant

Gibson, Falconer & Co , Merchants, Chisolm's Whf.

Gibson, George & Co., 240 E. Bay St.

Gibson, James, Coach Maker, Res. 138 Meeting St.

Gibson, Jane, Mrs., Teacher, W. End of Tradd St.

Gibson, Robert, 21 Friend St.

Gibson, William, Factor, Res. 20 Mazyck St

Gibson, William H., Tanner, 138 Meeting St

Gidiere, John Joseph, Merchant, 220 King St.

Gidiere, John Joseph, Merchant, 220 King St

Gidiere, John M., Merchant, 220 King St.

Gidiere, Philip N., Merchant, 220 King St

Gilberry, John B., Tailor, 16 Ellery St.

Gilbert, Seth H , Wharfinger, Res. 350 E. Bay St.

Gilchrist, E. L., Mrs., 12 King St.

Gilchrist, James, Bank Officer, 18 Cumberland St.

Gilchrist, Robert B., Attorney, Res. 18 Cumberland St.

Giles, Othniel J., Grocer, 19 Market St.

Gilfert, Charles, Manager of the Theatre, Res. at the Theatre

Gill, Charlotte, F.P.C., 3 Wall St.

Gilliard, William H., Merchant, Res. 176 cr. King & George Sts.

Gillon, Alexander, Teller, State Bank, Res. 2 Wall St

Gillon, P. Ann, Widow, 2 Wall St.

Gilman, Sally, Tailoress, 8 Back St.

Ginnis, Fortune, F.P.C., Market St.

Giraud, Francis, Merchant, 359 King St.

Gissendanver, Susannah, Widow, 37 Beaufain St.

Gitzinger, C. F., Widow, Boarding House, 130 Tradd St.

Gitzinger, John R., 129 Tradd St.

Givens, William, Shoemaker, 15 Elliott St.

Gladden, George, Butcher, Bridge St., Neck

Glanet, Louis, Vanderhorst St., Radcliffborough, Neck

Glatocar, Lewis, Painter, Anson St.

Gleize, Henry, M.D., cr. Anson & Market Sts.

Glen, John S., 53 Tradd St.

Glen, John, Teller, Planters' & Mechanics' Bank

Glen, Margaret, Widow, 53 Tradd St.

Glen, Tenah, F.P.C., 7 Linguard St.

Glover, Amos, 16 Chalmers Al.

Glover, Charles, Attorney

Glover, Elsy, F.P.C., 2 Parsonage Ln.

Glover, Henry E., M.D., 15 St. Philip's St

Glover, Joseph, M.D., cr. Wentworth & Rutledge Sts.

Glover, Margaret, Widow, 26 Anson St.

Glover, Wilson, 2 Meeting St.

Goash, Charles, Watchmaker, 65 E. Bay St.

Godard, Renne, 61 King St.

Godfrey, Catharine, Seamstress, 85 Tradd St.

Godfrey, Silvia, F.P.C., Cock Ln.

Godfried, John & Co., Grocers, cr. Anson & Laurens Sts

Goff, March, Shoemaker, 6 King St.

Goff, Margaret, Rutledge St

Goff, Mary, 2 Pitt St.
Goff, William, Painter, 52 Wentworth St.
Going, Sarah, F.P.C., 39 Wentworth St.
Golden, Palmer, Painter, 69 Market St
Goldsmith, Abraham, Clerk to the Synagogue, 2 Hasell St.
Goldsmith, Henry, Deputy Register in Equity, 2 Hasell St
Goldsmith, Isaac M., Vendue Cryer, 1 Hasell St.
Goldsmith, Morris, Deputy Marshal, Court House
Good, Francis, Shopkeeper, cr. Mary & Meeting Sts., Wraggsborough, Neck
Good, Sarah, Miss, 45 King St.
Goodman & Weyman, Merchants, 201 King St., Neck
Goodman, Duke, Factor, Duncan's Whf.
Goodman, Duke, Factor, Hudson St., Wraggsborough, Neck
Goodon, Sib, F.P.C , E Bay St.
Goodsell & Hitchcock, Chair Makers, Meeting St. Road, Neck
Gordet, John, Shopkeeper, Cannon & Borough Sts., Neck
Gordon, Charles P., 15 Cumberland St.
Gordon, Edward William, Shopkeeper, cr. Meeting & Mary Sts , Neck
Gordon, John, Bricklayer, 36 Meeting St.
Gordon, Martha, Widow, 10 Parsonage Ln
Gordon, -----, Widow, cr. King & Berresford Sts.
Gosprey, Francis, Carpenter, 206 King St., Neck
Gotton, Mary, F.P.C., Nurse, 63 Anson St.
Gough, Emma, Widow, Meeting St.
Gould, Sarah, Widow, Seamstress, Boundary St.
Gouldsmith, Richard, Cabinet Maker, 104 King St.
Goure, S., Widow, Fancy Store, cr. King & Broad Sts.
Gourley, U , Wharfinger, 9 Wall St
Gowan, Peter, Watchmaker, 38 Meeting St.
Graddock, Richard, Blacksmith, 391 King St.
Graham, Fanny, F.P.C., Beaufain St.
Graham, Peggy, F.P.C., Washer, 9 Pinckney St.
Graham, Thomas, Cabinet Maker, 58 King St.
Grainger, James, Painter, Henrietta St., Wraggsborough, Neck
Gran, John, Tailor, King St.
Grandis, Elector, Seamstress, College Yard
Grant & M'Guffie, Merchants, 111 Broad St
Grant, James, Printer, Res. 5 Wall St.
Grasier, C. J., Merchant, Res. 10 Tradd St.
Graves, Anthony, 54 Tradd St.
Graves, Charles & Son, Factors, Chisolm's Whf.
Graves, Charles, Res. 54 Tradd St.
Graves, Sarah, Widow, 4 Gibbes St.
Gray & Corby, Blacksmiths, Pritchard's Whf.
Gray, Alexander, Merchant, 181 King St.
Gray, Frances, Seamstress
Gray, H., Magistrate, 23 Ellery St
Gray, James W., Attorney, 228 Meeting St.
Gray, James W , Attorney, 7 Boundary St.
Gray, John, Boarding House, 4 Bedon's Al.
Gray, Ruth, Seamstress, 2 Whim Court
Gray, William, Blacksmith, E. Bay St.
Gready, Andrew P , Domestic Warehouse, 294 King St
Green, Daniel, Grocer & Carpenter, cr. Swinton's Ln & Archdale St.

Green, Elizabeth, Widow, cr. Broad & E. Bay Sts.
Green, James, Accountant, 33 Society St.
Green, Mary, Widow, cr. Church & Cumberland Sts.
Green, T P., Clerk, 121 Broad St
Greenhill, Hume, 4 Friend St.
Greenlan, George, 94 Tradd St
Greenland, Benjamin R., M.D., Res. S. End of Meeting St.
Greenland, William, Factor, Res S. End of Meeting St
Gregorie, Mary, Widow, 26 Anson St.
Gregson, Thomas, Assistant Clerk, State Bank, 39 Coming St.
Griffin, Susannah, Widow, Nurse, 58 Anson St
Grille, Claude, Hat Store, 137 Queen St.
Grimke, John F., Judge, 153 E. Bay St.
Grimke, Thomas S., Attorney, 3 St. Michael's Al.
Gripon, Delia, 10 Linguard St.
Groning, Lewis, Merchant, Res. 9 New St.
Groning, Simmons, F P.C., 4 Magazine St.
Gros, John, Cabinet Maker Warehouse, 82 Meeting St.
Gros, John, Hardware Store, 92 Meeting St.
Grove, John A., 11 Laurens St.
Grove, Lucretia, Mantua Maker, 14 Wentworth St
Groziant, Benjamin, Shoemaker, 7 Church St.
Gruber, George, Bricklayer, Meeting St near Boundary St., Neck
Gruber, Jacob, Bricklayer, 73 Wentworth St
Gruber, Margaret B., Widow, Meeting St. Road, Neck
Gue, John Francis, Tin Plate Worker, 42 Market St
Guellett, Hellen, Seamstress, 19 Coming St.
Guenveur, John M., French Teacher, 39 Meeting St
Guerin, Joseph, Grocer, St. Philip's St.
Guerin, Mary, Widow, 15 Pinckney St.
Guerin, Robert W., Tailor, 108 St. Philip's St.
Guerry, Grandison, Accountant, 8 Society St.
Guilbert, Eugene, Professor of Music, cr. Wall & Laurens Sts.
Guiness, Mary, Miss, Fruit Shop, 89 Queen St.
Guy, James, Taylor, 54 Boundary St , Neck
Guy, John, Carpenter, Vanderhorst St., City Lands, Neck
Guy, Joseph, Carpenter, 224 Meeting St., Neck
Gyles, John, 74 E. Bay St.
Hacke, Henry, Shopkeeper, 197 King St., Neck
Hackness, Mary Ann, Widow, 26 Wall St.
Haeket, Charles, Dry Goods Store, 128 E Bay St
Hagen, Christian, Corn Store, cr. of Wentworth & Rutledge Sts.
Hagen, Rosanna, Widow, Dry Goods Store, 129 King St.
Haig, David, Cooper, Res. 150 Meeting St.
Haig, James, Attorney, 150 Meeting St.
Haig, James, F.P.C , Shoemaker, 1 Archdale St
Haig, Susannah S., Widow, 4 New St.
Hair, Mary, Widow, 175 King St , Aged 92
Hall, Ann, Widow, 122 E. Bay St.
Hall, D W. & Co., Merchants, 235 E Bay St
Hall, David, 69 Market St.
Hall, Elizabeth, 155 Church St.
Hall, Ellinor, F.P.C., 17 Clifford St.
Hall, George & Co., Merchants, 104 Broad St.
Hall, George, M.D., 9 Meeting St.
Hall, Harriet, Widow, Wentworth St.

Hall, Jane, Widow, 155 Church St.
Hall, Sabina, Mrs., Plantress, cr. of Church & Amen Sts.
Hall, Sarah, Miss, 396 King St.
Hall, Susan, Widow, 2 State St.
Hall, William, M.D., 122 E. Bay St.
Halliday, Ellinor, 147 Church St.
Ham, Thomas, Clerk in Ordinary's Office, cr. Wolf & Nassau Sts., Neck
Hamble, Mary, Nurse, Nassau St.,Wraggsborough, Neck
Hamilton, Clarinda, F.P.C., Nurse, Anson St.
Hamilton, Euphame, Widow, Teacher, Seminary, cr Queen & Meeting Sts.
Hamilton, John, Ship Carpenter, 7 Anson St.
Hammet, Benjamin, Merchant., Res. Reed St., Neck
Hammett, Charlotte, Widow, 14 Guignard St.
Hammett, Thomas, Collector, 117 Wentworth St.
Hammond, Joseph, Tailor, 20 Friend St.
Hanahan, Thomas, Vanderhorst St , City Lands, Neck
Hancock, George, Clerk, cr. Bull & Rutledge Sts.
Hancock, John F., Merchant, 49 E. Bay St.
Hannahan, Hannah, F.P.C., Philadelphia St.
Happoldt, Christopher, Butcher, Cannon St., Cannonborough, Neck
Happoldt, John, Butcher, Hampstead, Neck
Happoldt, John G., Butcher, Cannon St., Cannonborough, Neck
Harbert, John & Co., 98 King St.
Harbus, John R., Grocer, cr. of Wentworth & Society Sts.
Harby, Isaac, School Master, 88 Tradd St.
Hard, Benjamin F., 27 Society St.
Harden, Tissey, F.P.C., Washer, 2 Beaufain St.
Hare, Francis, Widow, State St.
Harleston, Edward, Planter, 41 Boundary St.
Harleston, Edward, Planter, Smith's Ln.
Harleston, Elizabeth, Miss, cr. Church & Cumberland Sts.
Harleston, Nicholas, Planter, Alexander St., Mazyckborough, Neck
Harleston, William, Mrs., Widow, 72 Broad St.
Harman, Henry, Grocer, 294 King St.
Harper, James, Baker, State St.
Harper, James, Store, 42 Tradd St.
Harper, Jobit, F.P.C., College Green
Harris, Hyam, Merchant, 291 King St.
Harris, Jacob, Jr., Store Keeper, 274 King St.
Harris, Rebecca, Widow, 52 Wentworth St.
Harris, Tucker, M.D., 78 King St.
Harrison & Trowbridge, Merchants, 7 Vendue Range
Harrison, D. W., Clerk, 15 Broad St.
Harrison, Francis, Grocer, cr. of King & Queen Sts.
Harrison, James, Shoemaker, 41 Beaufain St
Harrison, Jared, Coach Maker, 178 Meeting St.
Hart & Hammet, Merchants, King St ,Road, Neck
Hart, Bella, Widow, 72 E. Bay St.
Hart, Jacob, Boarding House
Hart, Moses, St. Philip's St.
Hart, Nathan, Merchant, 139 King St.
Hart, S. M., Dry Goods Store, 205 King St., Neck
Harth, William, Lumber Merchant, 1 Gibbes St
Hartley & Magwood, Merchants, King St. Road, Neck
Harvey, Josiah R., Planter, cr. Bridge & Thomas Sts.,

Islington, Neck
Harvey, Mary, Widow, 35 Society St.
Harvey, Samuel, Ship Master, 129 E. Bay St.
Harvey, Susannah F., Widow, cr Bridge & Thomas Sts , Islington, Neck
Harvey, Thomas, Clerk, 35 Society St
Hasall, William, Charlotte St., Mazyckborough, Neck
Haskell, E., Maj., Planter, 155 E. Bay St.
Haskett, John, Saddler, Res. 46 Queen St.
Haslett, John, Merchant, 31 E Bay St.
Hatch, James R., Ship Master, 15 Pinckney St.
Hatch, Mary, Widow, 15 Pinckney St.
Hatch, Prince H., Boat Builder, 15 Pinckney St.
Hatfield, John, Grocer, 82 Church St
Hattier & Rame, Confectioners, 158 King St.
Hayden, Jane, Widow, cr. Blake & Drake Sts, Neck
Hayne, R. Y., Col., Attorney, cr. Pinckney & Cannons Sts., Cannonborough, Neck
Haynes, -----, Mrs, Widow, Plantress, St. Philip's St., Neck
Henry, Charles, Carpenter, Boundary St., Mazyckborough, Neck
Heriott, Benjamin, Factor, 126 Tradd St.
Hewitt, Thomas, Glass Store, 209 King St., Neck
Hill & Burn, Painters, 17 Cumberland St.
Hill, Asa, Painter, 69 Market St.
Hill, Henry D., Ship Master, 98 E. Bay St.
Hill, Keziah, Widow, 6 Magazine St.
Hill, Margaret, 3 French Al.
Hill, Martha, Widow, 15 Parsonage Ln.
Hill, Mary, Store, 88 King St.
Hill, Paul, Clifford St.
Hillegas, Sarah, Widow, School Mistress, 18 Berresford St.
Hilliard, Nathaniel, Ship Master, Res. 2 Laurens St.
Hilliary & Blanchard, Confectioners, 169 King St.
Hillman, Ann, Widow, 40 E. Bay St
Hinckley, J. C., Store Keeper, 66 King St.
Hinson, Sarah, Seamstress, Lodge Al.
Hippias, Phoebe, Widow, 26 King St.
Hislop, Hannah, Widow, 98 E. Bay St.
Hix, Joseph, Carpenter, cr. of Church & Market Sts.
Hoalton, Elizabeth, Pastry Cook, 8 Cumberland St.
Hodges, W. George, Soap Chandler, St. Philip's St., Radcliffborough, Neck
Hodges, W. George, Soap Chandler, King St Road, Neck
Hodgson, -----, Mrs., Boarding House, cr. of Gadsden's Al & Elliott St.
Hoff, John, Booksellers, 117 Tradd St.
Hoff, John M., Grocer, 20 Market St.
Hoffman, George, Grocer, 46 Church St.
Hoffmann, Jacob, Grocer, King St. Road, Neck
Hogarth, John, Shoemaker, 15 Beaufain St.
Hogarth, Mary, Widow, 30 Wall St.
Hogarth William, Shoemaker, 1 Boundary St.
Holbrook, Moses, M.D., 18 Elliott St.
Holland, Edwin C., Editor, Times, Res. 7 Legare St.
Holland, John, Boarding House, 118 Tradd St.
Holland, John, Carpenter, cr. of George & Coming Sts.
Hollowell, Richard, Carpenter, 13 Berresford St.
Hollowell, Thomas, Packet Man, 16 Lynch's Ln

45

Holmes, Charles, Butcher, Hampstead, Neck
Holmes, Ellinor, F P.C , 66 Tradd St
Holmes, I. C., Attorney, 7 St. Michael's Al
Holmes, James, Accountant, 174 King St.
Holmes, James, Notary Public & Dutch Consul, 46 E. Bay St., Res. Guignard St.
Holmes, James V., Bricklayer, 9 Whim Court
Holmes, John B., City Recorder, 6 Meeting St.
Holmes, John, Grocer, 70 Market St.
Holmes, John, Planter, 63 Tradd St.
Holmes, Mary, Widow, 7 Church St.
Holmes, Mary, Widow, Lynch's Ln.
Holmes, Sandiford, (Mease & Holmes), 52 Queen St.
Holmes, William, Vendue Master, 46 Boundary St
Honour, John, Grocer, 6 Berresford St.
Hopkins, John M., Merchant, Vanderhorst's Whf.
Hopton, John, F.P.C., Carpenter, 75 Church St.
Horden, Eliza, Grocer, 11 Middle St.
Horlbeck, Catherine, Widow, Cumberland St.
Horlbeck, Henry, Bricklayer, 14 Cumberland St
Horlbeck, John, Bricklayer, 208 King St.
Horry, Augustus, Boat Builder, 18 Wentworth St.
Horry, Elias, cr. Meeting & Tradd Sts.
Horry, Harriett, Widow, 60 Tradd St.
Horry, Lynch E., Planter, 65 Broad St.
Horry, Thomas, Planter, 246 Meeting St
Horsey, Thomas J., (Read & Horsey), 308 King St.
Hort, Benjamin Simmons, Millwright, Boundary St. Cont'd , Cannonborough, Neck
Horwood, Mary, Nurse, Zigzag Ln.
Houseal, David, Bookkeeper, Mary St., near King St., Neck
Howard, Alexander, City Assessor, 1 Minority St.
Howard, Elizabeth, Widow, 53 Boundary St., Neck
Howard, John N, Bricklayer, 140 Meeting St.
Howard, Richard F , Cooper, Washington St., Mazyckborough, Neck
Howard, Richard F., Cooper, Gillon St.
Howard, Robert, Proprietor, Southern Patriot, 57 E. Bay St., Res 97 Meeting St.
Howard, William, Bank Officer, Bank of Discount & Deposit
Howe & Fitch, Merchants, 232 E. Bay St.
Howe, Michael, Stone Cutter, 12 S. Bay St.
Howe, Silas, Merchant, Charlotte St., Mazyckborough, Neck
Howie, William, Merchant, King St Road, Neck
Howland, ----- & Co., Merchants, 10 Crafts' N. Whf.
Howland, Benjamin J., Merchant, 135 King St.
Hrabowski, Richard, 9 Blackbird Al.
Huard, Stanislas, Druggist, 24 Broad St.
Hubbell, Sears, Ship Master, 157 E. Bay St
Hudson & Carter, Porterhouse, 128 E. Bay St.
Huff, Abigail, Miss, 4 Price's Al.
Huger, Betsy, F.P.C., Seamstress, Alexander St., Mazyckborough, Neck
Huger, Carlos, F.P.C., Tailor, 304 King St.
Huger, Charlotte, Miss, 89 St. Philip's St
Huger, Daniel, 82 Queen St.
Huger, Daniel E , Planter, 239 Meeting St

Huger, Jacob G., Carpenter, 10 Water St.
Huger, Mary, Widow, 2 Wentworth St
Huger, -----, Misses, Ratcliff St., Radcliffborough, Neck
Huger, -----, Mrs., Widow of John, 70 Broad St.
Huger, Rosanna, Seamstress, 24 Coming St.
Huger, Sarah, F.P.C., Church St
Hughes, B., Widow, 7 Lamboll St.
Hughes, Edward, Ladies' Teacher, 87 Tradd St
Hull, Latham, Merchant, 330 King St.
Humbert, John, Carpenter, Charlotte St., Wraggsborough, Neck
Hume, John, Planter, Wentworth St
Humphreys & Mathewes, Grocers, 38 E. Bay St.
Humphreys, Joseph, 347 King St.
Hunt, Benjamin F., Attorney, 89 Broad St.
Hunt, Joesph, Shipmaster, King St. Road, Neck
Hunt, Thomas, Commissioner in Equity, Office 86, Res. 41 Broad St
Hunter, Alexander, Church St. Cont'd.
Hunter, John, Milliner, 249 King St
Hunter, Kate, F.P.C., 10 Smith's Ln.
Huntingdon, Mary, Widow, E. Bay St
Hurd, Sarah, Widow, State St.
Hurlburt, M. L., Teacher, College, Res. 8 Montague St
Hurst, Charles, 71 Anson St.
Hussey, Bryant, Pilot, 6 Stoll's Al.
Huston, James, Tailor, 61 Church St.
Hutchin, Shabau, Merchant, 241 E. Bay St
Hutchinson, Ann, Widow, 12 Champney St.
Hutchinson, Elizabeth L., 47 Society St.
Hutchinson, Judah, F.P.C., Whim Court
Hutchinson, Mary, 27 Church St.
Hutchinson, Mary, 5 Friend St.
Hutchinson, Mary, F.P.C., George St
Hutton, James, Factor, 10 S. Bay St.
Hyams, Henry, 112 King St.
Hyams, Isaac, Watch Maker, 242 King St.
Hyams, Rebecca, Widow, 90 Queen St.
Hyams, Samuel, Vendue Master, cr. Market & Meeting Sts.
Hyams, Solomon, Merchant, 303 King St.
Hyams, -----, Widow of Mordecai, 174 King St
Hyer, Henry, Boundary St., City Lands, Neck
Hyer, John, Carpenter, Coming St., Radcliffborough, Neck
Hyslop, Christiana, Widow, 3 Guignard St.
Inglesby & Brown, Tailors, 112 Meeting St.
Inglesby, H. William, Attorney, Office, 214 Meeting St.
Inglesby, James, F.P.C., Shoe-black Maker, Magazine St.
Inglesby, John, Clerk, 9 Mazyck St.
Inglesby, Maria, Widow, 9 Mazyck St.
Inglis, James, Ship Carpenter, Price's Al.
Inglis, Thomas, F.P.C., Hair Dresser, 40 Meeting St.
Ingraham, Henry, Factor, D'Oyley's Whf., Res. cr. Smith & Wentworth Sts.
Ireland, Benjamin, Grocer, 25 Bull St.
Irvine, Matthew, M D., 96 E. Bay St.
Isaacs, Abraham, Commission Broker, 305 King St.
Ives, Jeremiah, Capt., Groceries & Lumber, cr. Boundary & Washington Sts., Neck
Ives, Sophia, F.P.C., School Mistress, 12 Archdale St

Izard, Hector, F.P.C , Jones' Lot, King St

Izard, Ralph, Planter, 79 Broad St.

Izzard, Isabella, F.P.C., Seamstress & Washer, Coming St., City Lands, Neck

Jacks, James, Merchant, 105 Broad St.

Jacks, James, Merchant. Res. Chapel St., Wraggsborough, Neck

Jackson, Betsy, F.P.C., Washer, Alexander St , Mazyckborough, Neck

Jackson, Charles, F.P.C., 34 Boundary St.

Jackson, Fanny, F.P.C., Seamstress, 90 Queen St.

Jackson, Martha, F.P.C., 21 Wentworth St.

Jackson, Patty, F.P.C., 2 Cock Ln.

Jackson, William, F.P.C., Carpenter, Alexander St., Mazyckborough, Neck

Jacobs, James R., Accountant, 2 Ellery St.

Jacobs, Kitty, F.P.C., Seller in Market, 28 Boundary St.

Jacobs, Lucy, Grocer, 67 Anson St

Jacoby, George, Grocer, 29 Church St.

Jahan, Joseph, Architect, 120 Meeting St Cont'd , Neck

James, Hannah, F.P.C., Washer, Boundary St., Wraggsborough, Neck

James, John, Inspector of the Customs, 12 Guignard St.

James, Maria, Widow, Boarding House, 37 Elliott St.

James, Robert, Slop Shop, 265 King St.

Jandrel, Rebecca, Widow, 129 E. Bay St.

Jaques, Mary, Widow, 110 Laurens St.

Jarey, A , 50 Wentworth St

Jarvis, John, Butcher, Henrietta St., Wraggsborough, Neck

Jasper, William, Cabinet Maker, 351 King St.

Javain, Peter, Grocer, 95 King St.

Jeannerett, Christopher, Teacher, 164 King St.

Jeffords, Elizabeth, Widow, 2 Zigzag Court

Jeffords, J. H., Sail Maker, 71½ Anson St.

Jeffords, John, Fisherman, 71½ Anson St

Jenkings, Elias, Bricklayer, 11 Liberty St

Jenkings, Eliza, F.P.C., 1 Swinton's Ln.

Jenkings, Micah, Planter, 3 Legare St

Jenkins, Benjamin, Planter, W. Side, Pinckney St., Cannonborough, Neck

Jenkins, Harriett, F.P.C , 1 Swinton's Ln.

Jenkins, Maria, F.P.C , Washer, Motte's Ln

Jenkins, Molly, F.P.C., Boundary St.

Jenner, William & Co., Merchants, Chisolm's Whf.

Jenner, William, Merchant, Res. at Mrs. Woodrouff's Vanderhorst's Whf.

Jenneret, Mary T., Widow, Zigzag Court

Jennings, William, 126 E. Bay St.

Jervey, James, Clerk, Federal Court, State House, Res. E. Bay St.

Jimerson, John, Blacksmith, Cannon St., Cannonborough, Neck

Johnson & Fordham, Blacksmiths, 4 Gillon St.

Johnson & Maynard, Druggists, 5 Broad St.

Johnson, Alexander, Boarding House, 8 Bedon's Al.

Johnson, Andrew, Grocer, cr. Wentworth & Coming Sts.

Johnson, Ann, Grocer, Henrietta St., Wraggsborough, Neck

Johnson, Burnett, Grocer, 30 Bull St

Johnson, Caty, F.P.C., Seamstress, 72 Church St.

Johnson, D. W., Saddlery Store, 188 King St., Neck

Johnson, Delia, F.P.C., 5 Church St.

Johnson, Edward, 23 State St.

Johnson, Elizabeth, Widow, Dry Goods Store, 43 King St

Johnson, George, F.P.C., Wheelwright, St Philip's St.

Johnson, Hagar, F P.C , Washer, Meeting St.

Johnson, Issac A., Dr., cr. St. Philip's & Vanderhorst Sts , Neck

Johnson, Jabez, Watch & Clock Maker, 163 King St

Johnson, James S., Student at Law, cr Guignard & Anson Sts

Johnson, James, Soap Chandler, Chapel St., Wraggsborough, Neck

Johnson, Jane, Mrs., Dry Goods Store, 226 King St.

Johnson, John & John Owen, Commission Merchants, Fitzsimmons' Whf.

Johnson, John, Blacksmith & Founder, Director, Planters' & Merchants' Bank, Neck

Johnson, John, Grocer, cr. Beaufain & St. Philip's Sts.

Johnson, Joseph, M.D., Church St

Johnson, Louisa, Clear Starcher, 359 King St.

Johnson, Nancy, F.P.C., Washer, 35 Boundary St

Johnson, Nels, 20 King St.

Johnson, Sarah, F.P.C., Seamstress, 29 Anson St.

Johnson, Sarah, Mantua Maker, 10 Beaufain St

Johnson, Sarah, Widow, cr. Guignard & Anson Sts

Johnson, T. W., Grocer, 41 Elliott St.

Johnson, Thomas, Dry Goods & Groceries, King St Road, Neck

Johnson, William, Judge, Supreme Court of the U S , N E Side Pinckney St., Cannonborough, Neck

Johnson, William, Rigger, 122 Wentworth St.

Johnstock, Ann, Widow, 4 King St.

Johnston, Peter, Printer, Amen St.

Johnston, William, Planter, W. Side Pinckney St., Cannonborough, Neck

Jones, Abner, Tailor, 357 King St.

Jones, Abraham, Cabinet Maker, 5 Beaufain St

Jones, Barney, Carpenter, N. Side Vanderhorst St., Radcliffborough, Neck

Jones, Benjamin, F P.C., Tailor, Jones' Lot, King St.

Jones, Blanchey, F.P.C., 30 Boundary St.

Jones, David, F.P.C., Tailor, Meeting St., near Cumberland St

Jones, Edward, Dr., 37 St. Philip's St., Radcliffborough, Neck

Jones, Emanuel, Painter, 64 Tradd St.

Jones, Henry, Ship Carpenter, Aged 77, 20 Pinckney St.

Jones, Jehu, Jr., F.P C., Tailor, 34 Broad St.

Jones, Jehu, Sr., Boarding House, 36 Broad St.

Jones, John, cr. of Wentworth & Coming Sts.

Jones, John, Grocer, 25 Mazyck St.

Jones, John Henry, Merchant, 5 Crafts' Whf.

Jones, John S , Wire Worker, 122 Church St.

Jones, Joseph, Carpenter, Blackbird's Al.

Jones, M William, S.E. Side Coming St., Radcliffborough, Neck

Jones, Margaret, Widow, 30 King St

Jones, Mary, Widow, Seamstress, 42 Boundary St.

Jones, P , Mrs , 12 King St

Jones, Peter, F.P.C., Tailor, 41 Church St.
Jones, Sally, F.P.C., Lynch's Ln.
Jones, Thomas, Grocer, 380 King St.
Jones, Thomas, Merchant, 12 Tradd St
Jones, Thomas, President, Bank of S. C , Res. cr. of Anson & Guignard Sts
Jones, -----, Widow of Samuel, 1 Guignard St.
Jones, William, Carpenter, 30 King St
Jones, Wiswald, Merchant, 211 Meeting St.
Jordan, Christopher, Coach Trimmer & Painter, Res. 23 Ellery St.
Joseph, Joseph, Merchant, 222 King St
Joseph, Moses, Grocer, 3 St. Philip's St.
Joyner, David, Armorer, U. S. Arsenal, Doughty St., Cannonborough, Neck
Judah, Harriott, F.P C., Elizabeth St., Mazyckborough, Neck
Just, George, Wharf Builder, cr. Washington & Inspection Sts.
Kahnle, Harman John, Wood Measurer, 38 Boundary St.
Kallner, John, Shopkeeper, cr. Coming & Boundary Sts , Neck
Kamra, Richard, Block Maker, 25 Wall St.
Kanady, Peter, Grocer, 52 Tradd St.
Kannapaux, William, Goldsmith & Jeweller, 296½ King St.
Karey, William, Grocer, 7 Elliott St.
Kay, Mary, Widow, 110 Tradd St.
Keckley, George, Dry Goods Store, Brownlee's Row, King St., Neck
Keckley, John, Cabinet Maker, 12 Archdale St.
Keenan, George, Merchant, King St., near the Lines, Neck
Keife, Honour, Widow, 353 King St.
Keith, J., Merchant, Lothrop's Whf.
Keith, Sylvanus, Private Boarding House, cr King & Wentworth Sts.
Kelly, John, Merchant. King St. Road, Neck
Kelly, Joseph, Factor & Commission Merchant, 10 Chisolm's Upper Whf., Res. 4 Boundary St.
Kelly, Marcus Nelson, at Dr. Prioleau's Office, cr. Meeting & George Sts.
Kelly, Margaret, Widow, 12 Parsonage Ln.
Kelly, Mary, Widow, 129 King St.
Kelly, Mary, Widow, Nurse, 28 Ellery St.
Kelly, Michael, Ironmonger, 52 E. Bay St.
Kelsay, Matthew, Grocer, E Bay St.
Kemp, William, House Carpenter, Chalmers Al.
Kenedy, James, Capt., 24 Coming St.
Kenedy, James, Gauger, 136 Queen St.
Kennedy, Edward, Custom House Officer, 22 Mazyck St.
Kennedy, Frances, Coach Maker, 34 Wentworth St.
Kennedy, James, Merchant, 47 E. Bay St.
Kennedy, John, Grocer, 4 Market St.
Kennedy, Lionell H., Attorney, Office, 4 St. Michael's Al.
Kennedy, William, Glove Maker, 55 Anson St.
Keowin, John, 43 Boundary St
Keown, Robert, 22 Society St.
Ker, J. C , Merchant, 321 King St
Ker, John, 388 King St.
Kerr, Andrew, Broker, Cannon St., Islington, Neck

Kerrison, Elizabeth, Widow, School Mistress, Res. 12 Society St
Kershaw & Lewis, Factors, 264 E. Bay St
Kershaw, Charles, Factor, 238 Meeting St
Kewing, Elizabeth, Widow, 43 Boundary St.
Kidd, George, Grocer, 213 Meeting St.
Kiddell, Charles, Ironmonger, 17 Broad St.
Killian & [?], Clothing Store, 100 Broad St
Kimball, Daniel, Commission Merchants, Kunhardt & Leavitt's Whf
Kimble, Daniel, Mariner, 22 Guignard St.
King & Jones, Merchants, Counting House, Crafts' S Whf
King, Benjamin, Carpenter, Warren St., Radcliffborough, Neck
King, Elizabeth, Mrs., Umbrella Maker, 208 Meeting St.
King, John, Merchant, 96 Church St.
King, Joseph R., Baker, 42 Queen St.
King, Mary, Miss, 150 Church
King, Mary, Mrs., Grocer, 23 King St.
King, Mitchell, Attorney, 2 Meeting St., Office, 4 St. Michael's Al.
Kingdom, Henry, Millwright, College St.
Kingman, Hannah, Ladies Boarding House, State St
Kingman, John, School Master, 84 Wentworth St.
Kinloch, George, Grocer, 20 Ellery St.
Kinnicutt, Simon, Boot & Shoe Store, 117 King St.
Kinnier, Sarah, Mrs., Milliner & Mantua Maker, 138 King St
Kiol, Peter, Mariner, 28 Anson St.
Kippenberg, Andrew, Grocer, 37 Queen St
Kirk, John D., Grocer, 1 New St.
Kirk, John, Shop Keeper, cr. Maiden Ln. & Pinckney St.
Kirk, John, Union Bank
Kirkland, William, M.D., 107 Church St
Kirkpatrick, Douglas & Hall, Merchants, Duncan's Whf
Kittleband, David, Carpenter, 14 Logan St.
Kline, Henry, Vanderhorst St., City Lands, Neck
Klint, Nicholas, 2 Smith's Ln.
Knieff, Frances, Grocer, cr. Boundary & Anson Sts.
Knox, Jane, Widow, Alexander St., Mazyckborough, Neck
Knox, John F., Firm of Pritchard & Knox, Pritchard & Knox's Whf.
Knox, Walter, House Carpenter, 3 Green St.
Knust, Henry, Grocer, 65 Broad St.
Koffskey, Ann Catharine, Widow, 97 King St.
Kohler, Frederick, Tanner & Currier, John St., Wraggsborough, Res. at his Store, King St. Road, Neck
Kohne, Frederick, 66 Broad St.
Kounne, Dianna, College St.
Kugley, John, Carpenter, 17 Mazyck St.
Kunhardt & Leavitt, Factors, Kunhardt & Leavitt's Whf.
Kunhardt, William, Merchant, George St
Kurtze, Ludolph F., Alexander St., Mazyckborough, Neck
L'Eugle, Susan, 11 Philadelphia St.
L'Herminier, M.D., 78 Meeting St.
Laats, James, Grocer, 8 Archdale St
Labarben, A. D., Teacher, 48 King St.
Labaussay, Pire, Baker & Shopkeeper, King St. Road, Neck
Laboarde & Harde, Livery Stables, 24 Society St

48

Lachs, John, Grocer, 1 Market St.
Lacombe, Stephen, M.D., 13 Ellery St.
Lacompte, John, Druggist, 76 E. Bay St.
Lacoste, Augustus, Merchants' Clerk, cr. King & Mary Sts, Neck
Lacoste, Charles, Merchant, 246 & 72 King St.
Lacoste, Stephen, cr. King & Ann Sts., Neck
Ladaveze, Raymond, Merchant, 94 King St
Ladaveze, Victor, Merchant, 59 King St.
Ladson, Judith, Widow, 3 New St
Ladson, William, 3 New St.
Lafar, Catharine, Widow, 107 Queen St.
Lafar, David B., Cooper, Magwood's Whf., Res. 107 Queen St
Lafar, John J., City Marshal, 107 Queen St.
Lafars, Mary Louisa, F.P.C., Cook, Alexander St., Mazyckborough, Neck
Lafene, Frances, Shop Keeper, 3 West St.
Laffitean, Stanislas, Merchant, Res. 46 Anson St.
Lafilly, Martha, Teacher, 17 Wentworth St.
Lafon, John, Cooper, cr E. Bay St. & Fitzsimons' Whf.
Lahenth, Mary, Widow, 15 Magazine St.
Lamb, David, Merchant, 14 Kunhardt & Leavitt's Whf., Res. 104 Tradd St.
Lamb, James, Merchant, 16 Kunhardt & Leavitt's Whf., Res. 104 Tradd St.
Lambert, Francis, Boarding House, 125 Tradd St.
Lamboll, Rebecca, F.P.C., 6 Smith's Ln.
Lance, J. G., M.D., 86 Queen St.
Lance, Sarah, Widow, 82 Queen St.
Lance, William, Attorney, 81 Queen St., Office, St. Michael's Al.
Landri, Elizabeth, Widow, Seamstress, 21 Wentworth St.
Lane, Louisa, Widow, 96 Tradd St
Lang, J. H., Merchant, E. Bay St.
Langford, Ann R., Widow, 12 Liberty St.
Langley, William, Merchant, 147 Church & 26 Queen Sts.
Langlois, Maria, Widow, 383 King St.
Langstaff, Ann, Widow, 141 Meeting St.
Langstaff, John, Accountant, 141 Meeting St.
Langstaff, Robert, Accountant, 141 Meeting St
Langton, John, 361 King St.
Lankester, Jacob, Grocer, 66 E. Bay St
Lanneau, Bazile, 1 Pitt St.
Lanneau, Peter, Capt., 16 Elliott St.
Laporte, Rene, Meeting St. Road
Lappenne, John A., Dry Goods & Groceries, King St. Road, Neck
Lappenne, John Joseph, Merchant, King St. Road, Neck
Larbe, Joseph, Shoemaker, Chalmers Al.
Laroach, Mary, Widow, Plantress, Hudson St., Cannonborough, Neck
Laroache, Elizabeth, Widow, 43 Beaufain St.
Laroache, John, Clerk, 44 Beaufain St
Larousseliere, Francis, Merchant, Queen St.
Larousseliere, Louis, Druggist, 90 King St.
Latham, Daniel, Distiller, 2 Hasell St.
Laurans, Peter, Wine Merchant, 3 Lothrop's Whf., Res. cr St. Philip's & George Sts.
Laurence, Elizabeth, Widow, 28 Ellery St

Laurens, Henry, Planter, 169 E. Bay St.
Laval, Jacint, Jr., Factor, Mey's Whf., 2 Pinckney St.
Laval, Louis, 1 George St.
Lavauden, Paul, Merchant, 327 King St.
Lawerence, Mary Ann, F.P.C., Washer, Charlotte St., Wraggsborough, Neck
Lawincendiere, Michel, Cigar Maker, 7 Wentworth St
Lawrence, Elizabeth, Widow, 162 E Bay St
Lawton, Mary, Widow, 6 Lamboll St.
Lazarus, C. & R., Millinery Store, 140 King St
Lazarus, Henry, Merchant., Meeting St. Road, Neck
Lazarus, Jacob, Merchant, Chisolm's Whf., Res. 323 King St.
Lazarus, Mark, 49 Tradd St.
Lazarus, Michael, Merchant, 263 E. Bay St.
Leach, Sally, Lynch's Ln.
Leary & Thomas, Tanners & Curriers, cr. King & Warren Sts., Neck
Leary, Charles, cr. King & Warren Sts., Neck
Leaumonte, Margaret, Widow, cr Middle & Minority Sts
Leaycraft, -----, 349 King St.
Lebby, William, Ship Carpenter, Amen St.
Lecair, Pebarte V., Widow, 38 Tradd St.
Lecat, Francis, Music Master, 5 Ellery St
Lechels, Anna, Widow, cr. St. Philip's & Vanderhorst Sts., Neck
Ledbether, Agness, Widow, 9 Liberty St.
Lee, Charles, Saddler, cr. Wentworth & Meeting Sts.
Lee, Dorothea, Widow, 43 Broad St.
Lee, Elizabeth, Teacher, 9 Blackbird Al.
Lee, Elsy, Confectioner, 395 King St.
Lee, Elsy Frost, 4 Queen St.
Lee, Francis J., 35 Hasell St.
Lee, John, Tailor, 28 Broad St.
Lee, Thomas, Merchant, Duncan's Whf., Res. 3 Gibbes St.
Lee, Timothy, Factor, Res. 3 Wentworth St.
Lee, William, 14 St. Philip's St.
Lee, William, F.P.C., Jones' Lot, King St
Lee, William, Ship Carpenter, E. Bay St.
Leech, Catharine, Widow, 37 Society St.
Leech, Thomas, Millwright, Charlotte St., Mazyckborough, Neck
Leefe, Benjamin, Notary Public, 49 E. Bay St., Res. 46 Church St.
LeFransway, Merchant, 26 Queen St.
Lefurne, Thomas, Grocer, 37 & 39 King St.
Legare, Harriet, F.P.C., Boundary St.
Legare, James, Planter, 3 New St.
Legare, Joe, F.P.C., Boundary St.
Legare, John Berwick, Attorney, 44 Meeting St., Res S Bay St.
Legare, Mary, Plantress, 116 Wentworth St.
Legare, S & Co., Factor, Chisolm's Whf.
Legare, Sarah, Plantress, 23 Anson St.
Legare, Solomon, Factor, Res. 22 Friend St.
Legare, Tener, F.P.C., Washer, Charlotte St., Wraggsborough, Neck
Legare, Thomas, Planter, 1 S. Bay St
Leger, Elizabeth, Widow, 47 Society St.
Legge, Ann, Widow, 130 Wentworth St

49

Legrand, Lewis, Hairdresser, 121 King St.
Lehre, Thomas, Planter, 37 King St.
Leitch, Duncan, Grocer, 283 King St
Leland, A. W., Rev., 32 Tradd St.
Leland, Joseph & Brothers, Merchants, 89 E. Bay St.
Lemaitre, John B., Merchant, Fitzsimons' Whf, Res. 77 King St.
Leman, James, Shopkeeper, King St. Road, Neck
Leprince & Dumont, 342 King St.
Lequeux, Martha, Widow, cr. Anson & George Sts.
Leris, Susan, Mrs., Cumberland St
Leroy, Francis, M.D., 162 Meeting St
LeSeiguare, -----, M.D., 307 King St
Lesesne, Hannah, Widow, 16 Society St
Lesesne, Isaac, Chairman of Port Wardens, 249 E Bay St., Res. 16 Society St.
Leslie, Henry, Capt., cr. Anson & Pinckney Sts
Letchmore, Maria, Widow, 3 Smith's Ln.
Leuden, Francis, Confectioner, 102 Church St.
Levin, Eliza, Store Keeper, Widow, 221 King St
Levin, Lewis, Merchant, 223 King St.
Levingston, Henry, Shopkeeper, 3 Bridge St., Islington, Neck
Levy, George, cr. King St. & Parsonage Ln.
Levy, I. C., 144 E. Bay St. Cont'd.
Levy, Lyon, Boot Maker, Synagogue Yard, Hasell St.
Levy, Lyon, State Treasurer, 278 King St.
Levy, Moses C., Merchant, 110 King St
Levy, Nathan, Merchant, 131 King St.
Levy, Reuben, Broker, 7 Mazyck St
Levy, Simon, Merchant, 150 King St.
Levy, Solomon, cr. Broad & King Sts.
Lewis, Ann, Widow, 32 George St.
Lewis, David, Dry Goods & Second Hand Furniture, 200 King St , Neck
Lewis, Elijah, Saddler, 224 King St
Lewis, Elizabeth, Widow, 121 Wentworth St.
Lewis, James, Carpenter, 52 Wentworth St.
Lewis, John, Grocer, cr. Market & E. Bay Sts.
Lewis, John, Merchant, 2 Fitzsimons' Whf.
Lewis, Joseph, King St. Road, Neck
Lewis, Lydia, 5 King St.
Lhote, Pierre. Gardener, near Meeting St. & the Lines, Neck
Lightly, -----, Widow of James, Pitt St
Lightwood, Elizabeth, Widow, cr Meeting St. & Lynch's Ln
Lilley, Stephen, Distiller, 18 Society St.
Limehouse, Robert, Planter, 63 Tradd St
Lincoln, Benjamin, F.P.C., Tailor, 151 King St
Lincoln, Spenser, Boarding House, op. Pork Market
Lindenboom, Peter, U S. Arsenal, Coming St., Neck
Lindershine, John C., Carpenter, Charlotte St., Wraggsborough, Neck
Lindsay, Mary, Widow, 18 Tradd St
Lindsay, William, Merchant, Res. 267 E Bay St
Ling, John, Grocer, 101 E. Bay St.
Ling, Philip, Coachmaker, 13 Guignard St
Ling, Robert, Chairmaker, 41 Market St.
Linning, Charles, 6 Legare St

Linning, -----, Widow of Charles, 6 Legare St.
Linsey, Sarah, F.P C., 120 Wentworth St.
Linssor, Lewis, John, Cannon St , Cannonborough, Neck
Lipman, Abraham, Watchmaker, 152 King St.
Lipman, Jacob, 38 King St.
Lishman, Sarah, Widow, Boarding House, cr Amen & State Sts.
Liston, Henry, F.P.C., Cooper, near the Market
Liston, Rosanna, Seamstress, 43 Beaufain St
Little, Robert, Lumber Merchant, Chisolm's Upper Whf.
Little, Robert, Lumber Merchant., Charlotte St., Mazyckborough, Neck
Little, Thomas & John, Saw Gin Makers, 88 Meeting St.
Livingston, Jane, Widow, 40 Pinckney St.
Livingston, John, Tailor, 241 King St.
Livingston, R.Y., Bookkeeper, Union Bank, St Philip's St., Neck
Livingston, S. M., Grocer, 135 E. Bay St
Livingston, Sophia, Mantua Maker, 62 Queen St
Lizar, Eleazer, Lynch's Ln.
Lloyd, Dianna, F.P.C., Lynch's Ln.
Lloyd, Esther, Widow, 55 King St
Lloyd, John, 18 Bull St.
Lloyd, John P., Venetian Blind Maker, 111 Meeting St.
Lloyd, Joseph, Merchant, 55 King St.
Lloyd, Mary, F P C , Seamstress, 9 Pinckney St
Lloyd, Robert, Mariner, 32 Chalmers Al.
Lloyd, Widow, 37 Church St.
Loasdale, James, Carpenter, 383 King St.
Lochart, John, Grocer, 207 Meeting St.
Lockwood, Israel R., Carpenter, 12 Magazine St.
Lockwood, Joshua, Bookkeeper in State Bank, Res. Smith's Ln.
Logan, George, M.D., 9 West St
Logan, William, Librarian, Charleston Library Society, W. Side Pinckney St , Cannonborough, Neck
Long, Felix, Tanner, 1 Pitt St.
Long, John, F.P.C., Carpenter, 41 St. Philip's St.
Long, Robert S., Mariner, 7 Wall St
Longsdon, William, Merchant, 259 E. Bay St
Longworth, Henry, Grocer, 131 Tradd St.
Loomis, Henry, Hardware Merchant, 164 King St.
Lopez, Catharine, F.P.C., Seamstress, Jones' Lot, King St.
Lopez, Priscilla, Dry Goods Store, 336 King St
Lord, Archibald, Porter, Bank of Discount & Deposit, Over the Bank
Lord, Jacob N., Shoe Store, 186 King St., Neck
Lord, Samuel, Merchant, 231 E Bay St., Res. 11 Broad St
Lorent & Wulf, Merchants, cr. E. Bay St. & Martin's Whf.
Lorrimore, Ann, Widow, 3 Beaufain St.
Lorrimore, Sarah, Widow, cr. E. Bay St. & Vendue Range
Lothrop, Samuel H., Merchant, Lothrop's Whf., Res 228 E Bay St.
Lott, -----, Mr , Sausage Maker, Church St
Lovell & Paine, Ship Chandlers, 42 E Bay St.
Lovell, Stargis Josiah, Ship Chandler, N.E. Side Pinckney St., Neck
Loveman, Elisha, Painter, 82 Church St
Lowden, John, Merchant, 259 E. Bay St.
Lowe, John, Beer House, 204 Meeting St.

Lowndes, James, Planter, Meeting St.
Lowndes, Jane, Widow, Plantress, 45 Anson St
Lowndes, Thomas, Planter, Broad St.
Lownds, Amy, F.P.C , Washer, 79 Tradd St.
Lowrey, Charles, Grocer, 74 Queen St
Lubat, Charles, Baker, 26 Ellery St
Lubet, Amelia, F.P C., Mantua Maker, 16 Berresford St.
Lubet, Bon, F P.C., Washer, 8 Wentworth St.
Lucas, Jonathan, J., Planter, Boundary & Lucas Sts., Neck
Luce, Francis, Coffee House, cr Queen & State Sts.
Ludlow, Robert M. C , Merchant, Magwood's Whf., Res. 28 King St.
Lukens, John, Cashier, Planters' and Mechanics' Bank, Res. 16 Hasell St.
Lusher, George, 92 E. Bay St
Lushington, Betty, F.P.C., Washer, Henrietta St., Wraggsborough, Neck
Lyle & Davis, Merchants, 226 E. Bay St.
Lyles, Mary, F.P.C., Seamstress & Washer, Charlotte St , Wraggsborough, Neck
Lynah, Edward, M.D., cr. Montague & Pitt Sts.
Lynch, Esther, Miss, Plantress, 195 E. Bay St.
Lynch, Henry, Blacksmith & Farrier, Radcliff St., Neck
Lynch, Jane, Widow, Fruit & Toy Shop, 47 Broad St
Lynn, John, Accountant, 5 Boundary St.
Lynn, John S , Accountant, 5 Boundary St
Lynn, William S., Accountant, 5 Boundary St
Lyons, Emanuel Joseph, Porter House, 163½ King St.
Lyons, Isaac, Mineral Water House, 63 E. Bay St., Res 80 King St
Lyons, Mary, Miss, 4 Clifford St.
Lyons, Oliver, Shoe Store, 253 King St.
Macauley, George F., Merchant, 15 Broad St.
Macauley, George, Merchant, 119 Church St.
Mack, Lilly, F.P.C., 29 Anson St.
Mackay, Catharine, 43 Beaufain St
Mackay, John, School, St. Michael's Al.
Mackenzie, Patience, F P C., 32 Anson St.
Mackey, Charles, Accountant, 101 Wentworth St.
Mackey, Elijah, F.P.C., 2 College Green
Mackey, James, Cutler, 109 Wentworth St
Mackinza, William, Carpenter, cr. Reed & Nassau Sts., Hampstead, Neck
Maclish, Frances, Miss, 17 Elliott St
MacNeill, Daniel, Shipmaster, Doughty St., Neck
Macualey, Daniel, cr. Broad & State Sts.
Madelmond, John, Teacher, 97 Queen St.
Magee, Caroline, Miss, 20 Archdale St.
Magle, Francis, Mariner, French Al.
Magness, Emanuel, Grocer, cr. Amen & State Sts.
Magrath, John, Merchant, Duncan's Whf., Res. 107 Meeting St
Magson, S. J. & Co., Merchants, 28 E. Bay St.
Maguan, James, Dry Goods Store, King St Road, Neck
Maguire, Hugh, Merchant Tailor, 93 E. Bay St.
Magwood & Patterson, Merchants, Magwood's Whf
Magwood, James H. & Co., Merchants, 15 Kunhardt & Leavitt's Whf
Magwood, James W., Merchant, 76 Tradd St.
Magwood, Simon, (& Patterson), Res 79 Queen St

Maile, Peter, Jeweller, 87 King St.
Maillard, John, Grocer, cr. Wall & Boundary Sts
Main, William, Ship Carpenter, Smith's Whf., Mazyckborough, Neck
Maine, James, Cabinet Maker, 32 Broad St
Mair, Alexander, Shoe Store, 53 King St.
Mair, James, Planter, 5 Rutledge St.
Mairs, Simon, Merchant, 3 State St
Majors, -----, Mrs., Boarding House, 99 Broad St.
Malcom, Thomas, Bank Clerk, 77 Queen St.
Malcomson, James H. B., Physician, 26 St. Philip's St.
Man, John, Bricklayer, 22 Boundary St.
Man, Rebecca, F.P.C., 57 St. Philip's St.
Manigault, G. A., Planter, Meeting St
Manigault, Joseph, Planter, cr. Meeting & John Sts , Neck
Manning, Joseph, M D., cr. E. Bay & Society Sts.
Mansery, Mary, Widow, Baker, 141 E Bay St
Mansise, Cornelius, Capt., 257 King St
Manson, Andrew, Merchant, 61 King St., Res. New St.
Manuel, Philip, F.P.C., 8 Clifford's Al.
Marchant, Peter T., Planter, 142 King St.
Marion, Ann, Confectioner, State St
Markley & Rose, Factors, Duncan's Whf.
Markley, Abraham, Planter, 14 St. Philip's St.
Markley, B. A., Factor, Res. 110 Meeting St.
Marks, D., Miss, Dry Goods Store, 133 King St
Marks, Humphrey, Meeting St. Road, Neck
Marks, Joseph, Grocer, cr. Amen & State Sts.
Marley, Peter, Deputy Sheriff, cr. Archdale & Boundary Sts.
Marmigur, Elijah, 42 Beaufain St.
Marr, Ellen, Widow, Alexander St., Mazyckborough, Neck
Marsena, Mary F., F P.C., 36 St. Philip's St.
Marsh, James, Ship Builder, Gadsden's Whf.
Marsh, Moses, Merchant, 245 E. Bay St.
Marshall, Dorothy, Widow, Beaufain St.
Marshall, Henry, Grocer, 10 Back St
Marshall, John, Merchant, 262 E. Bay St.
Marshall, John, Oyster House, 216 Meeting St.
Marshall, Mary S., Widow, 55 Broad St.
Marshall, Thomas C , Accountant, 55 Broad St.
Marshall, Thomas, Merchant, Res. 161 E Bay St.
Marshall, William, Vendue Master, 229 E. Bay St., Res. 8 Queen St.
Marshburn, Nicholas, Carpenter, 6 Market St.
Marston, Benjamin, Clerk, Amherst St., Hampstead, Neck
Martin, Christian, Grocer, cr. Wall & Boundary Sts.
Martin, Dinah, F.P C., 58 Market St
Martin, James, Cooper, E. Bay St.
Martin, James, Merchant, Chisolm's N. Whf.
Martin, John N , Bricklayer, Wentworth St.
Martin, Joseph, F.P.C , Zigzag Ln.
Martin, Lewis, Bricklayer, 132 Meeting St
Martin, Patrick, Grocer, 31 Guignard St.
Martin, Richard, Grocer, King St. Road, Neck
Martin, Robert, Merchant, King St. Road, Neck
Martin, Sarah F., Widow, 43 Anson St.
Martin, Thomas, Wharf Owner, 54 Broad St.
Martindale, James C., Planter, King St. Road, Neck
Martinier, Julin, 55 Church St.

51

Mason, George, Bank Clerk, 10 Lynch's Ln
Mason, Sarah, Widow, Seamstress, Chapel St.,
 Mazyckborough, Neck
Masquito, Raphael D , Teacher, 163 Meeting St.
Massias, Solomon, Teacher, 38 King St.
Massot, H., Watchmaker, 6 Queen St.
Matheizon, Alexander, Merchant, 154 E. Bay St ,
 Kunhardt & Leavitt's Whf.
Mathews & Bonneau, Factors, Martin's Whf.
Mathews, Benjamin, Capt., Stoll's Al.
Mathews, David, Shoemaker, 24 St. Philip's St.
Mathews, George, F.P C., Carpenter, Tradd St.
Mathews, Henry, F.P C , Boundary St
Mathews, Henry, Grocer, 49 Elliott St
Mathews, James, Factor, 22 Anson St.
Mathews, John R , Planter, 20 Bull St.
Mathews, Mary, F.P.C., 2 Clifford St.
Mathews, Peter, F P.C., Shoemaker, 30 Boundary St
Mathews, Sarah, F.P.C., Boundary St.
Mathews, Sarah, Widow, cr. Wentworth & Rutledge Sts
Mathews, Thomas, Painter, 10 Clifford St
Mathews, Thomas W , Planter, Orange St.
Mathewson, C. J., Dry Goods Store, 17 Queen St.
Matthewes, William, Planter, Charlotte St.,
 Mazyckborough, Neck
Matthis, Molly, F.P.C , Midwife, Charlotte St., near
 Flinn's Church, Neck
Mattuce, George, Butcher, 20 Wall St.
Mauger, John J., Attorney, Office, State House Sq
Mauger, -----, Widow, Broad St
Maw, John F., Accountant, 13 Guignard St
Maxey, Ann, 38 Beaufain St
Maxton, John, Baker, 199 King St., Neck
Maxwell, Amelia, 14 Magazine St.
Maxwell, Robert, Merchant, 268 E. Bay St., Res. 8
 Meeting St
May & Munro, Cabinet Makers, 29 Queen St.
May, Ann, 38 Beaufain St
Mayberry, Thomas, Col., 51 Broad St.
Mayer, J G , Attorney & Quorum Unis, 45 St. Philip's St
Mayer, J. R., Blacksmith, Market St
Maynard, Richard, M.D., 5 Broad St
Mazyck & Gaillard, Factors, Chisolm's Whf.
Mazyck, Charlotte E , 102 Meeting St.
Mazyck, M., Widow, 18 Church St.
Mazyck, Nathaniel B., Merchant, Res 101 Meeting St.
Mazyck, P. P., M.D., cr Archdale & Queen Sts.
Mazyck, William, Factor, 3 Archdale St
Mazyck, William, M.D , 7 West St.
M'Afee, Jane, Widow, Dry Goods Store, 385 King St
M'Beath, Eliza, F.P.C., 8 Logan St.
M'Beath, James, Merchant, 5 Lamboll St
M'Beath, John, Grocer, 150 Market St.
M'Bride, Dasha, F.P.C , 16 Parsonage Ln
M'Bride, Eleanor, Widow, 44 Society St
M'Bride, Mary, Widow, 138 Church St.
M'Caffray, Hugh, Shoemaker, 134 King St.
M'Call & Hayne, Attorneys, 115 Church St.
M'Call, Beekman, Bank Clerk, cr. E. Bay & Hasell Sts.
M'Call, Caty, F.P.C., Henrietta St , Wraggsborough, Neck

M'Call, Elizabeth, Widow, 14 Church St.
M'Call, Hext, Attorney, 48 Church St
M'Call, James, Planter, King St., near the Lines, Neck
M'Call, John W , M.D , 14 Church St.
M'Call, Joseph P., Accountant, 14 Meeting St.
M'Call, M , Widow, 132 Church St.
M'Cartney, Samuel, Merchant, 115 Broad St.
M'Carty, C , Grocer, cr Magazine & Mazyck Sts
M'Carty, Clothier, 4 Broad St.
M'Carty, John, 18 Tradd St.
M'Cauley, Daniel, Merchant, cr. State & Broad Sts.
M'Cimme, Peter, 11 Friend St.
M'Cleary, Samuel, Merchant, King St., Neck
M'Cleish, Mary, Widow, School Mistress, 17 Elliott St.
M'Cleod, George, Tailor, 18 Queen St.
M'Clove, Eliza, F.P C., 39 Beaufain St
M'Collins, -----, Grocer, S. Bay St.
M'Cormick, Peter, Turner, 42 King St.
M'Cormick, -----, Widow, Boarding House, 129 Tradd St.
M'Cormick, William, Grocer, 54 E Bay St.
M'Coul, Walter, Merchant, Duncan's Whf.
M'Cready, Jane, Widow, cr Guignard & Anson Sts
M'Cready, Mary Ann Wilson, Milliner, 184 King St., Neck
M'Daniel, Nancy, F P C., King St.
M'Dermul, Timothy, Carpenter, 42 King St.
M'Donald & Bonner, Cabinet Makers, 48 Broad St.
M'Donald, Andrew, Grocer, 368 King St.
M'Donald, Andrew, Grocer, 39 Tradd St.
M'Donald, Sarah, Widow, cr. Liberty & King Sts
M'Donald, Susan, Widow, Society St.
M'Donell, Edward, Boarding House, 13 Champney St.
M'Donough, James, Grocer, 116 E. Bay St.
M'Dow, James, Teacher, cr. Rutledge & Montague Sts.
M'Dowall & Black, Merchants, 70 King St.
M'Dowall, David, Grocer, cr. Society & Meeting Sts.
M'Dowall, James, Merchant, 5 Brownlee's Row, King St.,
 Neck
M'Dowall, John, 194 King St , Neck
M'Elmoyle, William, Grocer, cr. King & Tradd Sts
M'Farlane, Catharine, Widow, 43 Hasell St.
M'Farlane, Robert, Price's Al
M'Gann, Patrick, Watchmaker, E. Bay St.
M'Gill & Naylor, Merchants, 267 King St
M'Gillivray, Alexander H., Vendue Master, 12 Lynch's Ln
M'Ginn, -----, Watchmaker, 95 Tradd St.
M'Girlay, Samuel, Carpenter, 6 Price's Al
M'Grannaghan, William, Grocer, 49 Anson St
M'Gregor, Alexander L., Bricklayer, cr Vanderhorst St ,
 Radcliffborough, Neck
M'Gregor, Neill, Vanderhorst St , Neck
M'Innis, Joseph, Mill Wright, Charlotte St., Neck
M'Intire, Neel, Tobacconist, 24 Berresford St.
M'Intosh, Daniel, Carpenter, cr. Archdale & Clifford Sts.
M'Intosh, John, Cabinet Maker, 82 Meeting St
M'Intosh, John, Capt., Wentworth St.
M'Intosh, Milly, F.P C , 15 Swinton's Ln
M'Kay, George, 1 Parsonage Ln.
M'Kean, -----, Widow, 23 George St
M'Kean, William, Bricklayer, 23 George St.
M'Kean, William, Silversmith, 109 Wentworth St.

52

M'Kee, Abel, Ship Joiner, cr E. Bay & Meeting Sts.
M'Keller, John, Bricklayer, 9 Whim Court
M'Keller, John, Merchant, 75 Church St
M'Kendree, Eliza, Widow, Seamstress, Spring St., near King St., Neck
M'Kenzie, Catharine, F.P.C , 6 Clifford St
M'Kenzie, Elizabeth, Widow, cr. Anson & Pinckney Sts.
M'Kenzie, Haugh, F P C , Zigzag Al. & 61 Queen St
M'Kenzie, John, Saddler, 40 Broad St.
M'Kenzie, T G , Saddler, 172 King St.
M'Kinlay, L., Widow, Grocer, 5 Water St.
M'Kinne, Ludlow & Co., Merchants, Magwood's Whf
M'Lachlin, Smith & Co., Merchants, 4 Tradd St.
M'Lachlin, Thomas, Grocer, 1 King St.
M'Lane, Elizabeth, 3 Logan St.
M'Lane, Lorton, 3 Logan St.
M'Lane, Susanna, Widow, cr Lowndes & Boundary Sts., Neck
M'Lean, Andrew, Capt., 37 Tradd St
M'Lean, Margaret, Widow, 4 Boundary St
M'Leod, Catharine, F.P.C., 6 Broughton's Court
M'Leod, H. C., Vendue Master, 24 Church, Res 3 Pinckney St.
M'Lure, Charles, Merchant, 174 King St.
M'Millan, Thomas, Carpenter, 24 Cumberland St.
M'Millen, Richard, King St., near Boundary St., Neck
M'Namara, J., Vendue Master, 25 Broad St.
M'Namee, James, Shoemaker, 22 Broad St
M'Neall & Co., Grocers, cr. Broad & Church Sts.
M'Neall, Archibald, 41 St. Philip's St
M'Nellage, John, Sail Maker, 7 Kunhardt & Leavitt's Whf.
M'Owen, Patrick, Vendue Master, Res. 386 King St.
M'Phail, James, Archdale St.
M'Pherson, D., Merchant, 370 King St.
M'Pherson, J. E., cr E. Bay & Laurens Sts.
M'Pherson, Laura, Widow, Broad St
M'Pherson, Peter, Tallow Chandler, Boundary St., Wraggsborough, Neck
M'Sheely, Edward, Merchant, 290 King St
M'Vicar, Archibald, Butcher, Nassau St., Wraggsborough, Neck
Meachen, Thomas, Grocer, cr Market & Church Sts
Mead, James, Grocer, cr. Hasell & Anson Sts.
Mealy, John, Grocer, 2 St. Philip's St
Mease & Holmes, Merchants, 78 King St.
Meeds, William, Boarding House, 41 Bay
Mellish, Phineas, Grocer, 1 Queen St.
Menude, John, Planter, Wappoo
Merkie, Ellen, Widow, Wentworth St.
Merrett, James H., Factor, Magwood's Whf
Messervey, P., Capt., 19 Berresford St.
Meurset, Ann, Widow, 6 Water St
Mey, Charles H., Merchant, 51 Pinckney St.
Mey, Florian C , Merchant, 51 Pinckney St
Mey, John H., Merchant, 51 Pinckney St
Mialle, Simon, Shoemaker, 75 Church St.
Michel, Frederick, Clerk of the Market, Wentworth St.
Michel, Henry, F P C , Livery Stables, Parsonage Ln
Michel, John E., Goldsmith, 152½ King St., Res. 348 E. Bay St.

Michel, John, Grocer, 45 E. Bay St.
Michel, Mary, Widow, 17 Coming St
Michel, Pierre, Hatter, 208 King St., Neck
Michel, -----, Widow, 22 Tradd St.
Michel, William, M.D , 17 Coming St.
Middleton, Arthur, Planter, 10 New St.
Middleton, John, Planter, cr. Society & Anson Sts.
Middleton, Mary, F P C., 16 Wall St.
Middleton, Mary, Widow, Parsonage Ln.
Middleton, Solomon, Tailor, 252 King St
Miles, George, F.P.C , Elizabeth St., Neck
Miller & Browne, Merchants, 217 E. Bay St
Miller, A. E., Printer, 101 Queen St
Miller, Abraham, Bank Clerk, 23 Society St.
Miller, Ann, Widow, Boundary St., Mazyckborough, Neck
Miller, Catharine, Widow, 23 Society St
Miller, Elizabeth S., Widow, 142 Meeting St.
Miller, Ezra L., Merchant, cr. Liberty & King Sts
Miller, F. J., Accountant, 52 Anson St.
Miller, Frederick, Butcher, cr. King & Wolf Sts., Neck
Miller, George, Merchant, 3 Brownlee's Row, King St., Neck
Miller, Jacob, Rope Maker, Vanderhorst St., City Lands, Neck
Miller, James A., Clerk to the Board of Health, 20 Magazine St.
Miller, James, Merchant, 52 Anson St
Miller, Jane, Widow, Wall St.
Miller, Job, Bricklayer, 38 King St
Miller, John, Accountant,142 Meeting St.
Miller, John B., Accountant, Boundary St., Mazyckborough, Neck
Miller, John, Clerk, 108 Queen St.
Miller, John M., Baker, 17 Society St
Miller, John, Merchant, 23 Society St
Miller, Lydia, Widow, 33 St Philip's St
Miller, Samuel Stent, Printer, 101 Wentworth St.
Miller, William, Bank Clerk, 23 Society St
Miller, William C., Merchant, 142 Meeting St.
Miller, William H., Merchant, 52 Anson St
Miller, William H., Tailor, 252 King St.
Miller, William, Jeweller, 326 King St
Miller, William, Steam Engineer, 35 Anson St.
Milligan, Jane, Nurse, 42 Beaufain St.
Milligan, Margaret, Widow, Charlotte St., Mazyckborough, Neck
Milligan, William, Tallow Chandler, Henrietta St., Wraggsborough, Neck
Milliken, Primerose & Co., Vendue Masters, Vendue Range
Milliken, Thomas, Commission Merchant, Charlotte St , Mazyckborough, Neck
Milliner, George, F.P.C., 4 Swinton's Ln
Mills, Ann L , Widow, 1 Legare St.
Mills, Harriet, F.P.C , Seamstress, Neck
Mills, John, Bookseller, 107 Broad St
Mills, Mary, Mrs., Spring St., Neck
Mills, William, Tailor, 21 Wentworth St.
Minot, William, Planter, 4 Gibbes St.
Minson, Ann, Widow, 124 Wentworth St

Miot, C. H., Carpenter, 19 Society St.
Mishow, John, F P.C., Shoemaker, 70 Meeting St.
Misseldim, Robert, Book Binder, 5 Smith's Ln.
Missroon, James, Merchant, E Bay St
Mitchell, Abigail, F P C , Washer, Elizabeth St., Neck
Mitchell, Andrew, Plasterer, 12 Clifford St.
Mitchell, Ann H., Widow, cr. Pinckney St. & Maiden Ln.
Mitchell, Charlotte, F P.C, 16 Anson St.
Mitchell, Edward, Planter, cr. Gadsden & Montague Sts
Mitchell, Elizabeth, Grocer, 40 Elliott St.
Mitchell, Elizabeth, Widow, Aged 97, 19 Wentworth St
Mitchell, Henry, F P C , Magazine St
Mitchell, James, Block Maker, 110 Wentworth St
Mitchell, James, Block Maker, 3 Gillon St
Mitchell, James, Cooper, 48 E Bay St
Mitchell, James, Cooper, F P C , 6 West St
Mitchell, James, Cooperage, cr. E Bay St. & Martin's Whf
Mitchell, James D , Ordinary, Office in the Guard House
Mitchell, Jane, F P C., Ellery St
Mitchell, John, City Attorney, 38 Broad St , Res Guignard
St.
Mitchell, John, F.P.C , 111 Wentworth St.
Mitchell, John, F.P.C , 49 Broad St.
Mitchell, John H., Notary Public & Quorum Unis, 250 E
Bay St., Res Guignard St.
Mitchell, July, F P C , 2 Magazine St
Mitchell, Mary, F P C., Washer, Henrietta St ,
Wraggsborough, Neck
Mitchell, Mitchell, Factor, 135 Church St.
Mitchell, Nancy, F P C., Washer, 7 Cock Ln.
Mitchell, Robert, Merchant, Kunhardt & Leavitt's Whf
Mitchell, Susan, F P C., 17 Boundary St.
Mitchell, Thomas, Carpenter, 127 Wentworth St.
Moer, William, Planter, St Andrew's Parish,
Wraggsborough, Neck
Moffett, Andrew, Merchant, 306 King St
Moir, Henry, Grocer, 68 Queen St.
Moise, Aaron, Merchant, 63 King St
Moise, Benjamin, Accountant, cr. Market & Meeting Sts
Moise, S , Widow, 47 Tradd St
Moise, Sarah, Mrs., 384 King St
Moise, Sherry, Merchant, 62 King St
Moison, John, Jr., Smith, State St
Moles, Ellinor, Milliner's Shop, Wraggsborough, Neck
Moles, Margaret, Widow, Dry Goods Store, King St. Road,
Neck
Moncrieffe, Aron, F P C , Shoemaker, 13 Tradd St.
Moncrieffe John, Merchant, 13 Society St.
Mondoza, Moriah, Boarding House, 51 E. Bay St.
Monnar, Lewis, Hair Dresser, 134 Queen St
Monpoey, H., Factor, 6 Bull St.
Monpoey, Susan, Dry Goods Store, 301 King St
Montague, Richard, Merchant, 229 E Bay St.
Montague, Richard, Merchant, 8 Vendue Range
Montesquieu, Richard, Tinner, 12 Ellery St.
Montesquieu, Richard, Tinner, 184 Meeting St
Mood, -----, & Sons, Silversmiths, 318 King St.
Mood, Ann, Widow, Teacher, 133 Meeting St.
Mood, Christian, Silversmith, 3 Water St
Mood, John, Silversmith, Hasell St

Mood, Peter, Silversmith, 159 King St.
Moodie, Benjamin, British Consul, Meeting St.
Mooney, Ann, Millinery & Dry Goods Store, King St
Road, Neck
Mooney, Pat, 227 E. Bay St.
Moor, Ann, Widow, Nassau St., Wraggsborough, Neck
Moore, Catharine, F.P.C., Lynch's Ln.
Moore, James, Carpenter, Meeting St Road, Neck
Moore, James, Saddle, Cap & Harness Maker, 196 King
St., Neck
Moore, James, Saddler, 43 Broad St
Moore, Joseph P , Physician, 50 King St
Moore, Mary D., Miss, Dry Goods Store, 173 King St.
Moore, P., Watchmaker, 278 King St
Moore, Philip, Lumber Merchant, cr of Montague &
Gadsden Sts
Moore, Philip, Watchmaker, George St.
Moore, Richard, Painter, 52 Wentworth St.
Moore, Stephen W , Clerk, Union Bank, Res St. Philip's
St.
Mordecai, Joseph, Gunsmith, 42 Beaufain St.
Mordecai, Moses, Accountant, 21 Guignard St
Mordecai, Reinah, Widow, 21 Guignard St.
Morell, Mary Victor, Seamstress, 9 Cumberland St
Morford, E., Bookseller, 8 Broad St.
Morgan, Ann, Widow, 24 Archdale St.
Morgan, Benjamin, Capt , 16 Middle St
Morgan, Eliza, Widow, 92 Wentworth St.
Morgan, Isaac C., Carpenter, George St
Morgan, John, Carpenter, 26 Wall St
Morgan, Sarah, Widow, 26 Wall St
Morgan, William, Bricklayer, 60 Wentworth St.
Morgan, William, Capt., 6 Magazine St.
Morialty, Maurice, 287 King St.
Morris, C. G., Merchant, 257 E. Bay St.
Morris, Henry, Accountant, cr E Bay St & Wentworth
Sts.
Morris, James, Accountant, cr E Bay St & Wentworth
Sts
Morris, Simpson, Merchant, 268 King St
Morris, Thomas J., Lumber Merchant, 8 Wharf St.
Morris, Thomas, Merchant, 4 Chisolm's Upper Whf
Morris, Thomas, Notary Public, cr. Crafts' S. Whf. & E
Bay St.
Morrison, James, Cooper, 8 Price's Al
Morrison, James, Cooperage, Chisolm's Whf.
Morrison, John, Capt , 97 Tradd St
Morrison, John, Jr , Baker, 5 Bedon's Al
Mortimer, Edward, U S. Appraiser, 24 Anson St
Morton, Eliza, Widow, 136 Church St.
Moser, Philip, M.D., Drug Store, 103 Broad St., Res
12 Logan St
Moses, Elizabeth, Widow, 9 Beaufain St
Moses, Esther, Dry Goods Store, 132 King St.
Moses, Hester, Milliner, 20 Berresford St.
Moses, I. & Co , Vendue Masters, 42 Meeting St.
Moses, I. C., Vendue Master, 47 Tradd St
Moses, Isaac, 43 Beaufain St
Moses, Josiah, Planter, 293 King St
Moses, Levy, Merchant, 106 King St.

54

Moses, Lyon, 10 Swinton Ln.
Moses, Myer, Vendue Master, Res Meeting St
Moses, Rachel, Dry Goods Store, 71 E. Bay St.
Moses, Reuben, Dry Goods Store, 263 King St
Moses, Simon, Merchant, 193 King St., Neck
Moses, Solomon, Constable, 131 King St
Moses, Solomon, Jr., Dry Goods Store, 262 King St.
Mossiman & Co , Watchmakers, 42 Meeting St.
Motta, J A , Confectioner, 82 King St.
Motta, James, F P.C , Anson St
Motte, Abraham, 97 E. Bay St.
Motte, Elizabeth, Miss, Meeting St.
Motte, Francis, Factor, 152 Church St.
Mouatt, Mary, Widow, 19 Middle St
Moubray, Martha, Widow, 24 Church St.
Moubray, Martha, Widow, 3 Pinckney St.
Moulin, James, Dry Goods Store, 85 King St.
Moulin, Peter, Grocer, 18 State St
Moultrie, Alexander, Bank Clerk, 26 Cumberland St.
Moultrie, Bella, F.P C., Anson St
Moultrie, James, Jr., M D., 26 Cumberland St.
Moultrie, James, Sr., M.D , 26 Cumberland St.
Moultrie, John, Accountant, 26 Cumberland St.
Mourton, Martha, F.P.C , 9 Pitt St.
Mo[?]n, William, Shoemaker, 9 Archdale St.
Muck, Philip, Stationer, cr. Broad & King Sts.
Muckenfuss, Catharine, Miss, cr. Archdale & Beaufain Sts.
Muckenfuss, Elizabeth, Widow, King St.
Muckenfuss, Henry, Bricklayer, 75 Wentworth St.
Muggridge, Matthew, Blacksmith, Lucas St.,
  Cannonborough, Neck
Muir, Jane, Mrs., Boarding House, 112 Broad St.
Muirhead & Co., Merchants, Chisolm's Whf.
Muirhead, James, Accountant, 19 Market St.
Muller, Ferdinand, Factor, St. Philip's St. Cont'd., Neck
Mulligan, Barnard, Merchant, 178 King St
Munds, Albert, Rev., 6 Queen St.
Munds, Israel, Rev , Teacher, State St.
Mundy, Thomas, Coachmaker, Archdale St.
Mungies,-----, Stone Mason, Beaufain St.
Munro, Catharine, Midwife, cr. Hasell & King Sts.
Munro, John, Grocer, 56 Market St
Munro, Margaret, Boarding House, 36 Church St.
Murden, Jeremiah, Beaufain St.
Murley, Samuel, Factor, Martin's Whf.
Murley, Samuel, Merchant, Res Charlotte St.,
  Mazyckborough, Neck
Muroney, Phoebe, F.P.C., 5 King St
Murphy, John, Fisherman, Guignard St.
Murphy, Nancy, Smith's Ln
Murphy, Patrick, Grocer, 66 Anson St.
Murphy, Peter, Grocer, cr King & Beaufain Sts.
Murray, A. E., Dry Goods Store, cr. King & Beaufain Sts
Murray, Jeremiah, Boarding House, 19 Elliott St.
Mushington, William, Tailor, 1 Price's Al
Mussalt, Guerre, Widow, Pinckney St.
Mutze, Jacob, 8 West St
Myers, John, Clerk, cr Pinckney & Doughty Sts , Neck
Myers, Michael, Vendue Master, 28 Hasell St.
Mynott, B. C., Shoe Store, 27 Broad St

Myott, Edward, Boat Builder, Pritchard & Knox's Whf
M[?]lest, Andrew, Rigger, 8 Minority St.
M[?]r, Ann, Miss, 8 Mazyck St.
M[?]r, Thomas, Planter, Tradd St.
Naar, Moses, Peddler, 353 King St.
Nagle, Elizabeth, Widow, 143 Church St.
Naler, William, Merchant, Res. 27 Beaufain St.
Napier, Thomas & Co , Auctioneers, Vendue Range, Res
  105 Broad St.
Naser, Ann, Widow, Berresford St
Naser, Frederick, Clerk, Broad St.
Nash, William, 61 Church St.
Nathan, Henry, Cryer, 5 St. Philip's St.
Nathan, Henry, Store Keeper, King St Road, Neck
Nathans & Co., Merchants, 187 King St , Neck
Neale, Robert, Shopkeeper, cr. St Philip's & Vanderhorst
  Sts., Neck
Nell, Nancy, Seamstress, 9 Lightwood Al
Nelson, Christopher, Grocer, cr. St. Philip's & Green Sts
Nelson, George, Merchant, 9 Middle St.
Nelson, Harriet, F.P.C., Pastry Cook, 49 King St.
Nelson, James, Butcher, St. Philip's St., near the Lines,
  Neck
Nelson, William, Blacksmith, 22 Middle St
Neufville, Ann, Widow, 39 Anson St.
Neufville, John, Attorney, 39 Anson St
Neville, Henry, Cabinet Maker, 134 E. Bay St.
Neville, John & Son, Cabinet Makers, 79 Meeting St
Neville, John, Grocer, cr. Magazine & Mazyck Sts.
Newall & Thayer, Shoe Store, 324 King St.
Newall, Jonathan, Jr., Merchant, Kunhardt & Leavitt's
  Whf.
Newman, Mary, Widow, 8 Mazyck St.
Newton, Ann, Widow, 7 Gibbes St.
Newton, Anthony, Butcher, Cannon & Borough Sts., Neck
Newton, Cornelia, F.P.C., Seamstress, 18 Ellery St.
Newton, Elizabeth, F.P.C , Elizabeth St., Mazyckborough,
  Neck
Newton, Margaret, F.P.C., 126 Church St.
Newton, Mary, Widow, Dry Goods Store, 286 King St.
Newton, Susannah, F.P.C., Seamstress, 3 Parsonage Ln.
Newton, William, Accountant, 286 King St.
Nicholes, Elizabeth, Widow, W. Side Pinckney St., Neck
Nichols, Harriet, Mrs., 3 Friend St.
Nicholson, James, Factor, N.E. Side Pinckney St., Neck
Nicholson, Jane, Widow, 10 Pinckney St.
Nicholson, Robert, Merchant, cr. King & Cannon Sts ,
  Neck
Nicholson, Samuel & Co., Merchants, 234 E. Bay St
Nobbs, James S., cr St Philip's & Radcliff Sts., Neck
Noble, John & Co., Druggist, 179 King St.
Nolan, James, Boarding House, 35 Market St
Nolan, James, Carpenter, 3 Back St.
Norman, John, Mariner, 12 Parsonage Ln.
Norris, Agness, Miss, 16 Cumberland St.
Norris, Ann, Grocer, 82 E Bay St
Norris, James C., Cabinet Maker, 57 King St.
Norris, Martha, Widow, 57 King St.
Norris, Mary, Widow, Boarding House, Chalmers Al.
Norroy, Desere, Seamstress

Norroy, F. C., Dr., 18 George St.
Norroy, Nina, Seamstress, 33 Hasell St
North & Webb, Factors, Chisolm's Whf.
North, Edward, Factor, Res. W. End of Tradd St.
Norton, John L., Rice Mill, Gadsden's Whf.
Nowell, John, Cashier, Union Bank, Res 44 George St.
Nowell, Thomas S., Discount Clerk, Bank of S. C., Res Beaufain St, op. Coming St
Nuney, Francis, Mariner, Unity Al.
O'Donavan, Michael, Schoolmaster, 290 King St.
O'Driscoll, Matthew, M D., 392 King St.
O'Hara, Charles & Henry, Merchants, 274 E. Bay St.
O'Hara, Charles, Col., 9 Smith's Ln.
O'Hara, Henry, Merchant, 8 Church St.
O'Hear, John, Factor, cr. Montague & Rutledge Sts.
O'Hear, Joseph, Planter, cr. Montague & Rutledge Sts.
O'Rawe, John, Grocer, 74 Meeting St.
O'Relli, Peter, Merchant, 109 Broad St.
Oakes, Samuel, Grocer, Gadsden's Whf.
Oates, John, Beer House, 81 E Bay St
Oates, Mary, Widow, 14 Parsonage Ln.
Oeland, John, Merchant, 231 King St.
Ogden, Robert, Attorney, Office 3 State St., Res. 94 Wentworth St
Ogden, W George, Tailor, 69 E. Bay St.
Ogelvey, Andrew, F.P.C , 22 Cumberland St.
Ogelvey, Mary, F.P.C , Seamstress, 22 Cumberland St
Ogier, Lewis, Factor, Office, 21 E. Bay St., Res 2 Anson St.
Ogier, Thomas, Broker & Commission Merchant, 3 Broad St., Res. 121 Church St
Ohring, Catharine, Widow, Elizabeth St., Mazyckborough, Neck
Oleron, F. J., Confectioner, 114 Broad St.
Oliphant, David, Painter, cr. Society & Meeting Sts
Oliver, James, Butcher, St. Philip's St., near the Lines, Neck
Oneal, Charles & Richard, Merchants, King St. Road, Neck
Oneal, Edmund, cr. Cannon & Pinckney Sts, Neck
Oring, Catharine, Widow, 143 Church St.
Osborn & Waring, Factors, Chisolm's Whf
Osborne, Samuel, Saddlery Store, 216 cr. Boundary & King Sts., Neck
Oswald, James, Butcher, cr Mary & Elizabeth Sts., Neck
Otis, Richard W., Merchant, 14 Broad St., Counting House, Crafts' Whf.
Ottlingui, Abraham, 5 N. Side of Vendue Range
Otto, Charles, Butcher, 30 Society St.
Otto, John, 9 King St.
Owans, Thomas, Packet Man, Wall St.
Owen, Betsey, F P C , 59 Wentworth St.
Owen, Nancy, F.P C , Boundary St.
Owen, Smart, 5 Coming St.
O'Neale, James, Carpenter, 28 Mazyck St.
O'Neale, Joseph, F.P C., 9 West St.
Packard, Chisolm, Teacher, 42 George St.
Padaoone, Ann, F.P.C., Pastry Cook, Spring St., Neck
Padaoone, Robert, F.P.C., Carpenter, Spring St., Neck
Page, John, City Guard, 134 Meeting St

Page, Joseph, Merchant, Gibbes & Harper's Whf.
Paine, Joseph B., Ship Chandler, 42 E Bay St.
Paine, Martha, 6 Montague St.
Paine, Thomas, Jr., Lt., U. S Navy, 42 E Bay St
Paine, Thomas, Sr , Harbor Master, 42 E. Bay St.
Paisley, Robert A , Merchant, 12 Guignard St
Palmer, Benjamin, Rev., D. D., 100 Queen St.
Palmer, Edward, Teacher, 46 Beaufain St.
Palmer, Job, Carpenter, 98 Wentworth St.
Parisen, W T., Portrait Painter, 67 Church St
Parish, Miller & Co., Merchants, 97 Broad St.
Parker, Ann, Widow, 21 Tradd St
Parker, Charles, City Surveyor & Engineer, 32 Meeting St
Parker, Edwin, 32 Meeting St.
Parker, Eliza M., F.P.C., Pastry Cook, 5 Short St.
Parker, Eliza, Widow, Rutledge St.
Parker, Florinda, Widow, 31 Guignard St
Parker, Isaac, Planter, 17 Legare St.
Parker, John, Planter, 13 Pitt St.
Parker, Martha, Widow, Plantress, John St., Mazyckborough, Neck
Parker, Mary, F.P C., Seamstress, 16 Wall St.
Parker, Mary, Miss, 12 Beaufain St.
Parker, Samuel, Planter, 43 George St
Parker, Sarah P , Meeting St.
Parker, Thomas, District Attorney, 32 Meeting St
Parker, Thomas, Jr., Attorney, 32 Meeting St.
Parker, William Henry, Factor, 32 Meeting St.
Parks, Josiah D , Merchant, State St., Store, 225 E. Bay St.
Parks, P. S. & Co., Merchants, 261 E Bay St.
Parsons, Isaac D., Teacher, 237 King St.
Parsons, Joseph, Blake St , Hampstead, Neck
Passailaigue, Lewis, Baker, cr. Washington & Boundary Sts
Patch, Nathaniel, Grocer, cr. Middle & Laurens St , Res. 4 Laurens St.
Paterson, Hugh, Auditor, Union Insurance Co
Patison, James, Grocer, 41 E. Bay St
Patrick, Cassimir, Leather Store, King St. Road, Neck
Patrick, Cassimir, Tanyard, Mary St., Wraggsborough, Neck
Patrick, Philip, Planter, 106 Meeting St
Patterson, James, Mariner, Lynch's Ln.
Patterson, Mary W., Widow, 116 King St.
Patterson, Samuel, Factor, 46 Hasell St.
Patton, William, Merchant, 19 Broad St.
Pawn, Bartholomew, Shoemaker, 44 Boundary St.
Paxton, H W , Factor, Magazine St , Res. Harleston's Green
Payenneville, Stephen, Merchant, 9 Wall St
Payne, John W , Capt , Broker & Vendue Master, Res 59 Broad St
Payne, William & Son, Broker & Vendue Masters, 110 Broad St.
Payne, William, Broker & Vendue Master, Res. 110 Broad St
Payne, William, Stone Cutter, 41 St Philip's St.
Peake, John S., Merchant, E. Bay St., near Tradd St., Res 107 Broad St.
Pearce, Lindy, F.P C., Archdale St

Pearce, Richard, 85 Meeting St.
Pearce, Samuel, Carpenter, Henrietta St.,
    Wraggsborough, Neck
Pearce, Thomas, Carpenter, 6 Mazyck St
Peardon, Louisa, F.P.C., Seamstress, 70 Church St.
Pease, Elizabeth, Widow, cr Pinckney & Anson Sts
Peck, Elizabeth, Widow, 24 George St
Pecon, Amy, F.P.C., Linguard St.
Peirl, Peter & Co., Grocers, 21 Queen St.
Pelzer, Anthony, Teacher, German Friendly Society, 7
    Archdale St.
Pemble, David, Tailor, 98 E. Bay St , Res. 2 Market St.
Penington, Ann Elizabeth, Widow, 9 Blackbird Al
Pennall, James, Merchant, cr. King & Warren Sts., Neck
Penott & Co., Shoe Store, 80 King St.
Pepoon, Benjamin F., Attorney, 287 Meeting St., Res.
    14 Queen St.
Pepoon, Benjamin, Grocer, cr. E. Bay & Queen Sts , Res.
    14 Queen St.
Percival & Johnson, Drs., Brownlee's Row, King St., Neck
Percy, William, Rev., D. D., 18 Tradd St.
Perdrieu, Isabella, Widow, 4 Maiden Ln.
Perman, George, Grocer, 35 & 36 E. Bay St.
Permekief, Frances, Widow, 116 King St.
Peronneau, Henry W., Planter, 4 S. Bay St.
Peronneau, Jane & Sisters, F.P.C., 59 Wentworth St.
Peronneau, John, Hair Dresser, 304 King St.
Peronneau, William, Planter, 4 S. Bay St.
Peronone, Elizabeth, Widow, Dry Goods Store, 343 King
    St.
Perry, Ann D., Widow, cr. Bull & Lynch's Sts.
Perry, Emanuel, Grocer, 75 Market St.
Perry, Isabella, Widow, Midwife, 102 Queen St.
Perry, Mary, Dry Goods Store, 108 King St.
Perry, Peter S , 123 E. Bay St.
Perry, Stephen, Accountant, State St.
Pesson, Joseph, Grocer, 2 State St.
Petch, Francis, Shoemaker, King St.
Peterie, George, 20 Society St.
Peters, Jane, Widow, 378 King St.
Peters, Mary, Broad St.
Peters, Vincent, Grocer, 22 Church St.
Petsch, Julius, Book Binder, 50 Church St., Res. 6 George
    St.
Peussi, John, Merchant, 365 King St.
Pezant, John L., Grocer, cr. Washington & Boundary Sts.
Pezant, Lewis, Grocer, 197 E. Bay St.
Phelon, Edmond M., Grocer, cr. Meeting & Queen Sts.
Phillips, Alexander, Ship Carpenter, 15 Pinckney St
Phillips, Ann, F.P.C., Philadelphia St.
Phillips, Benjamin S., Merchant, State St.
Phillips, Benjamin, Shoemaker, 119 Tradd St.
Phillips, Daniel, Grocer, cr. Amen & Church Sts.
Phillips, Dorothy, Widow, 75 Queen St.
Phillips, John, Grocer, 12 Chalmers Al.
Phillips, John, Painter, cr. E Bay & Pinckney Sts.
Phillips, Kitty, F.P.C., 8 Linguard St.
Phillips, Mathias, Grocer, 66 King St
Phillips, Odet, Cigar Maker, 80 E. Bay St.
Phynnea, Joseph, Pilot, 6 Lynch's Ln.

Pickenpack, John, Porter, Union Bank, Res. Bank Yard
Pidge, David, Ship Master, 29 Guignard St.
Pierce, Edward, Stoll's Al.
Piere, Peter, King St. Road, Neck
Pierson, Catharine, Widow, Boarding House, 44 Church
    St.
Piestor, Sarah, Widow, Seamstress, 42 Beaufain St.
Piezant, Peter, Ship Master
Pillot, John, Grocer, Meeting St. Road, Neck
Pilsbury & Hillard, Merchants, Crafts' S. Whf.
Pilsbury, Moody, Merchant, Crafts' Whf., Res. 4 Anson St.
Pilsbury, Rebecca, Widow, Nurse, 42 Boundary St
Pilsbury, Samuel, Export Officer of Customs, 9 Anson St
Pinceel, Elizabeth, F.P.C., Seamstress, 14 Berresford St
Pinceel, Margaret, F.P.C., Elizabeth St., Mazyckborough,
    Neck
Pinceel, William, F.P C., Tin Plate Worker, 43 Meeting St
Pinckney, Charles C , Attorney, Pinckney St.,
    Cannonborough, Neck
Pinckney, Charles Cotesworth, Gen., E. Bay St., above the
    Market
Pinckney, Charles, Planter, 6 Church St.
Pinckney, Eliza, F.P.C., Seamstress, 12 Berresford St.
Pinckney, Frances Susannah, Widow, 28 St. Philip's St
Pinckney, Henry L., 11 Legare St.
Pinckney, L , Widow, Pitt St.
Pinckney, Roger, Planter, 28 Legare St.
Pinckney, Thomas, Gen., 41 George St.
Pitts, Peter, F P C., Mariner, 24 Pinckney St.
Plissonan, John, Dry Goods Store, 44 E. Bay St
Plumeau, John Francis, Secretary, S. C. Insurance Co.,
    Res 350 King St.
Plunkett, P. C , Shopkeeper, E. cr. St. Philip's & Warren
    Sts., Neck
Pogson, -----, Rev., cr. Wentworth & Pitt Sts.
Pohl, Elias & Son, Merchants, Chisolm's Whf
Pohl, Elias, Merchant, Store, Chisolm's Whf., Res 76 King
    St.
Poineigson, P. A., Tin Plate Worker, 12 Queen St
Poineigson, Solomon, Tin Plate Worker, 12 Queen St
Poinsett, Joel Robert, N E. Side Pinckney St., Neck
Pollock, Levy, Dry Goods Store, 277 King St.
Pontoo, Nancy, F.P.C., Market St.
Poor, H., Mazyck St
Portas, Ann, F P.C., Seamstress, Henrietta St.,
    Wraggsborough, Neck
Porter, Benjamin R., Cabinet Maker, 352 King St.
Porter, John, Saddler, 189 King St., Neck
Porter, Lewis M., Rigger, E. Bay St
Porter, Peter, Blacksmith, 39 King St.
Porter, Sarah, Confectioner, cr. Lynch's Ln. & Church St.
Porter, William L., Accountant, 19 Meeting St
Postell, William, Planter, Charlotte, Elizabeth & John Sts
    Mazyckborough, Neck
Potter, John, Merchant, Res. 32 Society St.
Potter, -----, Widow of Washington, 23 E. Bay St.
Poujaud, Augustus, Merchant, 45 E. Bay St.
Poulton, Edward, Capt., 139 Church St.
Powell, John, F.P.C., 9 Cock Ln.
Powell, Martha

Power, Caroline, Widow, Dry Goods Store, 343 King St
Power, E , Ship Chandler, 217 E. Bay St.
Power, James, Painter, 18 Magazine St.
Poyas, John E., M.D., 26 Meeting St
Preble, Mary, Widow, 50 Church St.
Prele, Ann L., Widow, 192 Meeting St.
Prentiss, Anna R., Widow, Plantress, Cannonborough, Neck
Prescott, George W., Merchant, Magwood's Whf., Res. State St.
Pressly & Mandeville, Merchants, cr. Wolf & King Sts., Neck
Pressly, -----, Misses, Mantua Makers, 19 Blackbird Al.
Prevost, Mary, Widow, 192 E. Bay St.
Price, Ann, Widow, Grocer, 159 Church St.
Price, Charlotte, Widow, Cannon St., Neck
Price, Maria, Seamstress, Rutledge St.
Price, Thomas, Accountant, Society St.
Price, Thomas William, Planter, 39 George St.
Price, William, Jr , Planter, 2 Legare St.
Price, William, Planter, 2 Orange St.
Primrose, Catharine, Widow, 167 E Bay St.
Primrose, Diana, F.P.C., 14 Clifford St.
Primrose, Robert, Auctioneer, Res. 16 E. Bay St.
Prince, Bella, F.P.C., Seamstress, 32 Anson St.
Prince, Charles, Jr., Dry Goods Store, 345 King St.
Prince, Charles, Tin Plate Worker, 344 King St.
Prince, Herriot, Widow, 11 Bull St.
Prince, J. R., Planter, Broad St.
Prince, John, Porter & Transfer Clerk, Planters' & Mechanics' Bank, Res. Bank Yard
Prince, Mary, F.P C , Washer, 32 Anson St.
Pringle, George, Merchant., King St. Road, Neck
Pringle, Jane, Widow, 4 Archdale St.
Pringle, John J., 101 Tradd St.
Pringle, -----, Misses, Plantress, 98 Tradd St.
Prioleau & Pinckney, Attorneys, 111 Church St.
Prioleau, Jane B., Widow, Teacher, cr. Ellery St. & Maiden Ln.
Prioleau, John C., Factor, Res. 226 Meeting St.
Prioleau, Philip G., M.D., cr. Meeting & George Sts.
Prioleau, Samuel, Attorney, Res 28 Bull St.
Prioleau, Thomas G., M.D., 38 Queen St
Prioleau, -----, Widow of Samuel, 28 Church St.
Pritchard, Joseph, Merchant, 45 Society St.
Pritchard, Paul, Ship Carpenter's Yard, Gadsden's Whf., Res. 44 Hasell St.
Pritchard, Susannah, Widow, Plantress, 50 Anson St.
Pritchard, William, Jr., Ship Carpenter, 28 Pinckney St
Pritchard, William, Sr , Ship Carpenter, Res 1 Pinckney St.
Proctor, Mary C , Seamstress, Cock Ln.
Proctor, William & Co., Shoe Store, 24 Meeting St.
Puglia, James, Sworn Interpreter, State St.
Purce, William, Watchmaker, 96 Broad St.
Purcell, Ann, Widow, cr. Green & Bull Sts
Purcly, -----, Miss, Widow, 16 Mazyck St.
Pynt, H., Widow, 27 Church St
Quash, Robert, 73 Broad St.
Quin, Thomas F., Grocer, cr. Boundary & Meeting Sts., Neck
Quinby, Elizabeth, Widow, Store 5 Pinckney St
Quinby, Henry M., 5 Pinckney St.
Quinby, Joseph, Carpenter, 5 Pinckney St.
Quinland, Michael, 77 Wentworth St.
Quinman, Barbary, Widow, store 141 Pinckney St.
Quisgin, Mary, Widow, 39 St. Philip's St.
Raba, Susan, Widow, 11 Philadelphia St.
Radcliff, John W., Tailor, 125 Queen St.
Rade, J. E., M.D., 366 King St.
Railly & Gahan, Grocers, cr. Anson & Ellery Sts.
Raine, Thomas, Meeting St. Road, Neck
Ramsay, David, Attorney, Office, 88 Broad St., Res. Hampstead
Ramsay, David, Attorney, Res. Wraggsborough, Neck
Ramsay, James, M.D., 87 Broad St.
Ramsay, John, M.D., 1 Anson St.
Ranall, Peter, Comb Maker, 125 King St.
Randall, John P., Grocer, 117 E. Bay St.
Randall, Stephen, F P.C., Boundary St
Randall, William, Grocer, 6 Market St.
Rantin, William, King St. Road, Neck
Rasdale, Frederica, Widow, Meeting St. Road, Neck
Ratcliff, L. C., Widow, cr. Meeting & George Sts.
Ratlert, E. A., 6 King St.
Ravanell & Stephens, Factors, Vanderhorst's Whf.
Ravanell, Catharine, Widow, 94 Broad St.
Ravanell, Daniel, Attorney, 44 Society St.
Ravanell, Henrietta, Widow, 44 Society St.
Ravina, Joseph D., 31 St. Philip's St.
Raworth, George F., Saddler, 8 St. Philip's St.
Rawson, Edward D., 85 Meeting St
Rawson, William R., Cabinet Maker, Meeting St.
Ray, James, Factor, Vanderhorst's Whf.
Raymond & Motte, Merchants, 168 King St.
Raynay, Bauseyere, Carpenter, cr. Warren & Coming Sts., Neck
Read & Horsey, Merchants, cr. Wentworth & King Sts
Read, William, M.D., Logan St.
Readhimer, Christiana, Widow, Spring St., Neck
Rechon & Byrne, Sail Makers, Chisolm's Upper Whf.
Rechon, Daniel, Tailor, 1 Berresford St.
Rechon, Lewis, Sail Maker, Res. 6 Meeting St.
Redder, Eliza, Widow, Seamstress, Meeting St. Road, Neck
Redman, James, Blacksmith, Daniell's Whf.
Reed & Cooper, Shoe Store, cr. King & Queen Sts.
Reed, Bullen & Co , Shoe Store, 163 King St
Reeves, Aeneas S., Master Work House, 5 Back St.
Reeves, Samuel, Carpenter, 34 King St.
Regaud, Peter, Tallow Chandler, Henrietta St., Wraggsborough, Neck
Reid, Alexander, Watchmaker, 260 King St.
Reid, Ann M., Widow, 51 Wentworth St.
Reid, Elizabeth, Widow, 196 Meeting St.
Reid, Ellen, Miss, Wentworth St.
Reid, George, Bookkeeper, Bank of S. C., Res. 29 E. Bay St
Reid, Harleston, Planter, Montague St.
Reid, Jacob, Planter, Montague St.

58

Reid, John, Wheelwright, 10 Cumberland St.
Reid, Mary, Miss, Wentworth St.
Reid, -----, Widow of George, 29 E. Bay St.
Reigne, John, Baker, 105 E Bay St
Reilly & Barnard, Grocers, cr. State & Queen Sts.
Reilly, James, Coachmaker, 97 Church St.
Reilly, James, Grocer, 110 Church St.
Reilly, -----, Misses, Dry Goods Store, 170 King St
Reilly, Robert, 18 Mazyck St.
Remley, Mary, Widow, Vanderhorst St., City Lands, Neck
Remmington, Sarah, Mrs, Cannon & Borough Sts., Neck
Remoussin, Plutong, 45 Beaufain St.
Remoussin, -----, Widow of Daniel, 16 George St.
Renauld, John, Grocer, 84 Church St.
Renea, Ann, Widow, 5 Meeting St.
Revell, Hannah, Widow, 48 Anson St.
Reynolds & Bullock, Grocers, 127 Church St.
Reynolds, George N. C., Coachmaker, Meeting St.
Rhind, Elizabeth, Widow, Wentworth St
Rhodes & Applegate, Boarding House, Martin's Whf.
Rhodus, John S., Butcher, Coming St., City Lands, Neck
Ricard, Frances, F P.C., 58 E. Bay St.
Rice, O'Brien Smith, King St. Road, Neck
Richardin, Achelaus, Hatter, 13 Ellery St.
Richards, Abraham, F.P.C., Carpenter, Liberty St.
Richards, Charles, Bricklayer, 5 Blackbird Al.
Richards, Dinah, F.P.C., 56 Anson St.
Richards, Frederick, Bricklayer, 7 Liberty St.
Richards, Samuel, Grocer, 35 Elliott St.
Richards, Samuel, Quorum Unis, 253 E Bay St.
Richardson & Bennett, Attorneys, Office, State House Sq.
Richardson, Ann, Widow, Smith St.
Richardson, Colin, Silversmith, 109 Wentworth St.
Richardson, D., Planter, 160 E. Bay St.
Richardson, Henry, Dr., Planter, Charlotte St., Mazyckborough, Neck
Richardson, J. S., State Attorney General, Pinckney St., near Cannonsbridge, Neck
Richardson, Mary, Widow, 128 Queen St.
Righton, Elizabeth, Widow, 3 Water St.
Righton, Flora, Widow, 46 E. Bay St.
Righton, John M., M.D., Drug Store, 76 E. Bay St.
Righton, Joseph, Cooper, cr. E. Bay & Water Sts.
Riley & O'Hear, Factors, 276 E. Bay St.
Riley, John, Factor, Res. Boundary St., Neck
Ring, David, Painter, 2 Broad St., Res. 4 Meeting St.
Ritchie, M., Nurse, 26 King St.
Rivere, John Peter, Merchant, 312 King St.
Rivers, Elizabeth, Widow, 11 Stoll's Al.
Rivers, George, Planter, Tradd St.
Rivers, John, Grocer, cr. St. Philip's & Liberty Sts , Res. 4 Liberty St
Rivers, John, Ship Carpenter, 6 Water St.
Rivers, Mary G. W., Widow, 64 Queen St.
Rivers, Samuel, Ship Carpenter, 6 Water St.
Rivers, Thomas, 118 Wentworth St
Rix, Susan, 9 Pinckney St.
Roach, Nash, Teller, Planters' & Mechanics' Bank, Res Boundary St., City Lands, Neck
Roach, William, Jr., Clerk to Council, 3 Society St.

Roach, William, Sr., City Treasurer, 3 Society St.
Robcon, Elizabeth, Widow, 9 Berresford St.
Roberts, Catharine, F.P.C., 11 Archdale St.
Roberts, Catharine, Widow, 34 Wentworth St.
Roberts, Eliza S., Widow, 13 Cumberland St.
Roberts, Francis, Saddler, 140 King St
Roberts, Francis, Saddler, 198 King St., Neck
Roberts, Harriet, Widow, 9 Linguard St.
Roberts, Rina, F.P.C., 15 Middle St
Roberts, William, Inspector, Custom House, Res. 128 Wentworth St.
Robertson, Ann, Mrs., Vanderhorst St., Neck
Robertson, Francis, Grocer, 12 Champney St.
Robertson, Harriet, F.P.C., 45 Anson St.
Robertson, James, F.P.C., 27 Bull St.
Robertson, John, Baker, 151 Church St
Robertson, John, Merchant & Navy Agent, 8 Crafts' S. Whf , Res. 16 Meeting St.
Robertson, -----, Widow of Samuel, Vanderhorst St., op Orphan Church, Neck
Robertson, William, Boundary St.
Robertson, William, Grocer, cr Beadon's Al. & Elliott St
Robertsons, -----, Misses, Charlotte St., Wraggsborough, Neck
Robin, Antoniette, Widow, 115 Wentworth St.
Robinson & Carter, Merchants, 5 Crafts' S. Whf
Robinson, Alexander, 89 Broad St.
Robinson, Helen Mary, School, 89 Broad St.
Robinson, John, Factor, 8 Duncan's Whf
Robinson, John, Factor, Res. St. Philip's St., Neck
Robinson, Randal, Merchant, 76 Tradd St.
Rochacblanche, Louis, 64 Anson St.
Roche, John, 59 Queen St.
Roche, John, Grocer, 51 Church St.
Roddy, Martin, Grocer, Gibbes & Harper's Whf
Roddy, Mary, Widow, 26 Church St.
Rodericks, Anthony, Grocer, cr. Beaufain & Coming Sts.
Rodgers, Allice, Widow, Wentworth St.
Rodgers, Ann, Widow, 20 Friend St.
Rodgers, Christopher, 23 Tradd St.
Rodgers, John, Baker, 74 Wentworth St.
Rodgers, Joseph, Amen St
Rodgers, Lewis, Wheelwright, 2 Bull St.
Rodgers, Susannah, 74 Wentworth St.
Rodriguez, Jean, 226 E. Bay St.
Rogers, Elizabeth, Widow, 134 Meeting St.
Rogers, John Ralph, Ship Chandler, 60 E. Bay St.
Roh, Jacob Frederick, Blacksmith, cr. Cumberland & Church Sts.
Rohmer, John, Billiard Table, cr. Cumberland & Church Sts.
Rolando, Widow, 7 Cumberland St.
Romanzoff, Mary, Mrs., & Romanzoff, Christopher, Milliner, 154 King St.
Romo, Baptist, 203 Meeting St.
Roper, H., Widow, 22 E. Bay St
Roper, Thomas, Planter, 39 E. Bay St.
Roper, William, Planter, 22 E. Bay St.
Roper, William, Planter, 89 E. Bay St
Rose & Rogers, Ship Chandlers, 60 E. Bay St.

Rose, Arthur A., Assistant Clerk, Bank of Discount & Deposit, 75 George St
Rose, Christopher, Grocer, 367 King St.
Rose, Henry, Factor, Res. 254 King St.
Rose, Hugh, Planter, 15 Bull St.
Rose, John S., Accountant, Green St.
Rose, Mary, Friend St.
Rose, Nancy, F.P.C , Mantua Maker, Jones' Lot, King St
Rose, Rebecca, Widow, 9 Smith's Ln.
Ross, David, cr. E. Bay & Wentworth Sts
Ross, Margaret, Widow, Ellery St.
Ross, Thomas, Capt., Revenue Cutter, cr Anson & Ellery Sts
Roturnau, Charles, Planter, 126 King St
Rou, George D., Cabinet Maker, Warren St., Wraggsborough, Neck
Roulain, Catherine, 53 Meeting St.
Roumillatt, John & Son, Confectioners, 38 Meeting St.
Roun, Charles, Planter, 6 Short St.
Rouse, Christopher, Shoemaker, 14 Society St.
Rouse, William, Col., 37 Market St.
Rouse, William, Jr., 37 Market St
Rout, Catharine, Widow, 19 Friend St.
Rout, William George, Outdoor Clerk, Bank of Discount & Deposit
Roux, Lewis, Quorum Unis, 58 E Bay St
Rowe & White, Stone Cutters, cr. Church & Market Sts.
Roye, Francois, Grain Store, cr. Anson & Wentworth Sts.
Ruddock, Samuel, Surveyor, 20 King St.
Runciman, John K. N., Cannon St., Neck
Rush, Mary, 132 Church St.
Russell, Daniel, 123 Tradd St.
Russell, Elizabeth, Widow, 35 Guignard St.
Russell, John, Blacksmith, 124 Wentworth St
Russell, Nathaniel, 22 Meeting St.
Russell, Rachel, Widow, Charlotte St., Mazyckborough, Neck
Russell, -----, Widow, S W. cr. St. Philip's & Radcliff Sts , Neck
Russell, William, F.P C., Mariner, Longitude Ln
Rutledge, Charles, M.D., Wentworth St.
Rutledge, Frederick, Planter, 60 Tradd St
Rutledge, John, Gen., cr. Society & Meeting Sts.
Rutledge, John, Jr , cr Society & Meeting Sts
Rutledge, State, Planter, 155 E. Bay St.
Rutledge, William, 1 George St
Ryakbosch, -----, Mrs., Upholsterer, 4 Beaufain St.
Ryan, Elizabeth, Widow, 99 Wentworth St
Ryan, John, Merchant, 2 Chisolm's St
Ryan, Lawrence, Attorney, 5 St Michael's Al.
Safford, Isabella, Widow, cr. E Bay & Minority Sts.
Salter, Thomas R., Joiner, cr Amen & State Sts.
Salters, Francis & Son, Factors, 266 E. Bay St.
Salters, Francis, Capt , Factor, S. Bay St.
Salters, Francis, Ship Chandler
Salters, Pricilla, F.P C , Nurse, Jones' Lot, King St.
Salters, Samuel, F.P.C., Carpenter, Jones' Lot, King St.
Sammers, Susan B., Widow, 13 Coming St.
Samory, C., Store, Queen St.
Sampson, Henry, Dry Goods Store, 261 King St

Sampson, Joseph, Merchant, 266 King St.
Sandford, John, Dry Goods Store, Queen St
Sanford, John, Grocer, 110 E. Bay St.
Sarazin, Catharine, Miss, 56 Wentworth St
Sarazin, Mary, Miss, 56 Wentworth St.
Sargeant, John H., Attorney, 16 State St
Sarjeant, Duraquer, Shoemaker, 65 Church St.
Sarzadas, David, Auctioneer, 65 Queen St
Sass, Edward G., Warehouse, 99 Queen St., Res. 38 Queen St.
Sass, Jacob, Col., 39 Queen St
Sass, William H., Teller, Bank of Discount & Deposit, Res. 39 Queen St.
Satorias, John, 376 King St
Saunders, John, Grocer, cr. Rutledge & Montague Sts.
Savage, Ann, Mrs., Fancy & Millinery Store, cr King St & Clifford's Al.
Savage, Arthur, Merchant, Duncan's Whf
Savage, Mary, F P.C., cr. Elizabeth & Henrietta Sts , Wraggsborough, Neck
Savage, -----, Mrs , 9 Legare St
Savage, Patsey, F.P.C., Seamstress, 5 Swinton's Ln
Sawyer & Steele, Merchants, cr. King & Boundary Sts.
Sax, Henry, Grocer, 86 Church St.
Sayre, Eliza, 13 King St.
Scaeb, Emeline, F.P.C , 53 Wentworth St
Schelling, Daniel E., 179 Meeting St.
Schenck & Turner, Booksellers, Stationers & Book Binders, 15 Broad St.
Schmidt, Elizabeth, Widow, 2 Montague St.
Schmidt, John W., Dr., 3 Bedon's Alley
Schneider, Christian, Grocer, cr Wall & Minority Sts
Schnell, John J., Grocer, 74 Church St.
Schnirle, John, Carpenter, 6 Friend St.
Schroder, John A., Grocer, cr. Anson & Hasell Sts.
Schroder, John, Grocer, 10 Market & 25 Queen Sts
Schults & Ripley, Merchants, 278 King St.
Schultz, William, Mattress Maker, Boundary St , Mazyckborough, Neck
Schutt & Budd, Hardware Store, 51 E. Bay St
Schutt, Lewis H. E., Merchant, Res. cr. Meeting & S. Bay Sts
Schwartz, John, Grocer, 149 Queen St.
Scot, Abraham, F.P C , Boundary St
Scot, James, Merchant, 20 Elliott St
Scot, Thomas, Broad St.
Scot, William M., Quorum Unis, Office, 229 E. Bay St., Res Boundary St.
Scott, Andrew William, Carpenter, King St. Road, Neck
Scott, Rebecca E , Widow, 130 Meeting St., Neck
Scouder, Jane, Widow, 25 Pinckney St.
Scriven, Rebecca, Miss, 12 Lynch's Ln.
Scriven, -----, Widow, 137 Church St.
Seabrook, Benjamin, Planter, 23 St Philip's St.
Seabrook, Thomas B., Planter, cr. Bull & Rutledge Sts.
Seignious, John, 134 E Bay St
Selah, William, Printer, W. End of Tradd St.
Senet, Joseph, 317 King St.
Senet, Mary Ann, Widow, 59 King St.
Sensallary, Mary, F P.C., Fruit Shop, 71 Church St

60

Sever, Abraham, Carpenter, 42 Pinckney St.
Sexias, Isaac M., Crockery Store, 340 King St.
Seyden, Henry, Grocer, 9 Pitt St.
Seyle, Samuel, Saddler, 289 King St
Seyler, Pricilla, Widow, Shopkeeper, King St., Neck
Seymour, Eliza, F.P.C , Mantua Maker, 92 Tradd St.
Seymour, Sally, F.P.C., Pastry Cook, Tradd St. near King St.
Seymour, William, F.P.C , Carpenter, 92 Tradd St.
Shackleford & Middleton, Factors, Vanderhorst's Whf.
Shackleford, William, Factor, Res. 197 Meeting St.
Shally, Margaret, Mrs., Grocer, 355 King St.
Shand, Robert, Custom House Officer, 14 Pinckney St.
Sharp, John, Block & Pump Maker, cr Guignard St. & Maiden Ln.
Shatobla, Munra, F.P.C., 7 Logan St.
Shaw, Margaret, 43 Boundary St.
Shea, Richard, Grocer, Henrietta St., Wraggsborough, Neck
Shecut, J. L E W., M.D., 79 King St.
Shepard, Christiana, Widow, Pinckney St.
Shepard, James, Harness Maker, Coming St., Res. 276 King St.
Shepard, -----, Mrs., 41 Beaufain St
Shepard, Rachael, Widow, Rutledge St.
Sherwin, Hannah, F.P C., Nurse, Wraggsborough, Neck
Shewel, John, Rigger, 1 Bedon's Al.
Shields, Henry, Grocer, 239 King St
Shields, Mary, F.P.C., 26 Wentworth St.
Shirer, John, Carpenter, 26 Archdale St.
Shirer, John, Gunsmith, 188 Meeting St.
Shirer, Michael, 26 Archdale St
Shirtliff, William Lee, F P.C., Carpenter, Boundary St., Neck
Shively, Charles, 137 Meeting St.
Shively, John, Painter, 137 Meeting St
Shively, Mary, Widow, Seed Store, 137 Meeting St.
Sholtus, Abraham, Blacksmith, 18 Lynch's Ln.
Shorthouse, Thomas, Merchant, cr. Boundary & King Sts., Neck
Shotes, George, Ship Carpenter, 11 Amen St.
Shouldsbread, James, Planter, 12 Lamboll St
Shrewsbury, Edward, Ship Carpenter, 363 King St.
Shrewsbury, Jane M , Widow, 13 Linguard St.
Shrewsbury, Mary, F.P.C., Meeting St.
Shriven, Thomas, Planter, Res. on the Green, Hampstead, Neck
Shroder, F , Grocer, 121 Queen St.
Shroder, T. J., Grocer, cr. Philadelphia & Queen Sts.
Shubert, J H., 7 Stoll's Al
Shultz, John, Factor, 10 Fitzsimons' Whf., Res. Church St. Cont'd.
Shultz, Sarah, Miss, 16 Mazyck St.
Shwarts, Frederick, Butcher, Cannonborough, Neck
Sibley, George B. R., Washington St.
Sifley & Mimtzing, Saw Pit & Lumber Yard, W. End of Queen St.
Sifley, Henry, Lumber Merchant, Res. 44 Market St
Sifley, John, Bricklayer, 44 Market St.
Sifley, Susannah, Widow, Dry Goods Store, 44 Market St.

Sigwall, Thomas, 52 Wentworth St.
Silliman, John H., Shipmaster, Charlotte St , Mazyckborough, Neck
Sillings, Sarah, Widow, 8 Lowndes St , Neck
Silvia, Dominique, Mariner, 3 French Al.
Simmons, Susannah, Widow, 96 Meeting St
Simmons, William, Butcher, Neck
Simons & Hasell, Factors, D'Oyley's Whf.
Simons & Waring, Attorneys, 28 Meeting St.
Simons, Benjamin, M D., 55 Meeting St
Simons, Charles Ingraham, Engraver, 252 E. Bay St.
Simons, Edward P., Attorney, 5 Laurens St.
Simons, Edward, Planter, 156 E. Bay St
Simons, Gaines, 12 Bull St.
Simons, Hannah, Widow, 39 Coming St.
Simons, Harleston, Widow, cr. Cumberland & Church Sts
Simons, Joseph, Grocer, cr. Broad & E. Bay Sts.
Simons, Joseph, M.D., 25 Society St.
Simons, Keating & Sons, Factors, D'Oyley's Whf.
Simons, Keating, Factor, Res. Orange St
Simons, Keating Lewis, Attorney, 45 Broad St.
Simons, Lewis, Factor, D'Oyley's Whf , Res 12 Bull St.
Simons, Maurice, Factor, Res. 1 Middle St.
Simons, Orphy, Seamstress, George St.
Simons, R., Widow, Meeting St., near Hasell St.
Simons, Rebecca, Seamstress, 26 Wentworth St.
Simons, Samuel, Merchant, 281 King St.
Simons, Sarah, F P.C., Washer, 5 Broughton's Lot
Simons, Sarah T., Widow, 31 Beaufain St.
Simonton, C S. & Co., Merchants, King St. Road, Neck
Simpson, John, 66 Tradd St.
Simpson, Lydia, Seamstress, 12 Bedon's Al
Simpson, Michael, Merchant, 107 King St.
Simpson, Peter, F.P.C., Shopkeeper, cr. Elizabeth & Boundary Sts., Neck
Simpson, Preson, Dr., Dentist, Cannonborough Mill Pond, Neck
Simpson, Sarah, Mrs , 10 Market St
Simpson, Smart, F.P.C., Carpenter, 74 Church St.
Sims, William, Capt., Hudson St., Wraggsborough, Neck
Simson, William, Planter, 2 Minority St.
Simth, Henrietta, Widow, 16 Beaufain St
Sinclair, Alexander, Merchant, 26, Res. 75, E. Bay St.
Sinclair, John, 226 E. Bay St.
Singleton, Abigail, Seamstress, 24 Wentworth St.
Singleton, John, Tailor, 41 Queen St.
Singleton, Sarah, Widow, 50 Boundary St , Neck
Singleton, Tabitha, Seamstress, 24 Wentworth St
Sisk, Susannah, 12 Philadelphia St.
Skinner & Whilden, Editors, City Gazette, 146 E Bay St
Skirvin, Jane, F.P.C., 32 Anson St.
Slairs, Samuel, Pilot, 20 State St.
Slate, Ashbell, Grocer, 6 Middle St
Slawson, Nathaniel, Baker, 100 King St
Sledge, Mary Ann, Widow, 8 Coming St.
Slowick, John, Grocer, 10 King St.
Slowman, Abraham, Dry Goods Store, King St. Road, Neck
Smart, John T, Deputy Sheriff, 52 Meeting St.
Smerdon, P., Widow, Boarding House, 54 Church St

Smile, Martha, Widow, 27 St. Philp's St

Smith & Olds, Shoe Store, 258 King St

Smith, Agness, Widow, 11 George St.

Smith, Agness, Widow, 389 King St

Smith, Agness, Widow, 7 Broad St.

Smith, Ann, Widow, Plantress, Hudson St , Cannonborough, Neck

Smith, Ann, Widow, Plantress, Wraggsborough, Neck

Smith, Ann, Widow, Seamstress, 4 Berresford St.

Smith, Benjamin, Painter, E. Bay St., near the Custom House

Smith, Benjamin, Planter, Church St Cont'd.

Smith, Benjamin, Planter, Hudson St., Cannonborough, Neck

Smith, Charlotte, Widow, 29 Pinckney St.

Smith, Daniel W., Copper Plate Printer, 252 E. Bay St.

Smith, Eliza, Miss, 2 Mazyck St.

Smith, Eliza, Mrs , Dry Goods Store, 218 King St.

Smith, Elizabeth, Widow, 2 Blackbird Al.

Smith, Frederick, Shoemaker, King St Road, Neck

Smith, George, Carpenter, 9 Wall St

Smith, George E., Carpenter, 12 Parsonage Ln.

Smith, George, Grocer, cr. of Boundary & Anson Sts.

Smith, Gray, F.P.C , 6 Coming St.

Smith, Hamilton Q., Cooper, Res. Washington St., Neck

Smith, Hester, Mrs., cr of Beaufain & St Philip's Sts.

Smith, Hugh, Merchant, 7 Broad St., Res. Ladson's Court

Smith, James, 155 E. Bay St.

Smith, James, 4 Laurens St.

Smith, James, Boarding House, 37 Chalmers Al.

Smith, James, Grocer, cr. Meeting & Reed Sts., Neck

Smith, John, Boarding House, 11 Bedon's Al.

Smith, John L., Artist, Residence, 22 Pinckney St.

Smith, John, Upholsterer, cr. of Magazine & Mazyck Sts.

Smith, Jonathan, Measurer, Amen St

Smith, Josiah, (aged 88) 49 Anson St

Smith, Linda, F.P.C., Fruit Shop, Henrietta St., Mazyckborough, Neck

Smith, Louisa, F.P.C., Water St.

Smith, Lucretia, Mantua Maker, 218 Meeting St.

Smith, Mary, F.P.C , Washer, 42 Hasell St.

Smith, Mary, Widow, 37 Coming St.

Smith, Mary, Widow, Boarding House, 42 Elliott St.

Smith, Mary, Widow, Nurse, 20 Pinckney St.

Smith, Mary, Widow, Seamstress, Chapel St., Mazyckborough, Neck

Smith, Mills & Co., Merchants, 5 Vendue Range

Smith, N., Miss, 36 Coming St.

Smith, Paul, Grocer, 31 Coming St.

Smith, Peet & Co., Saddlery Warehouse, cr. of King & George Sts

Smith, Peter, Grocer, 43 Elliott St.

Smith, Peter, Lumber Merchant, 27 Mazyck St.

Smith, Peter, Sr., Capt., S. Bay St

Smith, Press M , Factor, D'Olyley's Whf , Res. cr. of St. Philip's & Boundary Sts.

Smith, R. M., Office, D'Oyley's Whf.

Smith, Richard, Cabinet Maker, 28 Broad St.

Smith, Robert, Glass Factory, 211 King St , Neck

Smith, Robert, Planter, 145 Meeting St.

Smith, Rosanna, F.P C , Washer, 36 St. Philip's St.

Smith, Samuel, Boarding House, 14 Champney St.

Smith, Samuel, Boot Maker, 13 Parsonage Ln.

Smith, Samuel, Factor, Res. 42 Broad St.

Smith, Sarah Ann, Anson St.

Smith, Susan, Widow, Plantress, cr. of Hasell & Meeting Sts

Smith, Susannah, F.P.C., 70 Church St.

Smith, Theodore, 22 Pinckney St.

Smith, Thomas, Planter, Meeting St.

Smith, Thomas Y , Capt., Planter, 10 Wall St

Smith, Whiteford, Grocer, 69 Church St.

Smith, William, Clerk, 27 Mazyck St.

Smith, William, Jr., Shipwright, Director, Union Insurance Office, E Side Washington St , Neck

Smith, William, Judge, 36 Queen St.

Smith, William Mason, Planter, Meeting St.

Smith, William S., Prothonotory, Office, State House, Res Laurens St.

Smith, William, Sr., Factor, Washington St., Neck

Smylie, Andrew, Port Inspector, Merchandise & Seed Store, cr. of Meeting & Hasell Sts.

Smythe, Charles, F.P.C., Hair Dresser, Church St

Smythe, Hellen, Widow, 13 Liberty St.

Smythe, John, Planter, 80 Queen St.

Smythe, Robert, F.P.C., Carpenter, 6 Bull St.

Snardi, Mary, F.P.C., Meeting St Road, Neck

Snipes, Eliza, Widow, 16 George St.

Snow, Lydia, Widow, 22 Society St.

Snowden, J. L., 149 E. Bay St.

Snowden, Sarah, Widow, 7 Pinckney St

Snowden, William E., Merchant, 149 & 214 E. Bay St.

Sobieski, Thaddeus, Engineer for the Government, Hampstead, near the Lines, Neck

Sollee, F. W , Merchant, 273 E. Bay St.

Sollee, John, 214 Meeting St.

Solomons, Aaron, Dry Goods Store, 244 King St.

Solomons, Alexander, Merchant, 146 King St

Solomons, Catharine, Widow, 379 King St

Solomons, Sarah, Store, 79 E. Bay St.

Solomons, Solomon, 195 King St., Neck

Sompayrac, Theodore, Merchant 5 Fitzsimons' Whf

Souche, Alexander, Fruit Shop, 109 Queen St

Southwork, Rufus, Teacher, 88 Tradd St.

Sparks, Rachael, Widow, 44 Queen St.

Sparrow, James, Butcher, cr. Nassau & Reed Sts , Hampstead, Neck

Sparrow, James, Butcher, Smith St., Cannonborough, Neck

Spears, George F., (of Dart & Spears), Res. 42 Society St

Spears, James H., Merchant, 316 King St

Spencer, Rose, F.P.C., Washer, Meeting St. Road, Neck

Spiddle, John G., Carpenter, 24 Archdale St.

Spinner, Michael, Planter, Linguard St.

Spissager, John, Musical Instrument Maker, cr. Hasell & Anson Sts.

Spitz, A 1., Glass & Crockery Store, cr Wentworth & King Sts.

Sprague, Boswell, Boarding House, 115 Church St

Sprigg, E. D., 9 Friend St.
Spring, John, Wraggsborough, Neck
St. Amand, J. S , Coachmaker, Meeting St., Res. Wentworth St
Stacks, Mary, Widow, Wraggsborough, Neck
Stagg, J. D., Merchant, 215 E. Bay St , Res. cr. E. Bay & Laurens Sts.
Stanyarne, Ann, Plantress, 25 King St.
Stark, Benjamin, Shipmaster, Charlotte St., Mazyckborough, Neck
Starkey, Susannah, Mrs., Vanderhorst St., City Lands, Neck
State, Christiana, Grocer, cr. Wentworth & Pitt Sts.
Stead, -----, Widow of Ralph, 7 New St.
Steedman, Elizabeth, Boarding House, 113 E. Bay St.
Steel, Gordon, Grocer, 44 Elliott St.
Steel, W. G., Lumber Merchant, Beaufain St.
Steele, John A., Discount Clerk, Planters' & Mechanics' Bank, Radcliffborough, Neck
Steele, John, Dry Goods Store, Wagon Yard & Stables, 212 King St., Neck
Steele, John, Grocery, Crockery, Grain & Salt Store, cr. Tobacco & Lowndes St., Neck
Steinmeyre, George W , 37 Boundary St
Steinmitz, Barron, F.P.C , Market St.
Stent, John, Carpenter, 4 Back & 23 Mazyck Sts.
Stent, Phillis, F.P.C , Nurse, 49 King St.
Stent, Robert N., 12 Coming St.
Stephens, Elizabeth, 39 Market St.
Stephens, Thomas, Teller, United Bank, Res. Vanderhorst's S Row
Stephens, William C., Custom House Officer, 7 Middle St.
Stevens, Daniel, Intendant of the City, 31 George St.
Stevens, Joel, Clerk at James Adgers, Upper End King St.
Stevens, Mary, Widow, 9 Bedon's Al.
Stevens, William Smith D. N., 15 King St.
Steward, Sally, F.P.C., Shopkeeper, King St. Road, Neck
Steward, Tom, F.P.C., Carpenter, King St. Road, Neck
Stewart, Adriana, Widow, 44 Wentworth St.
Stewart, Catherine, Widow, Seamstress, 3 Beaufain St.
Stewart, Lettia, Widow, 26 Wall St.
Stewart -----, Misses, Boarding School, 5 Wentworth St.
Stewart, Robert, 3 Beaufain St.
Stewart, York, Sail Maker, Cock Ln
Stiles, Copeland, Planter, 74 Wentworth St.
Stiles, Susan, F.P.C., Pastry Cook & Seamstress, Logan St.
Stilman, James, Grocer, 77 E. Bay St.
Stock, Ann, Widow, 7 Meeting St.
Stocker, Henry, Boat Builder, E. Bay St., near Market St., Res. Daniell's Whf.
Stoll, Catharine, Widow, 19 Magazine St.
Stoll, James G , Clerk, 19 Magazine St.
Stoll, Martha, Mrs., Society St.
Stoll, Smart, Tailor, 15 Tradd St
Stoll, W. F., Outdoor Clerk, Bank of S. C., Res. 19 Magazine St.
Stoll, William, Accountant, 116 King St
Stone, Elizabeth, Teacher, cr of Anson & George Sts
Stone, Isabella, Widow, 35 Guignard St
Stone, John T., 35 Guignard St.

Stone, Thomas, Bricklayer, 35 Guignard St.
Stone, Timothy, Coach Maker, 43 Wentworth St.
Stoney, John, Merchant, 3 Chisolm's Upper Whf., Res. 150 E. Bay St
Storne, Joseph, 81 Cumberland St.
Straeel, -----, Madam, 118 E. Bay St.
Street, H., Beer House, 95 E Bay St.
Street, Timothy & Co., Merchants, 238 E. Bay & cr Hasell & Meeting Sts.
Strobel, Benjamin, Merchant, E. Bay St., Res. 10 Liberty St.
Strobel, Jacob, Grist Mill, Market St , near Beef Market, Res. 117 King St.
Strobel, John, 33 Boundary St.
Strobel, John N., Accountant, 33 Boundary St.
Strobel, Martin, Attorney, 119 Meeting St.
Strobel, Martin, Steam Mill, Harleston Green
Strobel, Tom, F.P.C , Carter, near Fresh Water Pond, Neck
Strohecker, John, Blacksmith, 91 Meeting St. Res. 23 Cumberland St
Stroub, Jacob, Carpenter, 7 Blackbird Al.
Stuart, Robert, Planter, 7 Friend St
Sturges, Josiah, Planter, 8 S. Bay St.
Suaney, Esther, Widow, Seamstress, 4 Lynch's Ln.
Suar, Peter, Merchant, Lothrop's Whf., Res. 21 Magazine St.
Suares, Isaac, 112 Queen St.
Suares, Jacob, 112 Queen St.
Suares, Rachael, 15 Philadelphia St.
Suder, Ann, Widow, 21 Society St ,
Sudor, Betsy, F.P.C., Alexander St., Mazyckborough, Neck
Sullivan, O. Charles, Painter, 47 Anson St.
Sullivan, Timothy, Auctioneer, cr. E Bay St. & Vendue Range
Sullivan, Timothy, Auctioneer, N. Side Vanderhorst St., Radcliffborough, Neck
Summers, Rose, Seamstress, 11 Lynch's Ln.
Sutcliff, Annet, Mrs , Ellery St
Sutcliff, Elizabeth, Widow, 26 Guignard St.
Sutcliff, James, Baker, 38 Market St
Sutton, John, Grocer, 43 Hasell St.
Swain, Benjamin, Carpenter, 5 Stoll's Al
Swain, Luke, Pilot, 5 Stoll's Al.
Swain, Mark, Carpenter, 5 Stoll's Al.
Swain, Primus, Pilot, F.P.C., Church St.
Swain, Rebecca, Widow, 5 Stoll's Al
Sweeney, James, 66 Church St.
Sweeney, Margaret, Widow, Hudson St., Cannonborough, Neck
Sweeney, -----, Widow, 67 Church St
Sweney, Dinah, F P.C., Washer, Henrietta St., Wraggsborough, Neck
Swift, David D , Trunk Maker, 230½ King St.
Swift, William, Merchant, 30 King St.
Swinton, Susannah, Widow, 8 Meeting St.
Syfan, Charles, Carpenter, Coming St., Cannonborough, Neck
Syfan, John, Butcher, Coming St., Cannonborough, Neck
Symmes, Robert, Rev., D.D., 27 Coming St
Taggart, Mary, Widow, 17 Meeting St.

63

Talvand, Andrew, Boarding School, 51 Meeting St.
Talvand, -----, Mrs., Boarding School, 51 Meeting St.
Tastet, Eugene & Co., Merchants, 389 King St.
Tate, James, Mariner, 121 Queen St.
Tavel, Frederick, Wharfinger, 10 Anson St.
Taviesky, John, Painter, 7 King St
Taylor, Alexander, Capt , Custom House Officer, 11
   Middle St.
Taylor, Edward, Coach Maker, cr. of Meeting &
   Wentworth Sts.
Taylor, John, Factor, 13 Logan St.
Taylor, Joseph, Master, U. S Navy Yard, Res. 33
   Guignard St.
Taylor, Joseph, Ship Carpenter, 12 Anson St.
Taylor, Margaret & Daughter, Seamstresses, 8
   Blackbird Al.
Taylor, Mary, F.P C., Alexander St., Mazyckborough,
   Neck
Taylor, Mary, Shop Keeper, 2 Queen St.
Taylor, Mary, Widow, 12 Anson St.
Taylor, Paul, Mrs., Cannonborough, Neck
Taylor, William, Ship Carpenter, Res. Harleston's
   Green
Teasdale, -----, Mrs., Widow, cr. Vanderhorst's Whf. &
   E. Bay St.
Teasdale, Richard, Grain Store, 5 & 6 Martin's Row,
   Chisolm's Whf., Res.Vanderhorst's Whf.
Tebault, Clair, Widow, 128 E. Bay St.
Tebout, Judith, Miss, 55 Broad St.
Techester, Nancy, F P.C., Seamstress, Wraggsborough,
   Neck
Tediman, Philip, M D , 85 Wentworth St
Telfer, Robert, State St.
Tener, Mary, Seamstress, 127 Wentworth St.
Tenhet, John, Shoemaker, 82 Church St.
Tennant, Moses, Clerk to D. Goodman, cr St. Philip's
   & Radcliff Sts., Neck
Tennant, Thomas, Cabinetmaker, Amen St.
Tesia, -----, Madam, Widow, 106 Queen St.
Tesport, Peter, Grocer, 109 E. Bay St.
Teul, Christopher, Tanner, 82 Meeting St.
Tew, Charles, Quorum Unis & Notary Public & Teacher,
   92 Wentworth St.
Thackam, Francis, Carpenter, Meeting St Cont'd., Neck
Thackam, Judith, Widow, Seamstress, 124 Meeting St ,
   Neck
Thackam, Thomas, Carpenter, 113 Meeting St.
Thayer, Abenezar, Bookseller, 25 Broad St., Res. 48
   Tradd St.
Thayer, Abenezar, Jr. Wharfinger, 96 Wentworth St
Thayer, Seth, Boot & Shoe Store, 299 King St.
Thesserepe, Hannah, Confectioner, 40 Church St.
Theus, Charlotte, Mantua Maker, 28 Archdale St.
Theus, Simeon, Jr., Custom House Officer, 12 Hasell St.
Theus, Simeon, Sr., Collector of the Port, Res. King St.
Thomas, Barack G., Steam Engineer, Mazyckborough,
   Neck
Thomas, Emanuel, 202 Meeting St.
Thomas, Francis, Clerk, Bank of Discount & Deposit,
   30 Beaufain St

Thomas, James, 625 E. Bay St., Res. George St.
Thomas, James, Carpenter, 15 Wall St.
Thomas, John, Boarding House, Bedon's Al.
Thomas, John, Carpenter, 2 Clifford St
Thomas, John, Grocer, Market St.
Thomas, John, Measurer, 202 Meeting St.
Thomas, Mary, Widow, 44 Meeting St.
Thomas, Peter, Mechant, 315 King St
Thomas, Sarah, Widow, 19 Linguard St.
Thomas, Stephen, cr of Anson & Liberty Sts.
Thompson, Alexander, Bricklayer, 30 St. Philip's St
Thompson, Ann, F P C., King St.
Thompson, Anna, Widow, F.P.C., 2 State St.
Thompson, Elizabeth, Widow, 10 Church St.
Thompson, Francis, Shipmaster, Pritchard's Whf.
Thompson, George, Bricklayer, 12 Church St.
Thompson, Hannah, Grocer, 50 Elliott St.
Thompson, James, Boarding Officer, Customs, Res. Hasell
   St.
Thompson, James H., Cabinet Maker, St Philip's St.,
   Radcliffborough, Neck
Thompson, John, Black & White Smith, 14 Ellery St.
Thompson, John, Coach Maker, 218 E. Bay St
Thompson, Patty, F.P.C., 28 Ellery St.
Thompson, William, Ship Chandler, 218 Ellery St
Thomson, Nathan, Grocer, King St. Road, Neck
Thorne, John G., 5 Cumberland St.
Thorne, John S., Sailmaker, Loft, 271 E. Bay St , Res.
   5 Cumberland St.
Thornhill, Catharine, Dry Goods Store, 285 King St.
Thornton, Catharine, Widow, 35 St. Philip's St.
Thredcraft, Harriett, F.P C., Washer, Lowndes St., Neck
Thwing, Edward, Merchant, Vendue Range, Res. State St.
Tideyman, Hester, Widow, 22 Coming St.
Tift, Amos, Capt., Grocer, 223 E. Bay St
Tift, Solomon, Grocer, Gadsden's Whf.
Timme, Elizabeth, Widow, Seamstress, King St., near
   Boundary St , Neck
Timmons, George, Auctioneer, 8 Vendue Range
Timmons, William, Hardware Store, 90 E. Bay St
Timothy, Peter, Attorney, Office, 88 Broad St.
Timrod, William H., Bookbinder, 346 King St
Tinkham, Clark, Shipmaster, Elizabeth St.,
   Mazyckborough, Neck
Tobey, Elsha F., Shoe Store, 33 Church St.
Tobias, Abraham, Accountant, 57 Beaufain St.
Tobias, Susan, Widow, 166 Church St.
Todd, Jane, 4 Savage St.
Todd, John, 7 Church St.
Todd, John, Teacher, cr. of Coming & George Sts
Todd, Richard, 15 Legare St.
Todd, Robert A., Merchant, King St Road, Neck
Todd, Ruth, 5 Legare St.
Tomtis, Mary, Widow, 2 Wentworth St.
Toohey, Michael, Millinery Store, 236 King St.
Toomer, Anthony V., Dr., Planter, Chapel St.,
   Wraggsborough, Neck
Toomer, H. B , Broker, 67 E. Bay St., Res Hasell St
Toomer, Joshua W., Attorney, 9 St. Michael's Al , Res.
   169 E. Bay St

64

Torlay, Peter, Watchmaker, King, Res 24 Hasell St
Torre, Charles D., Merchant, 16 Broad St.
Torrey, Ann, Widow, Boarding House, 11 Broad St.
Torrey, Ezekiel, Block Maker, 6 Wentworth St.
Tourrette, Thomas, Cigar Maker, cr. Cumberland &
    Meeting Sts
Tonsegger, Eliza, 5 Water St.
Tousseger, Joseph, Carpenter, 7 Water St
Tovey, Henry, Block Maker, 7 S. Bay St , & 219 E.
    Bay St
Townsand, Tener, F.P.C , 136 E. Bay St.
Townsend, Daniel, Planter, cr Lucas & Boundary Sts.,
    Neck
Townsil, Affa, F P C , Washer, Charlotte St.,
    Wraggsborough, Neck
Townsil, Sebrena, F.P.C , Washer, Charlotte St.,
    Wraggsborough, Neck
Trapman, Jahncke & Co , Merchants, Chisholm's Whf
Trapman, L., Merchant, Res. Wentworth St.
Trenholm, William, Grain Store, 4 Boundary St
Trescot, Caroline, Widow, 4 George St.
Trescot, John, M.D., 107 Tradd St.
Trescot, Joseph, Merchant, 6 Vendue Range, Res. 95
    Meeting St
Trescott, Catharine, Plantress, E. End South St.,
    Hampstead, Neck
Trezvant, Dianna, F.P C , 49 King St.
Trezvant, Harriett, F P.C., 5 Broughton's Lot
Trezvant, John F , Attorney, Water St.
Trezvant, Peter, Registering Clerk of Customs, Res. Stoll's
    Al.
Trouch, Adelade, Widow, 115 Wentworth St.
Truxton, Eliza, Confectioner, 6 King St.
Tucker, Charles S., Register of Mesne Conveyance, Office,
    State House, Res 135 Church St.
Tucker, Samuel, Drayman, Rutledge St
Tucker, Sarah, Widow, 135 Church St.
Tunis, Charles H., of Brown & Tunis, S End of E. Bay St.
Tunno, Adam, Merchant, E. Bay St.
Tunno, Adam, Merchant, Res. Charlotte St., Neck
Tunno, Rosetta, Seamstress, 78 Tradd St.
Tunno, William, Charleston Auction Establishment, 99 E.
    Bay St.
Tunny, Susannah, Widow, 166 Church St.
Tupper, Henry D., 2 Kunhardt & Leavitt's Whf.
Tupper, T. & H , Merchants, 239 E. Bay St.
Tupper, Tristram, Merchant, 239 E. Bay St.
Ture, Peter, Boarding House
Turnbull, James, Carpenter, S. Bay St.
Turnbull, Robert J., Planter, 1 Logan St
Turner, Charles H , Factor, E. Bay St.
Turner, George R., Shipmaster, 2 Anson St.
Turner, John, Grocer, cr. of Meeting & Wentworth Sts
Turner, Philada, F P.C , Seamstress, Jones' Lot
Turner, Sarah, F.P.C., Parsonage Ln.
Turpin, Amelia, F.P.C., 16 Anson St.
Turpin, William, Planter, 180 King St
Tuttle, Joseph, Ellery St
Tweed & Pennall, Grocers, 225 King St.
Tyler & Hough, Merchants, 233 E. Bay St

Tyrell, Walter, Grocer, 4 Wentworth St.
Ulmo, Anthony, M D., 20 Queen St
Ummensetter, John, Tanner, 22 Beaufain St.
Uneacke, Honel, Boarding House, 21 Chalmers Al
Urquhart, Charles, Merchant, cr. Gillon St.
Utt, John, Upholsterer, 16 Queen St
Vale, -----, Mrs., 1 Cannon St., Islington, Neck
Valenchia, Moses, Fruit Shop, 93 King St
Valk, Jacob R., Merchant, 267 E Bay St. Res. 2 New St.
Van Rhyan, A. E., Miss, Storekeeper, 115 Broad St
Vance, William, Planter, W. Side Pinckney St.,
    Cannonborough, Neck
Vanderburg, John, Master Rigger, 30 Anson St.
Vanderford, Henry, Mariner, 32 Chalmers Al
Vanderhoff, Catherine, Widow, 22 Wentworth St.
Vanderhorst, M., Col , Tradd St.
Vanderhorst, Richard W., Planter, Hampstead, Neck
Vanderhost, A , Planter, 32 Wall St
Vanderlip, John, Shopkeeper, 41 St. Philip's St
Vandle, Sarah, Teacher, Lynch's Ln.
Vandyne, Branson, Boarding House, 260 King St.
Vanholten, Tunis, Grocer, cr. Amen & State Sts
Vanisaro, Elizabeth Mary, Widow, Grocer, 33 Archdale
    St.
Vanvelsy, William, Wheelwright, 32 St. Philip's St.
Varatwer, Rose, Widow, 11 St. Philip's St.
Vardel, Robert, Bricklayer, George St.
Vardel, Thomas A , Bricklayer, 27 Berresford St.
Varlnat, Mary, Widow, Mazyckborough, Neck
Varner, Arnold, City Guard, 20 Boundary St.
Varner, Henry, City Guard, 22 Wall St.
Varner, Samuel, Tailor, 54 Meeting St
Vause, John J., Grocer, State St.
Veith, William, Druggist, 96 King St.
Velles, Peter, Confectioner, 59 E. Bay St.
Venning, Jonah, M D , Williams' Whf , Res. 2 Society St
Venning, Robert, Factor, Williams' Whf , Res. 2 Society
    St.
Verdier, -----, Madam, 118 E. Bay St.
Vernon, Nathaniel, Jeweller, 83 Broad St.
Vernugh, James, Grocer, 11 King St.
Verree, Joseph & Samuel, 10 Church St.
Verree, Polurt, 5 Water St.
Very, Nathaniel, Grocer, Boundary St , Mazyckborough,
    Neck
Vesey, Charles M , Clerk, 21 Anson St.
Vesey, Joseph, Capt., 41 Anson St.
Vezieu, -----, Widow, 5 Maiden Ln.
Vhihart, Peter, Grocer, 114 E. Bay St.
Vidal, John, Store, E. Bay St.
Villalobas, Antonio A., Spanish Consul, 167 Meeting St.
Villepique, Paul, Baker, 126 King St.
Villers, Frances, F.P.C., 63 Anson St.
Vincent & Hotchkiss, Merchants, 4 Brownlee's Row, King
    St. Road, Neck
Vincent, Charles, Capt , 225 E Bay St
Vincent, Hugh G., Capt., 154 Church St.
Vinrose, Sarah, Widow, 121 Wentworth St
Vion, Elizabeth, Dry Goods Store, 93 King St.
Vogler, Henry, Butcher, Elizabeth St., Wraggsborough,

65

Neck
Vonderworth, Henry, Grocer, cr of Market & Church Sts
Vonhagan, Sarah, Widow, Elizabeth St., Mazyckborough, Neck
Votee, Charles, Shipmaster, 223 E. Bay St.
Wade, Job, Carpenter, 4 Amen St
Wadsworth, William, Grocer, 15 Archdale St.
Wagner & Cowing, Merchants, cr. King & Ann Sts , Neck
Wagner & Deming, Saddlers, 230 King St.
Wagner, Ann, Widow, 24 St. Philip's St
Wagner, Effingham, Merchant, 13 Cumberland St.
Wagner, George, Merchant, 100 E. Bay St
Wagner, Mary, Widow, 17 Pinckney St.
Wagner, Paul, Grocer, 52 King St.
Wagner, S. J., Inspector of Customs, 28 Broad St.
Wainwright, Ann, Widow, cr King & Tradd Sts.
Wainwright, Joseph, Painter, 8 Cock Ln.
Wakefield, Sarah & Elizabeth, Misses, 2 Lynch's Ln.
Walker, -----, Accountant, 106 Queen St.
Walker, Caleb, Carpenter, 12 Magazine St
Walker, Joseph, Boat Builder, 36 Society St.
Walker, Maria, F P.C., Boundary St
Walker, Mary, 17 Lynch's Ln.
Walker, Mary, Widow, 36 Society St.
Walker, Mercy, Widow, Seamstress, Boundary St., Mazyckborough, Neck
Walker, Richard, Bricklayer, 12 Pinckney St.
Walker, Robert, Cabinet Maker, 53 Church St.
Walker, Thomas, Stone Cutter, 38 Wentworth St
Wall, Eliza, Mrs , Seamstress, 4 King St
Wall, Richard, Grocer, cr. King & Queen Sts.
Wall, Robert, Plasterer, 1 Society St.
Wallace, Agnes, Widow, 10 Tradd St.
Wallace, Ann, Widow, 111 Church St
Wallace, James, cr. Lowndes & Boundary Sts., Neck
Wallace, Robert, Brass Founder, 393 King St.
Wallace, William, Carpenter, Coming St., Cannonborough, Neck
Waller, Charlotte, Widow, 8 Anson St.
Waller, William, Saddler, 51 Broad St
Walley, Betsy, F.P.C., 4 Swinton's Ln.
Wallis, John, Shopkeeper, Charlotte St., Mazyckborough, Neck
Walter, Jerry, Fish Store, State St.
Walters, Daniel, Rigger, Henrietta St., Wraggsborough, Neck
Walton, Elizabeth, Widow, King St., near Boundary St., Neck
Wansley, Joseph, Rigger, 21 Wentworth St
War, Elizabeth, Widow, Linguard St
Ward, F. S., Clerk City Court, 8 Anson St.
Ward, James, Attorney, cr Longitude Ln. & Church St.
Ward, Mary G., Widow, 55 Broad St.
Ward, Mary, Miss, Plantress, Rutledge St
Ward, Rosetta, F.P.C., Boundary St
Ward, Sarah, Widow, 233 Meeting St
Ward, Susan, Widow, 8 Anson St.
Warham, Mary, Widow, 7 Tradd St
Warham, William G., Accountant, 7 Tradd St.
Waring, Harriett, Widow, Washington St ,

Mazyckborough, Neck
Waring, Horatio, M.D., 95 Wentworth St
Waring, Jennings, Attorney, 45 George St.
Waring, John, Ship Carpenter, Washington St , Mazyckborough, Neck
Waring, Mary, F P C., 4 Wall St
Waring, Morton, 272 E. Bay St.
Waring, Morton A., Federal Marshall, Office, Court House, St. Philip's St., Neck
Waring, Morton, Factor, 82 Tradd St
Waring, Richard, Factor, 33 Wall St.
Warly, Elizabeth, Widow, 19 Market St.
Warner, Penelope, 228 Meeting St.
Warnock, Harris, 9 Magazine St.
Warren, Elizabeth, Widow, Ellery St.
Warren, Russell, Carpenter, 11 Wall St
Washington, -----, Widow of Gen. William, 20 Church St
Wasor, Joseph, Saddler, 257 King St.
Watkuyer, Frances, Widow, 76 King St
Watson, Alexander, Accountant, 134 E Bay St.
Watson, James, Capt., 44 Tradd St.
Watson, James, Mariner, 22 Chalmers Al.
Watson, Lydia, F.P.C., 8 Friend St.
Watson, Matthew, 7 Bull St.
Watson, Thomas, 61 Church St.
Watters, William, Hat Store, 174 King St.
Watts, James, Grocer, 151 Church St.
Waugh & Herriott, Merchants, 255 E. Bay St
Waugh, A. B., Merchant, 4 Logan St.
Weathers, Thomas & George, Boat Builders, 7 Cock Ln.
Webb, Charles, Clerk, 74 Wentworth St.
Webb, Daniel, Factor, N.W. cr Pinckney & Cannons Sts., Neck
Webb, William, Merchant, 218 E Bay St , Res. 5 Cumberland St.
Webber, Samuel, Droger, Pritchard's Whf.
Weed & Baldwin, Hat Store, cr. King & George Sts
Weenges, Joham H , Baker, 139 Meeting St
Weissinger, Magdelen, Widow, King St., near the Lines, Neck
Welch, George, Cabinet Maker, Charlotte St., Wraggsborough, Neck
Welch, John, Cabinet Maker & Superintendant, City Burial Ground, Cannonborough, Neck
Welling & Ballentine, Coach Makers, 65 Meeting St.
Wells, Martha, F.P.C , 9 Swinton's Ln.
Wells, Richard, Capt., 191 E. Bay St.
Wells, Sarah, Widow, 65 Meeting St
Wells, Thomas B., Accountant, 18 Archdale St.
Wellsman, James, Capt., 15 Lynch's Ln.
Welsh, James, 3 Logan St.
Welsh, Moses, F P C , Shoemaker, 34 Beaufain St.
Welsh, Thomas G., Carver, 14 Beaufain St.
Werderman, J. G., Store Keeper, 133 Queen St
Werderman, -----, Mrs., Store Keeper, 22 Cumberland St
Werner, John M., Cabinet Maker, Pinckney St.
Werner, William, Grocer, 43 Tradd St.
Wertenberg, Catherine, Widow, 72 Meeting St.
Wesner, Frederick, Carpenter, Shop, 8 New St., Res 73 Queen St.

66

West, Mary, Milliner, 204 King St., Neck
West, Nicholas, Currier, 204 King St., Neck
West, S G., Painter, cr. Broad & Savage Sts.
Westendorff, C. P. L., Merchant & Portuguese Consul, 230 E. Bay St.
Weston, John, F.P.C., Butcher, cr. Alexander & Mary Sts., Neck
Weston, Paul, Dr., near the River, Hampstead, Neck
Weston, Plowden, Planter, 35 Queen St.
Weston, Sarah, F.P.C., Seamstress, cr. Alexander & Mary Sts., Neck
Weyman & Co., Merchants, cr E. Bay & Wentworth Sts.
Weyman & Hall, Clothing Store, 71 E. Bay St.
Weyman, Catharine, Widow, cr. Meeting & Reed Sts , Neck
Wharton, Samuel, Merchant, cr. King & Mary Sts., Neck
Whatt, Bridget, Widow, 39 Queen St.
Wheeler, E P., Merchant, 279 King St.
Wheeler, Henry & Co., Merchants, 238 E. Bay St.
Wheeler, Henry, Merchant, Res. 99 Queen St.
Wheeler, J. P., Merchant, Magwood's Whf.
Wheeler, Joseph, Vendue Master, Vendue Range, Res. 136 Meeting St.
Whilden, Joseph, Editor, City Gazette, Res. 13 Magazine St.
Whipple, Solomon, Coach Maker, Maiden Ln.
White, Ann Sarah, Mrs , Meeting St. Road, Neck
White, Beford, F.P.C., Boundary St.
White, George, Factor, cr. of Beaufain & Mazyck Sts.
White, Gottlieb, Cabinet Maker, 75 Church St.
White, James, Work House, 10 Stoll's Al.
White, John & Co , Factors, Chisolm's Whf.
White, John B., Attorney, 85 Broad St.
White, John, Factor, Res. 144 Meeting St.
White, John P., Attorney, 44 Pinckney St.
White, Joseph F., Merchant cr. Bridge & King Sts. Road, Neck
White, W., Grocer, 59 Market St.
Whitehurst, James, Carolina Coffee House, Tradd St.
Whiting, John, Turner & Grocer, 103 Meeting St.
Whitney & Parsons, Merchants, 234 King St.
Whitney, Jedediah, Carpenter, 35 St. Philip's St.
Whitney, Mary, Widow, cr. of Church & Cumberland Sts
Whitney, Thomas, Store Keeper, 3 Market St.
Whitridge, Joshua B., M.D. 194 Meeting St.
Wienges, Conrad, Grocer, cr of St. Philip's & Wentworth Sts.
Wigfall, Constantia, Widow, 45 George St.
Wigfall, Robert, Coloured, Vanderhorst St., Radcliffborough, Neck
Wigfall, Tenner, F.P.C., Mazyckborough, Neck
Wigfall, Thomas, Planter, Charlotte St., Mazyckborough, Neck
Wightman, J. T., Turner, 193 Meeting St.
Wightman, Peggy, F.P.C., College Green
Wightman, W., Jr., Painter, cr. of Society & Meeting Sts.
Wightman, William, 210 Meeting St.
Wilbur, W. B., Comb Maker, 159 King St.
Wilcox & Son, Painters, 12 Broad St.
Wilcox, Jeremiah, Painter, Montague St.

Wilcox, S. W., Accountant, 13 Broad St.
Wildman & Starr, Hatters, 269 King St.
Wilhelmi, A. W. M., Widow, St. Philip's St., Neck
Wilkie, W B., Bank Clerk, 15 Church St.
Wilkinson, Grace, F.P.C., Zigzag Al.
Wilkinson, John, Fisherman, 2 Market St
Wilkinson, Susan, Widow, 13 Coming St.
Will, Robert, Bricklayer, 16 Pitt St.
Willams, Stephen, Shoemaker, Boundary St., Mazyckborough, Neck
Williams & Son, Merchants, Chisolm's Upper Whf.
Williams, Isham, Planter, Williams' Whf.
Williams, John, Rigger, 15 Clifford's Al.
Williams, Mary, Widow, Boundary St.
Williams, Rebecca, F.P.C., 360 King St.
Williams, Simpson, Capt., 134 Church St.
Williams, Susan, F.P.C., 2 Cock Ln.
Williams, William, Tailor, 91 Meeting St.
Williamson, Elizabeth, Widow, 91 King St.
Williamson, Mary, F.P.C., College Green
Williman, Christopher, Planter, 6 S. Bay St.
Williman, Ellinor, Broad St.
Williman, Jacob, Planter, 2 Monatague St.
Willington, A. S., Editor, Courier, cr. E. Bay St & Williams' Whf.
Willis, Henry, Carpenter, 7 St. Philip's St.
Willis, J. H., Broker, 118 Meeting St.
Wilmans, A., Grocer, cr. of Pinckney & E Bay Sts.
Wilson & Dubois, Blacksmiths, 3 Blackbird Al.
Wilson, A., 19 Ellery St.
Wilson, Cate, F.P.C., 13 Logan St.
Wilson, Hugh, Sr , Planter, N.E. Side Pinckney St., Neck
Wilson, Issac M., M.D. 69 Meeting St.
Wilson, James, 10 Mazyck St.
Wilson, John, Carpenter, 127 Meeting St., Neck
Wilson, John, Planter, 29 Bull St.
Wilson, John, State Engineer, 12 Friend St.
Wilson, Margaret, Seamstress, 2 Prices Al.
Wilson, Penelope, F.P.C., French Al.
Wilson, Robert, Carpenter, Ellery St.
Wilson, Robert, M.D., 38 Meeting St.
Wilson, Robert, Military Store Keeper, 3 Hasell St
Wilson, Samuel & Son, M.D., 31 Magazine St.
Wilson, Samuel, M.D., cr. of Archdale & Magazine Sts.
Wilson, Sylvia, Seamstress, 3 Pitt St.
Wilson, W. H , 201 Meeting St.
Wilson, William, Butcher, near the Lines, Neck
Wim, Jacob, Blacksmith, 20 Boundary St.
Wincey, Mary Ann, Widow, 26 Ellery St
Winchester, Jonathan, Carpenter, cr. Coming & Cannon Sts , Neck
Windstanly, Harriot, F.P.C., Seamstress, Alexander St , Mazyckborough, Neck
Wing, Sarah, Widow, Boarding House, 54 E. Bay St
Winges, Jacob, Grocer, 17 Church St.
Winstanly, Thomas, Attorney, 104 E. Bay St.
Winthrop & Ladson, Factors, 9 Crafts' Whf.
Winthrop, Joesph A , Factor, 32 E. Bay St
Winthrop, Joseph, 87 Tradd St.
Wish, Ann, Widow, 34 Elliott St

Wish, Robert S., Saddler, Smith's Ln.
Withington, Samuel, Shoe Store, 345 King St.
Wittlebraud, D., Carpenter, 14 Logan St.
Wodropp, John, Merchant, 20 Bay
Wolf, Dinah, F.P.C., Philadelphia St.
Wood, Absalom, Grocer, State St
Wood, Emily, Widow, Boundary St
Wood, Emily, Widow, Mantua Maker, Cannon St., Neck
Wood, G E., Merchant, 2 Kunhardt & Leviett's Whf.
Wood, James, Engraver, cr. Warren & St Philip's Sts.,
    Neck
Wood, John, Butcher, Wolf St., Hampstead, Neck
Wood, William, Shopkeeper & Rigger, Charlotte St.,
    Wraggsborough, Neck
Woodrouffe, Widow, Boarding House, cr. E. Bay St. &
    Vanderhorsts' Whf.
Woodruff, Joseph, U. S. Paymaster, 8 Bull St.
Woodward, E S., Widow, 96 Wentworth St
Woodward, Hester, Widow, Wentworth St
Woodworth, George, Mariner, 50 Tradd St.
Wooley, Thomas, Merchant, King St. Road, near the
    Lines, Neck
Wotherspoon, Robert, cr. Gadsden's Al. & Elliott St.
Wotten, A. S., Accountant, 227 E. Bay St.
Wotton, Christopher, Pilot, Wentworth St.
Wotton, Cloe, Widow, College Yard
Wragg & Parker, Factors, D'Oyley's Whf.
Wrainch, John, Teacher, Meeting St

Wright, John Izzard, St. Philip's St. Cont'd., Neck
Wright, Robert, Carpenter, 6 Rutledge St
Wrighton, Molly, F P.C., 13 Middle St.
Wyatt, Eliza, Widow, 73 Church St
Wyatt, I. K., Ship Carpenter, 73 Church St.
Wyatt, Peter, Lumber Merchant, Lynch's Ln
Yates, Ann, Widow, 7 Zigzag Al.
Yates, Deborah, Widow, 2 Fort St
Yates, Elizabeth, Widow, 6 Zigzag Al.
Yates, Jeremiah, Planter, Ladson's Court
Yates, Joseph, Cooper, E. Bay St., Res. Meeting St.
Yates, Samuel, Ship Chandler, 48 E. Bay St.
Yates, T. R., Carpenter, 7 Back St.
Yeadon, Richard, Officer, Bank of S C., Res. 19 King St
Yeadon, William, City Sheriff, 4 Hasell St.
You, John C., School Master, 33 Archdale St
Young & Glass, Booksellers, 64 E. Bay St.
Young, J. P., 79 King St.
Young, Joseph, Ship Chandler, 211 E. Bay St., Res cr.
    Hasell & E. Bay Sts.
Young, Nancy, F.P.C., French Al.
Young, W. P., Printer, 44 Broad St
Young, William, Counting House, 12 Champney St.
Young, William, Soap Chandler, Smith St.,
    Cannonborough, Neck
Zeely, Ann, 32 King St.
Zylolraw, H. I., Smith's Court, Meeting St.

The 1822 Directory

This directory was published by James R Schenck with the title of *The Directory and Stranger's Guide for the City of Charleston. Also a Directory for Charleston Neck Between Boundary-Street and the Lines; Likewise for the Coloured Persons Within the City, and Another for Coloured Persons residing on the Neck, for the Year 1822. To Which is Added an Almanac; The Tariff of Duties on All Goods Imported into the United States; and the Rates of Wharfage, Weighing, Storage, Dockage and Drayage, &c.* (Charleston: Archibald E. Miller, 1822). It has 3,706 entries. As the title indicates, Schenck divided people into four groups; however, they have been combined into one here with the Free Persons of Color being identified by F.P.C and those living above Boundary (Calhoun) St. having "Neck" added after their entries

Aaron, Moses, Clerk, 22 Anson St
Aberegg, Gotleib & Co., Grocers, 36 Archdale St
Aberegg, John, Cigar Manufacturer, 10 Blackbird Al.
Abino, James, Stone Cutter, 40 Coming St.
Abrahams, Elias, Merchant, 300 King St.
Abrahams, Judith, Widow, 34 Guignard St.
Abrams, Henrietta, Charlotte St., Mazyckborough, F.P.C , Neck
Adams & Milligan, Factors, 28, 30, 32 E. Bay St.
Adams, David, 1 Anson St., cr. Ellery St.
Adams, David, Jr , Factor, Charlotte St., Mazyckborough, Neck
Adams, David L., Factor, 28 E. Bay St , Res Wraggsborough
Adams, William, Planter, cr. Pinckney & Cannon Sts., Neck
Addison, Henry, Blacksmith, 84 Wentworth St.
Addison, James, Blacksmith, 29 Boundary St.
Addison, Joseph, Ship Carpenter, 31 Pinckney St.
Addison, Robert, Capt., 9 Magazine St.
Addison, Thomas, Merchant, King St. Road, Neck
Adger & Black, Shipping Merchants, 130 E. Bay St.
Adger, James & Co. Hardware Merchants, 130½ E Bay St.
Adger, James, Merchant, King St. Road, Neck
Aiken, William, Merchant, King St. Road, Neck
Aimar, Sebastian, Grocer, 201 E Bay St
Airs, Charles, Shoemaker, 12 Anson St.
Airs, Thomas, Boat Builder, 65 Wentworth St
Akin, Ann, Widow, 11 Cumberland St.
Akin, Thomas, Physician, 11 Cumberland St.
Albanac, Peter, Tailor, 2 Queen St
Aldridge, Robert, Wharfinger, Chisholm's Whf , Res. 15 Tradd St.
Alexander, Abraham, Dry Goods Store, 299 King St
Alexander, Alexander, Dry Goods Store, 381 King St., Neck
Alexander, David, President, Union Insurance Co., 7 Logan St.
Alexander, Samuel, Bank Coffee House, 129 E. Bay St.
Allan, Thomas, Planter, 22 Pinckney St , cr Anson St.

Allan, William, Factor, D'Oyley's Whf., Res. 46 Tradd St.
Allen, William, Merchant, 5 Champney St., Res. 109 Tradd St.
Alston, William, Planter, Hudson St., Cannonborough, Neck
Ambar, Sebastiao, Fish Store, op. Fish Market
Ancrum & Chiffelle's Steam Mill, 94 E. Bay St , op Wentworth St.
Anderson, Abigail, Washer, 7 Wall St., F.P.C
Anderson, Isabella, Widow, 99 Market St.
Anderson, Robert, Dry Goods Store, 294 King St
Anderson, Samuel, Grocer, Coming St., Neck
Anderson, William, Stay Maker, 3 Clifford's Al
Andrews, Moses, Mast, Pump & Block Maker, 268 E. Bay St., Res. 35 Hasell St.
Angel, Justus, Planter, 126 Tradd St.
Anney, Thomas, Cooper, 10 Lynch's Ln.
Anthony, I. C., Tallow Chandler, Mary St., near Fresh Water Pond, Neck
Anthony, John, Mariner, 17 Pinckney St.
Anthony, Mary, Widow, Pinckney St., Cannonborough, Neck
Applewood, Charles, Grocer, 48 Pinckney St
Armstrong, William, Clerk, Ordinary's Office, 49 Society St.
Arnold, Amos, 30 Pinckney St.
Arnold, Louisa, 20 Archdale St.
Arnold, Mary, Widow, 50 Church St.
Arnold, Theresa, Fruiterer, 105 Church St.
Artman, Peter, Coach Maker, 29 Archdale St.
Artopee, E., Mrs , Columbus St., Neck
Ash, Allen, 12 Philadelphia St., F P.C
Ash, Betsey, Zigzag Al., F.P.C.
Ash, Elizabeth, Widow, 9 Lamboll St.
Ash, John, Planter, 10 S. Bay St
Ashe, Andrew, Read St., Neck
Ashe, Samuel, Meeting St. Road, Neck
Assalitt, Ferdinand, 69 Tradd St.
Assalitt, Joseph, Teacher, 42 Tradd St
Astare, Elizabeth, Fruiterer, 193 & 239 King St.
Atchison, John, Livery Stables, 158 Church St.
Aubin, Joseph, Porter, Vault, 183 E. Bay St.
Augustine, Joseph, Read St., F.P.C., Neck
Aussten, James, House Carpenter, 121 E. Bay St.
Austen, Samuel W., House Carpenter, 121 E. Bay St
Avery, Prentice, Merchant, 132 E. Bay St.
Axon, Ann, Widow, 31 Cumberland St.
Axon, Elizabeth, Widow, 43 King St.
Axon, Jacob, Jr., Attorney, 43 Meeting St., Res. 70 King St.
Axon, John, Planter, Charlotte St , Mazyckborough, Neck
Ayres, Mary, Widow, 27 Archdale St.
Babcock, William R., Bookseller, 329 King St.
Bachman, John, Rev , Pastor, German Church, Res. cr. Pinckney & Hudson Sts., Neck
Bacon, Charles, Merchant, 253 King St
Bacot, Daniel D., Bookkeeper, S C. Bank, 94 Church St
Bacot, Henry H., Attorney, 49 Tradd St.
Bacot, Peter, Cashier, Bank of Discount & Deposit, 22 Society St

69

Bacot, Thomas W., Jr., Assistant Post Master, 94 Church St.
Bacot, Thomas W., Sr., Cashier, Bank of S. C., 94 Church St.
Badger, Daniel, Painter
Badger, Elizabeth, Widow, 1 Bull St.
Badger, James, Clerk, Planters' & Mechanics' Bank, Res. 6 Green St.
Bailey, David, Planter, 2 Green St., cr. St. Philip's St.
Bailey, Mary, Widow, 10 Wall St.
Bailey, William E., Teacher, 32 Wentworth, Res. 10 Wall St.
Baker, Ann, Widow, Plantress, 15 St. Philip's St.
Baker, Elias, Dyer, 169 Meeting St.
Baker, Francis Y., Milliner, 247 King St.
Baker, Joseph, Carpenter, 87 Boundary St.
Baker, Noah D., Porter House, 24 Market St.
Baker, Priscilla, 22 Church St., F.P.C.
Baker, R. B., Custom House Weigher, 17 Legare St.
Ball, Ann, Miss, Seamstress, 67 Church St.
Ball, Isaac, Planter, 1 Vernon St.
Ball, John, Planter, 27 Hasell St.
Ballantine, Sylvia, 2 Whim Court, F.P.C.
Ballund, Alexander, Merchant, 133 King St.
Ballund, Margaret, Grocer, 133 King St.
Bamfield, George, Butcher, Alexander St., Mazyckborough, F P.C., Neck
Bamfield, Maria, Teacher, 42 Society St.
Bampfield, James, Custom House Officer, 16 George St.
Bampfield, Thomas, Accountant, 16 George St.
Banks, Charles, 118 Tradd St.
Barbot, Anthony, Grocer, 81 Church St., cr. Tradd St.
Barelli, Kitty, Confectioner, 189 King St., Res. 17 Berresford St., F.P.C.
Barguet, John P., Stick & Umbrella Maker, 113 Meeting St., F.P.C.
Barker & Trescot, Attornies, 70 Broad St.
Barker & Watson, Grocers, 134 Meeting St , cr Market St.
Barker, J. Sandford, 18 Society St.
Barker, James, Truss Maker, 28 Pinckney St.
Barksdale, Thomas, Planter, 13 Washington St.
Barksdale, William B , Custom House Officer, 65 Anson St
Barnard, Horace, Merchant, 136 E. Bay St , Res. 275 State St.
Barnett, Abraham, Shopkeeper, King St. Road, Neck
Barnwell, Nancy, 34 King St., F P C.
Barre, John P., Merchant, 88 Queen St.
Barre, -----, Madam, 28 Guignard St.
Barre, Vincent, Brass Founder, 2 Amen St.
Barreilli, Torre & Co., Merchants, 65 Broad St.
Barrelli, Anthony, Grocer, 181 Church St
Barrett, Esther, Crockery Store, 182 Meeting St.
Barrett, Isaac, Auctioneer & Commission Merchant, 30 Vendue Range
Barron, Elizabeth, Widow, 115 Tradd St.
Barron, John, 26 Society St.
Barron, -----, Widow of Alexander, 99 Broad St.
Barrow, Ele, Confectioner, 102 Wentworth St.
Barry, Peter, Last Maker, 28 State St

Barten, John B., 8 Lowndes St., Neck
Bartless, Henry, Blacksmith, 33 Market, Res. 3 Anson St
Barton, Aaron, Grocer, 26 Archdale St.
Barton, Selena, Seamstress, 18 Cumberland St.
Bason, William P., Bookseller & Stationer, 317 King St.
Bass, Job, Dry Goods Store, 152 King St
Bass, Thomas T., 26 Cumberland St
Basset, John, Grocer, 32 Coming St
Bassett, C. I., Painter, Alexander St., Mazyckborough, Neck
Bateman, Edward, Hair Dresser, 226 E. Bay St., F.P.C
Bateman, Isaac, 54 Boundary St , F P C., Neck
Battker, John Andrew, Fruiterer, Market St.
Bauxbaum, John, Physician, 120 Queen St.
Baxter, Elizabeth, 109 King St.
Bay, Andrew, 16 Logan St.
Bay, Elihu H., Judge, 16 Logan St.
Bay, John, Merchant, Res. 72 King St., cr. Tradd St.
Bayard, Peggy, Washer, 121 Wentworth St., F.P.C.
Beach, May L., 23 King St.
Beach, Rebecca, Fruiterer, 7 King St., F.P.C.
Beale, Ann, Widow, 125 King St
Bean, Charles, Mariner, 98 Market St., F.P.C.
Beard, Frederick, Grist Mill, Boundary St , Neck
Beard, Frederick, Teller, Bank of S. C., Res. Boundary St.
Beard, -----, Mrs , 51 Wentworth St.
Beard, William, Bank of S. C., Res. 121 Church St
Beasden, Elizabeth, Seamstress, 4 Ellery St.
Beaudrot, Joseph, Bookkeeper, 106 Market St.
Beaufort, Charles, Butcher, Pinckney St., Neck
Beause, John A., Grocer, 9 Pinckney St.
Becais, Mary, Widow, 224 E. Bay Bay St
Becais, Peter, Mariner, 129 E. Bay St.
Bee, Barnard E., Planter, 114 Tradd St
Bee, Eliza, Widow, 31 Cumberland St.
Bee, Frances Caroline, Widow, 12 Coming St.
Bee, John Simmons, Vendue Master, State St., Res 51 Beaufain St.
Bee, Thomas, 76 Church St
Beeket & Davis, Merchants, 57 E. Bay St
Beekman, Adolph, Painter & Paper Hanger, 131 Meeting St
Beekman, Ann, Widow, 24 Hasell St.
Beekman, Francis D., Painter & Glazier, 125 Meeting St , Res. 14 Pitt St.
Beile, John C., Merchant, 164 King St
Bekofshey, Henry, Grocer, 21 S. Bay St.
Belcher, Elijah, Capt , 39 Tradd St.
Belcher, Manning, 8 Beaufain St., Res. 231 King St.
Belknap, Moses P., Saddler, Trunk Maker & Nine Pin Alley, cr King & Ann Sts., Neck
Bell, Alexander N., Carpenter, 3 Society St
Bell, David, Accountant, 23 Society St
Bell, Margaret Ann, Miss, King St. Road, Neck
Bell, Reuben, Drayman, 39 Magazine St., F.P.C.
Bell, -----, Widow, Nurse, 2 Ellery St
Bell, William, Bricklayer, 46 Society St
Bellamy, Adam, Cartman, Henrietta St., F P C , Neck
Bellanton, Fillett, Fruiterer, 237 E. Bay St , F.P.C.
Bellinger, Rebecca, Mrs , Plantress, 5 Minority St.

Belshaw, Robert, Merchant, at the Lines, King St., Neck
Benedict & Clark, Hatters, 376 King St., Neck
Benjamin, Philip, Dry Goods Store, 165 King St
Benjamin, -----, Shipmaster, 52 E. Bay St.
Bennett & Hunt, Attornies, 1 State House Sq.
Bennett, I S. K., Attorney, 1 State House Sq., Res 38 Bull St.
Bennett, John H., Grocer, 19 Market St.
Bennett, John, Jr., Merchant, 142 King St.
Bennett, John S., Auctioneer, 17 Vendue Range, Res. 127 E. Bay St.
Bennett, Joseph, Grocer, 12 S. Bay St
Bennett, Margaret, Boarding House, 5 Clifford's Al.
Bennett, Thomas, 5 Clifford's Al., F.P C
Bennett, Thomas, Governor, 19 Lynch St.
Bennett, -----, Widow of Thomas, 22 Montague St
Bennett, William S., 72 Tradd St.
Benson, Lavenia, 360 King St
Benson, Lawrence, Dry Goods Store, 324 King St.
Bentham & Parker, Attornies, 4 State House Sq.
Bentham, Mary, Mary, 6 King St.
Bentham, Robert, Attorney, 4 State House Sq., Res. 6 King St.
Bentham, William, Capt., 6 King St.
Berbant, Samuel, Tailor, 405 King St., Neck
Bernard, John, Confectioner, 77 Meeting St.
Berret, William H., Bookseller & Stationer, 14 Broad St.
Berry, Alexander, Clerk, D'Oyley's Whf., Res 16 Water St.
Bertham, Charles & Co , Grocers, 138 King St.
Beswick, Sophia, Teacher, 14 Broad St., Res. 331 King St.
Bethune, Margaret, Widow, 78 Broad St.
Betsy, Mary, Seamstress, Nassau St., F.P.C., Neck
Bevin, J K., Silversmith, King St. Road, Neck
Bezual, Julian, Grocer, E. Bay St
Biedenham, Joseph, Grocer, 200 King St.
Bigelow, Elizabeth, Widow, 265 King St., Neck
Biggar, John, Grocer, 5 Elliot St.
Billings, John, Public Stables, 122 Church St., Res. 17 Chambers St.
Bingley, David P., Blacksmith, Market Whf , Res. 182 E. Bay St.
Bird, John, Looking Glass Store, 41 Broad St
Birnie, William & George, Hardware Store, 21 Broad St.
Birnie, William, Merchant, 21 Broad St , Res. 4 Church St.
Bise, Daniel, Carpenter, St. Philip's St , Neck
Bishop, Otis, Printer, 51 Broad St.
Black, Alexander, Grocer, 30 Elliot St., cr. Gadsden's Al.
Black, Alexander, Merchant, 145, Res. 172 King St.
Black, Christopher, Attorney, Office 57½ Meeting St.
Black, Hester, Miss, 12 Church St.
Black, James, Boot Maker, 36 Broad St.
Black, James, Merchant, 130 E. Bay St , Res 9 Anson St.
Black, John, 21 Broad St.
Black, Robert, Tailor, 191 King St , Res. 12 Orange St.
Blackman, Joseph, Ship Master, 243 E. Bay St.
Blackwood, John, Merchant, King St. Road, Neck
Blackwood, Thomas, President, Planters' & Mechanics' Bank, 18 Pitt St.
Blain, Andrew, Wheelwright, Meeting St Road, Neck
Blair, Susan, 8 Mazyck St.

Blake, John H., Crafts' Whf., Res 28 Archdale St.
Blake, Margaret, Widow, 28 Archdale St
Blamyer, Caroline & Harriet, Misses, Boarding School, 54 St. Philip's St.
Blamyer, William, Factor, Alexander St., Mazyckborough, Neck
Blamyer, William, Office, D'Oyley's Whf.
Blanche, Christian, Gauger of Liquors, 24 Berresford St
Blandiford, Charlotte, 27 Beaufain St , F.P.C.
Blewer, Elizabeth, Widow, cr. Spring & Meeting Sts., Neck
Blewer, John G., Wagon Yard, King St. Road, Neck
Block, Sarah, Boarding House, 48 Elliot St
Blondeau, Stephen, Hat Store, 153 King St.
Blum, Frederick, Butcher, N. Side Cannon St., Neck
Blum, Mary, Widow, King St Road, Neck
Boggs, Simon, Musician, 7 Berresford St., F.P C.
Bolles & Bloshfield, Grocers, 74 Market St.
Bolles, Abiel, Teacher, College Yard
Bolles, Celina, Seamstress, 20 Berresford St., F.P C.
Bollough, Elias, Custom House Officer, 17 Mazyck St.
Bollough, James K., Teacher, 123 Church St., Res. 17 Mazyck St.
Bones, William, Merchant, 39 Broad St
Bonneau, John E., 13 Church St.
Bonneau, Sims, Attorney, 53½ Meeting St., Res 13 Church St.
Bonnell & Saltus, Ship Chandlers, 59 E. Bay St.
Bonnell, John, Ship Chandler, 59 E. Bay St , Res. 14 Lynch's Ln.
Bonner, John, Cabinet Maker, 85 Broad St.
Borch, Peter, 25 Boundary St., cr. Wall St.
Borduck, Emma, Teacher, 8 Whim Court, F.P.C.
Borno, Josephine, Seamstress, 87 Wentworth St., F.P C
Boston, Catharine, 36 Pinckney St., F.P.C.
Boudo, Louis, Manufacturer, Gold & Silver Ware, 160 King St.
Boullen, Enlorge & Peter, 193 E. Bay St.
Boullen, Peter, Shoemaker, 68 Queen St.
Bounetheau, Banbury, Bricklayer, 34 Cumberland St
Bounetheau, Edward W., House Carpenter, 84 Wentworth St.
Bounetheau, Elizabeth, Widow, 34 Cumberland St.
Bounetheau, Henry, Clerk, 34 Cumberland St.
Bounetheau, James W., Printer, 34 Cumberland St
Boutan, Peter, Radcliff St., Neck
Boutang, P. B., Baker, King St. Road, Neck
Bouvie, -----, Billiard Tables, King St Road, Neck
Bow, Ann, Widow, 174 Church St.
Bowen, -----, Rt. Rev., Bishop, Thomas St., Islington, Neck
Bowles, Caty, St. Philip's St., F P.C , Neck
Bowman, Charles A., Ship Carpenter, 81 Anson St.
Bowman, -----, Miss, 225 E. Bay St.
Boyce, Ker, Factor, Kunhardt's Whf.
Boyce, Ker, Merchant, 382 King St., Neck
Boyce, Robert, Millinery Store, 284 King St.
Boyd & M'Cullock, Porter House, 178 E Bay St
Boyd, Alexander, Watchmaker, 5 Broad St.
Boyle, Patrick, Hairdresser, 26 Queen St

71

Boylston, H., Physician, 49 King St , Res. 99 Wentworth St
Bradley, E B., Grocer, cr. Meeting & Hasell Sts.
Bradley, Solomon, Carpenter, 6 Clifford's Al.
Bradshaw, Elizabeth, Fruiterer, 32 Pinckney St
Bradshaw, James, Merchant Tailor, 146 King St
Braid, Matthew, Carpenter, 67 Tradd St.
Brailsford, Amelia, Widow, 35 E. Bay St.
Brailsford, Edward, Physician, 57 Church St.
Brailsford, Elizabeth, Miss, 34 Hasell St.
Brailsford, Elizabeth, Widow, 12 Hasell St.
Brailsford, Mary, Widow, 41 Tradd St.
Brandon, L., 93 Church St.
Braselman, Isabella, Mantua Maker, 6 Archdale St
Breammer, Mann, 102 Queen St.
Breen, Michael, Glass Cutter, 351 King St.
Brelett, Peter, Painter & Glazier, 250 E. Bay St
Bremar, Henry, Dentist, 13 Maiden Ln , cr Guignard St.
Bremar, Sarah, 19 Mazyck St., F P.C
Brenan, Richard, 99 Boundary St.
Brennon, Francis, Baker, 191 Elliot St.
Bretau, L, Tailor, 157 Church St.
Brett, Henry, Merchant, 178 E. Bay St.
Breville, Lewis, 395 King St., Neck
Brewster, Edward, Boarding House, 14 Bedon's Al.
Brian, Zebulon, Carpenter, 88½ Wentworth St.
Bright, Robert, Chemist, 11 Broad St., Res. 4 Lynch's Ln.
Bringlow, Richard, Boat Builder, 10 Stoll's Al.
Brisbane, John, Planter & Factor, Res Duncan's Mill Dam
Brisbane, William, Planter, 29 Meeting St.
Brisbet, Joseph, Ship Master, 29 Anson St.
Brittan, Samuel, Clerk, 13 Bull St
Broadfoot & M'Neel, Counting House, 72 E. Bay St., Res. 2 Laurens St.
Broadfoot, Frances, Widow, 7 Tradd St.
Broadfoot, William, Merchant, 72 E Bay St., Res. 2 Laurens St.
Brockway, Mary M , Widow, Seamstress, 26 Beaufain St
Brodie, M , Widow, Chapel St., Mazyckborough, Neck
Brodie, Robert, Jr., 12 Friend St.
Brodie, Robert, Sr , Lumber Measurer, 112 Tradd St
Broer, Martha, Widow, Alexander St , Neck
Brooks, Ann, Widow, 8 Lowndes St., Neck
Brooks, Rachel, Widow, Seamstress, 22 Blackbird Al
Broughton, Ann, Miss, 49 Anson St.
Broun, Archibald, Mrs., 97 Boundary St.
Brounger, Edward, Boarding House, 52 Elliot St.
Brown & Tunis, Factors, D'Oyley's Whf.
Brown, -----, 52 Queen St.
Brown, Alexander, Merchant, King St. Road, Neck
Brown, Charlotte, 106 Wentworth St., F.P.C.
Brown, George, at Robertson's Rope Walk, Neck
Brown, Jackson, Printer, Tradd St.
Brown, James, Butcher, Hampstead, Neck
Brown, John, 7 Whim Court
Brown, John, Grocer, 6 Archdale St., cr. Berresford St.
Brown, John, Ship Master, 47 State St.
Brown, Joshua, Boarding House, 53 E. Bay St., cr. Crafts' S. Whf.
Brown, Lavinia, Widow, Plantress, Washington St ,

Mazyckborough, Neck
Brown, Magdalene, Widow, Market St
Brown, Mary, Mrs., 22½ Wentworth St.
Brown, Mary, Seamstress, 9 Clifford's Al., F.P.C
Brown, Morris, Shoemaker, Wentworth St., cr Anson St., F P.C.
Brown, Moses, Hair Dresser, 5 Tradd St., F.P.C.
Brown, Nicholas, Grocer, 247 E. Bay St
Brown, Peter, Hair Dresser, 18 Elliott St., F P.C.
Brown, Robert C., Tailor, Tradd St.
Brown, Robert, Factor, D'Oyley's Whf., Res. 79 Church St
Brown, Samuel, Mariner, 58 Maiden Ln., cr. Market St
Brown, Samuel Scott, Surveyor, 8 Orange St.
Brown, -----, Widow of Moses, 1 Price's Al., F.P C.
Brown, -----, Widow of Peter, 25 Lynch's Ln.
Brown, William, Capt , 32 Church St.
Brown, William, Grocer, 58 Maiden Ln., cr. Market St
Browne, Adam J., 37 St Philip's St.
Browne, Anna, Widow, Milliner, 21 Amen St.
Browne, Edward, Merchant, 46, Res 29 E Bay St
Browne, Elizabeth, Widow, 67 Wentworth St.
Brownlee, John, cr. Meeting & Hudson Sts , Wraggsborough, Neck
Bryan, Jonathan, Merchant, 326 King St
Bryan, Lydia, Widow, Plantress, 16 Hasell St., cr. Anson St
Bryant, C. H., 70 Meeting St.
Bryce, Henry, Grain Store, 8 & 10 Tradd St., Res 52 King St.
Buchan, John, Rev., 9 Lynch St.
Buchanan, Ann, Widow, 257 Meeting St., Neck
Buchanan, Wood & Co., 39 E. Bay St
Buckle, Maria, 63 State St., F.P.C.
Buckley, Elizabeth, Widow, 48 Montague St
Buckmyer, Isaac, Butcher, 26 Blackbird Al., F P C
Budd, Abigail, Widow, 52 Tradd St.
Budd, William, Merchant, Lothrop's Whf., Res. 78 King St.
Buerhaus, Herman D., Tailor, 11 Queen St.
Buist, Arthur, Rev., 12 Meeting St
Buist, Mary, Widow, 5 Church St.
Bulet, Peter, Mount Pleasant Coffee House, cr. Mary & Meeting Sts., Neck
Bulkley, Ashbel, Merchant, 261 King St.
Bulkley, Erastus, Dry Goods Store, 261 King St
Bulkley, Stephen, 261 King St
Bull, Elizabeth, Widow, 8 Lamboll St.
Bull, Harry, 8 Swinton's Ln., F.P.C.
Bull, John, Grocer, 19 Market St.
Bull, Mary, Zigzag Al., F.P.C.
Bull, William, Grocer, 18 S. Bay St.
Bullen, Samuel, Shoe Store, 26½ King St.
Bulow, Charles W , Planter, 209 Meeting St.
Bulow, John J., 14 Montague St.
Bunch, Joshua, King St. Road, Neck
Bunells, -----, Misses, Seamstresses, 243 E. Bay St.
Burckmyer, Ann Mary, Widow, 118 Wentworth St.
Burckmyer, Charles, Merchant, 140 E. Bay St , Res. 118 Wentworth St.
Burckmyer, J. C & C , Commission Merchants, 140 E

72

Bay St.

Burckmyer, John C., Merchant, 140 E Bay St., Res. 30 Meeting St.

Burdell, John E., Carpenter, 49 Pinckney St., Res 16 Wentworth St.

Burden, Kinsey, Planter, 10 Short St

Burdon, Sophia, Nurse, Anson St.

Burg, Charles, Merchant, Vanderhorst's Whf.

Burger, Samuel, Tax Collector, over Bank of State S. C.

Burgoyne, William, Druggist, 2 Broad St., Res. E. Bay, cr. Water St

Burie, Daniel, Blacksmith, 6 Pitt St.

Burke, John, Rigger, 16 Stoll's Al.

Burminster, -----, Fruiterer, 36 King St.

Burn, G. A., Painter, Cannon St., Neck

Burn, John, 22 Washington St.

Burn, William, Carpenter, Cannon St., Neck

Burnet, Foster, Grocer, 2 Vendue Range

Burney, Mary, Mrs , 173 Meeting St.

Burns, James, Pilot, 12 Amen St.

Burns, John M., Shoe Store, 102 Church St.

Burrell, E., Merchant, 91 Church St.

Burrell, John E., Merchant, 4 Crafts' Whf , Res. 12 Lamboll St., cr. Logan St.

Burrell, William, Book Maker, 108 Church St., Res. 45 Broad St.

Burrows, Mary, Widow, 11 Wentworth St.

Bush, Mary, Fruiterer, 308 E. Bay St., F.P C.

Bussaker, Charles, Dry Goods Store, 107 King St.

Busse, John, Shop, King St. Road, Neck

Butler, Robert, Inspector, Union Insurance Co., 1 Laurens St.

Byrd John, Wharfinger & Grocer, Magwood's Whf., Res 60 King St.

Byrd, Orran, Merchants Hotel, 141 E. Bay St.

Cabueil, Lewis, Tailor, 98 Church St.

Cadiz, Michael, Mariner, 65 State St.

Cafrel, -----, Madame, 8 Berresford St.

Calder, Alexander, Jr., Baker, Lodge Al.

Calder, Alexander, Planters' Hotel, Church St., cr Queen St.

Calder, James, Cabinet Maker, 116 Meeting St.

Calder, James, Merchant, Chisolm's S. Whf., Res. 16 Broad St.

Caldwell, John, 27 Vendue Range

Caldwell, Robert, Merchant, King St. Road, Neck

Caldwell, William A. & Co., Auctioneers, 27 Vendue Range

Caldwell, William A., Auctioneer, 107 Meeting St.

Callaghan, John, Grocer, 8 Coming St

Callender, Joseph, Capt , 26 King St.

Calvert, Elizabeth, Widow, St. Philip's St , Neck

Cameron, -----, Widow, Boarding House, 17 Tradd St

Cammer, James, Blacksmith, 64 Market St.

Cammer, William, Carpenter, 24 St. Philip's St.

Campbell & Wightman, Commission Merchants, Napier's New Range, Dewees' Whf.

Campbell, Alexander, Clerk, Hampstead, Neck

Campbell, Ann, Alexander St., Mazyckborough, Neck

Campbell, I. M , Physician, 95 Broad St

Campbell, John, Commission Merchant, Napier's New Range, Res. 171 Meeting St

Campbell, Mary, Elizabeth St., Mazyckborough, F.P C , Neck

Campbell, Matthew, Stone Cutter, 16 Ellery St.

Campbell, -----, Mrs., 114 Meeting St

Campbell, P., Porter House, 133 E. Bay St.

Campbell, Peter, Porter House, 270 King St.

Campbell, Samuel & Co., Hair Dresser, 102 King St., F.P.C.

Campbell, -----, Widow of Alexander, 14 Maiden Ln

Campbell, William, Hair Dresser, 216 King St., F.P.C

Campbell, William S., Attorney, 69 Meeting St , Res. 4 George St.

Canaday, Henry, Grocer, 97 Tradd St , cr Legare St.

Cannon, Mary, Seamstress, 38 Coming St., F.P.C.

Cannon, William & Co., Stock & Exchange Broker, 117 E Bay St.

Canter, Emanuel, Glass & Crockery Warehouse, Vendue Range & 292 King St., Res. 306 King St.

Canter, John, Limner, 116 Queen St., cr. Archdale St.

Canter, Joshua, Limner, 121 Broad St

Canter, Rebecca, 121 Broad St.

Cantey, Ann, Widow, 96 Meeting St

Canty, Catharine M., Miss, Milliner, King St. Road, Neck

Canuet, William, Soap & Candle Manufactory, Henrietta St., Wraggsborough, Neck

Cape, Brian, 3 Bull St.

Carden, Louis J., Tallow Chandler, Meeting St Road, Neck

Cardo, Lewis, 13 Logan St., F P.C.

Cardoza, David, Measurer of Coal & Salt, Custom House, Res. 85 King St.

Cardoza, Isaac, Clerk, Southern Patriot, 99 E. Bay St., Res 85 King St.

Cardoza, Jacob, Editor, Southern Patriot, 99 E Bay, Res. 85 King St.

Cardoza, Joseph, Ship Master, 1 Pritchard's Whf.

Carevin, Joseph, Ship Master, 124 King St.

Carivenc, P., Baker, Meeting St.

Carman, Maria, Milliner, 296 King St.

Carmand, Francis, Merchant Tailor, 86 Queen St.

Carmele, John, Butcher, Meeting St. Road, Neck

Carnechan, Richard, Merchant, Crafts' S. Whf.

Carnighan, John, Custom House Officer, 29 Elliot St.

Carpenter, Joseph E., Boundary St , Neck

Carr, Ann, Seamstress, 33 King St.

Carr, Hester, Fruiterer, 31 State St., F.P.C.

Carr, Mary, Mrs., Boarding House, 8 Queen St.

Carr, Robert, Druggist, 381 King St , Res. 8 Green St

Carrendeffez, Alexis, Physician, 96 King St.

Carrero, Charles, Professor of Languages, 109 Broad St.

Carroll, Bartholomew, W. End Boundary St., Neck

Carroll, Charles H , Commission Merchant, Kunhardt's Whf., Res. 173 E. Bay St.

Carroll, Thomas, Painter, 4 Queen St.

Carroll, -----, Widow of James P., Plantress, Boundary St., Neck

Carson, Elizabeth, Mrs., 90 Tradd St.

Carson, William A., Planter, 90 Tradd St.

73

Carson, William, Grocer, 67 E. Bay St., cr. Tradd St
Carsten, John, City Scavenger, Elizabeth St.,
　Wraggsborough, Neck
Cart, John, Jr., Bookkeeper in Planters' & Mechanics'
　Bank, 41 George St.
Cart, John, Lumber Measurer, 28 Bull St
Cart, Sarah, Widow, Philadelphia St.
Carters, -----, Misses, Dry Goods Store, 394 King St.,
　Neck
Carvalho, D. N., Watchmaker & Jeweller, 333 King St.
Carvin, Elizabeth, Mrs., Milliner, 147 King St.
Cason, James, Grocer, 62 Market, Res. 23 Guignard St.
Castagnon, Mary Emily, Dry Goods Store, 131 King St.
Catherwood, J. J., Watchmaker, 63 Broad St.
Cato, Susan, Milliner, 24 Archdale St.
Catonet, Peter, Mrs., Dry Goods Store, 31 Queen St.
Cauchois, Courdier, Mrs., 14 Berresford St.
Caught, Thomas, 296 E. Bay St.
Causee, Amy, Widow, Pinckney St., Neck
Chabert, Frances, Nurse, 91 Wentworth St., F.P.C.
Chadwick, Samuel, 13 Meeting St.
Chalmers, Elizabeth, Widow, Whim Court
Chalmers, Henry J., Planter, 8 West St.
Chamberlin, Jacob, Agent, New England Glass Co., 127
　King St.
Champlin, Samuel, 14 Magazine St.
Champney, George, 9½ Wentworth St., F.P.C.
Chanet & Duquercron, Merchants, 398 King St., cr.
　Tobacco St., Neck
Chanet, Anthony, Merchant, Chisolm's Upper Whf., Res.
　19 Tradd St.
Chanler, Charles, Waiter, 10 Linguard St., F.P.C.
Chanlotte, -----, Widow, Seamstress, 22 Anson St.
Channer, Christopher J., Tailor, 10 Maiden Ln.
Chapman, Thomas, Factor, Edmondston's Whf., Res. 63 E.
　Bay St.
Charles, Silvey, 65 Tradd St., F.P.C.
Charnock, George, Turner, 37 Anson St.
Charnock, Mary, 36 Mazyck St., F.P.C.
Charnock, Thomas, Cabinet Maker, 37 Anson St., F.P.C.
Chartrent, Caroline, Seamstress, 8 Wall St.
Chasteau, Charles Rene, Physician, 194 Meeting St.
Chatelin, Mary Ann, Fruiterer, 256 King St.
Chatters, Henry, Carpenter, 8 Pitt St., F.P C.
Chazel, Frances, Fruiterer, 12 Lauren St.
Cheesbrough, J. W. & Co., Commission Merchant,
　Vanderhorst's Whf., Res. 7 Water St.
Cheney, Ebenezer, Jr., Merchant, 138 E. Bay St., Res. 26
　Broad St.
Cherier, Lewis, Pastry Cook, 59 Queen St.
Chevillion, Lewis, Grocer, 293½ King St.
Chiffelle, Thomas, Custom House Officer, 31 Coming St
Chio, Anantine Maillay, Washer, Coming St., F.P.C , Neck
Chisolm & Taylor, Factors, Chisolm's S. Whf.
Chisolm, Alexander, Planter, 10 Montague St.
Chisolm, George, Factor, Chisolm's S. Whf., Res. 25 E.
　Bay St.
Chisolm, Mary Ann, Widow, Hampstead, Neck
Chisolm, Robert, Planter, 6 Montague St.
Chisolm, Robert T , Chisolm's Upper Whf.

Chitty, C. C., Attorney, 85 Broad St., Res. 32 George St
Chitty, -----, Mrs., Widow, State House Yard
Chitty, Thomas J., Shopkeeper, King St., Neck
Chitty, William John, Jr., Porter & Collection Clerk, State
　Bank, Res. St. Philip's St., Neck
Choate, Catharine, Widow, 53 Wentworth St.
Chreitzburg, George, Baker, 87 Queen St.
Chreitzburg, Thomas, Grocer, 72 Market St.
Christian, Alexander B., 107 Church St.
Christie, Alexander, 98 Church St.
Christie, Edward, Dry Goods Store, 38 Tradd St , cr.
　Church St.
Chupein, Lewis, Mineral Water House, 13 Broad St.
Chur, George, Grocer, 78 Market St
Church, Bethel, Pitt & Boundary Sts.
Church, Margaret, Mrs., Umbrella Maker, 18 St. Philip's
　St
Church, Mary, Widow, Seamstress, 21 St. Philip's St
Clancy, John, Grocer, cr. Coming & Vanderhorst Sts.,
　Neck
Clark, Bartholomew, Merchant, 140 King St., Res. 163
　King St.
Clark, Elizabeth, Widow, 16 Church St.
Clark, George W., Ship Chandler, 71 E Bay St.
Clark, James, Tailor, 103 Church St.
Clark, Joseph, Attorney, 85 Meeting St.
Clark, Mary Eddy, Seamstress, 11 Zigzag Al.
Clark, Richard, Capt., Pilot, 47 Church St.
Clark, William, Tailor, 17 Archdale St., F.P.C.
Clarkson, William, Factor, Kunhardt's Whf., Res. 2 Bull St.
Clastrie, Stephen, 392 King St., Neck
Clay, William, Mariner, 13 Zigzag Al.
Clayton, Jane P., King St. Road, Neck
Cleapor, Charles, Sail Maker, Lothrop's Whf.
Cleary, Catharine, Widow, 34 Hasell St.
Cleary, Nathaniel G., Attorney, 145 King St.
Clemens, Daniel L., Ship Carpenter, 13 Price's Al.
Clement, Louis, Vanderhorst St., Neck
Clements, Sarah, 101 Queen St.
Cleveland, Cloe, Whim Court, F.P.C.
Clifford, Henry, Factor, Mey's Whf., 28 Middle St.
Cline, Jacob, State Constable, 75 Tradd St
Clissey, L., Dry Goods Store, 178 King St.
Cloughs, Phillis, Boarding House, 46 Elliot St.
Coates, Catharine, Widow, 16 Pinckney St.
Coates, Stephen S., Steam Saw Mill, Washington St.,
　Mazyckborough, Neck
Cobetyzer, Phillis, 11 College St., F.P.C.
Cobia, Ann, Miss, Teacher, Meeting St. Road, Neck
Cobia, D., Grocer, 7 Legare St.
Cobia, Dinah, Widow, 18 Montague St.
Cobia, Francis, Carpenter, 16 Berresford St.
Cobia, Francis J., Butcher, Reed St., near Meeting St.,
　Neck
Cobia, Nicholas, Planter, 124 Wentworth St
Coburn, Ann, Mrs., 21 George St
Cochran, Charles B., 24 Society St.
Cochran, Jane, Widow, Grocer, 87 King St.
Cochran, Margaret, Dry Goods Store, 120 King St.
Cochran, Robert, 24 Society St.

Cochran, Robert E., 85 Wentworth St.
Cochran, Samuel, Tailor, E. Bay St., F.P.C.
Cochran, Sophia, Grocer, 69 Queen St., F.P.C.
Cochran, Thomas, Broker & Auctioneer, 6 Broad St., Res. Cannon St.
Cocks, John S. H., Ship Master, 245 E Bay St.
Coe, -----, Widow of Richard, St Philip's St., Neck
Cogdell & Gilchrist, Attornies, 46 Meeting St.
Cogdell, John S., Naval Officer, 46 Meeting St.
Cogdell, Mary Ann Elizabeth, Widow, 5 St. Michael's Al.
Cogdell, Richard W., Teller, Bank of State S. C., 7 St. Michael's Al.
Cohen, Mordecai, 103 Broad St.
Cohen, Moses, Merchant, 222 King St.
Cohen, Philip, 2 Orange St.
Cohen, Rebecca, Widow, 10 Elliot St.
Cohen, Samuel, Shopkeeper, King St. Road, Neck
Cohen, Solomon, Dry Goods Store, 316 King St.
Colberg, Christopher, Grocer, 76 Tradd St.
Colburn, James S., Dry Goods Store, 86 Broad St., cr King St.
Colcock, Charles, Judge, 11 Lamboll St
Colcock, M., Widow, 11 Lamboll St.
Cole, Joseph, Shoemaker, 16 Tradd St.
Cole, Thomas, Carpenter, 17 Archdale St., F.P.C.
Coll, John, Butcher, Hampstead, Neck
Collier, William, Custom House Officer, 14 Wentworth St.
Collins, Catharine, Mantua Maker, 105 Queen St.
Collins, Mary, Widow, 33 Hasell St.
Colman, Solomon, Dry Goods Store, 316 King St
Colongin, -----, Gunsmith, 27 Queen St.
Colzy, -----, Widow of Charlemagne, Tailoress, 111 Church St.
Condie, David, Tanner, D. Cruckshank's Tanyard, Hampstead, Neck
Condy, Jeremiah, Merchant, 122 E. Bay St , Res. 100 Meeting St.
Condy, Thomas D., Attorney, 100 Meeting St.
Conklin, -----, Grocer, 70 Wentworth St.
Conner, John, Saddler, 384 King St , Neck
Connoly, Jeremiah, Capt., 33 Meeting St.
Connor, Samuel, Corn Store, 7 Martin's Row
Conover, Eliza, Widow, 50 Anson St.
Constantine, Peter, Boarding House, 33 State St.
Conte, Caroline T., Meeting St. Road, Neck
Conyers & Lambard, Commission Merchants, 128 E. Bay St.
Conyers, William A., 34 Pinckney St.
Coogly, Jacob, Butcher, Hampstead, Neck
Cooke & Martin, Shoe Store, King St. Road, Neck
Cooke, Eliza, Mrs., Boarding House, 100 E. Bay St.
Cookson, John, Shoemaker, 108 Meeting St.
Cooper, Ann, Grocer, 22½ George St.
Cooper, Mary, Mrs., 306 E. Bay St.
Cooper, Nathaniel, Merchant, Res. 64 Anson St.
Corby, John, Blacksmith, Eason's Whf., Res. Vernon St.
Corker, Thomas, Ship Carpenter, 26 Pinckney St.
Cornea, Francis, Ship Carpenter, 18 Wall St
Cormick, Thomas, Factor, Vanderhorst's Whf., Res. 72 Broad St

Cornell, Benjamin, Grocer, 5 Longitude Ln
Cornell, Gardener T., Baker, 35 Wall St.
Corning, Jasper, Dry Goods Store, 56 Broad St., Res. 47 E. Bay St.
Cornwell, Sarah, Seamstress, 11 Philadelphia St., F.P.C
Corr, Charles, Tailor, 28 Coming St., F.P.C
Corum, Ann, Widow, 150 Queen St.
Coste, Louis, Crockery Store, 63 Queen St.
Coste, Phillis, Shopkeeper, 20 St. Philip's St., F.P.C
Cotes, C., Teacher, 193 Broad St.
Counard, -----, Madam, 66 Wentworth St.
Course, Isaac, Factor, 12 Vendue Range, Res. 220 E. Bay St.
Courtenay, Edward S., Teacher, 38 St. Philip's St
Courtney, Humphrey, Wine Merchant, 47 E. Bay St
Courtois, Anthony, Grocer, 215 E. Bay St
Couturier, Eliza Maria, Widow, 2 State House Sq.
Coventry, Alexander, Dyer, 58 Tradd St.
Cowan, John, Cabinet Maker, 123 Meeting St.
Cowan, John, Clerk, 105 Boundary St.
Cowan, -----, Widow of John, 9 Minority St.
Cox, George, Seedsman & Florist, 212 King St
Cox, Juliet, 79 Boundary St , F.P.C.
Cox, Thomas, Coach Maker, 53 Broad St
Crafts & Eckhard, Attornies, 104 Church St.
Crafts, -----, Widow of William, 52 Beaufain St.
Crafts, William, Attorney, 104 Church St., Res. 52 Beaufain St.
Cramer, George, Grocer, 16 Hasell St. & 18 Linguard St.
Cramer, John, Church St
Cranston, James, Broker, Unity Al., 31 Mazyck St.
Crask, Philip, Painter, 51 Pinckney St.
Crawford, J., Butcher, Henrietta St , F.P.C., Neck
Crawford, John, Wharf Holder, Vanderhorst's Whf., Res. 6 Friend St.
Crawford, -----, Widow of Gabriel, 21 Pinckney St
Crawley, -----, Widow of Charles, 76 Broad St.
Craysack, Adelaide, 158 Meeting St
Cregier, Peter, Constable, 37 Wall St.
Creighton, -----, Barber, 197 E. Bay St , Res. 83 Anson St., F.P.C
Creighton, Grace, 66 State St., F.P.C
Crocker, D. & Co., Merchants, Magwood's Whf.
Crocker, Doddridge, Merchant, Magwood's Whf., Res. 23 Tradd St.
Croft, Arnold, Millinery, 245 King St
Croft, George, Capt., 77 Tradd St.
Croft, -----, Widow of Peter, Nassau St., Wraggsborough, Neck
Cromwell, Charles, Capt , 6 Stoll's Al.
Cromwell, Samuel, Bricklayer, 7 Back St.
Crone, Harman, Grocer, 2 Wall St.
Cropsey, William, Porter House, 104 Queen St
Crosby, Hannah, Widow, 111 Church St.
Cross & Gray., Attornies, 44 Meeting St., cr Tradd St.
Cross & Poincignon, Blacksmiths, 4 Amen St.
Cross, Ann, Fruiterer, 64 State St., F.P.C.
Cross, George W., Attorney, 44 Meeting, cr. Tradd St
Cross, Henry, Blacksmith, 4 Amen St., Res 37 State St
Cross, Phoebe, Lowndes St., F.P.C., Neck

Cross, Sarah, Widow, 6 Philadelphia St.
Cross, William, Bricklayer, 37 State St
Crouch, Abraham, Notary Public, Custom House, Res 247 Meeting St.
Crovat, Peter, Grocery & Dry Goods Store, 297 & 281 King St.
Crow, Edward, Printer, 100 Market St.
Cruckshanks, Amos, Painter, 67 Boundary St., F.P.C
Cruckshanks, Daniel, Shoemaker, 22 Queen St.
Cruckshanks, Daniel, Tanyard, Hanover St., Hampstead, Neck
Cruckshanks, R., Tailor, 170 Meeting St.
Cruckshanks, William, King St., Neck
Cruger, Elizabeth, Widow, 57 Meeting St.
Cruse, Amey, Widow, Seamstress, 29 Mazyck St.
Cruse, Englehart, Millright, Markley's Mills, Beaufain St
Cubie, John, Grocer, 127 Tradd St.
Cucko, William, Pilot, 65 Church St.
Cudworth, William, Chair Maker, Charlotte St., Mazyckborough, Neck
Cummens, William, Teacher, 190 King St., Res. 29 Broad St.
Cunningham, John, Tailor, 33 Pinckney St.
Curran, William, Bricklayer, 21 Beaufain St.
Curtis, Aaron, Saddler, 288 King St.
Curtis, Francis S., 13 Mazyck St
Cuthbert, John, Gen., 32 Society St.
D'Oyley & Legare, Attornies, 57 Meeting St
D'Oyley, Charles W , Attorney, 57 Meeting St., Res 7 St. Philip's St.
Dabriskey, John, Painter, 58 King St.
Dagleish, George, Bricklayer, Mazyck St.
Dalcho, Frederick, Rev. Dr., 39 Meeting St.
Dalton, James, Dr., Druggist, 87 Church St., cr. Tradd St
Darby, John, Silversmith, 27 Archdale St.
Darby, Mary, Widow, 84 Tradd St
Dare, Ann, Widow, Mantua Maker, 224 Ellery St.
Darr, Peter, Coach Maker, 21 Coming St.
Darrell, Edward, Accountant, 216 Meeting St.
Darrell, John S., Custom House Store Keeper, 205 King St
Darrell, Josiah J., Factor, Res. E. Bay St., cr. Vanderhorst's Whf.
Darrill, Molly, 11 E. Bay St., F.P.C.
Dart, Benjamin S., 55 Tradd St.
Dart, Isaac M., Factor, Crafts' Whf., Res. 42 Montague St.
Dart, Isabella, Mantua Maker, 19 Berresford St., F.P.C.
Dart, John S., 55 Tradd St.
Datty, Julia, Miss, School, 94 Wentworth St.
Datty, Mark, 94 Wentworth St
Davega, Isaac, Factor, 87 Meeting St.
David, Peter Bene, Store Keeper, 356 King St.
Davidson, Gilbert, Planter, 154 Wentworth St.
Davidson, James, Capt., 48 Elliot St.
Davis & King, Grocers, 13 Chalmers Al.
Davis, Alexander, Mrs., Mazyckborough, Neck
Davis, Catharine, Radcliff St., Neck
Davis, Elizabeth, Seamstress, 38 Guignard St.
Davis, George, Mariner, 13 Chalmers Al.
Davis, George Y., Merchant, 57 E. Bay St.

Davis, Henry, Hat Store, 285 King St.
Davis, J. M., Quorum Unis & Notary Public, Upper Side Pinckney St., Cannonborough, Neck
Davis, Jacob, Painter Oil & Color Store, 81 Queen St.
Davis, John M., Notary Public, 81 E. Bay St., Res. Cannonborough
Davis, Joseph, Cannon St., Neck
Davis, Martha, Seamstress, 45 Anson St., F.P.C.
Davis, Mary, Seamstress, 19 Boundary St
Davis, Sarah, Widow, 8 Philadelphia St.
Davis, Thomas, Capt., 8 Stoll's Al
Davis, -----, Widow of John, King St., near the Lines, Neck
Davis, William, 166 Church St.
Davis, William, Grocer, 3 Tradd St.
Dawes, Hugh P , Store, Lothrop's Whf., Res. 19 Hasell St.
Dawson, Ann, Widow, 4 Montague St.
Dawson, John & Co., Factors, Crafts' S. Whf.
Dawson, John, Cashier, State Bank, 34 Bull St.
Dawson, John, Factor, Gadsden's Whf., Res. 5 Montague St.
Dawson, John, Merchant, King St., near the Lines, Neck
Dawson, Rhoda, Fruiterer, St Philip's St., cr. Liberty St., F.P.C.
Dawson, William, Planter, 5 New St
Day, E. S., Shop, 373 King St., Neck
Deas & Brown, Factors, 6 Smith's Whf.
Deas, Catharine, Vanderhorst St., Neck
Deas, Charles, 12 Wall St
Deas, David, Planter, 116 Tradd St.
Deas, Henry, Planter, 1 Friend St
Deas, Lucy, Pastry Cook, 23 Mazyck St., F.P.C.
Deas, Robert, Planter, 133 Queen St.
Deas, Thomas H. & Co., Commission Merchants, Chisolm's Upper Whf.
Deas, Thomas H., Merchant, 8 King St.
Debarree, Mary, Widow, Henrietta St., Neck
Debeere, -----, Monsieur, Wolf St., Neck
Debo, John Frederick H., Grocer, 152 Wentworth St
Debow, John, Coach & Chair Maker, cr. King & Radcliff Sts., Neck
DeBow, Garret, Merchant, 53 State St., Res. 10 Amen St.
DeCampe, -----, Monsieur, Broker
Defrand, German, 13½ Logan St.
Dehon, Sarah, Widow, 43 Meeting St.
Deignan, Francis, Grocer, 25 Elliot St.
DeLaMotta, Judith, Mrs., 149 Queen St
Delaney, Ann, Widow, Seamstress, 2 Blackbird Al
Delaney, Michael, Pilot, 2 Stoll's Al
DeLattere, Albert, Capt., 14 Hasell St
DeLavincendiere, H., 13 Wentworth St.
Delcol, Celestine, Confectioner, 242 Meeting St , F.P.C.
DeLeon, Jacob, Vendue Range, Res. 14 Beaufain St
DeLeon, M. H., Auctioneer & Commission Merchant, Vendue Range, Res. 271 King St.
DeLiesseline, F. A., Planter, 240 E. Bay St.
DeLiesseline, F. G., Sheriff, Charleston District, 240 E Bay St.
Deming & Bulkley, Cabinet Warehouse, 231 King St.
Dempsey, Miles, Grocer, 3 Queen St. & 151 E Bay St.
Dempsey, Thomas, Porter House, 9 E Bay St

Dener, Christiana, Widow, 31 Mazyck St.
Denny, Mary, Widow, 24 Guignard St.
Denton, Eliza, Miss, cr. Cannon & Coming Sts , Neck
Depau, L. B., Merchant, 172, Res. 174 E. Bay St.
Deponte, Louisa, 5 Beaufain St , F.P C.
Dereef, R. W., King St. Road, F.P C., Neck
Derineau, Abraham, Dry Goods Store, 71 King St., cr
    Tradd St.
Deromas, Jane, Cigar Maker, 172 Meeting St
Desel, Charles L., Physician, 90 Wentworth St.
Desir, Joseph, 18 Berresford St., F.P.C.
Desportes, Peter, Grocer, 199 E. Bay St.
Despraugh, Ann Catharine, Milliner & Dry Goods, 357
    King St., Neck
Dessaussure, Henry, Attorney, 81 Broad St., Res. 35
    Meeting St.
Dessony, Harriet, 16 Wentworth St.
Devaga, Isaac, 375 King St , Neck
Deveaux, -----, Widow of Thomas, Boundary St., Neck
Deversiea, Andraise, Washer, 20 St. Philip's St., F.P C.
Deversiea, Priscilla, 9 Coming St., F.P C.
Devierre, -----, Meeting St. Road, Neck
DeVillers, Lewis, Stationer, 91 King St., cr. Broad St. &
    Grocery Store, cr. Church & King Sts
Dewees, John, Factor, Smith's Whf.
Dewees, John, Mary St., Mazyckborough, Neck
Dewees, Mary Ann, 31 Cumberland St.
Dewees, William & Sons, Dewees' Whf.
Dewees, William, Factor, cr. Alexander & Charlotte Sts.,
    Neck
Dewees, William, Jr., Dewees Whf., Res. cr. Wall &
    Minority Sts.
Dexter, Samuel W., Grocer, 15 King St.
Deye, Benjamin, Grocer, 17 S. Bay St
Dickinson, Elizabeth, Widow, Doughty St., Neck
Dickinson, Francis, Attorney, 71 Broad St
Dickinson, Samuel, Vendue Master, 32 Vendue Range
Dickson, John & Co , Soap & Tallow Chandlers, King St.
    Road, Neck
Dickson, John, Teacher, 76 Res 69 Meeting St.
Dickson, Mary, Widow, 50 St. Philip's St.
Dickson, Samuel, Grocer, 205 E. Bay St
Dickson, Samuel H., Physician, 361 King St.
Dile, Jane, Dry Goods Store, 177½ King St.
Dill, Eliza, Miss, 50 King St.
Dill, Jane Eliza, Widow, Lamboll St.
Dill, Joseph, Physician, 27 Hasell St.
Dillon, Jane, 32 Wentworth St.
Dixon, Robert, Butcher, Hampstead, Neck
Dobson, Oliver L , Grocer, 65 E. Bay St., cr. Tradd St.
Dodd & Barnard, Commission Merchants, 136 E. Bay St.
Dodd, Ann, Fruiterer, 109 Church St.
Dodd, William, Merchant, 136 E. Bay St.
Doggett, John, Tin Plate Worker, 83 King St
Dogherty, Joseph, Grocer, 25 S. Bay St.
Don, Alexander, Carpenter, 38 Society St.
Donegan, James, Shoe Store, 124 Church St.
Donnelly, James, Boarding House, 9 Gillon St.
Donnelly, William, Ship Master, 9 Gillon St.
Dorrill, Robert, Factor, Williams' Whf., Res. 35 State St

Dorrill, Rose, Fruiterer, 20 Pinckney St
Douein, Morrill, Painter & Glazier, 37 Wentworth St.
Dougherty, John, Plasterer, Wall St., cr. Boundary St
Doughty, James, Dr., Pinckney St , Neck
Douglass, C., Grocer, 141 Meeting St., cr. Market St.
Dove, William P., Ship Joiner, Prichard & Knox's Whf.,
    Res. 44 State St.
Dowling, Archibald, Grocer, 5 King St
Dowling, Daniel, Bricklayer, 9 Amen St.
Dowling, Edward, Widow, 17 Society St
Dowling, Mary, 65 State St , F.P.C
Downie, Robert, Tinner, 59 Broad St
Doyle, Thomas, Grocer, Daniell's Whf.
Drayton, Hannah, 5 Price's Al., F P.C.
Drayton, Henry, John St., Wraggsborough St., F.P.C.,
    Neck
Drayton, John, District Judge, 24 Friend St.
Drayton, John, Mrs., 49 Bull St
Drayton, Susan, 22 Berresford St., F.P.C
Drayton, William, City Recorder, 6 Gibbes St
Drege, Mary, 157 E. Bay St., cr. Queen St.
Drege, Peter, Clothier, 157 E. Bay St., cr Queen St.
Drewes, Henry, Grocer, 196 Meeting St.
Drummond, James, Shoemaker, 29 State St., cr Queen St.
Dubert, F., cr. Spring & King Sts., Neck
Duboc, Francis, Merchant, 181 King St.
Dubois, Lewis, Upholsterer, 90 Queen St.
Dubois, Narcisse, Fruiterer, 34 Market St.
Dubois, Peter, Carpenter, 14 Cannon St., Neck
Duffus, John, Accountant, 4 Short St
Dufort, John, Baker, 46 Queen St.
Duggan, Thomas, Plasterer & Stucco Man, St. Philip's St.,
    near the Lines, Neck
Duhadway, C. B., Milliner, 142 King St.
Duke & Browne, Printers, 9 Broad St.
Duke, Francis, Shop, King St. Road, Neck
Duke, John C., Printer, 6 Amen St.
Dukes, William C., Merchant, King St. Road, Neck
Dulaney, Mary, Widow, Seamstress, 24 Beaufain St.
Dullus, Amelia, 21 Friend St., F P.C.
Dumont, -----, Fancy Store, 118 King St.
Dumont, -----, Madam, 31 Wall St
Dumoutet, Julia, 52 Broad St
Duncan, John, Merchant, 6 Bull St
Duncan, Patrick, Pinckney St., Neck
Duncan, Phillis, Fruiterer, 20 Pinckney St., F.P.C
Duncan, Robert, Fisherman, 2 Zigzag Al., F.P.C.
Duncan, Samuel, Porter House, 139 E. Bay St
Dunkin & Campbell, Attornies, 69 Meeting St.
Dunn, D., Grocer, Charlotte St., cr. Washington St., Neck
Dunn, John & Co., Blacksmiths, Chalmers St., cr. State St.
Dunn, Thomas, St. Philip's St., Neck
Duplan, Leon, Hair Dresser, 15 Market St.
Dupont, J. B., Widow, Boarding House, 67 Market St
Dupont, Joseph, Crockery, 90 Meeting St. & Queen St.
Duport, R., 38 Elliot St.
Duprat, Hannah, 37 Market St., F.P.C.
Dupre, Cornelius, 19 E. Bay St., Res. Boundary St.
Dupre, Cornelius, Factor, Res. Boundary St.,
    Cannonborough, Neck

77

Dupuy, Francis, 31 Guignard St.
Durban, A., Hat Store, 67 Queen St.
Duroeck, Emanuel, Grocery & Corn Store, King St , Neck
Durrse, Lorent, Accountant, 75 Boundary St
Duryea, Jacob, Boarding House, 51 State St.
Dutton, Martin F., Fruit Shop, 69 King St
Duval, Peter, Shop, Cannon St., Neck
Dwight, Eliza, Pastry Cook, 34 Meeting St., F.P.C.
Dwight, Rebecca, Pastry Cook, 143 Church St., F.P.C.
Dymoody, Henrietta, Widow, 28 Anson St.
Dyott, John, Druggist, King St., cr. Market St.
Eager, George, Bricklayer, Philadelphia St.
Eager, Robert, Merchant, 37 George St.
Eager, Sarah, Widow, William's Whf.
Eason, -----, Mrs., Boarding House, 162 E. Bay St.
Eason, Robert, Shipwright, Reaper's Al.
Easterby, George, Ship Master, 19 Pinckney St
Easton, Anthony, Carpenter, 12 Savage St., F.P.C.
Easton, Dorothy, Widow, 273 E Bay St , cr. Wentworth
   St.
Eckhard, George B , Attorney, 105 Church St., Res. 87
   Tradd St.
Eckhard, Jacob, Jr., Teacher of Music, 114 Wentworth St.
Eckhard, Jacob, Sr., Organist, 87 Tradd St.
Eckhard, John F., Organist, 87 Tradd St.
Eckhoff, George H., Grocer, 158 Meeting St., cr. 158
   Guignard St.
Eden, Jonah, Carpenter, 3 Wentworth St.
Edmondson, Charles, Factor, Edmonston's Whf., Res 75
   Church St.
Edwards, Edward H., Attorney, 4 St. Michael's Al., Res 4
   Meeting St.
Edwards, George, Planter, 14 Legare St.
Edwards, Hannah, Widow, 25 Friend St.
Edwards, Harry, John St., Mazyckborough, F.P C., Neck
Edwards, James F., Planter, 27 Wall St.
Edwards, Jane, Washer, 23 Wentworth St
Edwards, Robert B., Stock & Exchange Broker, 105½ E.
   Bay St., Res 61 Anson St.
Edwards, Thomas S., 25 Friend St.
Eggart, Jacob, Grocer, 41 St. Philip's St., cr. George St.
Egleston & Heriot, Attornies, 12½ St. Michael's Al.
Egleston, George W., Attorney, Office, St. Michael's Al.
Egleston, John, Grocer, Market St., cr. E. Bay St.
Ehney, Catharine, Widow, Magazine St.
Ehney, George, Carpenter, 61 King St.
Ehney, William, Tailor, 33 George St.
Elder, Cloe, 9 College St., F.P.C.
Elfe, Benjamin, Bricklayer, 14 Washington St.
Elfe, Benjamin, Nassau St., Hampstead, Neck
Elfe, John P., Accountant, 39 Wall St.
Elfe, Robert, Attorney, 76 Broad St.
Elfe, Thomas, Lumber Measurer, 39 Wall St.
Elfe, William, Factor, Chapel St., Mazyckborough, Neck
Elford, James M., Mathematical & Navigation School,
   Store, 119 E. Bay St.
Eliss, Myer J., Grocer, 211 King St.
Eliss, Thomas, Tailor, 13 Pinckney St.
Ellard, Michael, Carpenter, 199 George St.
Elliot, Aramintha, 16 Legare St.

Elliot, Benjamin, 20 Legare St.
Elliot, Benjamin, Register in Equity, Office, State House
Elliot, Charles P., Merchant, Res 4 New St
Elliot, Juliet Georgiana, Widow, Plantress, 33 George St.
Elliot, Stephen, President, Bank of the State of S C., 97
   Boundary St.
Elliot, Thomas O., Attorney, 7 St. Michael's Al., Res. 4
   New St
Elliot, Thomas, Planter, 2 Gibbes St.
Elliott, George, Alexander St., Wraggsborough, Neck
Ellis, Ann, Widow, 84 Anson St.
Ellis, David R., Carver, 84 Anson St.
Ellis, Moses J , Dry Goods Store, 304 King St
Ellis, Nancy, Seamstress, 10 Market St
Ellis, Thomas, Jr., Carver, 84 Anson St.
Ellison, Mary, 10 Ellery St.
Elms, Charles, King St. Road, Neck
Elsworth, John, Gauger, 13 Boundary St.
Elwig, Peter, 14 Smith St., F.P.C.
Emanuel, Isaac, Broker & Auctioneer, 304 King St.
Emanuel, Sylvia, 11 Clifford's Al., F.P C.
Emery, Jonathan, Capt., Unity Al.
Emily, Cate, Zigzag Al., F.P.C.
England, Alexander, Baker, 54 Tradd St.
England, John, Rt. Rev., 86 Wentworth St.
English, James, Ship Carpenter, 29 S. Bay St., Res. 9
   Price's Al.
Enslow, Joseph L., Cooper, Res 89 E. Bay St.
Enslow, Mary, Widow, 89 E Bay St.
Esnar, Jane, Fruiterer, 31 St. Philip's St., F.P C.
Esnare, Peter, Clerk, 38 King St.
Evans, Charles, Turner, Swinton's Ln
Evans, John, Custom House Officer, 78 Anson St.
Evans, Leacraft, Carpenter, 98 King St.
Evans, Susan, Miss, 58 Anson St.
Evans, Timothy, Shoe Store, 268 King St.
Evans, William, Watchmaker, 299 King St.
Eveleth & Thayer, Merchants, 8 Gillon St.
Eveleth, William, Shoe Store, 319 King St.
Everard, William, Dyer, 44 Society St
Everingham, John, 247 E. Bay St.
Everingham, Rebecca, 247 E Bay St
Evo, Louisa, Fruiterer, 34 Ellery St., F.P.C.
Eyland, James & Co., Fancy Store, 142 King St.
Faber, C. H., Widow, Charlotte St., Mazyckborough, Neck
Faber, Christian H., 296 King St.
Faber, Philip A., Dr., 102 Meeting St
Faber, -----, Shopkeeper, St. Philip's St., Neck
Fagan, Barney, Grocer, 221 E. Bay St.
Fair, John, Shoemaker & Baker, 401 King St , Neck
Fair, William, 110 Wentworth St., cr. Coming St.
Fairchild, Aaron, Clerk, Military Stores, 3 Pritchard's Whf.
Fairchild, Alexander, 6 Beaufain St
Fairchild, Lyon & Co., Saddlery Warehouse, 321 King St.
Fairfield, Rufus, Shoe Store, 204 King St.
Faith, John, Corn Mill, 54 State St.
Faree, Felicity, Widow, Columbus St., Neck
Farmer, H. T., Physician, cr. Hudson & King Sts., Neck
Farr, John E., Planter, Hampstead, Neck
Farrell, Darley, Grocer, 12 King St

Faulkner, William, Carpenter, 18 Cumberland St.
Faures, John A., Milliner, 24 Cumberland St.
Faust, J., Grocer, 228 E. Bay St., cr. Pinckney St.
Fayolle, Peter, Dancing Master, 80, Res 82 King St.
Fayssoux, J. H., Physician, John St., Neck
Fell, Thomas, Tin Plate Worker, Shop 114 Church St., Res. 101 Market St.
Fenwick, -----, Rev., 86 Wentworth St.
Fenwick, Susan, Seamstress, 9 Middle St., F.P.C.
Ferguson, Ann, Widow, Planter, 5 Liberty St.
Ferguson, James, Planter, 5 Liberty St.
Ferguson, John, 32 Broad St
Ferguson, John, Tailor, 12 Orange St.
Ferguson, Sarah, Amen St., F.P.C.
Ferret, John F., Fruit Shop, 121 Church St.
Ferret, Josephine, Baker, 24 George St.
Ferret, Maria L., Cake Baker, 31 George St.
Fiche, Peter, Gilder, 82 Queen St., 250 King St
Fick, Charles, Grocer, 57 St. Philip's St., cr. Boundary St.
Fife, James, Merchant, 75 E. Bay St., Res. 72 Church St.
Fife, Mary, Widow, 72 Church St.
Figures, Peter B., Widow, 2 Guignard St.
Fillette, Francis, Dry Goods & Crockery Stores, 148 King St. & Meeting St., cr. Queen St.
Findley, -----, Widow of James E B., 1 Legare St.
Finklea, Elizabeth, 13 Middle St.
Firmon, Anthony, Henrietta St., Neck
Fisk, Horace, Shoe Store, 78 Church St.
Fitzsimons, Charles, Grocer, 111 King St., Res. 44 Tradd St.
Fitzsimons, Christopher, Planter, 18 Hasell St.
Fitzsimons, Dolly, 39 Magazine St., F.P.C.
Flagg, Eliza, Widow, 30 Tradd St.
Flanagan, Thomas, King St., Neck
Flemming & Ross, Merchants, 148 E. Bay St., cr. Vendue Range
Flemming, J. S. & J., Dry Goods Store, 313 King St.
Flemming, James, Grocer, 176 King St., cr. Cumberland St.
Flemming, John H., Carpenter, 40 Wentworth St.
Flemming, R., Merchant & Wagon Yard, cr. King & Spring Sts., Neck
Flemming, Thomas, Merchant, 148 E. Bay St., Res. 18 George St.
Flinn, -----, Widow of Andrew, 4 S. Bay St.
Flint, -----, Mrs , 23 State St.
Floderer, John, Grocer, 69 Church St.
Florence, Levy, Merchant, 250 King St.
Florence, Zachariah, Dentist, 170 King St.
Florrin, Ann, Vanderhorst St., Neck
Flory, Joseph, Carpenter, 14 Laurens St.
Flud, Daniel, Planter, 2 Lamboll St., cr. King St.
Fogartie, Christiana, Miss, Teacher, 23 Wall St.
Fogartie, James, Teacher, 23 Wall St.
Folker, Rebecca, Widow, 2 Beaufain St
Folker, Thomas, Druggist, 106 Church St., cr Elliot St.
Follin, Augustus, Snuff Manufacturer, 152 Meeting St.
Follin, Firmin, Snuff Manufacturer, 166 Meeting St.
Foot, Peter D., 8 Anson St.
Footman, John W., Broker, 107 Boundary St

Forbes, John, Tin Plate Worker, 11 Tradd St.
Forbes, William, Tin Plate Worker, 305 King St
Ford & Dessassure, Attornies, 81 Broad St.
Ford, Jacob, Attorney, 81 Broad St.
Ford, Timothy, Attorney, 42 Meeting St.
Fordham, John G., Superintendent, Lucas & Norton's Mill, Res. Daniell's Whf.
Fordham, Richard, Blacksmith, 6 Gillon St.
Forester, Stephen, Confectioner, 171 King St.
Forrest, Charity, Widow, 6 Hasell St.
Forrest, Thomas H., Cooper, Chisolm's Whf., Res. 83 Tradd St.
Forshaw, William, Bricklayer, 48 Montague St.
Fortuna, Alla, Miss, 10 Clifford's Al.
Foster, Henry, Boarding House, 4 Elliot St.
Foster, Henry, Bookkeeper, Bank of the State, Res 2 Boundary St.
Foster, Jonathan, Teacher, 62 Broad St
Fourgeaud, Arnold, Baker, 36 Guignard St.
Fowler, Andrew, Rev., Teacher, 115 Queen St.
Fowler, Mary Porter, 49 Boundary St., F.P.C.
Fox, Patrick, Merchant, Res. 10 Pinckney St.
Fox, William, Merchant, N.W. cr. King & Spring Sts., Neck
Francis, John, Upholsterer, 99 King St., F.P.C
Francis, John V., Carpenter, 10 Smith's Ln., F.P.C
Francks, John, Grocer, Hudson St., Cannonborough, Neck
Fraser & Son, Carpenter & Boat Builders, Daniell's Whf.
Fraser, Charles, Attorney, 47 Tradd St., Res. 57 King St.
Fraser, Elizabeth, 53 King St.
Fraser, Frederick G., Planter, 99 Tradd St.
Fraser, John & Co., Factors, D'Oyley's Whf., Res 41 E. Bay St.
Fraser, John, Carpenter & Boat Builder, Daniell's Whf
Fraser, John, Factor, 4 E. Bay St.
Fraser, Susannah, 53 King St.
Fraser, T. L. S., Washington St., Mazyckborough, Neck
Fraser, William, Boat Builder, Daniell's Whf.
Frean, William, 49 State St.
Freeman, Henry, Mariner, French Al., F P.C.
Freeman, Luther, Grocer, 115 E. Bay St.
Frierson, John, Planter, Doughty St., Neck
Frobus, John, Bricklayer, 4 Wall St.
Frobus, Rebecca, Widow, 4 Wall St.
Fronty, Michael, Physician, 186 King St.
Frost, Elizabeth, Widow, 23 Archdale St.
Frost, Henry R., Physician, 36 Society St., Res 23 Archdale St.
Fry & Gregory, Hat Store, 296 King St.
Fuller, Benjamin, Planter, cr. Boundary & Coming Sts , Neck
Fuller, Oliver, Inspector, Fire & Marine Insurance Co , Res. 105 Meeting St.
Fulmer, John, Chair Maker, 41 Hasell St.
Furman & Hibbens, Attornies, 100 Church St
Furman, Josiah B., Factor, Chisolm's S. Whf., Res 100 Church St.
Furman, Richard, Jr , Physician, 100 Church St
Furman, Richard, Rev., D. D., 100 Church St.
Furr, Jacob, Thomas St., Neck

79

Futerrel, James, Teller, Bank of S. C , 121 Church St.
Gabeau, Anthony S., Ship Master, 285 King St
Gabeau, Anthony, Tailor, 285 King St.
Gabriel, P , Paper Hanger, 103 Meeting St.
Gadsden & Edwards, Attornies, 4 St. Michael's Al.
Gadsden & Holmes, Lumber Merchants, Gadsden's Whf.
Gadsden & Ogden, Attornies, 6 St. Michael's Al.
Gadsden, Chloe, Meeting St. Road, F.P.C., Neck
Gadsden, Christopher E., Rev., D. D., 214 Meeting St.
Gadsden, J. W., Widow, Plantress, 124 Queen St.
Gadsden, John, Attorney, St. Michael's Al., Res. 11
Meeting St.
Gaillard, Bartley, Thomas St., Neck
Gaillard, Daphne, Widow, 245 Meeting St., F.P.C., Neck
Gaillard, Mazyck & Sons, Factors, Chisolm's Whf.
Gaillard, Peter, Capt., 300 E. Bay St.
Gaillard, Samuel, Carpenter, 3 Wentworth St., F.P.C.
Gaillard, Theodore, Factor, Lynch St., cr. Montague St.
Gaillard, Theodore, Judge, 39 Society St.
Gaillard, -----, Widow of Peter, Boundary St.,
Cannonborough, Neck
Gallagher, Michael, Druggist, 45 Broad St., cr. Church St.
Gallagher, -----, Rev. D. D., 16 Magazine St.
Galliot, Claude M., Cigar Maker, 13 Elliot St.
Galloway, James, Porter House, 70 Queen St.
Gamage, Edward, Merchant, Res. 3 Friend St
Gandet, John, 52 Boundary St., Neck
Gandouin, Isidore, Hat Store, 111 E. Bay St.
Gantt, Thomas J., Attorney, 74 Broad St.
Garden, Alexander, Maj., 8 Short St.
Garden, John, Planter, Pinckney St., Cannonborough, Neck
Garden, Molly, Alexander St., Mazyckborough, F.P.C.,
Neck
Gardner, Henry, Blacksmith, 19 Amen St
Gardner, Jack, 15 Swinton's Ln., F.P.C.
Gardner, John & Son, Blacksmiths, cr. E. Bay & Market
Sts.
Gardner, John, Blacksmith, 207 E. Bay St., Res. 10 Society
St.
Gardner, Margaret, 49½ Meeting St.
Gardner, Sophia, Seamstress, 41 Society St., F.P.C.
Gardner, Susannah, Seamstress, 11 Anson St.
Gardner, Tenah, Washer, 13 Pinckney St., F.P.C.
Garesche, Paul, Commission Merchant, 170 E. Bay St.
Garner, Ann, Widow, 76 Wentworth St.
Gary, Eufemy, Meeting St. Road, F.P.C., Neck
Gates, Jane, Widow, King St. Road, Neck
Gates, -----, Teacher, 114 Queen St
Gates, Thomas & John, Butchers, cr. Cannon & Coming
Sts., Neck
Gates, Thomas, Rev., Charlotte St., Mazyckborough, Neck
Gaujan, Theodore, Planter of St. Domingo, Meeting St.,
Neck
Gauvin, Rose, 21 Friend St.
Geddes, G. W., cr. Mary & King Sts., Neck
Geddes, James, 263 Meeting St., Neck
Geddes, James, Attorney, 72 Broad St.
Geddes, John, Gen., 54 Broad St.
Geddes, John, Jr., Attorney, 72 Broad St.
Geddes, Sarah, Baker, 4 Linguard St., F P.C.

Geddes, -----, Widow of Robert, Plantress, St. Philip's St.,
Neck
Gefkin, Christiana, Widow, 21 Society St.
Gefkin, Henry C., Carpenter, 49 George St
Gell, John, Livery Stables, 127 Church St.
George, James, Shipwright, 256 E Bay St.
George, John, Grocer, 119 E. Bay St.
Gerard, -----, 115 Meeting St.
Gest, William, Radcliff St., Neck
Getty, Samuel, Grocer, 348 King St
Geyer, John, Capt., 16 Lynch's Ln.
Geyer, John S , Factor, Mey's Whf., Res. 16 Lynch's Ln
Ghnesh, Charles D., Watchmaker, 62 Broad St.
Ghnesh, Elizabeth D., Dry Goods Store, 62 Broad St.
Gibbon & Co., Commission Merchants, 124 E. Bay St.
Gibbs & Harper, Counting House, Gibbs & Harper's Whf.
Gibbs, Elizabeth, Seamstress, 67 Church St.
Gibbs, G. & J., Bakers, 44 Elliot St.
Gibbs, George, 4 State St.
Gibbs, Robert, Jr., Planter, John St., Wraggsborough,
Neck
Gibbs, Robert R., Planter, cr. Meeting & John Sts., Neck
Gibbs, William H., Master in Equity, 87 Meeting St., cr.
Queen St.
Gibson, Alexander, Merchant, 31 E. Bay St.
Gibson, Calaghan Thomas, Accountant, 10 Friend St.
Gibson, Falconer & Co., Merchants, Chisolm's Whf.
Gibson, James, Coach Maker, 228 Meeting St.
Gibson, Mary, Seamstress, Swinton's Ln.
Gibson, Robert, 10 Friend St
Gibson, William, Factor, Res. 22 Mazyck St.
Gibson, William H., Tanner, 228 Meeting St
Gidiere, John Joseph, Merchant, 358 King St.
Gidiere, John M., Merchant, 358 King St.
Gidiere, Margaret, Widow, Dry Goods Store, 358 King St.
Gidiere, Philip N , Merchant, 358 King St.
Gilberry, John C., Tailor, 36 Ellery St.
Gilbert, George B. & Co., Commission Merchants, 7
Vendue Range
Gilbert, Seth H., Accountant, 253 E. Bay St
Gilchrist, E. L., Mrs., 23 King St.
Gilchrist, James, Bank Officer, 18 Cumberland St
Gilchrist, Martha, Elizabeth St., Mazyckborough, F.P.C.,
Neck
Gilchrist, Robert C., Attorney, Res. 18 Cumberland St.
Giles, Othniel J., Clerk, Commission, Streets & Lamps, 52
Wentworth St.
Gilfert, Charles, Manager of the Theatre, 125 Broad St
Gilliland, William H., Merchant, 320 King St., cr. George
St.
Gillman, L. & Co., Shoe Store, 139 Meeting St., cr. Market
St.
Gillman, Sally M., Widow, Tailoress, 29 Mazyck St
Gillman, Zadock, Merchant, 139 Meeting St., Res. 15
Anson St.
Gillon, Alexander, Teller, State Bank, Res 3 Wall St
Gillon, P. Ann, Widow, 3 Wall St.
Gilman, Samuel, Rev., Pastor, 2d Independent Church,
Res. Pinckney St., Neck
Gissendanner, Susannah, Widow, 36 Beaufain St

Gitzenger, Benjamin, Printer, 6 Tradd St
Gitzenger, John R., Porter House, 6 Tradd St
Gladden, George, Butcher, Coming St , Neck
Gleize, Henry, Physician, 122 Meeting St
Glen, James S , Planter, 25 Legare St.
Glen, John S , Planter, 97 Tradd St
Glen, John, Teller, Planters' & Mechanics' Bank, Res. 108 Wentworth St.
Glen, Margaret, Widow, 97 Tradd St.
Glover, Henry C., Physician, 39 St. Philip's St
Glover, Joseph, Physician, Wentworth St., cr Rutledge St.
Glover, Lydia, Mrs., 72 Meeting St.
Glover, Wilson, 3 Meeting St
Godard, Rene, Merchant, 166 E Bay St , Res. 127 King St.
Godefroy, Louis, Painter & Glazier, 250 E Bay St
Godfrey, Sarah, Widow, 137 Queen St.
Godfried, John, Grocer, Anson St., cr. Laurens St
Going, Christiana, 8 Whim Court, F.P.C.
Goldsmith, Abraham, Clerk to the Synagogue, 36 Hasell St
Goldsmith, Frances, 156 Meeting St
Goldsmith, Henry, Deputy Register in Equity, 36 Hasell St.
Goldsmith, Isaac M , Vendue Crier, 36 Hasell St
Goldsmith, Morris, Deputy Marshal, Court House, Res. 37 Hasell St
Gonsels, Emanuel, Cigar Maker, 73½ State St.
Good, Francis, Grocer, cr. Wolf & Meeting Sts., Neck
Good, Sarah, Miss, 95 King St.
Goodman, Duke, Factor, 1 Champney St , cr Edmondston's Whf.
Goodman, Duke, Factor, Res. Hudson St , Neck
Gorden, James, Carpenter, 12 Logan St , F.P.C.
Gordon, Charles P , Clerk, Bank of Discount & Deposit, 27 King St.
Gordon, John, Bricklayer, 209 Meeting St
Gordon, Martha, Widow, 103 Market St.
Gordon, Samuel, Coach & Chair Maker, John St , Wraggsborough, F P C , Neck
Gordon, -----, Widow, 189 King St , cr Berresford St
Gordon, William E., Deputy Keeper, Work House, Magazine St.
Gorth, Peter, Warren St., Neck
Gosprey, Francis, 392 King St , Neck
Gough, Emma, Widow, 18 Meeting St.
Gould & Riley, Printers, 41 Broad St.
Gould, Sarah, Widow, 17 Coming St.
Gouldsmith, Richard, Cabinet Maker, 203 King St.
Gourdine, Samuel, Planter, 20 Pitt St., cr Bull St
Gouverneur, John, Dyer, 73 Meeting St
Gowen, Peter, Watch Maker, 73 Meeting St.
Gradick, C. C , Grocer, 82 Church St.
Gradick, Richard, Blacksmith, 18 King St , Res. Smith's Ln
Graeser, C. J , Notary Public, Crafts' Whf., Res. 38 Archdale St.
Graham, Charlotte, Coming St , F.P.C., Neck
Graham, Fanny, 7 Beaufain St
Graham, Michael, Grocer, cr Boundary & Meeting Sts., Neck

Graham, Prince, Drayman, 11 Coming St , F.P.C
Gramley, John, Importer of Hardware, Kunhardt's Whf., Res 20 Tradd St.
Grand, Lydia, 6 Guignard St.
Grant, John, Tailor, 32 State St.
Grant, -----, Widow of James, 9 Wall St
Graves, Anthony, 103 Meeting St
Graves, Anthony, Factor, Res. Mary St , Neck
Graves, Charles & Son, Factors, Chisolm's Whf , Res 103 Meeting St
Graves, Lucinda, Washer, 46 Guignard St., F.P C.
Graves, Massy, Widow, 2 Smith's Ln.
Graves, S. Colleton, 94 Broad St.
Gray, Alexander, Merchant, 363 King St , cr. Boundary St
Gray, H., Magistrate, 32 Ellery St.
Gray, James W , Attorney, 44 Meeting St
Gray, John, Boarding House, 7 Bedon's Al
Gray, Sarah W., Miss, Teacher, 27 Middle St.
Gray, Sylvanus, Merchant, Magwood's Whf , Res. 24 Broad St.
Gray, Yancy, Widow, 195 Meeting St.
Gready, Andrew P , Northern Warehouse, 207 King St
Green, Benjamin, Grocer, 19 Rutledge St
Green, Christopher R., Planter, 96 Tradd St.
Green, Thomas P., Druggist, 187 E. Bay St
Green, -----, Widow of Edmund, Boundary St , Neck
Greenhill, Hume, 1 Greenhill St
Greenland, Benjamin R , Physician, 47 Beaufain St.
Greenland, Elizabeth, Widow, 74 Tradd St.
Greenland, William P , Factor, 21 Meeting St
Greenwood, William, 54 Beaufain St.
Gregorie, Mary C , Widow, 67 Anson St
Gregson, Thomas, Assistant Clerk, State Bank, 28 Magazine St.
Greig & Calder, Bakers, Lodge Al.
Greig, Alexander, Baker, Lodge Al
Grenan, Alexander H., Grocer, 8 Archdale St.
Grille, -----, Mrs., Widow of Claude, Hat Store, 17 Broad St.
Grimball, P C , Planter, Vanderhorst St., Neck
Grimke, John, Physician, 4 Friend St.
Grimke, Thomas S., Attorney, 9 St Michael's Al.
Grimke, -----, Widow of John F., 299 E. Bay St.
Gripon, Delia, 7 Linguard St.
Groning, Lewis, Merchant, 69 E Bay St.
Groning, Simmons, 7 Magazine St., F.P.C
Gross, John, Cabinet Warehouse, 191 Meeting St.
Groves, Elizabeth, Boarding House, 42 State St
Groves, Lucretia, Mantua Maker, 14 Wentworth St
Gruber, Charles, Capt., Powder Receiver, 128 Wentworth St.
Gruber, George, Bricklayer, 53 George St
Gruber, Jacob, 392 King St , Neck
Gruber, Jacob, Bricklayer, 126 Wentworth St
Gue, John Francis, Tin Plate Worker, 18 Market St
Guellet, Helen, 1 Archdale St.
Guerineau, Louisa, 7 Liberty St.
Guerry, Grandison, Accountant, 1 West St
Guilbert, Eugene, Professor of Music, Wall St , cr. Laurens St

81

Gunther, Sophia D., Milliner, 15 Middle St.
Gurfin, Mary Ann, Boarding House, 13 Bedon's Al.
Guy, James, Tailor, 90 Boundary St., Neck
Guy, John, Bricklayer, 11 Minority St.
Guy, William, Saddler, 241 King St.
Habert, John, Carpenter, 26 Pinckney St.
Hagood, Elizabeth, 6 Magazine St.
Hahnbaum, George E., 1 Bull St.
Haig, David, Cooper, 204 Meeting St.
Haig, James, Attorney, 53½, Res. 204 Meeting St.
Haig, James, Shoemaker, 41 Anson St., F.P.C.
Haines, Mary Ann, 63 George St., F.P C.
Halbert, John, Carpenter, 26 Pinckney St.
Hale, George, Merchant, 296 King St.
Hall, Charlotte, Seamstress, 44 Guignard St., F.P.C.
Hall, D. W., Merchant, 18 Vendue Range
Hall, Eleanor, 2 Clifford's Al., F.P.C.
Hall, Harriet, Widow, Wentworth St.
Hall, James, Stone Cutter, 51 Coming St.
Hall, Mills & Co., Merchants, 18 Vendue Range
Hall, Sabina, Widow, 20 Queen St.
Hall, Susannah, Widow, 2 State House Sq.
Hall, William, Physician, 297 E. Bay St.
Halsall, Margaret, Read St., Neck
Halsall, William, Elizabeth St., Mazyckborough, Neck
Ham, J. R., cr. Wolf & Nassau Sts., Hampstead, Neck
Ham, T. & J. R., Auctioneers, Factors & Commission
 Merchants, 87½ E. Bay St.
Ham, Thomas, cr. Wolf & Nassau Sts., Hampstead, Neck
Hamilton & Pettigru, Attornies, 16 St. Michael's Al.
Hamilton, Alexander, Coach Trimmer, 190 Meeting St.
Hamilton, Clarinda, Nurse, 155 Meeting St., F P C.
Hamilton, Euphame, Widow, Teacher, Seminary, 78
 Queen St.
Hamilton, James, Jr., Intendant, Coming St., cr. Bull St.
Hamilton, John, Ship Carpenter, 17 Anson St.
Hammell, Mary, Widow, Nurse, 16 Wall St.
Hammersley, David, Shoemaker, 314 King St.
Hammett, Benjamin, Merchant, King St. Road, Neck
Hance, Phoebe, 110 King St.
Hanckel, Christian, Rev., Pastor, St. Paul's Church, Res.
 Doughty St., cr. Pinckney St., Neck
Hancock, George, Warren St., Neck
Hancock, James, Clerk, 12 Clifford St.
Handy, Sarah, 43 State St.
Happoldt, Christian, Butcher, Bridge St , near the Lines,
 Neck
Happoldt, Christopher, Butcher, Cannon St., Neck
Harber, John R., Grocer, 107 King St.
Harby, Isaac, Teacher, 86 Tradd St.
Hard, Benjamin F , Livery Stables, 50 & 56 Society St.
Harden, William, Boarding House, 4 Chalmers Al.
Hardy, Betsey, Miss, 49 E. Bay St.
Hardy, John, Mariner, 21 Philadelphia St.
Hare, Frances, Widow, 21 State St.
Harkwood, Paul, Bricklayer, 29 Beaufain St.
Harleston, Alexander, Drayman, 37 Wentworth St., F.P.C.
Harleston, Edward, Planter, 91 Boundary St.
Harleston, Nicholas, Planter, Alexander St.,
 Mazyckborough, Neck

Harleston, -----, Widow of William, 110 Broad St.
Harper, James, Baker, 70 King St., cr. Tradd St., Res. 48
 State St.
Harper, Rose, Washer, Zigzag Al., F P.C
Harris, Hyam, Merchant, 216 King St.
Harris, Jacob, Jr., Clothing Store, 203 E. Bay St
Harris, Rebecca, Widow, 122 King St.
Harrison, D. W., Bookseller, 29 Broad St.
Harrison, Francis, Grocer, 17 Champney St., Res. 48
 Wentworth St.
Harry, Susannah F., Widow, cr. Bridge & Thomas Sts.,
 Neck
Hart, Napthalia H., China & Glass Store, 156 King St.
Hart, Nathan, Hardware Merchant, 206 King St., cr.
 Market St.
Hart, S. M., Merchant, 369 King St., Neck
Harth, William, Lumber Merchant, 1 Gibbes St.
Hartman, Justus, Grocer, 12 Beaufain St.
Harvey, Edward T., Grocer, 81 Wentworth St.
Harvey, Samuel, Ship Master, 11 Anson St.
Harvey, -----, Widow, 30 Society St.
Hase, Jacob, King St. Road, Neck
Hasell, Adam, St. Philip's St., F.P.C., Neck
Hashagen, B., Grocer, 4 Bull St.
Haskell, Elnathan, Maj., Planter, 303 E. Bay St.
Haslett, John, President, F M. & L. I. O., Res 7 Longitude
 Ln.
Hassan, Moses & David, Shoemakers, 42 Beaufain St.
Hatch, Mary M., Widow, Boarding House, 27 Pinckney St.
Hatch, Prince H., Boat Builder, 1 Ellery St.
Hatch, -----, Widow of James R., 27 Pinckney St.
Hatfield, John, Grocer, 1 Coming St., cr. Beaufain St
Hattier & Rame, Confectioners, 309 King St.
Hattier, William, Confectioner, 217 King St.
Hauck, John, Grocer, 23 Market St., cr State St.
Haven, C. C., Merchant, 3 Crafts' S. Whf., Res. 8 New St.
Hawes, Thomas, Ship Carpenter, 11 S. Bay St., F.P.C.
Hayden, Jane, Widow, cr. Blake & Drake Sts., Neck
Hayford, Ann, Mrs., Milliner, King St. Road, Neck
Hayley, John, Henrietta St., Neck
Hayne, Robert Y., Attorney, 117½ Church, Res. 8 New St.
Hayne, William, Accountant, 20 George St.
Hayward, China, 5 Clifford's Al., F.P.C.
Hayward, Richard, Grocer, 6 Chalmers Al.
Hazlehurst, George A., Factor, 55 E. Bay St.
Hazlehurst, Robert, Merchant, 55 E. Bay St., Res. 10
 Meeting St.
Heath, Nancy, Mrs., 6 Wentworth St
Hedderly, William, Bell Hanger, 117 Meeting St., Res. 147
 Queen St.
Heery, Thomas, Grocer, 1 Market St.
Helfred, John, Grocer, 14 Tradd St.
Helfred, John, Jr., Grocer, 14 Tradd St
Hendericks, Frederick, 88 Boundary St., Neck
Henderson, Robert, Corn Store, 63 Tradd St.
Henricks, John, Grocer, 22 Market St.
Henry, Alexander, Carpenter, 77 Anson St.
Henry, Alexander, Cashier, Bank of State of S. C., 136
 Wentworth St
Henry, Amelia, Midwife, 130 Meeting St

Henry, Charles, Carpenter, Vanderhorst St , Neck
Henry, Julian, Cabinet Maker, 130 Meeting St.
Henson, Thomas, Carpenter, 91 Berresford St.
Henwood, Samuel, Merchant, 8 Water St.
Heriot, Benjamin D., Merchant, 72 E. Bay St., Res. 28 S. Bay St.
Heriot, Roger, Merchant, 55 E. Bay St.
Herron, Charles, Tailor, 44 Pinckney St
Herron, -----, Widow of John, 40 Pinckney St.
Hertz, Alexander, King St. Road, Neck
Hertz, H. M., Merchant, King St. Road, Neck
Hertz, Jacob, Dry Goods Store, 36 King St.
Hevey, James, Grocer, 274 King St.
Heynes, James, 52 Church St.
Heyward, Charlotte, Widow, Plantress, 4 Hasell St.
Heyward, Hannah, Mrs., 21 Legare St.
Heyward, Nathaniel, Planter, 275 E. Bay St., cr. Society St.
Heyward, Susan, Widow, 30 S Bay St
Hicks, -----, Carpenter, 177 Church St.
Higham & Fife, Merchants, 75 E. Bay St.
Higham, Thomas, Merchant, 75 E. Bay St.
Hill, Francis C., Painter, 1 Clifford St.
Hill, Mary, 88 King St.
Hill, Paul, Painter, 1 Clifford St.
Hillegas, Sarah, Widow, School Mistress, 133 Meeting St.
Hilliard, Nathaniel, Ship Master, Res. 3 Laurens St.
Hillman, Ann, Widow, Boarding House, E. Bay St.
Hills, William E., Shoe Store, 151 Church St., cr. Queen St.
Hilson, John, Grocer, Henrietta St., Neck
Hinson, Thomas, Carpenter, 9 Berresford St.
Hippias, Phoebe, Widow, 5 Tradd St.
Hitchcock, Leonard, Tin Plate Worker, 71 Market St.
Hodgson, -----, Mrs., Boarding House, 32 Elliot St., cr. Gadsden's Al.
Hoff, John, Bookseller, 10 Broad St.
Hoff, John M., Clerk, Market, 10 Berresford St
Hoff, Philip, Bookseller, 10 Broad St
Hoffman, George, Grocer, 117 Church St.
Hogart, William, Vanderhorst St., Neck
Hogarth, Mary, Widow, 16 Wall St.
Holbrook, John M., Merchant, King St., cr. Broad St
Holbrook, Moses, Physician, 7 Broad St.
Holland, James, Sail Maker, 3 Wentworth St.
Holland, John, Carpenter, Coming St., Neck
Holland, John, Mrs., Boarding House, 28 Tradd St.
Hollowell, Thomas, 46 Church St.
Holmes, Charles, Butcher, Hampstead, Neck
Holmes, Charles R., Surveyor, 14 Water St., Res. 9 E. Bay St.
Holmes, Eleanor, 2 Clifford's Al., F.P.C.
Holmes, Harriet, Widow, 8 Lynch's Ln.
Holmes, I. E., Attorney, 3 St. Michael's Al., Res. 9 E. Bay St.
Holmes, J. B., Merchant, Napier's New Range, Res. 175 Meeting St.
Holmes, John B., 9 E Bay St.
Holmes, John, Bricklayer, 6 Whim Court
Holmes, John, Planter, 117 Tradd St., cr Greenhill St.
Holmes, Mary Ann, 21 Middle St.

Holmes, Sandiford, Merchant, 151 King St.
Holmes, William, Physician, 14 Water St., Res 9 E. Bay St.
Holton, Elizabeth, Widow, Nurse, 15 Cumberland St
Honour, John, 15 Beaufain St.
Hood, Thomas, Grocer, 168 Meeting St., cr Pinckney St
Horden, Eliza, Grocer, 7 Middle St.
Horlbeck, Henry, Bricklayer, 23 Cumberland St.
Horlbeck, John, 241 Meeting St., cr. Boundary St.
Horry, Elias, Meeting St., cr. Tradd St.
Horry, Harriet, Widow, 111 Tradd St.
Horry, Lynch E., Planter, 124 Broad St
Horsey, Thomas J., Merchant, 363 King St.
Hort, B. S., Millwright, Hudson St., Cannonborough, Neck
Horwood, Mary, Nurse, 13 Zigzag Ln.
Hosier, James H., Brewer, 49 Queen St
Houston, James, Carpenter, 20 Wall St.
Hovar, Connrad, Grocer, Gadsden's Whf.
Howard, Alexander, City Assessor, 236 Meeting St.
Howard, Elizabeth, Widow, Seamstress, 5 Maiden Ln.
Howard, Richard F., Cooper, Washington St., Mazyckborough, Neck
Howard, Robert F., Cooper, Chisolm's Upper Whf.
Howard, Robert, Proprietor, Southern Patriot, 99 E Bay St., 97 Meeting St., cr. George St.
Howe, John W., Grocer, 73 Tradd St.
Howe, Mary, Widow, 16 S. Bay St.
Howe, S., 139 Meeting St.
Howie, William, Merchant, King St. Road, Neck
Howland, Benjamin J., Merchant, 263 King St., Res. 58 Beaufain St.
Howley, William, Grocer, 2 Elliot St
Howren, James, Capt., Shop, 387 King St., Neck
Hoyt, Eli T. & Co., Hat Store, 315 King St.
Huard, Stanislas, Druggist, 49 Broad St.
Hubbell, S., Capt., E. End Boundary St., Neck
Hubert, John, Carpenter, Pinckney St.
Huff, Abigail, Miss, 7 Price's Al.
Huger, Benjamin T., Tailor, 192 King St., F.P.C.
Huger, Charlotte, Miss, 27 St. Philip's St
Huger, Daniel, Broker & Vendue Master, 4 State St., Res. 67 Coming St.
Huger, Daniel E., Judge, 28 Meeting St.
Huger, -----, Misses, Radcliff St., Radcliffborough, Neck
Huger, Rosanna, Seamstress, 42 Coming St.
Huger, -----, Widow of John, Broad St.
Hughes, Edward, Teacher, 88 Tradd St., cr Orange St.
Hughes, Mary, Widow, 5 Wentworth St.
Hughes, -----, Widow of Bulow, 5 Lamboll St.
Hull, Latham, Dry Goods Merchant, 48 & 54 Broad St
Hull, William, Merchant, 54 Broad St.
Humburt, John, Carpenter, 142 Wentworth St.
Hume, John, Planter, 17 Wentworth St., cr. Rutledge St.
Humphreys, Richard W., Capt., 101 E. Bay St.
Humphries, Joseph, Tailor, 93 Queen St., F.P.C.
Hunt, Benjamin F., Attorney, 1 State House Sq.
Hunt, Joseph, Ship Master, King St. Road, Neck
Hunt, Solomon, 15 Clifford's Al
Hunt, Thomas, Register in Equity, 70 Broad St., Res. 211 Meeting St.

83

Hunter, John, 277 King St.
Hunter, Thomas, Blacksmith, Radcliff St., Res. Warren St., Neck
Huntington, Mary, Widow, 26 E. Bay St
Huntscomb, Thomas, Planter, 113 Tradd St.
Hurd, Sarah, Widow, 43 State St.
Hurlburt, M. L., Teacher, College, Res. 14 Society St.
Hurst, Charles, Custom House Officer, 12 Blackbird Al.
Husser, William, Pinckney St., Neck
Hussey, Bryant, Pilot, 9 Stoll's Al
Hutchins, Nancy, Mrs., 9 Wentworth St.
Hutchins, Shubael, Merchant, 142, Res 37 E. Bay St.
Hutchinson, Ann, Widow, 8 Champney St.
Hutchinson, Charlotte, 9 Friend St
Hutchinson, Elizabeth L., 8 Society St.
Hutchinson, Judah, 1 Whim Court, F P.C.
Hutchinson, Leger, Mrs., 251 E. Bay St.
Hutchinson, Mary, 25 George St., F P.C.
Hutchinson, Mary, 9 Friend St.
Hyams, Henry, Dry Goods Store, 199 King St.
Hyams, Isaac, Clothing Store, 215 King St.
Hyams, Samuel, Keeper of Jail, Magazine St.
Hyams, Solomon, Merchant, 104 King St.
Hyde, David, Grocer, Meeting St Road, Neck
Inglesby & Browne, Tailors, 78 Meeting St.
Inglesby, H. William, Attorney, Office, St. Michael's Al., Res. 43 Tradd St.
Inglesby, Henry, Merchant Tailor, 76 Meeting St.
Inglesby, John, Clerk, Lynch's Ln., cr. Church St.
Inglesby, Maria, Widow, Lynch's Ln., cr Church St
Inglesby, William, 43 Tradd St.
Inglis, Thomas, Hair Dresser, 75 Meeting St., F.P.C.
Ingraham, Henry, Factor, D'Oyley's Whf., Smith St., cr. Wentworth St.
Ingraham, -----, Widow of Nathaniel, 7 Church St.
Ireland, Benjamin, Mrs., Grocer, 24 Bull St
Irvin, Moses, Shoemaker, 11 Logan St., F.P.C.
Irvine, Matthew, Physician, 57 Tradd St.
Isaman, Peter, Grocer, cr. Coming & Boundary Sts., Neck
Ives, Jeremiah, Capt., Washington St., Mazyckborough, Neck
Ives, Sophia, Teacher, 25 Archdale St., F.P.C
Izard, Elizabeth, Widow, 90 Broad St.
Izard, Henry, 3 Meeting St.
Jacks, James, Merchant, 38 Broad St.
Jacks, James, Merchant, Res. Chapel St., Wraggsborough, Neck
Jackson, Edmund & Co., Soap & Candle Manufactory, St Philip's St., Neck
Jackson, Fanny, Seamstress, 2 Berresford St., F P.C.
Jackson, Moses, Barber, 9 Elliott St., F.P.C.
Jackson, Patty, 5 Motte's Ln., F.P.C.
Jackson, Rachel, 5 Magazine St., F P.C.
Jackson, Robert, Grocer, 22 Coming St.
Jacobs, Cecilia, Dry Goods Store, 15 Queen St
Jacoby, George, Grocer, 83 Church St
Jahan, Joseph, Architect, 247 Meeting St., Neck
Jameison, John, Blacksmith, 18 Meeting St.
James, Catharine, Widow, 15 Guignard St.
James, Henry, Tailor, 328 King St., F.P C.

James, Robert, Slop Shop, 272 King St.
Jandrel, Rebecca, Widow, 243 E. Bay St
Jaques, Mary, Widow, 33 Wall St.
Javain, Peter, Grocer, 187 King St.
Jay, William, Architect, 59 Church St
Jeannerett, Christopher, Teacher, 21 Bull St.
Jeffords, John, Grocer, 11 Middle St.
Jencks, F. A., Blacksmith, 190 Meeting St.
Jenkins, Benjamin, Planter, Pinckney St., Cannonborough, Neck
Jenkins, Elias, Bricklayer, 6 Liberty St
Jenkins, Joseph, Capt., Planter, 9 Smith's Ln
Jenkins, Joseph, Jr., Carpenter, 33 Montauge St.
Jenkins, Micah, Planter, 11 Legare St
Jenkins, Richard, Mariner, 25 Archdale St., F.P.C
Jennings, William, 12 Wentworth St
Jequel, Elizabeth, Widow, Grocer, 69 State St.
Jervey, James, Clerk, Federal Court, State House, Res 1 Laurens St.
Jervey, Thomas, Capt , Surveyor & Inspector of Customs, Res. 51 Church St.
Johnson & Fordham, Blacksmiths, 4 Gillon St
Johnson & Maynard, Druggists, 1 Broad St.
Johnson, Alexander, Mariner, 12 Bedon's Al
Johnson, Allan, Mariner, 39 State St., F.P.C.
Johnson, Andrew, Grocer, 20 Meeting St.
Johnson, Ann, Widow, Grocer, 55 State St.
Johnson, Benjamin, Grocer, 14 Market St
Johnson, Bennett, Grocer, 22 Bull St.
Johnson, Betsey, 6 Linguard St , F P.C
Johnson, Clarissa, 22 Wentworth St., F.P.C
Johnson, D. W., 154 Meeting St
Johnson, Edward, Chairmaker, 176 Church St.
Johnson, Eleanor, Milliner, 323 King St
Johnson, Eleanor, Widow, 101 Queen St.
Johnson, Elizabeth, Widow, Dry Goods Store, 91 King St.
Johnson, Emily, 4 Whim Court, F.P.C.
Johnson, Isaac A , Physician, cr. St. Philip's & Warren Sts., Neck
Johnson, Jabez W., Watch & Clock Maker, 323 King St
Johnson, James, Blacksmith, 4 Washington St.
Johnson, James S., Attorney, 30 Queen St., Res 4 Anson St.
Johnson, James, Soap Chandler, Chapel St , Wraggsborough, Neck
Johnson, Jane, Mrs., Hardware Store, 344 King St.
Johnson, John & John Owen, Commission Merchant, Fitzsimons' Whf
Johnson, John, Barber, King St. Road, Neck
Johnson, John, Blacksmith & Founder, Washington St , Neck
Johnson, John, Grocer, 38 Mazyck St
Johnson, Joseph, Physician, 49 Church St.
Johnson, Nancy, Washer, 77 Boundary St., F.P.C.
Johnson, Neils, Grocer, 36 Tradd St
Johnson, Peter, Printer, 13 Amen St.
Johnson, Sarah, Mantua Maker, 75 Wentworth St , F.P.C
Johnson, Sarah, Widow, 4 Anson St., cr. Guignard St.
Johnson, Thomas, Shoemaker, Meeting St. Road, Neck
Johnson, William, Judge, U. S Supreme Court , E. Side

Pinckney St., Cannonborough, Neck
Johnson, William, Planter, Pinckney St , Cannonborough, Neck
Johnston, Thomas, Merchant & Wagon Yard, King St. Road, Neck
Jones, Abraham, Cabinet Maker, 13 Beaufain St.
Jones, Cuba, Carpenter, 14 Smith's Ln , F.P.C
Jones, Edward, Dr , 37 St Philip's St , Neck
Jones, Edward, Dr , Seminary, Warren St , Neck
Jones, Elias, Charlotte St , Mazyckborough, Neck
Jones, Emanuel, Painter, 124 Tradd St.
Jones, Evan D., Debenture Clerk, Custom House, Res 27 State St., cr Queen St.
Jones, Henry, Ship Carpenter, 37 Pinckney St
Jones, Jehu, Jr., Tailor, 61 Broad, F.P.C
Jones, Jehu, Sr., Boarding House, 67 Broad, F.P C.
Jones, Jenny, Jones' Lot, King St., F.P.C
Jones, John C., 112 Wentworth St , cr Coming St.
Jones, John Henry, Merchant, 45 E. Bay St , Res 101 Broad St.
Jones, John S., Wire Worker, 92 Church St.
Jones, Lewis, 2 Longitude Ln., F P C
Jones, P , Mrs., 23 King St.
Jones, Peter, Tailor, 97 King St., F P C.
Jones, Sally, 6 Lynch's Ln., F.P.C.
Jones, Sarah, Seamstress, Henrietta St., Mazykborough, F.P.C., Neck
Jones, Thomas, President, Bank of S C., 3 Anson St., cr Guignard St.
Jones, -----, Widow, 1 Guignard St.
Jones, -----, Widow of Abner, Grocer, 83 King St
Jones, William, Carpenter, 57 King St.
Jones, Wiswald, Merchant, 34 E. Bay St., Res. 80 Meeting St.
Jordon, Christopher, Coach Trimmer & Painter, Res. 2 Ellery St
Joseph, -----, Fruiterer, 43 State St
Joseph, Joseph, Merchant, 332 King St
Joseph, Moses, Grocer, 24 Beaufain St.
Joyner, George, Meeting St. Road, Neck
Just, George, Wharf Builder, 12 Washington St.
Kahnle, Harman John, Wood Measurer, 85 Boundary St.
Kain, James, Rigger, 4 Smith's Ln., F.P.C.
Kain, Paul, 11 E. Bay St , F P C.
Kane, Francis, Clerk, 9 State St.
Kanuff, Mary, Widow, Meeting St Road, Neck
Keckley, George, Merchant, King St Road, Neck
Keckley, John, Cabinet Maker, 42 Meeting St.
Keenan, George, Merchant, near the Lines, King St Road, Neck
Keils, Christian, 392 King St., Neck
Keith & Miller, Merchants, Lothrop's Whf.
Keith, Carey M., Teacher, 190 King St.
Keith, Hannah, Widow, 12 Lowndes St., Neck
Keith, Rebecca, 8 Linguard St., F.P C
Keith, Sylvanus, Boarding House, King St., cr Wentworth St.
Keith, -----, Widow of Isaac S., 15 Meeting St , cr. Smith's Ln.
Kellin, Charles, Grocer, Boundary St , Mazyckborough,

Neck
Kellner, John, 56 Boundary St , Neck
Kelly, Bernard R , Shoemaker, French Al.
Kelly, Fanny, Gardener, St Philip's St., F P C , Neck
Kelly John A., Millinery Store, 251 King St.
Kelly, Joseph, Grain Store, Chisolm's Upper Whf , Res 57 Boundary St.
Kelly, Marcus Neilson, Physician, 20 King St
Kelly, Mary, Widow, 151 King St.
Kelly, Michael, Ironmonger, 353 King St.
Kelser, Robert, Butcher, King St. Road, Neck
Kenedy, James, Capt , 54 Society St
Kenedy, James, Gauger, 28 Cumberland St
Kennedy, Edward, Custom House Officer, 18 Mazyck St
Kennedy, Francis, Coachmaker, 10 Clifford St
Kennedy, James, Capt , Planter, 27 Mazyck St.
Kennedy, James, Grocer, 117 Queen St.
Kennedy, James P , Broker, 9 State St.
Kennedy, Jane, Seamstress, 18 Chalmers St.
Kennedy, John, Carpenter, Jones' Lot, King St.
Kennedy, John, Grocer, 198 Meeting St
Kennedy, Lionel H., Attorney, 7 St Michael's Al.
Kennedy, Peter, Grocer, 95 Tradd St.
Kennedy, William, Glove Maker, 31 King St
Ker, John, 55 King St
Ker, John C , Merchant, 162 King St
Ker, Joseph, Merchant, Chisolm's Whf.
Ker, Maria, Miss, Teacher, 55 King St.
Kershaw & Lewis, Factors, 56 E. Bay St
Kershaw, Charles, Factor, 56 E. Bay St , Res. 30 Meeting St.
Kershaw, Newman, Factor, 5 Crafts' S Whf , Res 15 Church St.
Kiddell, Arthur, Clerk, 210 Meeting St.
Kiddell, Charles, Merchant, 35 Broad St.
Killam & Hills, Clothing Store, 50 Broad St.
Kimbal, Daniel, Commission Merchant, 116, Res. 56 E. Bay St.
Kimbal, Daniel, Mariner, 22 Guignard St.
Kimberly & Moody, Hat Store, 240 King St , cr Hasell St
Kinder, John G., Shoemaker, 141 Church St.
King & Jones, Merchants, 134 E Bay St.
King, -----, Alexander St , Mazyckborough, Neck
King, Benjamin, Carpenter, Warren St , Radcliffborough, Neck
King, Elizabeth, Mrs , Umbrella Maker, 86 Meeting St.
King, John, 27 Wentworth St.
King, John, Jr., Commission Merchant, 144 E Bay St
King, John, Merchant, 138 Church St.
King, Joseph, Mariner, 13 Chalmers Al.
King, Joseph R., Baker, 35 Wall St.
King, Katy, 4 Whim Court, F P C
King, Mary, Miss, 33 Anson St
King, Mary, Mrs , Grocer, 45 King St.
King, Mitchell, Attorney, 66 Meeting St., St. Michael's Al
Kingdom, Henry, Millwright, 34 Coming St
Kingman, Eliab, Sr., Orphan House., Neck
Kingman, Hannah, 139 Church St.
Kingman, John, School Master, 53 Coming St
Kinloch, George, Grocer, 65 Market St

85

Kint, Nicholas, 10 Smith's Ln
Kippenberg, Andrew, Grocer, 75 Queen St.
Kirk, Alexander, Druggist, 173 King St
Kirk, John, at the Union Bank
Kirk, John D , Grocer, 115 Broad St
Kirkland, William, Physician, 118 Church St
Kirkpatrick, John, Merchant, 4 Meeting St.
Kirkpatrick, Maria, 9 West St , F P C
Kitchburn, Joel, Dry Goods Store, 325 King St.
Kittleband, David, Carpenter, 6 Logan St
Knappo, Joseph, Shoemaker, 194 Meeting St
Knauff, Conrad, Saddler, King St Road, Neck
Knieth, John, Grocer, 28 State St.
Knight Nancy, Washer, 1 Magazine St., F P C.
Knox, John F., Pritchard & Knox's Whf
Knox, Walter, House Carpenter, 12 Green St
Knust, -----, Widow of Henry, Grocer, 119 Broad St., cr Logan St
Kohler, -----, Widow of Frederick, John St., Neck
Kohne, Frederick, 120 Broad St.
Kugley, -----, Widow of John, 34 Mazyck St
Kunhardt, William, Factor, Kunhardt's Whf., Res 34 George St
Kyall, Peter, 71 Anson St.
Laats, James, Apothecary, 15 Archdale St.
Labarben, A , Teacher, 90 King St.
Labatore, John, Fruiterer, 226 E Bay St , F.P.C.
Labatt, Catharine, Widow, Shopkeeper, 172 Church St
Labattue, Z., 261 Meeting St., Neck
Labaussay, Pierre, Baker & Grocer, King St Road, Neck
Laborde, Harriet, Fruiterer, 102 King St , F.P C.
Lacompte, John, Druggist, 137 E Bay St
Lacoste, Charles, Merchant, 149 King St.
Ladaveze, Victor, Merchant, 185 King St
Ladson, James H , Factor, Crafts' S Whf., Res Church St.
Lafar, Catharine, Widow, 58 Queen St
Lafar, David B , Cooper, Magwood's Whf., Res. 58 Queen St
Lafar, John J , City Marshall, 58 Queen St
Laffiteau, Stanislas, Clerk, 24 Mazyck St
Lafon, Francis, Mariner, 5 Whim Court, F.P.C.
Lafon, John, Cooper, 190 E Bay St., cr Fitzsimons' Whf.
Lamb & Robertson, Merchants, 51 E. Bay St
Lamb, David, Merchant, 4 King St
Lamb, James, Merchant, 51 E. Bay St , Res. 61 Tradd St.
Lambard, Allen, Merchant, 128 E Bay St., Res. 26 Broad St.
Lambert, Eleanor, Boarding House, Unity Al
Lance, Francis, Planter, 23 Friend St
Lance, J G., Physician, 59 State St , Res. 108 Queen St
Lance, Sarah, Widow, 108 Queen St
Lance, William, Attorney, 108 Queen St., 22 St. Michael's Al
Landey, Elizabeth, Widow, Seamstress, 33 Wentworth St
Landreth, D & C , Seed Store, 228 King St
Lang, Jacob H., Hardware Merchant, 78 E Bay St., Res 1 Church St
Langford, Ann R , Widow, 4 Liberty St.
Langley, Susan, Seamstress, 14 Philadelphia St
Langley, William, 57 Queen St

Langlois, Maria, Widow, Teacher, 28 King St
Langton, John, Broker & Notary Public, 10 State St , Res 76 King St
Lankester, Jacob, Grocer, 113 E Bay St
Lanneau, Bazile, 1 Pitt St
Lanneau, Peter, Capt., 33 Elliott St
Lapenne, John A , Merchant, King St Road, Neck
Lapenne, Joseph J , Merchant, King St. Road, Neck
Lapotte, Rene, Dancing Master, 6 St Philip's St
Laroache, Elizabeth, Widow, 24 Beaufain St.
Laroache, John, Clerk, 24 Beaufain St
Larousseliere, Francis, Merchant, 29 St. Philip's St
Larousseliere, Louis, Druggist, 180 King St.
Latham, Daniel, Distiller, 1 Hasell St
Lauraine, Edward, Teacher, 42 King St
Laurens, Henry, Planter, 290 E. Bay St
Laurens, Peter, Wine Merchant, 3 Lothrop's Whf., 42 St Philip's St , cr George St.
Laval, Jacint, Jr , Factor, William's Whf , Res. 2 Pinckney St
Laval, William, Factor, Williams' Whf , Res. 10 Anson St
Lawton & Reilly, Grocers, 3 Vendue Range
Lawton, Charles, Merchants Whf , Res. Carolina Coffee House
Lawton, J. & C , Merchants, Kunhardt's Whf , Res. E. Bay St , cr Amen St
Lawton, Mary, Widow, 3 Lamboll St
Lawton, Roger B , Grocer, 3 Vendue Range, Res 187 E Bay St
Lawton, S. H , Teacher, 37 Meeting St.
Lazarus, C & R., Millinery Store, 273 & 282 King St
Lazarus, Jacob, Merchant, Chisolm's Whf , Res 156 King St.
Lazarus, Mark, 93 Tradd St
Lazarus, Michael, Merchant, 7 Champney St , Res. 103 Broad St
Leary & Thomas, Tanners & Curriers, cr King & Warren Sts , Neck
Leary, Charles, cr. King & Warren Sts , Neck
Leaumonte, Margaret, Widow, Middle St , cr Minority St
Lebby, William, Ship Carpenter, 14 Amen St
Lebreton, John, Mrs , 108 Meeting St.
Lecair, -----, Widow of Pebarte V., 71 Tradd St.
Lecat, Francis, Professor of Music, 7 Ellery St
Lechais, Ann, Widow, cr St. Philip's & Vanderhorst Sts., Neck
Lechmere, Maria, 3 Church St
Lee, Dorothea, Widow, 75 Broad St
Lee, John, Tailor, 87 Broad St , F.P.C
Lee, Joseph, 49 Beaufain St.
Lee, Sarah, Midwife, 43 Society St
Lee, Thomas, 22 Pitt St
Lee, William F , Physician, 22 Pitt St
Lee, William P , Pilot, 1 Longitude Ln
Lee, William, Ship Carpenter & Grocer, 269 E Bay St
Lee, William, Tailor, 5 Laurens St., Res Jones' Lot, King St., F.P.C
Lee, William, Teller, Bank State of S C , 46 Coming St
Leech, Catharine, Widow, 28 Society St.
Leefe, -----, Widow of Benjamin, 5 Greenhill St.

86

Legare & Gibbs, Attornies, 83 Meeting St.
Legare, Ann H , Cumberland St , F P C
Legare, Francis Y , Planter, 26 S Bay St
Legare, Hugh, Planter, 32 Bull St
Legare, Isaac, Mrs , Plantress, 15 Wentworth St
Legare, J Berwick, Attorney, 83 Meeting St , Res 1 Guignard St
Legare, James, Planter, 7 New St.
Legare, S & Co., Factors, Chisolm's Whf , Res. 1 S. Bay St
Legare, Solomon, Factor, Res 12 Friend St.
Legare, Thomas, Jr., Physician, 89 Boundary St.
Legare, Thomas, Planter, 1 S Bay St
Lege, John M , Dancing Master, 62 Queen St
Leger, Elizabeth, Widow, 8 Society St
Legge, Ann, Widow, 4 Wentworth St.
Lehre, Ann, Widow, Plantress, 96 Tradd St
Lehre, Thomas, Col., Planter, 54 King St
Leitch, Duncan, Grocer, 232 Tradd St.
Leitch, Henry, Cooper, King St. Road, Neck
Leland, Joseph & Brothers, Merchants, 159 E. Bay St.
Leland, Joseph, Merchant, 159 E Bay St., Res 180 Meeting St , cr. Hasell St.
Lemaitre, John B , Merchant, 177 E. Bay St
Lemar, Mary, Nurse, Whim Court, F P.C.
Lemon, James, Grocer, 136 Meeting St , cr. Market St
Lemount, Robert, Physician, 5 Cumberland St
Lepiere, Amy, Seamstress, 5 Cumberland St , F P C.
Leprince & Dumont, Merchants, 118 King St
Leprince, A., Fancy Store, 118 King St
Leroiy, Francis, Madam, 184 Meeting St
LeSeigneur, Physician, 48 Church St
Lesesne, Hannah, Widow, 45 Society St.
Leuder, Francis, Confectioner, 128 Church St.
Levin, Lewis, Merchant, 352 King St
Levy, Hayman, Dry Goods Store, 214 King St.
Levy, I C., 279 E Bay St
Levy, Lyon, 244 King St
Levy, Moses C., Merchant, 213 King St
Levy, Nathan, Merchant, 255 King St
Levy, Reuben, Broker, 40 Anson St
Levy, Simon, Merchant, 295 King St
Levy, Solomon, 88 Broad St , cr. King St
Lewis, David, Dry Goods & Second Hand Furniture, 403 King St , Neck
Lewis, Eliza, Widow, Store Keeper, 352 King St.
Lewis, Elizabeth, Widow, 121 Wentworth St.
Lewis, Florence, Fruiterer, 33 St. Philip's St , F P.C
Lewis, Isaac, 36 Wentworth St.
Lewis, Jacob, Dry Goods Store, 308 King St
Lewis, John, Factor, 56 E. Bay St & Meeting St.
Lewis, John, Grocer, 207 E Bay St., cr. Market St.
Lewis, John, Merchant, Fitzsimons' Whf , Res. 12 Church St.
Liblong, Henry, Shoemaker, 16 Liberty St.
Liddle, John, 106 Market St.
Lieure, Peter, Grocer, 62 State St.
Lightwood, Elizabeth, Widow, 18 Meeting St , cr Lynch's Ln
Lightwood, Lucy, Zigzag Al., F P C.

Limehouse, Robert, Planter, 123 Tradd St
Linch, Henry, Boarding House, 18 State St.
Lincoln, Benjamin, Tailor, 8 Clifford's Al., F P C
Lincoln, Elizabeth, Widow, 10 Liberty St.
Lindenboom, Peter, U S. Arsenal, Coming St , Neck
Lindershine, J C , Carpenter, Charlotte St., Neck
Lindsay, William, Merchant, Res 50 E. Bay St
Lines, Richard, 18 Market St
Ling, Philip, Coachmaker, 82 Market St , Res. 21 Guignard St.
Ling, Robert, Chair Maker, 84 Market St
Lining, Charles, Clerk, Bank of Discount & Deposit, 17 Legare St.
Lining, Edward B , Planter, 17 Legare St
Lining, -----, Widow of Charles, 17 Legare St.
Linsey, Sarah, 41 Wentworth St , F P C.
Linsor, John Lewis, Cannon St., Cannonborough, Neck
Lishman, Sarah, Widow, Boarding House, 58 State St., cr Amen St
Liston, Henry, Cooper, 6 Market St , Res 24 Beaufain St., F P C.
Litel, Jane, Widow, Saw Gin Maker, 159 Meeting St
Little, Cyrus, 15 Philadelphia St., F P C.
Little, Robert, Lumber Merchant, Chisolm's Upper Whf
Little, Robert, Lumber Merchant, Charlotte St , Mazyckborough, Neck
Livingston,-----, Grocery, King St Road, Neck
Livingston, John, Tailor, 316 King St , F P C
Livingston, Robert Y , Accountant, 26 Elliott St
Livingston, Sophia, Mantua Maker, 127 Queen St
Lloyd, Diana, 26 Lynch's Ln., F P C
Lloyd, Esther, Widow, 117 King St.
Lloyd, John, Mrs , 101 Meeting St.
Lloyd, John P , Venetian Blind Maker, 205 Meeting St
Lloyd, Joseph, Merchant, 117 King St
Lloyd, Mary, Mrs , 36 Bull St.
Lochart, John, Grocer, 86 Meeting St.
Lock, George B , Grocer, Dewee's Whf
Lock, John, Cigar Maker, 89 Queen St
Lockwood, Joshua, Bookkeeper, State Bank, Res. 75 Broad St
Logan, C M , Broker & Notary Public, 8 Champney St , Res 34 Archdale St
Logan, George, Physician, 22 Beaufain St
Logan, -----, Widow of Honorio, 34 Archdale St
Logan, William, Librarian, Charleston Library Society, State House, Cannonborough, Neck
Long, Felix, Tanner, Upper End Beaufain St.
Long, Robert S., Ship Master, 13 Wall St.
Long, Thomas, Coachmaker, 161 Church St
Longsden, John & William, Merchants, 70 E. Bay St., cr. Crafts' N. Whf
Lopez, Catherine, Seamstress, Jones' Lot, King St , F.P C.
Lopez, John, Mariner, 10 Ellery St
Lopez, Priscilla, Dry Goods Store, 132 King St.
Lopez, William, Tailor, 87 Market St., Res Jones' Lot, King St., F.P C.
Lord, Archibald, Porter, Bank of Discount & Deposit, 2 State St.
Lord, Jacob N , Shoemaker, 371 King St , Res King St

Road, by the Fresh Water Pond, Neck

Lord, Samuel, Merchant, 16 Vendue Range, Res. 26 Broad St.

Lorent & Wulf, Merchants, 76 E. Bay St , cr. Smith's Whf

Lorent, J J., Merchant, 76 E. Bay St

Loring, Martin, Northern Warehouse, 30 State St

Lorrimore, Sarah, Widow, E Bay St , cr. Vendue Range

Lothrop, Samuel H., Lothrop's Whf , 34 Vendue Range, Res. E Bay St.

Lott, -----, Mr., Sausage Maker, 154 Church St.

Loud, John, Piano Forte Manufacturer, 29 Broad St., Res 160 E. Bay St

Lovegreen & Co., Grocers, 11 Elliott St.

Lovell, Frances, 2 Widow, 41 E. Bay St.

Loveman, Elisha, Painter, 87 Boundary St.

Lowden, John, Merchant, 66 E Bay St., Res 154 Meeting St.

Lowndes, Amy, Washer, 108 Tradd St , F P C.

Lowndes, James, Planter, 14 Meeting St

Lowndes, Jane, Widow, Plantress, 74 Anson St.

Lowndes, Peggy, 108 Tradd St., F.P.C.

Lowndes, Thomas, Planter, 112 Broad St.

Lowrey, Charles, Livery Stables, 136 Queen St

Lowry, J M., Planter, St Philip's St , Neck

Lubat, John, 92 King St

Lubbock, Henry, 4 Water St.

Lucas & Dotterer, Iron Foundery, Gadsden's Whf.

Lucas, J J., Planter, cr. Boundary & Lucas Sts , Neck

Lucas, John, near Charleston Bridge, Neck

Ludlow, Robert C , 111 Broad St.

Lukens, John, Cashier, Planters' & Mechanics' Bank, 164 Church St.

Lupp, -----, Widow, 171 Church St.

Lusher, -----, Widow of George, 169 E Bay St.

Lushington, Betty, Washer, Henrietta St., F P.C., Neck

Lyle & Davis, Merchants, 226 E Bay St

Lyles, Mary, Washer, Charlotte St., F.P C , Neck

Lynah, Edward, Auctioneer, 12 Pitt St , cr Montague St

Lynch, Esther, Miss, Plantress, 225 E. Bay St.

Lynch, Henry, Painter, 100 King St

Lynch, Jane, Widow, Boarding House, 83 Broad St.

Lynch, John, Baker, 6 Minority St.

Lynn, John S., Accountant, Markley's Mill, Beaufain St.

Lyon, George, Watch & Clock Maker, 97 E. Bay St.

Lyon, Moses Roderiguez, Merchant, 97 E. Bay St.

Lyon, William W., Shoe Store, 113 King St

Lyons, Jonathan, Shoe Store, 167 King St.

Lyons, Mary, Miss, 60 Clifford St.

Macauley, Daniel, 14 Broad St , State St

Macauley, George F., Merchant, 37 Broad St

Macauley, George, Merchant, 96 Church St.

Macbeth, John, Grocer, 132 Tradd St

Mack, Sylvia, 79 Anson St , F.P.C.

Mackay & Norris, Ship Joiners, 210 E Bay St.

Mackay, James, Cutler, 146 Wentworth St.

Mackay, John, Teacher, 117 Broad St.

Mackenzie, Patience, 85 Anson St., F.P.C.

Mackey, Catherine, 40 Beaufain St , F P C

Mackey, Eliza, Nurse, 5 Wall St., F.P C.

Magee, John, Bricklayer, 3 Bedon's Al

Magness, Emanuel, Grocer, 61 State St , cr. Amen St.

Magrath, John, Merchant, 1 Gillon St , Res 197 Meeting St

Magson, Saul I , Merchant, 47 E Bay St

Magwood & Patterson, Merchants, Magwood's Whf.

Magwood, Charles, Merchant, 114 Queen St

Magwood, Sandy, Drayman, 53 Boundary St., F.P.C

Magwood, Simon, 122 Queen St.

Mahon, James, Pilot, 65 Church St

Maillard, John, Grocer, 119 Queen St., cr Friend St

Main, James, Cabinet Maker, 63 Broad St.

Main, William, Ship Carpenter, 27 Wall St

Mair, James, Planter, 14 Rutledge St.

Mairs & Valentine, Merchants, 6 State St

Mairs, Simon, Merchant, 6 State St

Malcolm, Thomas, Clerk, Planters' & Mechanics' Bank, 126 Queen St.

Males, Margaret, Widow, Dry Goods Store, King St , Neck

Man, Jacob, Carpenter, 40 George St

Mangels, John & Co , Grocers, 15 Mazyck St.

Manigault, Henry G., Maj., Planter, 16 Meeting St.

Manigault, Joseph, Planter, cr Meeting & John Sts , Neck

Manson, Andrew, Keeper, St. Andrew's Hall, 96 Broad St.

Manson, Sarah, Widow, Seamstress, Chapel St., Mazyckborough, Neck

Manswey, Mary, Widow, Baker, 271 E Bay St

Marchant, Peter, Carpenter, 31 Beaufain St., F.P.C.

Marchant, Peter T., Planter, 49 Coming St

Marchant, Stephen, Shoemaker, 3 Coming St , F P.C.

Marineau, Polly, Widow, 47 George St

Marion, Ann, Confectioner, 34 State St.

Marion, Francis, Planter, Thomas St , Neck

Marion, Samuel, Planter, Hampstead, Neck

Markley, Abraham, Thomas St , Radcliffborough, Neck

Markley, B A., Thomas St , Radcliffborough, Neck

Marks, Humphrey, Shopkeeper, cr King & John Sts , Neck

Marks, Joseph, Merchant, 10 Queen St

Marks, Mark, Deputy Sheriff, 310 King St

Marr, Ann, Widow, 14 Church St

Marriner, William, Sailmaker, Fitzsimons' Whf., cr. E. Bay St

Marsh, Abraham, 109 Boundary St., F.P.C.

Marshall, Annette, 42 Wentworth St

Marshall, John Henry, Grocer, cr. Elizabeth & Charlotte Sts., Res. Elizabeth St., Neck

Marshall, Mary S., Widow, 97 Broad St.

Marshall, Robert, Grocer, 2 Anson St.

Marshall, Thomas C., Accountant, 97 Broad St.

Marshall, -----, Widow, Midwife, 1 Clifford St.

Marshall, -----, Widow of William, 45 State St.

Marston, Benjamin, Clerk, Amherst St , Hampstead, Neck

Martin, Elizabeth, 8 Whim Court, F.P.C.

Martin, Jacob, Blacksmith, 18 Blackbird Al.

Martin, James, Merchant, 2 Chisolm's Upper Whf.

Martin, James, Merchant, King St Road, Neck

Martin, John N., Bricklayer, 15 Hasell St.

Martin, Lewis, Tailor, 21 Queen St.

Martin, Patrick, Grocer, 202 King St.

Martin, -----, Physician, 39 Pinckney St

Martin, Robert, Merchant, King St. Road, Neck
Martin, Sarah, Washer, 61 Wentworth St., F.P C.
Martin, Thomas, 3 Middle St.
Martin, -----, Widow, 35 Cumberland St.
Martindale, Betsey, 2 Washington St , F P C.
Martindale, J. C , Capt., Planter, King St. Road, Neck
Martindale, Mary, 65 State St., F P C
Mashaw, John, Grocer, 231 E. Bay St.
Mashburn, Nicholas, Carpenter, 16 Cumberland St
Mason, George, Clerk, Union Bank, 22 Lynch's Ln.
Massot, Horatio, Watch Maker, 13 Queen St.
Masterson, Hugh, Bricklayer, 5 Swinton's Ln.
Mather, Lewis, Tailor, 145 Church St.
Mathewes, William, Planter, Charlotte St.,
   Mazyckborough, Neck
Mathews & Bonneau, Factors, Smith's Whf.
Mathews, Benjamin, Capt., 110 Tradd St
Mathews, Charlotte, 8 Logan St , F.P.C.
Mathews, David, Shoemaker, 75 Tradd St.
Mathews, George, Carpenter, 5 Friend St., F P C.
Mathews, Henry, Grocer, 24 Elliott St.
Mathews, Henry, Shoemaker, 20 St. Philip's St., F P C
Mathews, James, Factor, 59 Anson St.
Mathews, John B., Tailor, 65 Boundary St., F.P.C.
Mathews, John W., Planter, 12 New St
Mathews, Judah, 5 Coming St., F P C
Mathews, Lucy, 6 Clifford's Al , F.P.C.
Mathews, Martha Ann, 32 S Bay St
Mathews, Mary, 1 Clifford's Al., F.P.C.
Mathews, Peter, Shoemaker, 43 Boundary St , F P.C.
Mathews, -----, Widow of Thomas W., Planter, 12 Wall St.
Mathiessen, C F., Dry Goods Store, 34 Queen St
Mattis, Cumsey, Tin Plate Worker, 42½ King St., F P C.
Maull, Mary E , Widow, Seamstress, 38 Beaufain St.
Maxey, Ann, Widow, Seamstress, 58 St Philip's St.
Maxfield, -----, Grocer, 20 Market St.
Maxton, John, Baker, 91 Market St
Maxwell, James, Mrs , 91 Meeting St
Maxwell, Robert, Merchant, 48 E. Bay St , Res. 15
   Meeting St , cr. Smith's Ln.
Maxwell, William, 91 Meeting St.
Maxwell, William, Planter, Cannon St , Neck
May, John, Cabinet Maker, 61 Queen St
Maye, Caroline, Dry Goods Store, 37½ King St.
Maynard, James, Baker, 49 St. Philip's St., cr. Green St.
Maynard, Richard, Physician, 11 Broad St.
Mays, James, Grocer, 4 Tradd St.
Mazyck, M , Widow, 61 Church St.
Mazyck, Mary, 7 Mazyck St., F.P.C.
Mazyck, Nathaniel B., Meeting St.
Mazyck, Paul, 9 Archdale St.
Mazyck, Philip, Physician, 50 Wentworth St
Mazyck, William, Chisolm's Upper Whf , Res. 9 Archdale
   St
Mazyck, William, Factor, 50 Wentworth St.
M'Anally, John, Grocer, 115 King St
M'Arthur & C Duncan, Charleston Coffee House, 83 E.
   Bay St
M'Bride, Eleanor G , Widow, 287 E. Bay St , cr Laurens
   St.

M'Bride, Mary, Widow, Grocer, 55 George St.
M'Bride, -----, Widow, 64 Church St
M'Caffray, Hugh, Shoemaker, 12 Queen St
M'Call, Beekman, Clerk, State Bank, 259 E Bay St , cr.
   Hasell St.
M'Call, Caty, Henrietta St., Mazyckborough St , F P C ,
   Neck
M'Call, Elizabeth, Widow, 25 Meeting St
M'Call, Hagar, 9 King St., F P.C
M'Call, James, Mrs , Planter, King St Road, Neck
M'Call, John W., Physician, 25 Meeting St.
M'Call, Joseph P., 25 Meeting St.
M'Call, -----, Widow of John, 74 Church St
M'Calla, Sarah, Widow, 88 Anson St
M'Cannts, William, Planter, 10 Savage St
M'Cartney, Samuel, Merchant, 18 Broad St.
M'Cask, -----, Hardware Merchant, 130 E. Bay St.
M'Clane, -----, Billiard Rooms, 187 Church St
M'Clane, -----, Mrs., 240 Meeting St
M'Clane, William, Pump & Block Maker, Maiden Ln , cr
   Guignard St.
M'Clary, Samuel, Merchant, King St Road, Neck
M'Cleish, Mary, Widow, School Mistress, Tradd St
M'Clure, Eliza, Seamstress, 16 Swinton's Ln., F.P.C
M'Cormick, Peter, Grocer, 28 St Philip's St., cr. Liberty
   St.
M'Cormick, Thomas, Merchant, Vanderhorst's Whf.
M'Cormick, Timothy, 10 Hasell St.
M'Cormick, William, Grocer, 18 Tradd St. & 95 E. Bay
   St
M'Coy, Joseph, Baker, 36 Church St.
M'Cready, Mary Ann, Milliner, 367 King St Road, Neck
M'Cullum, James, Grocer, 3 King St
M'Cullum, Robert, Grocer, 33 S Bay St
M'Donald & Bonner, Cabinet Makers, 85 Broad St.
M'Donald, Allen, Cabinet Maker, 85 Broad St.
M'Donald, Christopher, Grocer, 60 King St.
M'Donald, Hugh & Alexander, Grocers, 312 King St
M'Donald, John, Planter, Saltus' Whf., Res. Mey's Whf
M'Donald, Sarah, Widow, 29 George St.
M'Dow, William, Teacher, 29 Coming St.
M'Dowall & Black, Merchants, 145 King St.
M'Dowall, Andrew, Merchant, 145 King St.
M'Dowall, David, Grocer, 206 Meeting St.
M'Dowall, Nancy, Fruiterer, 314 King St., F.P.C.
M'Dowall, -----, Widow of John, 391 King St., Neck
M'Dowall, William, Grocer, 244 Meeting St.
M'Dowell, James, Merchant, King St , Neck
M'Elmoyle, William, Grocer, 73 King St , cr. Tradd St.
M'Farlane, Catharine, Widow, 8 Hasell St
M'Farlane, Mary, Mrs., 96 Meeting St.
M'Gann, Patrick, Watchmaker, 86 E Bay St.
M'Ginley, Samuel, Carpenter, 74 Market St.
M'Ginnis, Elijah, Shoe Store, 230 King St
M'Govery, William, Grocer, 3 Market St.
M'Granagan, William, Grocer, cr Elizabeth & Boundary
   Sts., Neck
M'Guire, Hugh, 171 E Bay St., cr Lodge Al
M'Ilhenny, John, Shoemaker, 219 E. Bay St.
M'Innis, Joseph, Wheelwright, Charlotte St., Neck

M'Intosh, -----, 147 Meeting St.
M'Intosh, Milly 13 Swinton's Ln , F.P.C
M'Intosh, Rebecca, Widow, 1 Wentworth St.
M'Intosh, William, Shop, King St. Road, Neck
M'Intyre, Elizabeth, Widow, 13 Price's Al.
M'Kee, Abel, Ship Joiner, 206 E Bay St , Res 150 Church St.
M'Kegan, John, Blacksmith, Blackbird Al
M'Kendree, Eliza, Widow, Spring St., Neck
M'Kenzie, Elizabeth, Widow, Unity Al.
M'Kenzie, George T , 20 Broad St.
M'Kenzie, John, Saddler, 75 Broad St.
M'Kenzie, John, Wine Merchant, 44 Broad St.
M'Kenzie, Michael, Saddler, 20 Broad St.
M'Kewn, -----, Widow, 59 George St.
M'Kewn, William, Bricklayer, 59 George St.
M'Kimme, Clarissa, 22 Wentworth St
M'Kinna, Lawrence, Grocer, 7 Chalmers Al.
M'Lachlan, Archibald, 9 Tradd St.
M'Lachlan, Smith & Co., Merchants, 9 Tradd St.
M'Lane, -----, Livery Stables, 147 Church St
M'Lauchlin, A & Co., Grocers, 108 Tradd St.
M'Laughlin, Thomas, Grocer, 8 Smith's Ln.
M'Lean, Harriet, Widow, Mantua Maker, 25 Coming St
M'Leod, George, Tailor, 32 Broad St.
M'Leod, H. C., 69 Meeting St.
M'Millan, Daniel, Carpenter, 62 Beaufain St.
M'Millan, John, Dry Goods Store, 172 King St.
M'Millan, John, Merchant, King St Road, Neck
M'Millan, Richard, 376 King St., Neck
M'Millan, Thomas, Carpenter, 101 Meeting St.
M'Namara, John, Grocer, 8 Queen St.
M'Namee, James, Shoemaker & Grocer, 112 Church St.
M'Neil, Neil & Co., Grocers, 46 Broad St , cr Church St.
M'Neil, Neil, Capt., 41 King St.
M'Neil, Neil, Wine Merchant, 116 Church St
M'Neil, Samuel, Merchant, 72 E. Bay St., Res. 2 Laurens St.
M'Nellage, John, Sail Maker, Kunhardt's Whf.
M'Niel, Daniel, Ship Master, Doughty St , Neck
M'Owen, Patrick, 26 King St.
M'Pherson, D , Milliner, 56 King St.
M'Pherson, J E., 289 E. Bay St., cr. Laurens St.
M'Pherson, Laura, Widow, 94 Broad St
M'Shea, Mary, Dry Goods Store, 221 King St.
M'Vicar, Archibald, Butcher, Nassau, Wraggsborough, Neck
Meacher, Thomas, Grocer, 47 Church St , cr. Market St.
Mealy, John, Grocer, 13 St. Philip's St.
Mease & Holmes, Merchants, 151 King St
Meeds, -----, Widow of William, Boarding House, 71 E. Bay St.
Menude, John, Planter, 8 Liberty St.
Mercier, Margaret, Widow, Washington St., Mazyckborough, Neck
Meredith, William, Grocer, 18 Guignard St.
Merritt, James H., Factor, Kunhardt's Whf , Res. 87 Bull St.
Messervy, Philip, Capt., 120 Meeting St.
Meucci, Antoine, Miniature Painter, 157 King St

Meukens, H , Grocer, 397 King St., Neck
Mey, Charles H., Merchant, 2 Pinckney St , Res 218 E. Bay St
Mey, Florian C , Merchant, 2, Res 4 Pinckney St
Mey, John H., Merchant, 2, Res. 4 Pinckney St
Mialle, Simon, Shoemaker, 179 Church St.
Michael, Henry, Jr., Livery Stables, 28 Mazyck St , F.P.C.
Michael, Henry, Sr., Livery Stables, 36 Mazyck St , F P.C.
Michael, Maria, 7 Mazyck St., F.P.C.
Michael, Maria, Teacher, 2 Zigzag Al , F.P.C.
Michel, Frederick, Assistant Clerk, Market, 100 Wentworth St.
Michel, John E., Goldsmith, 303 King St.
Michel, Mary, Widow, 35 Coming St.
Michel, Pierre, Hatter, 388 King St., Neck
Michel, Thomas, Ship Carpenter, 8 Wentworth St.
Michel, William, Physician, 51 Anson St
Middleton, Arthur, Planter, 294 E Bay St.
Middleton, John, Planter, 42 Bull St.
Middleton, Maria, Boarding House, 22 Chalmers Al
Middleton, Thomas, Factor, Crafts' S. Whf., Res. 11 George St.
Miles, Ann L., Widow, 3 Legare St.
Miles, Edward, Mariner, 3 Linguard St
Mill, John, Bookseller, 34 Broad St
Miller, Abraham, Clerk, State Bank, 53 Society St
Miller, Andrew, Boarding House, 15 Elliot St
Miller, Ann, Widow, 20 Middle St
Miller, Archibald E., Printer, 4 Broad St
Miller, Catharine, Widow, 53 Society St
Miller, Charles, Hay Merchant, Lothrop's Whf., Res. 18 Beaufain St.
Miller, Elizabeth S., Widow, 142 Meeting St.
Miller, Ezra L , Merchant, 265 King St , cr. Wentworth St.
Miller, Frederick J., Accountant, 33 Anson St.
Miller, George, King St. Road, Neck
Miller, Jacob, Rope Maker, Vanderhorst St., Neck
Miller, James A., Clerk, Board of Health, 10 Magazine St
Miller, James A., Clerk, 53 Society St
Miller, Jane, Widow, Baker, 143 Meeting St
Miller, Job P., Bricklayer, 81 King St.
Miller, John, Accountant, 212 Meeting St.
Miller, John C., Factor, William's Whf., Res. 65 Anson St.
Miller, Lydia, Widow, Seamstress, 30 St Philip's St
Miller, M. John, Dry Goods Store, 112 King St.
Miller, Magdalen, Widow, 56 Queen St., cr. George St.
Miller, Mary, Widow, 33 Anson St.
Miller, Matthew, Goldsmith & Jeweller, 150 King St.
Miller, Peter C., Grocer, 2 Middle St., cr. Laurens St
Miller, Samuel Stent, Printer, 20 Middle St.
Miller, -----, Widow of John M., Ladies' Dress Maker, 9 Wentworth St.
Miller, William C., Merchant, Vanderhorst's Whf., Res 212 Meeting St.
Miller, William, Clerk, 53 Society St.
Miller, William H., Merchant, Chisolm's Lower Whf , Res 33 Anson St.
Miller, William H., Tailor, 56 Queen St.
Miller, William, St. Philip's St., Neck
Milligan, Joseph, Charlotte St , Mazyckborough, Neck

Milligan, Joseph, Factor, 28 E. Bay St., Res. Mazyckborough
Milliken, Primerose & Co , Auctioneers, 21 Vendue Range
Millken, Thomas, Auctioneer, Res. Charlotte St., Neck
Mills, Harriot, Seamstress, Charlotte St , Mazyckborough, F P C , Neck
Mills, Mary, Widow, Spring St., Neck
Milne, Andrew & Co , Merchants, 66½ E. Bay St.
Milne, Andrew, Merchant, 66½ E. Bay St., Res Stoll's Al
Milton, William H., 7 Legare St
Milward, Eliza, Widow, Meeting St. Road, Neck
Minot, William, Planter, 8 Savage St.
Minsey, Ann, Widow, 35 Wentworth St
Miot, Charles H., Boarding House, King St., cr Society St.
Miot, -----, Livery Stables, 55 Society St.
Mishaw, John, Shoemaker, 127 Meeting St., F P.C.
Missidine, Robert, Bookseller & Bookbinder, 134 King St
Missroon, James, Merchant, 26 E Bay St
Mitchel, John, 35 Coming St.
Mitchell, Andrew, Plasterer, 9 Mazyck St.
Mitchell, Ann H., Widow, 17 Guignard St.
Mitchell, Charles, Mariner, 12 Bedon's Al.
Mitchell, Elizabeth, Widow, 9 Wentworth St.
Mitchell, James & Co , Cooperage, 74 E Bay St., cr Smith's Ln.
Mitchell, James, Block Master, 4 Washington St.
Mitchell, James, Cooperage, 27 E. Bay St., cr. Smith's Whf , Res. 87 E Bay St.
Mitchell, James D., Ordinary, Office, Guard House, Res. 134 Wentworth St.
Mitchell, Jane, Washer, 8 Ellery St., F P.C.
Mitchell, John H., Notary Public & Quorum Unis, 88 E. Bay St., Res. 42 Guignard St.
Mitchell, John, Musician, 38 Wentworth St., F P C.
Mitchell, John, Tailor, 92 Anson St., F.P.C.
Mitchell, John W., 88 E Bay St., Res 42 Guignard St
Mitchell, -----, Widow of John E., 45 Tradd St.
Mitchell, -----, Widow of Thomas, Charlotte St , Mazyckborough, Neck
Modern, James, Boat Builder, 210, Res 240 E Bay St.
Moffatt, Peter, Grocer, 20 S. Bay St
Moffett & Calder, Dry Goods Store, 177 King St.
Moffett, Andrew, Merchant, 177 King St.
Mohr, Henry, Grocer, 141 Queen St.
Moise Aaron, Clerk, Beaufain St.
Moise, Benjamin, Accountant, 28 Hasell St
Moise, Cherry, Clerk, 129 King St.
Moise, Sarah, Mrs , 2 Clifford St
Moisson, John, Gunsmith, 16 State St.
Monar, Lewis, Hair Dresser, 134 Queen St.
Moncrieffe, Aaron, Shoemaker, 38 Tradd St., F.P.C
Mondoza, Mary, Widow, 14 Anson St.
Monefeldt, Maria, Widow, Teacher, 51 Coming St.
Monpoey, H., Factor, 40 Bull St
Monpoey, Susan, Dry Goods Store, 198 King St.
Montague, Richard, Merchant, 18 Vendue Range
Montesquieu, Rene, Tin Plate Worker, 142 Meeting St., Res. 42 Ellery St.
Montgomery & Platt, Commission Merchant, 15 Vanderhorst's Whf

Montross, Nathaniel, Hat Store, 229 King St.
Mood, Peter, Silversmith, 166 King St
Moodie, Benjamin, British Consul, 95 Meeting St.
Moon, James, 173 Church St
Mooney, Ann, Widow, Millinery & Dry Goods, King St., Neck
Mooney, John, Mariner, 30 Pinckney St
Mooney, Patrick, 21 Cumberland St
Moore, Ann, Miss, 21 Mazyck St.
Moore, Catharine, 9 Lynch's Ln , F P.C
Moore, J., Jr., Dry Goods Store, 306 King St.
Moore, Joseph P , Physician, 105 King St
Moore, Philip, Lumber Merchant, cr Montague & Gadsden St
Moore, Robert, Shopkeeper, 54 Church St.
Moore, Stephen West, Clerk, Union Bank, Vanderhorst St., Neck
Moore, William, 128 Meeting St
Mordecai, Joseph, Cutler, 25 Beaufain St.
Mordecai, Moses, Accountant, 34 Guignard St.
Mordecai, Reinah, Widow, 34 Guignard St.
Morford, E., Bookseller, 112 E. Bay St., Res 40 Broad St
Morgan, Ann, Widow, 3 Cumberland St.
Morgan, Benjamin, Capt , 14 Middle St.
Morgan, Eliza, Widow, 82 Wentworth St.
Morgan, Isaac C , Carpenter, 36 George St
Morgan, John, Carpenter, 29 Wall St.
Morgan, Samuel, Constable, 37 Elliott St.
Morgan, Susannah, Widow, 29 Wall St.
Moriarty, Maurice, Dry Goods Store, 224 King St.
Morris, Christopher G., Merchant, 80 E. Bay St., Res. 2 Wentworth St
Morris, Henry, Meeting St. Road, Neck
Morris, Simpson, Crockery Store, 264 King St.
Morris, Thomas, Jr., 4 Chisolm's Upper Whf., Res. 2 Wentworth St
Morris, Thomas, Quorum Unis & Notary Public, 68 E. Bay St., cr. Crafts' Whf , Res 2 Wentworth St.
Morrison, J., Jr , Capt., Alexander St , Mazyckborough, Neck
Morrison, -----, Widow of James, Cooper, 4 Price's Al
Morrison, -----, Widow of John, 70 Tradd St.
Mortimer, Edward, U. S. Appraiser, 13 Champney St , Res 63 Anson St
Moser, Philip, 10 Logan St.
Moses, Abigail, Widow, 18 Swinton's Ln
Moses, Esther, Dry Goods Store, 280 King St.
Moses, Hester, Milliner, 276 King St
Moses, Isaiah, Planter, 226 King St.
Moses, Israel, Auctioneer & Commision Merchant, 15 Vendue Range.
Moses, Jacob, Dry Goods Store, King St Road, Neck
Moses, Levy, Merchant, 83 Wentworth St.
Moses, Myer, Auctioneer, Vendue Range, Res 65 Meeting St.
Moses, Rachel, Dry Goods Store, 123 E Bay St
Moses, Reuben, Dry Goods Store, 278 King St.
Moses, Simon, Dry Goods Store, 385 King St., Neck
Moses, Solomon, Constable, 255 King St.
Moses, Solomon, Jr , Deputy Sheriff, 4 Clifford St.

Mosiman, J., Watchmaker, 79 Meeting St
Moss, Joseph, Tailor, 295 King St.
Motta, J. A., Confectioner, 169 King St.
Motte, Abraham, 17 Wentworth St
Motte, Catharine, Seamstress, Jones' Lot, King St., F P C.
Motte, Darilla, Pastry Cook, 75 Anson St , F.P C
Motte, Francis, Factor, 34 Church St
Motte, Isaac, Mrs , 24 Meeting St.
Motte, Jacob, 75 Anson St., F.P.C.
Moubray, Martha, Widow, 30 Hasell St.
Moulin, Peter, Grocer, 72 State St.
Moultin, Martha, Seamstress, 19 Pitt St , F P.C
Moultrie, Alexander, Clerk, Union Bank, 12 Cumberland
  St
Moultrie, James, Jr., Physician, 12 Cumberland St.
Moultrie, James, Sr., Physician, 12 Cumberland St.
Moultrie, John, Accountant, 12 Cumberland St.
Moultrie, Robert, Bricklayer, 128 Boundary St , F P C
Moutang, Joseph, Tailor, 257 King St., F.P.C.
Mouzon, Charles, Shoemaker, 4 St Philip's St., 141
  Church St.
Muck, Philip, Stationer, 91 Broad St , cr. King St., Res 90
  King St.
Muckenfuss, Henry, Bricklayer, 120 Wentworth St
Muggridge, Mathew, Blacksmith, Hudson St.,
  Cannonborough, Neck
Muggrude, Mathew, Blacksmith, Ellery St., Res. 1 Maiden
  Ln
Muir, Jane, Mrs , Boarding House, 24 Broad St.
Muller, Jane, Dry Goods Store, 201 King St
Mulligan & M'Cready, Saddlers, 33 Broad St.
Mulligan, Barnard, Merchant, 357 King St
Mullings, John, Pilot, 15 Zigzag Al.
Mulloy, James, Grocer, 21 Market St.
Munds, Israel, Rev , Teacher, 41 State St.
Munro, Catharine, Midwife, 38 Hasell St
Munro, Margaret, Boarding House, 95 Church St
Munro, Martin E , Wharfinger, 29 Mazyck St.
Murden, Jeremiah, Corn Store, Kunhardt's Whf., Res 8 S.
  Bay St
Murley, Samuel, Factor, 68 E Bay St., Res. 68 Wentworth
  St
Murphy, John, 141 Church St.
Murphy, Patrick, Grocer, 16 Anson St.
Murphy, Peter, Grocer, 223 King St , cr. Beaufain St
Murphy, Sarah, Widow, Shopkeeper, 91 Church St
Murray & M'Leod, Merchant Tailors, 32 Broad St.
Murray, Ann E , Dry Goods Store, 196 King St
Murray, John M., Grocer, 1 King St.
Murray, -----, Widow of Jeremiah, Boarding House, 17
  Elliot St.
Murrell, John J., Planter, 23 Middle St.
Mushington, William, Mariner, 101 King St., F.P C.
Mussault, Ann, Mrs , 301 E Bay St
Myatt, Edward, Boat Builder, Johnson's Whf., Res Cox's
  Ln.
Myers, John & Co., 26 Church St.
Myers, Michael, Vendue Master, 38 Hasell St
Myles, Jane, Mrs., Midwife, 180 Meeting St.
Myles, Levi, Grocer, 180 Meeting St

Mynarts, M., Limner, 57 Queen St.
Myning, Francis, Grocer, 73 State St.
Mynott, Baxter O., Commission Merchant, 142 E. Bay St.,
  Res. 115 Church St.
Napier, Nancy, 10 Washington St , F.P.C.
Napier, Rapelye & Bennett, Auctioneers, 17 Vendue
  Range St
Napier, Thomas, 17 Vendue Range, Res. Ladson's Whf.
Nash, Levi, Merchant, King St. Road, Neck
Nathan, Henry, Cryer, 50 Boundary St., Neck
Nathans, Nathan & Co , Merchants, King St., Neck
Nayler, Sarah, Dry Goods Store, 266 King St , cr
  Wentworth St
Neill, Susan, Widow, Plantress, 98 Tradd St
Neilson, George, 35 State St.
Neilson, William A , Grocer, 67 King St
Nell, Jesse, Rope Maker, near the Lines, Neck
Nell, Maria, Teacher, 26 Lynch's Ln., F P.C
Nell, Nancy, Seamstress, 26 Lynch's Ln , F.P.C
Nelson, Christopher, Porter House, 153 E Bay St.
Nelson, Dinah, Pastry Cook, 36 Coming St., F.P C.
Nelson, James, Butcher, St. Philip's St., Neck
Nelson, John, Blacksmith, 29 Wall St.
Nelson, William, Blacksmith, 4 Middle St
Nesbit, Maria, Mrs., 6 S. Bay St.
Nesbit, William, Grocer, 31 Elliott St.
Neufville, Ann, Widow, 86 Anson St
Neufville, John, Attorney, 59½ Meeting, Res 86 Anson St
Nevill, John, Grocer, 13 Magazine St , cr. Mazyck St.
Neville, Henry, Cabinet Maker, 260 King St.
Neville, Joshua & Co., Cabinet Makers, 260 King St
Newell & Peck, Grocers, 289 King St , cr Liberty St
Newell, Jonathan A., Grocer, 289 King St.
Newhall & Thayer, Shoe Store, 154 King St.
Newhall, Edward, 154 King St., Res. 103 Queen St
Newhall, Jonathan, Jr , Merchant, Kunhardt's Whf.
Newton, Anthony, Butcher, Cannon St., Neck
Newton, Cornelia, Seamstress, 7 Cumberland St , F.P C.
Newton, Elizabeth, Elizabeth St., Mazyckborough, F P.C ,
  Neck
Newton, Elizabeth, Mantua Maker, 1 Market St., F P.C
Newton, Susannah, Seamstress, 11 E Bay St., F P C
Nichola, Louisa, 43 George St., F.P.C.
Nichols, Harriet F , 108 King St.
Nicholson & Holmes, Merchants, Napier's New Range,
  Gibbes & Harper's Whf.
Nickerson, W , Shopkeeper, Meeting St Road, Neck
Nicks, Joseph D., Teacher, 339 King St.
Niles, Roxanna, Cook, 13 Philadelphia St., F.P.C
Nix, Benjamin, Tailor, 12 Orange St.
Nobbs, -----, Mrs., cr. St. Philip's & Radcliff Sts., Neck
Noise, Henry, Capt , Cannon St , Neck
Nolan, John M , Merchant, Tailor, 43 Broad St
Nolen, James, Carpenter, 5 Back St
Norman & Jones, Grocers, 27 Tradd St.
Norman, George A , Grocer, 25 Tradd St.
Norris, Agness, Miss, 2 West St.
Norris, James C , Cabinet Maker, 119 King St
Norris, Martha, Widow, 33 Cumberland St.
Norroy, Mary Magdalen, 47 George St

North, Edward W., Physician, 74 Queen St , Res. 89 Meeting St

North, Richard, Factor, Chisolm's Whf , Res 7 Greenhill St

North, Webb & Osborn, Factors, Chisolm's Whf

Northrop, David A., Merchant Tailor, 27 Broad St.

Norton, Lucas, Rice Mill, Gadsden's Whf.

Novelle, Mary, 15 College St., F P.C.

Nowell, John, Cashier, Union Bank

Nowell, Thomas S , Discount Clerk, Bank of S C, Res 55 Wentworth St

Nugent, John, Shoemaker, 40 Queen St

Nuney, Francis, Mariner, 10 Philadelphia St.

Nurse & Wood, Shoe Store, 310 King St

O'Brien, Matthew, Grocer, 12 Market St

O'Callaghan, Patrick, Grocer, 193 King St.

O'Connor, Matthew, Grocer, 7 Elliot St

O'Dare, Janty, Confectioner, 81 Anson St.

O'Farrell, Michael, Grocer, 6 Champney St

O'Hara, Arthur H., Attorney, 70 Meeting St.

O'Hara, Charles & Henry, Factors, 45 E. Bay St.

O'Hara, Charles, Col., Factor, 6 Smith's Ln , Res 45 E Bay St.

O'Hara, Daniel, 20 King St.

O'Hara, Henry, Broker & Vendue Master, 5 Broad St., Res. Mazyck St

O'Hear, James, Factor, D'Oyley's Whf., Res. 7 Smith St

O'Hear, Joseph, Planter, 7 Smith St., cr Montague St

O'Neale, Charles, Merchant, King St. Road, Neck

O'Neale, Edmund, Merchant, King St Road, Neck

O'Neale, Richard, Merchant, King St. Road, Neck

O'Neil, Patrick, Grocer, cr Boundary & Washington Sts., Mazyckborough, Neck

O'Rawe, B , Grocer, 377 King St , Neck

O'Rawe, John, Grocer, 137 Meeting St.

O'Sullivan, F , Painter & Glazier, 190 Meeting St.

Oakes, Samuel, Grocer, Gadsden's Whf

Oakley Robert S., Druggist, 117 King St

Oates, John, Beer House, 147 E. Bay St

Oates, Mary, Widow, 8 Stoll's Al.

Ogden, George W., Tailor, 109 E. Bay St

Ogden, Robert, Attorney, 6 St Michael's Al

Ogier, John, Factor, 38, Res. 305 E. Bay St.

Ogier, Thomas, Broker & Commission Merchant, 7 Broad, Res 188 E Bay St.

Olden, Patty, 13 Philadelphia St , F P C

Olds, Liberty, Shoe Store, 53 Broad St.

Oleron, F J ,Boarding House, 23 Queen St

Oliphant, David, Painter, Meeting St , cr. Society St

Oliver, James, Cannon St , Neck

Oliver, William, Butcher, Meeting St. Road, F P.C , Neck

Oneale, James, Carpenter & Clerk, St Michael's Al., Res. 26 Magazine St.

Oring, Catharine, Widow, 30 Anson St

Orsborn, Catharine, 32 S. Bay St.

Ortega, Juan G., Spanish Vice Consul, Office 14 Queen St.

Osborn, Richard, Factor, 32 S. Bay St

Osward, Rebecca, Widow, Butcher, cr Mary & Elizabeth Sts , Neck

Otis, Richard W & Co , Commission Merchant, 87 E. Bay St., Res. 29 Broad St

Ottolingui, Abraham, Auctioneer, 28 Vendue Range

Owen, Smart, Shoemaker, 13 Coming St., F P C.

Oxlade, Thomas, Painter & Glazier, 15 State St., cr. Chalmers St.

Packard, Chilion, Shoe Store, 288 King St , Res 8 George St.

Paddock, G H , Exchange Office, 110 E Bay St , cr. Gillon St.

Page, John, Jr , Commission Merchant, Res 160, 138 E Bay St.

Paine, Joseph B., 42 E Bay St

Paine, Thomas, Jr., Lt , U. S. Navy, 42 E Bay St

Paine, Thomas, Laborer, 21 Hasell St , F P.C.

Paine, Thomas, Sr., Harbor Master, 42 E. Bay St.

Paisley, Robert A , Merchant, 2 Minority St.

Palmer, Benjamin, D. D., Rev., 76 Queen St.

Palmer, Edward, Mrs , Teacher, 7 State St

Palmer, Job, Carpenter, 64 Wentworth St

Palmer, Sarah, Widow, Boarding House, Edmonston's Whf., cr Champney St.

Parish, D & Co , Wholesale Dry Goods Merchants, 56 Broad St.

Parish, Daniel, Merchant, 56 Broad St , Res 95 Church St

Parker & Brailsford, Factors, Vanderhorst's Whf.

Parker, Amy, Miss, 257 Meeting St.

Parker, Ann, Widow, Tradd St., cr. Church St

Parker, Charles, City Surveyor & Engineer, 2 New St

Parker, Edwin, 61 Meeting St.

Parker, Henry, 44 Church St

Parker, Isaac, Planter, 11 Legare St.

Parker, James, Porter House, 125 Church St.

Parker, John, Thomas St , Islington, Neck

Parker, Martha, Widow, Plantress, John St , Mazyckborough, Neck

Parker, Mary, Miss, 27 Coming St.

Parker, Samuel, Planter, 6 George St.

Parker, Sarah P., 18 Meeting St

Parker, Thomas, Attorney, State House Sq., Res Meeting St

Parker, -----, Widow of Thomas, 61 Meeting St.

Parker, William, 18 Meeting St.

Parker, William Henry, Factor, 61 Meeting St.

Parkinson, John, 102 Market St

Parks, Josiah, Merchant, 169 E. Bay St., Res 135 Church St.

Parlour, Peter, Drayman, 5 Magazine St., F.P C

Parsons, Isaac D , Teacher, 66 Church St.

Parsons, Joseph, Blake St., Hampstead, Neck

Passailaigue, Lewis, Baker, Washington St., cr Boundary St.

Patch, Nathaniel, Grocer, 29 Pinckney St , cr Anson St

Paterson, Hugh, Auditor, Union Insurance Co., Res 7 Laurens St

Patrick, Cassimer, Leather Store, King St Road, Tanyard, Mary St , Wraggsborough, Neck

Patterson, Alexander, Grocer, 5 Vendue Range

Patterson, James, Mariner, 19 Washington St

Patterson, Samuel, Factor, Magwood's Whf., Res 2 Hasell St

93

Patton, Jane, 98 Queen St
Patton, William, cr King & Spring Sts , Neck
Patton, William, Merchant, 108 Church St
Paul, Isaac, Shoemaker, 235 E Bay St
Paul, J & Dunbar, Grocers, 47 Broad St., cr. Church St
Payenneville, Maria C., 13 Berresford St
Payne, John W., Broker & Vendue Master, Res 107 Broad St
Payne, William & Sons, Brokers & Vendue Masters, 28 Broad St
Payne, William, Broker & Vendue Master, Res. 28 Broad St
Pearce, Richard, 153 Meeting St.
Pearce, Samuel, Carpenter, Henrietta St , Wraggsborough, Neck
Pearson, Benjamin, Capt., 249 Meeting St., Neck
Pease, Hannah, Nurse, 7 Clifford's Al., F.P.C.
Peck, Elizabeth, Widow, 61 George St.
Peck, Samuel H., Grocer, 289 King St
Peckerd, Job, Baker, 401 King St , Neck
Peel, Charles, Saddlery Warehouse, 302 King St
Pellot, O , Grocer, 342 King St.
Pelmoine, Francis, Barber, 33 State St
Pelzer, Anthony, Teacher, German Friendly Society, 13 Archdale St
Pemble, David, Tailor, 161 E Bay St., Res. 8 Market St
Pendleton, Martha, Seamstress, 6 Berresford St., F P.C.
Penington, Ann Elizabeth, Widow, 22 Blackbird Al
Pennal, Robert, Grocer, 386 King St., Neck
Penott & Co., Shoe Store, 80 King St
Penson, Margaret, Fruiterer, 18 Archdale St , F.P C
Pepoon, Benjamin F , Attorney, Meeting St., Res 23 Beaufain St.
Pepoon, -----, Widow of Benjamin, 23 Beaufain St.
Percival & Johnson, Physicians, Brownlee s' Row, King St., Neck
Perdriau, Isabella, Widow, 7 Maiden Ln.
Perman, George, Grocer, 61 & 63 E Bay St
Peronneau, William, Planter, 34 S. Bay St.
Perony, Charles, Fencing Master, 6 Anson St.
Perry, Ann D., Widow, Bull St , cr. Lynch St.
Perry, Edward, Planter, Vanderhorst St , Neck
Perry, Flora, Hampstead, F.P.C., Neck
Perry, Isabella, Widow, Midwife, 72 Queen St
Perry, Peter S., Millinery Store, 276 King St
Perry, Stephens, Accountant, 8 Water St
Peschoder, Solomon, 36 Hasell St
Petch, Francis, Shoemaker, 7 Berresford St
Peters, James, Teacher, 30 Cumberland St.
Peters, Mary, Mrs., Boarding House, E Bay St , cr. Crafts' S.Whf.
Peters, Mary, Widow, 111 Broad St
Peters, -----, Mrs , Boarding House, 60 E Bay St.
Peterson, John, Grocer, 233 E Bay St.
Peterson, Joseph, Grocer, 16 Market St.
Peterson, Oliver, Mariner, 12 Bedon's Al
Petrie, George, 47 Society St.
Petsch, Jane, Widow, Teacher, 14 Liberty St
Pettet, Robert, Grocer, French Al
Pettigru, James, Attorney, 16 St Michael's Al , Res. 5 S

Bay St
Pezant, John L , Grocer, cr Washington & Boundary Sts
Pezant, Lewis, Grocer, 9 Boundary St
Pezant, Peter, Mariner, 16 Washington St.
Phelon, Edmond M., Grocer, 88 Meeting St., cr Queen St.
Phillipe, Odet, Cigar Maker, 103 E. Bay St
Phillips, Ann, 16 Philadelphia St., F.P C
Phillips, Benjamin, Shoemaker, 26 Tradd St.
Phillips, -----, Capt , 102 Church St
Phillips, Dorothy, Widow, 132 Queen St.
Phillips, John, Grocer, 2 Lynch's Ln.
Phillips, John, Painter, 61 Pinckney St., cr E. Bay St
Phillips, Kitty, 4 Philadelphia St , F P.C
Phillips, Margaret, Seamstress, 2 Guignard St
Phillips, Rosetta, 3 Linguard St., F.P.C
Phillips, St. John, Physician, 6 Pinckney St , cr E Bay St.
Phynnea, Josiah, Pilot, 11 Zigzag Al.
Picault, Hyacinth, Boarding House, 7 Queen St
Pierce, Edward, 15 Tradd St
Pierson, Catharine, Widow, Boarding House, 50 Broad St
Pillot, -----, Widow of John, Meeting St., Neck
Pilsbury, Moody, Merchant, 13 Anson St
Pilsbury, Rebecca, Widow, Nurse, 27 Pinckney St.
Pilsbury, Samuel, Export Officer of Customs, 23 Anson St
Pincel, William, Tin Plate Worker, 81 Meeting St , F P.C.
Pinckney, Charles Cotesworth, Gen., 223 E. Bay St.
Pinckney, Charles, Planter, 9 Church St.
Pinckney, Eliza, Seamstress, 26 Berresford St , F P C
Pinckney, Frances Susannah, Widow, 40 St. Philip's St
Pinckney, Hannah, 45 Boundary St , F.P.C.
Pinckney, Hannah, 6 Ellery St., F.P C.
Pinckney, Henry L , 4 New St
Pinckney, L., Widow, 25 Pitt St
Pinckney, Roger, Planter, 40 St. Philip's St.
Pinckney, Thomas, Gen., 10 George St
Pine, -----, Widow of John, 79 Broad St.
Pitray & Viel, Merchants, 167 E. Bay St.
Pitray, L. A , Merchant, King St. Road, Neck
Pitts, Peter, Mariner, 54 Church St , F P C
Platt, George, Commission Merchant, Vanderhorst's Whf , Res. 71 E. Bay St
Platt, John T , Corn Store, Edmondston's Whf
Plissonau, John, Dry Goods Store, 44 E Bay St
Plumeau, John Francis, Secretary, S C. Insurance Co., 62 E. Bay St.
Plunkett, L. C., Shopkeeper & Billiard Tables, N.E. cr St , Philip's & Warren Sts., Neck
Pogson, Milward, Rev , 130 Wentworth St , cr. Pitt St.
Pohl, Joseph & Son, Merchants, 53 E Bay St
Pohl, Joseph, Merchant, 53 E. Bay St
Poincignon, Peter A., Tin Plate Worker, 19 Queen St.
Poinsett, Harry, Henrietta St , F P.C , Neck
Pont, Anthony, Shoemaker, 308 King St
Popenheim, Barbary, Widow, 234 Meeting St.
Porcher, Philip, Mrs., Plantress, Alexander St., Mazyckborough, Neck
Portas, Ann, Seamstress, Henrietta St., F.P.C., Neck
Porter, Benjamin R , Cabinet Maker, 14 King St
Porter, Lewis M., Ship Master, 12 Tradd St
Porter, Peter, Blacksmith, 15 King St.

94

Porter, Sarah, Confectioner, 12 Church St

Porter, William L., Accountant, 13 Champney St., Res 22 S. Bay St.

Portrener, Stephen, 14 Lowndes St., Neck

Postell, William, Planter, cr. Charlotte St., Res. Elizabeth & John Sts , Wraggsborough, Neck

Potter, John, Merchant, Res. 40 Society St.

Potter, -----, Widow of Washington, 37 E. Bay St.

Power, -----, Widow of Edward, 27 Guignard St

Powers, Sabina, Washer, 25 Wentworth St , F P C.

Poyas, James, Jr., Gunsmith, 84 Meeting St.

Poyas, James, Sr., Shipyard, 35 S. Bay, Res 49 King St.

Poyas, John E., Physician, 49 Meeting St.

Prary, Manuel, Grocer, 2 Market St.

Pratt, John, Capt., 5 Laurens St.

Prele, Ann L , Widow, 118 Meeting St.

Prele, Frederick, 118 Meeting St

Prentis, Anna R., Widow, Plantress, Cannonborough, Neck

Prescott, George W., Merchant, Magwood's Whf., Res 10 State St.

Pressly, -----, Misses, Mantua Makers, 6 Blackbird Al.

Price, Ann, Widow, Grocer, 30 King St., cr. Whim Court

Price, O'Brian Smith, Planter, King St. Road, Neck

Price, Thomas, Bookkeeper, Union Bank, Res. 15 Society St.

Price, Thomas William, Planter, 12 George St

Price, William, Jr , Planter, 116 Broad St.

Price, William, Planter, 3 Orange St

Price, William S , Physician, King St. Road, Neck

Primerose, Catharine, Widow, 294 E. Bay St.

Primerose, Robert, Auctioneer, Res. 294 E. Bay St.

Prince, Charles, Tin Plate Worker, 114 King St.

Prince, John, Porter & Transfer Clerk, Planters' & Mechanics' Bank, Res. Bank Yard

Pringle, George, Merchant, King St. Road, Neck

Pringle, James R , Collector of Customs, Res. 101 Tradd St.

Pringle, John J., 62 Tradd St.

Pringle, Mary, Widow, 90 Broad St.

Pringle, -----, Misses, Plantress, 60 Tradd St.

Prioleau & Pinckney, Attornies, 108 Church St.

Prioleau, Catharine, Widow, 102 Tradd St.

Prioleau, John C., Factor, 9 Vendue Range, Res. 50 Meeting St.

Prioleau, Philip G., Physician, 220 Meeting St., cr George St

Prioleau, Samuel, Attorney, 108 Church St., Res 12 Bull St

Prioleau, Thomas G., Physician, 135 Meeting St.

Pritchard, Joseph, Merchant, 8 Society St.

Pritchard, Paul, Ship Carpenter's Yard, Gadsden's Whf., Res. 6 Hasell St

Pritchard, William, Sr., Ship Carpenter, Res. 1 Pinckney St.

Proctor, William, Shoe Store, 213 King St.

Provost, Camilla, Seamstress, 13 Berresford St.

Provost, Mary, 15 Philadelphia St., F.P C.

Provost, Phillis, Seamstress, French Al , F.P C.

Purcell, Harriet, Whim Court, F.P.C.

Purse, Thomas, Watchmaker, 43 St Philip's St.

Purse, William W., Cabinet Maker, 241 King St , Res 40 Liberty St.

Purse, William, Watchmaker, 58 Broad St

Quash, Francis D., 307 E Bay St.

Quash, Robert, 108 Broad St

Quin, Thomas F , Grocer, cr Boundary & Meeting Sts., Neck

Quinby, Elizabeth, Widow, 11 Pinckney St.

Quinby, Joseph, Carpenter, 4 Minority St

Quinlan, Michael, 8 St Philip's St.

Quinn, Aeneas, Grocer, 13 Hasell St., cr. Anson St.

Quinnan, Barbary, Northern Warehouse, 275 King St

Rabb, J., Block Master, 206 E. Bay St., Res State St.

Rain, Elizabeth, Miss, Teacher, 6 Orange St.

Raine, Thomas, Meeting St. Road, Neck

Ramsay & Gantt, Attornies, 74 Broad St

Ramsay, David, Attorney, 74 Broad St., Res 109 Queen St.

Ramsay, James, Physician, 74 Broad St

Ramsay, John, Physician, 1 Anson St.

Ramsay, Judith, Fruiterer, 32 Guignard St., F.P.C

Ramsay, -----, Misses, Seminary, 74 Broad St.

Ranall, Peter, Comb Maker, 243 King St.

Randall, Ann, 104 Tradd St.

Rapelye, Jacob, Auctioneer, 17 Vendue Range, Res. 38 Broad St.

Rapp, Catharine, Milliner, King St. Road, Neck

Rasher, Elizabeth, Widow, Hampstead, near Meeting St , Neck

Ratcliffe, John W , Tailor, 30 Wentworth St

Ravenel & Stevens, Factors, Vanderhorst's Whf.

Ravenel, Catharine, Widow, 64 Broad St

Ravenel, Daniel, Attorney, 47 Meeting St.

Ravenel, Edmund, Physician, 30 Tradd St., Res 64 Broad St.

Ravenel, Henrietta, Widow, 287 E Bay St cr. Laurens St.

Ravenel, Henry, Surveyor, 27½ St. Michael's Al , Res 64 Broad St.

Ravina, J. D., Teacher of Languages, Church St.

Raworth, George F., Saddler, 161 Meeting St , Res 12 Liberty St.

Ray, Constance, Seamstress, 31 Coming St , F P C

Ray, Eliza, Seamstress, 10 Philadelphia St , F.P.C

Ray, James, Factor, 2 Smith's Whf.

Raymond, Napoleon, Porter House, 179 E. Bay St

Raymond, William H., Merchant, 331 King St.

Raynay, Bauseyere, Carpenter, cr. Warren & Coming Sts , Neck

Read & Horsey, Merchants, 265 King St., cr. Wentworth St.

Read, Benjamin, Wheelwright, Elizabeth St , Wraggsborough, F.P.C., Neck

Read, William, Physician, 14 Logan St.

Readlimer, Christiana, Widow, Spring St., Neck

Rechon & Byrne, Sail Makers, Chisolm's Upper Whf.

Rechon, David, Tailor, 241 King St.

Rechon, Lewis, Sailmaker, Chisolm's Upper Whf., Res. 229 E. Bay St.

Redfern, John, Shoemaker, 34 King St.

Redman, James, Blacksmith, Daniell's Whf., Res 32

95

Beaufain St.

Redman, Matthew, Carpenter, 25 Market St.
Reed & Cooper, Shoe Store, 143 King St., cr Queen St
Reed, Betty, Seamstress, St. Philip's St , F P C., Neck
Reeves, Abraham P., Carpenter, 202 Meeting St
Reeves, Aeneas S., Master, Work House, 1 Lynch St.
Reeves, Solomon, Carpenter, 8 Clifford St
Reid, Ann M , Widow, 10 Laurens St
Reid, Betsey, 8 Logan St., F.P.C.
Reid, E. S., Widow, Milliner, King St. Road, Neck
Reid, Elizabeth, Widow, 104 Meeting St.
Reid, George, Bookkeeper, Bank of S. C., 49 E Bay St.
Reid, George, Rev., 169 E. Bay St.
Reid, James, Blacksmith, 17 Cumberland St
Reid, James, Wheelwright, 106 Meeting St.
Reilly & Barnard, Grocers, State St , cr Queen St.
Reilly, Bernard, Grocer, 17 Queen St.
Reilly, Bernard, Jr , Grocer, 191 King St.
Reilly, Charles, Grocer, 3 Vendue Range
Reilly, -----, Widow of James, 64 Queen St
Remoussin, Tissy, Fruiterer, 3 Beaufain St., F.P.C
Ren, Martin, Grocer, 12 Elliott St.
Renaud, Mary, Seamstress, 8 Wentworth St.
Renauld, John, Fruiterer, 42 Anson St
Revell, Margaret, 242 E. Bay St
Reviere, John P., Dry Goods Store, 174 King St.
Reynolds, George N., Coach Maker, 117 Meeting St
Reynolds, Sarah, Mrs , 104 Wentworth St
Rhind, Elizabeth, Widow, Wentworth St.
Ribbecks, Frederick, Grocer, Boundary St , W. End, Neck
Ribboch, Frederick, Grocer, 129 Boundary St.
Ricard, Frances, Grocer, 95 E. Bay St., cr. Elliott St
Rice, A., Merchant, King St. Road, Neck
Richard, Charles, Bricklayer, 37 Coming St
Richards, Joseph, Boarding House, 4 Elliott St.
Richards, Martha, Widow, 16 Church St.
Richards, Samuel, Quorum Unis, 84 E Bay St., Res. 56
    Elliott St
Richardson, Ann, Widow, 12 Smith St
Richardson, Henry, Physician, 210 Meeting St
Richardson, J. S., Judge, Pinckney St , Cannonborough,
    Neck
Richardson, Louisa, Seamstress, 44 Beaufain St., F P.C
Richardson, Mary, Widow, 15 Smith St.
Ricketts, Lorens, Grocer, 6 Wall St., cr. Minority St.
Righton, Elizabeth, Miss, 66 Church St.
Righton, Elizabeth, Widow, 5 Water St.
Righton, Flora, Widow, 81 E Bay St
Righton, John M., Physician, Res. 15 George St.
Righton, Joseph, Cooper, 34 E Bay St , Res 5 Water St.
Riley, Catharine, Widow, 32 Mazyck St
Riley, William, Printer, 41 Broad St , Res 3 Back St
Ring, David A., Painter, 5 Broad St., Res. 33 Meeting St
Ripley, Tilson, Grocer, 20 & 22 State St
Rivers, George, Planter, 2 Greenhill St
Rivers, John, Grocer, 55 St Philip's St.
Rivers, Nelly, Zigzag Al., F.P.C.
Rivers, Susannah, 4 Whim Court, F P.C
Rivers, Thomas, 28 Ellery St.
Roach, William, Jr , Clerk to Council, 13 Society St

Roach, William, Sr , City Treasurer, 13 Society St
Robb, James, Grocer, 190 King St
Roberts, Catharine, 25 Archdale St., F.P.C.
Roberts, Catharine, Widow, Dry Goods Store, 110 King
    St.
Roberts, Martha, Widow, 399 King St., Neck
Roberts, Rosetta, 14 Clifford St., F P C
Roberts, Shelton, Grocer, 100 King St
Roberts, Stephen, Capt , 160 Church St.
Roberts, Thomas M , Watch Maker, 45 Broad St
Roberts, Venus, Fruiterer, 19 Beaufain St., F P C
Roberts, William, Inspector in Custom House, Res 6
    Wentworth St.
Robertson, Ann, Widow, Vanderhorst St , Neck
Robertson, Eliza & Ann, Grocers, 18 Pinckney St.
Robertson, James, 16 Bull St., F.P C
Robertson, James, Merchant, 51 E. Bay St.
Robertson, John, Grocer, 193 Meeting St.
Robertson, John, Merchant & Navy Agent, Crafts' S. Whf.,
    Res. 31 Meeting St.
Robin, Antoinette, Widow, 115 Wentworth St.
Robinson, Alexander, Secretary, F. M. I. Co., 85 Meeting
    St.
Robinson, Alexander, Sr., Watchmaker, 136 King St
Robinson, Betsey, Washer, Alexander St., Mazyckborough
    St , F P.C., Neck
Robinson, John, Factor, 15 Champney St., Res
    Wraggsborough
Robinson, John, Merchant, Res. John St., Wraggsborough,
    Neck
Robinson, Randall, Merchant, Kunhardt's Whf., 94 Tradd
    St
Robinson, Thomas H , Baker, 9 Bedon's Al.
Robinson, William, Grocer, 42 Elliott St.
Robinson, William, Planter, 81 Church St
Robiou, Elizabeth, Widow, 40 Beaufain St.
Roche, Edward L., Tailor, 140 King St.
Roche, John, Lodge Room, cr. Church & Chalmers Sts
Roddy, Martin, Grocer, 47 King St.
Rodericks, Anthony, Deputy Sheriff, 267 E Bay St
Rodgers, Abraham, Shoemaker, 18 Water St., F.P.C.
Rodgers, Joseph, 7 Amen St , F P.C.
Rodgers, Lewis, Wheelwright, 3 Bull St.
Rodgers, Sarah, Widow, 24 King St.
Rodgers, Susannah, 122 Wentworth St.
Rodgers, Willis, Shoe Store, 267, Res. 240 King St , cr
    Hasell St.
Rogers, Charles C., Custom House, Res. 29 Guignard St
Rogers, Christopher, 47 Tradd St.
Rogers, Elizabeth, Widow, 259 Meeting St., Neck
Rogers, John B , Merchant, cr. Crafts' Whf., Res. 122
    Wentworth St.
Rogers, John Ralph, Ship Chandler, 105 E. Bay St
Roh, Jacob Frederick, Blacksmith, 109 Meeting St., cr.
    Cumberland St.
Rohmer, John, Billiard Table, 140 Meeting St
Rolain, Catharine, 10 Archdale St.
Rolando, F. G., Attorney, Berresford St
Rolando,-----, Widow, 13 Cumberland St.
Roma, Janifer, Mariner, 9 Linguard St

96

Roper, Benjamin, Planter, 15 Legare St

Roper, H , Widow, 35 E Bay St.

Roper, Thomas, Planter, 163 E. Bay St.

Roper, William, Planter, 163 E Bay St

Roper, William, Planter, 35 E. Bay St.

Rose, Arthur G., Assistant Clerk, Bank of Discount & Deposit, 75 George St

Rose, Christopher, Grocer, 62 King St

Rose, Hugh, Planter, 15 Bull St.

Rose, James, Planter, 292 E. Bay St

Rose, John, Commission Merchant, 120 E Bay St., Res. 26 Broad St.

Rose, John S., Accountant, 4 Green St.

Rose, Nancy, Mantua Maker, 8 Zigzag Al , F.P.C.

Ross, David, Custom House Officer, Res. 9 Motte's Ln.

Ross, Eliza Ann, 4 Magazine St.

Ross, Hugh, Stone Cutter, 149 Meeting St.

Ross, James,Merchant, 148 E. Bay St , cr. Vendue Range

Ross, Thomas, 8 Liberty St.

Ross, William, Merchant, King St. Road, Neck

Rothwell, Jane, Boarding House, 2 Broad St , cr. E. Bay St.

Rotureau, Charles, Confectioner, 48 Tradd St.

Roumillant & Son, Widow of John, Confectioners, 71 Meeting St.

Roumillat, Joseph, Candle & White Wax Manufactory, cr. Columbus & Meeting Sts , Neck

Rouse, Christopher, Bricklayer, 43 Wentworth St.

Rouse, William, Jr., Col., 83 Market St.

Rouse, William, Tanner, 83 Market St.

Rouse, William, Tanyard, cr. King & Mary Sts , Neck

Rout, Catharine, Widow, 14 Friend St.

Rout, William George, Outdoor Clerk, Bank of Discount & Deposit, Res 14 Friend St.

Routledge, John, Merchant, King St. Road, Neck

Roux, Lewis, Quorum Unis, 101 E. Bay St , Res. 162 Meeting St.

Rowand, Charles E., Planter, 93 Meeting St.

Rowe & White, Stone Cutters, Church St , cr Market St

Rowe, George W., Shoemaker, 106 King St.

Rowe, James, Stone Cutter, 182 Church St.

Roye, Francois, Grain Store, 39 Anson St., cr Wentworth St.

Ruddock, Samuel H., Surveyor, 39 King St.

Rumpp, G. H., Grocer, cr Meeting & Wolf Sts., Neck

Runceman, John, Grocer, 8 Bull St.

Rush, Mary, Mrs., 26 Meeting St

Russ, Benjamin, Carpenter, 2 Society St.

Russell, Elizabeth, Widow, 8 Guignard St.

Russell, Margaret, 39 George St.

Russell, Robert, Zigzag Al , F.P C

Russell, Sarah, Washer, 2 Ellery St., F P.C.

Russell, Sarah, Widow, 11 Lynch's Ln

Russell, -----, Widow of Daniel, Unity Al., cr. State St

Russell, -----, Widow of John, 18 Wentworth St.

Russell, -----, Widow of Nathaniel, 48 Meeting St.

Rutledge, Frederick, Planter, 111 Tradd St.

Rutledge, John, Planter, 292 E. Bay St.

Rutledge, Mary, Widow, 66 Tradd St.

Rutledge, State, Planter, 303 E. Bay St.

Rutledge, -----, Widow of Charles, 2 New St.

Rutledge, William, 3 George St

Safford, Isabella, Widow, 295 E. Bay St , cr Minority St.

Saltar, Thomas R., Ship Joiner, Pritchard & Knox's Whf., Res 59 State St , cr. Amen St

Saltus & Blythewood, Factors, Vanderhorst's Whf

Saltus, Francis, Jr , Capt , Factor, S Bay St

Saltus, Francis, Sr., Ship Chandler, 59 E. Bay St , Res. 19 S. Bay St.

Samory, Claude, Upholstery Store, 50 Queen St.

Sampson, Henry, Dry Goods Store, 169 E. Bay St.

Sampson, Joseph, Merchant, 181 E. Bay St.

Sarazin, Catharine, Miss, 101 Wentworth St

Sarazin, Mary, Miss, 101 Wentworth St.

Sargent, J. H., Attorney, King St , near Vanderhorst St , Neck

Sarzedas, David, Jr , Auctioneer, Vendue Range, Res 3 Berresford St.

Sarzedas, David, Sr., Physician, 285 King St.

Sass, Edward G , Northern Warehouse, 77 Queen St.

Sass, Jacob, Col., 79 Queen St

Sass, Ludwig W., Grocer, Wentworth St., cr. Anson St.

Sass, William H., Teller, Bank of Discount & Deposit, Res. 79 King St.

Satorius, Catharine, Widow, 44 King St.

Saunders, Elizabeth B., Widow, Henrietta St., Neck

Savage, Ann, Mrs., Millinery Store, 179 King St , cr. Clifford Al

Savage, Arthur, Merchant, 16 Legare St.

Savage, Mary, cr. Elizabeth & Henrietta Sts., F.P.C., Neck

Savage, -----, Mrs , 16 Legare St.

Savage, -----, Widow of George, 14 Savage St.

Savenia, Joseph, Fruiterer, 74 State St.

Sawyer & Steele, Merchants, 364 King St., cr. Boundary St.

Sayrs, Francis, Carpenter, 26 Bull St.

Scanler, Jane, Grocer, Widow, 14 Maiden Ln.

Schaffer, Charles G., Printer, 21 Anson St.

Schenck, James R., Bookseller & Stationers, 23 Broad St

Schieffely, F., Professor of Modern Languages, 10 Coming St.

Schirmer, John E., Cooper, 8 Elliott St.

Schmidt, Elizabeth, Widow, 3 Montague St

Schmidt, John W., Physician, 5 Bedon's Al., Res. 53 Church St.

Schnell, John J., Grocer, 175 Church St.

Schnierle, John M , Carpenter, 11 Friend St.

Schriber, Nicholas, Boarding House, 56 State St.

Schrieder, Christian, Accountant, 53 State St.

Schroder, John, Grocer, 55 Queen St.

Schroder, Matilda, Dry Goods Store, 226 King St , Res 102 Meeting St.

Schults, W B , Baker, 188 Meeting St

Schults, William, Grocer, Henrietta St., Neck

Schultz, John, Factor, 40 Fitzsimons' Whf , 4 Laurens St.

Schutt & Budd, Hardware Store, 89 E Bay St.

Schutt, Lewis C., Merchant, 27 E Bay St., Res 2 Meeting St., cr. S. Bay St.

Schwartz, Frederick, Butcher, Cannonborough, Neck

Schwartz, Mary, Mrs., Coming St., Neck

Scot, Thomas, Clerk, 63 E Bay St , Res. 89 Tradd St

Scot, William M , Quorum Unis, 183 E Bay St., Res. 7 Pinckney St
Scott, Bridget, 225 King St.
Scott, Rebecca E., Widow, 265 Meeting St., Neck
Scriven, Amarintha, Widow, 62 Church St
Scriven, Jane, Nurse, 14 Stoll's Al , F.P.C
Scriven, Rebecca, Miss, 18 Lynch's Ln.
Scriven, Thomas, Planter, Hampstead, Neck
Seabrook, Benjamin, Planter, 15 Rutledge St.
Seabrook, Thomas B., Planter, 18 Rutledge St., cr Bull St
Seaver, Abraham, 12 Pinckney St.
Seaward, James, Clerk, U S Paymaster, 23 Pitt St.
Sebring & Ferguson, Merchant Tailors, 30 Broad St.
Sebring, Cornelius C , Printer, 44 Queen St.
Sebring, Edward, Merchant Tailor, 30 Broad St.
Seigling, J., Music Warehouse, 69 Broad St
Selah, William W., Printer, 172 Tradd St
Selean, Peter, Fruiterer, 185 Church St.
Selfe, James & Co., Shoe Store, 108 King St.
Senet, Joseph, Confectioner, 168 King St
Senet, Mary Ann, Widow, 123 King St.
Seran, Francis, Fruiterer, 47 Anson St
Seresy, Sarah, 92 Queen St.
Service, John, School Master, cr Cannon & Coming Sts , Neck
Sexias, Isaac M , 122 King St.
Sexton, Phineas, Trunk Maker, 93 Boundary St.
Seyle, Priscilla, Widow, Shopkeeper, King St , Neck
Seyle, Samuel, Saddler, 220 King St.
Seymour, Eliza, Mantua Maker, 80 Tradd St., F.P C
Seymour, Sally, Pastry Cook, 80 Tradd St., F.P.C.
Seymour, William, Carpenter, 80 Tradd St , F P.C.
Shackelford, Francis, Painter, 15 Archdale St., F.P C .
Shackleford, William, Factor, Res 52 Society St.
Shand, Robert, Custom House Officer, 25 Pinckney St
Sharp, John, Block & Pump Maker, Guignard St., cr Maiden Ln.
Shaw, Charles, Carpenter, 144 Meeting St.
Shaw, Margaret, 111 Boundary St
Shay, Frances, Milliner, 301 King St.
Shecut, J. L. E. W., Physician, 94 Meeting St.
Shegog, Joseph & George, Grocers, 293 King St
Sheldon, Henry & Co., Hardware Store, 335 King St.
Sheon, Caty, 2 St Philip's St., F P.C.
Shepard, James, Harness Maker, 248 King St., Res. 24 Coming St
Sherrer, John, Rigger, 1 Bedon's Al.
Shields, Henry, Grocer, 144 King St
Shields, Mary, 41 Wentworth St., F P C.
Shields, William, Portrait Painter, 36 Broad St
Shirer, John, Carpenter, 12 Archdale St.
Shirer, John, Gunsmith, 48 Queen St.
Shively, Charles, 230 Meeting St.
Shively, John, Painter, 230 Meeting St
Shively, Mary, Widow, Seed Store, 230 Meeting St.
Sholtus, -----, Widow of Abraham, 9 Mazyck St.
Shoolbred, James, Planter, 46 Montague St.
Shorthouse, Thomas, Hardware Merchant, 365 King St , cr. Boundary St., Neck
Shrewsbury, E., Ship Carpenter, Charlotte St.,

Mazyckborough, Neck
Shroudy, W. B T., Clerk, 176 Meeting St
Shults, Henry, Doughty St., Neck
Sibley & Jones, Commission Merchants, 183 E Bay St.
Sibley, George B. R., 183 E. Bay St.
Sifley & Mintzing, Saw Pit & Lumber Yard, W End Queen St.
Sifley, Henry, Lumber Merchant, Res. 44 Market St
Sifley, John, Bricklayer, 44 Market St.
Sifley, Susannah, Widow, Dry Goods Store, 86 Market St
Sigwall, Thomas, 52 Wentworth St.
Silivia, Dominique, Mariner, 3 French Al.
Silliman, John H., Ship Master, Charlotte St., Mazyckborough, Neck
Simmons, Clarissa, Fruiterer, 97 Wentworth St., F.P.C.
Simmons, Joseph, Grocer, cr. Broad & E. Bay Sts
Simmons, Orphay, Widow, 251 Meeting St., Neck
Simons & Waring, Attornies, 10 St. Michael's Al.
Simons & Waring, Factors, 8 Smith's Whf.
Simons, Anthony, Factor, 75 Wentworth St
Simons, Benjamin P., Painter, 88 Market St
Simons, Charles, Engraver, Columbus St , Neck
Simons, Edward, 2 Brownlee 's Row, King St., Neck
Simons, Edward P., Attorney, 5 Laurens St
Simons, Eliza, 17 St. Philip's St , F.P.C.
Simons, Francis, Widow, 107 Tradd St
Simons, Gains, 48 Bull St.
Simons, Hannah, Widow, 26 Coming St
Simons, Joseph, Physician, 103 Meeting St
Simons, Joseph W , Druggist, 359 King St.
Simons, K. L., Widow, Coming St., Neck
Simons, Keating & Sons, Factors, D'Oyley's Whf.
Simons, Keating, Factor, Res. 5 Orange St.
Simons, Lewis, Factor, D'Oyley's Whf.
Simons, Maria, 21 Middle St., F.P.C.
Simons, Maurice, Factor, Res. 1 Middle St.
Simons, Maurice, Jr., Planter, 24 Society St.
Simons, Rebecca, Seamstress, 26 Wentworth St
Simons, Samuel, Merchant, 236 King St
Simons, T., Physician, 164 Meeting St
Simons, Thomas Y., Physician, 15 Society St.
Simons, -----, Widow of Harleston, cr. Cumberland & Church Sts.
Simons, -----, Widow of Keating Lewis, 7 Orange St
Simpson, P., Dentist, 96 Meeting St.
Simpson, Peter, Shopkeeper, cr Boundary & Elizabeth Sts , F.P.C , Neck
Simpson, Smart, Carpenter, 152 Tradd St., F.P C
Sims, William, Capt., Hudson St., Mazyckborough, Neck
Simson, William, Planter, 3 Minority St.
Sinclair, Alexander, Merchant, 64, Res. 45 E Bay St.
Sinclair, William, Planter, Pinckney St , Neck
Sinclair, William, Purser, U. S Navy, Office, Crafts' S Whf.
Singleton, Abigail, Seamstress, 39 Wentworth St
Singleton, Sarah, Widow, 94 Boundary St , Neck
Sinmark, Elizabeth, Fruiterer, 18 Washington St., F P.C.
Sire, Joseph, 173 Church St.
Skinner, Samuel H., Printer, 85 Market St
Slade, Maria, Widow, 8 S Bay St.

Slate, Ashbell, Grocer, Gadsden's Whf.
Slawson, Nathaniel, Baker, 195 King St.
Slowick, John, Grocer, 19 King St.
Sluter, Jacob, Dry Goods Store, 238 King St , cr Hasell St
Small, Catharine, Seamstress, 7 Coming St., F.P.C.
Small, Thomas, Carpenter, 9 Swinton's Ln., F P C
Smallwood, Richard, Custom House Officer, 4 Guignard St
Smart, John T., Deputy Sheriff, 4 Minority St.
Smerdon, P., Widow, Boarding House, 131 Church St
Smile, Martha, Widow, 44 St. Philip's St.
Smith, Agnes, Widow, 389 King St
Smith, Ann, Miss, 36 Coming St.
Smith, Ann, Miss, Boundary St., Cannonborough, Neck
Smith, Ann, Widow, Henrietta St., Neck
Smith, Benjamin & Co., Ship Chandlers, 71 E. Bay St.
Smith, Benjamin, Painter, 2 Exchange St., Res 13 E Bay St.
Smith, Benjamin, Planter, 2 Church St.
Smith, Eliza, Cook, 10 Linguard St , F P.C.
Smith, Eliza, Mrs., Dry Goods Store, 362 King St.
Smith, Elizabeth, Widow, 15 Blackbird Al.
Smith, Elizabeth, Widow, 9 Montague St.
Smith, Grace, 15 Coming St., F P C
Smith, H. Q., Cooper, Washington St , Mazyckborough, Neck
Smith, Henrietta, Widow, 45 Beaufain St
Smith, Hester, 2 Savage St
Smith, Hugh, Merchant, Smith's Whf., Res. 15 Broad St
Smith, James, Clerk, 16 Beaufain St.
Smith, John A., Merchant, 1 Kunhardt's Whf.
Smith, John, Boarding House, 2 Bedon's Al.
Smith, John M., Mrs., Boarding House, 33 Broad St.
Smith, John, Upholsterer, 12 Magazine St , cr. Mazyck St
Smith, Joseph, Guardman, 17 Price's Al.
Smith, Josiah, 60 Anson St
Smith, Linda, Henrietta St., F.P.C., Neck
Smith, Lucretia, Mantua Maker, 235 King St.
Smith, Maria, Seamstress, 1 Swinton's Ln.
Smith, Mary, 3 Society St.
Smith, Mary, Elizabeth St., F.P.C., Neck
Smith, Mary, Widow, 14 Coming St.
Smith, Nancy, 30 Mazyck St., cr West St., F.P C.
Smith, Peter, Grocer, 16 Elliott St
Smith, Peter, Lumber Merchant, S. Bay St., Res. 4 Mazyck St
Smith, Press M., Factor, D'Oyley's Whf., Res. St Philip's St., cr Boundary St.
Smith, Quinton H., Cooper, Dewee's Whf
Smith, R. M , Widow, 14 Coming St.
Smith, Richard, Cabinet Maker, 55 Broad St.
Smith, Robert, Planter, 281 E. Bay St
Smith, Samuel, Boarding House, 5 State St
Smith, Samuel, Boot Maker, 104 Market St
Smith, Samuel, Factor, Res. 73 Broad St.
Smith, Susan E , Widow, Plantress, 183 Meeting St.
Smith, Theodore L., Notary Public, 49 Wentworth St.
Smith, Thomas, 4 Berresford St., F P C
Smith, Thomas, Planter, 10 Green St.
Smith, Thomas R , Planter, 1 Meeting St

Smith, Thomas Y., Capt , Planter, 11 Boundary St.
Smith, Whiteford, Grocer, 163 Church St.
Smith, -----, Widow of Michael, Columbus St , Neck
Smith, -----, Widow of William, 185 E. Bay St.
Smith, William, Boarding House, 15 Chalmers St.
Smith, William, Clerk, 4 Mazyck St
Smith, William, Grocer, 23 Rutledge St.
Smith, William J., Factor, Smith's Whf , Mazyckborough, Neck
Smith, William, Jr., Shipwright Director, Union Insurance Co., E . End Washington St , Mazyckborough, Neck
Smith, William, Judge, 73 Queen St.
Smith, William Mason, Planter, 10 Lamboll St
Smith, William, Merchant, 9 Tradd St
Smith, William S., Prothonotory, State House, Res. 11 Boundary St.
Smylie, Andrew, U. S Appraiser, 13 Champney St., Res 257 E. Bay St.
Smylie, Martha, Widow, 44 St Philip's St.
Smylie, Susannah, Widow, 18 Legare St.
Smythe, Robert, Carpenter, 15 Bull St , F.P.C
Snetter, Charles, Barber, 40 Guignard St
Snowden, Joshua L. & Co., Ship Chandlers, 186, Res. 241 E. Bay St.
Snowden, Sarah, Widow, 291 E. Bay St.
Snowden, William E., Factor, 291 E Bay St.
Sobieski, Thaddeus, Engineer for Government, at the Lines, Neck
Sollee, H. N., Widow, 101 Church St.
Solomon, Jonas, Shopkeeper, King St Road, Neck
Solomons, Aaron, 396 King St., Neck
Solomons, Alexander, Merchant, 287 King St
Solomons, Catharine, Widow, 40 King St.
Solomons, Chapman, Hardware Store, 290 King St
Solomons, Lewis, Watchmaker, 375½ King St., Neck
Solomons, Sarah, Clothing & Mattress Store, 143 E. Bay St.
Solomons, Solomon, Dry Goods Store, 393 King St , Neck
Sommers, John W , Accountant, D'Oyley's Whf., Res 3 Church St.
Sommers, Rose, Mantua Maker, 24 Lynch's Ln., F.P.C.
Sompayrac, Theodore, Merchant, 5 Fitzsimons' Whf.
Southworth, Rufus, Teacher, 17 Broad St., cr. Gadsden's Al.
Sparks, Rachael, Widow, 87 Queen St
Sparm & Dinkinns, Factors, Edmonston's Whf.
Sparneck, Henry, 23 Amen St., cr. Philadelphia St.
Sparrow, James, Mrs., Butcher, Cannonborough, Neck
Spears, Archibald, Clerk, Planters' & Mechanics' Bank, 15 Society St.
Spears, Mary, Widow, 15 Society St.
Speissegger, John, Musical Instrument Maker, cr Hasell & Anson Sts.
Spencer, Seth, 35 Elliott St.
Sprague, Boswell, Merchant, 10 Vendue Range, Res. 9 State St.
Spring, John, Wraggsborough, Neck
St Amand, J S., Coach Maker, Meeting St , Res 14 Mazyck St.
Stade, Christian & Co , Grocers, Rutledge St , cr

99

Montague St.
Stade, Christian, Grocer, 10 Wentworth St., cr Pitt St.
Stafford, James, Mariner, 17 Middle St.
Stall, Frederick, Grocer, 21 Pitt St , cr Montague St.
Stanley, Charles A., Comb Store, 327 King St.
Stanton, Sarah, Widow, 53 Wentworth St.
Stark, Charles, Grocer, 246 E Bay St.
Starr, Edward B , Ship Chandler & Commission Merchant, 146 E. Bay St.
Steedman, C. J., Meeting St. Road, Neck
Steedman, Elizabeth, Boarding House, 191 E. Bay St.
Steedman, J., Physician, 96 Wentworth St.
Steel, Elizabeth, Boarding House, 36 Elliott St.
Steel, Richard, Stone Cutter, 67 Market St
Steel, W. G., Lumber Merchant, Head of Beaufain St.
Steel, William, Dry Goods & Grocery Store, 354 King St.
Steele, J. A., Discount Clerk, Planters' & Mechanics' Bank, Res. Radcliffborough, Neck
Steele, John, Dry Goods Store, Wagon Yards & Stables, 380 King St , Neck
Steinmeyre, George W., 83 Boundary St.
Stellson, J., Millwright, King St Road, Neck
Stent, John, Carpenter, 1 Back St., Res. 37 King St.
Stent, Robert N., 12 Coming St.
Stephens, Thomas B., Printer, 17 Tradd St.
Stephens, Thomas, Teller, Union Bank, Res. at the Bank
Stephens, William S., Custom House Officer, 12 Middle St.
Stevens, Brown, Drayman, 124 Tradd St , F.P C.
Stevens, Daniel, Planter, 28 George St.
Stevens, Jervis H., cr. St. Michael's Al., Res. 118 Tradd St.
Stevens, Ratry, Pastry Cook, 27 Friend St , F.P C.
Stevens, Samuel S., Factor, Vanderhorst's Whf., Res. 29 King St
Stevens, William Smith, Physician, 29 King St.
Stewart, -----, 11 Linguard St , F P.C.
Stewart, Adriana, Widow, 73 Wentworth St.
Stewart, Angus, Carolina Coffee House, 20 Tradd St.
Stewart, Mary, Midwife, 13 Friend St.
Stewart, Robert N., Clerk, Bank of Discount & Deposit, 13 Friend St
Stiles, Copeland, Planter, 122 Wentworth St
Stiles, Samuel, Pilot, 17 E. Bay St., cr. Lynch's Ln.
Stille, Susan, Seamstress, 23 George St , F.P.C
Stillman, James, Public House, 343 King St.
Stock, Ann, Widow, 92 Wentworth St
Stocker, Henry, Boat Builder, 208 E Bay St., Res. Daniells' Whf
Stockin, Braddock, Dyer, 285 King St.
Stoddard, Elijah, Shoe Store, 121 E. Bay St
Stolan, Joseph, 228 King St.
Stoll, Catharine, Widow, 8 Magazine St.
Stoll, James G., Clerk, 8 Magazine St
Stoll, William F , Outdoor Clerk, Bank of S. C , Res 8 Magazine St.
Stone, Charles, 31 King St
Stone, Timothy, Coach Maker, 69 Wentworth St.
Stoney, Charles H., 23 E Bay St.
Stoney, John, Merchant, 3 Chisolm's Upper Whf., 293 E. Bay St

Street, H. G., New England Coffee House, 175 E Bay St
Street, Joseph, Wheelwright, 14 Swinton's Ln.
Street, Thaddeus, Merchant, 126 E. Bay St.
Street, Timothy & Co., Merchants, 126 E. Bay St.
Strobel, Jacob, 11 Back St.
Strobel, John, 55 Boundary St
Strobel, John N , Accountant, 55 Boundary St.
Strobel, Martin, 224 Meeting St
Strohecker, John, Blacksmith, 163 Meeting St., Res. 18 Cumberland St.
Stromer, Henry M., 25 Archdale St.
Stroub, Jacob, Carpenter, 14 Blackbird Al.
Strum, John, Saddler, 126 Church St.
Sturgis, Josiah, Planter, 24 S Bay St
Suau, Peter, Merchant, Lothrop's Whf , 20 Society St.
Suder, Ann, Widow, 49 Society St
Sullivan, Daniel, Shop, cr. Meeting & Henrietta Sts., Neck
Sullivan, Timothy, Auctioneer, cr E. Bay St & Vendue Range, Res. 66 Anson St.
Surat, Joseph, 390 King St , Neck
Sutcliff, Eli, 22 St. Philip's St.
Sutcliff, James, Baker, 219 King St.
Swain, Mark, Carpenter, 7 Stoll's Al.
Swain, Rebecca, Widow, 7 Stoll's Al
Sweeny, Dinah, Washer, Radcliffborough, F.P.C., Neck
Swift & Turnley, Clothing Warehouse, 16 Broad St
Swift, Samuel, Trunk Maker, 337 King St
Swift, William, Merchant, 336 King St
Swinton, Susannah, Widow, 21 Archdale St
Swords, John, 8 Lowndes St., Neck
Syfan, J. W., Butcher, Coming St. Cont'd., Neck
Symes, J T., 255 Meeting St , Neck
Symes, R. S., Rev., Cannon St., Neck
Taft, C. G., Grocer, 373 King St., Neck
Talvande, Andrew, Young Ladies Boarding School, 24 Legare St
Talvande, -----, Mrs., 100 Tradd St.
Tate, James, Mariner, 36 Queen St.
Taveau, Augustus, 9 Legare St.
Tavel, Frederick, Wharfinger, 15 Anson St.
Taylor, Elizabeth, Widow, near Meeting St , Hampstead, Neck
Taylor, George, Mrs., 96 Boundary St.
Taylor, James, Grocer, 54 Queen St
Taylor, John, Grocer, 130 Church St., cr. Chalmers St
Taylor, Joseph, Ship Carpenter, 262 E Bay St.
Taylor, Josiah, Factor, 4 Lamboll St.
Taylor, Margaret & Daughter, Seamstresses, 13 Blackbird Al.
Taylor, Mary, Shopkeeper, 5 Linguard St
Taylor, Richard, Boarding House, 181 E. Bay St.
Taylor, Thomas, Mariner, 22 Elliott St.
Taylor, Thomas S , Ship Yard, Johnson's Whf., Res. 19 Wall St.
Taylor, -----, Widow of Joseph, 12 Guignard St.
Taylor, William, Ship Carpenter, 26 Wentworth St.
Teachester, John, Cabinet Maker, 11 E. Bay St.
Teale, Mary Jane, Milliner, 252 King St.
Teasdale, Richard, Grain Store, 5 & 6 Martin's Row, Res 54 E. Bay St , cr Vanderhorst's Whf

Teasdale, -----, Widow, 54 E. Bay St., cr. Vanderhorst's Whf
Telfer, Robert, 35 State St.
Tenick, Carpenter, 38 George St
Tennant, Moses, 10 Stoll's Al.
Tennant, Thomas, Custom House Officer, 7 Maiden Ln
Tennant, William, Planter, 60 Anson St.
Tew, Charles, Quorum Unis, Notary Public & Teacher, 86 Wentworth St.
Thackam, Francis, Carpenter, 61 King St
Thayer, Ebenezer, Bookseller, 51 Broad St., Res. 91 Tradd St.
Thayer, Ebenezer, Jr., Teacher, 14 Chalmers St., Res. 62 Wentworth St.
Thayer, Isaac, Boot & Shoe Store, 8 Gillon St., Res 42 Broad St
Thayer, William, 154 King St , Res. 107 Queen St.
Theus, Samuel, Carpenter, John St., cr Elizabeth St , Wraggsborough, F.P.C , Neck
Theus, Simeon, Jr , Planter, 126 King St
Thomas, Barak G., Steam Engineer, 2 Ellery St.
Thomas, Emanuel, 96 Meeting St.
Thomas, Francis, Clerk, 50 Beaufain St.
Thomas, John, Cannon St , Neck
Thomas, John, Grocer, 26 Market St
Thomas, John, Measurer, 96 Meeting St.
Thomas, John, State Constable, 10 Bedon's Al.
Thomas, Joseph, Dry Goods Store, 242 King St.
Thomas, Mary, Widow, 96 Meeting St.
Thomas, Peter, Merchant, 244 King St.
Thomas, Sarah, Widow, 5 Linguard St.
Thomas, Stephen, Jr., 3 Brownlee 's Row, King St , Neck
Thomas, Stephen, Sr , Coming St., Neck
Thompson, Anna, 16 Mazyck St , F P.C
Thompson, Daniel, Custom House Officer, 99 Market St.
Thompson, Eliza Y , Widow, 12 Water St
Thompson, George, Bricklayer, 24 Blackbird Al.
Thompson, James, 8 Lowndes St., Neck
Thompson, James, Boarding Officer, 25 Hasell St.
Thompson, John, Black & White Smith, 48 Market St
Thompson, John, Coach Maker, 46 Beaufain St.
Thompson, John, Grocer, 16 Friend St.
Thompson, Rebecca, Widow, St. Philip's St., Neck
Thompson, Susan, Widow, 2 State House Sq.
Thompson, William, Ship Chandler, 160, Res. 20 Mazyck St.
Thorne, John S., Sail Maker, Loft, 42 E. Bay St., Res 22 Guignard St.
Thorne, -----, Widow of John G., 22 Guignard St.
Thornhill, Catharine, Dry Goods Store, 25 King St
Thorp, David, Coach Maker, 160 Meeting St., Res. 19 Coming St.
Thwing, Edward, Merchant, 16 Vendue Range, 19 State St.
Thynes, William, Planter, 57 Queen St.
Tidyman, Hester, Widow, 4 Short St
Tift, Solomon, Mrs., Grocer, Gadsden's Whf.
Timme, Elizabeth, Widow, Seamstress, 28 Beaufain St.
Timmons, George, Commission Merchant, 45 E. Bay St., Res. 6 Smith's Ln

Timmons, Hannah, 5 Price's Al., F.P.C.
Timmons, William, Hardware Store, 165 E Bay St
Timothy, Peter, Attorney, 50 Meeting St.
Timrod, William H., Book Binder, 112 King St.
Tobias, Abraham, Accountant, 124 King St.
Tobias, Susan, Mantua Maker, 46 King St , F P C
Todd, Jane, 4 Savage St.
Todd, John, Teacher, 20 Coming St , cr George St
Tonge, Susannah, Widow, 12 Church St
Toohey, Michael, Millinery Store, 322 King St.
Toole, John, Grocer, 4 Champney St.
Toomer, A V , Physician, Planter, Chapel St., Wraggsborough, Neck
Toomer, Ann, Widow, 32 Hasell St.
Toomer, H. B., Broker, 9 Broad St., Res. Coming St.
Toomer, H B , Broker & Auctioneer, Res Coming St., Neck
Toomer, Joshua W., Attorney, St Michael's Al., Res 290 E. Bay St.
Toppan, E., 306 King St.
Torrey, Ann, Widow, Boarding House, 26 Broad St.
Torrey, Ezekiel, Block Maker, 19 Guignard St.
Torrey, Penelope, Boarding House, 11 Bedon's Al.
Touchstone, Frederick, Planter, 3 College St.
Toumez, Peter, Grocer, 17 King St.
Tovey, Henry, Block Maker, 176, Res 285 E Bay St
Townsend, Daniel, Planter, cr. Boundary St. Cont'd. & Lucas St., Neck
Trapier & Smith, Factors, D'Oyley's Whf.
Trapier, Paul, Planter, 6 Short St.
Trapmann, Jahncke & Co., Merchants, 79 E. Bay St.
Trapmann, L., Merchant, Prussian Consul, 79 E Bay St , Res. 16 New St.
Treadway, W. R. H , Bookseller, 42 Broad St.
Trenholm, William, Jr., Merchant, 97 Market St.
Trenholm, William, Vendue Range
Trescot, Caroline, Widow, 16 College St.
Trescot, Henry, Attorney, 70 Broad St.
Trescot, Joseph, Merchant, 20 Vendue Range, 19 Maiden Ln
Trezvant, Peter, Notary Public & Quorum Unis, 84 E. Bay St., Res Stoll's Al.
Trouch, Adelade, Widow, 34 Wentworth St.
Trout, William, Pilot, 40 Church St.
Tschudy, Mary, Widow, Grocer, 19 Anson St.
Tucker, Charles S., Register of Mesne Conveyance, State House, Res. 68 Church St.
Tucker, Nicholas, Carpenter, 4 Hasell St
Tunno, Adam, Merchant, 77 E. Bay St.
Tunno, John C , Physician, 2 Short St
Tunno, Nancy, Fruiterer, Zigzag Al., F P C.
Tunno, William, Charleston Auction Establishment, 183 E Bay St.
Tupper & Kimball, Merchants, 116 E Bay St
Tupper, Tristam, Merchant, 116, Res. 128 E. Bay St.
Turnbull, James, Carpenter, Meeting St , near S. Bay St
Turnbull, Robert J., Planter, 1 Logan St.
Turner, Ann, Seamstress, 21 Berresford St
Turner, Ann, Widow, 10 Guignard St., cr. Anson St.
Turner, Eliza, Seamstress, 36 Anson St

Turner, William, Lamp Inspector, 23 Beaufain St
Turnley, George, Res. 37 Tradd St
Turpin, Amelia, 43 Anson St., F.P.C.
Turpin, Hagar, Zigzag Al , F P.C.
Tusha, Eliza, 20 Water St.
Tweedy, R & S. & Co., Hat Store, 220 King St.
Tyler, Joseph, Merchant, 138 E. Bay St., Res. 131 Queen St.
Tyler, Walter, Grocer, 34 Wentworth St.
Ulmo, Anthony, Physician, 45 Queen St.
Ummensetter, John, Tanner, 55 Beaufain St.
Urban, Joseph, Ship Broker, Maiden Ln.
Urquhart, Charles, Merchant, Gillon St., cr. Exchange St., Res. 39 Elliott St.
Usher, James, Jr., Merchant, Magwood's Whf.
Utly, Horace, 10 Vendue Range, Res. 45 State St
Valenchia, Moses, Fruit Shop, 93 King St.
Valentine, Ann, 65 King St , F.P.C.
Valentine, S., Merchant, 6 State St.
Valk, Jacob R , Merchant, Consul of Netherlands, 58 E. Bay St.
Vall, -----, Widow, Cannon St , Neck
Vanderhorst, Charlotte, Mantua Maker, 7 West St., F P.C.
Vanderhorst, R W., Planter, cr Judith & Alexander Sts., Mazyckborough, Neck
Vanderlippe, Frederick, 88 Wentworth St., cr. St Philip's St.
Vandyne, Bransom, Boarding House, 327 King St.
Vaner, Henry, 7 Swinton's Ln.
Vanhagan, Sarah, Widow, Pinckney St , Cannonborough, Neck
Vanhagen & Dye, Grocers, 81 Tradd St.
VanHolten, Tennis, Grocer, Amen St., cr. Philadelphia St.
VanRhyn, A E., Miss, Store Keeper, 22 Broad St.
VanRoven, John, Grocer, 2 Archdale St
Vanveazle, Levi, Barber, 155 Church St.
Vanvelsy, William, Wheelwright, 48 St. Philip's St.
Vardell, Thomas A., Bricklayer, Vanderhorst St., Neck
Varner, Samuel, Tailor, 11 Society St.
Vaughn, Ann, Boarding House, 349 King St
Vause, John T., 25 Mazyck St.
Veitch, William, Druggist, 223 King St.
Venning, Jonah M., Factor, William's Whf , Res. 25 St Philip's St.
Venning, Robert, Factor, William's Whf., Res. 7 Society St.
Verdier, John M , 9 Back St.
Vernagh, John, Grocer, 21 King St.
Vernon, Nathaniel, Jeweller, 84 Broad St.
Verree, Betsey, 7 West St , F P C
Verree, Joseph, 63 Church St.
Very, Nathaniel, Grocer, cr Alexander & Chapel Sts , Neck
Vesey, Charles M , Clerk, 82 Anson St.
Vesey, Denmark, Carpenter, 20 Bull St., F.P C.
Vesey, Joseph, Capt , 82 Anson St.
Vidal, John, Clothing Store, 217 E. Bay St.
Viel, Just, Merchant, 167 E Bay St.
Vieusse, Frances, Dry Goods Store, 121 King St.
Vincent, B , Merchant, 157 E Bay St

Vincent, Hugh, Ship Chandler, 85 E Bay St.
Vinrose, Sarah, Widow, Midwife, 28 Wentworth St.
Vinyard, John, Planter, Hampstead, Neck
Vion, Elizabeth, Dry Goods Store, 183 King St.
Votee, Charles, Ship Master, 106 King St.
Wadsworth, William, 36 Archdale St.
Wagner, Ann, Widow, 52 St. Philip's St.
Wagner, Effingham, Merchant, 19 Cumberland St.
Wagner, George, Merchant, 1 Orange St.
Wagner, John, Physician, 179 Meeting St., cr Hasell St
Wagner, Samuel J., Inspector of Customs, 118 Queen St., cr. Archdale St
Wakefield, Sarah, 7 Lynch's Ln.
Walker, J. F., Merchant, King St. Road, Neck
Walker, John C., Bookseller & Stationer, 15 Broad St.
Walker, Joseph, Boat Builder, 8 Maiden's Ln.
Walker, Mary Ancrum, 4 Orange St.
Walker, Mary, Widow, 12 Liberty St
Walker, Robert, Cabinet Maker, 139 Church St.
Walker, Samuel, 6 Zigzag Al , F P.C
Walker, Thomas, Stone Cutter, 149 Meeting St.
Walker, -----, Widow of Caleb, 24 Magazine St
Walker, William, Accountant, 27 George St.
Wall, Francis, Upholsterer, 37 Boundary St , F.P.C.
Wall, Richard, Grocer, 141 King St., cr. Queen St.
Wall, Robert, Plasterer, 2 Maiden Ln.
Wallace, Agnes, Widow, 88 Church St.
Wallace, James, Shopkeeper, Pinckney St , Neck
Wallace, John, Grocer, cr. Charlotte & Washington Sts , Mazyckborough, Neck
Waller, Charlotte, Widow, 22 Magazine St.
Waller, William, Saddler, 89 Broad St
Walter, Jerry, Fish Store, 24 & 26 State St.
Ward, F S , Clerk, City Court, 14 Cumberland St.
Ward, James, Attorney, Church St., cr. Longitude Ln
Ward, James, Grocer, Dewee's Whf.
Ward, James, Maj , Doughty St., Neck
Ward, Rosetta, 69 Boundary St , F P C.
Ward, Susan, Widow, 14 Cumberland St.
Ward, -----, Widow of Joshua, 50 Meeting St.
Waring, Daniel Jennings, Attorney, 2 George St
Waring, Edward, Bricklayer, 18 Middle St.
Waring, Horatio, Physician, 74 Wentworth St.
Waring, Mary, 90 Church St., F.P C.
Waring, Mary Ann, 7 Wall St., F.P C.
Waring, Morton A., Federal Marshal, Office, Court House, St. Philip's St., Neck
Waring, Morton, Factor, 40 E. Bay St , Res 36 Meeting St
Waring, Thomas, Mrs., 32 Meeting St.
Warley & Co , Factors, Chisolm's Whf.
Warley, Ann, Widow, 2 King St
Warley, Elizabeth & Mary, 30 Meeting St
Warley, William, Dr , 30 Meeting St.
Warner, Penelope, 4 Longitude Ln.
Warner, William, King St. Road, Neck
Warnock, Ann, Mrs , 10 Laurens St.
Warren, Elizabeth, Widow, 25 Middle St.
Warren, Russell, Carpenter, 34, Res 4 Ellery St
Washington, -----, Widow of Gen. William, 48 Meeting St
Washington, William, 1 Church St , cr. E. Bay St.

Waterhouse, B , Attorney, 55 Meeting St.
Watson, Betsey, 4 Whim Court, F.P C.
Watson, James, Capt., 16 Tradd St.
Watson, Lydia, 15 Friend St., F P.C.
Watson, Richard, 4 Whim Court, F.P.C.
Watton, J. A., Teacher, Free School No. 4, Hampstead, Neck
Watts, Bridget, Widow, 121 Queen St.
Watts, James, Grocer cr. Church St & Lynch's Ln.
Waugh, Alexander B., Merchant, 68 E Bay St., Res. 15 Legare St.
Webb, Daniel, Factor, N.W cr. Pinckney & Cannon Sts., Neck
Webber, Samuel, Dragger, Pritchard's Ln.
Weed, Joseph, Hat Store, King St , cr. George St., Res. 29 George St
Weissenger, Magdalen, Widow, King St., near the Lines, Neck
Welles, W. H., 21 Wall St.
Welling & Ballentine, Saddlery & Harness Makers, 119 Meeting St.
Wells, Peter, Tailor, Elizabeth St., Wraggsborough, F P C., Neck
Wells, Rachel, 46 Beaufain St., F.P.C.
Wells, -----, Widow of Thomas B., 30 Archdale St.
Wellsman, James, Capt , 12 Lynch's Ln.
Welsh, James, Boarding House, 21 Elliott St.
Welsh, Lewis, Factor, Gadsden's Whf.
Welsh, Nathaniel, Teacher, 142 Wentworth St
Welsh, Thomas G., Carver, 37 Beaufain St.
Welsh, -----, Widow of Edward, 5 Logan St.
Wenger, J , Upholsterer, 66 Queen St.
Wesner, Frederick, Carpenter, 138 Queen St., cr. Mazyck St
West, Charles, Charlotte St., Mazyckborough, Neck
West, Charles H., Ship Chandler, 79 E. Bay St., Res. 30 Elliott St.
West, Nicholas, Tanner, 265 E. Bay St.
Westendorff & Co., Merchants, 22 Vendue Range
Westendorff, C. P. L., Merchant & Portuguese Consul, Mey's Whf.
Weston, Elizabeth, Mantua Maker, 99 Meeting St , F P.C.
Weston, John, Butcher, Wolf St., Hampstead, F.P.C., Neck
Weston, Plowden, Planter, 70 Queen St.
Weston, Sarah, Mantua Maker, 99 Meeting St., F.P.C
Weston, Sarah, Seamstress, cr Alexander & Mary Sts , F.P.C., Neck
Weyman, Francis, Grocer, 38 Church St.
Weyman, Joseph T., Merchant, King & Vanderhorst Sts., Neck
Wharton, Samuel, Merchant, cr. King & Mary Sts., Neck
Wheeler, Henry, King St. Road, Neck
Whilden, Joseph, Editor, City Gazette, 114 East Bay St., Res. 22 Magazine St.
White, Felicity, Fruiterer, 34 Anson St., F.P.C
White, George K , Factor, 21 Anson St.
White, John & Co., Factors, Chisolm's Whf.
White, John B , Attorney, 78 Broad St.
White, John, Factor, Chisolm's Whf., Res. 216 Meeting St.
White, John, Planter, 24 Smith's Ln.

White, John, Stone Cutter, 35 Market St
White, Primus, 54 Church St., F P.C.
White, Sarah Ann, Widow, Nassau St , Neck
White, William, Grocer, 44 Market St.
Whiteheart, Peter, Grocer, 209 E. Bay St.
Whiting, John, Turner & Grocer, 189 Meeting St
Whitley, Michael, Grocer, 77 Market St.
Whitley, Thomas, Grocer, 24 Ellery St.
Whitney, Archibald, Grocer, 36 Market St.
Whitney, Mary, Widow, 160 Church St.
Whitridge, Joshua B , Physician, 139 Church St.
Wibur, W. B., Comb Maker, 311 King St
Wienges, Conrad, Grocer, 59 Church St.
Wienges, J H., Baker, 186 Meeting St
Wienges, Jacob, Grocer, 31 Archdale St., cr. Beaufain St.
Wigfall, Paul, Bricklayer, 10 Swinton's Ln , F.P C
Wigfall, Phillis, 5 Linguard St., F P.C
Wigfall, Robert, Vanderhorst, F.P C., Neck
Wigfall, Thomas, Washington St., Mazyckborough, Neck
Wiggins, Sylvia, 1 Whim Court, F.P.C.
Wightman, J. T., Turner, 114 Meeting St.
Wightman, Peggy, Pastry Cook, 23 Mazyck St., F P.C
Wightman, W., Jr , Painter, 199 Meeting St.
Wightman, William, 82 Meeting St.
Wilcox, Jeremiah, State Hotel, cr. Meeting St. & Berresford Al.
Wilcox, Samuel W., Merchant, 136 E Bay St., Res. 11 Price's Al
Wildman & Starr, Hatters, 286 King St., & 26 Broad St
Wiley, James, Grocer, 60 Elliott St
Wiley, Samuel & Co., Grocers, 27 Elliott St.
Wilhelmi, A. W. M., Widow, St. Philip's St., Neck
Wilkes, John, Merchant, 10 Crafts' Whf., Res. 18 Meeting St.
Wilkie, William B., Cashier, Union Bank, 55 Church St
Wilkinson, Grace, Zigzag Al., F.P.C.
Will, Robert, Bricklayer, 47 Pinckney St.
Williams, Hannah, Seamstress, 21 Boundary St.
Williams, Isham, Planter, William's Whf
Williams, John, Coach Maker, 190 Meeting St
Williams, John, Rigger, 15 Clifford Al
Williams, M. G., Grocer, 8 Market St.
Williams, Simpson, Capt., 70 Church St.
Williams, Susan, 5 Motte's Ln , F P C
Williams, Theophilus, Planter, 63 Wentworth St.
Williams, William, Tailor, 20 Guignard St.
Williamson, Elizabeth, Widow, Milliner, 6 Cumberland St
Williamson, Maria, Mantua Maker, 2 Clifford St.
Williamson, Nancy, Seamstress, 20 Pinckney St., F.P.C.
Williman, Christopher, Pinckney St., Neck
Williman, Ellinor, Widow, 111 Broad St.
Williman, -----, Mrs., Boundary St., Cannonborough, Neck
Willington, A. S., Editor, Courier, 220 E. Bay St., cr William's Whf.
Willis, Henry, Carpenter, 23 St. Philip's St.
Willis, John H., Broker, 77 Wentworth St.
Willis, William, Commission Merchant, 163 E. Bay St.
Wilson, Alexander, 14 George St
Wilson, Ann, 106 Queen St.
Wilson, Ann, 5 Amen St., F P C

Wilson, Anna, 9 Clifford's Al., F.P.C.
Wilson, Cate, 8 Logan St., F.P.C.
Wilson, Elizabeth, Mrs , 67 Meeting St.
Wilson, George, Blacksmith, 13 Archdale St., F.P.C.
Wilson, Hugh, Sr , Planter, Pinckney St., Neck
Wilson, Isaac M., Physician, 82 Broad St
Wilson, J. W. & Co., Grocers, 272 E. Bay St., cr.
Wentworth St.
Wilson, John, Butcher, near the Lines, Neck
Wilson, John H , Planter, 12 Pitt St
Wilson, John, Mariner, 90 Anson St.
Wilson, John, State Engineer, 106 Broad St., Res. 19
Friend St.
Wilson, Samuel & Son, Physicians, 80 Broad St.
Wilson, Samuel, Jr , Physician, 6 New St.
Wilson, Samuel, Physician, 11 Archdale St., cr Magazine
St.
Wilson, -----, Widow of Daniel, 30 Church St.
Wilson, -----, Widow of Hugh, Plantress, Pinckney St.,
Neck
Wilson, William H., Commission Merchant, 122 E. Bay
St., Res. 100 Meeting St.
Winchester, Mary, Widow, cr. Coming & Cannon Sts.,
Neck
Windsor, Elizabeth, Widow, Seamstress, 11 Maiden Ln.
Wing, Sarah, Widow, Boarding House, 95 E. Bay St., cr.
Elliott St.
Winn, Joseph D., Grocer, 349 King St
Winstanly, Thomas, Attorney, 193 E. Bay St.
Winthrop & Parker, Factors, 9 Crafts' Whf
Winthrop, Augustus, Attorney, 47, Res. 105 Tradd St.
Winthrop, Joseph A., Factor, 32 E Bay St.
Winthrop, Joseph, Consul, Norway & Sweden, 105 Tradd
St.
Wish, Ann, Widow, 58 Elliott St.
Wish, Richard S., Deputy City Sheriff, 30 Coming St
Wiss, Lewis M., Dry Goods Store, 242 King St.
Withington, Samuel, Shoe Store, 227 King St
Woddrop, John, Merchant, 43 E. Bay St.
Wood, James, Engraver, cr. Warren & St Philip's Sts ,
Neck
Wood, James, Mrs., Mattress Maker, Warren St., Neck
Wood, John, Butcher, Wolf St., Hampstead, Neck
Wood, Joseph, Tailor & Grocer, King St. Road, Neck
Wood, William, Grocer, cr. Henrietta & Elizabeth Sts.,
Neck
Woodward, E. S., Widow, 62 Wentworth St
Woodward, Hester, Widow, 62 Wentworth St.
Woodworth, George, Mariner, 23 Boundary St
Woolley, Thomas, Merchant, King St. Road, Neck
Wotton, Cloe, Widow, College Yard St
Wotton, -----, Widow of Christopher, 20 Pinckney St
Wrainch, John, Teacher, 177 Meeting St
Wright, Charles C., Engraver, 142 King St., Res. 51 State
St.
Wright, Henry, Grain Store, 38 Market St., cr. Anson St
Wright, John Izard, cr. Coming & Cannon Sts , Neck
Wright, Robert, Carpenter, Bennett's Mill, Res Rutledge
St.
Wulff, Jacob, Merchant, 76 E. Bay St , Res. 131 Church
St.
Wurdeman, Christiana, Dry Goods Store, 218 King St
Wurdeman, John G., Merchant, 14 Queen St
Wyatt, Ann, Widow, John St., Neck
Wyatt, Elizabeth, Widow, 173 Church St
Yates, Ann, Widow, 14 Zigzag Al.
Yates, Christiana, 97 Queen St.
Yates, Deborah, Widow, 3 S. Bay St.
Yates, Elizabeth, Widow, 12 Zigzag Al.
Yates, Jeremiah A., Planter, Ladson's Court
Yates, Joseph, Cooper, 83 E. Bay St , cr Smith's Whf.,
Res. 23 Meeting St.
Yates, T. H., Carpenter, 7 Lamboll St
Yates, -----, Widow of Samuel, 10 Water St.
Yeadon, Richard, Bank of State of S. C., Res. 35 King St.
Yeadon, William, City Sheriff, 77 King St.
York, Nicholas, Grocer, 27 Wall St., cr. Boundary St
You, Elizabeth, Widow, 4 Archdale St.
You, John C., School Master, 4 Archdale St
Young, Dinah, Widow, 77 Broad St
Young, Henry, Boarding House, 5 Chalmers Al.
Young, James, Book Binder, 127 E. Bay St.
Young, John P , Apothecary, 94 Meeting St
Young, Joseph, Ship Chandler, 194, Res. 263 E. Bay St
Young, Nancy, 6 Ellery St., F.P.C.
Young, William C., Printer, 77 Broad St
Zealy, Ann, 61 King St
Zealy, Joseph, Carpenter, 61 King St.
Zemes, Z., Locksmith, 153 Church St.
Zylstra, H. I., 34 Society St.

The 1825 Directory

This directory was published by William F. Shackleford using the title of *Directory and Stranger's Guide, for the City of Charleston; Also, for Charleston Neck, Between Boundary-Street and the Lines; To Which Is Added, An Almanac for the Year of Our Lord 1825; With Other Useful and Important Information* (Charleston: A. E. Miller, November, 1824). A notation beneath the title states that this directory was "compiled principally by the late Wm. F Shackeford, Esq. while taking a census of the city." It has 3196 entries Although the directory has the residents of the city divided into those who lived within the city and those who lived in the Neck area, the two groups have been combined here with the word "Neck" appearing after the entry for people living there. The Free People of Color are not listed in this volume.

Abbot, Samuel, Quorum Unis, 18 Broad St
Abrahams, Elias, Dry Goods Store, 300 King St.
Abrahams, Levy J., 9 Market St.
Adams, David, 28 Ellery St.
Adams, John, Grocer, S. Bay St.
Adams, William, Planter, Cannon St., Cannonborough, Neck
Addison, Henry, Blacksmith, 3 College St
Addison, James, Blacksmith, 29 Boundary St
Addison, Joseph, Shipwright, 35 Pinckney St
Addison, Robert, Sea Captain, 5 Price's Al.
Adger & Black, Merchants, 130 E. Bay St
Adger, James & Co., Hardware Store, 130 E. Bay St.
Adger, James, Merchant, King St Cont'd., Neck
Aiken, Catherine, Shopkeeper, King St. Cont'd Neck
Aiken, William, Merchant, cr. King & Ann Sts, Neck
Airs, David, 179 Church St.
Airs, Mary, Mrs , 27 Archdale St.
Aishar, S., Shopkeeper, 207 E Bay St.
Akin, Ann, Mrs., 11 Cumberland St.
Akin, Thomas, Physician, 11 Cumberland St.
Albagnac, Peter, Merchant Tailor, 2 Queen St.
Aldrich, Robert, Wharfinger, Chisolm's Whf., Res. 15 Tradd St.
Alexander, Abraham, Dry Goods Store, 228 King St.
Alexander, David, President, Union Insurance Co., Res. 3 Society St
Alexander, John J., Union Insurance Co , Res. 3 Society St.
Alexander, Samuel, Bank Coffee House, 129 E. Bay St.
Allan, William & Son, Factors, 2 D'Oyley's Whf
Allan, William, 46 Tradd St.
Allen, S M. & Co , Exchange Brokers, 6 Broad St.
Allen, William, Commission Merchant, Champney St., Res. 3 Pinckney St.
Alston, William, Planter, 25 King St
Ancrum, James, Mrs , 2 S Bay St
Anderson, Ricks, Shopkeeper, cr. Vanderhorst, & Coming Sts., Radcliffborough, Neck
Anderson, Robrt, Dry Goods Store, 222 King St
Anderson, William, 129 Queen St

Andrews, Moses, Pump & Block Maker, 34 Hasell St.
Angel, Justus, 124 Tradd St.
Angus, John, Blacksmith, Water St., Res 31 King St
Annelley, Thomas, Cooper, 54 E Bay St.
Anthony, J. C., Tallow Chandler, Mary St., Mazyckborough, Neck
Anthony, John, Mariner, 17 Pinckney St.
Anthony, William, Grocer, 108 Tradd St.
Antonie, John, 8 Hasell St.
Arms, Elizabeth, Nurse, Anson St.
Arms, William, Bricklayer, 56 St. Philip's St.
Armstrong, Archibald, Shipwright, 17 Middle St.
Armstrong, William, Ordinary's Office, Res. 49 Society St
Arnold, Amos, 30 Pinckney St.
Arnold, Louisa, Mrs., 20 Archdale St.
Arnold, Mary, Mrs., 30 Church St.
Artman, Peter, Coach Maker, 5 Archdale St
Artopee, George, Grocer, Nassau St., Wraggsborough, Neck
Artopee, Paul, Grocer, Nassau St., Wraggsborough, Neck
Arzeno, Lewis, 195 E. Bay St
Ashby, Thomas, Planter, 25 Friend St.
Ashe, John, Jr., Planter, 8 S. Bay St.
Ashe, John, Planter, 8 S. Bay St.
Ashley, Matilda, Mrs., 1 Berresford St.
Assalit, Andrew, Carpenter, Beaufain St.
Assalit, Joseph, Teacher of French, 42 Tradd St.
Astaix, Elizbeth, Mrs , 193 King St.
Atchison, John, Livery Stables, 158 Church St
Aubin, Joseph, Porter Cellar, 183 E Bay St.
Austin, Margaret, Miss, 117 E. Bay St.
Austin, Maria, Mrs., Alexander St., Mazyckborough, Neck
Austin, Michael, 18 Pinckney St
Avery, P., Grocer, cr. Exchange & Champney St.
Axson, Elizabeth, Mrs., 49 King St.
Axson, Jacob, Attorney, 7 St. Michael's Al., Res. 49 King St.
Axson, John, Planter, Charlotte St., Mazyckborough, Neck
Axson, Sarah, Mrs., 62 Wentworth St
Babcock, S & Co , Book Store, 329 King St.
Bachman, John, Rev., Pastor, German Church, Res., cr. Hudson & Pinckney Sts, Cannonborough, Neck
Bacon, E., Res. 69 E Bay St.
Bacot, D. D., Teller, S. C. Bank, Res. 11 Lamboll St
Bacot, Henry H., Attorney, 49 Tradd St
Bacot, Peter, Cashier, Office of Discount & Deposit, Res. 95 Meeting St.
Bacot, Thomas W., Jr., Assistant Post Master, 94 Church St.
Bacot, Thomas W., Post Master, Res. 94 Church St
Badger, James, Outdoor Clerk, Planters' & Mechanics' Bank, Res. cr Wentworth & King Sts.
Bagshaw, Robert, Carpenter, 12 Smith St
Bailey, A., Watchmaker, cr. King & Beaufain Sts
Bailey, David, Planter, 2 Green St.
Bailey, William, Teacher, 11 Wall St.
Baker, Elias, Dyer, 169 Meeting St.
Baker, Joseph, Carpenter, 87 Boundary St.
Baker, L., Clerk, cr. King & Hasell Sts.
Baker, Martha, Mrs., Dyer, 167 Meeting St.

105

Baker, Richard B., 17 Legare St
Baker, Sarah, Mrs., 3 St. Philip's St
Balentine, John, Grocer, 228 E Bay St
Ball, Isaac, Planter, cr. E Bay & Vernon Sts.
Ball, John, Planter, 21 Hasell St
Balland, Alexander, Lafayette Coffee House, E Bay St
Bampfield, James, 17 George St
Bampfield, Thomas, 14 George St
Bancroft, James & Co., Commission Merchants, 164 E. Bay St.
Banks, Charles, 64 Wentworth St.
Barbot & Esnard, Grocers, cr. Church & Tradd Sts.
Barbot, Anthony, 85 Church St.
Barker, J. S., 18 Society St.
Barker, James Truss Maker, 28 Pinckney St.
Barker, Samuel, Attorney, 18 Society St.
Barksdale, Thomas, Planter 13 Washington St.
Barnard, John, Confectioner, Meeting St
Barnes, Thomas, Wharf St.
Barnes, William B., Dyer 118 Meeting St.
Barre, Vincent, Brass Founder, 2 Amen St.
Barrelli, John, Merchant, 65 Broad St
Barrelli, Torre & Co., Fancy Store, 65 Broad St
Barrett, Esther, Mrs , 172 Meeting St.
Barrett, Isaac & Co., Commission Merchants, N. Vendue Range
Barrett, Isaac, 167 King St
Barrite, G. E , Cabinet Maker, 107 Church St.
Barron, John, 26 Society St.
Barron, Sarah, Mrs , 115 Tradd St.
Bartless, Henry, Blacksmith, 33 Market St
Bartless, Henry, Blacksmith, Charlotte St , Mazyckborough, Neck
Barton, Aaron, Carpenter, 20 Wall St.
Bason, William P., Book Store, 308 King St.
Bass, Job, Dry Goods Sore, King St.
Bassett, Cornelius, 33 Wall St.
Bassett, S., Mrs., Church St., near Market St.
Battee, Robert, Carpenter, Cannon St., Cannonborough, Neck
Bay, Andrew, Sheriff's Office, Res. 16 Logan St.
Bay, Elihu H , Judge, 16 Legare St
Bay, John, 14 New St.
Bayman, Charles, Shopkeeper, Meeting St. Cont'd., Neck
Beale, Abigail, Mrs., 127 King St.
Beard, Frederick, Teller, S. C. Bank
Beard, William, Porter, S. C. Bank, Res. 121 Church St.
Beaufort, Charles, Butcher, Pinckney St., Cannonborough, Neck
Beaufort, Frederick, Butcher, Pinckney St., Cannonborough, Neck
Beck, Rebecca, Mrs., Motte's Ln.
Beckett & Davis, Merchants, 57 E. Bay St
Beckmann, Adolph, Painter & Glazier, 149 Meeting St.
Beckmann, Christian, Grocer, 45 Pinckney St.
Beckmann, F. A., Grocer, cr. St. Philip's & Liberty Sts
Bee, Barnard E., Planter, 114 Tradd St.
Bee, Eliza, Mrs , 26 Cumberland St.
Bee, Frances C , Mrs.
Bee, James M , 96 King St

Bee, John S., 128 Queen St.
Bee, John S., Shipwright, 150 Wentworth St
Bee, Thomas, 76 Church St
Bee, William, Teacher, S C. Society School, 51 Meeting St.
Beekman, Ann, Mrs., 24 Hasell St
Beers & Bunnell, Exchange Brokers 105½ E Bay St
Beevans, John K., Goldsmith, Elizabeth St , Mazyckborough, Neck
Beile, John C., Dry Goods Store, 164 King St.
Belcher, Manning, Teacher, 17 Hasell St
Belin, Esther, Mrs., 64 Wentworth St
Belknap, Moses P , Church St., near Market St
Bell, David, Merchant, Kunhardt's Whf., Res. 23 Society St.
Bell, William Bricklayer, 46 Society St.
Bellinger, Joseph, Planter, 25 Pitt St.
Belser, Frederick S., Attorney, King St. Cont'd , Neck
Belser, -----, Mrs., King St. Cont'd., Neck
Bement & Whitney, Wholesale Grocery, cr State & Queen Sts.
Benjamin Ezra, Sea Captain, 52 E. Bay St
Benjamin, Philip, Dry Goods Store, 165 King St.
Bennett & Hunt, Attornies, State House Sq.
Bennett, Cooke & Co., Dry Goods Store, 142 King St.
Bennett, Isaac S K , Mrs , Widow, Charlotte St., Mazyckborough, Neck
Bennett, Joseph B., Grocer, 12 S Bay St.
Bennett, Joseph, City Treasurer, 10 New St.
Bennett, L M., Mrs., 97 Queen St
Bennett, Martha, Mrs., Boarding House, 4 Bedon's Alley
Bennett, Martha, Mrs., cr. Amherst & Hanover Sts., Hampstead, Neck
Bennett, Simons, Planter, 30 Bull St
Bennett, Thomas, Charleston Mill, Smith St.
Bennett, Thomas, Sr., Mrs., 126 King St
Bennett, William S., Mrs., 126 King St.
Benoist, -----, Madam, Confectioner, 118 Meeting St
Benson, Lavinia, Mrs., 360 King St.
Benson, Lawrence, Dry Goods Store, 324 King St.
Bentham & Dunkin, Attornies, 65 Meeting St.
Bentham, Robert, Attorney, 49 Coming St
Berbant, Samuel, Tailor, 351 King St.
Bermister, Jacob, 69 Beaufain St
Berney, Mary, Mrs., 134 Meeting St.
Berney, Rebecca, Mrs., 86 Boundary St.
Berney, Robert, Broker & Commission Merchant, 1 State St., Res 131 Meeting St
Berney, William R., 86 Boundary St.
Bernie, George & William, Hardware Store, 21 Broad St
Berrett, William H., Bookstore, 14 Broad St.
Berry, Alexander, Wharfinger, D'Oyley's Whf , Res 4 Water St.
Berry, John H., 106 Wentworth St.
Berry, Peter, Confectioner, 251 King St.
Bethume, Margaret, Mrs., 98 Broad St
Bettison, William R., Carpenter, 23 Rutledge St.
Beusse, John H , Shopkeeper, 9 Pinckney St
Bicaise, Frederick, Carpenter, 10 Anson St.
Bicaise, James, Cabinet Maker, 10 Anson St

106

Bicaise, Mary, Mrs., 10 Anson St
Bicaise, Peter B., Bank Coffee House, E Bay St
Bigelow & Birch, Wholeslae Dry Goods Store, cr. King &
　Society Sts.
Bigelow, Elizabeth, Meeting St., Mazyckborough, Neck
Bigelow, Elizabeth, Mrs , 265 Meeting St.
Biggs, Henry S , House & Sign Painter, 295 King St.
Billings, John, Livery Stables, 122 Church St.
Bingley, David P., Accountant, 77 Wentworth St.
Bird, John S., Hardware & Fancy Store, 51 Broad St , Res.
　73 King St.
Bird, William, Shipwright, 19 Pinckney St
Bishop, Otis, Printer, Church St., near Market St.
Bishop, Samuel N , Merchant, 65 Meeting St
Bize, Daniel, Carpenter, Mary St., Hampstead, Neck
Bizeul, Julien, Upholsterer, 135 E. Bay St
Black, Alexander, Grocer, 30 Elliott St.
Black, Alexander, Merchant, Wentworth St.
Black, James, 9 Anson St.
Black, James, Bootmaker, 36 Broad St.
Black, John, Merchant, 21 Broad St.
Blackwood, John, Commercial Merchant, Napier's Range,
　Res. 92 Wentworth St.
Blackwood, Thomas, President, Planters' & Mechanics'
　Bank, Res. 18 Pitt St
Blake & Robertson, Commission Merchants,
　Vanderhorst's Whf.
Blake, -----, Misses, 72 King St
Blakely, Elias, Coach Maker, Henrietta St.,
　Mazyckborough, Neck
Blakely, Seth, Tailor, Henrietta St., Mazyckborough, Neck
Blalock, Elizabeth, cr St. Philip's St. & the Lines, Neck
Blamyer & Middleton, Factors, D'Oyley's Whf.
Blamyer, -----, Misses, Academy, 3 King St Cont'd., Neck
Blamyer, William, 296 E. Bay St
Blanchard, John, Shoemaker, 40 Queen St.
Blane, Alexander, Wheelwright, Meeting St. Cont'd., Neck
Blaney, Joseph, 1 Cumberland St
Blewer, Elizabeth, Mrs., Hampstead, Neck
Blewer, John G , Grocer, King St Cont'd , Neck
Block, Sarah, Mrs., 1 Swinton's Ln.
Blondeau, S., Hat Store, 153 King St.
Bloomfield, John, Student at Law, 33 Meeting St.
Blum & Dickson, Commission Merchants, S Vendue
　Range
Blum, John A., Vendue Master, Res cr King & Wolf Sts.,
　Neck
Blum, Mary, Mrs , King St Cont'd , Neck
Blume, Wilhelmia, Mrs., Shopkeeper, cr. John & Elizabeth
　Sts , Mazyckborough, Neck
Boesdon, Henry, Baker, 89 Market St.
Boisseau, James E , 313 King St
Bolles, A., Female School, N. End of Charleston College
Bollough, Elias, 17 Mazyck St.
Bones, William, Dry Goods Store, 39 Broad St.
Bonneau, John E., 13 Church St
Bonneau, Symes, Office of Discount & Desposit, Res
　Zigzag Court
Bonnell, John, Sea Captain 14 Lynch's Ln
Bonner, John, Upholsterer, Queen St.

Borch, Peter, 1 Market St.
Borch, Peter, 237 Meeting St.
Bordenave, John, Hair Dresser, 76 Market St.
Bordenes, John, Grocer, 62 Anson St.
Bordoux, Joseph, 80 Anson St.
Bosquet, Peter, Dry Goods Store, 182 King St
Bosset, Vincent, Neck
Boucheneau, Charles, 29 King St
Boudo, Louis, Jeweller, 160 King St.
Bounetheau, Banbury B , Bricklayer, 34 Cumberland St.
Bounetheau, Edward W., Carpenter, 8 Green St.
Bounetheau, Elizabeth, Mrs., 34 Cumberland St
Bounetheau, Henry B Accountant, 34 Cumberland St.
Bounetheau, James W., Printer, 34 Cumberland St
Bourne, N. G., Baker, 20 Queen St.
Bours, Luke, Dry Goods Store, 268 King St.
Boutan, Peter B., Confectioner, King St. Cont'd , Neck
Bowen, Nathaniel, Right Rev., D D , Elliott St ,
　Cannonborough, Neck
Bowman, Charles A , Shipwright, 41 Laurens St
Bowman, -----, Widow, 24 Queen St
Boyce, Johnson & Henry, Factors, Kunhardt's Whf
Boyce, Ker, cr. King & Vanderhorst St
Boyce, Ker, Factor, Res. cr. Vanderhorst & King Sts,
　Radcliffborough, Neck
Boyce, -----, Mrs , Milliner & Fancy Store, cr. King &
　Society St.
Boyce, Robert, 284 King St
Boylston, Henry, Physician, Reid St., Hampstead, Neck
Bradley, E. B., Grocer, 119 Broad St
Bradshaw, James, Merchant Tailor, 30 Broad St
Braid, Matthew, Carpenter, 67 Tradd St
Brailsford, Alexander, 57 George St.
Brailsford, E., Miss, 30 S Bay St.
Brailsford, Edward, Physician, 39 Tradd St.
Brailsford, James, 57 George St
Brailsford, William, 4 Friend St.
Brandt, Ann, Mrs., Shopkeeper, 103 King St.
Bremar, Henry, Dentist, 13 Maiden Ln
Brenan, Richard, 53 Beaufain St
Breteau & Co., Dyers, 129 Meeting St.
Brewster, Ann, Boarding House, 13 Bedon's Al.
Bridgewood & Reeve, China & Glass Store, 281 King St.
Bridie, Robert, 149 E. Bay St.
Brisbane, John, Planter, Upper End Beaufain St.
Brisbane, Mary, Mrs., 29 Meeting St
Broaders, Frederick, New England Coffee House, 171 E
　Bay St.
Broadfoot, F., Mrs., 7 Tradd St.
Broadfoot, M'Neel & Co , Merchants, 72 E Bay St
Brocklebank, William, Plasterer, Upper End Beaufain St.
Brodie, Robert, 37 Meeting St
Brodie, Robert, Iron Founder, Chapel St., Mazyckborough,
　Neck
Broer, Martha, Mrs., Shopkeeper, King St., Neck
Brogan, John, Porter House, 65 Queen St
Broughton, Ann, Miss, 49 Anson St
Broughton, George, Rope Walk, Meeting St Cont'd ,
　Hampstead, Neck
Broun, A , Mrs., 97 Boundary St

107

Broun, J. D., 97 Boundary St.
Brown & Tunis, Factors, D'Oyley's Whf.
Brown, Alexander, Dry Goods Store, King St., Res St
  Phililp's St , Neck
Brown, Charles, 9 Society St.
Brown, Daniel, 91 E Bay St.
Brown, Edward, Planter 11 Church St
Brown, George, Rope Walk, Meeting St. Cont'd ,
  Hampstead, Neck
Brown, Jane, Mrs., 23 Berresford St.
Brown, Joseph, Rev., 115 E. Bay St.
Brown, Joshua, Mrs., 56 E. Bay St.
Brown, Lavinia, Mrs., Washington St., Mazyckborough,
  Neck
Brown, Magdalen, Mrs., 96 Market St.
Brown, Maria T , Mrs , Private Boarding House, 105 E
  Bay St.
Brown, -----, Mrs., 5 Guignard St.
Brown, Robert, 79 Church St.
Brown, Robert C , 47 Tradd St.
Brown, Samuel S., 327 King St.
Brown, Sarah, Mrs., Court House Yard
Brown, Stephen, Rope Walk, Meeting St. Cont'd.,
  Hampstead, Neck
Brown, William, 306 King St.
Brown, William, 58 Market St.
Brown, William H., Cabinet Maker, 53 Pinckney St.
Browne, A J., Planter 48 Beaufain St.
Browne, Elizabeth, Mrs., 38 St. Phlip's St.
Browne, John D , 38 St. Philip's St
Brownlee, John, cr. Meeting & Hudson Sts.,
  Wraggsborough, Neck
Bruce, Charles, 131 Church St.
Bruen, John, Teacher, 280 King Sf.
Bruen, Mary, Mrs., Milliner, 280 King St.
Brummer, Frances, Mrs , 102 Queen St
Bryan, John, Planter, 18 Hasell St.
Bryan, Jonathan, Dry Goods Store, 326 King St.
Bryant, Charles H., Ship Chandler, 105 E. Bay St.
Bryant, Jane, Mrs., 54 Tradd St.
Bryant, Z., Carpenter, 11 Berresford St.
Bryce, Henry, Merchant, 74 King St
Buckles, E., Mrs., Church St , near Market St
Buckner, Eliza, Mrs , 8 Montague St
Budd, Thomas, Sea Captain, Tradd St
Budd, William, Commission Merchant, Crafts' N. Whf.,
  Res. 78 King St.
Buerhaus, H D , Merchant Tailor, 21 Queen St
Buist, Arthur, Rev., Charlotte St., Mazyckborough, Neck
Buist, Mary, Mrs., 5 Church St
Bull, Elizabeth, Mrs., 8 Lamboll St
Bull, John, Grocer, 19 Market St.
Bull, Timothy, Grocer, 24 Church St.
Bullen, Samuel, Shoe Store, 261 King St
Bulow, John J., Planter, 16 Montague St.
Burch, Edward, 10 Savage St
Burckmyer, Cornelius, 118 Wentworth St.
Burckmyer, J C & C., Merchants, 140 E Bay St
Burckmyer, John C., cr. Wentworth & Coming Sts
Burdell, John E., Carpenter, 16 Wentworth St

Burdell, Robert F., Grocer, E. Bay St., cr. Gillon St
Burdell, Robert, Grocer, Res. King St Cont'd , Neck
Burden, Isaac, Carpenter, 33 Coming St.
Burden, K., Planter, 10 Short St
Burden, Thomas Carpenter, 33 Coming St.
Burger, Henry, Grocer, cr Rutledge & Montague Sts
Burger, Samuel, Tax Collector, 19 Broad St.
Burgess, Samuel B , Carpenter, 7 Guignard St
Burgoyne, William, Druggist, cr E Bay & Broad Sts.,
  Res cr. E. Bay & Water Sts
Burke, Alexander M'Neil, 238 Meeting St.
Burke, Michael, 35 Wentworth St
Burn, Jacob, Bricklayer, 20 Washington St.
Burnett, Elizabeth, Mrs., 38 Meeting St
Burnham, John, Carpenter, Boundary St., Radcliffborough,
  Neck
Burnham, William, Whitesmith, 17 College St.
Burns, James, 12 Lynch's Ln
Burns, John M., Bootmaker, 108 Church St
Burrell, James, 43 Church St
Burrell, William, Bootmaker, 45 Broad St.
Burrill, John E., 12 Lamboll St
Burrows, F., Pilot, 4 Stoll's Al.
Bussacker, Charles, Dry Goods Store, 307 Coming St
Bussacker, John P , Grocer 32 Coming St.
Butler, Charles P , Watch Maker, 135 King St
Butler, Robert, 25 Laurens St.
Buxbaum, John, Physician, 120 Queen St
Byange, -----, 4 Philadelphia St.
Byrd, John, Wharfinger, Magwood's Whf., Res. 128 E.
  Bay St.
Byrd, Mary, Mrs., Hotel, 183 E Bay St.
Byrne, Mary, Mrs., 23 Pinckney St.
Cabuel, Louis, Tailor, 99 Church St
Calahan, John, Carpenter, Berresford St
Calder, Alexander, Jr., Lodge Al
Calder, Alexander, Planters' Hotel, cr Church & Queen
  Sts
Calder, J. & J., Merchants, Chisolm's Whf.
Calder, James, Cabinet Maker, 116 Meeting St.
Calder, James, Merchant, Chisolm's Whf., Res. 88 Broad
  St
Caldwell, Robert, Dry Goods Store & Wagon Yard, King
  St Cont'd., Neck
Caldwell, William A., Vendue Master, S Vendue Range,
  Res. 107 Meeting St.
Callender, Joseph, Sea Captain, 5 Tradd St.
Cambridge, L., Mrs., Boarding House, 4 Kiddell's Whf
Cameron, Amelia, Mrs., 92 Church St.
Campbell, A. W., Factor, 63 Beaufain St
Campbell, Ann, Mrs., 95 Broad St.
Campbell, Dugald, 24 Market St.
Campbell, I. Motte, Physician, 95 Broad St
Campbell, John, Merchant & Grocer, 39 Market St
Campbell, M'Millan, Mrs., cr. Charlotte & Alexander Sts.,
  Mazyckborough, Neck
Campbell, Patrick, Hotel, 133 E. Bay St.
Campbell, Peter, Plasterer, 19 Beaufain St
Campbell, Peter, Porter & Beer House, 270 King St.
Campbell, Peter, Shopkeeper, cr. Meeting & Boundary

108

Sts., Neck
Campbell, -----, Porter House, Queen St.
Campbell, Thomas, Church St , near Market St.
Canady, Henry, Grocer, 97 Tradd St
Cane, Christian, 14 Market St.
Canter, Emanuel, Merchant, 5 Vendue Range, Res 4 Savage St
Canter, Joshua, 121 Broad St.
Cantwell, Patrick, Boundary St.
Cardozo, David, Measurer, Custom House, Res 99 E Bay St.
Cardozo, Isaac N , Southern Patriot Office, 99 E Bay St
Cardozo, Jacob N., Proprietor, Southern Patriot, 99 E. Bay St
Carew, Edward, Lumber Merchant, Gadsden's Whf , Res. 30 Laurens St.
Carivene, Anthony, Baker, 124 Meeting St.
Carmand, Francis, Woolen Draper & Men's Mercer
Carmer, George, Deputy Marshal, cr. Anson & Pinckney Sts.
Carmile, John, Butcher, Meeting St. Cont'd., Neck
Carminade, V , Mrs., 26 Meeting St
Carnes, D., Grocer, 74 Market St.
Carnighan, John, 21 Elliott St
Carnochan, Richard, Merchant, Craft's S. Whf., Res. 71 E. Bay St.
Carpenter, Joseph, Butcher, Cannon St., Cannonborough, Neck
Carpentier, -----, Teacher of French, 43 Coming St.
Carpentiere, Peter, King St. Cont'd , Neck
Carr, Ann, Mrs , 210 King St
Carr, James, 10 Berresford St.
Carrere, Charles, 109 Broad St
Carroll, Bartholomew, Vanderhorst St., Radcliffborough, Neck
Carson, Elisha, Dry Goods Store, King St Cont'd., Neck
Carson, Elizabeth, Mrs., 90 Tradd St.
Carson, William A., Planter, 90 Tradd St.
Carson, William, Grocer, 144 King St.
Carsten, John, City Scavenger, 30 Society St
Cart, John, Jr., Bookkeeper, Planters' & Mechanics' Bank, Res 51 Meeting St
Cart, John, Measurer of Lumber, 28 Bull St.
Cart, Sarah, Mrs , 2 Philadelphia St
Cart, Vernal, Attorney, 70 Broad St., Res 28 Bull St
Carter, E , Mrs , Dry Goods Store, 394 King St.
Carter, Elizabeth, Dry Goods Store, 394 King St Cont'd , Neck
Carter, Joseph, 243 E. Bay St.
Carter, William, 23 Coming St
Carvalho, D N., Watch Maker, 323 King St.
Carvin, E., Mrs., Milliner & Fancy Store, 147 King St
Carvine, M., Mrs , Milliner, 297 King St
Cason, Ann, Mrs., Baker, 54 State St.
Cason, James, Grocer, 62 Market St
Cassidy, George W , Dry Goods Store, cr. King St Cont'd , Neck
Cassin, Conly, Quorum Unis, 7 Queen St
Cassin, James, Boundary St.
Cassin, Mary, Mrs , 26 Laurens St

Castel, John, National Coffee House, 23 Queen St.
Catherwood, J. J , Watch Maker, 63 Broad St.
Cato, Susan, Mrs., 24 Archdale St.
Caught, Thomas, 269 E Bay St
Cause, Amey, Mrs., Henrietta St., Mazyckborough, Neck
Causse, Adolph, 236 Meeting St.
Causse, -----, Madam, School, 236 Meeting St
Cay, -----, Mrs , 18 Washington St
Chadwick, Samuel, Merchant, Craft's S. Whf., Res 13 Meeting St.
Chalmers, Catharine, Mrs., 46 St. Phililp's St.
Chalmers, E R., Mrs , Whim Court
Chamberlain, Jacob, Agent for New England Glass Co., 188 King St
Chanet, Anthony, Merchant, Chisolm's Upper Whf., Res. 19 Tradd St.
Channer, C. J , 10 Maiden Ln.
Chapman, William & Thomas, Factors, Edmondston's Whf., Res. 51 E Bay St.
Charriol, Peter, 75 State St
Chasteau, C. C., Physician, 128 Meeting St.
Chaulatte, H C , Mrs 44 Hasell St
Chazal, John P., Sea Captain, 7 Minority St.
Cheesborough & Campbell, Factors, 54 E Bay St
Cheesborough, John W , 305 E. Bay St.
Cheney, E , Jr , Commission Merchant, 138 E Bay St
Chiffelle, Thomas P , Custom House, Res 131 Queen St.
Chisholme, S , Charleston House, cr. King & George Sts
Chisolm & Taylor, Factors, Chisolm's S. Whf.
Chisolm, Alexander R., Planter, 10 Montague St
Chisolm, George, 25 E. Bay St.
Chisolm, George, Jr , 6 Montague St.
Chisolm, Robert, Mrs., 6 Montague St
Chisolm, William, Mrs , 3 George St
Chitty, Charles C., Attorney, 83 Broad St , Res 20 George St.
Choat, Catharine, Mrs., 43 Wentworth St.
Choate, Thomas, Sea Captain, 83 E. Bay St.
Chrietzberg, George, Baker 42 King St
Chrietzberg, Thomas, Grocer, 72 Market St
Christian, Ole, Grocer, Champney St.
Christie, Johanna, Mrs , 98 Church St
Christophersen, C., Grocer, 7 Legare St.
Chupein, Louis, Mineral Water Fountain & Dressing Room, 18 Broad St.
Chur, George, Grocer, 78 Market St
Church, Margaret, Mrs., Umbrella Maker, 16 St. Philip's St
Clancey, John, Grocer, King St., Neck
Clark, James, Tailor, 99 Meeting St
Clark, Joseph, Attorney, 79 Broad St.
Clark, Mary, Mrs , 104 Market St.
Clark, Richard, Pilot, 47 Church St.
Clarke, Bartholomew, Dry Goods Store, cr King & Queen Sts., Res. 163 King St
Clarkson, William, Kunhardt's Whf., Res 2 Bull St
Cleapor, Agnes, Mrs., 22 Ellery St
Cleary, Catharine, Mrs , 5 Greenhill St
Cleary, N. G., Sheriff, Charleston District, Res 145 King St

Clement, Sarah, Mrs , 101 Queen St.
Clement, Sarah, Mrs., 31 Coming St
Clements, Catharine, Mrs , 25 George St
Clifford, Henry, Factor, Mey's Whf , Res. 8 Middle St.
Clissey, Adelle, Miss, Dry Goods Store, 158 King St.
Clough, J B., Merchant, 188 E Bay St.
Coates, Catharine, Mrs , 16 Pinckney St
Coates, Christopher, Teacher, cr Broad & King Sts.
Coates, Thomas, 15 Hasell St.
Cobia, -----, 18 Montague St.
Cobia, Francis, Carpenter, 8 Smith St
Cobia, Francis J., Butcher, cr. Meeting & Reid Sts ,
    Hampstead, Neck
Cobia, N., Planter, 126 Wentworth St
Coburn, Ann, Mrs., 14 Beaufain St
Coby, Richard, Grocer, 8 Wall St
Cochran, Charles B., President, Union Bank, Res. 52
    Wentworth St.
Cochran, Jane, Mrs., 87 King St.
Cochran, Margaret, Mrs., 120 King St.
Cochran, Robert E , 29 Coming St.
Cochran, Thomas, Broker, Auctioneer, & Commission
    Merchant, 20 Broad St., Res 20 Rutledge St.
Cogdell & Gilchrist, Attornies, cr Meeting & Tradd Sts.
Cogdell, John S , Attorney, cr. Meeting & Tradd Sts.
Cogdell, M. A E., Mrs , Female Academy & Boarding
    School, 5 St. Michael's Al.
Cogdell, Richard W., Teller, Bank of the State of S C , 7
    St. Michael's Al
Cohen, Mordecai, 103 Broad St.
Cohen, Moses, Dry Goods Store, 100 King St., Res 32
    Cumberland St.
Cohen, Philip, Broad St.
Cohen, Rachael, Mrs., Dry Goods Store, 210 King St
Cohen, Samuel J., Grocer, cr. Boundary & Alexander Sts.,
    Mazyckborough, Neck
Cohen, Solomon J., Dry Goods Store, 356 King St.
Coit, Jonathan, Commission Merchant, Kiddell's Whf.
Colberg, Christopher, Grocer, 76 Tradd St
Colburn, James S., Dry Goods Store, cr Broad & King St.
Colcock, M., Mrs., 11 Lamboll St
Cole, Eliza, Mrs., 5 Tradd St
Cole, Joseph, Planter
Colhoun, William, Merchant, Chisolm's Upper Whf
Coll, John, Butcher, Hanover St., Hampstead, Neck
Collier, William, 14 Wentworth St.
Collin, Peter, 36 Market St.
Collins, Catharine, Miss, 105 Queen St
Collins, Mary, Mrs., 33 Hasell St.
Collins, Robert, 12 Society St.
Collins, Reddin, Butcher, Hanover St., Hampstead, Neck
Collins, Robert, Warren St., Radclilffborough, Neck
Colson, William, Tailor, 154 Meeting St.
Colzy, Angelica, Mrs., 33 Meeting St
Condy, Jeremiah, Hardward Store, 122 E Bay St., Res.
    100 Meeting St.
Condy, Thomas D., Attorney, 100 Meeting St.
Connelly, Elizabeth, Mrs., 10 Stoll's Al
Connelly, Mary, Mrs., 33 Meeting St.
Connelly, Matthew, Grocer, 5 Market St

Connelly, Richard, Grocer, 14 St Bay St
Conner & Wilson, Factors, Champney St
Conner, John, Saddler & Harness Maker, 375 King St
Conner, John, Saddler, 375 King St Cont'd , Neck
Connot, -----, Madam, 19 Anson St
Constamagne, Mary, Mrs , 10 Wentworth St
Contey, P., Jr., 265 King St
Conyers, William N., Merchant, 128 E Bay St , Res 34
    Pinckney St.
Cooke, Eliza, Mrs , Private Boarding House, 65 E. Bay St
Cooper, Mary, Mrs., 40 St. Philip's St
Cooper, Nathaniel, Shoe Store, cr King & Queen Sts
Copes, James, Pilot, 44 Church St.
Coram, Charlotte, Mrs., 3 Liberty St
Coram, Thomas, Mrs., 130 Queen St.
Corbet, James, Dry Goods Store, 350 King St.
Corbet, Richard, Physician, 59 State St.
Corbet, Thomas, Planter, cr. Lynch & Bull Sts.
Corby, John, Blacksmith, Vernon St.
Cordes, Rebecca, Mrs., Charlotte St., Mazyckborough,
    Neck
Corker, Thomas, Shipwright, 26 Pinckney St.
Corlis, Peter, Grocer, 6 Wall St.
Cormick, Thomas, Factor, Vanderhorst's Whf , Res. 72
    Broad St
Cormier, Francis, 308 E. Bay St.
Corneliuis, Michael, Grocer, 15 Elliott St.
Corning, Jasper, 84 Wentworth St.
Corrie, Samuel, Wheelwright, King St. Cont'd., Neck
Coste, Lucinda, Mrs , 114 Meeting St
Course, Isaac, Merchant, Vendue Range, Res. 281 E. Bay
    St.
Courtenay, Edward S., Attorney, 72 Broad St , Res. 40
    College St.
Courtenay, James, Teacher, Charleston College
Courtney, Humphrey, Private Boarding, 47 E. Bay St.
Couturier, Eliza M., Mrs., 3 State House Sq.
Coventry, C , Mrs , Dyer, 58 Tradd St.
Cowan, John, Accountant, 95 E Bay St.
Cowan, John, Cabinet Maker, 159 Meeting St
Cox, Abner, United States Coffee House, 8 Queen St.
Cox, George, Agriculture & Seed Store, 212 King St
Cox, John S. H., Sea Captain, 245 E Bay St.
Cox, Thomas, Coach Maker, 58 Broad St
Crafts, William, Attorney, cr. Church & Elliott Sts., Res.
    52 Beaufain St.
Crafts, William, Mrs., Coming St., Radcliffborough, Neck
Cramer, John, Livery Stables, 143 Church St.
Cranston, Mary, Mrs., 31 Mazyck St.
Crask, Philip, Painter, 41 Pinckney St.
Crawford, John, Vanderhorst's Whf., Res 5 Rutledge St.
Crawford, Susan, Mrs , 21 Pinckney St
Crawley, Hannah, Mrs , 76 Broad St.
Cripps, -----, Misses, 47 Meeting St
Crocker, D., Commission Merchant, Magwood's Whf.,
    Res. 23 Tradd St.
Crocker, E , Shoe Store, 275 King St.
Crocker, O. C., Carpenter, 30 State St
Croft, A., 245 King St
Croft, George, Sea Captain, 77 Tradd St.

Cromwell, Samuel, Bricklayer, 7 Back St
Crone, Harman, 10 Pitt St
Cross & Gray, Attornies, 44 Tradd St.
Cross, George W , Attorney, cr Meeting & Tradd Sts
Cross, Henry, Black & White Smith, 37 State St.
Cross, Sarah, Mrs , 6 Philadelphia St
Cross, William, Bricklayer, 10 Beaufain St.
Crouch, Abraham, Custom House, Res 3 Smith's Ln.
Crown, Peter, Dry Goods Store, 74 Wentworth St
Cruckshanks, D , Shoemaker, 22 Queen St.
Cruckshanks, Robert, Tailor, 259 King St
Cruger, Elizabeth, Mrs , 51 Meeting St
Crukshanks, Daniel, Tan Yard, Hanover St , Hampstead, Neck
Crukshanks, William, King St. Cont'd., Neck
Cruse, Engelhart, 35 Market St
Cubie, John, Grocer, 127 Tradd St.
Cudworth, William, 12 Wentworth St.
Cumming, E T., 272 E Bay St.
Cunningham, Andrew, Carpenter, 15 Beaufain St.
Cunningham, Richard, Planter, Charlotte St., Mazyckborough, Neck
Curtis, Aaron, Saddler, 39 Coming St.
Curtis, Ephraim, Carpenter, 22 Beaufain St
Curtis, F. C., Mrs., cr. Beaufain & Mazyck Sts.
Curtis, Joseph, Carpenter, 15 Beaufain St
Cuthbert, George, Planter, 20 Montague St
Cuthbert, James, Planter, 6 Smith St.
Cutting & Whittemore, Tallow Chandlers, St. Philip's St., Radcliffborough, Neck
Dalcho, Frederick, Rev , 39 Meeting St.
Daley, Wiklliam, Grocer, 16 Anson St
Dalgleish, George, Bricklayer, cr. Queen & Mazyck St.
Dalton, James, Druggist, cr. Tradd & Church Sts.
Dalton, Michael, Mariner, Charlotte St , Mazyckborough, Neck
Danelly, David, 401 King St.
Danley, David, Butcher, King St Cont'd Neck
Darby, John, Silversmith, Market St., Res. 27 Archdale St.
Darby, Mary, Mrs , 55 King St
Darrell, John S., Mrs., 281 King St.
Dart, Benjamin S., 55 Tradd St.
Dart, Isabella, Mrs., 44 Montague St
Dart, John S., 55 Tradd St
Dart, Peter, Coach Maker, 16 Pitt St.
Datty, Julia, Miss, Female Academy & Boarding School, 23 King St.
Davega, Isaac, 11 Linguard St
Davega, Moses, 21 Amen St
Davenport & Johnson, Shoe Store, 117 E Bay St
Davenport, S. & Co., Commission Merchants, Crafts' N Whf
David, David, Boarding House, 13 Elliott St.
David, Henry, Confectioner, 17 Tradd St.
David, John, Planter, Pinckney St., Cannonborough, Neck
Davidson, Eliza, Mrs , 98 Broad St
Davis & Duffus, Notary Publics & Insurance Brokers, 81 E. Bay St
Davis, Aimey, Mrs., 32 Anson St.
Davis, Eliza, Mrs , 8 Maiden Ln

Davis, G Y , Merchant, 57 E. Bay St.
Davis, Jacob, House & Sign Painter, 81 Queen St
Davis, Jane, Mrs., America St., Hampstead, Neck
Davis, John M , Broker, Cannon St , Cannonborough, Neck
Davis, John, Sea Captain, 7 Longitude Ln
Davis, Margaret, Mrs., 139 King St
Davis, Martha, Mrs , cr. Meeting & John Sts., Wraggsborough, Neck
Davis, Peter, 3 Maiden Ln.
Davis, Sarah, Mrs., 8 Philadelphia St.
Davis, Thomas, Sea Captain, 8 Price's Al.
Davson, John, Grocer, King St. Cont'd. Neck
Dawes, H P., Factor, D'Oyley's Whf , Res. 307 E Bay St.
Dawson & Mitchell, Attornies, Waring's Law Buildings, Meeeting St , op St Michael's Al.
Dawson, Ann, Mrs., 4 Montague St.
Dawson, Charles C , Teller, State Bank, Res 9 New St.
Dawson, John, Mrs., 34 Bull St.
Dawson, William, Mrs , 11 New St
Deas & Broun, Factors, Kiddell's Whf.
Deas, Charles, 382 King St
Deas, David, Mrs., 116 Tradd St.
Deas, Henry, Planter, 1 Friend St.
Deas, Robert, Planter, 133 King St.
Deas, Thomas H & Co , Merchants, Chisolm's Upper Whf.
Deas, Thomas H , 8 King St.
DeBerniere, William, 54 Wentworth St.
Debiere, Francis, Gardener, Wolf St , Hampstead, Neck
Debow, Garrett, 12 Anson St.
Debow, John, Coach Maker, 203 Meeting St
Debow, Lewis, 219 E. Bay St.
Decamps, James, Broker, 144 Meeting St
Decotte, -----, Madam, 20 Pinckney St.
Deglanne, Mary, Mrs , 75 Boundary St.
Degnan, Mary Ann, Mrs., Boundary St , Mazyckborough, Neck
Dehon, Sarah, Mrs., 43 Meeting St.
Delaire, Ann, Mrs , 10 Middle St
Delamotta, Jacob, Physician, 58 Wentworth St.
Delaney, Michael, Pilot, 2 Stoll's Al
Delap, E , Mrs., Church St.
Deleon, Jacob, 10 West St
Deliesseline, Francis A , City Sheriff, 256 E. Bay St.
Deliesseline, Francis G , 256 E. Bay St.
Deliesseline, William, Carpenter, 29 Boundary St
Demming & Bulkley, Cabinet Makers, 231 King St
Dempsey, M., Union Hotel, 147 E. Bay St
Dempsey, Thomas, Grocer, 90 E Bay St.
Dennehy, Jeremiah, Printer, 34 Laurens St.
Denny, Mary L , Mrs , 17 Guignard St.
Denny, Thomas, Musician, 134 Queen St.
Denoon, Henry P , Carpenter, Chapel St , Mazyckborough, Neck
Denoon, Margaret, Chapel St., Mazyckborough, Neck
Dent, Ann, Mrs., 59 Beaufain St.
Depass, Joseph, Beaufain St
Depras, C., Shoe Store, 55 Broad St.
Depray, John, 94 King St

111

Deromas, F , Cigar Maker, 170 Meeting St
Desaussure, Henry A , 35 Meeting St.
Desel, Charles L., 90 Wentworth St.
Desportes, Peter, Grocer, 199 E Bay St
Despraugh, Ann, Mrs , 303 King St.
Deveaux, Martha, Mrs., 34 Beaufain St.
Devillers, Louis, Book & Music Store, 91 Broad St.
Devineau, Abraham, Shopkeeper, 71 King St
Devix, D., 72 Queen St.
Devling, John, 250 E. Bay St
Dewees, John, Factor, 70 E. Bay St
Dewees, John., Factor, Mary St., Wraggsborough, Neck
Dewees, William, Factor, Dewees Whf.
Dewees, William, Sr., cr Charlotte & Alexander Sts.,
    Mazyckborough, Neck
Deweet, William, Collector, Elizabeth St ,
    Mazyckborough, Neck
Dews, J E., Mrs , 17 Bull St
Dexter, Samuel W , 10 King St.
Deye, Benjamin, Grocer, S Bay St.
Dickinson, Francis, Planter, Alexander St.,
    Mazyckborough, Neck
Dickinson, Jeremiah, Planter, Alexander St ,
    Mazyckborough, Neck
Dickinson, Samuel, Vendue Master, N. Vendue Range,
    Res 76 Broad St.
Dickson, John, Rev., Charleston College, Res. 59 St.
    Philip's St
Dickson, Mary, Mrs , 343 King St
Dickson, Samuel H , Physician, 54 St. Philip's St
Dill, Eliza, Miss, 50 King St.
Dill, Jane, Mrs., Dry Goods Store, 177 King St.
Dinkins, L. J., Factor, 8 Champney St
Disher, Lewis, Shopkeeper, King St Cont'd Neck
Disher, Susan, Mrs., 116 Meeting St
Dixon & Wilkinson, Tallow Chandlers, King St. Cont'd ,
    Neck
Dixon, O S , 118 Meeting St
Dixon, Robert, 31 Pinckney St.
Dobbin, John, Clerk, 95 E. Bay St.
Dobson, O. L., Grocer, cr. E. Bay & Tradd Sts., Res. 8
    Water St
Dodd & Barnard, Merchants, 136 E. Bay St.
Doggett, Samuel W., Teacher, 357 King St.
Don, Alexander, Printer, Courier Office, Res. 40 Society
    St.
Don, Ann, Mrs., 40 Society St.
Donaldson, David, Church St.
Donegan, John, Shoemaker, 5 Queen St.
Donnelly, James, Sign Painter, 33 State St.
Dorrill, Robert, Factor, Williams' Whf., Res. 35 State St.
Dougherty, John, Grocer, 27 S. Bay St.
Dougherty, John, Plasterer, 87 Anson St.
Douglas, Anthony, Accountant, 95 E. Bay St.
Douglas, Campbell, Grocer, cr Meeting & Market Sts.
Dove, William P , Joiner, 44 State St.
Dowling, Archibald, Grocer, 5 King St.
Dowling, E. A., Mrs 17 Society St.
Downie, Robert, Tin Plate Worker, 59 Broad St.
Drayton, -----, Misses, 30 Church St

Drayton, Rebecca, Mrs., 49 Bull St.
Drayton, Thomas, Planter, 78 Wentworth St
Drayton, William, City Recorder, 6 Gibbes St.
Drege, Peter, Clothing Store, cr. E Bay & Queen Sts
Dreher, Frederick, Currier & Tanner, John St.,
    Wraggsborough, Neck
Drews, Henry, Grocer, 196 Meeting St.
Drummond, James, Shoemaker, 38 Queen St.
Drummond, John, Shoemaker, 9 Maiden Ln
Dubert, Frederick, Spring St , Hampstead, Neck
Duboc, Francis, Dry Goods Store, 181 King St.
Dubois, Louis, Upholsterer & Paper Hanger, Queen St
Duboise, Peter, Carpenter, Cannon St., Cannonborough,
    Neck
Dubose, Henry, 122 Tradd St.
Duc, Francis, Shopkeeper, cr King & Columbus St., Neck
Duffie, Andrew, Grocer, 43 Church St.
Duffus, John, Notary Public, 81 E. Bay St , Res. 119
    Church St.
Dufort, John, Baker, 40 Queen St.
Duggan, Thomas, Plasterer, St. Philip's St., Neck
Duhadway, C B , Saddler, 142 King St.
Duke, John C., Printer, 6 Amen St.
Dukes, William C., Dry Goods Store, King St Cont'd ,
    Neck
Dumoutet, Elizabeth, Mrs., Jeweller, 52 Broad St
Duncan, A J. H , Physician, Boundary St.,
    Radcliffborough, Neck
Duncan, John, cr. Bull & Pitt St.
Dunkin, Benjamin F , Attorney, Warren St ,
    Radcliffborough, Neck
Dunlap, Samuel, 37 Elliott St.
Dunn, John, St. Philip's St., Neck
Dupass, Hannah, Mrs., 116 King St
Dupass, Jacob, Grocer, 25 S. Bay St
Dupont, Catharine, Mrs , 69 Market St.
Dupont, Joseph, Crockery Store, cr. Queen & Meeting Sts.
Duprat, Raymond, 37 Market St.
Dupre, James, Carpenter, Meeting St., Wraggsborough,
    Neck
Dupuy, Francis, Teacher, 31 Guignard St.
Duquercron, Francis, Grocer, 398 King St
Durban, A., Hat Store, 67 Queen St.
Durbec, Emanuel, Grain Store, 387 King St
Durbec, -----, Mrs , 67 King St.
Dursse, Lorent, 35 Cumberland St.
Duryea, Jacob, Private Boarding, 51 State St.
Dutreaux, C , 32 Archdale St.
Duvall, John, Tinner, King St. Cont'd., Neck
Duvall, Peter, Shopkeeper, Cannon St , Cannonborough,
    Neck
Dyott, John, Dentist & Druggist, cr. King & Market Sts.
D'Oyley & Legare, Attornies, Waring's Law Buildings,
    Meeting St., op St Michael's Al
D'Oyley, Charles W., Attorney, 3 St. Philip's St
Eager, Robert, Merchant, 33 George St.
Eason, Martha, Mrs., 24 Berresford St.
Eason, Robert, Shipwright, Reaper's Al
Eassterby, George, Boarding House, 95 E. Bay St.
Easton, D , Mrs., 45 Pinckney St.

112

Eckhard, George B., Attorney, Chalmers St , Res 31
  George St.
Eckhard, Jacob, Jr , Teacher of Music, 35 Societey St
Eckhard, Jacob, Teacher of Music, 31 George St
Eckhoff, George H., Grocer, 158 Meeting St
Edmondson, Charles, Merchant, Edmondston's Whf , Res
  77 Meeting St.
Edwards, Edward H , 11 Meeting St
Edwards, George, Planter 14 Legare St.
Edwards, James F , Planter, 22 Wall St.
Edwards, Thomas K., Mary St., Mazckborough, Neck
Eger, Charles, 16 Market St.
Eggart, Jacob, Grocer, cr. George & St Philip's Sts.
Egleston & Heriot, Attornies, St Michael's Al
Egleston, George W., Attorney, 31 Society St.
Egleston, Sarah, Mrs , Northern Stage Office, 196 E Bay
  Office
Ehney, William, 84 King St.
Elder, James, Tanner, Pitt St.
Eldridge, Ephraim, 6 Maiden St
Elfe, Bejamin, Bricklayer, Blackbird Al.
Elfe, Benjamin, Deputy Secretary of State, Amherst St ,
  Hampstead, Neck
Elfe, Benjamin, Sr., Planter, Hampstead, Neck
Elfe, George, Planter, cr. John & King Sts.,
  Wraggsborough, Neck
Elfe, Isaac, Factor, Fitzsimons' Whf
Elfe, Robert, Attorney, St Michael's Al.
Elfe, Thomas, Amherst St , Hampstead, Neck
Elfe, Thomas, Measurer of Mahogany, 383 King St.
Elfe, William, Clerk, Elizabeth St., Mazyckborough, Neck
Elford, James M., Mathematical Store & Navigation
  School, 119 E. Bay St.
Elliott, B., Mrs., cr George & St Philip's Sts.
Elliott, Benjamin, Commissioner in Equity, 22 Legare St.
Elliott, Mary, Miss, 2 Gibbes St
Elliott, Stephen, President, Bank of State of S C , Res. 7
  Archdale St.
Elliott, Thomas O., Attorney, St. Michael's Al., Res. 75
  King St
Ellis, Ann, Mrs , 84 Anson St.
Ellis, Mary, Mrs , 244 E. Bay St
Elsworth, John T , Gauger, 13 Boundary St.
Emanuel, Isaac, Auctioneer, 302 King St.
Embert, Mary, Mrs., 271 E. Bay St.
Emery, Jonathan Sea Captain, 2 Unity Al.
England, Alexander, Baker, 54 Tradd St.
England, John, Right Rev , 86 Wentworth St
English, James, Shipwright, 23 S Bay St.
Enslow, Joseph L , Cooper 85 E. Bay St
Enslow, Mary, Mrs., 85 E. Bay St.
Ertzberger, Jane, Mrs., 70 State St.
Esnard, Peter, Grocer, 38 King St.
Evan, William, Notary Public & Quorum Unis, Guard
  House, Res 89 E. Bay St
Evans, Charles, Turner, 3 Swinton's Ln
Evans, James, 40 Coming St.
Evans, John, 78 Anson St
Evans, Lecraft, Repairer of Musical Instruments, 98 King
  St

Evans, Susan, Miss, 25 Coming St.
Evans, William H., 33 Laurens St.
Eveleth & Thayer, Commission Merchant, Gillon St.
Everingham, John, 240 E Bay St.
Eyland, James & Co., Military & Fancy Store, 172 King St.
Faber, C. H , 296 King St.
Faber, C. L., Mrs., 2 Montague St
Faber, Henry C., Accountant, Charlotte St ,
  Mazyckborough, Neck
Faber, J C , Mrs., Charlotte St., Mazyckborough, Neck
Faber, P A., 102 Meeting St.
Fabian, Lucette, Mrs , Private Boarding, 97 Church St
Fable, John, Grocer, 81 Tradd St.
Fable, John, Grocer, cr St. Philip's & Bridge Sts ,
  Cannonborough, Neck
Fair, William, 2 West St
Fairchild, Alexander, 93 Market St
Fairchild, Lyon & Co , Saddlery, 321 King St.
Fairchild, Rufus, Shoe Store, 204 King St.
Fanning, F D , 276 King St
Farley, John, Teacher, 10 Liberty St
Farmer, Henry T , Physician, cr Hudson & King Sts , Neck
Farr, Catharine, Mrs., 16 Coming St.
Farrell, Bernard, Grocer, 2 Anson St.
Farrell, Darby, 12 King St
Fasbender, J. H , Watch Maker, 110 Meeting St
Fash, Leonard, Sea Captain, 23 Tradd St
Fayolle, Peter, Teacher of Dancing, 82 King St
Fayolle, Theodore, B , Teacher of Dancing, 80 King St.
Febve, Laura, Mrs., 173 Meeting St.
Fegan, Simon, Grocer, Williams' Whf.
Fell, Thomas, Tin Plate Worker, 100 Market St.
Fell, William, 128 Tradd St.
Feret, Charles, Tailor, 57 Wentworth St.
Ferguson, Eliza M , Mrs , 11 Lamboll St.
Ferguson, Hugh, 24 Tradd St
Ferguson, James, Planter, cr. King & John Sts , Neck
Ferguson, John, 32 Broad St.
Ferman, Anthony, Mariner, Henrietta St , Mazyckborough,
  Neck
Ferrett, John F , 121 Meeting St
Ferrett, John, Jeweller, 179 King St.
Ferrett, Josephine, Miss, 22 George St
Ferrett, M. R , Mrs , 219 King St.
Fields, Nathaniel, 22 Ellery St.
Fife, James, Merchant, 75 E. Bay St , Res 72 Church St.
Fillette, Francis, Dry Goods Store, 148 King St.
Finckley, Elizabeth, Mrs , 23 Guignard St
Finley, Mary, Mrs., 1 Legare St.
Finley, S B R., Physician, 1 Legare St
Finley, William P , Attorney, 70 Broad St.
Fisk, Thomas, Teacher, 141 E Bay St
Fitch, C H , Mrs , Private Boarding, 20 State St.
Fitch, Thomas, Commission Merchant, 138 E Bay St
Fitzsimons, Charles, Constable, 58 Elliott St.
Fitzsimons, Christopher, Planter, 20 Hasell St.
Fleming, James, Grocer, cr. King & Cumberland Sts
Fleming, John H , Carpenter, 24 Laurens St
Flemming & Co., Hardware Store, cr. King & George Sts.
Flemming & Ross, Merchants, cr E. Bay St & Vendue

Range
Flemming, Joseph, Merchant, 1 Liberty St
Flemming, Robert, Dry Goods Store, cr. King & Spring Sts., Neck
Flemming, Thomas, Merchant, cr. King & George Sts., Res. 16 George St.
Flinn, Elizabeth, Mrs., 4 S. Bay St.
Floderer, John, Grocer, 71 Church St.
Florence, R., Mrs, Dry Goods Store, 170 King St
Flyan, Edward P, Tailor, 278 King St.
Fogartie, D., 6 Minority St.
Fogartie, James, 23 Wall St
Fogartie, Susan, Mrs, 24 Hasell St
Foisson, Martha, Mrs, 114 Tradd St.
Foistier, Petant, Confectioner, 109 Church St.
Folker, E., Mrs, 8 St Philip's St
Folker, Thomas H., Druggist, cr. Church & Elliott Sts.
Follin, Augustus, Tobacconist, 150 Meeting St.
Follin, Firman, Tobacconist, 166 Meeting St
Foote, Peter D., Cooper, Exchange
Forbes, John, Tin Plate Worker, 16 Tradd St.
Forbes, William, Tin Plate Worker, 305 King St.
Ford & Desaussure, Attornies, 41 Broad St.
Ford, Henry, 127 E. Bay St
Ford, Jacob, Attorney, 81 Broad St.
Ford, Timothy, Attorney, 42 Meeting St
Fordham, John G., Vernon St.
Fordham, Richard, Blacksmith, 1 Exchange St.
Forrest, F, Mrs, 5 Hasell St.
Forrest, Thomas H, Cooper, 9 Water St.
Foster, Jonathan, 5 Berresford St.
Foster, William B, Bank of State of S C, Res. 121 Boundary St.
Fourgeaud, Arnold, Baker, 36 Guignard St
Fox, Ann, Mrs, 31 Hasell St.
Francis, Edward, Grocer, 130 Church St.
Francis, P, 47 State St
Francisco, Samuel, Painter, 20 Market St
Fraser, Charles, Attorney, St Michael's Al, Res. 53 King St.
Fraser, Frederick, Mrs., 99 Tradd St.
Fraser, James, Gardener, King St. Cont'd, Neck
Fraser, John & Co., Factors, 47 E. Bay St
Fraser, John, Factor, 41 E Bay St.
Fraser, John G., 41 E. Bay St.
Fraser, Thomas L S., Planter, John St, Wraggsborough, Neck
Frazer, John, 1 Society St
Frazer, John, Boat Builder, John St, Wraggsborough, Neck
Frazer, John M., 22 Laurens St
Frazer, Sarah, Mrs, 25 Society St
Frazer, William M., 22 Laurens Sts.
Frean, William, 49 State St
Freeman, Luther, Grocer, cr E Bay & Queen Sts, Res. 9 State St.
Freeman, William, Grocer, 1 Tradd St
Friel, Edward, Boarding House 1 Chalmers St
Friend, Ann, Mrs, 69 Anson St.
Frierson, John, Planter, E. Bay St, Hampstead, Neck

Fripp, Charles, 117 Tradd St.
Fritz, John, Gardener, Henrietta St, Mazyckborough, Neck
Fronty, Michael, Physician, 186 King St
Frost & Mazyck, Attornies, State House Sq.
Frost, Edward, Attorney, 23 Archdale St.
Frost, Elizabeth, Mrs, 23 Archdale St.
Frost, Henry R., Physician, 23 Archdale St.
Fry & Gregory, Hat Store, 318 King St
Fuller, Benjamin, Planter, cr. Boundary & Coming Sts, Radcliffborough, Neck
Fuller, Oliver, 105 Meeting St
Fulmer, John, Chair & Coach Maker, cr King & Spring Sts., Neck
Furman & Hibben, Attornies, 100 Church St.
Furman & Smith, Factors, 60 E. Bay St.
Furman, Charles M, Attorney, 100 Church St
Furman, Richard B., Physician, 100 Church St.
Furman, Richard, Rev., 100 Church St
Furr, Jacob, Radcliffborough, Neck
Fursman, James, 10 Clifford's Al
Gabeau, Anthony, 36 St Philip's St.
Gadsden, Christopher E., Rev., 67 Anson St
Gadsden, J & T., Attornies, St. Michael's Al.
Gadsden, John, Attorney, 28 Church St.
Gadsden, John, District Attorney for S. C., St. Michael's Al., Res. 11 Meeting St.
Gadsden, Mary, Mrs., 12 S Bay St.
Gadsden, Rebecca, Mrs., 124 Queen St.
Gadsden, Thomas, Attorney, 28 Church St
Gafkin, C, Mrs, 21 Society St
Gaillard, Alfred, Planter, Lynch St.
Gaillard, B B., Planter, Hudson St, Cannonbourgh, Neck
Gaillard, Daniel H., State House Sq
Gaillard, Mazyck & Sons, Factors, Chisolm's N Whf.
Gaillard, Peter, Planter, 300 E. Bay St.
Gaillard, Rebecca, Mrs, 121 Boundary St
Gaillard, Theodore, Judge, 5 Liberty St
Galbot, Alexis, Tobacconist, 125 Meeeting St
Galibau, Francis, 181 E Bay St.
Gallagher, Bridget Jane, Mrs., King St Cont'd, Neck
Gallett, Hellen, Miss, 1 Archdale St.
Galloway, Eliza, Mrs., Cannon St, Cannonborough, Neck
Galluchat, Joseph, Rev., 110 Wentworth St.
Galpin, L 327 King St.
Gamage, Edward, 3 Friend St.
Gandouine, Isidore, Clothing Store, 111 E Bay St.
Ganjan, Theodore, Meeting St., Wraggsborough, Neck
Gantt, Thomas J., Attorney, State House Sq
Gappin, William, Coach Maker, Boundary St., Neck
Garden, Alexander, Planter, 8 Short St
Gardner, John, Planter, Cannon St., Cannonborough, Neck
Garesche, P., Importer French Goods, 170 E Bay St.
Garner, Ann, Mrs., 76 Wentworth St.
Garner, Thomas, Gardener, Meeting St Cont'd., Neck
Garrard, Jacob, Planter, Washington St., Mazyckborough, Neck
Garrett, John, Planter, St. Philip's St, Radcliffborough, Neck
Garrett, William, Grocer, 14 Guignard St.
Gaskin, John, Carpenter, Charlotte St, Mazyckborough,

114

Neck
Gates, Jane, Mrs., King St. Cont'd , Neck
Gates, John, Butcher, Cannon St., Cannonborough, Neck
Gates, Thomas, Butcher, Cannon St., Cannonborough, Neck
Gates, Thomas, Rev , Charlotte St , Mazyckborough, Neck
Geddes, George W , cr. King & Morris Sts.
Geddes, John, 54 Broad St.
Geddes, John, Jr., 54 Broad St.
Gediere, Margaret, Mrs , Dry Goods Store, 358 King St
Gefkin, Henry C., Carpenter, 20 Bull St
Gelser, Robert, Planter, King St. Cont'd., Neck
Gentie, August, 83 Anson St.
George, Elizabeth, Mrs , 12 Guignard St
George, John, Grocer, 149 E. Bay St
Gervais, P. T., Rev , 8 New St
Getty, Samuel, Grocer, cr. King & Blackbird Al.
Geyer, John, Planter, 16 Lynch's Ln
Gibbes, Edwin, Book Store, 51 Broad St., Res. Upstairs
Gibbes, William H , Master in Equity, cr. Meeting & Queen Sts.
Gibbon, G & Co , Commission Merchants, 124 E Bay St.
Gibbs, Elizabeth, Mrs , 69 Church St.
Gibbs, George, Counting House, Gibbes' Whf , Res 4 State St
Gibbs, Josephn, Vanderhorst St , Cannonborough, Neck
Gibbs, M G , Attorney, 83 Meeting St., Res 51 Meeting St.
Gibbs, P. C , 4 State St
Gibbs, Robert, Jr , Planter, cr John & Elizabeth Sts , Mazyckborough, Neck
Gibbs, Robert R., Planter, cr. Meeting & Ann Sts , Wraggsborough, Neck
Gibbs, Susannah, Mrs , 51 Meeting St
Gibbs, William, Planter, cr. Warren & St. Philip's Sts., Radcliffborough, Neck
Gibson, Alexander, 31 E. Bay St.
Gibson, Falconer & Co., Merchants, Chisolm's Whf.
Gibson, James, Coach Maker, 226 Meeting St.
Gibson, William, Accountant, 13 Back St
Gibson, William H., Grocer, cr Anson & Guignard St
Gilbert, Catharine, Mrs , 17 Amen St.
Gilbert, Eugene, Teacher of Music, 1 Wall St.
Gilchrist, James, Clerk, S. C. Bank, Res. 52 Tradd St.
Gilchrist, Robert B., Attorney, 52 Tradd St.
Giles, O J., 4 Green St
Gilfert, Charles, Manager of Theatre, Broad St
Gillaspie, Thomas, Tavern, 70 Queen St
Gilliand, William H., 24 George St
Gilliland, Margaret, Mrs., 353 King St.
Gilliland, William H & Co., Dry Goods Store, 320 King St
Gilman, S , Mrs., 6 Mazyck St.
Gilman, S , Rev , Pinckney St., Cannonborough, Neck
Gilman, Z., Shoe Store, cr. Meeting & Market Sts , Res 15 Anson St.
Giraud, Francis, Merchant, 80 King St
Gissendanner, -----, Mrs , Nurse, 36 Beaufain St
Gitsinger, B. R., Printer, 6 Tradd St.
Gitsinger, E F., Mrs , 6 Tradd St

Gitsinger, John R., Porter House, 6 Tradd St.
Gitsinger, W. R S , Gilder, 155 King St.
Gladden, George, Butcher, Coming St , Cannonborough, Neck
Gleize, Louisa, Mrs , 122 Meeting St
Glen, Ann, Mrs , Baker, 361 King St
Glen, John S , Planter, 97 Tradd St.
Glen, John, Teller, Planters' & Mechanics' Bank, Res 108 Wentworth St.
Glen, Margaret, Mrs., 97 Tradd St
Glover, Joseph, Physician, cr Wentworth & Rutledge Sts.
Glover, Lydia, Mrs., 27 Mazyck St
Glover, Margaret, Mrs., 3 Meeting St.
Gnech, Charles D , Watch Maker, 62 Broad St
Godard, Rene, Merchant, 53 E. Bay St., Res 129 King St.
Godet, John, 39 Hasell St
Godfrey, Eleanor, Mrs., 63 Wentworth St
Godfrey, Richard, Coming St., Radcliffborough, Neck
Godfrey, Sarah, Mrs., 137 Queen St
Gold, Sarah, Mrs , Coming St
Goldsmith, Abraham, 36 Hasell St.
Goldsmith, M , Deputy U S. Marshal, 37 Hasell St.
Good, Francis, Shopkeeper, Res. cr Wolf & Meeting Sts., Neck
Gooddrich, Nathaniel, Butcher, Cannon St , Cannonborough, Neck
Goodman, Benjamin, Mrs., King St., Neck
Goodman, Duke, Factor, Edmondston's Whf.
Goodman, Duke, Hudson St., Wraggsborough, Neck
Goodwin, John, Bookkeeper, Courier Office, Res cr Broad & E. Bay St.
Gordon, Charles P., Clerk, Office of Discount & Desposit, Cannonborough, Neck
Gordon, John, Bricklayer, 218 Meeting St
Gordon, R., Mrs., 189 King St.
Gordon, William E , Master, Work House, 17 Magazine St.
Gorldon, Martha, Mrs., 27 Archdale St.
Gosprey, Francis, Carpenter, Coming St., Radcliffborough, Neck
Goteer, Felix, Teacher of French & Drawing, 2 Chalmers St.
Gough, Emma, Mrs , 18 Meeting St.
Goujan, Theodore, 263 Meeting St
Gouldsmith, Richard, Cabinet Maker, cr. King & Market Sts.
Gourdin, Samuel, Planter, 20 Pitt St
Gowan, Peter, Watchmaker 108 Meeting St
Gowdey, Margaret, Mrs., 28 Guignard St.
Grace, John, 16 King St.
Graddick, Charles, cr. Coming & Cannon Sts., Cannonborough, Neck
Graddick, Richard, Blacksmith, King St., Neck
Graeser, C J., Notary Public, Crafts' N Whf , Res. cr Beaufain & Archdale Sts.
Graham, Michael, Grocer, cr King & Boundary Sts
Grand, -----, Mrs., 6 Guignard St.
Grannis, George B. & Co , Shoe Store, 252 King St
Grant & M'Guffie, Merchants, 50 E Bay St.
Grantt, Ann, Mrs , 9 Wall St

115

Gravel, John, Grocer, cr Wentworth & Rutledge Sts.
Graves, Anthony, Brickmaker, Wolf St , Hampstead, Neck
Graves, Charles, Planter, 28 S. Bay St.
Graves, Massy, Mrs , 2 Smith's Ln
Graves, S. C., Mrs., 94 Broad St.
Graves, Sarah, Mrs , 8 Savage St
Gray & Ellis, Printing Office, 9 Broad St.
Gray, James, Attorney, 5 Pinckney St
Gray, Sarah W., Dry Goods Store, 372 King St., Neck
Gray, William H , Printer, 36 Coming St
Gready, A. P , 151 Meeting St.
Green, Christopher R , Planter, 96 Tradd St
Green, James, 9 Friend St.
Green, Thomas P., Druggist, 187 E Bay St
Greenhill, -----, Misses, 1 Greenhill St.
Greenland, B R., Physician, 47 Beaufain St
Greenland, Elizabeth, Mrs., 74 Tradd St.
Greenland, Esther, Mrs , 51 George St.
Greenland, William P., 21 Meeting St.
Greer, Benjamin, Grocer, 51 Bull St.
Gregorie, James, Broker, 9 State St., Res 283 E Bay St.
Gregorie, James L , Attorney, 9 State St
Gregson, Thomas, Clerk, State Bank, Res. 28 Magazine St
Greig, Alexander, Baker, Boundary St , Wraggsborough, Neck
Greneker, Margaret, Mrs , Boarding House, 83 E Bay St
Griffin, -----, Mrs , cr Cannon & Coming Sts., Cannonborough, Neck
Grimball, Paul C., Planter, Pinckney St., Cannonborough, Neck
Grimes, Michael, Farmer, 50 Boundary St , Mazyckborough, Neck
Grimke, John Physician, 23 Hasell St.
Grimke, Mary, Mrs., 299 E Bay St
Grimke, Thomas S., Attorney, 82 Broad St.
Grimkey, Legare & Grimke, Attornies, 82 Broad St
Groning, Lewis, Merchant, 112 Tradd St.
Gros, John, Cabinet Maker, 191 Meeting St
Gruber, Charles, 128 Wentworth St.
Gruber, Charles M , 19 Pitt St
Gruber, Margaret B., Mrs., Meeting St. Cont'd., Neck
Guangan, Eliza, Miss, 173 Meeting St
Guenveur, John M., Dyer, 73 Meeting St.
Guerard, Ann, Mrs , 115 Meeting St
Guerry, Grandison, 53 George St.
Guy, James, Tailor, 90 Boundary St , Neck
Guy, John, Bricklayer, 11 Minority St
Guy, William, Saddler, Beaufain St
Gyles, Mary R., Mrs., Milliner, Clifford St.
Hahnbaum, G. E , cr Montague & Pitt Sts
Hahnbaum, -----, Mrs., Female Academy, cr. Montague & Pitt Sts.
Haig, David, Cooper, 204 Meeting St
Haig, James, City Attorney, 58 Meeting St , Res. 204 Meeting St.
Hains, Samuel, Pilot, 35 Elliott St.
Hall & Mills, Commission Merchants, S. Vendue Range
Hall, Jane, Mrs., Dry Goods Store, cr King & Market Sts
Hall, Susannah, Mrs., State House Sq.
Hall, William, Physician, E. Bay St , Hampstead, Neck

Halliday, Eleanor, Mrs , 42 Church St.
Hallson, John, Grocer, Henrietta St , Mazyckborough, Neck
Halsam, John, Rev , Teacher, German Friendly Society School
Halten, J. C , Grocer, cr Meeting & Cumberland Sts
Ham, Thomas, Notary Public & Quorum Unis, 6 Broad St , Res 405 King St.
Hamilton & Brush, Hat Store, 327 King St.
Hamilton, Alexander, Coach Trimmer, 37 Laurens St
Hamilton, Euphame, Mrs., Female Academy, 97 Meeting St.
Hamilton, James, Jr., cr. Coming & Bull Sts.
Hamilton, James, Sr , 2 Church St
Hamilton, John, Shipwright, 17 Anson St
Hammersly, D., Shoemaker, 170 Meeting St.
Hammet, Benjamin, Store, King St Cont'd., Neck
Hammett, C., Mrs , 22 Anson St
Hance, Phoebe, Mrs., 141 King St
Hanckel, Christian, Rev , 115 Boundary St.
Hannah, William, 32 King St.
Hannahan, J C , 134 Tradd St
Hannanto, Teresa, Confectioner, 26 Tradd St
Hanscome, Thomas, Planter, 113 Tradd St
Hanson, John, Boarding House, 7 Bedon's Al.
Happoldt, Christian, Butcher, Cannon St., Cannonborough, Neck
Happoldt, Christopher, Butcher, Cannon St , Cannonborough, Neck
Harbers, John R., Grocer, 77 Market St
Harby, Henry, Blacksmith, 165 Church St.
Harby, Isaac, Teacher, 86 Tradd St.
Harcourt, Paul, Bricklayer, Smith St.
Hard, Benjamin F., Livery Stables, 50 Society St
Hardrion, William, 6 Middle St.
Hardy, John J , Mariner, 19 Philadelphia St.
Harleston, Edward, Planter, 91 Boundary St.
Harleston, Elizabeth, Miss, 2 Cumberland St
Harleston, Nicholas, Planter, Radcliffborough, Neck
Harleston, William, Mrs , 118 Broad St
Harper, William W., Baker, 79 Tradd St.
Harris, Hyam, 199 King St.
Harris, Jacob, Clothing Store, 203 E. Bay St.
Harrison, D. W., Book Store, 40 Broad St.
Harrison, Francis, Grocer, 178 Meeting St.
Hart, Nathan, Hardware Store, cr King & Market Sts
Hart, Richard, Res. Tobacco St., Neck
Hart, Richard, Wharfinger, Edmonston's Whf , Res. Tobacco St
Hart, Simon M , 23 Beaufain St
Harth, William, Lumber Merchant, 1 Gibbes St
Hartman, John P., Grocer, 5 Elliott St
Hartman, Justus, Grocer, cr. Beaufain & St. Philip's St.
Harvey, A M , 41 Beaufain St
Harvey, E , Dyer, 89 Queen St.
Harvey, Edward T , 79 Wentworth St
Harvey, S. F., Mrs., 9 Lynch St.
Harvey, Samuel, Sea Captain, 252 E Bay St
Harvey, Thomas P , City Sheriff's Office, Res. 54 Society St.

116

Hasel, Christopher, Planter, Charlotte St., Mazyckborough, Neck
Hasell, Hannah, Mrs, 12 S. Bay St.
Haskell, E., Planter, Upper End Wentworth St.
Haskell, -----, Planter, Boundary St., Cannonborough, Neck
Haslett, John, Merchant, 5 Longitude Ln.
Hatch, Mary, Mrs, 27 Pinckney St.
Hatfield, John, Grocer, 1 Coming St.
Hattier, Mary, Mrs., Confectioner, 309 King St.
Hauck, Henry, 58 Anson St.
Haven, C. C., Merchant, Crafts' S Whf, Res. 73 Church St.
Hawes, James, Cooper, 28 State St
Hayden, Jane, Mrs., America St., Hampstead, Neck
Hayden, Mary, Mrs., Shopkeeper, Meeting St. Cont'd, Neck
Hayes, James, Bricklayer, St. Philip's St, Neck
Hayne, Elizabeth, Mrs., 10 Water St.
Hayne, Robert Y., Ladson's Court
Hayne, William A., Bookkeeper, Bank of State of S. C., Res 30 St. Philip's St
Hayward, Richard, 14 Maiden Ln.
Hazard, R., Dry Goods Store, 333 King St.
Hazlehurst, G. A., Factor, Kiddell's Whf.
Heath, John D., Attorney, 179 E Bay St
Hedderley, William, Bell Hanger, 83 Tradd St.
Heery, Thomas, Grocer, 7 Market St
Heery, Thomas, Grocer, Cordes St.
Heilbron, James, Medical Steam Bath, 74 Church St.
Hely, John, 73 State St
Henderson, Alexander, Watch Maker, 84 Queen St
Henderson, Robert, Grain Store, 63 Tradd St.
Hendrick, John, 22 Market St.
Hendricks, Frederick & Co., Grocers, cr Boundary & Lowndes St.
Hendricks, Frederick, Grocer, 21 S. Bay St.
Henry, Alexander, Cashier, Bank of State of S. C, Res 136 Wentworth St.
Henry, Edward, Grocer, 18 Guignard St
Henry, George, cr. King & Vanderhorst Sts.
Henry, Jacob, Cabinet Maker, 130 Meeting St.
Henry, Thomas C., Rev, Charlotte & Alexander Sts., Mazyckborough, Neck
Henwood, Samuel, Accountant, 60 E Bay St.
Hepburn, John, 71 State St
Heriot, B. D, Factor, 72 E. Bay St., Res. 6 Water St
Heriot, -----, Mrs, Female Academy & Boarding School, 66 Church St.
Heriot, Roger, Accountant, 66 Church St
Herron, Charles, Tailor, 44 Pinckney St
Hertz, Jacob, Shopkeeper, 95 King St
Hesley, John, Butcher, Cannon St., Cannonborough, Neck
Heynes, James, 52 Church St
Heyward, Hannah, Mrs., 21 Legare St.
Heyward, Nathaniel, Planter, 277 E Bay St
Heyward, William, Mrs, 6 Friend St.
Hichborn, Catharine, Mrs, 30 Tradd St.
Hichborn, William C., 30 Tradd St.
Higham & Fife, Merchants, 75 E Bay St

Higham, Thomas, 75 E. Bay St.
Hill, C. G, Chair Factory, 386 King St.
Hill, Christopher G., King St. Cont'd., Neck
Hill, Francis C., Painter, 7 Clifford St.
Hill, Margaret, Mrs., 16 Anson St.
Hill, Mary, Miss, Fancy Store, cr King & Clifford Sts.
Hill, Paul, Distiller, 7 Clifford St.
Hillain, Ann E., Mrs, 175 Meeting St.
Hillbrand, Henry, 35 State St.
Hillegas, Sarah, Mrs., 133 Meeting St
Hillman, Ann, Mrs., Private Boarding, 69 E. Bay St.
Hindley, T H., Merchant, Chisolm's S. Wharf
Hinds, James, Boarding House, 14 Bedon's Al.
Hippins, P, Mrs, 5 Tradd St.
Hislop, C., Mrs., 51 Pinckney St.
Hislop, H, Mrs, 83 Boundary St.
Hislop, Robert, Rice Store, 24 State St.
Hoff, John M., Clerk of Market, 10 Berresford St
Hoff, Philip, Book Store, 10 Broad St.
Hoffman, George, Grocer, 117 Church St.
Hogarth, Mary, Mrs., 16 Wall St
Holbrook, J. E, Physician, 87 Tradd St.
Holbrook, Moses, Physician, 123 Church St.
Holland, John, 38 Tradd St.
Holmes & Waring, Attornies, St. Michael's Al.
Holmes, C, Justice of Peace, 45 State St.
Holmes, Charles R., Factor Vanderhorst's Whf.
Holmes, Isaac, Mrs, 81 Church St
Holmes, J. T. W., Accountant, 119 King St.
Holmes, John B., Bricklayer, Whim Court
Holmes, John B., Jr., 61 Beaufain St.
Holmes, John B., Planter, 7 E. Bay St.
Holmes, John, Mrs., 89 Tradd St.
Holmes, Margaret, Mrs., 354 King St.
Holmes, Mary Esther, Mrs., 77 Church St.
Holmes, Sandiford, Wholesale & Retail Dry Goods Store, 154 King St.
Holmes, W H., Factor, Washington St, Mazyckborough, Neck
Holwell, Thomas, 2 Guignard St
Honour, John, 17 Beaufain St.
Honour, John H, 29 St Philip's St
Hopkins, David, 35 Magazine St.
Hopkins, John M, 15 Wall St.
Horden, Eliza, Mrs., 4 Minority St.
Horlbeck, Alexander, 103 Boundary St
Horlbeck, Henry, Bricklayer, 23 Cumberland St.
Horlbeck, John, Bricklayer, 241 Meeting St
Horry, Elias Lynch, Planter, 124 Broad St.
Horry, Elias, Planter, 45 Meeting St
Horry, Harriet, Mrs., 111 Tradd St
Horry, Lucretia, Mrs., 99 Wentworth St
Horsey, Thomas J., 292 King St.
Hort, Benjamin, Millwright, Hudson St, Cannonborough, Neck
Houseal, David, School, Henrietta St., Mazyckborough, Neck
Housheldt, Peter, Grocer, cr. Washington & Charlotte Sts, Mazyckborough, Neck
Hover, Gunrod, Shopkeeper, Pinckney St.,

Cannonborough, Neck

Howard, Alexander, City Assessor, 88 St. Philip's St.

Howard, John, Bricklayer, Henrietta St., Mazyckborough, Neck

Howard, John, Rev., 37 George St.

Howard, Richard, Cooper, Washington St., Mazyckborough, Neck

Howard, Robert, 222 Meeting St

Howard, William, Mrs., School, 383 King St Cont'd., Neck

Howe, John, Grocer, 75 Tradd St

Howe, Mary, Mrs., 7 King St

Howe, Silas, 139 Meeting St.

Howland & Co., Merchants, Crafts' N Whf

Howland, B. J., Dry Goods Store, 263 King St.

Howland, William, Dry Goods Store, 220 King St

Howley, William, 12 Market St.

Hoyt, Eli T & Co, Hat Store, 315 King St

Huard, S., Hat Store, 17 Broad St.

Huard, Stanilaus, Druggist, 49 Broad St

Hubbel, Sears, Grocer, cr. Boundary & Washington Sts., Mazyckborough, Neck

Huchet & Roger, Merchants, 31 Queen St.

Huff, Abigail, Mrs, 7 Price's Al

Huger, Alfred, Planter, 114 Broad St.

Huger, Ann, Mrs, 114 Broad St.

Huger, Charlotte, Miss, 27 St. Philip's St.

Huger, Daniel, Broker & Auctioneer, 6 State St, Res 47 Coming St

Huger, Daniel E, Judge, 28 Meeting St.

Huger, John, Planter, 3 Meeting St.

Huger, -----, Misses, Radcliff St., Radcliffborough, Neck

Hughes, B, Mrs., 6 Lamboll St

Hughes, Edward, Notary Public & Quorum Unis, 28 Tradd St

Hume, Alexander, Planter, 96 Wentworth St.

Hume, John, Jr., Planter, cr. Wentworth & Smiths Sts.

Hume, John, Planter, cr. Wentworth & Smith St.

Hume, Robert, Planter, Lynch St.

Humphreys, John, Coach Trimmer, 20 Berresford St

Humphreys, Mary, Mrs., 101 E. Bay St.

Hunt, Benjamin F, Attorney, State House Sq.

Hunt, Hannah, Mrs., King St. Cont'd., Neck

Hunt, Thomas, Register in Equity, 211 Meeting St.

Hunter, John, 2 Beaufain St.

Hunter, Mary, Mrs., 12 Berresford St.

Hurd, Sarah, Mrs., 43 State Sts.

Hurlburt, M. L, 14 Society St

Hurlbut & Keith, Book Store & Bindery, 23 Broad St.

Hurst, B, 129 Tradd St

Hurst, Charles, 15 Blackbird Al.

Husser, William, Carpenter, Cannon St, Cannonborough, Neck

Hussey, Susan, Mrs, 9 Stoll's Al

Hutchinison, Ann, Mrs., 8 Champney St.

Hutchins, S., Merchant, 142 E. Bay St.

Hutchinson, Anna, Mrs., Mantua Maker, 29 Archdale St

Hutchinson, E. L, Mrs, 8 Society St.

Hutchinson, Legere, Mrs., 251 E Bay St

Hutton, Henry, Grocer, 80 Church St

Hutton, James, 132 Tradd St.

Hyams, Catharine, Mrs., Clothing Store, 194 King St.

Hyams, H., Mrs., Dry Goods Store, 217 King St.

Hyams, Henry, 282 King St.

Hyams, M. K., 19 Magazine St.

Hyams, Moses D, 16 S Bay St

Hyams, Rebecca, Mrs., Mantua Maker, 17 Swinton's Ln.

Hyams, Samuel, Jailor, 19 Magazine St.

Hynson, Thomas, Carpenter, 11 Berresford St.

Icarden, Lewis, Tallow Chandler, Meeting St. Cont'd., Wraggsborough, Neck

Inglesby, William H, Attorney, St. Michael's Al, Res 9 West St.

Inglis, Mary, Miss, 10 Lamboll St

Ingraham, Henry, Planter, cr. Wentworth & Smith Sts

Ingraham, Louisa, Mrs., 11 Smith's Ln

Irvine, Matthew, Physician, cr. King & Lamboll Sts.

Irving, John B, Physician, 2 Cumberland St

Iseman, P. H., Shopkeeper, cr. Coming & Boundary Sts, Radcliffborough, Neck

Ives, Jeremiah, Sea Captain, 5 Middle St.

Izard, Elizabeth, Mrs., 90 Broad St

Izard, Henry, Planter, cr. Meeting & S. Bay St.

Jacks, Elizabeth, Mrs, Chapel St, Mazyckborough, Neck

Jackson, James, Lynch St.

Jackson, Robert, 367 King St.

Jackson, Robert, Dry Goods Store, 367 King St. Cont'd, Neck

Jacob, Moses, Dry Goods Store, 273 King St.

Jacobs, Barnet, Mrs, 229 E. Bay St.

Jacobs, Hyman, 53 State St.

Jacobson, Caspar, Shopkeeper, cr Meeting & Reid Sts, Neck

Jacoby, George, Grocer, 83 Church St

Jahan, Joseph, 247 Meeting St.

Jameison, John, Blacksmith, 11 Market St

James, -----, Mrs., Clothing Store, 272 King St

Jaques, Ann, Mrs, 3 West St.

Javain, Peter, Grocer, 187 King St

Jeanerett, Christopher, 43 Society St

Jeffords, John H., 9 Minority St.

Jeffords, John, Shopkeeper, 11 Middle St.

Jenkins, Christopher, Planter, 9 Smith St.

Jenkins, Elias, Bricklayer, 6 Liberty St

Jenkins, Micha, Planter, 11 Legare Sts.

Jenkins, Richard, Mrs., 42 Bull St

Jervey, James, Clerk, Federal Court, 37 Laurens St.

Jervey, Thomas H, Custom House, Res 51 Church St.

Johnson & Maynard, Druggists, 11 Broad St.

Johnson, Andrew, Grocer, 119 Queen St

Johnson, Ann, Mrs., 55 State St.

Johnson, Archibald, Grocer, 135 Church St

Johnson, Bennett, Grocer, 22 Bull St.

Johnson, E. H, Mrs, 156 Meeting St

Johnson, Edward, 60 State St.

Johnson, Edward, Sea Captain 66 Wentworth St

Johnson, Elizabeth, Mrs., Shopkeeper, 91 King St.

Johnson, Isaac A, Physician, 52 Society St.

Johnson, J., Clothing Store, 169 E. Bay St.

Johnson, James, Blacksmith, 13 Amen St.

118

Johnson, James, Tallow Chandler, Chapel St ,
Mazyckborugh, Neck
Johnson, James W., Planter, Pinckney St., Cannonborough,
Neck
Johnson, John, 52 Broad St.,
Johnson, John, Grocer, 38 Mazyck St
Johnson, John, Jr , Iron Founder, 54 Wentworth St
Johnson, Joseph, Physician, 49 Church St.
Johnson, Nathaniel, Carpenter, 2 Blackbird Al
Johnson, Neils, Grocer, cr. Pinckney & E Bay Sts.
Johnson, Samuel, cr. King & Vanderhorst St.
Johnson, Sarah, Mrs , 22 Society St
Johnson, William, Judge, Pinckney St., Cannonborough,
Neck
Johnson, William, Planter, Pinckney St., Cannonborough,
Neck
Johnston, Jacob, Grocer
Johnston, Thomas, Dry Goods Store & Wagon Yard, King
St. Cont'd., Neck
Johnston, Thomas, Farmer's Hotel, 226 King St.
Johnston, Thomas, Shoemaker, cr King & Spring Sts.,
Hampstead, Neck
Jones, Abraham, Cabinet Maker, 13 Beaufain St.
Jones, Edward Simons, Physician, St. Philip's St ,
Radcliffborough, Neck
Jones, Evan D , Custom House, Res Lodge Al.
Jones, Gersham, 292 King St.
Jones, Henry, Notary Public, 84 Meeting St.
Jones, Henry, Shipwright, 37 Pinckney St.
Jones, John C., Grocer, cr. Wentworth & Coming St.
Jones, John S., Wire Factory, 145 E. Bay St.
Jones, Mary, Mrs., 1 Guignard St.
Jones, Thomas, 3 Guignard St.
Jones, Thomas Simons, Warren St., Radcliffborough, Neck
Jones, William, Carpenter, 57 King St.
Jones, William, Mrs , cr. Meeting & Reid Sts , Neck
Jones, Wiswall, Counting House, 134 E. Bay St., Res 80
Meeting St.
Joor, P. L., Cannon St., Cannonborough, Neck
Jorck, Nicholas, Shopkeeper, cr Boundary & Logan Sts
Neck
Jordan, Christopher, Coach Trimmer, 2 Ellery St
Josephs, Isaac, 49 Wentworth St
Josephs, Joseph, Dry Goods Store, 332 King St.
Joy, Daniel, 74 State St.
Joy, Daniel G , 89 Church St
Juhan, Joseph, Carpenter, Meeting St Cont'd., Neck
Just, George, Wharf Builder, 12 Washington St
Kahnle, John H., 85 Boundary St.
Kalorn, John, 95 Queen St.
Kanapaux, Joseph, Tobacconist, 164 Meeting St.
Kane, Francis W , Mary St., Wraggsborough, Neck
Kanuff, John, Saddler, cr. King & Spring Sts.
Kanuff, John William, Cabinet Maker, cr King & Spring
Sts., Neck
Keckeley, Michael, cr Boundary & Coming St.
Keckley, George, Dry Goods Store, cr. King & Morris Sts ,
Neck
Keckley, John C , Cabinet Maker, 12 Swinton's Ln
Keenan, Elizabeth, Mrs., 216 King St

Keiles, Christian, Shopkeeper, Warren St.,
Radcliffborough, Neck
Keith & Miller, Hay Merchants, Lothrop's Whf
Keith, Jane, Mrs , 15 Meeting St.
Keith, Matthew I , cr. King & Lamboll Sts
Keith, Susannah, Mrs , cr King & Lamboll Sts.
Keith, Sylvanus, 79 Broad St.
Kelly, Joseph, Corn Store, 392 King St Cont'd , Neck
Kelly, Joseph, Shopkeeper, 8 Bull St.
Kelly, Marcus, N., Physician, 20 King St
Kelly, Mary, Mrs., 22 Cumberland St
Kelly, Mary, Mrs , 253 King St
Kelly, Michael, Hardware Store, 117 E. Bay St., Res. 37
Tradd St.
Kelly, Patrick, 265 King St.
Kembell, Ann, Mrs., 114 Meeting St
Kenefeck, Daniel, Shopkeeper, Alexander St.,
Mazyckborough, Neck
Kennedy, Ann, Mrs., 19 George St
Kennedy, Edward, Custom House, Res. 18 Mazyck St
Kennedy, Frances, Mrs., Milliner, 123 King St
Kennedy, James, 27 Mazyck St.
Kennedy, James B., Gauger, 28 Cumberland St
Kennedy, James, Grocer, 117 Queen St
Kennedy, James P , Broker & Quorum Unis, 7 State St
Kennedy, John, Butcher, 198 Meeting St.
Kennedy, L. H., Attorney, St. Michael's Al., Res. 118
Tradd St
Kennedy, Thomas, Factor, 24 Guignard St.
Ker, John, Orange St
Kerr, Thomas J., Assistant Wharfinger, Edmondston's
Whf., Res 108 Church St
Kerrison, Elizabeth, Mrs., Matron, Orphan House
Kershaw & Lewis, Factors, 56 E. Bay St
Kershaw, Charles, Factor, 30 Meeting St.
Kershaw, Newman, 5 New St.
Ketchum & Ripley, Dry Goods Store, 330 King St.
Kiddell, Arthur, 2 Philadelphia St.
Kiddell, Charles, Merchant, Kiddell's Whf., Res. 35 Broad
St
Kilkeney, Timothy, Grocer, 95 Tradd St.
King & Barker, Attornies, St. Michael's Al
King, A. W , Grocer, 25 Market St
King, John, 22 Archdale St.
King, John, Commission Merchant, 138 Church St.
King, Leonard, Carpenter, 84 Meeting St.
King, Mary, Miss, 31 Beaufain St.
King, Mary, Mrs , 45 King St.
King, Mitchell, Attorney, cr. Meeting & George Sts
Kingdom, Henry, Millwright, 31 George St
Kingman, E., Steward, Orphan House
Kingman, Hannah, 20 State St
Kingman, John, Teacher, Orphan House, Res. 31 Coming
St
Kinloch, George, Grocer, 65 Market St.
Kinsey, Francis, Grocer, 247 King St
Kippenberg, Andrew, Grocer, 75 Queen St.
Kirk, Charles W., Bricklayer, 32 Laurens St.
Kirk, Henry, Sea Captain, 16 Church St.
Kirk, John, 131 E Bay St

Kirk, Sarah, Mrs., Grocery, cr Coming & George Sts.
Kirkland, William L., Physician, 118 Church St
Kirkland, William L., Physician, Alexander St.,
Mazyckborough, Neck
Kirkpatrick & Hall, Factors, Edmondston's Whf
Kirkpatrick, John, Factor, 4 Meeting St
Kittleband, David, Carpenter, 6 Logan St.
Klinck, John, Grocer, cr St. Phililp's & Liberty Sts.
Knauff, Conrad, 60 Market St.
Knauff, Conrad, Saddler, Henrietta St , Mazyckborough,
Neck
Knieff, Francis, Shopkeeper, cr Pinckney & Doughty Sts ,
Cannonborough, Neck
Knight, R & W , Commission Merchants, Edmondston's
Whf
Knight, Thomas, Wharfinger, Crafts' Whf., Res 45
Beaufain St.
Knight, W. K , City Guard, 45 Beaufain St.
Knox, John F., Shipwright, Pritchard & Knox's Whf.
Knox, Margaret, Mrs , Alexander St , Mazyckborough,
Neck
Knox, Walter, Carpenter, 12 Green St
Knust, Sarah, Mrs., 23 Coming St.
Knuth, John, Grocer, 18 State St.
Kohne, Frederick, 120 Broad St.
Kowing, John, 105 Boundary St
Krebs, Henry & Co., Grocers, cr Pitt & Montague Sts
Krohn, Peter, 92 Anson St.
Kugley, Martha, Mrs., 34 Mazyck St
Kunhardt, William, Factor, Kunhardt's Whf , Res. 32
George St
Kyall, Peter, 90 Anson St.
Labarben, A., Teacher of French, 90 King St.
Labat, Catharine, Mrs., 11 Linguard St
Labatut, Isedore, Teacher of Drawing, 261 Meeting St.
Labatut, Isidore, Painter, Meeting St Cont'd.,
Wraggsborough, Neck
Labausse, Mary, Mrs , Meeting St Cont'd , Neck
Laborde, Francis, cr. King & Society Sts.
Lacks, John, 13 Zigzag Al.
LaCoste, Charles, Fancy Store, 149 King St
Ladeveze, Victor, Dry Goods Store, 185 King St.
Ladson & Dawson, Factors, 62 E. Bay St.
Ladson, James H , Factor, 8 Meeting St
Lafar, David B., Cooper, Magwood's Whf , Res. 1 Maiden
Ln
Lafar, John J., City Marshal, 58 Queen St.
Laffiteau, Stanislaus, 50 Anson St.
Lafon, John, Cooper, 62 State St.
Laford, -----, Madam, 219 King St
Lagrave, C , Motte's Ln.
Lamb, James Merchant, 61 Tradd St.
Lamb, Jane, Mrs., Dry Goods Store, 173 King St.
Lance, Francis, Planter, 23 Friend St
Lance, William, Attorney, St. Michael's Al., Res. 108
Queen St
Landershine, John, Carpenter, Charlotte St.,
Mazyckborough, Neck
Lang, Jacob, Merchant, 78 E. Bay St., Res. 1 Church St.
Langley, William, 57 Queen St

Langlois, Maria, Mrs., 4 Clifford St
Langton, Susan, Mrs , 41 Market St.
Langton, William, 41 Market St.
Lankester, Joseph, Grocer, 113 E. Bay St.
Lanneau, Bazil, 1 Pitt St.
Lanneau, Peter, 33 Elliott St
Lapenne, John Joseph, Tallow Chandler, King St. Cont'd ,
Neck
Laporte, Rene, 26 Wentworth St.
Laroach, Mary, Mrs., Hudson St , Cannonborough, Neck
Laroche, John G., 24 Beaufain St
Larousseliere, Francis, Sea Captain, 13 Berresford St
Larousseliere, L., Druggist, 184 Meeting St.
Latham, Daniel, 1 Hasell St.
Laurain, Edward, Teacher of French, 176 Meeting St.
Laurans, Peter, Merchant, 27 George St
Laurence, Robert D , Accountant, State House Sq.
Laurence, Sarah, Mrs., 6 George St
Laurens, Henry, Mrs , 290 E Bay St.
Laurens, John B., Planter, 290 E. Bay St.
Laurimer, Ann, Mrs., 12 Liberty St.
Laval, Lewis, Reid St , Hampstead, Neck
Laval, William, Secretary of State, 3 Wall St.
Lavencendiare, M., Tobacconist, 13 Wentworth St.
Lawton & Reilly, Commission Merchants & Grocers, 5
Vendue Range
Lawton, J. & C., Merchants, 136 E. Bay St.
Lawton, Mary, Mrs., 3 Lamboll St.
Lawton, R. B., Grocer, 53 Market St.
Lawton, S H., Teacher, 44 Tradd St.
Lazarus, Benjamin D., Steam Boat Agent, Lothrop's Whf
Lazarus, Jacob, Crockery & Glass Store, 156 King St
Lazarus, Marks, 93 Tradd St.
Lazarus, Michael, Merchant, Champney St , Res 103
Broad St.
Leaders, Mary, Mrs , 3 Berresford St
Leavitt, Horatio, 2 Green St.
Lecat, Catharine, Mrs , 7 Ellery St.
Lecat, Francis, Musician, 16 Ellery St.
Lechemere, Maria, Miss, 3 Church St.
Lecompt, John, Apothecary, 40 State St.
Lecourtois, Anthony, Confectioner, 215 E Bay St.
Lee, Elizabeth B., Mrs., Cannon St., Neck
Lee, Francis, J., Custom House, Res 24 Hasell St
Lee, -----, Mrs., Midwife, 8 Clifford St
Lee, Stephen, Attorney, 75 Broad St.
Lee, Thomas, U. S Judge, 22 Pitt St.
Lee, William, Pilot, 7 Lynch's Ln.
Lee, William, Teller, Bank of the State of S C., Res 46
Coming St
Leefe, Benjamin, Mrs., 2 Mazyck St
Legare, Daniel, Physician, 3 Guignard St
Legare, Hugh S , Attorney, 32 Bull St.
Legare, James B., Attorney, 3 Gibbes St
Legare, James, Planter, 7 New St
Legare, Joshua, 18 Wall St.
Legare, Mary, Mrs., 32 Bull St.
Legare, Mary, Mrs., 5 Wall St.
Legare, Sarah, Mrs , 57 Anson St.
Legare, Sarah, Mrs., Jr., 88 Anson St.

Legare, Solomon, Factor, Chisolm's S Whf.
Legare, Solomon, Jr., 7 New St
Legare, Solomon, Sr , 8 Friend St.
Legare, Thomas, Physician, cr. Boundary & St. Philip's St
Legare, Thomas, Planter, 40 S Bay St
Legare, William B , Factor, Williams' Whf
Lege, John M., Teacher of Dancing, 62 Queen St.
Legg, Joseph, St Philip's St , Radcliffborough, Neck
Legge, Ann, Mrs., Private Boarding, 4 Wentworth St.
Lehre, Ann, Mrs., 96 Tradd St.
Lehre, Thomas, Planter, 54 King St
Lehre, Thomas, Tanner, cr. King & Warren Sts., Neck
Leitch, Duncan, Grocer, 232 King St.
Leland, Joseph & Brothers, Merchants, 159 E. Bay St.
Leland, Joseph, 10 State St.
Lemaitre, John B , Merchant, 180 E Bay St.
Lemman, James, Shopkeeper, Nassau St , Wraggsborough,
    Neck
Leon, L. F , Hair Dresser, 15 Market St.
LePrince, Achille, Dry Goods Store, 207 King St.
Leroy, Angelica, Mrs., 184 Meeting St.
Leseigneur, V , Physician, 48 Church St
Lesesne, Ann, Miss, 113 Boundary St.
Lesesne, Charles, Farmer, cr Bridge & Elliott Sts ,
    Cannonborough, Neck
Lesesne, Hannah, Mrs., 45 Society St
Lesesne, -----, Misses, 45 Society St.
Lesesne, Thomas, Mrs , 97 Boundary St.
Lester, Eliza D., Mrs , 179 E. Bay St.
Letch, Catharine, Mrs , 28 Society St
Leuder, Frances, Confectioner, 128 Church St.
Leveck, John C., Goldsmith, 191 King St
Levin, L., Jr , Dry Goods Store, 340 King St.
Levingston, Jane, Mrs , Mantua Maker, 7 West Sts.
Levingston, Mary, Mrs., 12 Blackbird Al.
Levy, Andrew, King St Cont'd , Neck
Levy, D C., Dry Goods Store, 242 King St.
Levy, D C , Grocer, 189 King St
Levy, Elias, Accountant, 11 West St.
Levy, George, Grocer, 23 Market St
Levy, J C , Broker, Auctioneer & Commission Merchant,
    Champney St., Res 279 E Bay St
Levy, L S., Hardware Store, 236 King St.
Levy, Lyon, State Treasury Office, Res 242 King St.
Levy, M C., 213 King St.
Levy, Reuben, Broker, 4 Blackbird Al.
Levy, Simon, 236 King St
Lewis, Daniel, 403 King St.
Lewis, David, Dry Goods Store, King St. Cont'd., Neck
Lewis, Isaac, 36 Wentworth St
Lewis, John, Factor, 12 Meeting St.
Lewis, John, Grocer, cr E Bay & Market Sts
Lewis, William H., Accountant, 35 George St.
Libby, Robert, John St , Neck
Liddle, John, 106 Market St.
Lieur, Peter, Shopkeeper, 221 E Bay St.
Lightwood, Eliza, Mrs., 18 Meeting St
Limbair, N., 3 Lingaurd St.
Limehouse, Robert, 123 Tradd St.
Lindeboom, Peter, St Philip's St , Neck

Lindsay, William, Merchant, Crafts' Whf., Res 50 E Bay
    St.
Lindsser, John L., Butcher, Cannon St , Cannonborough,
    Neck
Lines, Ann, Mrs., Beaufain St
Ling, Philip, Coach Maker, 82 Market St., Res. 21
    Guignard St.
Ling, Robert, Coach Maker, 84 Market St
Lining, Charles, Bookkeeper, Office of Discount &
    Deposit, Res 17 Legare St.
Lining, Edward B., Planter, 17 Legare St.
Lining, Thomas, Physician, 17 Legare St.
Little, James Cotton Gin Maker, 161 Meeting St. Res 30
    Archdale St.
Little, Robert, Lumber Merchant, Chisolm's Upper Wharf
Little Robert, Lumber Merchant, Charlotte St.,
    Mazyckborough, Neck
Livingston, R. Y., Accountant, 27 Middle St
Lloyd, Esther, Mrs., 117 King St.
Lloyd, John P , Blind Maker, 205 Meeting St
Lloyd, John, Printer, 71 Beaufain St.
Lloyd, Joseph, Clerk, Rope Walk, Meeting St Cont'd ,
    Hampstead, Neck
Lloyd, Mary, Mrs , 36 Bull St
Lloyd, S. P., 265 King St.
Lockart, John, Grocer, 86 Meeting St
Locke, George B & Co., Grocers, Dewees' Whf.
Locke, George B , 181 E Bay St
Lockwood, Israel, Carpenter, 24 Bull St.
Lockwood, Joshua, Bookkeeper, State Bank, Res 75
    Board St.
Logan, C M , Broker & Notary Public, 88 E. Bay St , Res
    34 Archdale St.
Logan, George, Physician, cr. Meeting & Hasell Sts
Logan, William, Librarian, Pinckney St , Cannonborough,
    Neck
Long, Felix, Accountant, King St Cont'd , Neck
Long, Robert, Butcher, Mary St., Wraggsborough, Neck
Long, Robert, Sea Captain, 11 Wall St
Longsdon, J & W , Merchants, 70 E Bay St.
Lonsdale, James, 10 Ellery St.
Lopez, P , Mrs , Dry Goods Store, 132 King St.
Lopez, Samuel, Dry Goods Store, 372 King St., Neck
Lord, Archibald B., Porter, Office of Discount & Deposit,
    Res. 2 State St.
Lord, Jacob N., Shoemaker, 371 King St
Lord, Richard, 54 Beaufain St.
Lord, Samuel, 27 Guignard St
Lothrop, Samuel H., Merchant, Lothrop's Whf., Res 101
    Tradd St
Lotte, Peter, King St. Cont'd., Neck
Lovejoy, Nathaniel, Painter, 85 Tradd St
Lovell, H. F , Mrs., 239 E Bay St.
Lovet, -----, Mrs., 5 Swinton's Ln
Lowden, John, Merchant, 66 E Bay St., Res. 56 Meeting
    St.
Lowndes, Charles, Mrs., 74 Anson St
Lowndes, James, Planter, 14 Meeting St
Lowndes, Thomas, Planter, 112 Broad St
Lowndes, William, Mrs., 1 Orange St

Lowrey, Charles, 217 E. Bay St
Lozier, John C , Sheriff's Office, Res Carolina Coffee House
Lubbock, Henry W., 1 S Bay St
Lucan, John, Charleston Mills
Lucan, William, Planter, cr Wentworth & Smith Sts
Lucas, Ellen, Mrs., Wharf St.
Ludlow, J R. & Co , Glass & Crockery Store, cr King & Wentworth Sts.
Ludlow, Robert C , 111 Broad St
Lufler, Margaret, Mrs , 4 Berresford St.
Lund, Christian, Boarding House, 17 Elliott St
Lundrey, Elizabeth, Mrs., 33 Wentworth St.
Lusher, Sarah, Mrs., Private Boarding, 169 E Bay St
Lynah, Edward, Planter, 89 Meeting St.
Lynch, Esther, Miss, 225 E Bay St
Lynch, James, Mrs., Private Boarding, cr Church & Queen Sts
Lynch, Thomas M., Confectioner, 45 Hasell St.
Lynn, F. S., Mrs., Cannonborough, Neck
Lynn, John, 46 Market St.
Lynn, John S., 1 Society St
Lyon, Aaron, Watch Maker, 97 E. Bay St.
Lyon, George, Watch Maker, 187 E. Bay St
Macaulay, Daniel, Merchant, cr. Broad & State Sts.
Macaulay, George, 96 Church St
Macaulay, George, Jr , Merchant, 37 Broad St
Mackey, John, Teacher, 29 Archdale St
Mackie, James, Notary Public & Quorum Unis, cr State & Chalmers Sts , Res Upper End Beaufain St.
Magill, Mary, Mrs., 44 Anson St.
Magness, Sarah, Mrs , Grocer, 61 State St
Magrath, John, Merchant, Edmondston's Whf., Res. 197 Meeting St.
Magson, Saul J , Merchant, 46 E Bay St.
Magwood & Patterson, Factors, Magwood's Whf.
Magwood, Charles, Factor, 11 Smith St
Magwood, Simon, Planter, 13 Smith St.
Maillard, John M , Factor, 11 S. Bay St.
Main, William, Shipwright, Wall St
Mairs & Valentine, Brokers, 6 State St.
Mairs, Simon, Broker, 6 State St
Malcom, Thomas, 96 Broad St.
Manigault, G. H., Planter, 16 Meeting St
Manigault, Joseph, Planter, Meeting St. Cont'd., Neck
Manlove, Edward, Clerk, 71 E Bay St.
Mann, Jacob, Carpenter, 10 St Philip's St.
Mann, John, Bricklayer, Boundary St , Neck
Manning, Joseph, Physician, 2 Soceity St
Manson, Andrew, Private Boarding, 50 Broad St.
Manson, George, Shipwright, John St , Wraggsborough, Neck
Manuel, Francis, 42 Anson St.
Marchant, Peter T., Planter, 17 Rutledge St
Mariner, William, Sail Maker, 267 E. Bay St.
Marion, Ann, Mrs , 12 Hasell St
Marion, Francis, Jr , Pinckney St., Cannonborough, Neck
Marion, Theodore S , Planter, E Bay St , Hampstead, Neck
Markley, Benjamin A , Radcliff St., Radcliffborough, Neck

Markley, John, Coach Maker, 67 Wentworth St.
Marks, Joseph, Merchant, 10 Queen St
Marks, Mark, 308 King St.
Marley, Peter, 34 Magazine St
Marr, Ann, Mrs , 14 Church St.
Marsh, James, Shipwright, Marsh's Whf
Marshall, Andrew, Grocer, 4 Bull St.
Marshall, Caroline, Mrs , 1 Minority St
Marshall, David, cr. Charlotte & Elizabeth Sts., Mazyckborough, Neck
Marshall, Dorothy, Mrs , 1 Beaufain St
Marshall, Mary S., Mrs , 97 Broad St.
Marshall, Robert, Grocer, 2 Anson St.
Martin, Charles, Blacksmith, Charlotte St , Mazyckborough, Neck
Martin, Christian, 26 Wall St.
Martin, Fanny, Mrs , Merchant Tailoress, 13 Queen St.
Martin, Jacob, Blacksmith, 20 Blackbird Al.
Martin, James, Merchant, King St. Cont'd., Neck
Martin, James, Notary Public & Broker, 7 State St
Martin, John N., Bricklayer, Bull St.
Martin, John, Physician, cr. Anson & Society Sts
Martin, P J., Grocer, 202 King St.
Martin, Robert, Merchant, King St Cont'd , Neck
Martin, Sarah, Mrs., Charlotte St., Mazyckborough, Neck
Martin, Thomas, 26 Laurens St
Martindale, J. C., Mrs., King St. Cont'd , Neck
Mson, George, Outdoor Clerk, Union Bank, Res Lynch St
Martineau, John, Columbus St , Hampstead, Neck
Massias, ------, Pay Master of this Division, U. S Troops, 78 Church St
Massot, Horatio, Watch Maker, 15 Queen St
Mathewes, Benjamin, Commander, U. S. Revenue Cutter, cr Water & Meeting Sts.
Mathews & Bonneau, Factors, Kiddell's Whf.
Mathews, David, Shoemaker, Boundary St., Wraggsborough, Neck
Mathews, George, Mrs , 29 E. Bay St
Mathews, Harriet, Mrs., 57 Church St
Mathews, James, 55 Anson St
Mathews, William, Planter, cr. Elizabeth & Charlotte Sts , Mazyckborough, Neck
Mattheisen, C. F., Dry Goods Store, 176 King St
Mattuce, John, Butcher, Henrietta St , Mazyckborough, Neck
Maull, Mary E., Mrs , 38 Beaufain St.
Maxton, John, Tailor, King St. Cont'd , Neck
Maxwell, H E , Mrs., 91 Meeting St
May, John, Cabinet Maker, 66 Queen St
May, Pleasant H , Attorney, 67 Meeting St., Res 2 Meeting St.
Maynard, James & William, Bakers, 43 Elliott St
Maynard, John, Baker, cr. St. Philip's & Green Sts
Mayrant, William, Planter, Vanderhorst St , Radcliffborough, Neck
Mays, James, Grocer, 20 Meeting St.
Mazyck, Edward, 7 Archdale St
Mazyck, Mary, Mrs , 61 Church St
Mazyck, ------, Misses, 187 Meeting St.
Mazyck, N B , Factor, Kunhardt's Whf , Res 7 Archdale

122

St
Mazyck, Paul, Planter, 7 Archdale St
Mazyck, Philip, 50 Wentworth St.
Mazyck, Stephen, Planter, 19 Society St.
Mazyck, William, Factor, Chisolm's Whf., Res. 7 Archdale St.
Mazyck, William, Jr., 50 Wentworth St.
M'Annally, John, Grocer, 115 King St
M'Arthur D., Commission Merchant, 162 E Bay St.
M'Beth, Catharine, Mrs., 1 Lamboll St.
M'Bride, Mary, Mrs., 55 George St.
M'Bridge, Mary, Mrs , 58 Church St.
M'Caffrey, H., Shoemaker, 68 State St.
M'Call, Beckman, Bookkeeper, State Bank, Res 159 E Bay St.
M'Call, John B , Attorney, cr. Meeting & Chalmers St
M'Call Joseph, P 27 Meeting St.
M'Call, Susan, Mrs , 18 Legare St.
M'Calla, Sarah, Mrs 88 Anson St.
M'Cants, Ann, Mrs., 10 Savage St.
M'Carter, James J , Book Store, 325 King St
M'Cartney & Gordon, Dry Goods & Hardware Store, 18 Broad St.
M'Cleary, Samuel, Dry Goods Store, King St Cont'd , Neck
M'Collin, Robert, Grocer, 33 S Bay St
M'Collum, John, 14 New St.
M'Cormick, Eliza, Mrs , 35 George St.
M'Cormick, William, Grocer, 95 E. Bay St
M'Cosh, Joseph, 130 E Bay St.
M'Cready, Edward, Attorney, 70 Broad St.
M'Cready, William, Saddler, 33 Broad St
M'Cullough, William, Shopkeeper, King St. Cont'd., Neck
M'Donald, Allen, Cabinet Maker, 153 Meeting St
M'Donald, H & A., Grocers, cr. King & George Sts
M'Donald, Hugh, Shopkeeper, Mill St , Cannonborough, Neck
M'Donald, Sarah, Mrs., City Hotel, 191 E Bay St
M'Dow, William, Teacher, 32 Hasell St.
M'Dowall, Andrew, Wholesale & Retail Dry Goods Store, 145 King St.
M'Dowall, -----, Mrs , Grocer, 244 Meeting St
M'Dowall, -----, Mrs., Grocer, 206 Meeting St.
M'Dowell, W A , Rev , 85 Wentworth St
M'Ehney, Peter, 25 Pinckney St
M'Elhaney, Susannah, Mrs., 46 Bull St
M'Elmoyle, William, cr King & Tradd Sts.
M'Encroe, John, Rev , 195 Meeting St.
M'Farlane, Catharine, Mrs., 8 Hasell St.
M'Farlane, Mary, Mrs , 38 State St
M'Gann, Patrick, Watch Maker, 68 E Bay Sts
M'Gill, Robert, 237 E. Bay St
M'Ginley, Samuel, Boarding House, 74 Market St.
M'Ginnis, E , Shoe Store, 230 King St.
M'Ginnis, Joseph, Millwright, Charlotte St., Mazyckborough, Neck
M'Granham, William, 231 E. Bay St
M'Gregor, -----, 6 Meeting St.
M'Gregor, Neill, Butcher, Cannon St , Cannonborough, Neck

M'Guffie, Anthony, 71 E Bay St.
M'Intire, Elizabeth, Mrs., 15 Price's Al
M'Intosh, Daniel, Shopkeeper, Charlotte St., Mazyckborough, Neck
M'Intosh, Rebecca, Mrs., 1 Wentworth St
M'Intosh, William, Shopkeeper, King St Cont'd , Neck
M'Intyre, John, Grocer, 47 King St
M'Kay, William, 20 Market St.
M'Kee, Abel, Carpenter, 150 Church St
M'Kee, John, Bricklayer, 3 Bedon's Al.
M'Kegan, John, Blacksmith, Blackbird Al.
M'Kendrie, Eliza, Mrs., Columbus St , Hampstsead, Neck
M'Kenzie, G. T. Saddler, 5 State St
M'Kenzie, James, Plasterer, 33 Broad St
M'Kenzie, John, cr. Broad & Church Sts.
M'Kenzie, Richard, Saddler, cr Broad & Church Sts
M'Kewn, William, Bricklayer, 59 George St
M'Kinney, Christopher, Teller, Office of Discount & Deposit, Res 8 West St.
M'Kinney, Laurence, 123 Queen St
M'Kinney, Mary Ann, Mrs , Shopkeeper, Columbus St , Hampstead, Neck
M'Laughlan & Gaffney, Grocers, 10 Tradd St.
M'Laughlan, Archibald, Merchant, 9 Tradd St
M'Lean, Mary, Mrs , 238 Meeting St.
M'Lelan, Jane, Mrs., 64 State St
M'Lenau, Sarah, Mrs., 91 Queen St.
M'Leod, H. C , Book Store, 221 King St
M'Leod, H C., Mrs., School, 41 George St.
M'Milan, Daniel C., Grocer, cr. Tradd & Church Sts
M'Millan, John, Dry Goods Store, 298 King St.
M'Millan, Richard, Boarding House, 376 King St
M'Millan, Thomas, Carpenter, 14 Washington St
M'Namee, James, Shoemaker, 110 Church St
M'Neill, Daniel, Sea Captain, Doughty St., Cannonborough, Neck
M'Neill, N & Co , Grocers, cr. Broad & Church Sts.
M'Neill, Neil, 112 Church St.
M'Nellage, Alexander, 77 Boundary St
M'Nellage, John, Sail Maker, 24 State St
M'Nish, Henry, City Scavenger, Vanderhorst St., Radcliffborough, Neck
M'Owen, Patrick, 26 King St
M'Pherson, Duncan, 56 King St.
M'Pherson, James, Planter 289 E. Bay St.
M'Pherson, Susan, Mrs , 94 Broad St
Meal, S , Confectioner, 345 King St.
Mealy, John, 13 St Philip's St
Mecune, John, Elizabeth St , Mazyckborough, Neck
Meeds, S , Mrs., Private Boarding, 71 E Bay St
Meetz, Jacob, 97 Market St
Memminger, G C , Charleston Mills
Menude, John, Planter, 8 Liberty St
Merritt, James, H , Kunhardt's Whf, Res. 5 Bull St
Messervey, Phillip, Sea Captain, 120 Meeting St
Metiviere, Francis, Baker, Wraggsborough, Neck
Mey, Charles S & J. H., Merchants, Mey's Whf
Mey, Charles S., 4 Anson St
Mey, Florian C , Merchant, 2 Pinckney St., Francis, 35 Coming St.

123

Michel, Frederick, Assistant Clerk of Market, Res 25 St. Philip's St.

Michel, John E., Goldsmith, 312 King St

Michel, John, Notary Public & Coroner, Parishes of St Philip's & St. Michael's, 84 E Bay St., Res. 173 Meeting St.

Michel, Mary, Mrs , 35 Coming St.

Michel, W., Physician, 183 Meeting St

Middleton, Arthur, Planter 38 S. Bay St.

Middleton, John, Planter, 185 E Bay St

Middleton, Thomas, Factor, Crafts' Whf , Res 38 S. Bay St.

Miles, Ann, Mrs., 68 Tradd St.

Miles, Edward, 29 Anson St.

Mill, John, Book Store, 34 Broad St.

Miller, A. E , Printing Office, 4 Broad St

Miller, Abraham, Outdoor Clerk, Bank of State of S. C., Res. 49 Society St

Miller, Ann, Mrs., 7 Wall St.

Miller, Catharine, Mrs , 49 Society St

Miller, Charles, 391 King St.

Miller, Charles, Hay Merchant, King St Cont'd , Neck

Miller, George, Dry Goods Store, King St. Cont'd , Neck

Miller, J. P , Bricklayer, 81 King St.

Miller, Jacob, Rope Maker, Vanderhorst St., Radcliffborough, Neck

Miller, James A., Accountant, 49 Society St.

Miller, James A., Clerk of Board of Health, 14 Mazyck St.

Miller, Jane, Mrs , Baker, 143 Meeting St.

Miller, John C , Factor, Williams' Whf

Miller, John M., Dry Good Store, 216 King St.

Miller, Lydia, Mrs , 30 St. Philip's St.

Miller, Mathew, Jeweller, 150 King St.

Miller, Samuel Stent, Printer, 7 Wall St.

Miller, Sarah, Mrs., Mantua Maker, 2 Wentworth St.

Miller, W. C., Factor, 212 Meeting St

Miller, W S. & Co , Wholesale Dry Goods Store, 310 King St

Miller, William, Accountant, St. Philip's St , Radcliffborough, Neck

Miller, William, H., Jr., Tailor, 56 Queen St.

Miller, William H , Merchant, Chisolm's Whf , Res 52 Anson St

Milligan, Joseph, Student of Medicine, King St Cont'd , Neck

Milligan, William, Tallow Chandler, Elizabeth St., Mazyckborough, Neck

Milliken, Thomas, Auctioneer, Charlotte St , Mazyckborough, Neck

Milliken, Thomas, Vendue Master, S Vendue Range

Mills, Drake, Merchant, 178 E Bay St.

Mills, Mary, Mrs., Spring St., Hampstead, Neck

Mills, Mary P., Mrs., School Mistress, Orphan House

Mills, O. & S , Commission Merchants, N Vendue Range

Mills, Otis, Merchant, 220 E. Bay St.

Mills, Robert H , Wharfinger, D'Oyley's Whf , Res 33 King St

Mills, Thomas, 90 Church St

Millward, Elizabeth, Miss, Wolf St , Wraggsborough, Neck

Milne, Andrew & Co , Merchants, 48 E Bay St.

Minos, Margaret E., Mrs., Lowndes St

Minot, William, Planter, Savage St.

Mintzing, Jacob F , 26 Friend St

Miot, Charles H., Merchants Hotel, cr King & Society Sts

Miscally, Daniel, Shopkeeper, 69 King St

Mishaw, John, Grocer, 14 Pinckney St.

Missroon, James, 26 E Bay St.

Mitchel, Mary, Mrs., Charlotte St., Mazyckborough, Neck

Mitchell & Dawson, Attornies, Waring's Buildings, Meeting St., op. St. Michael's Al.

Mitchell, Ann E., Mrs , 45 Tradd St.

Mitchell, Elizabeth, Mrs., 29 Wentworth St.

Mitchell, James, Cooper, 87 E. Bay St.

Mitchell, James D , Ordinary, Charleston District, 134 Wentworth St.

Mitchell, James, Pump & Block Maker, 4 Washington St.

Mitchell, John, 40 Wentworth St

Mitchell, John, Goldsmith, Henrietta St., Mazyckborough, Neck

Mitchell, John H., Quorum Unis & Notary Public, 88 E Bay St , Res. 42 Guignard St.

Mitchell, John, Mariner, 15 Bedon's Al.

Mitchell, Peter, Hat Sore, 388 King St

Mitchell, Thomas, Mrs , 11 Wentworth St.

Mitchell, William, Rev , 42 Guignard St.

Moffett & Calder, Dry Goods Store, 177 King St.

Mohn, Henry, Grocer, 141 Queen St

Moise & Shand, Attornies, Hunt's Law Buildings

Moise, Aaron, 33 Cumberland St.

Moise, Abraham, Accountant, 103 Market St.

Moise, Esther, Mrs., 11 West St.

Moise, Isaac, Accountant, 103 Market St.

Moise, Sarah, Mrs., 103 Market St

Moisson, John, Gunsmith, 16 State St.

Moles, Margaret, Mrs., Dry Goods Store, cr. King & Ann Sts , Neck

Monefeldt, Maria H , Mrs , School, 24 Hasell St

Monnar, Lewis, Hair Dresser, 12 Queen St.

Monroe, Robert, Attorney, St Michael's Al

Montesquieux, R , Tin Plate Worker, 142 Meeting St.

Montgomery & Platt, Commission Merchants, Vanderhorst's Whf.

Montgomery, Ann C , Mrs , cr Beaufain & Coming Sts

Montross, N , Hat Store, 329 King St.

Mood & Ewan, Goldsmiths, 203 King St

Moodie, James, 63 Meeting St.

Mooney, Patrick, Merchant, 21 Cumberland St

Moore, Frances, Mrs., 71 Broad St.

Moore, George, Saddler, 44 Wentworth St

Moore, James, Carpenter, Meeting St Cont'd., Neck

Moore, John, Merchant, 22 Bull St.

Moore, Peter Joseph, Physician, 105 King St.

Moore, Philip, Lumber Merchant, cr Montague & Gadsden Sts.

Moore, Richard, Painter, Meeting St. Cont'd., Neck

Moore, Thomas, Blind Maker, 14 Smith St.

Mordecai, Joseph, 50 Beaufain St

Mordecai, R., Mrs , 34 Guignard St

Morford, Edmund, Mercury Office, Res 120 Church St

Morgan, Benjamin, Sea Captain, 14 Middle St.
Morgan, Elizabeth, Mrs., 82 Wentworth St.
Morgan, Jane, Mrs., 34 George St.
Moriarity, Maurice, Dry Goods Store, 211 King St
Morley, Suran, Nurse, 75 E. Bay St
Morris, Christopher G , Merchant, 80 E Bay St
Morris, James, Accountant, 87 E. Bay St.
Morris, Simpson, 27 Laurens St.
Morris, Thomas, Jr., Merchant, 80 E Bay St.
Morris, Thomas, Notary Public & Quorum Unis, 87 E Bay
    St , Res. 2 Wentworth St
Morrison, Elizabeth, Mrs , 70 Tradd
Morrison, Elizabeth, Mrs , Lynch St.
Morrison, Jane D., Mrs , 51 King St.
Morrison, John B , Deputy Sheriff, S. Side Chalmers St.,
    Next to Church
Morrison, R. T., Planter, Mary St., Hampstead, Neck
Morrison, Simon, Cabinet Maker, 160 Meeting St.
Mortimer, Edward, 59 Anson St.
Moser, Philip, Physician, 10 Logan St.
Moses, Abigail, Mrs., 14 Berresford St.
Moses, Daniel L , 14 Berresford St
Moses, I. C., 6 Cumberland St.
Moses, Isaiah, Planter, 35 St. Philip's St
Moses, Israel, Auctioneer, Vendue Range, Res. 24
    Beaufain St
Moses, Jacob, State Constable, cr. Radcliffborough, Neck
Moses, Myer, cr Meeting & Hasell Sts.
Moses, Reuben, Clothing Store, 276 King St.
Moses, Simon, Dry Goods Store, 385 King St
Moses, Solomon, Jr , Deputy Marshal, 106 King St
Mosimann, Jacob, Watch Maker, 109 E. Bay St
Moss & Cassidy, Merchant Tailors, 311 King St.
Motta, J A., Confectioner, 169 King St.
Motte, Abraham, 17 Wentworth St.
Motte, Francis & Son, Factor, Chisolm's N Whf
Motte, Francis, 34 Church St.
Motte, Mary, Mrs , 24 Meeting St.
Motte, Mellish J., Rev., 17 Wentworth St.
Mouatt, Mary, Mrs , 10 Middle St.
Moulan, Peter, Grocer, 72 State St.
Moulin, Jane, Mrs., Dry Goods Store, 173 King St
Moultrie, Alexander, Attorney, 83 Meeting St.
Moultrie, James, Mrs., Physician, 4 Cumberland St.
Moultrie, James, Sr., 4 Cumberland St.
Mounsey, Thomas, Merchant, 151 E. Bay St., Res. 6
    Society St.
Mouzon, Charles, Shoemaker, cr Church & Chalmers Sts ,
    Res. 4 St. Philip's St
Mowry, Smith, Merchant, Res 141 Church St.
Moynan, Francis, 77 Meeting St.
Muck, Philip, cr. King & Broad Sts
Muckenfuss, Henry, Bricklayer, 120 Wentworth St.
Muir, Jane, Mrs., Private Boarding, 24 Broad St
Mulligan, James, Saddler, 7 Broad St.
Mullings, John, Pilot, 1 Stoll's Al.
Mulloy, James, Porter House, 21 Market St.
Munday, Thomas, Private Boarding, 83 Broad St.
Munds, Israel, Rev., 41 State St.
Munro, Catharine, Mrs , Midwife, Society St

Munro, Margaret, Mrs , Private Boarding, 95 Church St.
Murden, Jeremiah, 10 S Bay St
Murley, Samuel, Wine Merchant, 68 E. Bay St , Res. 68
    Wentworth St.
Murphy, John, 46 Guignard St
Murphy, Patrick, 16 Anson St.
Murphy, Peter, Grocer, cr. King & Beaufain Sts
Murphy, Sarah, 91 Church St.
Murray, A. E., Mrs., Dry Goods Store, 196 King St.
Murray, James, Clerk, Post Office
Murray, John M., Grocer, 1 King St
Murray, M P , Mrs , 23 Middle St.
Murray, R., Mrs., Grocery, 18 S. Bay St.
Murray, Robert, Merchant Tailor, 26 Broad St.
Murray, William, Planter, Lynch St.
Myatt, Edward, 29 Wentworth St
Myer, John, 29 Pinckney St.
Myers, John, 268 E Bay St.
Myers, John, Beaufain St
Myers, Michael, 38 Hasell St.
Myles, Jane, Mrs., Midwife, 12 Clifford St.
Mynott, Baxter O., Commission Merchant, 166 E Bay St
Napier, Thomas, Ladson's Court
Naser, Frederick, Lumber Merchant, Yard, cr Tradd &
    New Sts., Res. 29 Mazyck St.
Nathans, Henry, 26 Beaufain St
Nathans, Nathan, Dry Goods Store, King St. Cont'd , Neck
Nell, Stephen, Rope Walk, Meeting St. Cont'd , Neck
Nell, William, Rope Walk, Meeting St., Hampstead, Neck
Nelme, John W , Grocer, 41 Market St
Nelson, Christopher, State House Hotel, Meeting St.
Nelson, George, 41 Society St.
Nelson, James, Hanover St., Hampstead, Neck
Nelson, John, Blacksmith, 4 Middle St
Neufville, Ann, Mrs., 17 Anson St.
Neufville, Benjamin S., Printer, 86 Anson St
Neufville, John, 86 Anson St.
Neufville, William, 86 Anson St
Nevill, John, Grocer, 13 Magazine St.
Neville, James, Grocer, 114 King St
Neville, Joshua & Son, Cabinet Makers, 260 King St
Newbold, Samuel, Pilot, 11 Zigzag Al.
Newhall & Thayer, Shoe Store, 154 King St
Newhall, Edward, 103 Queen St.
Newhall, John M., Shoe Store, 285 King St.
Newton, Anthony, Mrs., Cannon St., Cannonborough,
    Neck
Newton, Mary, Mrs., Cannon St , Cannonborough, Neck
Newton, William, Merchant, Cannon St., Cannonborough,
    Neck
Neyle, Susannah, Mrs., 98 Tradd St
Nicholson, Warren, Shopkeeper, Hudson St ,
    Cannonborough, Neck
Nisbet, Maria, Mrs., Pinckney St , Cannonborough, Neck
Nobbs, Mary, Mrs., cr. St. Philip's & Radcliff Sts ,
    Radcliffborough, Neck
Nolan, John, 45 King St.
Nolan, John M , Merchant Tailor, 9 Broad St
Norman & Stinson, Dry Goods Store, 292 King St.
Norman, George E , Factor, 21 E Bay St.

North, Edward W., Physician, 103 Meeting St
North, Richard B., Factor, 103 Meeting St
North, Thomas S , Discount Clerk, S C Bank, Res. 218 E. Bay St.
North, Webb & Osborn, Factors, Chisolm's S. Whf.
Northrop, -----, Mrs., Boundary St., Radcliffborough, Neck
Nowell, Margaret, Mrs , 60 Wentworth St.
Noyse, Henry, Sea Captain, Cannon St , Cannonborough, Neck
Nuney, Francis, Mariner, 10 Philadelphia St.
Oakly, Robert S., Druggist, 152 King St.
Oaks, Samuel, Milton Ferry House, cr. E Bay & Market Sts.
Ogden, G W , Hard Alley
Ogier & Carter, Brokers & Auctioneers, 29 Broad St.
Ogier, John M., Accountant, Alexander St , Mazyckborough, Neck
Ogier, Susan, Mrs , Alexander St , Mazyckborough, Neck
Ogier, Thomas, 69 Meeting St.
Olds, Liberty, Shoe Store, cr. Church & St. Michael's Al
Olds, Welcome, Boot & Shoe Store, 228 King St
Oliphant, David, Painter, 208 Meeting St.
Oliver, Alias, Mrs., Spring St., Hampstead, Neck
Oneal, John, Butcher, Cannon St , Cannonborough, Neck
Oneale & Bird, Shipwrights, Pritchard's Whf
Oneale, Charles, Dry Goods Store, cr. King & Cannon Sts., Neck
Oneale, Edmund, Cannon St , Cannonborough, Neck
Oneale, John, 30 Magazine St
Oneale, John, 83 Broad St.
Oneale, Richard, Dry Goods Store, King St. Cont'd , Neck
Oneel, James, Carpenter, 26 Magazine St.
Oppenheim, H. W., Grocer, cr Church & Market Sts.
Osborn, Catharine, Mrs., 32 S. Bay St
Osborn, Richard, Factor, 32 S. Bay St.
Ottolengui, Abraham, Auctioneer, N Vendue Range
Overstreet, William & Co , Commission Merchants, Magwood's Whf.
Overstreet, William, 107 Broad St.
Owen, Ann, Miss, Milliner, 125 King St.
O'Callaghan & Johnson, Merchants, Fitzsimons' Whf.
O'Driscoll, Maria R , Mrs , 100 Tradd St.
O'Hara, Arthur H., Attorney, 61 Church St
O'Hara, Henry, Broker & Auctioneer, 5 Broad St , Res 23 Legare St.
O'Hear, James, Factor, D'Oyley's Whf., Res 7 Smith St
O'Hear, Joseph, Planter, 7 Smith St.
O'Rawe, John, Grocer, 137 Meeting St.
O'Riley, Eugene, Mrs., 124 Church St
O'Sullivan, Charles, Sign Painter, 52 Queen St.
O'Sullivan F., Coach Maker, 56 Wentworth St
Packard, C , 8 George St.
Paddock, G H , Exchange Broker, 6 Broad St.
Paduani, Lewis, Portrait & Miniature Painter, 198 King St
Page, Francis, 40 Anson St.
Page, John, Jr , Commission Merchant, 138 E Bay St
Page, Joseph W., Commission Merchant, N Vendue Range
Paine, Joseph B., 73 E Bay St
Paine, Thomas, Harbor Master, 73 E Bay St

Palmer, Benjamin M , Rev , Queen St.
Palmer, J., Sail Maker, 58 State St.
Palmer, Job, Carpenter, 62 Wentworth St.
Parish & Co., Wholesale & Dry Goods Store, cr. King & Wentworth Sts.
Parish, Thomas, 205 King St
Parker & Brailsford, Factors, Vanderhorst's Whf.
Parker, Arthur M., Factor, No 1 Kiddell's Whf.
Parker, Charles, City Surveyor, 2 New St.
Parker, F., Mrs , 16 Guignard St
Parker, George, Mrs., Chapel St , Mazyckborough, Neck
Parker, Henry, Pilot, 44 Church St
Parker, John, Jr., Planter, Warren St., Radcliffborough, Neck
Parker, John, Planter, St. Philip's St., Radcliffborough, Neck
Parker, Mary, Mrs., 25 Legare St.
Parker, Samuel, Planter, 6 George St.
Parker, William H., 25 Legare St.
Parker, William M., Planter, 4 Church St
Parker, William, Mrs , 4 Friend St.
Parsons, J. D., Teacher, 55 Queen St.
Parsons, -----, Mrs., Bull St., Hampstead, Neck
Pasley, Lewis, Baker, 1 Boundary St.
Paterson, Hugh, Office, Union Insurance Co., Res. 31 Laurens St.
Patrick, Cassimer, Tanner, Res. Mary St., Wraggsborough, Neck
Patterson, Alexander, Commission Merchant & Grocer, S Vendue Range
Patterson, James, 19 Chalmers St.
Patterson, Samuel, Factor, E. Bay St.
Patton, Isaac, Shoemaker, 235 E. Bay St.
Patton, William, Counting House, Fitzsimons' Whf , Res 108 Church St.
Paul, J. & D , Grocers, cr Broad & Church St
Paxton, H W., 24 Wentworth St
Payne, John W., 28 Broad St.
Payne, Josiah S., 2 Friend St.
Payne, William & Sons, Brokers, Vendue Masters & Commission Merchants, 28 Broad St
Pearson, Benjamin, 255 E. Bay St
Pecault, Adelle, Mrs., Union Hotel, 7 Queen St
Peigne, James L., 7 Cumberland St.
Peixotto, S E., Priest of the Synagogue, 26 Hasell St.
Pelmome, Francis, Hair Dresser, 33 State St.
Pelzer, Anthony, Teacher, 13 King St.
Pemble, David, Clothing Store, 161 E. Bay St.
Pennal, Robert, Grocer, cr. King & Boundary Sts
Pennington, Ann E., Mrs., 22 Blackbird Al.
Pennington, Martha, Mrs., 39 Pinckney St.
Penot, Charles, 13 Anson St.
Pepoon, Benjamin F , Attorney, 104 Church St.
Percival & Boag, Druggists, 355 King St
Perdrican, Isabella, Mrs., 7 Maiden Ln.
Perkins, D , Commission Merchant, 124 E Bay St
Perman, George & Co., Grocers, 63 E. Bay St.
Perman, George & Co , Grocers, 59 E Bay St.
Perman, George & Co., Grocers, 65 E Bay St
Perman, George, Ship Chandler, 61 E Bay St

Peronnean, William, Planter, 34 S Bay St.
Perry, Ann D., Mrs., 44 Bull St.
Perry, Edward S., Planter, Vanderhorst St , Radcliffborough, Neck
Perry, Peter S., 10 Coming St
Perry, Stevens, Attorney, Res 52 Broad St.
Peters, Cecilia, Mrs , Boarding House, 15 Chalmers St
Peters, George, Mrs , St Philip's St , Radcliffborough, Neck
Peters, James, Teacher of Music, 30 Cumberland St.
Peters, Mary, Mrs., 111 Broad St.
Peterson, Christian, Grocer, cr. Boundary & Smith Sts
Peterson, Jahncke & Co., Merchants, Crafts' S. Whf.
Peterson, John, Grocer, 233 E. Bay St.
Peterson, Joseph, 8 Market St.
Peterson, Mary, Mrs , Boarding House, 12 Bedon's Al
Petigru & Cruger, Attorneys, St Michael's Al.
Petigru, James L , Attorney General, 6 Orange St
Petit, M., 38 George St.
Petival, J B , Surveyor & Engineer, 42 Queen St
Petrie, George, 47 Society St
Petrie, Sarah, Miss, School, 47 Society St
Petsch, Jane, Mrs., School, 14 Liberty St.
Peyssou, M. L , Mrs , Milliner, 159 King St.
Pezant, John, Merchant, E. Bay St , Res cr. Washington & Boundary Sts
Pezant, Lewis, Grocer, 9 Boundary St.
Pezant, Peter, 16 Washington St
Phelon, Edmund M , Grocer, cr. Meeting & Queen Sts
Phelps, Mary E , Mrs , Sewing Mistress, Orphan House
Philipps, John, Sea Captain, 4 Lynch's Ln.
Phillips, Aaron, Dry Goods Store, 221 King St.
Phillips, Benjamin, Grocer, Vendue Range
Phillips, Dorothy, Mrs , 132 Queen St.
Phillips, Edward, Rev., 6 Pinckney St
Phillips, John, Jr., Attorney, 6 Pinckney St.
Phillips, John, Mrs , 2 Lynch's Ln.
Phillips, John, Painter, 6 Pinckney St.
Phillips, Margaret, Mrs , 42 Pinckney St.
Phillips, St John, Physician, 6 Pinckney St
Phinney & Scott, Grocers, 4 Tradd St.
Phinney, Josiah, 4 Tradd St.
Pienville, -----, Madam, 36 Ellery St.
Pierson, Catharine, Mrs , 52 Broad St
Pillans, John C., Carpenter, 43 King St.
Pillot, A P., Dry Goods Store, King St Cont'd , Neck
Pillot, Ome, Shopkeeper, Meeting St. Cont'd., Hampstead, Neck
Pilsbury, Samuel, Custom House, Res. 23 Anson St
Pinckney, C C , Jr , Attorney, George St.
Pinckney, Charles C., Planter, 223 E. Bay St.
Pinckney, Henry L., Proprietor of the Mercury Office, Res. 75 King St.
Pinckney, Lucia, Mrs , 25 Pitt St.
Pinckney, Thomas, Planter, 10 George St.
Pitray & Viel, Merchants, 167 E Bay St
Pitray, Lewis A., 12 George St
Place, Smith, Franklin Hotel, 30 Queen St.
Plumeau, John F., Accountant, 131 King St
Plumer, Benjamin, Bricklayer, 26 George St

Plunket, Patrick C , Billiard Tables, cr Warren & St Philip's Sts., Radcliffborough, Neck
Pogson, Milward, Rev., 130 Wentworth St
Pohl, E & Son, Merchants, 166 E Bay St.
Pohl, Elias, 175 E Bay St.
Poincignon, Jane, Mrs , 19 Queen St
Porcher, Catharine, Mrs., 15 Rutledge St
Porcher, Francis, Physician, 45 Queen St
Porcher, George, Mrs., 12 New St
Porcher, George, Mrs , Ann St , Wraggsborough, Neck
Porcher, Malsey, Mrs , Ann St., Wraggsborough, Neck
Porter, Benjamin R , 11 Water St.
Porter, Sarah, Mrs., 18 Middle St.
Porter, Peter, Black & White Smith, 14 Swinton's Ln.
Porter, William L., Grain Store, Chisolm's Whf., Res. 22 S. Bay St.
Porterino, Stephen, 14 Lowndes St., Neck
Potter, John, Planter, 42 Society St.
Potter, Perley & Co , Grocers, cr E Bay & Market Sts
Potter, Washington, Mrs , Private Boarding, 37 E. Bay St.
Poulnot, Joseph, Baker, cr. King & Reid Sts , Neck
Poulton, Richard, Mrs., 56 Church St.
Powers, James, Painter, 16 Swinton's Ln.
Poyas, Francis, Gunsmith, 119 Meeting St
Poyas, James, Shipwright, 4 Gibbes St.
Prary, Manuel, Grocer, 2 Market St
Pratt, John, 29 Laurens St
Prele, Ann, Mrs , 106 Meeting St.
Prele, John F , 106 Meeting St.
Prescott, Bishop & Gray, Merchants, Magwood's Whf
Prescott, George W., 29 Broad St.
Pressley, -----, Misses, 47 George St
Prevost, Joseph, Grocer, 9 Market St.
Price, Ann, Mrs , 30 King St
Price, Elizabeth, Mrs , 6 Queen St.
Price, O'Brien S., Planter, King St Cont'd., Neck
Price, Thomas, Bookkeeper, Union Bank, Res. 15 Society St.
Price, Thomas, Jr., Planter, 75 Church St
Price, William, Jr , Planter, 101 Tradd St.
Price, William S., Physician, King St. Cont'd , Neck
Prince, Charles, Tin Plate Worker, 114 King St
Prince, John, Clerk, Planters' & Mechanics' Bank
Pringle, George, Dry Goods Store, Res. Spring St., Hampstead, Neck
Pringle, James R , Collector of Customs, 3 Orange St
Pringle, John J., Planter, 62 Tradd St.
Pringle, Mary, Mrs , 90 Broad St.
Pringle, -----, Misses, 48 Meeting St.
Pringle, Robert A , Planter, 91 Meeting St
Pringle, Robert, Planter, 62 Tradd St.
Prioleau, Jane B., Mrs , 22 Guignard St
Prioleau, John C., Planter, cr. Society & Anson St.
Prioleau, Philip G., Physician, cr. Meeting & George St
Prioleau, Samuel, Attorney, Waring's Buildings, Meeting St., op. St Michael's Al , Res 2 Church St
Prioleau, Samuel, Mrs., State House Sq
Prioleau, Thomas G , Physician, 135 Meeting St
Pritchard, John, 7 Wentworth St.
Pritchard, Paul, Shipwright, 6 Hasell St.

127

Pritchard, William, Sr., Shipwright, 1 Pinckney St
Proctor, William, Shoe Store, cr Church & Queen Sts
Pundt & Myers, Grocers, 15 Mazyck St
Purcell, Ann, Mrs., 10 Green St.
Purcell, Sarah, Mrs. 3 Legare St.
Purse, Thomas F
Purse, William, Cabinet Maker, 21 Mazyck St.
Purse, William W., Cabinet Maker, 337 King St Cont'd.,
    Neck
Purse, William, Watch Maker 58 Broad St
Quash, Francis D., Planter, 306 E. Bay St.
Quash, Robert F., Planter, 108 Broad St.
Query, Honoria, Mrs., Private Boarding, 335 King St.
Quin, Francis, 19 Guignard St
Quinan, V, Mrs., 257 King St.
Quinby, Elizabeth, Mrs., 11 Pinckney St
Quinn, Thomas F, Shopkeeper, cr. Meeting & Boundary
    Sts., Neck
Rabb, Jacob, Pump & Block Maker, 206 E. Bay St, Res.
    Wentworth St.
Radcliffe, John, 116 Meeting St
Raine, Thomas, Shopkeeper, cr. Amherst & Nassau Sts.,
    Wraggsborough, Neck
Rame, C, Confectioner, 165 Meeting St
Ramsay, David, State Treasurer, 9 Meeting St.
Ramsay, James, Physician, 74 Broad St.
Ramsay, John, Planter, 1 Anson St.
Ramsay, -----, Misses, Female Academy, 74 Broad St.
Randolph, John, cr King & Society St.
Ransford, Henry, Painter, Blackbird Al.
Ravenel & Stevens, Factors, Chisolm's Whf.
Ravenel, Catharine, Mrs, 64 Broad St.
Ravenel, Daniel, Cashier, Planters' & Mechanics' Bank,
    Res 76 King St.
Ravenel, Edmund, Physician, 64 Broad St.
Ravenel, Henry, Surveyor, 64 Broad St
Ravina, J D., Teacher of French & Spanish, 174 Meeting
    St
Raymond, Mary, Mrs, 2 Beaufain St.
Raymond, Nap, Gillon St.
Raynal, Benjamin, Fancy Store, 243 King St.
Read, J. H, Planter, cr Wentworth & Rutledge St
Read, William, Planter, cr. Montague & Rutledge St.
Redder, Elizabeth, Mrs., Columbus St., Hampstead, Neck
Redfern, John, Shoemaker, 13 Tradd St.
Redman, James, Blacksmith, 32 Beaufain St
Redman, Matthew, Carpenter, 15 State St.
Reedy, James, Carpenter, 28 Hasell St
Reeves, Abraham P., Carpenter, 3 Back St.
Reeves, Solomon, Carpenter, 14 Pitt St
Reid, Elizabeth, Mrs., 104 Meeting St
Reid, George, Bookkeeper, S C. Bank
Reid, George, Mrs., 49 E. Bay St
Reid, George, Rev, Teacher, 155 Meeting St.
Reid, James, Wheelwright, 17 Cumberland St.
Reid, Moultrie, Post Office, Res. 49 E Bay St
Reid, William, 104 Meeting St
Reidhammer, Peter, Cabinet Maker, Columbus St.,
    Hampstead, Neck
Reigne, John, Baker, 197 E. Bay St.

Remley, Mary, Mrs., 70 Anson St
Remley, Paul, Bricklayer, 24 Ellery St
Renaud, John, 81 Anson St.
Rennay, Boissere, Carpenter, cr Coming & Warren Sts,
    Radcliffborough, Neck
Requier & Co, Confectioners, 106 Meeting St
Requier, Augustus, 106 Meeting St
Revell, Margaret, Mrs., 253 E Bay St
Reynolds, George N., Coach Maker, 117 Meeting St.
Reynolds, Susannah, Mrs, Washington St.,
    Mazyckborough, Neck
Ribbeck, Frederick, Grocer, 138 King St
Ricard, Francis, Grocer, 93 E. Bay St
Rice, A & Co, Merchants, 134 E Bay St.
Rice, Alanson, Merchant, King St Cont'd, Neck
Rice, William, Attorney, 76 Broad St
Rich, John, Coach Maker 123 Meeting St
Richards, Joseph, 40 Elliott St.
Richards, Samuel, Notary Public & Quorum Unis, 84 E
    Bay St., Res., 56 Elliott St.
Richardson, A., Slater, 68 Anson St.
Richardson, Henry, Planter 117 Boundary St.
Richardson, John S., Judge, Pinckney St., Cannonborough,
    Neck
Richardson, Mary, Mrs, 18 Queen St
Richters, John P C., Grocer, 12 Kiddell's Whf.
Rickets & Green, Grocers, 2 Middle St
Rickets, L, Grocer, 47 Market St.
Ridgeway, Benjamin J, 133 Tradd St.
Righton, Elizabeth P., Miss, 7 Water St.
Righton, F., Mrs., 81 E Bay St.
Righton, John M., Physician, 15 George St.
Rightson, Joseph, Cooper, 5 Water St.
Riley, H, Mrs, 16 Hasell St
Riley, William, Printer, 125 Church St.
Ring, David R., Paint & Oil Store, 23 Broad St., Res 41
    Tradd St.
Rion, James, 31 Elliott St
Ripley, William Y., 232 Meeting St
Rivers, Elizabeth, Mrs., 6 Stoll's Al
Rivers, George, Mrs, 2 Greenhill St
Rivers, H. S., 19 Cumberland St
Rivers, John, Shopkeeper, 55 St Philip's St.
Rivers, Samuel, Shipwright, 13 Water St
Rivers, Thomas, 21 Anson St.
Rivers, William H., Wentworth St.
Riviere, J P, Dry Goods Store, 171 King St.
Roach, Edward, 13 Society St. or City Hall
Roach, Henry, Grocer, cr. Boundary & Lowndes Sts.
Roach, Henry, Shopkeeper, King St. Cont'd., Neck
Roach, Mary, Mrs., 13 Society St.
Roach, William, Clerk of City Council, 13 Society St
Robb, James, Grocer, 190 King St.
Roberds, S, Painter, 100 King St.
Roberts, Stephen, Sea Captain, 14 Amen St
Roberts, William, 8 Wentworth St.
Robertson, Ann, Mrs., 54 St. Philip's St.
Robertson, James, Merchant, 51 E Bay St
Robertson, John, Merchant, Crafts' S Whf., Res. 31
    Meeting St

Robertson, William, Planter, 2 Short St

Robinson, Alexander, Secretary, Fire & Marine Insurance Co

Robinson, J W., Commission Merchant, 31 Meeting St

Robinson, John, Factor, Edmondston's Whf

Robinson, John, Merchant, Res Ann St , Wraggsborough, Neck

Robinson, Mary, Mrs , 6 Berresford St.

Robinson, Randel, Teller, Office of Discount & Deposit, Res. 10 Bull St

Robinson, Thomas H., 45 Market St

Robinson, William, Grocer, 81 Elliott St

Robiou, Elizabeth, Mrs , 40 Beaufain St.

Roca, Egnais, 32 Market St

Roche, E. L., Merchant Tailor, 141 King St.

Roche, John, 130 Church St.

Roddy, Martin, Grocer, cr Queen & State Sts

Roddy, Mary, Mrs., 1 Hasell St

Rodericks, Anthony, Deputy Sheriff, Vernon, St.

Rodgers, John B., Accountant, 124 Wentworth St

Rodgers, Lewis, Wheelwright, 1 Montague St

Rodgers, S., Mrs., 124 Wentworth St.

Rodgers, Spofford & Tiletson, Store, 335 King St

Rodrigues, Moses, 8 Orange St.

Rodtbert, E A P., 13 King St.

Rodus, John, 10 Blackbird Al

Rogers, Charles, 87 Tradd St.,

Rogers, Christopher, 47 Tradd St

Rogers, Francis, Grain Store, 39 Anson St.

Rogers, John R., Ship Chandler, 105 E. Bay St , Res 24 King St

Roh, Ann M., Mrs , 6 Wentworth St.

Rolando, Francis G., Cooperage, E. Bay St., Res 15 Cumberland St

Rolando, Isabella, Mrs., 126 Queen St

Rooney, Hugh, Grocer, 44 Market St.

Roper, Benjamin, Planter, 15 Legare St.

Roper, Thomas, Planter, 163 E Bay St.

Roper, William, Planter, 163 E. Bay St

Roper, William, Planter, 35 E. Bay St.

Rose, Arthur G , Office of Discount & Deposit, Res. 40 Bull St.

Rose, E. H., Mrs., 55 Wentworth St.

Rose, Hugh, Planter, 292 E. Bay St.

Rose, James, Planter, 292 E. Bay St

Rose, John, Merchant, 118 E Bay St.

Rose, -----, Misses, 18 George St

Rose, Rebecca, Mrs., 6 Smith's Ln.

Ross, David, Custom House, Res. Motte's Ln.

Rothwell, Jane, Mrs , Private Boarding, 25 Tradd St

Rotureau, Charles, Confectioner, 101 Meeting St.

Roumillat & Son, Confectioners, 71 Meeting St.

Roumillet, Joseph, Tallow Chandler, cr. Meeting & Columbus St , Neck

Rouse, Christopher, Shoemaker, 85 Market St

Rouse, James, 83 Market St.

Rouse, William, 83 Market St.

Rout, Catharine, Mrs., 14 Friend St

Rout, William G., Office of Discount & Deposit, Res. 14 Friend St

Routledge, John, Dry Goods Store, King St Cont'd , Neck

Roux, Lewis, Notary Public & Quorum Unis, 101 E. Bay St., Res. 162 Meeting St

Rowan, S & Co., cr. King & Wentworth Sts.

Rowand, Charles E., Planter, 93 Meeting St

Rowe & White, Stone Cutters, cr. Church & Market St

Ruddock, Samuel A , Surveyor, 39 King St.

Rumph, C. H , Shopkeeper, cr Meeting & Wolf Sts , Wraggsborough, Neck

Rush, Catharine, Mrs., 26 Meeting St

Russ, Benjamin, Carpenter, 18 Magazine St.

Russell, Elizabeth, Mrs , 8 Guignard St.

Russell, Margaret, Mrs , 39 George St.

Russell, Mary, Miss, 102 Tradd St.

Russell, Sarah, Mrs., 11 Lynch's Ln.

Russell, Sarah, Mrs , 20 Wentworth St

Russell, Sarah, Mrs., 43 Meeting St.

Rutledge, Frederick, Mrs , 111 Tradd St.

Rutledge, John, Planter, 292 E Bay St.

Rutledge, Mary, Mrs., 56 Tradd St

Rutledge, States, Planter, 10 College St.

Ryan, Elizabeth, Mrs , 65 Broad St

Ryan, L., Attorney, 226 King St

Ryan, Thomas, Grocer, 107 King St

Safford, Isabella, Mrs , 295 E Bay St.

Salinas, C. J., Grocer, 37 Boundary St.

Salomon, Sarah, Mrs., Clothing Store, 143 E. Bay St.

Saltar, Thomas R , Quorum Unis & Ship Joiner, 59 State St.

Saltus, Francis W., Factor, S Bay St.

Salvo, Corado, 94 King St

Samory, -----, Mrs , Upholsterer, 50 Queen St

Sampson, Henry, Grocer, 207 E Bay St.

Sampson, Joseph & Co., Clothing House, cr. E Bay St & Market St.

Sampson, Joseph, 181 E. Bay St.

Sampson, Samuel, 205 E Bay St

Sanders, William, Planter, Nassau St., Hampstead, Neck

Sanford, C , Mrs., 3 Cumberland St

Sarizin, Catharine, Miss, 99 Wentworth St.

Sarzedas, David, Auctioneer, 25 Beaufain St.

Sass, Edward G., Northern Ware House, 77 Queen St

Sass, Jacob, Cabinet Maker, 79 Queen St.

Sass, L W , Grocer, 38 Anson St

Sass, William H , Bookkeeper, Office of Discount & Deposit, Res 79 Queen St.

Satorious, Catharine, Mrs , 44 King St

Savage, Ann, Mrs , Milliner, 1 Clifford St

Savage, -----, Miss, cr. Broad & Savage Sts

Saviske, Peter, 84 Boundary St.

Savisky, Peter, Boundary St., Neck

Sawyer, William, Dry Goods Store, 366 King St.

Sax, Henry, Grocer, cr. Anson & Society Sts.

Saylor, S S , Factor, Kunhardt's Whf.

Schaffner, Frederick, Grocer, 16 Queen St.

Schenck, James R , 23 Broad St.

Schmidt, Elizabeth, Mrs., 5 Montague St.

Schmidt, John W., Physician, 53 Church St

Schneider, Christian J., 19 Anson St

Schnell, John J , Grocer, 175 Church St

Schnierlie, John M., Carpenter, 11 Friend St.
Schroder, T. J., Gauger, 102 Meeting St.
Schroeder, Thomas W , 255 King St.
Schulte, Henry, Grocer, 56 Meeting St
Schulte, J. H., Grocer, 66 Market St
Schults, William B., Auction Establishment, 205 King St
Schultz, John, Factor, Fitzsimons' Whf., Res. 28 Laurens St.
Schutt, John G , Hardware Store, 89 E Bay St.
Schwartz, Frederick, Butcher, Henrietta St., Mazyckborough, Neck
Schwartz, Mary, Mrs., Coming St., Radcliffborough, Neck
Scott, Charles, Mrs., Private Boarding, cr Amen & State St
Scott, George, St. Philip's St., Neck
Scott, Margaret B., Mrs., 99 Market St.
Scott, Rebecca E., Mrs., 265 Meeting St.
Scott, Rebecca, Mrs., Meeting St., Wraggsborough, Neck
Scott, Robert J., Accountant, 4 Magazine St.
Scott, Thomas, 39 E. Bay St.
Scott, Thomas, Accountant, 26 Broad St
Scott, William M , Notary Public & Quorum Unis, 151 E Bay St., Res. 7 Pinckney St.
Scriven, Rebecca, Miss, 18 Lynch's Ln.
Scriven, Thomas, Planter, America St., Hampstead, Neck
Seabrook, Thomas B., Planter, 18 Rutledge St
Sears, Francis, Carpenter, 26 Bull St.
Seaver, Abraham, 12 Pinckney St.
Sebring, Cornelius C., Printing Office, 44 Queen St., Res 32 Broad St
Sebring, Edward, Woolen Draper & Men's Mercer, 32 Broad St
Seigling, John, Music & Musical Instrument Store, cr. Meeting & Cumberland Sts
Seixas, Isaac M., 122 King St.
Senet, Joseph, Lt., City Guard, Confectioner, 168 King St.
Service, John, cr. Warren & St. Philip's Sts., Wraggsborough, Neck
Seyle, Samuel, Masonic Hall, 220 King St.
Shackelford, Elizabeth, Mrs., Mary St , Wraggsborough, Neck
Shaffer, Elizabeth, Mrs , 21 Anson St
Shaffer, Frederick J., Carpenter, 13 Bull St
Shaw, Charles, Carpenter, Boundary St., Neck
Shea, Richard, Grocer, Berresford St.
Shecut, John L. E. W., Physician, 20 Coming St.
Shegog, J. & G., Grocers, cr. King & Liberty Sts.
Sheldon, Henry, Hardware Store, cr King & Liberty Sts
Sheppard, James, Saddler, 24 Coming St
Sheppard, William, Saddler, 30 Coming St
Sherreson, John, Grocer, 19 Rutledge St
Shievely, M A , Mrs., 230 Meeting St
Shirer, John, Gunsmith, 48 Queen St.
Shoolbred, James, Planter, 46 Montague St.
Shoolbred, John, Planter, Warren St., Radcliffborough, Neck
Shorters, Margaret, Mrs., 8 Zigzag Al.
Shorthouse, Thomas, cr King & Boundary St
Shrewsbury, Edward, Shipwright, Charlotte St , Mazyckborough, Neck

Shroudly, W B T., Accountant, Courier Office, Res 15 Archdale St.
Sibley, G. B. R., 366 King St
Siddon, Joseph, Carpenter, 92 King St.
Sieluff, Charles W., Grocer, 36 Archdale St.
Sifly & Mintzing, Lumber Merchants, Head of Queen St
Sifly, Henry, 24 Friend St.
Sifly, John, Bricklayer, 86 Market St
Sigwald, Thomas, 91 Wentworth St
Sillman, John H., Charlotte St., Mazyckborough, Neck
Simons, Edward, Planter, King St Cont'd., Neck
Simmons, Joseph, Grocer, cr. East Bay & Broad Sts
Simon, Moses, 19 Mazyck St.
Simonds, J. W., Druggist, 359 King St
Simons, Anthony, Factor, 75 Wentworth St.
Simons, Benjamin B., Physician, 303 E Bay St
Simons, Charles, Engraver, 82 Queen St.
Simons, Francis, Mrs , 107 Tradd St.
Simons, George W., Tin Plate Worker, 43 Broad St.
Simons, Jane, Mrs., Coming St., Radcliffborough, Neck
Simons, Keating & Sons, Factors, D'Oyley's Whf.
Simons, Keating, President, S. C Bank, Res. 5 Orange St
Simons, Maurice, 1 Middle St.
Simons, S L., Factor, 150 Montague St.
Simons, Thomas G., Factor, 48 Bull St.
Simons, Thomas Y., Physician, 171 Meeting St.
Simonton, C. S., Dry Goods Store, King St. Cont'd., Neck
Simpson, Preston, Dentist, Bridge St., Cannonborough, Neck
Simpson, William, 3 Minority St.
Sinclair, Alexander, Merchant, 64 E. Bay St , Res. 12 State St.
Sinclair, William, Purser, U. S Navy, Crafts' S. Whf
Singleton, Lucy, Mrs., 39 Wentworth St.
Singleton, Mary, Mrs , 94 Boundary St.
Sirrau, Francis, 47 Anson St.
Sivil, Alexander, 37 Wall St.
Skirving, -----, Mrs., Pinckney St., Cannonborough, Neck
Slawson, Nathaniel, Baker, 195 King St
Slowick, John, 52 Boundary St., Neck
Slowman, Eliza, Mrs., 73 Boundary St
Sluter, Jacob, Dry Goods Store, cr King & Hasell Sts
Smallwood, Richard, Custom House, 33 Pinckney St.
Smallwood, Richard, Jr., 33 Pinckney St.
Smart, John T., 24 Ellery St
Smerdon, Pricilla, Mrs., Private Boarding, 131 Church St
Smith & Robbins, Hardware Store, 313 King St.
Smith, Agnes, Mrs., 15 Broad St
Smith, Agnes, Mrs., 22 King St
Smith, Ann, Mrs , 14 Logan St.
Smith, Ann, Mrs., 2 State St.
Smith, B. & Co., Ship Chandlers, 71 E. Bay St
Smith, B R., Commission Merchant, Vanderhorst's Whf.
Smith, B S., Dry Goods Store, 215 King St
Smith, Benjamin, House Painter, 13 E. Bay St
Smith, Daniel, Grocer, 23 Rutledge St
Smith, Edward, Attorney, 55 Meeting St.
Smith, Edward, Attorney, Washington St , Mazyckborough, Neck
Smith, Eliza, Miss, 28 Wentworth St

Smith, Eliza, Mrs., Shopkeeper, 29 Wall St ,
Smith, Elizabeth, Mrs , 48 Wentworth St
Smith, George E., 11 Wentworth St.
Smith, George, Rigger, 19 Mazyck St.
Smith, Henrietta, Mrs., 45 Beaufain St.
Smith, James, 16 Beaufain St.
Smith, James H., Attorney, St. Michael's Al., Res. 154
  Wentworth St
Smith, John, 17 Price's Al.
Smith, John, Cabinet Maker, Henrietta St., Mazykborough,
  Neck
Smith, John, Carpenter, Henrietta St , Mazyckborough,
  Neck
Smith, John, Grocer, 248 E Bay St
Smith, John, Upholsterer, 12 Magazine St.
Smith, Josiah, 60 Anson St
Smith, Mary, Mrs , 14 Coming St.
Smith, Mary, Mrs , 76 Broad St.
Smith, Moses, Carpenter, 46 Pinckney St.
Smith, -----, Mrs., Hanover St , Hampstead, Neck
Smith, Quinton H., Washington St., Mazyckborough, Neck
Smith, Richard, Cabinet Maker, 57 Broad St
Smith, Robert, Planter, 209 Meeting St
Smith, Robert, Upholsterer, 224 E. Bay St
Smith, Rosella, Mrs , 73 Queen St
Smith, Samuel, 73 Broad St.
Smith, Samuel, Shoemaker, 104 Market St.
Smith, Sarah Ann, Mrs., Henrietta St , Mazyckborough,
  Neck
Smith, Theodore L, Accountant, 49 Hasell St
Smith, Thomas, Jr , 10 Green St
Smith, W L., Mrs., 130 Wentworth St
Smith, Whiteford, Grocer, 163 Church St
Smith, William, 9 Tradd St.
Smith, William John, Factor, Smith's S Whf ,
  Radcliffborough, Neck
Smith, William, Jr., Shipwright, Washington St.,
  Mazyckborough, Neck
Smith, William M , Planter, 22 Meeting St.
Smith, William S., Clerk, Court of Common Pleas, Res 35
  Laurens St
Smoke, John B., Bridge St., Cannonborough, Neck
Smylie, Andrew, U. S. Appraiser, 257 E. Bay St.
Smyth, John, 120 Queen St
Snowden, Joshua L. & Co., Ship Chandlers, 186 E. Bay St
Snowden, William E., Merchant, Fitzsimons' Whf., Res
  291 E. Bay St
Sobieski, Thaddeus, Surveyor & Engineer, Bull St.,
  Hampstead, Neck
Solice, Harriet, Mrs , 101 Church St.
Sollee, F W , Factor, Edmondston's Whf , Res. 45 E. Bay
  St.
Solomon, Chapman, Dry Goods Store, 290 King St
Solomons, Aaron, Dry Goods Store, 396 King St
Solomons, Aaron, Dry Goods Store, 370 King St. Cont'd.,
  Neck
Solomons, Alexander, Store, 287 King St
Solomons, S., Dry Goods Store, 75 Market St
Sompayrac & Petipain, Merchants, 174 E Bay St

Southworth, Rufus, Teacher, St. Michael's Al
Spann, W T , Factor, Edmonston's Whf
Sparks, Rachel, Mrs., 87 Queen St
Speaks, John, Hanover St., Hampstead, Neck
Spears, Archibald, Clerk, Planters' & Mechanics' Bank
Spears, C P , Mrs , 15 George St
Spears, James H., Wharfinger, Kiddell's Whf.
Spears, Mary, Mrs., 15 Society St
Speissegger, John, Musical Instrument Maker, 11 Hasell
  St
Spencer, Ruth, 283 E Bay St.
Spidle, John G , Carpenter, 14 Archdale St
Spiller, William, Comedian, 65 Church St.
Spring, John, cr Cannon & Elizabeth Sts.,
  Wraggsborough, Neck
Springer, Samuel, Grocer, 137 E Bay St
St Amand, J A., Coach Maker, 277 King St.
St John & Phelps, Commission Merchants & Grocers, S
  Vendue Range
Stafford, James, Sea Captain, 80 Anson St
Stall, Frederick, Shopkeeper, Cannon St., Cannonborough,
  Neck
Starr, Edwin P., Merchant, Edmondston's Whf., Res. 4
  Society St.
State, Asal, Boundary St.
Steedman, Charles John, Washington St., Mazyckborough,
  Neck
Steedman, E , Mrs , Private Boarding, Queen St
Steedman, Thomas, Accountant, John St., Wraggsborough,
  Neck
Steel, Elizabeth, Mrs., Grocery, 36 Elliott St.
Steel, Richard, Stone Cutter, 147 Meeting St
Steel, William, Dry Goods Store, 354 King St
Steele, John A., Discount Clerk, Planters' & Mechanics'
  Bank, Radcliff St , Radcliffborough, Neck
Steele, William G , 67 Beaufain St.
Steinmeyer, G. W., 6 Blackbird Al
Stent, John, Carpenter, 37 King St
Stephens, James R., Shoe Store, 331 King St.
Stephens, Thomas, Teller, Union Bank, 131 E Bay St
Stephens, William, Custom House, 16 Middle St.
Stevens, Daniel, Planter, 28 George St.
Stevens, J H., Coroner for Charleston District, 118 Tradd
  St
Stevens, William S., Physician, 29 King St.
Stewart, Adrianna, Mrs., 73 Wentworth St
Stewart, Angus, Carolina Coffee House, 20 Tradd St.
Stewart, Ann, Miss, 10 Clifford St
Stewart, Mary, Mrs., Midwife, 13 Friend St
Stewart, R L., Clerk, Office of Discount & Deposit, Res.
  13 Friend St
Stewart, Robert, Carpenter, 7 Beaufain St.
Stewart, William, Merchant, Chisolm's N. Whf., Res. 4
  King St
Stiles, Copeland, Planter, 49 Beaufain St.
Stilman, James, Auctioneer & Commission Merchant, S.
  Vendue Range, Res. 14 Amen St.
Stock, -----, Mrs , Montague St.
Stocker, Henry, Boat Builder, 26 Laurens St.
Stoll, Catharine, Mrs , 8 Magazine St

Stone, Charles, 31 King St.
Stone, Thomas, Bricklayer, 8 Guignard St
Stone, Timothy, Coach Maker, 69 Wentworth St.
Stone, William, Carpenter, 34 St. Philip's St
Stoney, John, Merchant, Chisolm's Upper Whf., Res 293
  E. Bay St
Stoppelbien, L., Grocer, 63 State St
Storn, Joseph, 42 Wentworth St.
Strayn, James, Beaufain St.
Street, H G., Commercial Coffee House, 141 E. Bay St
Street, Timothy & Co., Merchants, 28 Coming St.
Street, Timothy, 126 E. Bay St
Streets, Joseph, Wheelwright, 23 Coming St.
Strobel, Jacob, Steward, Marine Hospital, 5 Back St.
Strobel, John, Poor House
Strobel, Martin, Attorney, Archdale St.
Strobel, Mary G , Mrs , Matron, Poor House
Strohecker, John, Blacksmith & Hardware Store, 167
  Meeting St , Res. 20 Cumberland St
Stroub, Jacob, Carpenter, 14 Blackbird Al.
Strum, John J , Confectioner, 126 Church St.
Suares, Judith, Mrs., 114 Queen St.
Suares, Judith, Mrs , Henrietta St., Mazyckborough, Neck
Suau, Peter, 71 Beaufain St
Suder, Ann, Mrs., 49 Society St
Sullivan, Daniel, 43 Pinckney St.
Sullivan, Jeremiah, Shopkeeper, cr. Coming & St. Philip's
  Sts., Radcliffborough, Neck
Sullivan, Timothy, Broker & Vendue Master, 72 Anson St.
Summers, Thomas, Grocer, 26 Elliott St
Surau, Joseph, Shoemaker, 381 King St Cont'd., Neck
Surtis, Thomas, Pilot, 40 Church St.
Sutcliffe, Elizabeth, Mrs., 26 Guignard St.
Sutcliffe, James, Baker, 83 Queen St.
Sutton, Benjamin, Sea Captain, 8 Anson St.
Swain, Rebecca, Mrs., 7 Stoll's Al.
Sweegan, Matthew, Grocer, 1 Market St.
Sweeney, Ann, Mrs., 11 Elliott St.
Swift, William, Dry Goods Store, 336 King St.
Swint, Charlotte, Mrs , Nurse, 6 Archdale St.
Swinton, Ann, Mrs , 4 St. Philip's St.
Swinton, -----, Misses, 21 Archdale St.
Syfan, John, Butcher, Coming St., Cannonborough, Neck
Sykes, Walter G., Sheriff's Office, Res 7 Queen St
Syme, John T., Tailor, Lowndes St.
Syme, John T., Tailor, 10 Lowndes St , Neck
Symmes, Robert, Rev., 234 Queen St.
Symmes, Thomas, Dry Goods Store, 253 King St
Talvande, Andrew, 24 Legare St.
Talvande, -----, Madam, Female Academy & Boarding
  School, 24 Legare St
Talvande, Rose, Mrs , 100 Tradd St.
Tanswell, William N., Lock Smith & Bell Hanger, 79
  Meeting St
Taste, Peter, Teacher of Dancing, 162 King St
Tate, James, Sea Captain, 36 Queen St.
Taveau, Augustus, 9 Legare St.
Taylor, G. A., Mrs., 11 Anson St.
Taylor, George, Mrs., 37 St. Philip's St
Taylor, J. & Co., Grocers, 197 King St

Taylor, John, 37 Anson St.
Taylor, Joseph, Shipwright, 262 E Bay St.
Taylor, Josiah, Factor, 6 Lamboll St.
Taylor, Margaret, Mrs., Lowndes St
Taylor, R A., Mrs , Private Boarding, 179 E. Bay St.
Taylor, Robert A., Broker & Commission Merchant, 179
  E. Bay St.
Taylor, Thomas, Mariner, 9 Bedon's Al.
Taylor, Thomas, Pump & Block Makers, 12 Wall St
Taylor, Thomas R., Shoe Store, 173 King St
Teasdale, George, Bricklayer, 218 Meeting St.
Teasdale, Richard, Factor, Gadsden's Al.
Tennent, Frances, Mrs , 4 Swinton's Ln
Tennent, Thomas, Custom House, 29 Guignard St
Tennet, Charles, 60 Anson St.
Tew, Charles, Teacher, 80 Wentworth St.
Thayer, Ebenezer, Teacher, 80 Queen St.
Thayer, Heyward, Planter, 6 King St.
Thayer, William, 85 Meeting St
Theus, Benjamin, Printer, 7 Friend St
Thomas, B. G., 3 Greenhill St.
Thomas, Eliza, Mrs , Boarding House, 10 Bedon's Al.
Thomas, James, Accountant, 95 Broad St.
Thomas, Mary G., Mrs , 13 George St.
Thomas, Mary, Mrs., 96 Meeting St.
Thomas, Peter, Dry Goods Store, 244 King St
Thomas, Sarah, Mrs , 5 Linguard St.
Thomas, Stephen, Coming St., Radcliffborough, Neck
Thompson, Ann, Mrs., State House Sq
Thompson, E. Y., Mrs., 12 Water St.
Thompson, George, 273 E. Bay St.
Thompson, George, Bricklayer, 48 Wentworth St.
Thompson, John, Blacksmith, 183 Church St
Thompson, John, Grocer, 82 Church St.
Thompson, Mary, Mrs., 19 Hasell St.
Thompson, Rebecca, Mrs., St. Philip's St.,
  Radcliffborough, Neck
Thompson, Robert, Accountant, State House Sq
Thompson, William, Dry Goods Store, 214 King St
Thomson, John, Coach Maker, 39 Wall St
Thornhill, C , Mrs , Dry Goods Store, 225 King St.
Thwing, Edward, Merchant, N Vendue Range, Res 19
  State St
Tiddyman, Esther, Mrs , 4 Short St.
Tift, A , Grocer & Fish Store, cr E. Bay & Market Sts.
Timme, Elizabeth, Mrs., 28 Beaufain St.
Timmons, George, 19 Meeting St.
Timmons, William, Hardware Store, 165 E. Bay St
Tobias, Abraham, Auctioneer, N. Vendue Range, Res 85
  King St
Todd, Jane, Miss, 2 Savage St.
Todd, John, 61 George St.
Toilington, George, Grocer, Boundary St.
Tomkins, H., Watch Maker, 299 King St
Tonge, Thomas, Dyer, 250 King St.
Toohey, -----, Mrs., Milliner, 322 King St
Toole, John, Grocer, Champney St.
Toomer, A N., Physician, John St , Mazyckborough, Neck
Toomer, Ann, Mrs., 181 Meeting St.
Toomer, Henry B., Broker & Vendue Master, 10 State St.

132

Toomer, Joshua W , Attorney, St. Michael's Al , Res 297 E. Bay St.
Topham, Edward, Dry Goods Store, 267 King St.
Topham, Elizabeth, Mrs , 228 Meeting St
Torlay, Peter, 179 King St
Torre, Antonie, Merchant, 65 Broad St.
Torrey, Ann, Mrs., Private Boarding, New St.
Torrey, Eliza, Mrs , 37 Laurens St.
Torrington, John, King St. Cont'd , Neck
Toussiger, Eliza, Mrs., 20 Water St.
Tovey, Henry, Pump & Block Maker, E Bay St , Res. 285 E Bay St.
Towers, George M., 11 Back St.
Town, Susan, Mrs., 12 Church St.
Tracey, Carlos, Commission Merchant, Edmondston's Whf , Res. 32 Society St.
Trapier, Paul, Mrs., 6 Short St.
Trapmann, Lewis, Merchant, 16 New St
Trapmann, Schmidt & Co., Merchants, 79 E Bay St.
Treadway, W R. H , Book Store, 42 Broad St.
Trenholm, George A., Accountant, 39 E. Bay St., Res 26 Society St.
Trescot, Edward, 19 Maiden Ln.
Trescot, Henry, 5 Society St.
Trescot, Joseph, Merchant, N. Vendue Range, Res 19 Maiden Ln.
Trescot, William, Mrs., Boundary St., Radcliffborough, Neck
Trezvant, Peter, Notary Public & Quorum Unis, 84 E. Bay St., Res 5 Stoll's Al.
Trouche, Augustus, Clerk, Hudson St., Cannonborough, Neck
Trout, William, Pilot, 10 Lynch's Ln.
Truesdell, David, New York Oyster House, 32 Queen St.
Tucker, Charles S., Register of Mesne Conveyance, 68 Church St.
Tucker, Sarah, Mrs., 68 Church St.
Tunno, Adam, Merchant, 77 E Bay St
Tunno, John C , Planter, 7 Church St.
Tunno, Sarah, Mrs , 7 Church St
Tupper, Tristam, Merchant, E. Bay St., Res 54 State St
Turnbull, Robert J , Planter, 1 Logan St
Turner, E., Mrs., Boarding House, 167 Church St.
Turner, George R , Sea Captain, 10 Guignard St.
Turner, William, Inspector of Lumber, 33 Boundary St.
Tweed, Eleanor, Mrs., 2 Liberty St.
Tyler, Joseph, Merchant, E. Bay St., Res 7 State St
Ulmer, Michael, Shopkeeper, 3 King St
Ulmo, Anthony, Physician 157 King St.
Ummensetter, John, Tanner, 55 Beaufain St.
Urban, Joseph, 15 Maiden Ln
Urquhart, Charles, Merchant, Gillon St., Res 39 Elliott St
Utley, Horace, Notary Public & Quorum Unis, Register's Office for Seamen, 115 E. Bay St
Vale, Elizabeth, Mrs., cr. Cannon & Elliott Sts., Cannonborough, Neck
Valk, Jacob R., Merchant, 58 E. Bay St.
Vallenet, S., Mrs , Milliner, 314 King St
Vanbrunt, R., Book Store, 259 King St., Bindery, 5 Broad St

Vanderhoff, Catharine, Mrs., 11 Wentworth St
Vanderhorst, Arnoldus, Planter, Charlotte St , Mazyckborough, Neck
Vanderhorst, Richard W , Planter, cr Alexander & Judith Sts., Mazyzkborough, Neck
Vanderlippe, F , Grocer, cr Wentworth & St. Philp's Sts
Vandyne, B., Private Boarding, 330 King St.
Vanhagan, John, 10 Smith's Ln.
Vanholten, T., Grocer, 25 Boundary St.
VanRhyn, A. E , Miss, Dry Goods & Fancy Store, 22 Broad St
Vanruver, John, Grocer, 12 Tradd St
Vanvelsen, William, Wheelwright, 48 St. Philip's St.
Vardell, Thomas A , Bricklayer, Vanderhorst St , Radcliffborough, Neck
Varner, H , Grocer, 2 Archdale St
Varner, S., 37 Coming St
Vaughn, Ann, Mrs , 349 King St.
Vause, John T., 25 Mazyck St.
Veitch, William, Druggist, 223 King St.
Venning, Jonah M., Factor, 44 Anson St.
Venning, Robert M , 7 Society St.
Verdier, John M., 9 Back St.
Vernon, Nathaniel, Jeweller, 84 Broad St.
Veronnee, William, Tinner, King St Cont'd., Neck
Very, Nathaniel, Sugar Store, 53 Queen St.
Vesey, Joseph, 80 Anson St.
Veusse, Frances, Mrs., Dry Goods Store, 162 King St.
Vincendiere, H., Mrs , Shopkeeper, King St Cont'd., Neck
Vincent, H. E., Ship Chandler, 91 E Bay St.
Vinro, -----, Mrs., Wentworth St.
Vinyard, John, Planter, Drake St., Hampstead, Neck
Wadsworth, -----, 36 Archdale St.
Wagner, Ann, Mrs., 52 St Philip's St
Wagner, E., 53 E. Bay St
Wagner, George, Factor, cr. Alexander & John Sts , Mazyckborough, Neck
Wagner, Samuel J., Custom House, 118 Queen St
Wakefield, Sarah, Miss, cr Wentworth & Pitt Sts.
Waldo, Thomas, 106 Queen St
Walker, Ann, Mrs., 24 Magazine St.
Walker, J , Book Store & Reading Room, 15 Broad St
Walker, John, 95 Church St.
Walker, John F , Planters' & Mechanics' Bank, 23 State St.
Walker, John J., Dry Goods Store, 294 King St
Walker, Joseph, Carpenter, 40 Pinckney St.
Walker, Mary, Mrs , 40 Pinckney St.
Walker, Thomas, Stone Cutter, 145 Meeting St.
Walker, William, Accountant, 1 Bedon's Al
Wall, Richard, 92 Queen St.
Wallace, Christiana, Shopkeeper, Pinckney St., Cannonborough, Neck
Wallace, William, Butcher, Coming St., Radcliffborough, Neck
Waller, C , Mrs., 22 Magazine St.
Waller, William, Saddler, 89 Broad St
Wallis, John, Shopkeeper, cr Alexander & John Sts , Mazyckborough, Neck
Walter, Jerry, Commission Merchant, N. Vendue Range,

Res 26 State St

Walton, Elizabeth, Mrs., 378 King St

Ward & Yeadon, Attornies, Meeting St., Next to Guard House

Ward, James, Grocer, Cordes St.

Ward, James M., Mrs., 94 Tradd St

Ward, Joshua, 94 Tradd St.

Ward, S Francis, Attorney, 3 Middle St

Ward, Sarah, Mrs., 40 Meeting St

Ward, Susannah, Mrs., 3 Middle St

Waring, Daniel J., Attorney, 2 George St.

Waring, Edward, Bricklayer, Washington St., Mazyckborough, Neck

Waring, H. S., Physician, 83 Wentworth St.

Waring, Jane L., Mrs., 32 Hasell St.

Waring, Morton A., Marshal, St Philip's St., Radcliffborough, Neck

Waring, Morton, Factor, 4 George St.

Waring, Thomas, Mrs , 32 Meeting St.

Warley, Ann, Mrs., 2 King St.

Warley, Charles, Factor, 36 E. Bay St.

Warley, -----, Misses, 30 Beaufain St.

Warner, P., Mrs., 4 Tradd St.

Warner, Russel, Carpenter, Ellery St.

Warren, James, Boarding House, 16 Bedon's Al.

Washington, William, Mrs., 2 S. Bay St.

Washington, William, Planter, 40 Church St.

Watson, Henry, Grocer, cr. Meeting & Market Sts.

Watson, James, Price's Al.

Watson, Mary, Mrs., 22 Chalmers St.

Watson, Mary, Mrs., 38 Elliott St.

Watson, Stephen, Merchant, 71 E. Bay St.

Watt, James, Grocer, 36 Church St

Watton, Eliza, Mrs., Nurse, 53 Anson St

Wattong, John A., Teacher, 357 King St.

Waugh, Alexander B., 13 Legare St.

Webb, Daniel C., Factor, cr. Pinckney & Cannon Sts., Cannonborough, Neck

Webber, Samuel, Hard Al.

Weed, Joseph, 24 Blackbird Al

Weissinger, L., 294 King St.

Welch, James, 20 Cumberland St.

Welch, Jane, Mrs., 5 Logan St.

Welch, Patrick, Private Boarding, 116 Queen St.

Welch, Thomas G., Carver, 37 Beaufain St.

Welling & Ballantine, Harness Makers, 119 Meeting St.

Welling, Charles, Accountant, 119 Meeting St.

Wells & Cone, Commission Merchants, 151 E. Bay St

Wells, S., Mrs., 102 Market St.

Welsby, John, Merchant, Crafts' N., Whf., Res. 55 Church St.

Welsman, James, Sea Captain, 88 Church St

Wesner, Frederick, Carpenter, cr. Queen & Magazine Sts.

West, Anthony, 52 Elliott St.

West, Charles, Accountant, Washington St , Mazyckborough, Neck

West, Charles H., Ship Chandler, 79 E. Bay St.

Westendorff, C. P. L., Wine & Liquor Store, 177 E. Bay St

Weston, Paul, Planter, cr. America & Columbus Sts.,

Hampstead, Neck

Weston, Plowden, Planter, 71 Queen St.

Weyman, Francis, Grocer, 38 Church St.

Weyman, J. T , Merchant, cr. E Bay St. & Vendue Range

Weyman, Joseph T., Merchant, cr. Meeting & Charlotte Sts., Mazyckborough, Neck

Wharton, Samuel, Dry Goods Store & Wagon Yard, King St. Cont'd., Neck

Wheeler, Henry, Merchant, 144 E. Bay St., Res. 33 Queen St.

Wheeler, M. J., Shoe Store, 304 King St.

Wheeler, S. C , Dry Goods Store, 328 King St , Res. 353 King St.

Whilden, Elias, Planter, 10 Society St.

Whilden, John, 70 Anson St.

Whilden, Joseph, 22 Magazine St

Whitaker, Joseph, Shopkeeper, Elizabeth St., Mazyckborough, Neck

White, George K., Factor, 21 Anson St.

White, John & Co., Factors, Chisolm's N. Whf.

White, John B., Attorney, 78 Broad St.

White, John, Factor, 216 Meeting St.

White, John, Planter, Smith St.

White, John, Stone Cutter, 40 Market St.

White, William, Cabinet Marker, cr. Reid & Hanover Sts., Hampstead, Neck

White, William, Grocer, 44 Market St.

Whiteheart, Peter, Grocer, 211 E. Bay St.

Whiting, John, Turner, 189 Meeting St.

Whitney, Archibald, Notary Public & Collector of Accounts, St. Michael's Al. or 9 Society St.

Whitney, J , Carpenter, 24 St. Philip's St.

Whitney, Mary, Mrs., 28 Queen St.

Whitridge, J. B., Physician, 136 Church St

Whittencamp, Ann, Mrs., Confectioner, 28 Tradd St.

Wigfall, Thomas, Planter, Washington St., Mazyckborough, Neck

Wightman, John T , Turner, 112 Meeting St

Wightman, William, 82 Meeting St.

Wightman, William, J., Merchant, 173 E. Bay St.

Wightman, William, Painter, 199 Meeting St.

Wilbur, William W., Comb Manufacturer, 166 King St.

Wilcox, S. W., 11 Price's Al.

Wildman & Starr, Hat Store, 279 King & 27 Broad Sts

Wiley, James, Grocer, 60 Elliott St

Wiley, Samuel, Grocer, 29 Elliott St.

Wilhelmi, M. W. A., Mrs., Private Boarding, 28 Tradd St.

Wilkes & Wilkins, Merchants, 6 Crafts' S. Whf

Wilkes, John, 18 Meeting St.

Wilkie, William B., Cashier, Union Bank, 32 Church St.

Wilkie, William, Church St., near Market St

Wilkins, Martin, S. Bay St.

Will, Robert W., Bricklayer, 46 Anson St.

Williams, Isham, William's Whf.

Williams, James G., Coach Maker, 53 Anson St.

Williams, John, Riggger, 15 Clifford's Al.

Williams, Simpson, Pilot, 113 Church St.

Williams, William, Tailor, 101 Boundary St

Williamson, E., Mrs., Milliner, 121 King St.

Williamson, John, 69 E. Bay St

Williman, A. E., Mrs., 111 Broad St.
Williman, Christopher, Planter, cr. Pinckney & Bridge Sts., Cannonborough, Neck
Williman, -----, Mrs., Boundary St., Radcliffborough, Neck
Willington, A. S., Proprietor, Charleston Courier, Res. 281 E. Bay St
Willis, Henry, Carpenter, 23 St. Philip's St.
Willis, John H., 36 Bull St.
Willis, William, Oil Merchant, 163 E. Bay St.
Wilson, Alexander B., Planter, St. Philip's St., Radcliffborough, Neck
Wilson, Elizabeth, Mrs., 67 Meeting St.
Wilson, Isaac M., Physician, 116 Broad St.
Wilson, James, Seed Store, 193 King St.
Wilson, John, Carpenter, 16 Blackbird Al.
Wilson, John, Civil Engineer & Surveyor, 12 Coming St.
Wilson, John W., Shoemaker, 200 Meeting St.
Wilson, Judith, Mrs , 104 Wentworth St.
Wilson, Mary C., Mrs., 30 Church St.
Wilson, Mary, Mrs , Meeting St. Cont'd., Neck
Wilson, Robert, Boarding Officer, Custom House, 5 Hasell St.
Wilson, Samuel, Jr., Physician, 6 New St.
Wilson, Samuel, Physician, 9 Archdale St.
Wilson, William H., Clerk, City Court, 100 Meeting St.
Windsor, Elizabeth, Mrs., 40 Anson St.
Wing, Sarah C , Mrs., 89 Boundary St.
Winges, Conrad, Grocer, 59 Church St.
Winges, Jacob, Grocer, cr. Beaufain & Archdale Sts.
Winges, John H., Baker, 186 Meeting St.
Winne, John, Tailor, 58 Elliott St.
Winslow, Edward, Factor, Craft's N. Whf.
Winstanley, Thomas, 193 E. Bay St.
Winthrop & Parker, Factors, 3 D'Oyley's Whf.
Winthrop, Joseph, 105 Tradd St.
Winthrop, Joseph, Jr., Factor, 109 Tradd St.
Wish, Ann, Mrs., 27 Coming St.
Wish, Richard S., Deputy Marshall, Res 135 Queen St.
Wislon, John, 24 Society St.
Withers, Margaret, Mrs , Amherst St , Hampstead, Neck
Withers, Margaret, Mrs., Dry Goods Store, 370 King St.
Woddrop, John, Merchant, 43 E. Bay St.
Wolf, Isaac, Shoopkeeper, King St Cont'd., Neck
Wood, Francis, Shopkeeper, cr. Henrietta & Elizabeth Sts., Mazyckborough, Neck
Wood, John, Butcher, Amherst St., Hampstead, Neck
Wood, Mary, Mrs., Elizabeth St , Mazyckborough, Neck
Woolf, Isaac, Dry Goods Store, 370 King St.
Wotherspoon, Robert, 70 Church St.
Wotton, John A., Schoolmaster, King St. Cont'd., Neck
Wragg, E., Miss, 130 Wentworth St.
Wragg, Samuel, Cashier, State Bank, Lower End Meeting St.
Wrainch, John, Teacher, 95 Market St.
Wray, Sarah D., Mrs., 11 Wentworth St.
Wright & Meacher, Commission Merchants, 3 Anson St.
Wright, Alexander, 1 George St
Wright, John, Attorney, St. Michael's Al.
Wright, John I., 73 State St.
Wulff, Jacob, Merchant, 76 E. Bay St., Res. 131 Church St.
Wurdemann, C. D., Mrs., Dry Goods Store, 218 Queen St.
Wurdemann, John C., Dry Goods Store, 218 Queen St
Wyatt, E., Mrs., 173 Church St.
Wyatt, John R., Shipwright, 173 Church St
Wyatt, Violetta, Mrs., John St., Hampstead, Neck
Yates, Ann, Mrs., 13 Wall St.
Yates, D., Mrs., 3 S. Bay St.
Yates, Eliza Jane, Mrs., Water St.
Yates, Jeremiah A., Planter, Ladson's Court
Yates, Thomas, Carpenter, 27 King St.
Yeadon & Lewis, Collection Office, Meeting St., Next to State Arsenal
Yeadon, Richard, Bank of State of S. C., Res. 35 King St.
Yeadon, Richard, Jr , Attorney, Meeting St., Next to State Arsenal
Yeadon, William, Attorney, 30 Archdale St.
You, John C., Teacher, 4 Archdale St.
Young, Dinah, Mrs., 77 Broad St
Young, John P., 167 King St.
Young, Joseph, Ship Chandler, 194 E. Bay St., Res., 263 E. Bay St.
Young, William, Baker, 36 Church St
Zealy, Joseph, 61 King St
Zylstra, John, 33 Society St

135

The Directory for 1829

The directory for 1829 was published by O Cromwell under the title of *Directory of Guide to the Residences and Places of Businesses of the Inhabitants of the City of Charleston and Its Environs; Prefaced with a Description of Our Various Public Buildings and Other Local Information* (Charleston: James S Burges, 1828). It has 2,681 entries An Oliver Cromwell was listed in the directories of 1803-1809 as an attorney or sheriff. This may be a son by the same name. The directory lists white residents north of Boundary (now Calhoun) St., the area known as the Neck, separately but does not include Free People of Color Here those living in the Neck have been combined with the residents of the city with the word "Neck" appearing after their entries.

Abrahams, E., Wholesale Dry Goods Store, 300 King St.
Abrahams, I , Widow, 33 Meeting St
Abrahams, M , Store, 193 E. Bay St
Adams, Jasper, Rev., D D , President, Charleston College, Radcliffborough, S W. End, Neck
Addison, Joseph, Grocer & Cabinet Maker, S W. cr Pitt & Montague Sts
Adger & Black, Merchants, N. cr E Bay St. & Kiddell's Whf
Adger, James, Merchant, Firm of Adger & Black, King St , E. Side, btw. Wolf & Spring Sts., Neck
Aiken, William, Jr., S cr King & Ann Sts., Neck
Aiken, William S., cr King & Ann Sts , Neck
Aimer, S., Grocer, 199 E Bay St.
Ainger, Joseph M., Cooper, 12 Amen St
Airs, Ann, Widow, 85 Meeting St.
Airs, Mary, Widow, 27 Archdale St.
Akin, Ann, Widow, 11 Cumberland St
Akin, Thomas, M.D , 11 Cumberland St
Aldrich, Robert, 15 Tradd St., op Bedon's Al
Alexander, Abraham, Store, King St., W Side, 2nd Door N of Mary St , Neck
Alexander David, President, Union Insurance Co , 7 Logan St
Alexander, J J., 14 Hasell St.
Alexander, Samuel, Harbor Master, 90 King St
Allan, Robert M , Factor, 46 Tradd St
Allan, Sarah, 46 Tradd St.
Allan, William & Son, Factors, S C Insurance Co. Whf.
Allen, Ellener, Nurse, Beaufain St
Allen, S & M Co , Exchange Brokers, 6 Broad St.
Allen, Thomas, John St., S. Side, Neck
Alston, William, N cr Washington St & Smith's Whf , Neck
Alston, William, Planter, 25 King St
Ancrum, Jane, Widow, N.W cr Church & S Bay Sts
Ancrum, William Washington, N.W cr Church & S. Bay Sts
Anderson, E K , Accountant, at Mrs Muir's, 24 Broad St
Anderson, Robert, Dry Goods Stores, 222 & 360 King St , Res 222
Andrews, Louisa, 35 Hasell St
Andrews, Warren, Factor, Kunhardt's Whf

Annely, T. S , cr. Vanderhorst's Whf. & E. Bay St
Anthony, J. C , Tallow Chandler, Mary St., near King St , Neck
Arden, Thomas, Cabinet Maker, Vanderhorst St., Neck
Ardrion, William, State Constable, 250 E Bay St
Arms, Catharine, Store 194 King St.
Arms, Elizabeth, Widow, 44 Anson St
Arms, William, Bricklayer, Radcliff St., S. Side, Neck
Armstrong, William, Accountant, Ordinary's Office, Res Wentworth St., near Meeting St.
Arnold, J. J. B., Tailor, 84 Broad St
Arnold, L., E. Bay St., cr Magwood's Whf.
Artman, Peter, Coachmaker, 5 Archdale St
Artope, George, Nassau St., Neck
Ash, John, Boarding House, 17 Elliott St.
Ash, John, Planter, 8 S. Bay St.
Ashby, John, Boarding House, 20 Elliott St
Ashby, Thomas, Planter, King St., E. Side, 2nd Door Above Hudson St., Neck
Ashe, Richard, Planter, 8 S. Bay St
Assalit, J , Teacher of Languages, 7 Orange St.
Astaix, Elizabeth, Widow, 193 King St.
Atchison, John, Stables, Church St., a Little N of Saint Philip's Church
Aubin, Joseph, Porter Cellar, 183 E Bay St , op Chisolm's Upper Whf.
Audler, E , Surgeon Dentist, 110 Meeting St.
Auld, Donald, Wentworth St., near Meeting St
Aveilhe, Louisa, Widow, W. cr. Boundary & Middle Sts.
Avery, P., Grocer, E. cr. Champney & Exchange Sts
Axson, Ann, Widow, 85 Meeting St.
Axson, Jacob, Attorney, 19 Meeting St.
Axson, John, Planter, S. Side Charlotte St , Mazyckborough, Neck
Axson, Sarah, Private Boarding House, N cr Church & Cumberland Sts.
Babcock, S & Co Booksellers, 321 King St.
Babson, Anna R , cr. Church & Linguard Sts.
Backman, John, Rev., Pastor, Lutheran Church, Pinckney St., W. Side, Cannonborough, Neck
Bacot, D D., Teller, S. C. Bank, Res 11 Lamboll St
Bacot, Henry H., 95 Meeting St.
Bacot, Peter, Cashier, Branch Bank of U S , Res N. cr Magazine & Archdale Sts.
Bacot, Thomas W., Jr Assistant Postmaster, Res N.E cr King & Tradd Sts.
Bacot, Thomas W., Sr., Postmaster & Cashier, S C Bank, Res. N E. cr. King & Tradd Sts.
Badger, James, Clerk, Circular Church, 45 Wentworth St.
Bailey, A., Watchmaker, N. cr. King & Beaufain Sts.
Bailey J. S., Accountant, S cr. Chisolm's Lower Whf
Bailey, William E , Professor, Charleston College, Res. 8 Guignard St
Baird, John B., Wolf St., Hampstead, Neck
Baker, Gregory & Co., Hat Store, N.E. cr King & George Sts.
Baker, Martha, Dyer, 167 Meeting St.
Baker, R. B., Jr., Custom House, Res. 16 Legare St
Baker, R E , Planter, 16 Legare St.
Baker, R. S , N.E. cr Broad & Friend Sts.
Ball, John, Planter, 27 Hasell St

136

Ball, -----, Misses, Church St., op Stoll's Al

Ball, -----, Widow of Isaac, N. cr E Bay & Vernon Sts

Ballantine, Jane, Widow, 45 Tradd St.

Bampfield, James, 17 George St

Bampfield, M. B., 52 Society St

Bampfield, T, Broker, Res. 16 George St

Bancroft, James, Merchant, 164 E. Bay St

Barbot, Anthony, Merchant, 55 E. Bay St.

Barguet, John P., Umbrella Manufactory, Meeting St., One Door N. of Cumberland St

Barit, G. E., Grocer, cr King & Smith Sts.

Barker & Watson, Grocers, N E. cr. Market & Meeting Sts.

Barker, J S, 18 Society St

Barker, James, Truss Maker, 28 Pinckney

Barker, Samuel G., Attorney, Charlotte St., N Side, Neck

Barksdale, Thomas, 83 Wentworth St.

Barnes, Hannah, Widow, 118 Meeting St.

Barnes, Thomas, Miller, Lucas' Mills, Cannonborough, Neck

Barnes, W. B, 118 Meeting St.

Baron, Elizabeth, Widow, E. cr. Tradd & Greenhill Sts.

Baron, Sarah, Widow, 99 Broad St.

Barre, John, Fruit Store, 46 Market St.

Barrelk, Torre & Co., Fancy Store, 65 Broad St.

Barrelli, John, Merchant, 65 Broad St.

Barrelli, Joseph, Merchant, 13 Champney St.

Barrett, Isaac, Factor, Kunhardt's Whf, Res N.E. cr King & Boundary Sts.

Barron, Peter & Brothers, Hair Dressers, 1 Tradd St.

Bartlett, Hiram, Shoe Store, S.W. cr. King & Market Sts.

Bateman, Edward, Hair Dresser, 224 E. Bay St.

Bay, Andrew, 16 Logan St.

Bay, Elihu Hall, Hon., Senior Judge, Court of Common Pleas, Res.16 Logan St

Beattie, James, Accountant, W. End Beaufain St

Beckmam, C J., Grist Mill, Boundary St., N. Side, btw. Coming & St Philip's Sts., Neck

Beckman, A., Painter & Glazier, 151 Meeting St

Beckman, G, Grocer, N cr Coming & George Sts

Bee, Barnard E., Capt., Guard, 115 Tradd St

Bee, Francis, Seamstress, Pitt St

Bee, James, 4 Friend St.

Bee, James M., Accountant, Church St, W Side, near Chalmers St.

Bee, Joseph F., Planter, 87 Boundary St

Bee, Price, Cooper, S. C Society Hall, Meeting St.

Bee, R. R., Cooper, near Exchange, Res 48 E. Bay St

Bee, Thomas, St. Michael's Al.

Bee, W C., Accountant, 4 Friend St

Bee, William, S C. Society Hall, Meeting St.

Behrman, Charles, Store, S.W. cr. Church & Market Sts

Beile, J. C., Agent For Roorback, 296 King St

Belcher, Manning, Instructor, 1 Bull St.

Bell, Ann, 55 Society St

Bell, David, 23 Society St.

Bell, David, Jr., 21 Society St.

Bell, John L, 23 Society St

Bell, W., Bricklayer, 46 Society St

Bellinger, Elizabeth B., S.E. cr. Boundary & Coming Sts.

Bellinger, John, M.D., 37 St. Philip's St.

Bellinger, Joseph, Hon., Planter, 20 Pitt St

Belsen, Mary, Widow, King St, E. Side, btw Wolf & Spring Sts, Neck

Bement, Edward, Wholesale Grocery, 130 E Bay St, cr Magwood's Whf.

Bennett, Catherine E, Widow, S Side Charlotte St, Mazyckborough, Neck

Bennett, Hannah, Widow, S cr Amherst & Wolf Sts, Hampstead, Neck

Bennett, John, Teller, Planters' & Mechanics' Bank, Beaufain St., op. Pitt St.

Bennett, Joseph, Attorney & City Treasurer, 10 New St

Bennett, Joseph W., 10 New St.

Bennett, L. M, Boarding House, E cr Archdale & Queen Sts.

Bennett, Thomas, Lumber Mills, Cannonborough, Neck

Bennett, Thomas, Sr., Mrs, King St, near Quaker Meeting House

Bennett, -----, Widow of W. S., King St, near Quaker Meeting House

Bennett, William J., Cannonborough, Neck

Benoist, John B., Baker, N cr. Reid & King Sts, Neck

Bentham, Robert, Attorney, 49 Coming St.

Berbant, Samuel, Tailor, 352 King St

Bernard, F., 15 Market

Berney, Alfred, 45 Society St

Berney, Mary, Widow, 45 Society St.

Berney, Robert, Broker, 1 State St, Res 45 Society St

Berney, William, Merchant, 65 E. Bay St., Res. 45 Society St.

Berrett, William H., Bookseller & Stationer, 14 Broad St.

Berry, Alexander, 14 Water St.

Berry, Peter, Confectioner 251 King St.

Berry, R. H., Dry Goods Store, 261 King St

Bessent, P. G., N.E cr. Wentworth & Coming Sts

Beusse, John H, Store, 223 E Bay St.

Bicais, P P., Tavern, 127 E Bay St.

Bigelow & Birch, Northern Dry Goods Store, 270 King St

Bigelow, Lyman, Tallow Chandler, St. Philip's St., W. Side, btw. Warren & Radcliff Sts., Neck

Bird, John Stiles, Fancy Store, 22 Broad St., Res 49 King St.

Bird, Sarah F., Widow, Burns Ln.

Bird, William, Shipwright, 20 Pinckney St

Birmingham, John, Rev., N E. cr. Broad & Friend Sts

Birnie, W. & G., Merchants, 21 Broad St.

Bishop, S N., 118 Church St.

Black, Alexander, Maj, 102 Wentworth St

Black, Alexander W., Store, 105 E. Bay St.

Black, Elizabeth, Widow, Coming St, E Side, N. St Paul's Church, Neck

Black, James, Bootmaker, 36 Broad St

Black, James, Merchant, Firm of Adger & Black, S. Side Spring St., Neck

Black, W P., Accountant, 195 King St.

Black, William, 11 Queen St.

Blackwood, John, Merchant, Chisolm's Lower Whf, Res 10 Montague St

Blackwood, S. C., 18 Pitt St.

Blackwood, Thomas, President, Planters' & Mechanics' Bank, 18 Pitt St.

Blain, W S., Male & Female Seminary, 26 State St.
Blair, Andrew, Wheelwright, S. cr. Meeting & Henrietta Sts., Neck
Blair, William, Merchant, N.E. cr. Church & Broads Sts.
Blake, Edward, U. S. Branch Bank, 8 King St.
Blake, John, Tanner, John St , N. Side, btw King & Meeting Sts., Neck
Blanchard, John, Shoemaker, 135 E. Bay St.
Blaney, Joseph, Constable, 15 Chalmers St.
Blewer, John G., Store, King St., E Side, btw Wolf & Spring Sts., Neck
Bloomfield, John, Instructor, 118 King St
Blum, F., Carpenter, btw. Mary & Cannon Sts., Neck
Blum, Mary, Widow, King St., W Side, btw Mary & Cannon Sts., Neck
Blumon, J., Carpenter, 109 Church St
Boag, W. S & Co. Wholesale Druggists, 285 King St.
Bock, Henry, S.E. cr. Coming & Vanderhorst Sts., Neck
Bohlen, J., Grocer, 79 Archdale St.
Boisdon, H , Baker, 124 Meeting St.
Bolds, Selina S., Mantua Maker, Mazyck St.
Bolles, A , Female Academy, College St , near Charleston College
Bones, W , Merchant, 39 Broad St
Bonnea, H , 109 Church St.
Bonneau, John E., 13 Church St.
Bonneau, S., U. S. Branch Bank, Res. 7 Church St
Bonner, E M., Mrs., Milliner, S.W. cr King & Clifford Sts.
Bonner, John, Cabinet Maker, 1 Clifford St
Borch, Peter, Grocer, 211 E Bay St.
Bordenave, John, Hairdresser, 150 Meeting St
Bosset, Vincent, Billiard Room, King St., W. Side, btw. Mary & Warren Sts., Neck
Boucheneau, C., Customs House, Res Magazine St., near Jail.
Boudo, -----, Widow of L., Jewellery, 156 King St.
Bounetheau, B B Bricklayer, 5 State St.
Bounetheau, Edward, Carpenter, N. Side, btw. Pitt & Coming Sts , Neck
Bounetheau, H. B , Accountant, 5 State St.
Bounetheau, J. W , Printer, 5 State St.
Bounetheau, John, Accountant, King St , W Side, btw. Vanderhorst & Coming Sts., Neck
Bours, Luke, 58 Wentworth St.
Bousquet, Peter, Store, 183 King St
Boutan, Peter B , Baker, King St., W. Side, btw. Vanderhorst & Warren Sts , Neck
Bowen, Nathaniel, Right Rev., Bishop, Protestant Episcopal Church of S C , Elliott St , W. Side, Cannonborough
Bowman, S , Grocer, N. cr. Boyce & Henry, Factors, Fitzsimons' Whf.
Boyce, Ker, W. cr. King & Boundary Sts
Boyce, R., Millinery, King St., op. Liberty St
Boyle, A., Mazyck St.
Boyle, Alexander, Lucas' Mills, Cannonborough, Neck
Boylston & Douglass, Apothecaries, 118 Church St.
Boylston, Henry, M.D , Druggist, N. cr. King & Hudson Sts., Neck
Bradley, H , Burns Ln.

Bradley, J. C. Blacksmith, Burns Ln
Brady, J., Grocer, 16 Anson St.
Braid, Matthew, Church St
Brailsford, Edward, M.D., 39 Tradd St.
Brailsford, Eliza, 12 Hasell St.
Brailsford, Elizabeth, 31 S. Bay St
Brailsford, John, Roper's Whf., Res E Bay St.
Brailsford, W. M., 39 Tradd St
Brailsford, W. R., Factor, Roper's Whf., Res. 68 Tradd St
Brandt, Ann F., Widow 254 E. Bay St
Brandt, Mary Ann, Coming St., near Boundary St
Brase, Peter, Grocer, 108 Tradd St
Bremar, Henry, Dentist, 20 Pickney St.
Bremer, John, Grocer, W. cr Charlotte & Elizabeth Sts , Neck
Brenan, Hannah, Milliner, 282 King St
Brewster, James & Co., Coachmakers, Wentworth St , 1 Door E. of King St
Bridgwood, T , Wholesale Crockery, S. cr. King & Beaufain Sts
Bright, R., 11 Broad St.
Bringloe, Richard, Boatbuilder, 65 Church St
Brisbane, Mary, Widow, 29 Meeting St
Brodie, Robert, Accountant, 39 Meeting St.
Broughton, A., 15 George St.
Broughton, G. S., Rope Maker, N. cr. Meeting St. & Lines, Neck
Broughton, Mary, Miss, Boundary St., N. Side, btw Pitt & Coming Sts , Neck
Broughton, Mary, Widow, S Side Boundary St., op. Orphan House
Brow, Harriet, Widow, 91 Church St.
Brown & Weissinger, Store, King St , E. Side, btw. Cannon & Bridge Sts., Neck
Brown, A. H., N. cr. E. Bay St. & Vanderhorst's Whf.
Brown, Alexander, St. Philip's St., E. Side, btw. Cannon & Mary Sts., Neck
Brown, Charles T , Planter, S cr. Anson & George Sts
Brown, Edward, 12 Church St.
Brown, J. A , Hairdresser, 72 Queen St.
Brown, J. F., 79 Church St.
Brown, J. M., Planter, 79 Church St
Brown, James, N. cr. E. Bay St. & Vanderhorst's Whf
Brown, John, Cabinet Maker, 84 King St.
Brown, Joseph, Rev , Pastor, Mariner's Church, Res W cr. Church & Cumberland Sts
Brown, Joshua, Mrs., N. cr. E. Bay St. & Vanderhorst's Whf.
Brown, Lavinia, Widow, N. cr. Smith's Whf. & Washington St., Neck
Brown, Malcom, Boot Maker, 45 Anson St
Brown, Moses, Hairdresser, 109 Church St
Brown, Peter, Hairdresser, 24 Elliott St
Brown, R. E., Factor, 79 Church St.
Brown, Robert, Factor, 79 Church St.
Brown, Tunis & Co., Factors, Roper's Whf
Brown, W. G., Planter, 79 Church St.
Brown, William, 4 Minority St.
Browne, A. J , 22 Society St.
Browne, Elizabeth, Widow, 22 Society St.
Browne, G. W., 22 Society St.

Browne, H. N , Bricklayer, 22 Society St.
Browne, James, Butcher, Wolf St , Hampstead, Neck
Browne, John Davies, Instructor, 22 Society St.
Browne, R. C , 47 Tradd St.
Browne, R. J., Block & Pump Maker, 267 E Bay St.
Bruce, Charles, Merchant, 18 Vanderhorst's Whf.
Bruen, John W., 282 King St.
Bruen, Mary E., Milliner, 282 King St.
Bruorton, J. A., Tavern & Store, E. cr. Broad & Logan Sts.
Brush, John, Hat Store, 263 King St.
Bryan, John, Planter, N.W. cr. Hasell & Anson Sts.
Bryan, Johnathan, Dry Goods Store, 335 King St.
Bryant, C. H., Wharfinger, 29 King St
Bryce, Mary E., Widow, 74 King St
Buckheister, John A., Accountant, Henrietta St., Neck
Budd, T. S., Mariner, 52 Tradd St
Buerhaus, H. D., Tailor, 142 King St.
Buist, Arthur, Rev., Pastor, First Presbyterian Church, 45 Tradd St
Buist, Edward T., 5 Church St.
Buist, Henry, M.D., 119 Church St
Buist, Mary, Widow, 5 Church St
Bull, Elizabeth, Widow, 8 Lamboll St
Bullen, S., Shoe Store, 271 King St.
Bulow, John J., Maj., Planter, N cr. King & Cannon Sts., Neck
Burch, Edward C., Accountant, 128 Queen St.
Burch, Sarah, 232 Meeting St.
Burckmyer, Cornelias, 25 Cumberland St.
Burckmyer, J. C. & Co., Merchants, 140 E. Bay St
Burckmyer, J. C., 24 Society St.
Burdell, R F., Store, N. cr. Tradd & E Bay Sts , Res. near W End Beaufain St
Burden & Ioor, Factors, Chisolm's Lower Whf.
Burden, Kinsey, Jr , Factor, N. cr. Smith's Ln. & Meeting St
Burden, Kinsey, Planter, N. cr. Smith's Ln. & Meeting St
Burdges, S B., Oyster House, N.E cr. Queen & State Sts.
Burger, Samuel, Tax Collector, Fire Proof Building, Res. Broad St., W cr. Gadsden's Al.
Burges, James S., Printer, 44 Queen St
Burgoyne, William, Druggist & Apothecary, N. cr. Broad & E. Bay Sts , Res. N. cr. Water & E. Bay Sts
Burie, Daniel & Son, Blacksmiths, 127 Meeting St.
Burke, Alexander M'Neile, Meeting St., 2 Doors Above Boundary St.
Burke, J. H., 65 Church St
Burke, Mercy, Widow, 8 Mazyck St.
Burn, William, Keeper, New Bridge Ferry, N.W. End Cannonborough, Neck
Burnham, Robert W., Accountant, N. Side Boundary St , btw. St. Philip's & Coming Sts., Neck
Burnham, Thomas, Carpenter, N. Side Boundary St , btw St. Philip's & Coming Sts., Neck
Burnham, W., Locksmith, 126 Pinckney St.
Burns, James, Pilot, 12 Lynch's Ln.
Burns, John M., Shoemaker, 108 Church St
Burrage, L., Grocer, N.E cr. Rutledge & Wentworth Sts.
Burrell, W., Bootmaker, 52 Broad St.
Burrows, F., Pilot, S. cr. Water & Meeting Sts.
Burrows, James T , Carpenter, S cr. Water & Meeting Sts.

Burrows, S. S., cr Water & Meeting Sts.
Bussacker, Charles, Dry Goods Store, 307 King St
Bussey & Hawley, Grocers, Vendue Range
Butler, C. P , Silversmith, 135 King St.
Buxbaum, John C., M.D., 10 Friend St.
Byrd, J. J., S E. cr Middle & Minority Sts.
Byrd, Mary, Boarding House, 188 E. Bay St.
Bythewood, M. W , Rev , Philadelphia St.
Cabeuil, L., Merchant Tailor, 99 Church St.
Calder, Alexander, S Side John St., btw. Meeting & King Sts., Neck
Calder, J. & J. Merchants, Chisolm's Lower Whf
Calder, James, Grocer, Church St , near St. Philip's Church
Calder, James, Merchant, 38 Broad St
Calder, William, Store, 61 Meeting St.
Caldwell, W. A., Auctioneer & Commission Merchant, S Side Vendue Range, Res. 107 Meeting St.
Callender, Joseph, 5 Tradd St.
Came, William, Shoemaker, Beaufain St
Cameron, Amelia, 92 Church St
Campbell, A W., Factor, Res. 14 New St.
Campbell, Alexander, Grocer, 168 King St.
Campbell, J. M., M.D , 95 Broad St
Campbell, John, S.E cr. Ann & Meeting Sts., Neck
Campbell, Peter, Hotel, 246 King St.
Campbell, Peter, Tailor, Henrietta St., Neck
Campbell, Samuel, Hairdresser, 245 E. Bay St
Canaday, H. E., cr Tradd & Legare Sts.
Canter, Emanuel, Jr., Accountant, Coming St , E. Side, near Vanderhorst St., Neck
Canter, Emanuel, N. Side Columbus St , near Tivoli Garden, Neck
Cantwell, P., Factor, Gadsden's Whf.
Capers, L. G & Co. Store, 338 King St
Capers, William, Rev., N.E. cr. Boundary & Pitt Sts., Neck
Cardozo, David, Editor, The Southern Patriot, 99 E. Bay St.
Cardozo, Isaac N , Patriot Office, 99 E. Bay St.
Cardozo, J. N , Customs House, Res. 99 E. Bay St.
Carew & Childs, Lumber Mills, N. End Washington St , Mazyckborough, Neck
Carew, Edward, E. cr Wall & Laurens Sts
Carey, Eugene, Accountant, N. cr. King & Hudson Sts , Neck
Cariven, L., Widow, King St , W. Side, btw. Vanderhorst & Warren Sts., Neck
Carman, M., Milliner, 301 King St.
Carmand, Francis, Wollen Draper, Men's Mercer, Etc , 86 Queen St.
Carmille, John, Butcher, Meeting St., W Side, btw Columbus & Wolf Sts., Neck
Carnochan, Richard, 1 Crafts Whf.
Carpenter, James, Butcher, Cannon St., S Side, Neck
Carr, C. D., Boarding House, cr. State & Amen Sts
Carr, James, 10 Berresford St.
Carr, Robert, Mary St., N. Side, btw. King & Meeting Sts , Neck
Carrere, C J., E cr. Friend & Broad Sts
Carrere, Charles, E. cr. Friend & Broad Sts.
Carrere, W J., E cr Friend & Broad Sts.
Carroll, B , Jr., Radcliffborough, N W End, Neck

Carroll, Bartholomew, Radcliffborough, N W End, Neck
Carroll, Charles Rivers, Attorney, Radcliffborough, N.W End, Neck
Carson, Elisha, Merchant, King St., E. Side, btw Wolf & Spring Sts., Neck
Carson, Elizabeth, 90 Tradd St.
Carson, W., Grocer, 144 King St.
Carson, William, Planter, 90 Tradd St
Carsten, John, City Scavenger, 30 Society St
Cart, John, Jr., Bookkeeper, Planters' & Mechanics' Bank, Res Meeting St , nearly op St Michael's Al.
Cart, John, Measurer of Lumber, 28 Bull St.
Cart, Vernal, Attorney, 28 Bull St.
Carter, Elizabeth, Store, King St , E Side, btw. Ann & Mary Sts., Neck
Carter, Elizabeth, Widow, 352 King St
Carter, William, Broker & Auctioneer, 2 Logan St.
Caskin, John, Carpenter, Charlotte St , Neck
Catherwood, J. J., Watchmaker, 63 Broad St
Caulfield, S., Cabinet Maker, Philadelphia St.
Causse, Adolphe, S W. cr. Smith & Montague Sts
Chadwick, Samuel, Merchant, Crafts' S Whf
Chamberlin, J. & Co., Wholesale Crockery, 277 King St.
Champlin, Jane, School, Beaufain St.
Chancey, W., N.E. cr Broad & Friend Sts.
Chanlat, Harriet, Widow, 69 Tradd St
Chapeau, J B , Confectioner, 128 Church St.
Chapman, Eliza, S.W. cr. Broad & King Sts.
Chapman, James, 76 King St
Chapman, Thomas, 51 E. Bay St.
Chapman, W. & T , Factors, Edmondston's Whf.
Chapman, W , 51 E. Bay St.
Charrol, P., 72 State St
Chartrand, Philip, Tivoli Garden, S E. cr Columbus & Meeting Sts., near the Lines, Neck
Cheesborough & Campbell, Factors, S. cr. E Bay St & Vanderhorst's Whf
Cheesborough, J. M , E Bay St , near Boundary St.
Chew, Thomas R , Blacksmith, Lucas St., Cannonborough, Neck
Chiffelle, Thomas, Custom House, 131 Queen St.
Child, Hail, Mariner, 24 State St.
Childs, Robert, Baker, Meeting St., 1 Door N of Market St
Childs' Mills, Neck
Chisolm & Taylor, Factors, Chisolm's Lower Whf.
Chisolm, A. H., Wharfinger, Chisolm's Upper Whf
Chisolm, George, Factor & Wharfinger, 23 E Bay St
Chisolm, Mary Ann, Widow, 17 King St.
Chisolm, Robert, Planter, S E. cr S Bay & Meeting Sts.
Chisolme, S., Charleston House, S W cr King & George Sts.
Chitty, C. C , Attorney, Res 20 George St.
Chitty, J W., Court House Sq., Meeting St.
Chitty, Richard, Butcher, cr Nassau & Wolf Sts , Neck
Chrietzburg, C , 35 King St.
Chrietzburg, George, Baker, 42 King St
Christian, Ann, Boarding House, 3 Champney St.
Christie, Johanna, Widow, 98 Church St.
Chupein, Louis, Mineral Water Establishment, 13 Broad St

Chur, George, Store, 26 Market St
Church, Margaret, Umbrella Maker, 16 St. Philip's St
Clancy, John, Grocer, King St., W. Side, btw Vanderhorst & Warren Sts , Neck
Clark, B & Co , Dry Goods Store, 163 King St
Clark, James, Tailor, 99 Meeting St
Clark, William, Carpenter, 33 Beaufain St
Clarke, Charles, Grocer, S cr. E Bay & Tradd Sts
Clarke, Richard, Mariner, 46 Church St.
Clarkson, -----, Mrs. Widow, 2 Bull St.
Cleapor, & Fields, Sail Makers, Lothrop's Whf
Cleary, N. G., Late High Sheriff, Charleston District, Res Broad St., op Roman Catholic Cathedral
Clement, Sarah, Widow, 101 Queen St
Clements, -----, Mrs , N.E. cr. Boundary & Coming Sts., Neck
Clifford, Henry, Factor, Mey's Whf., Res 8 Middle St
Clissey, A., Miss, Store, 180 King St
Clough, J B., Merchant, 188 E. Bay St
Cloves, P , 45 State St.
Clyde, Thomas M., Tanner, Amherst St , N Side, Hampstead, Neck
Coates, C., Instructor, Queen St., op Friend St
Coates, Pinckey, Miss
Cobia, Ann, Mrs. School, Reid St., S. Side, btw. King & Meeting Sts., Neck
Cobia, D , Meeting St , E Side, btw Wolf & Columbus Sts , Neck
Cobia, Francis J., Butcher, Reid St , S. Side, btw. King & Meeting Sts., Neck
Coburn, Anna, Widow, 1 George St
Cochran, Charles B , Charleston College, 14 Society St
Cochran, Charles B., cr. Archdale & Magazine Sts
Cochran, Henry, Attorney, 14 Society St
Cochran, John C., Planter, W End Cannon St., Cannonborough, Neck
Cochran, R E., Jr., 14 Society St.
Cochran, Robert, 14 Society St
Cochran, Thomas, Notary Public, W. End Cannon St., Cannonborough, Neck
Cochrane, M., Widow, 120 King St.
Coffin, Louisa M., Widow, N cr. Water & Meeting Sts
Cogwell, H & Co Northern Dry Goods Store, 324 King St.
Cohen & Mordecai, Auctioneers & Commission Merchants, N. cr E. Bay St & Vendue Range
Cohen, David, Planter, 103 Broad St
Cohen, Hyam, Accountant, 8 Orange St
Cohen, J I., Jr. & Brothers, Lot. & Exchange Brokers, 199 E. Bay St.
Cohen, M. M , 86 Tradd St.
Cohen, Mordecai, 103 Broad St
Cohen, N. A , Store, 169 E Bay St
Cohen, P. M , 86 Tradd St
Cohen, P S , 356 King St.
Cohen, S I , Store, 356 King St
Cohrs, H A , Linen & Dry Goods Store, 322 King St.
Colburn, F A. & Co., Merchants, 234 King St
Colburn, J. S., Dry Goods Store, N E. cr. Broad & King Sts.
Colcock, -----, Mrs 11 Lamboll St

Cole, John, Painter, 7 Tradd St., at Mrs Watson's
Coleman, Eliza, Widow, N. cr Magazine & Mazyck Sts
Coleman, L. N., cr. King & Society Sts.
Colhoun, Isabelle, Widow, Meeting St , op. St. Michael's Al.
Collier, W R., Millwright, 14 Wentworth St.
Collier, William, Custom House, Res 14 Wentworth St.
Collins, John, 169 Meeting St
Colzy, A , 111 Church St.
Coming, R.C , St. Philip's St., W. Side, near Lines, Neck
Condy, Jeremiah, Merchant, 122 E. Bay St., Res. Meeting St., 2 Doors S. of Circular Church
Condy, Thomas Doughty, Attorney, 9 Church St.
Connelly, Catherine, 26 S Bay St.
Connelly, Elizabeth, Store, 26 S. Bay St.
Conner, H. W., Factor, Edmondston's Whf., Res. 96 Church St.
Conner, John, Saddlery, 349 King St.
Conner, Samuel, Corn Mill, Ellery St., Res. 32 Hasell St.
Cook, Daniel, Grocery & Wagon Yard, E. Side, btw Mary & Reid Sts., Neck
Cook, J. A , Grocery Stores, S.E cr. Coming & Vanderhorst Sts. & S.E. cr. Pinckney & Cannon Sts., Neck
Cooper, G. W., 25 St. Philip's St., op. Liberty St.
Cooper, Henry P., N E. cr. Warren & St. Philip's Sts., Neck
Cooper, Mary, Mrs., 25 St. Philip's St., op. Liberty St.
Cooper, N., Shoe Store, N.W. cr. King & Queen Sts.
Cooper, T J., Boot Maker, 87 Broad St.
Cooper, William, Bootmaker, 64 King St.
Corbett, James, Dry Goods Store, 330 King St.
Corbett, John H., S.W cr. Lynch & Bull Sts.
Corbett, Mary, S. Bay St.
Corbett, Thomas, Planter, S.W. cr. Lynch & Bull Sts.
Corby, John, Blacksmith, O'Neal & Bird's Whf., Res cr. Vernon & Washington Sts
Corcoran, Jane, 49 King St.
Cordes, Rebecca, Widow, Charlotte St., N. Side, Neck
Corker, Thomas, Boat Builder, 26 Pinckney
Corleis, P., Grocery, cr. Montague & Bull Sts.
Cormick, Thomas, Factor, Vanderhorst's Whf., Res. 66 Church St.
Corniskey & Cubie, Grocers, New St., near Theatre
Corrie, Samuel, Wheelwright, King St , E. Side, btw. John & Ann Sts., Neck
Cortee, H. C., Grocer, Edmondston's Whf.
Cournand, C., Widow, 234 Meeting St.
Course, Isaac, Merchant, Vendue Range, N. Side
Courtenay, Edward S., Magistrate & School, 4 Brownlee's Range, King St., W. Side, Above Hudson St., Neck
Courtenay, James, Charleston College, Res. St. Philip's St., nearly op. Liberty St.
Cowan, Elizabeth, Widow, 32 Pinckney St.
Cowan, Maria, Clear Starcher, 32 Beaufain St.
Cox, O. W , Accountant, King St., E. Side, btw. Wolf & Spring Sts., Neck
Crafts, Margaret, Miss, 19 Bull St
Crafts, William, Sr., Mrs., Coming St., E Side, btw. Vanderhorst & Boundary Sts., Neck
Craig, Mary, Milliner, King St., W Side, btw Mary &

Warren Sts , Neck
Craig, Mary, Widow, N cr Burns Ln. & Meeting St
Cramer, George, Deputy City Marshal, 243 E. Bay St.
Crandal, Ann, Widow, S Side Spring St., Neck
Cranston, Mary, Widow, 31 Mazyck St.
Crawford, Grace, Widow, 4 Magazine St.
Crawford, John, Wharf Holder, Vanderhorst's Whf. Res. 1 Lynch St
Crecac, Adelaide, Widow, Meeting St., E. Side, btw Wolf & Columbus Sts., Neck
Cregier, Thomas, Coachmaker, Henrietta St., Neck
Crocker, D. & Co., Merchants, Magwood's Whf.
Crocker, D., Merchant, 23 Tradd St.
Crocker, E., Store, N.W cr Wentworth & King Sts.
Croft, George, 13 Cumberland St
Cromwell, Clara, Widow, 4 West St
Cromwell, Samuel, Bricklayer, 7 Back St.
Cross, Charles, at Smith's Store, E Bay St., near Exchange
Cross, George Warren, Attorney, S.E. cr. Meeting & Tradd Sts
Cross, William, Bricklayer, 6 Beaufain St.
Crovat, L J., Merchant, 172 E. Bay St.
Crovat, P., Sr., Store, 269 King St.
Crowby, T., Blacksmith, King St., E. Side, btw. Ann & Mary Sts., Neck
Crowly, Hannah, Widow, 76 Broad St
Crozier, William, Grocery, N. cr. Washington & Charlotte Sts., Neck
Cruger, Henry, Attorney, Short St
Cruger, Lewis, Attorney, 82 Broad St
Cruickshanks, D , Bootmaker, 22 Queen St.
Cruickshanks, William, King St., E. Side, btw. John & Hudson Sts., Neck
Cruse, Amey, Widow, 8 Mazyck St
Cudworth, John, Printer, 49 Society St.
Cunningham, A., Carpenter, 2 Beaufain St
Cunningham, A. F., Printer, 36 Queen St.
Cunningham, A. J., Watchmaker, 219 King St.
Curtis, E. M., Carpenter, 22 Beaufain St
Cuthbert, James, Planter, 6 Smith St
Cutting & Whittemore, Soap & Candle Manufactory, N.W. cr Radcliff & St. Philip's Sts , Neck
Cutting, John, Tallow Chandler, W. Side St. Philip's St , btw. Warren & Radcliff Sts., Neck
Dalcho, Frederick, Rev. Dr., Assistant Minister, St. Michael's Church, at Mrs. Torre's, 4 New St.
Daley, William, Store, 156 Meeting St.
Dalgliesh, H., Bricklayer, S.W. cr. Queen & Mazyck Sts.
Dalton, James, Apothecary, 78 Queen St.
Darby, A. E., Mrs., Milliner, 333 King St.
Darby, Mary, Widow, 64 Tradd St.
Darevedo, Rachel, Toy Store, 169 King St
Dart, B. S., Factor, 55 Tradd St.
Datty, J., Miss, Female Academy, 83 King St.
Davega, Abraham, Store, King St., E Side, btw. Reid & Wolf Sts , Neck
Davenport & Co., Merchants, 6 Crafts' S. Whf.
Davenport & Rice, Wholesale Shoe Store, 303 King St
Davenport, Charles, at Mrs. Davis', 25 Tradd St.
Davis, George Y., Merchant, 52 E. Bay St.
Davis, Jacob, House & Sign Painter, 34 Tradd St.

Davis, Jane, Private Boarding House, 25 Tradd St.
Davis, John, Mariner, 37 E. Bay St
Davis, John S., N W. cr. John & Meeting Sts., Neck
Davis, Martha, Widow, N.W cr. John & Meeting Sts , Neck
Davis, Mary Eliza, Widow, N W. End Cannonborough, Neck
Davis, Thomas, Mariner, 1 Door S. of Baptist Church, Church St.
Dawes, H. P , Lumber Yard, Roper's Whf., Res. 71 Church St.
Dawson, J. H., Factor, 10 Meeting St
Dawson, John Drayton, N.E. cr. Bull & Rutledge Sts.
Dawson, John, Jr , Custom House, Ann St., op. Public Mall, Neck
Dawson, John, Mrs., N E. cr Bull & Rutledge Sts.
Day, F., Mrs , Millinery, S. cr. King & Society Sts , Upstairs
Day, F , S cr King & Society Sts
Day, Zelotes, Agent for J Brewster & Co , Wentworth St., 1 Door E of King St., S Side
Deas & Broun, Factors, 6 Kiddell's Whf
Deas, David, 116 Tradd St., E. cr Logan St
Deas, E. Horry, M.D., 1 Friend St.
Deas, Henry, 116 Tradd St., E. cr. Logan St.
Deas, Henry, Hon , State Senator, 1 Friend St.
Deas, J. Miles, M D., S. cr. Minority & E. Bay Sts.
Deas, John, 116 Tradd St., E cr Logan St.
Deas, Lynch Horry, M.D., 1 Friend St.
Deas, Thomas H., Broker & Auctioneer, 5 Broad St., Res. N.W cr Pitt & Montague Sts.
DeBow, John, Coachmaker, 202 Meeting St.
DeBow, Mary B., Widow, 12 Amen St.
DeBow, William, Distillery, 53 State St
Degaffarelly, A., Instructor, 5 Stoll's Al.
Deglaune, C. A., Miss, Corset Maker, King St., E. Side, btw. John & Ann Sts , Neck
Dehon, Sarah, Widow of Bishop Dehon, N cr. Meeting St. & Price's Al
DeLaMotta, J., M.D 58 Wentworth St
DeLange, Lucas, 26 State St.
Delany, Michael, Pilot, S. cr. Stoll's Al. & Church St.
DeLaunay, Victor, Merchant, Edmondston's Whf.
Deliesseline, F. G , Attorney, 78 Broad St.
DellaTorre, A., Merchant, 65 Broad St.
DeLorme, A., Store, 21 Market St
Deming & Bulkley, Furniture & Carpet Warehouse, 205 King St.
Dempsey, Miles, Tavern, 147 E. Bay St
Dener, Christiana, Widow, 31 Mazyck St.
Denny, M. L., Mrs., 17 Guignard St.
Denny, Thomas S , 17 Guignard St
Denny, W., Accountant, 17 Guignard St.
Dent, Ann, Widow of Com Dent, 99 Wentworth St.
DeSaussure, Henry A., Attorney, 35 Meeting St.
DeSaussure, William H , Factor, 35 Meeting St.
Descamps, J., 5 West St
Descoudres & Co., Store, 281 King St.
Desgraves, Peter, Farmer, Bee St , Cannonborough, Neck
Deveaux, Caroline, Miss, 29 Meeting St.
DeVeaux, Jane, Widow, Meeting St., W Side, btw. Wolf

& Reid Sts., Neck
DeVeaux, Portius, Accountant, Meeting St , W. Side, btw. Wolf & Reid Sts., Neck
DeVeaux, Thomas E., Attorney, Meeting St., W Side, btw Wolf & Reid Sts., Neck
DeVillers & Poirier, Store, N E cr. Queen & Church Sts
DeVillers, Louis, Bookstore, S.E. cr King & Broad Sts.
Devineau, E., Accountant, 103 King St.
Devineau, Elizabeth, Store, 103 King St.
Dewees, John, Factor, Mary St., Wraggsborough, Neck
Dewees, Joseph, S.E. cr. Charlotte & Alexander Sts
Dewees, W., Factor, Dewees' Whf
Dexter, M., Elliott St.
Dexter, Samuel W., Grocer, 12 King St
Dibble, A. C , Hat Store, 31 Broad St
Dibble, P V , 31 Broad St.
Dick, James, Merchant, 121 Church St.
Dickson, John, Rev., 31 Coming St.
Dickson, Samuel Henry, M D., Professor of Medicine, Medical College of S. C., N. cr Hudson & Meeting Sts
Dill, Eliza, Miss, 50 King St.
Dixson, Robert, Bricklayer, 31 Pinckney St.
Dobson, O L., 8 Water St.
Dodd & Barnard, Merchants, 136 E. Bay St.
Donegan, J., Shoemaker, 237 King St
Dorrill, Robert, 35 State St.
Dotterer, Thomas, Foundary, Eaton's Whf.
Dougherty, J., Store, 25 S. Bay St.
Dougherty, John, Plasterer, W. cr. Anson & Boundary Sts.
Doughty, James, M.D., Planter, W. cr. of Elliot & Bridge Sts., Cannonborough, Neck
Doughty, William, W. cr. Pinckney & Bridge Sts Cannonborough, Neck
Douglas, Campbell, Store, N.W. cr. Meeting & Market Sts.
Douglass, Ann, Widow, 102 Church St.
Douglass, Benjamin, M.D., 102 Church St
Douglass, John, Accountant, 232 Meeting St
Dowling, A., Store, 3 King St.
Dowling, Elizabeth Ann, Widow, 17 Society St.
Dowling, Felix, Bricklayer, 17 Society St.
Downie, Robert, Tin Plate Worker, 59 Broad St., N Side
Drayton, Charles, M.D , Planter, W End Montague St , N. Side
Drayton, -----, Misses, at Mrs. Tidyman's, N W. cr. Wentworth & Rutledge Sts.
Drayton, William, Hon , U S. Representative, Gibbes St., Extreme W. End
Drege, Peter, Clothing Store, N. cr. E. Bay & Queen Sts., Res. 49 State St
Drewes, Henry, S.E. cr. Meeting & Wentworth Sts
Drummond, James, Bootmaker, 123 King St
Dubert, Frederick, Spring St , S Side, Neck
Duboc, A , Tailor, 328 King St
Duboc, Francis, Store, 187 King St.
Duboc, P., 62 State St.
Dubois, Eleanor, Upholsterer, Etc., 88 Queen St
Dubois, Peter, Carpenter, Cannon St , Cannonborough, Neck
Duff, Elizabeth, Widow, Meeting St , W. Side, btw Columbus & Wolf Sts., Neck

Duff, John, Shoemaker, 148 Meeting St.
Duffie, James, Store, 23 S Bay St.
Duffus, John, Notary Public, 87 E Bay St., Res. Meeting St., 1 Door S. of Circular Church.
Duggan, T., Bricklayer, St. Philip's St , W Side, near Lines, Neck
Duhadway, C. B , Saddler, 106 King St
Duhadway, -----, Mrs., Millinery, 106 King St.
Duke, John C , Printer, 6 Amen St.
Dukes, Francis, Grocery, S. cr. King & Columbus Sts , Neck
Dukes, William C , Neck
Dunkin, Benjamin F., Attorney, Radcliffborough, Neck
Dunlap, W., Bird's Store, 22 Broad St
Dunn, Joseph, 20 Market St
Dupre, -----, Meeting St , E Side, btw. Mary & Ann Sts., Neck
DuPre, -----, Mrs., Widow, E cr. Tradd & Orange Sts
Duquercron, Francis, Merchant, Chisolm's Upper Whf , Depau's Range, Res 19 Tradd St.
Durand, Victor, Clothing Store, S. cr. E. Bay & Queen Sts Res. 36 Queen St
Durban, A., Hat Store, 67 Queen St
Dursse, L., Commercial Coffee House, 149 E Bay St.
Duryea, E. S., Printer, 5 Queen St
Duryea, -----, Mrs., Boarding House, 5 Queen St.
Duryea, P , Tavern, 152 E Bay St.
Dutland, Peter, Fruit Shop, 312 King St.
Dutrieux, C., Snuff Maker, 191 King St.
Duval, John, Tinner, King St., W Side, btw Vanderhorst & Warren Sts., Neck
Duval, Peter, Grocer, Cannon St., S. Side, Neck
Eager, James, near S W. cr Coming & Wentworth Sts
Eager, Robert, Merchant, near S.W. cr. Coming & Wentworth Sts.
Eason, Dorothea, Widow, 37 Hasell St.
Eason, Robert, Shipwright & Wharf Owner, Eason's Whf., Res. 36 Anson St.
Easterby, George, Capt , 87 E Bay St.
Eckhard, George, B., Attorney, 31 George St.
Eckhard, Jacob, Jr., Teacher of Music, 37 Society St.
Eckhard, Jacob, Sr. Teacher of Music, 31 George St
Eckhard, John, 31 George St.
Eckhoff, G. H , Grocery, Henrietta St , Neck
Edmondston, Charles, Merchant & Wharf Owner, Edmondston's Whf., Res 3 E Bay St
Edwards, Edward H , Maj., 11 Meeting St
Edwards, George B., 14 Legare St.
Edwards, James F , Planter, 22 Wall St
Egleston, George W., Attorney, Radcliffborough, Neck
Egleston, Sarah, Private Boarding House, 85 Society St.
Ehney, Mary, E. cr. Magazine & Wilson Sts
Ehney, William, Tailor, Charlotte St , Neck
Elder, James, Tanner, John St , N Side, btw King & Meeting Sts , Neck
Elfe, William, Chapel St , E End, near Carew & Childs Mills, Neck
Elford, Ann Louisa, Widow, S E. cr. Meeting St & Lines, Neck
Elford, Ann, Store, 64 State St
Elford, James M , Mathematical Store & Nautical School, 119 E. Bay St.
Elford, Thomas, 119 E. Bay St
Elliott, Barnard, Mrs , Widow, 10 George St
Elliott, Benjamin, Attorney, 22 Legare St.
Elliott, Stephen, Bank of State of S. C., 7 Archdale St
Elliott, Stephen, Jr., Attorney, 7 Archdale St
Elliott, T O., Attorney, 65 King St.
Elliott, William, 22 Legare St.
Ellis, Mary, Widow, 10 Stoll's Al.
Ellis, Moses, St. Philip's St , nearly op Liberty St.
Emanuel, Isaac, Book Auction Establishment, 302 King St , Res 6 Liberty St
Emanuel, J. D., 6 Liberty St
Emery, Elizabeth, Widow, Unity Al.
England, Alexander, 54 Tradd St.
England, John, Right Rev , Roman Catholic Bishop of Charleston, N E. cr. Wentworth & St. Philip's Sts
English, James, Shipwright, 23 S Bay St
Enslow, Joseph, L. Cooper, Vanderhorst's Whf
Estill, William, Bookbinder, 75 Queen St
Evans, C., Turner, Swinton's Ln.
Evans, James, 40 Coming St.
Evans, L , Cutler, 81 Queen St.
Evringham, John, 240 E. Bay St.
Ewan, J , Silversmith, 214 King St
Eyland, James, Jewellery, & Military Store, 172 King St
Faber, Henry F., Factor, N Side Charlotte St , Mazyckborough, Neck
Faber, Joseph W , N. Side Charlotte St., Mazyckborough, Neck
Fable, John, Grocer, S W. cr. St. Philip's & Cannon Sts., Neck
Fairchild, Lyon & Co., Saddlery, N. cr King & Society Sts
Farmer, -----, Mrs. Widow, Pinckey St.
Farr, Catharine, Widow, Coming St., op Montague St
Farr, Elizabeth, 1 Greenhill St
Fasbender, J H., Watchmaker, 111 Meeting St
Fash, L., Grocer, 148 Meeting St.
Fayolle, Peter, Assembly Room, 82 King St
Fayolle, Theodore B., Teacher of Dancing, 180 King St
Fell, Thomas D., Tin Plate Worker, 110 Market St
Fell, W., Mrs , Private Boarding House, 50 E Bay St
Fenn, Townsend & Hull, Dry Goods & Fancy Store, 244 King St.
Ferguson & Taylor, Merchant Tailors, 23 Broad St.
Ferguson, Ann, Widow, N cr King.& John Sts , Neck
Ferguson, James, Planter, N cr. King & John Sts., Neck
Ferret, Charles, Tailor, 44 Coming St.
Fetchman, John, Grocer, Smith's Ln
Fields, N., Sailmaker, 27 Laurens St
Filey, W. Peronneau, Attorney, 69 Broad St.
Fillette, Francis, Fancy Store, 159 King St
Fink, Clas P , Grocer, E. cr Mazyck & Beaufain Sts
Finkley, J. G., Harness Maker, 14 Wentworth St.
Finley, James E B., 69 Broad St
Finley, Mary, Widow, 69 Broad St
Finley, S B. Rush, M D , 69 Broad St
Fishburn, F B., 20 Pitt St
Fitzsimons, C , Hasell St , op Maiden Ln
Fitzsimons, Charles, Constable, 58 Elliott St
Flagg, Henry C , Attorney, Meeting St , E. Side, btw. Mary

& Reid Sts., Neck

Fleming, J , Grocer, S E. cr E Bay & Pinckey Sts

Flemming, Robert, Jr., Merchant, E. Side King St., btw. Wolf & Spring Sts., Neck

Flemming, Ross & Co., Merchants, S.E. cr. E. Bay St. & Vendue Range

Flemming, Thomas, Wholesale Dry Goods Store, S.W. cr. George & King Sts , Res 18 George St.

Flint, Jane, Widow, 23 State St.

Floderer, John, Store, 69 Church St

Foissin, Martha, Widow, 115 Tradd St.

Folker, E., Mrs., 3 St Philip's St.

Folker, T H., Mrs , Widow, N. cr. Church & Elliott Sts.

Follin, Augustus, N.E cr Meeting & Columbus Sts., Neck

Follin, Augustus, Tobacconist, 152 Meeting St

Follin, Joseph, Tobacconist, 219 E Bay St.

Footman, Elizabeth, Magazine St.

Footman, Harriet, Magazine St.

Forbes, J., Tin Plate Worker, 14 Tradd St.

Forbes, W , Tin Plate Worker, 241 King St.

Ford, F. A , Attorney, N.W. cr. Meeting & Society Sts.

Ford, Jacob, Attorney, N.W. cr. Meeting & Society Sts

Ford, Timothy, Attorney, 42 Meeting St.

Fordham, Richard, Blacksmith, Washington St., nearly op. Charlotte St., Neck

Fougeres, -----, Marquis de, Consulate of France, 31 Queen St

Fowler, Andrew, Rev., 115 Queen St.

Fox, William, 12 Liberty St.

Frampton, Eliza, S W. cr King & Broad Sts

Francies, John, Hairdresser, 312 King St.

Francis, Edward, Stables, 120 & Planters Hotel, Church St.

Fraser, Charles, Attorney, 53 King St.

Fraser, J. G., Factor, 41 E Bay St

Fraser, James, King St., W. Side, op Ann St, Neck

Fraser, John & Co., Factors & Merchants, 39 E. Bay St.

Fraser, John, Factor, 41 E. Bay St.

Fraser, John, Hairdresser, Church St , near St. Philip's Church

Fraser, Mary, Widow, 99 Tradd St.

Frazer, C P., Wood Factor, Res Laurens Whf.

Frazer, J. J., Wood Factor, Laurens Whf

Frazer, Rebecca, Widow, Laurens St

Frazer, W M., Notary Public, 81 E Bay St., Res. Laurens St.

Freeman, W., Grocer, 3 Tradd St.

Friel, Edward, Blacksmith, 17 Chalmers St.

Frierson, -----, E. End Hampstead, Neck

Fripp, Charles E., Planter, N cr Short & Mazyck Sts

Fronty, M , Physician, 48 Church St.

Frost, Edward, Attorney, 23 Archdale St.

Frost, Henry R , M.D , 23 Archdale St.

Fulda, Frederick W., Store, 181 Tradd St

Fuller, B., Jr., Montague St.

Fuller, B , Planter, Montague St

Fuller, Oliver, 105 Meeting St.

Fulmer, John, Chairmaker, King & St Philip's St., Neck

Furman, C. M., Treasurer, Lower Division, Fire Proof Building

Furman, H H., Factor, N. cr. E Bay St & Long. Ln.

Furman, R. B., M D., 186 King St

Furman, Thomas, N. cr E. Bay St & Longitude Ln

Gabeau, Anthony, 36 St. Philip's St.

Gadsden, Christopher E , Rev., D D , Rector, St Philip's Church, 28 Church St.

Gadsden, Fisher, Factor, Gadsden's Whf

Gadsden, James, Accountant, 124 Queen St

Gadsden, John, Hon , Intendant & U. S District Attorney, 11 Meeting St

Gadsden, Rebecca, Widow, 124 Queen St.

Gadsden, Thomas, Attorney, 28 Church St.

Gadsden, Thomas N , Accountant, 124 Queen St

Gaffney, J., Jewelry, 242 King St.

Gaillard, A T., Factor, 6 New St

Gaillard, Daniel S., U. S. M. Storekeeper, 2 State House Sq.

Gaillard, John, U. S. Appraiser, Office, Gillon St , Res. 5 Liberty St

Gaillard, Peter, Sr., 300 E. Bay St.

Gaillard, Sextus T., Factor, Chisolm's Lower Whf

Gaillard, Theodore, Accountant, 5 Liberty St.

Gaillard, Theodore, Hon., Judge, Court of Common Pleas, 5 Liberty St.

Galliot, C., Cigar Manufactory, E cr Elliott St & Gadsden's Al.

Galluchat, Virginia, N E. cr. St. Philip's & George Sts

Galpin, L., Hat Store, 263 King St.

Gandouin, Isidore, Store, 441 E Bay St

Gantt, Thomas John, Register in Equity, 2 State House Sq.

Garden, Alexander, Maj., 8 Short St

Garden, John, Planter, E Side Pinckney St., Cannonborough, Neck

Gardner, Jack, Stables, Chalmers St

Gardner, Margaret, Widow, 6 Society St.

Garrett, Ann, Widow, 115 Meeting St.

Garrett, W. W., Grocer, King St., E Side, btw. Spring & Columbus Sts., Neck

Gary, R , Accountant, King St., W Side, op Wolf St , Neck

Gates, John, Butcher, S Side Cannon St , Cannonborough, Neck

Gates, Thomas, Butcher, S Side Cannon St., Cannonborough, Neck

Gates, Thomas, Rev , D. D., S Side, Charlotte St , Mazyckborough, Neck

Gaugan, Eliza, S W. cr Anson & Pinckney Sts.

Gaylord, Norman, Boarding House, 38 Elliott St

Geddes, G W , N W. cr. King & Mary Sts , Neck

Geddes, Gilbert C , 34 Society St.

Geddes, James, Attorney, N.W cr King & Mary Sts , Neck

Geddings, Eli, M.D , 63 Meeting St

Gelzer, John, King St., W. Side, op. Columbus St , Neck

George, Rachael, Hotel, 149 E Bay St

Gerard, Mary, Widow, 38 State St.

Gerard, Peter Grandin, Merchant Tailor, 80 Queen St

Gerkin, C , Grocer, W. cr. Friend & Queen Sts.

Gervais, Paul T., Rev , 8 New St

Getty, Samuel, Store, S.W. cr. Meeting & Society Sts.

Geyer, R. C., 18 Lynch's Ln.

Gibbes & Waring, Factors, 3 Roper's Whf.

Gibbes, Arthur S , S. cr. Meeting & Ann Sts., Neck
Gibbes, Benjamin S , Factor, N.W. cr. Elizabeth & John Sts , Neck
Gibbes, Edwin, Bookstore & Circulating Library, 48 Broad St
Gibbes, John R., Planter, St. Philip's St , W. Side, btw. Warren & Radcliff Sts., Neck
Gibbes, Robert, Planter, Meeting St., W Side, 2d Door Below Ann St., Neck
Gibbes, Robert R., Planter, S. cr Meeting & Ann Sts , Neck
Gibbes, William Hasell, Late Master In Equity, 81 Broad St.
Gibbon, George & Co , Merchants, 8 Gillon St.
Gibbs, Elizabeth, Church St., op. Stoll's Al.
Gibbs, George, Wharf Owner, 4 State St
Gibbs, Mathurin G., Attorney, 49 Meeting St.
Gibbs, Paul G., Wharf Owner, 17 Meeting St.
Gibson, Alexander, Merchant, 3 Crafts' Whf., 69 Meeting St
Gibson, James, 226 Meeting St.
Gibson, William H , Merchant, N. cr. Elliott & E. Bay Sts
Gibson, William, Jr., Col., 13 Back St.
Gidiere, J. J., 358 King St
Gidiere, J. M., Music Store, 192 King St
Gidiere, Margaret, Dry Goods Store, 358 King St
Gidiere, P N., 358 King St.
Gilbert, Catharine, 9 Water St.
Gilchrist, James, S. C Bank
Gilchrist, Robert B , Attorney, 3 Society St.
Gildersleeve, B., Rev., Editor, Charleston Observer, Chalmers St , op City Sq.
Giles, O J., C C. Streets, Beaufain St., op. Coming St
Gilliand, W. H , Merchant, N E cr. King & George Sts.
Gillon, Ann P., Widow, Cannon St , Cannonborough, Neck
Gilman, Sally M., Widow, 8 Mazyck St.
Gilman, Samuel M , 8 Mazyck St.
Gilman, Samuel, Rev., 28 Archdale St
Gilmar, M., Store, King St., W. Side, btw. Bridge & Lines, Neck
Giraud, -----, Mrs., Teacher of Music, 80 King St.
Gissendanner, S., Nurse, 38 Beaufain St
Gist, Sarah B., Widow, 7 S. Bay St.
Gitsinger, B. R., Printer, Mercury Office
Gleason, H. B. & Co., Crockery & Glass Warehouse, S.E. cr. King & Wentworth Sts.
Glen, J. S., 97 Tradd St.
Glen, John, Planters' & Mechanics' Bank, N.W. cr. Reid & Meeting Sts., Neck
Glen, John, Teller, Planters' and Mechanics' Bank, 108 Wentworth St.
Glen, Margaret, Widow, 97 Tradd St
Glover, Henry C., M D , 52 Society St
Glover, Joseph E , 7 Rutledge St.
Glover, Joseph, M.D., 7 Rutledge St.
Glover, Lydia, Widow, 14 Cumberland St.
Glover, Margaret, Widow, 3 Meeting St
Gnech, C D , Watchmaker, 62 Broad St
Gnech, Elizabeth, Fancy Store, S.E. cr King & Cumberland Sts
Godard, Rene, President, Union Bank, 129 King St.

Godet, John, Cutler, 41 Hasell St.
Godet, -----, Mrs. Widow, King St , E Side, btw John & Ann Sts., Neck
Godet, P , Saddler, 41 Hasell St
Godet, P., Saddler, King St., E. Side, btw. John & Ann Sts , Neck
Godfrey, W. W , 252 E Bay St.
Goldsmith, M., Deputy U. S Marshal, S.E cr. Anson & Pinckney Sts.
Gonzalez, B., Merchant, Edmondston's Whf.
Gonzalez, John, King St., W. Side, btw. Radcliff & Mary Sts., Neck
Good, Francis, Grocer, S.E. cr Meeting & Wolf Sts., Neck
Goodman & Miller, Factors, 1st Floor Scale House, Edmondston's Whf.
Goodwin, Elizabeth, Private Boarding House, 26 Broad St
Gorden, W E., Master, Work House, W. cr Lightwood's Al. & Meeting St
Gordon, John, Bricklayer, 218 Meeting St.
Gough, Emma, Mrs , Widow, S. cr. Lightwood's Al & Meeting St.
Gouldsmith, Richard, Cabinet Maker, N. cr Meeting & Ellery Sts.
Gourdin & Smith, Merchants, 44 E. Bay St.
Gourdin, Henry, Merchant, 44 E. Bay St.
Gourley, Mary Ann, Widow, Meeting St.
Gowan, Peter, Watchmaker, N. cr. Meeting & Chalmers Sts
Graber, -----, Mrs., Widow, 128 Wentworth St.
Gradick, C., Grocery, S W. cr. Elizabeth & John Sts., Neck
Graham, C., Store, 5 Market St.
Graham, Catharine, 15 Bedon's Al.
Granby, George, 252 King St.
Granniss, George B. & Co., Shoe & Comb Store, 240 King St., N. cr. Hasell St.
Graves, Anthony, 28 S Bay St.
Graves, Charles, Planter, 28 S. Bay St.
Graves, Daniel D., M.D , 28 S. Bay St.
Graves, Massy, Widow, Smith's Ln.
Gray, Albert, Accountant, 3 Anson St
Gray, Francis M., Carpenter, Henrietta St., S Side, Neck
Gray, James, Accountant, 3 Anson St
Gray, James W , Attorney, N. cr. Williams Whf & E Bay St
Gray, John B., Instructor, 32 Wentworth St.
Gray, Ruth, Widow, Henrietta St., S Side, Neck
Gray, W. H., Printer, Coming St
Gready, A P., Northern Warehouse, 199 King St
Green, C. F. & Co., Grocers, E. cr Laurens & Middle Sts.
Green, James, 32 Cumberland St.
Green, -----, Mrs , Widow, 113 Boundary St.
Green, -----, Mrs., Widow, Washington St., Neck
Green, Sarah, Widow, 10 Stoll's Al.
Green, Thomas P., Druggist, 187 E Bay St
Greenhill, -----, Misses, 1 Greenhill St.
Greenland, Benjamin R , M.D., 6 Back St.
Greenland, Eliza, Widow, 74 Tradd St.
Greenland, W. P., 21 Meeting St
Gregor, Thomas, Merchant, N.E. cr. Anson & Guignard Sts.
Gregorie, Richard, Carpenter, Meeting St., E. Side, btw.

145

Boundary & Henrietta Sts., Neck
Gregson, Thomas, State Bank, E. cr Magazine & Wilson Sts
Greneker, Thomas, 60 King St.
Grierson, John C., Custom House, 20 Wall St.
Grimball, Paul C., Planter, W. Side Cannonborough, near Bennett's Mills, Neck
Grimke, Henry, Attorney, 299 E Bay St
Grimke, John, M.D., St Philip's St., op. Charleston College
Grimke, Mary, Mrs., Widow, 299 E Bay St.
Grimke, Thomas S., Hon., State Senator, 2 S Bay St.
Gros, J., Cabinet Maker, 191 Meeting St.
Gruber, M. B., Widow, Meeting St., E. Side, btw. Wolf & Columbus Sts., Neck
Grumball, J. B., Planter, 4 S. Bay St
Gue, V. A , Tin Plate Worker, 90 Market St.
Guerry, G., Shoe Store, 217 King St
Gunemer, G., N. cr. Meeting St. & Columbus Sts., Neck
Gunther, F G. H., 3 West St
Gunther, S. D., Mrs, Widow, 3 West St
Gurang, Eupheme, Widow, Meeting St., E Side, btw Boundary & Henrietta Sts., Neck
Guy, William, Saddler, 29 Archdale St.
Hadler, J., Grocer, N W cr. Meeting & Cumberland Sts.
Hahnbaum, -----, Mrs., Female Boarding House, Academy, N.E. cr Montague & Pitt Sts.
Haig, David, Cooper, 304 Meeting St
Haig, James, Attorney, 304 Meeting St.
Hall, James, Boarding House, 6 Elliott St
Hall, Jane, Mrs., Store 183 King St.
Hall, John, Late Major of Marines, 146 Wentworth St.
Hall, Susannah, Mrs , Widow, 2 State House Sq
Hall, William, M.D., E. Side Hampstead, Neck
Hamilton, Alexander, Coach Trimmer, 25 Archdale St.
Hamilton, Henrietta R., Widow, Bee St., N.W. End Cannonborough, Neck
Hamilton, James, Sr., Maj., Extreme S. End Church St.
Hamilton, John, Shipwright, 12 Guignard St
Hamilton, -----, Mrs., Female Academy, 97 Meeting St.
Hamje, C. H., Grocer, 18 Market St.
Hammersley, D., Shoemaker, 170 Meeting St.
Hammet, Thomas, Instructor, 240 Meeting St.
Hammill, Thomas, Wheelwright, Church St., N. of St. Philip's Church
Hammond, Ogden, Merchant, Crafts' Whf, 14 Legare St.
Hanckel, Christian, Rev., Rector, St. Paul's Church, 115 Boundary St.
Hannahan, J. C., 131 Tradd St.
Hanscome, Thomas, Planter, 111 Tradd St.
Happoldt, Albert, Butcher, S. Side Cannon St , Neck
Happoldt, Christian D., Butcher, S. Side, Cannon St., Neck
Happoldt, Christopher, Mrs , Widow, S Side Cannon St, Neck
Happoldt, J. M. Gunsmith, 117 Meeting St
Harby, Henry, Blacksmith, Church St., near St. Philip's Church
Harby, Rebecca, Widow, 86 Tradd St
Harckenrath & Lowndes, Merchants, 8 Crafts' S. Whf.
Hard, Benjamin F., Livery Stables, 50 Society St.
Harlow, Rebecca, Widow, 8 Mazyck St

Harlston, John, Planter, Charlotte St., Mazyckborough, Neck
Harlston, N., Planter, Radcliffborough, Neck
Harper, Peter, Tanner, N Side Reid St , Neck
Harper, William, Hon., Attorney, 110 Broad St.
Harper, William W , Baker, S E cr. King & Tradd Sts
Harris, Elizabeth, Clothing Store, 203 E. Bay St
Harris, Rebecca, Widow, 122 King St
Harrison, D. W., Bookseller, 40 Broad St.
Harrison, James, Bootmaker, 35 Beaufain St.
Harrison, John, Bootmaker, 1 West St.
Harrisson, Harriet Ann, Mantua Maker, 35 Beaufain St
Harrisson, J., Oil & Paint Store, 207 E. Bay St.
Hart, Alexander, Accoutant, 23 Beaufain St.
Hart, Bella, Widow, 122 Meeting St
Hart, Nathan, Ironmonger, S.E cr. King & Market Sts
Hart, Philip, Accoutant, 23 Beaufain St.
Hart, Richard, Wharfinger, Edmondston's Whf
Hart, S. M., 23 Beaufain St.
Harth, William, Lumber Yard, 1 Gibbes St.
Harts, S. H., Wood Yard, Harleston's Green
Harvey, Ann, Widow, 252 E Bay St
Harvey, E. T., Wharfinger, 10 Queen St.
Harvey, S F., Widow, 9 Lynch St.
Harvey, T. Pinckney, Accountant, 15 Anson St.
Hasell, C G , Planter, 12 Berresford St.
Hasell, Hannah, Mrs., E. cr. King & S. Bay Sts.
Hasell, Thomas. M., Merchant, E. Bay St., Res 71 Church St.
Hasgill, -----, Mrs. Widow, S. cr. Archdale & Mazyck Sts
Haskett, J., Saddler, 224 King St.
Haskins, James, Bricklayer, St Philip's St., East Side, near Lines, Neck
Haskins, Sarah, Widow, 3 Berresford St
Haslett, John, President, Charleston Fire, Marine & Life Insurance Co., N.W. cr. Church & Water Sts.
Hatch, Mary M., Widow, E. cr. Pinckney St. & Goodby Al
Hatch, W. W., Shipwright, E. cr. Pinckney St. & Goodby Al.
Hatfield, John, Grocer, W. cr. Beaufain & Coming Sts
Hattier, W. H., Fruit Store, 197 King St.
Haunato, Therese, 26 Tradd St
Hauschildt, P., Grocery Stores, E Bay St., N. cr. Unity Al. & S.W. cr. King & Queen Sts.
Hayden, Jane, Mrs., America St., Hampstead, Neck
Hayden, N., Accountant, 172 King St.
Hayferd, G., Carpenter, 95 King St.
Hayne, Arthur P., Col., King St., cr. Whim Court
Hayne, Elizabeth, Widow, 10 Water St.
Hayne, Robert Y , Hon., U. S. Senator, Ladson's Court
Hayne, William E., Bank of the State, S.W cr. St Philip's & Vanderhorst Sts , Neck
Hazlehurst, G A., Planter, Anson St., op. Laurens St.
Hedley, J., Boundary St., N. Side, btw. Pitt & Coming Sts., Neck
Hedley, John L Accountant, 29 King St.
Hedley, William, Accountant, Boundary St., N. Side, btw. Pitt & Coming Sts., Neck
Heilbron, James & Co., Druggists & Sulphur Bath, 74 Church St., Res. 72 Church St
Henderson, T., Watchmaker, 229 King St.

Hendricks, F., Grocer, N. cr. King & Warren Sts , Neck

Hendricks, J., King St., W. Side, btw Radcliff & Mary Sts., Neck

Henry, Alexander, Cashier, Bank of State of S. C., Res. N.E. cr. Smith & Wentworth Sts.

Henry, George, Factor, Firm of Boyce & Henry, 3 Liberty St.

Henry, Jacob, Cabinet Maker, Charlotte St., op. Flinn's Church, Neck

Henry, Robert, Merchant, Firm of Fleming, Ross & Co., N.E. cr. Smith & Wentworth Sts

Hepburn, John, Cabinet Maker, 71 State St.

Heriot, Benjamin D., Maj., Factor, Kunhardt's Whf., Scale House, Res. Beaufain St., W End

Heriot, Roger, Notary Public & Quorum Unis, 87 E. Bay St., Res. 108 Church St.

Hernandes, P., Shoemaker, W. cr. John & Elizabeth Sts., Neck

Hertz, Jacob, Store, 97 King St.

Hervey, Edward, Dyer & Scourer, 87 Queen St.

Hervey, George, Merchant

Heyns, James, Price's Al

Heyward, Arthur, Planter, S. cr. Society & E. Bay Sts.

Heyward, Charles, Planter, S cr. Society & E. Bay Sts

Heyward, Hannah, Widow, 21 Legare St.

Heyward, Nathaniel, Planter, S. cr. Society & E. Bay Sts.

Hichborn, W. C., Merchant, 38 Tradd St.

Higham & Fife, Merchants, 75 E. Bay St.

Hill, C. G., Chairmaker, E Side Coming St., near St. Paul's Church, Neck

Hill, Francis C., Drawing School, 7 Clifford St.

Hill, Mary, Mrs., Fancy Store, cr King & Clifford Sts.

Hillard & Nelme, Grocers, Vendue Range 5 & 7

Hillegas, Philip, Military & Fancy Store, 165 King St.

Hillman, Ann, Mrs., Private Boarding House, 69 E. Bay St.

Hinson, Thomas, Carpenter, 9 Berresford St.

Hinton, James, Meeting St., btw Columbus & Wolf Sts., Neck

Hislop, George, Accountant, N.E. cr. Pinckney St. & Maiden Ln.

Hislop, Hannah, Widow, N.E. cr. Pinckney St. & Maiden Ln.

Hislop, Robert, Cooper, N.E. cr. Pinckney St. & Maiden Ln.

Hitchingham, Thomas, Grocer, 27 Market St.

Hobart & Jones, N.W cr. Market & King Sts.

Hodgson, Elizabeth, Store, 32 Market St.

Hoff, John C., Bookseller, 84 Queen St

Hoff, John M., Clerk of Market, George St., near Meeting St.

Hoff, Philip, Printer & Bookseller, 10 Broad St.

Hohn, C. F., Grocery, E. cr Market & State Sts.

Holbrook, J. Edwards, M.D , N.E. cr. Tradd & Meeting Sts.

Holbrook, Moses, M.D., 64 Queen St

Holloway, Richard, 33 Beaufain St

Holmes, Cato, Henrietta St., Neck

Holmes, Charles Rutledge, Factor, Vanderhorst's Whf., Res. E. cr. Tradd & Logan Sts

Holmes, H. P., Planter, 10 West St.

Holmes, Harriet, Widow, 7 Water St.

Holmes, Issac Edward, Attorney, 1 E. Bay St , near Battery

Holmes, J. T. W. & Co., Fancy Dry Goods Store, 161 King St.

Holmes, James G., Attorney, 1 E. Bay St., near Battery

Holmes, John Bee, Mrs., Widow, 1 E. Bay St., near Battery

Holmes, John L , Accountant, Pinckney St , near Mey's Whf.

Holmes, John, Lumber Yard, Gadsden's Whf

Holmes, Margaret, Store, 354 King St

Holmes, -----, Mrs., Widow, Pinckney St., near Mey's Whf.

Holmes, William, Factor, Gadsden's Whf., Res. 113 Boundary St.

Holmes, William, M.D., 1 E. Bay St., near Battery

Holton, Elizabeth, Nurse, 15 Cumberland St

Holton, John, Tailor, 15 Cumberland St.

Holton, Margaret, Pastry Cook, 15 Cumberland St

Holton, Thomas, Mariner, 77 Tradd St.

Holton, Thomas, Tailor, 15 Cumberland St.

Holwell, T., Market St., op. Beef Market

Honour, J., Rev., 7 Mazyck St.

Honour, John H., 7 Mazyck St

Honour, T., 7 Mazyck St

Hopkins, John M., 15 Wall St.

Horlbeck, Daniel, 23 Cumberland St.

Horlbeck, Elias, M.D., 23 Cumberland St.

Horlbeck, John, Bricklayer, S W cr. Meeting & Boundary Sts.

Horlbeck. Henry, Bricklayer, 23 Cumberland St.

Horry, Elias Lynch, 124 Broad St , W. End, near Theatre

Horry, Elias, Planter, N W. cr. Tradd & Meeting Sts

Horry, Harriot, Widow, 117 Tradd St.

Horry, Lucretia, Widow, 99 Wentworth St

Horry, T. L., N.W. cr. Tradd & Meeting Sts.

Horsey, Thomas J., 30 Cumberland St.

Hort, E. B., Millwright, 8 Society St

Howard, Alexander, City Assessor, Pitt St., E. Side, 2d House Above Wentworth St.

Howard, J., Bricklayer, N. Side Henrietta St., near Meeting St., Neck

Howard, James, Sailor's Boarding House, 48 State St.

Howard, Richard F., Cooper, Washington St , W. Side, Neck

Howard, Robert, 78 Wentworth St.

Howard, T., Shipwright, N Side Henrietta St., near Meeting St., Neck

Howard, William, S cr King & Wolf Sts , Neck

Howe, Mary, Store, 8 King St.

Howe, Silas, 133 Meeting St.

Howland, B. J., Merchant, 14 Queen St.

Howland, Ward & Spring, Merchants, S.E. cr Vendue Range & E. Bay St.

Howland, William & Co , N.E. cr King & Market Sts

Huard, Stanislaus, Druggist, 34 Broad St.

Hubbell, Sears, Grocery, E End Boundary St., N. Side, Neck

Huger, Alfred J., Planter, E cr. Mazyck & Broad Sts

Huger, Benjamin, M.D , 110 Broad St.

Huger, Benjamin T , Tailor, 110 King St

Huger, D. Elliott, Hon., Judge, Court of Common Pleas, 28 Meeting St

Huger, D. Elliott, Jr., Attorney, 28 Meeting St

147

Huger, Daniel, Broker, 6 State St., Res. 47 Coming St.

Huger, John, Mrs , E. cr Mazyck & Broad Sts.

Hughes, Edward, 151 King St

Hughes, -----, Mrs Widow, 83 King St.

Hume, Alexander, M.D., Planter, near W. End Wentworth St.

Hume, John, Planter, S.W. cr. Wentworth & Smith Sts

Hume, Robert, Planter, Lynch St., near Wyatt's Mill

Hume, William, M.D., N.W. cr Rutledge & Montague Sts.

Humphreys, Hannah, Mantua Maker, 112 Queen St.

Humphreys, Mary, Mrs., 101 Queen St

Humphries, Joseph, Tailor, 112 Queen St.

Hunt, Benjamin F., Attorney, Meeting St., op. Municipal Guard House, Neck

Hunt, Randall, Attorney, 211 Meeting St

Hunt, Theodore G., Attorney, 211 Meeting St

Hunt, Thomas, Commissioner in Equity, 211 Meeting St.

Hurlburt, M L., Principal, S C Society School, Meeting St.

Hurst, C. W., Blacksmith, Charlotte St., op. Flinn's Church, Neck

Husser, M. W., Carpenter, 1 Door S W cr Cannon & Pinckney Sts., Neck

Hussey, Susan, Widow, 9 Stoll's Al

Hutchins, & Lanneau, Merchants, 142 E. Bay St.

Hutchinson, Anna W., Widow, 16 New

Hyams, Samuel, Jailor, Charleston District, Charleston Jail, Magazine St

Hyer, J., Carpenter, S.W cr. Radcliff & St. Philip's Sts., Neck

Icarden, Louis, Tallow Chandler, E. Side Meeting St., N. of Mary St., Neck

Inglesby, J. S., M.D., 89 Church St., near cr. Tradd St.

Inglesby, William H., Attorney, 41 Tradd St.

Inglis, Thomas, Hairdresser & Perfumer, 83 Meeting St.

Ingraham, George, Factor, 28 Laurens St.

Ingraham, Henry, Planter, S.E cr. Smith & Wentworth Sts.

Ingraham, Louisa, Widow, 28 Laurens St

Ioor, William, M.D., N. cr. Water & Meeting Sts

Irvine, William, Hairdresser, 198 King St.

Ivers, Sophia, 114 Wentworth St.

Izard, Claudia S., Widow, 25 Legare St.

Jacks, Elizabeth, Mrs., N Side Chapel St., Mazyckborough, Neck

Jackson, George, Mariner, 4 Longitude Ln.

Jackson, J. A., Saddler, N.W. cr King & George Sts

Jackson, John H., Hotel, 83 E. Bay St.

Jackson, R., Mrs , Millinery, 342 King St

Jackson, Robert, Accountant, 342 King St

Jacobs, M., Clothing Store, 254 King St.

Jacoby, George, Grocery, 83 Church St.

Jarcke, N., Grocer, S.E. cr. Wentworth & Pitt Sts.

Javain, Peter, Farmer, W. cr. St. Philip's St. & Lines, Neck

Jeannerette, C., 164 E. Bay St.

Jeannerette, M. T , Widow, 68 Church St.

Jeffords, John, Store, 44 Middle St.

Jenkins, Christopher, Planter, N.W. cr. Smith & Montague Sts.

Jenkins, Elizabeth, Widow, 6 Liberty St.

Jenkins, James, 6 Liberty St

Jenkins, John H., Factor, 72 Church St.

Jenkins, John W., Rutledge St , near Bull St.

Jenkins, Micah, Planter, 11 Legare St

Jenkins, Thomas, 6 Liberty St.

Jennings, David, Tailor, 20 Market St

Jervey, James, Clerk, U. S. District Court, 37 Laurens St.

Jervey, Thomas Hall, Custom House, Res 51 Church St

Johnson, Ann M., Matron, Marine Hospital, 5 Back St.

Johnson, Ann, Widow, 55 State St.

Johnson, Bennett, Grocer, N Side Boundary St , btw. Meeting & Elizabeth Sts., Neck

Johnson, Delia, Nurse, Wentworth St.

Johnson, H., Shoe Store, 330 King St., at the Bend

Johnson, I. A., M.D., S.E. cr. Warren & St. Philip's Sts., Neck

Johnson, J. A., Tailor, Wentworth St.

Johnson, James S., Corn Store, W. cr Anson & Market Sts., Res. N. E. cr. Ellery & Anson Sts.

Johnson, James, Tallow Chandler, Chapel St., Neck

Johnson, Jane, Miss, S. cr King St. & Burns Ln.

Johnson, John, 9 Magazine St

Johnson, John, Jr., Iron Foundry, Johnson's Whf., E. Bay St., Res. 4 Society St.

Johnson, John, Tailor, S.E. cr. Church & Chalmers Sts., Upstairs

Johnson, Joseph, M.D., Druggist Establishment, 11 Broad St.

Johnson, Joseph, M.D., President, U. S. Branch Bank, Res Church St.

Johnson, Loring, Shoe Store, 117 E. Bay St.

Johnson, N., Boarding House, 12 Market St

Johnson, T. W., Store & Tavern, King St., W. Side btw Radcliff & Mary Sts., Neck

Johnson, William, Hon., Judge, U. S. Supreme Court, E Side Pinckney St., Cannonborough, Neck

Johnston, Alexander, Shoemaker, 13 Tradd St.

Johnston, Archibald, Grocery, S W. cr. Meeting & Wentworth Sts.

Johnston, C., Accountant, 8 Mazyck St

Johnston, Camilla, Pastry Cook, 129 King St.

Johnston, David C., M D., 101 Queen St

Johnston, E., Chairmaker, 76 State St.

Johnston, Eleanor, Widow, 101 Queen St

Johnston, Elizabeth, Store, 91 King St.

Johnston, J. J M. C. 101 Queen St.

Johnston, T., Farmer's Hotel, 226 Bend of King St.

Jones, Abraham, Cabinet Maker, 13 Beaufain St.

Jones, Christiana, Widow, 36 Market St.

Jones, Edward, M.D., Planter, S W. cr St. Philip's & Warren Sts., Neck

Jones, Elias J., Meeting St., E. Side, near Public Mall, Neck

Jones, Elias, Rice Mill, Belvidere Farm, Res. Meeting St., near Public Mall, Neck

Jones, Henry, Notary Public, 57 Tradd St.

Jones, J. C., Grocery, N.W. cr. Wentworth & Coming Sts

Jones, J. S., cr Boundary & Washington Sts., Mazyckborough, Neck

Jones, Jehu, Hotel, Broad St., 1 Door E St. Michael's Church

Jones, Jehu, Jr , Tailor, 27 Beaufain St

Jones, John S , Wire Manufactory, 145 E Bay St.,

Grocery, S.W cr. Market & Queen Sts
Jones, Mary, Widow, W. cr. Reaper's Al. & Guignard St.
Jones, Thomas L., Attorney, 256 E. Bay St.
Jones, W., House Carpenter, 57 King St.
Jones, William, Mrs., S.E. cr. Meeting & Reid Sts., Neck
Jones, Wiswald, Commission Merchant, 15 Vendue Range, Res. 80 Meeting St.
Joseph, J. J , Store, King St , W Side, btw Radcliff & Mary Sts., Neck
Joshua, P., Grocery, 203 E. Bay St.
Joye, D. G., Grocery, N. cr. Church St & St Michael's Al.
Joyner, Catherine, Widow, N.W. End Cannonborough, Neck
Joyner, J , 73 Boundary St.
Kanapau, Charles, Superintendent, Lucas' Mills, Cannonborough, Neck
Kanapaux, J., Shoemaker, 164 Meeting St.
Kane, W. D., Shoemaker, Church St., near Market St.
Kay, Ann, Beaufain St.
Keckeley, M. W., cr. Boundary & Coming Sts.
Keehl, Henry & Co , Grocery, N.W cr. St. Philip's & Vanderhorst Sts., Neck
Keenau, Elizabeth, Widow, 43 Society St.
Keils, George M., Coming St , E Side, Above St. Paul's Church, Neck
Keith, Jane, Widow of Late Rev. Dr. Keith, W End Magazine St.
Keith, Matthew Irvine, Master in Equity, W cr. Broad & Mazyck Sts.
Keith, Susannah, Widow, N cr. King & Lamboll Sts
Keller, Jacob, Grocer, 20 Market St.
Kelly, Edwin H., 37 Tradd St
Kelly, Mary, Millinery, 190 King St.
Kelly, Michael, Ironmonger, 149 E. Bay St., Res 87 Tradd St.
Kennedy, Ann, Mrs., 19 George St.
Kennedy, Ann, Widow, 39 Market St.
Kennedy, Edward, Custom House, 18 Mazyck St.
Kennedy, James, Grocer, 117 Queen St.
Kennedy, Lionel H., Attorney, W. cr Logan & Tradd Sts.
Kennedy, Mary E., Widow, 27 Mazyck St.
Kennedy, Thomas, Accountant, 145 King St
Ker, J. Cessford, Merchant, E. Bay St., Res. 66 Queen St
Kerr, George, Wharfinger, 24 Laurens St.
Kerr, Susan, Seamstress, 26 Beaufain St.
Kerr, Thomas J., Wharfinger, 24 Laurens St.
Kerrison, Elizabeth, Private Boarding House, 131 Church St.
Kershaw, Charles, Factor, 30 Meeting St.
Kershaw, George, Wharfinger, 74 Church St.
Kershaw, Lewis & Co., Factors, N. cr. Vanderhorst's Whf. & E. Bay St.
Kershaw, Newman, Roper's Whf., Res. 5 New St.
Kershaw, Thomas, Accountant, 30 Meeting St.
Ketchum, J. & Son, Dry Good Store, 332 King St.
Kidd, C., Grocer, 14 Market St.
Kiddell, Charles, Wharf Owner, Res. 35 Broad St.
King, Ann, 36 Elliott St.
King, John, 138 Church St.
King, John, Jr , 138 Church St.
King, Leonard, Carpenter, 84 Meeting St

King, Mary, 31 Beaufain St.
King, Mitchell, Attorney, N.W. cr. Meeting & George Sts
Kingdon, H., Millwright, 123 Boundary St.
Kingman, Eliab, Steward, Orphan House
Kingman, John, Teacher, Orphan House
Kingman, Samuel, Accountant, W. Side King St , op Wolf St., Neck
Kinloch, Frederick, at Mrs. Langlois, 128 Queen St
Kinloch, George, Groceries, Market St & N. cr. Lightwood's Al & Meeting St.
Kirkpatrick, J. & Co., Merchants, Edmonston's Whf.
Klinck, John, Grocery, S. cr St. Philip's & Liberty Sts.
Knauff, Conrad, S. cr. King & Spring Sts., Neck
Knauff, John H , Accountant, King St., E Side, btw Wolf & Spring Sts., Neck
Knauff, John, King St., W Side, near Lines, Neck
Knauff, John W., King St., W. Side, near Lines, Neck
Knee, -----, Grocer, S.E. cr. Meeting & Boundary Sts.
Knepley, S., Blacksmith, 13 Chalmers St.
Knight, James D., Lt., U S. Navy, 252 E. Bay St
Knight, Thomas, Wharfinger, Crafts' Whf.
Knight, W. K., Lt., Guard, Bank Coffee House, E Bay St
Knox, J. F., Shipwright, Pritchard & Knox's Whf., Res. 12 Anson St.
Knox, Jane, Widow, Alexander St., Neck
Knox, Walter, Carpenter, 12 Green St.
Kohlman, J. H. & Co Grocers, 67 Tradd St.
Koster, C., Grocer, N cr. Amen & State Sts
Kugely, Jacob, Butcher, E End Hampstead, Neck
Kugley, Martha, Mrs., 34 Mazyck St
Kunhardt, William, Factor, Kunhardt's Whf., Res. W. cr. George & College Sts
Labatt, Catharine, Widow, 175 Church St.
Labatt, Issac C., King St. Road, Neck
Labatut, Isidore, S.W. cr. Meeting St. & Lines, Neck
Lacoste, Charles G A., Fancy Store, 149 King St.
Ladeveze, Victor, Fancy Store, 185 King St.
Laffan, Edmund, Firm of John Fraser & Co , 41 E Bay St
Lafon, John, Cooper & Grocery, 198 E. Bay St
Lafourcade & Prele, Confectioners, 309 King St
Lamb, James, Merchant, 51 E. Bay St., Res. 61 Tradd St.
Lance, Francis, Broker & Auctioneer, 7 State St., Res. Friend St., op. Roman Catholic Cathedral
Lance, Maurice H , Rev., Late Rector, Prince George, Winyaw, E. Side Pinckney St., Cannonborough, Neck
Lance, William, Attorney, 108 Queen St.
Landreth, R. Seed Store, 216 King St
Landreth, Robert, N., cr. Pinckney & Cannon Sts , Neck
Lang, Jacob, 1 Church St.
Langlois, L , Miss, 128 Queen St.
Langlois, Maria, Widow, Private Boarding House, 128 Queen St
Lanneau, Basil, 1 Pitt St., W. cr. Beaufain St.
Lanneau, C. H , Tanner, 1 Pitt St., W cr. Beaufain St.
Lanneau, Peter, 33 Elliott St
Laporte, R., Farmer, Bee St., Cannonborough, Neck
LaRousseliere, F., 32 Cumberland St
LaRousseliere, L., Druggist, 186 Meeting St.
Latham, Daniel, Distillery, 1 Hasell St.
Lauder, F., Widow, 128 Church St.
Laudershine, C., Widow, cr. St. Philip's & Mary Sts., Neck

Lauraine, E., Teacher of Languages, 6 St. Philip's St

Laurence, Robert D , Accountant, 39 Tradd St.

Laurence, Sarah, Widow, 6 George St.

Laurens, Edward R., Planter, E. Bay St , S. cr Laurens' Whf.

Laurens, Henry, Mrs., 290 E. Bay St. S. cr. Laurens' Whf

Laval, Lewis, Reid St., Hampstead, Neck

Laval, William, City Sheriff, West St., Next to M'Dowell's Church

Lawton, J. & C , Merchants, 136 E Bay St.

Lawton, Mary, Widow, 3 Lamboll St.

Lawton, William M., Factor, Chisholm's Lower Whf.

Lawton, Winburn, Planter, S. Bay St.

Lazarus, B D., Merchant, Champney St , Res. 93 Tradd St

Lazarus, Marks, 93 Tradd St.

Lazarus, Michael, Merchant, Champney St , Res. 103 Broad St.

Lea, William, Pilot, 46 Tradd St

Leader, Mary, Widow, 16 Berresford St

Leake, R., Attorney, 8 Orange St.

Lebby, Frances S., Widow, 16 Amen St.

Lebleux, F., Dying Establishment, 92 King St.

LeCaron, Charles, Merchant, Scale House, Upstairs, Edmonston's Whf.

Lee & Dewitt, Steam Saw Mill, cr. Beaufain & Lynch Sts., near Harleston Green

Lee, Edward, Hairdresser, 51 Broad St.

Lee, Elizabeth, B., Widow, W Side St. Philip's St., btw. Mary & Cannon Sts., Neck

Lee, Elizabeth, Pastry Cook, 78 Tradd St.

Lee, Elsey, Pastry Cook, 53 Wentworth St.

Lee, F J , Custom House 24 Hassell St.

Lee, J. M., Attorney, 22 Pitt St.

Lee, John, Tailor, 78 Tradd St

Lee, Joseph T., 22 Pitt St

Lee, Paul S. H , Broker, Broad St , Res. 103 Meeting St.

Lee, Stephen, Professor, Charleston College, Radcliff St., near N.W. End Radcliffborough, Neck

Lee, Thomas, Hon., U. S. District Judge, 22 Pitt St.

Lee, Thomas, Jr , 22 Pitt St

Lee, W., Bank of the State of S. C., Res. College St., near Charleston College

Leefe, Benjamin, Accountant, Queen St., near the Circus

Leefe, Harriet, Widow, Queen St., near the Circus

Leefe, John H., N.E. cr. King & Queen Sts., Res. Queen St., near the Circus

Legare, Daniel, M D., Planter, S.E. cr. Anson St. & Guignard Sts.

Legare, Hugh S., Attorney, 32 Bull St.

Legare, J. B , Attorney, 19 Hasell St

Legare, James C. W., 7 New St.

Legare, James, Factor, E. End Hampstead, Neck

Legare, James, Sr., Planter, 6 New St.

Legare, Mary, Mrs , Widow, 32 Bull St.

Legare, S & J., Factors, Chisolm's Lower Whf.

Legare, Solomon, Factor, 3 Gibbes St.

Legare, T , M.D., N.E. End Vanderhorst & St. Philip's Sts, Neck

Legare, Thomas, Planter, 1 S Bay St

Legg, Joseph, Farmer, near Wachington Race Course, Neck

Legrix, John P., Clothing Store, 127 E. Bay St.

Lehre, Ann, Widow, 95 Tradd St.

Lehre, Thomas, Col., Planter, 54 King St.

Leitch, Jane, Grocery, 232 King St.

Leland, J. & Brothers, Merchants, 159 E. Bay St.

Lemaitre, John B., Wine Store, 152 King St.

Leon, L. F., 73 State St.

LePrince, A., Store, 218 King St

Lesesne, Ann, 39 Society St.

Lesesne, Ann, Widow, 39 Society St

Lesesne, W. J., 39 Society St.

Levy, Emanuel, Store, 245 King St.

Levy, J. C., Merchant, Edmondston's Whf., Res. 279 E. Bay St.

Levy, Solomon, N.W. cr. King & Broad Sts.

Lewis, C. H., Grocery, N.W. cr. Market & E Bay Sts

Lewis, John, Bootmaker, 7 Liberty St

Liaumant, Margaret, Widow, N.W. cr Middle & Minority Sts.

Lieure, Peter, Clothing Store, 103 E Bay St

Limehouse, Robert, W. End Tradd St.

Ling, Philip, Chairmaker, 82 Market St.

Ling, Robert, Chairmaker, 84 Market St.

Lining, Charles, U. S. Bank, 18 Legare St.

Lining, Richard H., Planter, Res. 18 Legare St

Liston, Henry, Cooper, Amen St.

Litle, James, Cotton Gin Maker, 161 Meeting St.

Little, James, Grocer, 76 Tradd St.

Little, Robert, Lumber Merchant, Chisolm's Upper Whf.

Little, Robert, N Side Charlotte St., Mazyckborough, Neck

Lloyd, John, South St., Hampstead, Neck

Lloyd, William, Auctioneer, 33 Broad St.

Lloyd, William, Venetian Blind Maker, 144 Meeting St

Lockwood, Eliza, Widow, 17 Back St.

Lockwood, Joshua, 75 Broad St.

Lockwood, Joshua W., 75 Broad St.

Logan, C. M., Broker, 18 Queen St., Res. N. cr Market & Archdale Sts.

Logan, G. W., Attorney, Wentworth St., near St Philip's St

Logan, George, M.D., Wentworth St , near St. Philip's St.

Logan, William L. C. L., S.W. Side Pinckney St., Cannonborough, Neck

Lopez, -----, Mrs. Widow, 8 Stoll's Al.

Lopez, S., Tin Plate Worker, King St., 1 Door S. of Boundary St.

Lord, Jacob N., 75 Boundary St

Lord, Richard, 19 Berresford St.

Lord, Samuel, 47 State St.

Lordan, Patrick, Grocer, E. cr. Boundary & Wall Sts

Lovegreen, Andrew A , 298 King St.

Lowden, John, Merchant, Crafts' N. Whf., Res N cr. Meeting St. & St. Michael's Al.

Lowe, R. C., Sailmaker, Fitzsimons' Whf., 14 Amen St.

Lowndes, C. T., Merchant, 112 Broad St.

Lowndes, E. T., 112 Broad St.

Lowndes, Elizabeth, Widow of Hon. William, 15 Legare St.

Lowndes, Jacob, 112 Broad St

Lowndes, James, Planter, 14 Meeting St.

Lowndes, T. Pinckney, 15 Legare St.
Lowndes, Thomas, Planter, 112 Broad St
Lowndes, W. P., 112 Broad St.
Lowry, Charles, 12 State St.
Lowther, Thomas, Carpenter, 57 State St.
Lubkin, L., Grocer, cr. Anson & Boundary Sts.
Lucas, Jonathan, Jr., Merchant, Chisolm's Lower Whf., Scale House
Lynah, E. T., M.D., Alexander St., Neck
Lynah, Edward, M.D., Alexander St , Neck
Lynch, James, Planter, Upper End St. Philip's St., Neck
Lynes, Charity, Seamstress, Beaufain St.
Lyon, George, Watchmaker, 137 E. Bay St.
Macauley, Daniel, W. cr. Broad & State Sts.
Macauley, George, 37 Broad St.
Macbeth, Charles, Attorney, S cr. King & John Sts., Neck
Macbeth, James, Accountant, S cr. King & John Sts., Neck
Macbeth, -----, Mrs., Widow, S. cr. King & John Sts., Neck
Macbride, Ellener, Mrs., Widow, N.W. cr. Anson & Society Sts.
Mackay, Frances, 60 Tradd St.
Mackay, John, Teacher, 16 Mazyck St.
Mackey, John, Instructor, E. Side Coming St., near Vanderhorst, Neck
Mackie, Hervey & Co. Merchants, 48 E. Bay St., N cr. Chisolm's Lower Whf
Mackie, James, Notary Public, 6 Mazyck St.
Macnamara, J., Commission Merchant, 30 Vendue Range, Res. N. W. cr. Anson & Guignard Sts.
Magee, John, Mariner, Whim Court
Magrath & Fitzsimons, Merchants, Fitzsimons' Whf
Magrath, Edward, Butcher, Cannon St., Neck
Magrath, John, Merchant, 197 Meeting St.
Maille, P. A., Goldsmith, 114 Meeting St
Main, A. R., 215 King St.
Mair, Thomas, Merchant, 60 E. Bay St.
Mairs, Levi, Linen Store, 117 King St.
Mairs, Simon, 117 King St.
Mallery, L. & Co., Bootmakers, 97 E. Bay St.
Manigault, Charles D., Attorney, 124 Broad St , W. End, near the Theatre
Manigault, Gabriel, Planter, S.E. cr. Meeting & John Sts. Neck
Manigault, Henry, Maj., 16 Meeting St.
Manigault, Joseph, Planter, S.E. cr Meeting & John Sts. Neck
Manigault, Peter, Attorney, S E cr. Meeting & John Sts., Neck
Manley, Basil, Rev., Pastor, Baptist Church, Res. 85 Tradd St.
Manning, Joseph, M.D , 2 Society St.
Manson, Andrew, Tradd St., op Orange St.
Marion, F. B., Accountant, Pinckney St., Neck
Marion, Maria, Widow, Pinckney St., Neck
Markey, John, Coachmaker, 205 Meeting St. & Porter House, 6 Market St.
Markley, John, Coachmaker, 103 Broad St.
Marks, Joseph, Store, 10 Queen St
Marshall, John, Wood Factor, Gadsden's Whf.

Marshall, -----, Mrs. Widow, Back St
Marshall, -----, Mrs. Widow, E. cr Broad & Orange Sts
Marshall, Thomas C., Wharfinger, Crafts' Whf, Res. 74 Tradd St
Martenaru, John, Farmer, S Side Columbus St., Neck
Martigniat, J., Store, E. cr. Meeting & Hasell Sts.
Martin, Charles W., Blacksmith, Meeting St., E. Side, btw. Boundary & Henrietta Sts , Res America St , Hampstead
Martin, Charlotte, Widow, 6 Friend St.
Martin, J. H., Tailor, 61 Wentworth St.
Martin, Jacob, Blacksmith, 300 Meeting St.
Martin, John N., King St., E. Side, btw. Reid & Wolf Sts., Neck
Martin, Lewis V., Bricklayer, Coming St., E. Side, btw. Vanderhorst & Boundary Sts., Neck
Martin, Robert & Co., Factors, 7 Kiddell's Whf.
Martin, Thomas, 6 Friend St.
Mashburn, N., Carpenter, 55 Anson St.
Mason, George, Out Door Clerk, Union Bank
Massias, A. A., Maj., Paymaster, U. S. Army, Office, 5 Waring's Row, Meeting St , Res S. cr. E. Bay St. & Laurens
Massot, Horatio, Watchmaker 11 Queen St.
Masterson, M., Grocery, 15 Market St.
Mathews & Bonneau, Factors, 22 Kiddell's Whf.
Mathews, B., Commander, U. S. Revenue Cutter Gallatin, 26 Meeting St
Mathews H., Bootmaker, Beaufain St
Mathews, Harriet, Mrs., Widow, 56 Church St
Mathews, Henry, Shoemaker, 9 St. Philip's St.
Mathews J B., Tailor, 65 Boundary St.
Mathews, Martha Ann, Mrs., E. cr. S. Bay & Legare Sts.
Mathews, William, 36 Church St.
Mathy, C., Watchmaker, 171 King St.
Matthews, David, Shoemaker, Boundary St., N. Side, btw Meeting & Elizabeth Sts , Neck
Matthews, William, Planter, S.E cr. Elizabeth & Charlotte Sts., Neck
Matthiessen, C. F , 175 King St
Matthiessen, J. S., W. cr Pinckney & E. Bay Sts.
Maull, C., Janitor, Medical College, 38 Beaufain St
Maull, Mary, 38 Beaufain St.
Maxwell, H. E., Mrs., Widow, 91 Meeting St.
May, John, Cabinet Maker, 66 Queen St.
May, Margaret, Widow, S W. cr. Radcliff & St Philip's Sts., Neck
Maybank, Mary S , Widow, N. cr Nassau & South Sts , Hampstead, Neck
Maynard, Gabriel, Baker, 17 Tradd St
Maynard, John, Baker & Store, N. cr. St. Philip's & Green Sts., near Charleston College
Mayrant, C., Attorney, S. cr Lucas & Pinckney Sts., Neck
Mazyck, Alexander, Attorney, 96 Wentworth St.
Mazyck, Alexander S., Planter, cr. Church & Water Sts.
Mazyck, Edward, 96 Wentworth St
Mazyck, Gaillard & Mazyck, Factors, Chisolm's Lower Whf
Mazyck, Mary, Widow, cr. of Church & Water Sts.
Mazyck, -----, Misses, 188 Meeting St
Mazyck, N B., 186 Meeting St.

Mazyck, Paul, 96 Wentworth St.
Mazyck, William, Factor, 96 Wentworth St
Mazyck, William, Factor, E. End Judith St., Neck
M'Alister, J., Carpenter, near Lucas' Mills,
Cannonborough, Neck
M'Alpin, Mary, Widow, Beaufain St., op Coming St
M'Anally, John, Store, S W. cr. King & Broad Sts.
M'Beth, Robert, 35 King St.
M'Bride, Mary, Mrs , Widow, 58 Church St., near Water
St.
M'Burney, John R., Merchant, Sign of the Keys, S. cr.
King St. & Bridge, Neck
M'Call, Beekman, S. cr. Hasell & E. Bay Sts.
M'Call, Joseph P , 27 Meeting St.
M'Calla, Sarah, Mrs., Anson St.
M'Carter, J. J., Bookstore, 308 King St
M'Cartney & Gordon, Hardware Store, 18 Broad St.
M'Clain, J., 9 Bedon's Al.
M'Clain, James, Billiard Room, 99 Church St.
M'Clair, Butcher, Cannon St., Neck
M'Cleary, Samuel, Merchant, E. Side King St., btw.
Columbus St & the Lines, Res. Spring St , Neck
M'Cormick, John & Co. Dry Goods Store, 249 King St.
M'Cormick, Thomas, Factor, Vanderhorst's Whf , Res.
Church St., Near Stoll's Al.
M'Cormick, Timothy, Accountant, Price's Al.
M'Crady, Edward, Attorney, Meeting St., op. Circular
Church
M'Crady, Jane, Mrs , Widow, Meeting St., op. Circular
Church
M'Cure, John, Elizabeth St., Neck
M'Donald, Alexander, S E. cr. King & George Sts
M'Donald, C., 60 King St.
M'Donald, H. & A., Store, S.E cr. King & George Sts.
M'Donald, Hugh, City Hotel, 191 East Bay St.
M'Donald, Sarah, Mrs., City Hotel, 191 E Bay St.
M'Dow, William, Instructor, 98 Wentworth St.
M'Dowall, Andrew, Stores, 145 King & 58 E. Bay Sts
M'Dowall, John, Accountant, 145 King St.
M'Elheney, James, Attorney, N. cr Bull & Lynch Sts.
M'Elheney, Susannah, Mrs., N. cr. Bull & Lynch Sts.
M'Elmoyle, William, N W. cr Tradd & King Sts.
M'Encroe, John, Rev., N.E. cr. Broad & Friend Sts.
M'Feeters, Andrew, 2 Liberty St.
M'Gann, P., Watchmaker, 24 Queen St
M'Gillivray, A. H., Broker, 13 Chalmers St., Res. 16
Lynch's Ln.
M'Ginnis, Elijah, Store, W. Side King St , btw. Radcliff &
Mary Sts., Neck
M'Gowan, A., King St , 1 Door N of Spring St , Neck
M'Gregor, Alexander, 54 Church St.
M'Innes, Joseph M., Millwright, S Side Charlotte St ,
Neck
M'Intosh, D., W. Side King St., btw. Radcliff & Mary Sts ,
Neck
M'Intyre, Elizabeth, Widow, Smith's Ln
M'Kee, A., Carpenter, 150 Church St.
M'Kee, D. G., 3 Bedon's Al.
M'Kee, John, Bricklayer, 3 Bedon's Al.
M'Keegan, Daniel, Store, 61 Market St
M'Keegan, John, Blacksmith, Burns Ln.

M'Kendree, Eliza, Widow, W. Side King St., btw. Radcliff
& Mary Sts , Neck
M'Kenrue, Ann, Widow, S cr. Reid & Amherst Sts., Neck
M'Kenzie, Eliza, Widow, Unity Al.
M'Kenzie, R., Saddler, S.W. cr. Church & Chalmers Sts.
M'Kinney, Christopher, First Teller, U S. Branch Bank,
Res. 8 West St.
M'Kinney, L., Wheelwright, 121 Queen St
M'Mahon, Owen, N.E. cr. Friend & Broad Sts.
M'Millan, Thomas, Carpenter, Washington St.
M'Namee, James, Shoemaker, 112 Church St
M'Neill & Blair, Merchants, N.E cr. Broad & Church Sts
M'Neill, Daniel, Capt., Doughty St., Neck
M'Neill, Henrietta, Widow, 41 King St.
M'Neill, John, Accountant, E. Side King St., 1 Door S. of
Columbus St., Neck
M'Neill, Neill, Merchant, N.E. cr. Broad & Church Sts.
M'Nellage, John, Sail Maker, Kunhardt's Whf , Res. 1
Reaper's Al.
M'Owen, P , St. Philip's St , near George St
M'Pherson, James E , Planter, N. cr. E. Bay & Laurens
Sts
M'Pherson, -----, Mr., 53 King St.
M'Pherson, S., Mrs., Widow, Broad St , Next Door, E
Side, to St. Andrew's Hall
M'Whinnie, William, Merchant, 71 E. Bay St
Meacher, T., Grain Store, S.E. cr E. Bay & Market Sts ,
Res. 5 Pinckney St.
Mealy, Harriet, Widow, 13 St. Philip's St.
Mealy, John, Planter, 19 St Philip's St.
Mease, C. B., Stores, 151 King St. & 50 E. Bay St.
Meeds, S., Mrs., Private Boarding House, E Bay St
Meeker & Ward, Coachmakers, Meeting St., nearly op.
Wentworth St
Meeker, Willaim, 57 Wentworth St.
Melrose, Mary, Mrs., Widow, 6 Minority St
Menlove, Edward, Merchant, 7 Fitzsimons' Whf.
Merchant, C., Grocery, 19 Market St.
Merchant, Peter, Planter, E. End Hampstead, Neck
Merritt, J H., Merchant, 112 E Bay St
Messervey, Sophia, 120 Meeting St.
Mey, Charles S , Merchant, Mey's Whf , Res N cr
Guignard & E. Bay Sts.
Mey, Florian C., Mey's Whf
Meynardie, Bernard, Cabinet Maker, 38 Beaufain St.
Meynardie, Elias, Cabinet Maker, 38 Beaufain St
Michau, John, Bootmaker, 125 Meeting St.
Michel, John, Notary Public, St. Philip's St , W Side, op
Orphan House, Neck
Michel, John, Notary Public & Quorum Unis, 90 E Bay
St.
Michel, Peter, Hat Store, 351 King St
Michel, W., M.D., 183 Meeting St.
Middleton, Arthur, Planter, 251 E. Bay St
Middleton, Francis, Grocer, S. cr. Elliott & Church Sts
Middleton, John Izard, Planter, E. Bay St , S. cr Vernon
St.
Middleton, R. N , 251 E Bay St.
Middleton, Thomas, Factor, 251 E Bay St.
Mignot, R., Confectioner, 170 King St
Miles, Mary Ann B., Widow, 112 Tradd St.

152

Miller, A. E., Printer, 4 Broad St.
Miller, Abraham, Bank of State of S. C.
Miller, Catherine, Widow, Mary St., E. Side, Neck
Miller, Charles, 52 Anson St.
Miller, Charles, Radcliffborough, Neck
Miller, George A , 16 Wentworth St
Miller, George, Merchant, E. Side King St., btw. Wolf & King Sts , Neck
Miller, George, Merchants Hotel, N. cr. King & Society Sts
Miller, Horatio, Merchants Hotel, N. cr. King & Society Sts.
Miller, James A., Accountant, Edmondston's Whf
Miller, James A., Charleston Theater, btw. Broad & New Sts.
Miller, James, Factor, Vanderhorst St , Neck
Miller, Job P., Bricklayer 7 Orange St.
Miller, John C., Mary St., E. End, Neck
Miller, John M., 56 Queen St.
Miller, L., Widow, Whim Court
Miller, M., Mrs., Widow, 56 Queen St.
Miller, Matthew, Jewelry & Fancy Store, 150 King St.
Miller, -----, N. cr. Reid & Amherst Sts., Neck
Miller, Ripley & Co., Wholesale, 310 King St.
Miller, Robert S., Baker, 143 Meeting St
Miller, W. S., Merchants Hotel, N. cr. King & Society Sts.
Miller, William H., Merchant, Chisolm's Lower Whf., Res. 52 Anson St.
Miller, William H., Tailor, 56 Queen St.
Miller, William, Hampstead, Neck
Milliken, Gilliland & Co. Auctioneers, Vendue Range
Milliken, Thomas, Auctioneer & Commission Merchant, Charlotte St., near Elizabeth St., Neck
Mills, Eliza D., Mrs., Private Boarding House, N.E. cr. Church & Tradd Sts.
Mills, O & S., Corn Merchants, Napier's Range, Gibbes Whf.
Mills, Otis, 150 King St.
Mills, Samuel S., Commission Merchant, Vendue Range
Milne, Andrew, 14 Rutledge St
Minott, Charles, Savage St
Minott, William, Planter, Savage St
Mintzing, Jacob F., 26 Friend St.
Minus, Margaret, Widow, Henrietta St., Neck
Miot, Charles H , Merchants Hotel, N. cr. King & Society Sts.
Miscalley, D.W., Orderly Sergeant, Picket Guard House
Missron, James, E. Bay St., near the Battery
Mitchell, Ann E., Widow, 222 Meeting St.
Mitchell, Ann, Mrs., 29 Archdale St.
Mitchell, F , Fruit Store, 181 E. Bay St.
Mitchell, J. W., Attorney, 42 Guignard St.
Mitchell, James, Cooper, 50 Meeting St.
Mitchell, James D , Ordinary, Charleston District, Fire Proof Building, Res. W. End Wentworth St.
Mitchell, John H., Notary Pubic & Quorum Unis, 84 E. Bay St., Res. 42 Guignard St.
Mitchell, Martha, 29 Archdale St.
Mitchell, W. H., Rev., Rector, St. James' Santee, Res. 42 Guignard St
Moffett & Calder, 35 Broad St & 177 King St.

Mohr, Henry, Store, S.W. cr. Queen & Mazyck Sts.
Moise, Aaron, Accountant, Courier Office, Res Church St., near Meeting St.
Moise, Abraham, Attorney, 86 Tradd St.
Moise, Abraham, Church St., near Market St.
Moise, Columbus, Post Office, Church St , near Market St
Moise, Theodore, Accountant, Stoll's Al.
Moise, Warren, Post Office, Stoll's Al.
Moisson, John, Gunsmith, 10 State St.
Moles, M., Store, N. cr. King & Radcliff Sts., Neck
Moncrieff, Aaron, Shoemaker, N. Side Boundary St., Neck
Monefeldt, -----, Mrs. & Misses, Female Seminary, cr Beaufain & Coming Sts.
Monies, Jane, 2 Bedon's Al.
Monnar, Lewis, Hairdresser, 12 Queen St.
Monpoey, Honore, Factor, 40 Bull St.
Montesquieuu, R., Tin Plate Worker, E. Bay St., 2 Doors above Amen St.
Montgomery & Platt, Commission Merchants, Vanderhorst's Whf
Montgomery, R., Tin Plate Worker, 189 E. Bay St.
Mood, C. A., Coming St.
Mood, Peter, Silversmith, 134 King St.
Mood, W. G. K., Accountant at M'Dowell's Store, 145 King St.
Moodie, James G , 73 Queen St.
Moore, Ann, Elizabeth St., Neck
Moore, Ellen S., Widow, S. Side Vanderhorst St., Neck
Moore, James C., Carpenter, E. Side Meeting St., btw. Reid & Mary Sts., Neck
Moore, Philip, cr. Montague & Gadsden Sts.
Moore, Richard, N.W. cr Boundary & St Philip's Sts., Neck
Moorhead, James & Co , Grocery, S. cr King & Society Sts.
Morang, B., Widow, 36 King St
Mordecai, J., Accountant, 33 Meeting St.
Mordecai, J., Store, 234 King St.
Mordecai, M. C., Commission Merchant, 89 Market St
Mordecai, R., Mrs., Widow, 33 Meeting St.
Moreland, Andrew, Factor, Magwood's Whf., S. Bay St.
Morgan, Benjamin, Sea Captain, Middle St
Morgan, Elizabeth, Mrs., Widow, 82 Wentworth St.
Moriarty, Maurice, Dry Goods Store, 224 King St.
Morison, Simon, Cabinet Maker, 174 Meeting St.
Morison, T., Cabinet Maker, 107 Church St
Morris, C. G., Merchant, 80 E. Bay St
Morris, Thomas, Notary Public, 89 E. Bay St , Res N. cr Wentworth & E. Bay Sts.
Morris, Thomas, S. C. Bank
Morrison, Elizabeth, Widow, Tradd St.
Morrison, John, 60 Wentworth St
Mortimer, Edward C., Anson St , op. Laurens St.
Mortimer, Samuel, Anson St., op. Laurens St.
Mortimer, Samuel H., Accountant, Anson St., op. Laurens St.
Moser, Philip, Hon. 12 New St.
Moses, Isaiah, Planter, E Side King St., btw John & Hudson Sts., Neck
Moses, Israel, Auctioneer, 87 Market St.
Moses, Jacob, State Constable, 129 King St.

Moses, Levi, Merchant, Coming St., near St. Paul's Church, Neck

Moses, R. F., Mrs , Upholsterer, 55 Queen St.

Moses, R., Store, 276 King St.

Moses, Simon, Store, 340 King St.

Moses, Simon, Store, E Side King St., btw. John & Ann Sts., Neck

Moses, Solomon, Deputy City Marshall, Wentworth St., near King St.

Mosimann, J., Watchmaker, 86 Queen St

Moss & Cassidy, Tailors, 311 King St.

Mosseau, L , 25 Society St.

Motta, J A., Fancy Store, 121 King St.

Motte, Dorilla, Pastry Cook, N Side Boundary St., btw. Meeting & Elizabeth Sts., Neck

Motte, Jacob, N. Side Boundary St , btw. Meeting & Elizabeth Sts., Neck

Motte, Jane, Mrs., 24 Meeting St.

Moulin, Jane, Store, W. Side King St., btw. Vanderhorst & Warren Sts., Neck

Moultrie, James, Jr., M.D , 12 Cumberland St

Moultrie, James, Sr., 12 Cumberland St

Moultrie, John, 12 Cumberland St.

Mounsey, J., Merchant, 178 E. Bay St

Mouzon, C., Bootmaker, 4 St. Philip's St.

Mowry, Smith, Merchant, 134 E. Bay St.

Moynan, Ann, Store, State St., cr. Linguard St.

Muckinfuss, B S. D., 120 Wentworth St.

Muckinfuss, H. W., 120 Wentworth St.

Muckinfuss, Henry, 120 Wentworth St.

Muckinfuss, James C., 26 Friend St.

Muggridge, M., Globe Tavern, 202 King St.

Muir, Jane, Mrs., Private Boarding House, 24 Broad St.

Muller, -----, Mrs. Widow, 9 Back St.

Mulligan, J., 249 King St.

Munds, Israel, Rev., Instructor, 41 State St.

Munds, James T., Paint & Oil Store, 69 E. Bay St.

Munro, C., Mrs., Midwife, Society St

Munro, J. W., Carpenter, 8 Mazyck St.

Munro, M. E , Corn Merchant, 4 Vendue Range, Res. 8 Mazyck St.

Munro, Margaret, Mrs., Private Boarding House, 95 Church St.

Munro, -----, Mrs. Widow, 8 Mazyck St

Munson, Jesse, Inspector of Lumber, 14 Pitt St.

Murden, Jeremiah, 67 Wentworth St.

Murden, -----, Mrs. & Daughters, Female Seminary, 67 Wentworth St.

Murphy, Sarah, Mrs., 91 Church St.

Murray, Ann, Widow, 81 King St

Murray, Charles, Accountant, 81 King St.

Murray, J. M., Store, 4 King St., near S. Bay St.

Murray, James, 81 King St.

Murray, Robert, Tailor & Draper, 26 Broad St.

Murray, William, Planter, cr. Beaufain & Lynch Sts.

Murreil, Martha M , Mrs., 6 Stoll's Al.

Murreil, Martha P., Mrs., 23 Middle St.

Myers, David, Capt., S. Side Charlotte St , Neck

Myers, John, 8 Pitt St.

Myers, S., Store, 280 King St.

Myles, Jane, Mrs., Midwife, 105 Queen St.

Napier, James, Merchant, 167 E. Bay St.

Napier, Thomas, Ladson's Court, Lower End Meeting St

Nathans, Nathan & Co., Store, E. Side King St , btw. Hudson & John Sts , Neck

Nauman, W., 292 King St.,

Nedderman, F S., Oil Store, 104 Market St

Nell, Stephen, Accountant, Hampstead, Neck

Nell, Ursula, Widow, Hampstead, Neck

Nell, William, Grist Store, E. Side Henrietta St , Neck

Neufville, Benjamin S., Printer, 86 Anson St.

Neufville, P. M S., Printer, 86 Anson St.

Neufville, William, Librarian, F L. S , 86 Anson St.

Neve, William, Grocery, 76 Tradd St

Neville, Henry W , Cabinet Maker, 64 Wentworth St

Neville, James, Grocer, 110 King St

Neville, Joshua, Cabinet Maker, 64 Wentworth St

Newbold, S., Pilot, 12 Water St

Newhall, Edward, Dry Goods Store, Firm of J. T. W. Holmes & Co., 161 King St.

Newton, Mary, Widow, Cannon St., Neck

Newton, William, Merchant, Cannon St., W. End, Neck

Newton, William, Merchant, S cr. Chisolm's Upper Whf. & E Bay St.

Nichols, Harriet, Widow, 108 King St.

Nickerson, Warren, Grocery, near Lucas' Mills, Cannonborough, Neck

Nickolson, James, E. Side, Pinckney St., Cannonborough, Neck

Nobbs, James S., S.E. cr. Radcliff & St. Philip's Sts., Neck

Nolan, John, Grocer, S. cr King St & Price's Al.

North, Edward W., M.D., N.W. cr. Montague & Rutledge Sts., Meeting St., op. Circular Church

North, James R., N.W. cr. Montague & Rutledge Sts

North, Richard B., Factor, Archdale St , op. West St

North, Richard, N.W. cr. Montague & Rutledge Sts

North, Webb & Co., Factors, Chisolm's Lower Whf.

Notta, Louisa, 103 King St.

Nowell, John L., Planter, E. Side Alexander St., Neck

Nowell, Lionel C., Planter, E Side Alexander St., Neck

Nowell, Margaret, Widow, E. Side Alexander St., Neck

Nowell, Thomas S., S. C. Bank, N.W. cr. Meeting & Queen Sts

Numan, Elizabeth, 44 Anson St

O'Hara, Henry, Broker & Auctioneer, 5 Broad St., Res. 23 Legare St.

O'Hear & DeSaussure, Factors, 6 Roper's Whf

O'Hear, James, Factor, 9 Cumberland St.

O'Hear, John S., M.D , 9 Cumberland St.

O'Neale & Bird, Shipwrights & Wharf Owners, O'Neale & Birds Whf

O'Neale, C., Merchant, W. Side King St., op. Wolf St, Neck

O'Neil, James, Carpenter, Back St., op. Jail

O'Neill, Edmund, Grocery, 62 Market St

O'Neill, Edmund, S. Side Cannon St., Cannonborough, Neck

O'Neill, Jeremiah, Rev., N.E. cr. Broad & Friend Sts.

O'Neill, John, Butcher, S. Side Cannon St., Cannonborough, Neck

O'Neill, Patrick, Butcher, S. Side Cannon St , Cannonborough, Neck

O'Toole, Patrick, Tailor, 60 State St.
Oakes, Samuel, Sugar Store, 53 Queen St
Oakes, Z. B., Store, 117 Broad St.
Oakley, R. S , Druggist, 152 King St
Oakley, William C., Dry Goods Store, 220 King St.
Odena, John C , Saddler, E. Side King St., Above John St., Neck
Ogden, W S., Accountant, E Side King St., btw Columbus St. & Lines, Neck
Ogier, Bee & Carter, Brokers & Auctioneers, 29 Broad St.
Ogier, Thomas, Broker, Firm of Ogier, Bee & Carter, 36 Beaufain St.
Ohlsen, C. & Co., Grocers, N.W. cr. Church & Chalmers St
Olds & Howe, Shoe Store, S. cr. Church St. & St Michael's Al
Oliphant, David, N.E. cr. Meeting & Society Sts.
Oliver, -----, Mrs., E. Side Coming St , near St. Paul's Church, Neck
Oppenheim, H W., Grocery, S.E cr. Church & Market Sts
Ottolengui, A., Fancy Store, 91 Market St
Page, Jane, Widow, Cannon St., Neck
Page, John, W. Side King St., near Lines, Neck
Palmer, Benjamin M., Rev., D., D., Pastor, Independent Congregationalist Church, 72 Queen St.
Palmer, Job, Carpenter, 62 Wentworth St.
Pane, William, Grocery, E cr. Bedon's Al & Elliott St.
Parish, D. & T. & Co. Wholesale Dry Goods Store, S.W cr. King & Wentworth Sts.
Parker & Bailsford, Factors, 13 Roper's Whf.
Parker, Ann, Widow, 68 Tradd St.
Parker, Charles, City Surveyor, 6 St. Michael's Al., Res. Anson St., op. Laurens St.
Parker, Elizabeth, 19 Legare St.
Parker, John, Jr , S. Side Ann St., Neck
Parker, John, Sr., Planter, E. Side St. Philip's St., btw. Cannon & Mary Sts., Neck
Parker, Peter G., Accountant, Chapel St., Neck
Parker, Robert, Planter, Chapel St , Neck
Parker, Samuel D., 6 George St.
Parker, Samuel, Planter, 6 George St.
Parker, William M., Planter, Extreme W. End Tradd St.
Parsons, Isaac D., Instructor, S cr. Church St. & Longitude Ln.
Paterson, Hugh, Secretary, Union Insurance Co., Res. 31 Laurens St.
Paterson, William, Accountant, 31 Laurens St.
Patrick, Casimer, E. cr. Beaufain & Coming Sts.
Patrick, J., 65 Boundary St.
Patrick, Philip, 37 State St.
Patterson & Jenkins, Factors & Grocers, 73 E. Bay St.
Patterson & M'Whinnie, Grocers & Wine Dealers, 71 E. Bay St
Patterson, George H., 42 Church St
Patterson, Mary W , School, S. Side Radcliff St., Neck
Patterson, Samuel, Merchant, 20 Rutledge St.
Patton, William, Merchant, Fitzsimons' Whf , Res. W. cr. Middle & Laurens Sts.
Paul & Brown, Merchants, S.W cr Broad & Church Sts
Paxton, Henry W , Accountant, Lynch's Ln.

Payne, Josiah S., 28 Broad St.
Payne, R K., Surveyor, Hampstead, Neck
Payne, Robert K., Surveyor, N.W. cr. Friend & Broad Sts.
Payne, William & Son, Brokers & Auctioneers, 28 Broad St.
Payne, William, Sr., 28 Broad St
Pearse, T. S., Carpenter, 26 Beaufain St
Peart, J S., Ship Joiner, Pritchard's Al
Peigne, James I., 195 E. Bay St.
Peixotto, J., Store, 180 Church St
Pelzer, A., Mrs., Boundary St
Pemble, D., Clothing Store, 161 E. Bay St.
Pendergrast, Eliza, cr. State & Amen Sts.
Pendergrast, M., Orderly Sergeant, Main Guard House
Penington, Ann E., Burns Ln.
Penington, Charles, Carpenter, Burns Ln
Pennal, Robert, Grocery, King St., near Boundary St.
Pennington, Martha, Mantua Maker, 114 Queen St.
Pepoon, Benjamin F., Attorney, Bank Coffee House, E. Bay St.
Pereira, M., Grocer, 2 Market St.
Perinchief, Francis, S. Side Radcliff St., Neck
Perman & Bacon, Store, 63 E. Bay St.
Peronneau, Edward, Attorney, W. cr S. Bay & Legare Sts
Peronneau, Henry W., Attorney, 101 Tradd St.
Peronneau, James F., M.D., W. cr. S Bay & Legare Sts
Peronneau, William, Planter, W. cr. S. Bay & Legare Sts.
Perry, Julia, Mrs., W. cr. Beaufain & Mazyck Sts.
Perry, Stevens, Attorney, Mazyck St., op. Magazine St.
Perry, William, Baker, 20 Queen St.
Peters, James, Teacher of Languages & Music, Price's Al.
Petigru, James L., Attorney General of S. C., S.W cr Friend & Broad Sts.
Petit, Florial, Stores, 162 King St. & 188 Meeting St.
Petrie, G. H. W., 47 Society St.
Petrie, George, 47 Society St.
Petsch, Jane H., Widow, 14 Liberty St.
Petsch, Julius D., Engineer, 14 Liberty St.
Petsch, William, 14 Liberty St.
Peuot, R., Shoe Store, 63 Broad St.
Peysson, Mary Louise, Store, 159 King St.
Pezant, John L., Merchant, Lothrop's Whf., Res cr. Boundary & Washington Sts.
Pezant, Louis, Grocer, W. cr. Boundary & E. Bay Sts
Phelon, Edmund M , Grocery, S.E. cr Meeting & Queen Sts.
Phillips, Aaron, Grocery, S.W. cr Church & Tradd Sts.
Phillips, B., Grocer, Vendue Range, E End, N Side
Phillips, Dorothy, Widow, 132 Queen St.
Phillips Edward, Rev., Pastor, St. Stephen's Chapel, 52 Beaufain St., op. Mazyck St.
Phillips, Eliza, Mrs., 52 Beaufain St., op Mazyck St
Phillips, John, Attorney, 52 Beaufain St., op Mazyck St.
Phillips, John, Mrs., Lynch's Ln
Phillips, Otis, 52 Beaufain St., op. Mazyck St.
Phillips, P., S.W. cr Church & Tradd Sts
Phillips, S.W. cr. Church & Tradd Sts.
Phillips, St. John, M.D., 52 Beaufain St., op. Mazyck St
Phynney, Eliza, 62 Tradd St.
Pickenpack, J. N., W. cr. St. Philip's & Vanderhorst Sts , Neck

Pierce, James, 103 Queen St.
Pierce, P , Ice House, Meeting St , near Market St.
Pierson, Catharine, Mrs., S.W cr. Broad & King Sts
Pillans, John C., Carpenter, 43 King St
Pilsbury, -----, Mrs. Widow, 23 Anson St.
Pinckney, C. C., Planter, N. cr. Elizabeth & Chapel Sts., Neck
Pinckney, H. L., Editor, Charleston Mercury, 123 E. Bay St , Res. King St
Pinckney, Lucia, Widow, E. cr. Boundary & Coming Sts
Pinckney, -----, Misses, S. cr. E. Bay & Guignard Sts
Pinckney, R Q., Surveyor, 5 State St., Cannonborough, near Bennett's Mills, Neck
Pinckney, Roger, Planter, 23 Smith
Pinckney, Thomas, Planter, Broad St., near Roman Catholic Cathderal
Pitray & Viel, Merchants, N. cr. Lothrop's Whf & E. Bay St.
Pitray, L A , Merchant, 12 George St
Plumeau, J. F., Fancy Store, 167 King St.
Plunkett, P C., Grocer, N E. cr. Warren & St. Philip's Sts., Neck
Pogson, Milward, Rev , N.W. cr. Pitt & Montague Sts
Poigncignon, E.,Tin Plate Worker, 19 Queen St.
Poissonau & Co., Brass Founders, Amen St., near E. Bay St.
Poland, Oliver, Boarding House 52 Elliott St.
Porcher, Francis Y., M.D , 45 Queen St.
Porcher, Harriet, Mrs., 31 S. Bay St.
Porcher, Mary, Widow, Boundary St., Neck
Porcher, Peter, M.D., St Philip's St., op Green St., near Charleston College
Porcher, Philip J , Planter, St. Philip's St., op. Green St., near Charleston College
Porter, Eliza, 38 Tradd St.
Porter, William L., Grocery, 47 E Bay St.
Postell, William D., S.E. cr. Charlotte & Alexander Sts, Neck
Potter, John, Planter, 42 Society St.
Poyas, Catharine, Widow, 49 Meeting St
Poyas, Elizabeth Ann, Widow, 67 Tradd St.
Poyas, F D., Gunsmith, 63 Queen St
Poyas, James, Shipwright, S. Bay St., Res. 4 Gibbes St.
Pratt, John, 4 Church St.
Pratt, John, Capt , Edmondston's Whf., Res. 8 Church St.
Pratt, John, M.D., 4 Church St., S. End
Prentiss, -----, Mrs. Widow, Radcliffborough, Neck
Preston, James, Merchant, 175 E Bay St.
Preston, John, Grocery, S.E. cr. Church & Chalmers Sts.
Price, Philip, Planter, S E cr. St. Philip & Radcliff Sts., Neck
Price, Rachael, 95 Wentworth St
Price, Thomas, Union Bank, 5 Society St.
Price, William Smith, M.D., N.E. cr. Mary & St. Philip's St., Neck
Prince, Charles, Jr., Tin Plate Worker, 235 King St.
Prince, Charles, Tin Plate Worker, 114 King St.
Prince, Edward, Shipwright, 114 King St.
Prince, John, Planters' & Mechanics' Bank
Prince, Joseph, 114 King St.
Prince, William, 114 King St.

Pringle, E. J., Planter, 62 Tradd St.
Pringle, G., Store, W Side King St , btw Bridge & Lines, Neck
Pringle, James R., U. S. Collector, 3 Orange St
Pringle, John J J., 90 Broad St.
Pringle, John Julius, Late Attorney General of S C., 52 Tradd St.
Pringle, Mary, Widow, 90 Broad St
Pringle, -----, Misses, 48 Meeting St.
Pringle, R. A., Planter, 91 Meeting St
Pringle, Robert, Planter, 62 Tradd St.
Prioleau, John C., Planter, 131 Meeting St
Prioleau, Mariane, Widow, 131 Meeting St.
Prioleau, Philip Gendron, M.D., 220 Meeting St., S E. cr George St.
Prioleau, Samuel C., M.D., 131 Meeting St.
Prioleau, Samuel, Hon., Recorder, City Court, Res. Church St , Extreme S. End
Prioleau, Samuel, Mrs , W. cr. Broad St. & State House
Prioleau, Thomas G , M.D., 135 Meeting St
Pritchard, David H., 12 Anson St.
Pritchard, Paul & Son, Shipwrights, Pritchard's Whf , Res 6 Hasell St.
Pritchard, W. J., Shipwright, 12 Anson St.
Pritchard, William, Sr., 1 Pinckney St.
Pult, Francis, Grocer, 1 Elliott St.
Pundt, John, Grocery, 1 Door E. of cr. Bull & Smith Sts.
Purcell, Ann, Widow, 10 Green St
Purse, Isaiah, Accountant, 58 Broad St.
Purse, Robert, 205 King St.
Purse, Thomas F., Accountant, 82 Meeting St.
Purse, W. H., Accountant, 58 Broad St
Purse, William, Cabinet Maker, Liberty St.
Purse, William, Jr., N cr. Columbus & Nassau Sts., Neck
Purse, William, Watchmaker, 58 Broad St.
Purvis, J. & R., Factors, 5 Kiddell's Whf.
Quash, Francis D., Planter, Washington St., 2 Doors S. of Boundary St.
Quash, Robert H., Factor, 4 Kiddell's Whf, Res. Boundary St., op. Lowndes St
Query, Honoria, Mrs., Private Boarding House, 281 King St
Quinby, Thomas, Carpenter, 8 Minority St.
Rain, Eliabeth, 110 Tradd St
Raine, Thomas, Grocer, N cr. Wolf & Nassau Sts., Neck
Rame, Claude, Confectioner, 165 Meeting St.
Ramsay, James, M.D., 181 Meeting St.
Ramsay, Mary, Widow, 74 King St.
Ramsay, -----, Misses, Female Seminary, 74 Broad St
Rast, John, Dry Goods Store, 329 King St.
Ravenel & Stevens, Factors, Chisolm's Lower Whf
Ravenel, C , Mrs., Broad St., Adjoining City Sq.
Ravenel, D. E., 54 Meeting St.
Ravenel, Daniel, Cashier, Planters' & Mechanics' Bank, 54 Meeting St.
Ravenel, Edmund, M.D., 42 Meeting St
Ravenel, Henry, 37 Meeting St.
Ravenel, John, Factor, Broad St , Adjoining City Sq
Ravenel, William, Broad St., Adjoining City Sq.
Ravina, J. D , Teacher of Languages, 18 Queen St.
Rawrth, George F., Superintendant, City Burial Ground, N

cr. Doughty & Thomas Sts., Cannonborough, Neck
Raynal, -----, Mrs. Milliner, King St.
Raynal, W. T., Store, 341 King St.
Read, John Harleston, Planter, S E. cr Wentworth &
  Rutledge Sts.
Read, Sarah, Widow, 1 Minority St
Read, William, M.D., 31 Meeting St.
Readhimer, Peter, Farmer, N. Side Spring St., Neck
Rechon, L., Sailmaker, Swinton's Ln.
Redfern, John, Shoemaker, 9 Tradd St
Redman, J. & Co , Porter House, 72 Market St.
Redmond, M., Grocer, N. cr. State & Chalmers St.
Reeves, Abraham P., Architect, Meeting St., op. St.
  Michael's Al.
Reeves, Eliza, Widow, 10 Back St.
Reid, Ann, Widow, 49 E. Bay St.
Reid, George B., S. C. Bank, 49 E. Bay St.
Reid, James, Wheelwright, Meeting St., 1 Door N. of
  Circular Church, Shop, cr. Cumberland St.
Reid, Sarah, Widow, 95 King St.
Reid, W M., Post Office, 49 E. Bay St.
Reigne, John, Baker, 195 E. Bay St.
Remly, Mary, Widow, Amherst St., Hampstead, Neck
Remoussin, Mary, Widow, S E. cr. Ann & Meeting Sts.,
  Neck
Requier, A., Confectioner, 108 Meeting St.
Revell, George, Accountant, Anson St.
Revell, Margaret, Widow, Anson St.
Rice, William, Attorney, 76 Broad St.
Rich, C. T., Ladies Fancy Shoe Store, 268 King St.
Richards, Martha, Widow, 13 Amen St.
Richards, Mary, Boarding House, 37 Elliott St.
Richards, Samuel, Notary Public & Quorum Unis, 56
  Elliott St.
Richardson, J. S., Hon., Judge, Pinckney St.,
  Cannonborough, Neck
Richardson, R , Bellhanger, 92 Queen St.
Richters, J., Jr., Grocery, N.W. cr Pinckney & E. Bay Sts.
Righton, Joseph, Cooper, 5 Water St.
Riley, William, Printer, 110 Church St.
Ring, David A., Paint Store, 1 Broad St., Res. 133 Queen
  St.
Ripley, S. P., Merchant, 15 George St.
Ritcha, E., 53 Tradd St
Rivers, John, Shipwright, 15 Water St.
Rivers, Martha, Widow, N.E. cr. Montague & Wentworth
  Sts.
Rivers, Samuel, 15 Water St.
Rivers, Thomas, 22 Anson St.
Rivers, W. H , Printer, Wentworth St., near Smith St.
Riviere, J P., Store, 169 King St.
Roach, Edward, Pinckney St
Roach, H., Grocer, E. Side King St., btw. John & Ann Sts ,
  Neck
Roach, William, Clerk, Council, Society St., near Anson
  St
Robb, James, Grocery, 190 & Provision Store 192 King
  St
Roberds, S., Painter & Glazier, 119 King St.
Roberts, J. S., Grocer, N.W. cr. Anson & Pinckney Sts
Robertson, Alexander, Accountant, 71 Broad St.

Robertson, James, Merchant, 64 E. Bay St., Res. 7
  Meeting St.
Robertson, William, Planter, 71 Broad St.
Robinson, Alexander, Secretary, Charleston Fire, Marine
  & Life Insurance Co , 23 E Bay St.
Robinson, J , 49 Tradd St.
Robinson, J. A., Accountant, 23 E. Bay St.
Robinson, John & Co., Factors, Edmondston's Whf
Robinson, John, Factor, Judith St., N. Side, Neck
Robinson, Martha, Miss, Hudson St., N. Side, Neck
Robinson, S. T., Judith St., N. Side, Neck
Robinson, William, Attorney, Judith St , N. Side, Neck
Robinson, William, Grocery, S. cr. Elliott & E. Bay Sts.
Roche, Edward L., Draper & Tailor, 30 Broad St.
Roddy, Martin, Grocery, S.E. cr. Queen & State Sts.
Roddy, Mary, Widow, 1 Hasell St.
Rodgers, John B., Wentworth St.
Rodrigues, Moses, 103 King St.
Roe, James, 36 Queen St.
Rogers, John R. 24 King St.
Rogers, Sarah, Widow, 24 King St.
Rolando, J , Widow, 71 Tradd St.
Roorbach, O. A., Half Price Book Store, 296 King St
Rose, Arthur G., U. S Branch Bank, Bull St., N Side, btw
  Pitt & Smith Sts.
Rose, Eliza H., Widow, 55 Wentworth St.
Rose, Henry, Accountant, 5 Smith's Ln.
Rose, Hugh, Planter, N. cr. E. Bay St. & Lauren's Whf
Rose, J. & H., Merchants, Kunhardt's Whf.
Rose, J., 55 Wentworth St.
Rose, James, Planter, N. cr. E. Bay St. & Lauren's Whf.
Rose, -----, Misses, 13 George St.
Rose, Rebecca, Widow, 6 Smith's Ln.
Ross, Eliza, 4 Magazine St.
Ross, James, Merchant, 167 E Bay St.
Roulain, Catharine, 99 King St.
Roumillat, A., 71 Meeting St.
Roumillat, G. W., Confectioner, 71 Meeting St.
Roumillatt, E., Saddler, S cr. Meeting & Wolf Sts., Neck
Roupell, Mary, Miss, E cr. Tradd & Friend Sts.
Rouse, James, 81 Market St.
Rouse, William, Sr., 81 Market St
Rout, Catharine, Widow, 14 Friend
Rout, William George, U S. Branch Bank, 14 Friend St.
Roux, L., Coroner, Charleston District, 101 E. Bay St ,
  Res 162 Meeting St.
Rowan, Samuel, Store, N.E cr. King & Wentworth Sts.
Rowan, William, Store, S.E. cr. King & Queen Sts.
Rowand, Charles E., Jr., 93 Meeting St.
Rowand, Charles E , Sr., Planter, 93 Meeting St
Rowand, John S., 93 Meeting St.
Rowand, Robert, 93 Meeting St
Rowe, George R., Shoe Store, 140 King St.
Roye, F., Fruit Store, 92 Market St
Ruddock, Susannah, 39 King St.
Rumph, G. H., Grocery, S.E. cr. Meeting & Wolf Sts ,
  Neck
Russ, B., Carpenter, 16 Beaufain St
Russel, Sarah, Widow, 43 Meeting St.
Rutledge, F. E., Rev , cr. Magazine & Mazyck Sts
Rutledge, Frederick, Planter, 117 Tradd St.

Rutledge, Harriet P., Widow, 117 Tradd St
Rutledge, John, Planter, N. cr E. Bay St. & Laurens Whf
Rutledge, Mary, Widow, N. cr. Lamboll & Legare Sts.
Rutledge, Sarah, N. cr Lamboll & Legare Sts.
Ryan, James, Boarding House, 31 Elliott St.
Ryan, John, Grocery, King St., op. Price's Al
Ryan, Lawrence, Attorney, 66 Church St.
Ryan, Thomas, 22 State St.
Safford, Isabella, Mrs., Widow, S. cr E Bay & Minority Sts.
Safford, John, Mariner, S. cr. E. Bay. & Minority Sts.
Salin, Peter, Grocery, N. cr. Meeting & Reid Sts., Neck
Salin, Peter, Store, 33 Market St.
Salomon, Sarah, Cloathing Store, 143 E. Bay St
Salter, Thomas R., Quorum Unis & Shipjoiner, S. cr. Amen & State Sts.
Saltus, F W., Back St , op. Medical College
Salvo, Corado, Fruit Store, 95 King St.
Sampson, A., Store, 205 E. Bay St.
Sampson, Jane, Store, 201 E. Bay St
Sampson, Joseph, Clothing Stores, 163 & 203 E. Bay St.
Sanders, William, Farmer, Nassau St., Neck
Sass, E. G., Northern Warehouse, 77 Queen St.
Sass, Jacob, Cabinet Maker, 79 Queen St.
Savage, Ann, Milliner, 179 King St.
Savage, Margaret, Widow, 22 Legare St.
Sawyer, William, Dry Goods Store, S.E. cr. King & Boundary Sts.
Saylor, Samuel S., Factor, Kunhardt's Whf., Res. 37 Meeting St.
Schirer, Mary C , Gunsmith Shop, 48 Queen St.
Schmidt, E , Mrs., 5 Montague St.
Schmidt, John W., Physician, 53 Church St.
Schnierle, John M., Carpenter, 11 Friend St.
Schreiner, J. H., Merchant, Kunhardt's Whf.
Schroeder, C., N cr Meeting & Reid Sts., Neck
Schroeder, -----, Mrs. Milliner, King St.
Schulte, Henry, Grocery, N.W. cr Magazine & Mazyck Sts.
Schultz, J G , Planter, S.E. cr. Meeting & S Bay Sts.
Schwartz, J G., Rev., E. Side Coming St., near Boundary St , Neck
Schwartz, Mary, Widow, Coming St., E Side, near Boundary St., Neck
Scott, Henry, Carpenter, 17 Friend St
Scott, Jane, Mrs , 4 Magazine St.
Scott, Louisa A., Widow, 4 Magazine St.
Scott, Morgan, Grocery, 87 King St.
Scott, William M., Notary Public, E. Bay St., Res. 7 Pinckney St.
Scriven, Rebecca, Miss, 18 Lynch's Ln.
Seabrook, Thomas B., Planter, S.E cr. Rutledge & Bull Sts
Sebeck, C , Grocery, S. cr. Archdale & Berresford Sts.
Sebring, E., Woollen Draper & Men's Mercer, 32 Broad St.
Segelke, J. F , Grocery, S.W. cr. Anson & Society Sts
Seguines, John, Engineer, 272 E Bay St
Seigling, John, Music Warehouse, S W. cr. Meeting & Cumberland Sts
Seignious, John, Mary St., E of Meeting St , Neck

Senet, Joseph, Lt., Guard
Seyle, Samuel, Masonic Hall, Etc., 224 King St
Seymour, Mary Ann, 135 Queen St.
Seymour, R. W., Attorney, 57 King St.
Shackelford, Eliza A., Widow, 48 Society St.
Shaffer, C. G., Printer, 186 Meeting St.
Shaffer, Frederick J., Carpenter, 11 Bull St.
Shand, Peter J., Attorney, 38 Bull St
Shannon, John, Store, 102 Church St.
Shea, Richard, Grocer, Henrietta St., Neck
Shecut, J. L. E. W., M.D , 160 King St.
Shegog, W. & Co., Grocers, Market St
Shelton, L. N., Merchant, N cr. Kunhardt's Whf & E. Bay St.
Sheppard, J., Saddler, 248 King St , Res. 30 Coming St.
Sheridan, J. J , Upholsterer & Cabinet Maker, 153 Meeting St.
Shievely, C. G , Paint & Oil Store, 238 Meeting St
Shinie, Alexander, Millwright, Gadsden's Whf.
Shirer, M , Accountant, S cr. King & Cannon Sts , Neck
Shoolbread, John G., M.D., near St. Paul's Church, Radcliffborough, Neck
Shoolbred, James, Planter, 46 Montague St.
Shoulters, Margaret, Nurse, Pitt St.
Shrewsbury, Edward, Shipwright, Charlotte St , Mazyckborough, Neck
Shroudy, W. B. T. Courier Office, Archdale St , nearly op. Berresford St
Sifly & Mintzing, Lumber Yard, W. End Queen St , near Medical College
Sifly, Henry, 24 Friend St.
Sikes, Walter G., Commission Merchant, 2 Queen St.
Silliman, John H., Capt., Charlotte St., Mazyckborough, Neck
Simmons, Joseph, Store, S. cr. Broad & E. Bay Sts
Simmonton, Charles, 169 E Bay St.
Simms, William G., Jr., E. Side King St , btw. Ann & Mary Sts., Neck
Simonds, Joseph W., Druggist, 359 King St.
Simons, B. P., Painter & Glazier, 3 Queen St.
Simons, Benjamin B., M.D., 303 E. Bay St., Middle St , in the Rear of Residence 303 E. Bay St.
Simons, Edward, Planter, Maiden Ln.
Simons, Harleston, Mrs., 2 Friend St
Simons, Keating & Sons, Factors, 4 Roper's Whf
Simons, Keating Lewis, Mrs., Widow, 5 Orange St.
Simons, Keating, President, S. C. Bank, 6 Orange St.
Simons, Maurice, Register of Mesne Conveyance, Fire Proof Building
Simons, Robert Dewar, 2 Friend St.
Simons, Sedgwick Lewis, Factor, 42 Bull St
Simons, Thomas Grange, Factor, 50 Bull St
Simons, Thomas Y., M.D., Meeting St., Tradd St., 1 Door E. Of Meeting St
Simpson, Martha, Cannonborough, near Lucas' Mills, Neck
Sinclair, Alexander, Merchant, Kiddell's Whf.
Sinclair, William, U. S Navy Agent, 9 State St
Skrine, M. G., Mrs., 50 King St.
Slawson, N., Baker, 195 King St ,
Sluter, Jacob, Dry Goods Store, S cr King & Hasell Sts.

Small, Ann, Mrs , Milliner, 203 King St.
Small, Robert, Accountant, 203 King St.
Smith & Robins, Hardware Store, 313 King St.
Smith & Wright, Saddlery, N.W. cr. King & George Sts.
Smith, Aaron C , Union Bank, 26 Cumberland St.
Smith, Agnes, Widow, 22 King St.
Smith, Ann S., Widow, S. cr. Legare & Gibbes Sts.
Smith, Benjamin R., Merchant, Vanderhorst's Whf
Smith, Benjamin S , Dry Goods Store, 221 King St.
Smith, Charlotte W., Widow, S. cr. E. Bay & Amen Sts.
Smith, Cyrus, Beer Shop, S. cr. Chalmers & State Sts.
Smith, Edward, Attorney, S. cr. Smith's Whf &
  Washington St., Neck
Smith, Elizabeth, Miss, Amherst St , Hampstead, Neck
Smith, G. W. & Co , 313 King St.
Smith, H. W., Sailmaker, 23 Mazyck St
Smith, J M., Hotel, 85 E Bay St.
Smith, James, Accountant, Beaufain St.
Smith, John, 10 Friend St
Smith, John, Upholsterer, N. cr. Magazine & Mazyck Sts.
Smith, Joseph Allen, Planter, W. cr. Meeting & S. Bay Sts.
Smith, Joseph S., Shipwright, S. cr. Smith's Whf. &
  Washington St., Neck
Smith, Louisa, Nurse, Wentworth St
Smith, Moses, Carpenter, 155 Meeting St.
Smith, -----, Mrs , Broad St., op. State St
Smith, Quinton H., W. Side Washington St , Neck
Smith, Rosella B., Widow, 73 Queen St.
Smith, Samuel, 73 Broad St.
Smith, Samuel, Bootmaker, 104 Market St.
Smith, Susan E., Widow, 124 Wentworth St.
Smith, Theodore L., Editor, City Gazette
Smith, Thomas, Jr , Planter, Green St., near Charleston
  College
Smith, Thomas, Tailor, Wentworth St.
Smith, W. J., N. cr. Magazine & Mazyck Sts.
Smith, W. Wragg, S. cr. E Bay & Amen Sts.
Smith, Whiteford, E. cr. Beaufain & Archdale Sts.
Smith, William, 15 St. Philip's St.
Smith, William, Factor, 10 Logan St.
Smith, William J., Wood Factor, Smith St., cr Smith's
  Whf. & Washington St., Neck
Smith, William, Jr , Shipwright, S cr. Smith's Whf &
  Washington St , Neck
Smith, William L., Planter, 124 Wentworth St.
Smith, William M., Planter, 22 Meeting St
Smith, William S., Clerk, Court of Common Pleas, Res. 35
  Laurens St
Smylie, Andrew, U S. Appraiser
Snetter, Charles, Hairdresser, 93 Market St.
Snowden, William E., Store, 200 E. Bay St.
Sollee, Arthur, Accountant, 101 Church St
Sollee, F W , 101 Church St.
Sollee, Harriet, Widow, 101 Church St.
Sollee, Henry, Accountant, 101 Church St.
Solomon, Alexander, Store, 287 King St
Solomons, Joseph, Store, W. Side King St., btw. Radcliff
  & Mary Sts., Neck
Solomons, Solomon, Store, 73 Market St.
Somers, J W., 3 Church St
Southworth, Edward, Male Seminary, 91 Queen St.

Sparks, R., Widow, 87 Queen St
Spears, Archibald D , Planters' & Mechanics' Bank, 5
  Orange St.
Spears, Margaret, Widow, 5 Orange
Spencer, Joseph, Accountant, 25 Queen St.
Spencer, Maria, Widow, 93 King St.
Spencer, -----, Mrs. Widow, 25 Queen St
Spofford, Charles N , 303 King St
Springer, Samuel C., Shop, W. End Tradd St., Res 57
  King St.
St. Amand, J. A., Coachmaker, 205 Meeting St.
Stall, Frederick, Grocer, Thomas St., Cannonborough,
  Neck
Stark, Charles, Store, Kiddell's Whf
Starr, Edwin P., Courier Office, 203 Meeting St.
Steedman, Charles John, Sheriff, Charleston District,
  Office, Court House, Down Stairs, Res. Near Carew &
  Childs' Mills, Neck
Steedman, Thomas, Elizabeth St., Neck
Steel, William, Dry Goods Store, 354 King St.
Steele, John A., Planters' & Mechanics' Bank, N. End
  Smith St , Neck
Steele, William G., Lumber Yard, W. End Beaufain St
Stent, John, Carpenter, W. End Queen St., Res. 37 King St
Stephens, Thomas, Teller, Union Bank, 26 Cumberland St
Stevens, Daniel, Col., Planter, 28 George St.
Stevens, J. R., Dry Goods Store, 213 King St.
Stevens, James R , Shoe Store, 271 King St.
Stevens, Joel & Co., Hardware Store, 101 E Bay St.
Stevens, Samuel N , Factor, Firm of Ravenel & Stevens,
  Magazine St., W. End
Stewart, Angus, Carolina Coffee House, 20 Tradd St
Stewart, James, Shoemaker, 167 Meeting St.
Stewart, Robert, Carpenter, Burns Ln.
Stewart, Robert L., U. S. Branch Bank, 13 Friend St.
Stewart, William, Merchant, E. Bay St., E. Side, btw
  Crafts S. & N. Wharves
Stock, Margaret, Widow, S. cr Legare & Gibbes St
Stocker, W. J., Boat Builder, E. Bay St., near Market St.
Stockfleet, John, Grocer, cr. Elizabeth & Henrietta Sts ,
  Neck
Stoddard & Davis, Shoe Store, 272 King St
Stoll, J. T., Turner, 123 Meeting St.
Stoll, Justinus, Grocery, Market St.
Stoll, Smart, Tailor, 27 Tradd St.
Stoll, William, Accountant, N. cr. King & Society Sts.
Stoney, John, Merchant, S cr. Fitzsimons' Whf. & E. Bay
  St., Res. 293 East Bay St.
Stoppelbein, L., Grocery, N.W. cr. Boundary & Coming
  Sts , Neck
Storne, Joseph, Confectioner, 228 King St
Street, H. G , Planters' Hotel, S.W. cr. Queen & Church
  Sts
Street, T. & T. & Co., Merchants, 126, E Bay St
Streets, Joseph, Wheelwright, Wentworth St., near King St
Strobel, B. B., M.D., 151 Meeting, W Side, Above Market
  St.
Strobel, Jacob, Steward, Marine Hospital, 5 Back St.
Strobel, John, Meeting St.
Strobel, M.D., Archdale St , Yard of the German Friendly
  Society.

159

Strobel, Martin, Attorney, Archdale St., Yard of the German Friendly Society
Strobel, Stephen, 5 Back St.
Strober, N. M., M D., Druggist, N.W. cr King & Tradd Sts.
Strohecker, C. C , Attorney, 20 Cumberland St
Strohecker, John, Ironmongery, 163 Meeting St., Res 20 Cumberland St.
Sturkes, Henry, S.E. cr. Pinckney & Cannon Sts., Neck
Suares, Abraham, Accountant, Henrietta St., Neck
Suares, Judy, Widow, Henrietta St., Neck
Suder, Ann, Widow, 49 Society St
Suder, P. J., Carpenter, 49 Society St.
Sullivan, Timothy, Broker & Auctioneer, 72 Anson St
Summers, P., 26 Elliott St.
Suou, Peter, 180 E. Bay St
Surau, J , Bootmaker, E. Side King St., near Ann St., Neck
Sutcliffe, James H., Baker, 75 Market St
Sweegan, M., Store, 7 Market St.
Swift, William, Dry Goods Store, 336 King St.
Swindersine, A. W., Planter, 44 St. Philip's St.
Swiney, Edward, Rev., N.E. cr. Friend & Broad Sts
Swinton, -----, Misses, 21 Archdale St.
Symmes, Charlotte, Widow, 134 Queen St.
Symmes, T., Dry Goods Store, 250 King St.
Talman & Gantz, Merchants & Grocers, Vendue Range
Talvande, Andrew, 24 Legare St.
Talvande, -----, Madame, Female Boarding Seminary, 24 Legare St.
Tanswell, W N., Locksmith & Bell Hanger, 54 Queen St.
Taveau, Augustus, E. Bay St., near Boundary St.
Tavel, Julius, Accountant, N. cr. Lothrop's Whf. & E Bay St.
Taylor, Josiah, Factor, 4 Lamboll St
Taylor, R Rivers, Accountant, 4 Lamboll St.
Taylor, T R., Shoe Store, S W. cr King & Clifford Sts.
Taylor, T. S., Mast, Block & Pump Maker, S. cr. Johnson's Whf & E. Bay St.
Teasdale, George, Factor, 1 Orange St.
Telfer, Robert, Gauger, 123 King St
Tennent, Charles, Planter, Anson St., op. George St.
Tennent, William M., Anson St , op George St
Tew, Charles, Accountant, 82 Wentworth St.
Tew, E., Mrs , Widow, 80 Wentworth St.
Tew, Henry J., Accountant, N. cr. Fitzsimons' Whf. & E. Bay St.
Tew, William M., Carpenter, St. Philip's St., near George St
Thayer, Catharine S., Widow, Tradd St., nearly op. Orange St
Thayer, E , Instructor, 79 Broad St
Thayer, T W., 54 Wentworth St
Thayer, William, Accountant, Tradd St., op. Orange St.
Theus, Benjamin T., Printer, 84 King St
Theus, Susannah B , Widow, W. Side St. Philip's St., btw. Vanderhorst & Boundary Sts , Neck
Theus, Thomas H., Farmer, near Washington Race Course, Neck
Thomas, J., 65 Boundary St.
Thomas, J M., Cabinet Maker, Minority St
Thomas, Mary, Mrs., 96 Meeting St.

Thomas, Samuel, E. Side Coming St., Btw.Vanderhorst & Boundary Sts , Neck
Thomas, Stephen, E. Side Coming St., btw. Vanderhorst & Boundary Sts , Neck
Thompson, Ann, Mrs., 2 Court House Sq.
Thompson, Frances, Widow, 43 Society St.
Thompson, George, Grocer, S. cr. Wentworth & E. Bay Sts.
Thompson, George, Store, E. cr. Tradd St. & Bedon's Al.
Thompson, Henry, Merchant, E. Side King St., btw. John & Hudson Sts., Neck
Thompson, J , Blacksmith, 52 Market St
Thompson, James, Attorney, 98 Church St.
Thompson, James, Blacksmith, 37 State St
Thompson, R. H., Factor, Chisolm's Lower Whf., Res. 2 Court House Sq.
Thompson, W., Bootmaker, 10 Market St.
Thompson, William, Boarding House, 13 Elliott St
Thompson, William, Dry Goods Store, 164 King St.
Thorn, Elizabeth, Boarding House, 25 Elliott St.
Thorn, James D., Boarding House, 48 Elliott St
Thornhill, Catharine, Fancy Store, 225 King St
Thrving, Edward, Commission Merchant, Vendue Range
Tiddyman, E., Mrs , N.W cr. Wentworth & Rutledge Sts
Timme, Elizabeth, Seamstress, 28 Beaufain St.
Timmons & Graveley, Hardware Store, 165 E Bay St
Timmons, George, 3 Legare St.
Timmons, William, 165 E. Bay St
Timrod, William, Book Binder, 114 King St.
Tobias, Abraham, Auctioneer, Vendue Range
Todd, Jane, Miss, 2 Savage St.
Tolck, David, Grocer, Elliott St.
Tonssiger, Eliza, Miss, Water St.
Toole, Dalk, 60 State St.
Toomer, A. V., M.D., Planter, Chapel St., Neck
Toomer, Henry B., Broker, Green St., op. Charleston College
Toomer, Henry B., Jr , Accountant, Green St , op Charleston College
Toomer, Joshua W., Attorney, S E. cr Pitt & Bull Sts
Toppan, E., Store, N.W. cr. King & Wentworth Sts.
Torre, Ann, Merchant, 55 Broad St.
Torre, Anne, Mrs., Private Boarding House, 4 New St.
Tovey & Son, Block & Pump Makers, 176 E. Bay St
Townsend, Mary, Widow, 23 Mazyck St
Trapier, B F , Planter, N.E. cr. Elizabeth & Judith Sts , Neck
Trapier, Paul, 6 Short St
Trapier, Sarah A., Widow, 6 Short St.
Trapman, L & Co., Merchants, 79 E Bay St
Trapman, L., Merchant, E Side Pinckney St., Cannonborough, Neck
Trenholm, George A., Accountant, 27 Mazyck St.
Trescot, Amelia, Widow, S.E. cr Broad & Friend Sts.
Trescot, Caroline M., Widow, E Side, btw. Vanderhorst & Boundary Sts., Neck
Trescot, Edward, Accountant, 5 Anson St.
Trescot, Henry, Attorney, Meeting St , op. Circular Church
Trescott, Caroline C., Widow, S.E. cr Broad & Friend Sts.
Trott, J. W., 42 Society St
Trouche, P. Augustus, Accountant, Smith St.

Trout, Thomas, 42 Broad St.
Truesdell, D , Oyster House, 30 Queen St
Tucker, John H., Planter, Extreme N E. End Hampstead, Neck
Tucker, Sarah, Widow, 68 Church St.
Tunno, Adam, Merchant, 77 E. Bay St.
Tunno, Sarah, Widow, 5 Meeting St.
Tupper & Kimball, Merchants, 116 E Bay St
Turnbull, Robert J., Planter, 1 Logan St.
Turner, George R., Sr., Doughty St., Cannonborough, Neck
Turner, Philledy, Seamstress, Wentworth St.
Tweed, Ellen, School, Charlotte St., Mazyckborough, Neck
Tyler, J M , 62 Wentworth St.
Tyler, Joseph & Son, Merchant, 183 E. Bay St., Res. 62 Wentworth St.
Ulmo, Anthony, M.D., Druggist, 92 Meeting St.
Ulmo, E , Shoe Store, cr. Hasell & Meeting Sts.
Ulmo, F. J., Accountant, cr. of Hasell & Meeting Sts.
Ummensetter, John, 55 Beaufain St., N cr Wilson St.
Utley, Horace, Notary Public, 89 E. Bay St.
Valentine, S., 117 King St.
Valk, Jacob R , 65 Meeting St.
Vallinet, Sophia, Milliner, 196 King St.
Vanbrunt, R., Bookbinder, 10 Broad St.
Vanderhorst, R. W., Col , Planter, cr. Alexander & Judith Sts. Neck
Vanderlippe, F., Grocery, N.W. cr. St Philip's & Wentworth Sts.
Vanghan, Ann, Widow, Burns Ln.
Vanroven, M. E., Grocer, 10 Tradd St.
Vardell, Thomas A., Mrs., Widow, Vanderhorst St., near St Paul's Church, Neck
Vardell, Thomas R., Bricklayer, Vanderhorst St., near St. Paul's Church, Neck
Varre, Vincent, Grocer, N. cr King & Ann Sts., Neck
Vause, J T., Deputy Sheriff, 25 Mazyck St.
Veitch, William, Druggist, 223 King St
Venning, J. M., Factor, Charlotte St., Mazyckborough, Neck
Venning, R. N., Factor, William's Whf., Res 9 Society St.
Vernon, N., Harleston's Green
Veronee, William, Grocery, N.E. cr Meeting & Wentworth Sts.
Vesey, Sarah, Store, 44 Market St.
Vieusse, Frances, Store, S. cr. King & Berresford Sts
Vincent, Hugh E., Ship Chandlery, 91 E. Bay St.
Vincent, William, Broker, 61 Meeting St.
Vinro, J. W., 6 Wentworth St.
Vinro, Sarah, Midwife, 6 Wentworth St
Vinyard, John, Planter, Hampstead, E. End, Neck
Wagner, Ann, Mrs., St. Philip's St , op Green St
Wagner, Effingham, 53 E. Bay St.
Wagner, George, 6 Friend St.
Wagner, H. S., Wentworth St., near St. Philip's St
Wagner, John, M.D , Professor, Medical College of S. C., S.W. cr. Meeting & Queen Sts.
Wagner, P , Tavern, 152 E Bay St.
Waistcoat, J., Butcher, N. cr. Amherst & Wolf Sts., Neck
Walker & M'Kenzie, Dry Goods Store, N cr. Liberty & King Sts

Walker, Ann, Widow, Magazine St , op Work House
Walker, -----, Book Binder, 44 Queen St., Res. 15 Broad St.
Walker, H. D , Carpenter, Magazine St., op Work House
Walker, J. C., Stationer, 15 Broad St., op. State St.
Walker, J. F , Factor, 23 State St
Walker, John, George St., N. Side, 2d Door W. of Meeting St.
Walker, Mary, Widow, E. Side King St., 2d Door S of Lines, Neck
Walker, Thomas, Stone & Marble Yard, 145 Meeting St.
Wall, Richard, 95 Queen St.
Wallace, Agnes, Widow, 18 Friend St.
Wallace, James, 17 St. Philip's St.
Wallace, Thomas, Accountant, 18 Friend St.
Waller, Charlotte, Mrs , 22 Magazine St.
Waller, William, Saddler, 89 Broad St. near King St.
Wallis, John, Grocer, N.E. cr Charlotte & Alexander Sts., Neck
Walpole, Horace, Planter, Gibbes St
Walter, E. W., Accountant, 33 Queen St.
Walter, Jerry, Commission Merchant, Vendue Range, S Side, Res. 33 Queen St.
Walton, A. Y. & Co. Wholesale Hardware Store, 314 King St.
Walton, Elizabeth, Widow, 62 Wentworth St
Wanless, Archibald, Saddler, 122 Church St.
Ward, Francis S., Clerk, City Court
Ward, Harriet, Widow, 94 Tradd St.
Ward, John, 91 Tradd St.
Ward, M., Coachmaker, 57 Wentworth St
Ward, Sarah, Widow, 40 Meeting St.
Waring, D. Jennings, Attorney, 42 George St.
Waring, Francis M., Factor, 29 Hasell St.
Waring, H. S., M.D., Wentworth St., near St. Philip's St.
Waring, Jervey & Blake, Brokers & Auctioneers, Broad St.
Waring, Morton, 40 George St.
Waring, Morton A., U. S. District Marshall, W. Side St. Philip's St., Near Cannon St., Neck
Waring, -----, Mrs. 15 Friend St.
Waring, Sarah, Widow, 76 Wentworth St.
Warley, Charles, Factor, Edmondston's Whf , Res N E cr Tradd & Meeting Sts.
Warley, Elizabeth, Miss, 30 Beaufain St.
Warley, Mary, Miss, 30 Beaufain St
Warren, P M., Grocery, N.W. cr Boundary & College Sts
Warren, P., Mrs., 4 Tradd St.
Washington, Jane, Widow of Gen William Washington, N.W. cr. Church & S. Bay Sts.
Washington, William, Jr., N. cr Lamboll & Legare Sts
Washington, William, Planter, N cr. Lamboll & Legare Sts.
Waters, John, Private Boarding House, 10 Bedon's Al.
Waters, Willaim, Accountant, 38 George St.
Watson, Lydia, 15 Friend St.
Watson, Mary, Private Boarding House, 7 Tradd St.
Watson, S., Importer & Merchant, 66 E. Bay St.
Waugh, Alexander B., Notary Public & Quorum Unis, cr of E. Bay St. & Crafts' N. Whf., Res. 13 Legare St
Wayne, Jacob, Accountant, N. Side Wolf St., btw. King & Meeting Sts., Neck

161

Webb, Daniel C., Factor, Firm of North, Webb & Co., N.W cr. Pinckney & Cannon Sts., Cannonborough, Neck
Weed & Benedict, Hat Store, 315 King St.
Weissinger, L., Farmer, W. Side King St., near Cannon St., Neck
Welch, Mary, St. Philip's St., near Beaufain St.
Welch, Thomas B., St Philip's St., near Beaufain St.
Welling, & Ballantine, Harness Makers, 119 Meeting St
Wells, J T., Merchant, 151 E. Bay St
Welsh, James, Grocery, 59 Elliott St.
Welshman, James, Mariner, 88 Church St
Wesner, Frederick, Carpenter, N.E. cr. Queen & Mazyck Sts.
West, Charles H., Ship Chandlery, 79 E. Bay St.
Westendorff, C. P. L , Gauger, 23 Mazyck St
Western, Julia, Mantua Maker, Wentworth St.
Westfeldt, C., Merchant, Chisolm's Lower Whf.
Weston, George H., M.D., Planter, E. Side Hampstead, Neck
Weston, -----, Mr. Planter, 71 Queen St.
Weston, Sarah, Mantua Maker, 106 Queen St.
Weyman, F., Grocery, N cr. Lightwood's Al. & Church St
Whilden, Elias, Planter, Cannonborough, near Bennett's Mills, Neck
White, John & Co. Factors, Chisolm's Lower Whf.
White, John, Stone Cutter, 40 Market St.
White, William H., Grocery, 44 Market St.
Whiting, John, Turner, 189 Meeting St
Whitney, Archibald, Notary Public & Collector of Accounts, 9 Society St.
Whitney, Mary, Mrs., Private Boarding House, W cr. Amen &Philadelphia Sts.
Whitridge, J. B., M.D , 93 Church St
Whittaker, William, Grocer, S. cr. Elizabeth & Henrietta Sts , Neck
Whittemore, Cephas, Tallow Chandler, W. Side St Philip's St., Btw Warren & Radcliff Sts , Neck
Wienges, Jacob, Grocery, W. cr. Archdale & Beaufain Sts.
Wienges, R , Widow, 186 Meeting St.
Wigfall, Paul, Bricklayer, Beaufain St.
Wigfall, Samuel, Planter, Washington St., near E End Boundary St., Neck
Wigfall, T., Sen., Planter, Washington St., near E. End Boundary St., Neck
Wigfall, William M., Planter, Washington St., near E. End Boundary St., Neck
Wightman, W., Jr., Painter, S.W cr. Meeting & Society Sts.
Wilbur, W. W , Comb Manufactory & Store, 166 King St
Wildman, N. H. & Co , Hat Store, 279 King St
Wildren, Joseph, Printer, 22 Magazine St.
Wiley, James, Grocery, 15 Elliott St.
Wiley, Samuel, Grocery, W cr Bedon's Al & Elliott St
Wiley, Thomas, 55 Elliott St.
Wilkes & Wilkins, Merchants, Crafts' N. Whf.
Wilkes, John, Merchant, 18 Meeting St.
Wilkie, W. B. & G W., Shipchandlery, 61 E. Bay St
Wilkie, William B., Cashier, Union Bank, 91 Church St
Wilkins, M L., Merchant, 4 S. Bay St
Wilkinson, Willis, M.D., S.E. cr. Montague & Lynch Sts.

Williams, George P., Watchmaker, 69 Market St.
Williams, Isham, William's Whf , E Bay St.
Williams, James T., Coachmaker, Beaufain St.
Williams, John O., Coachmaker, 25 Archdale St
Williams, Paris, Hairdresser, Society St., near S. cr. King St.
Williams, T. S., Pilot, 115 Church St.
Williamson, E , Mrs., Milliner, 116 King St.
Willington, A S., Editor, Charleston Courier, 107 E. Bay St., Res. 281 E. Bay St.
Willis, Henry, Carpenter, Mary St., Neck
Willis, Mary H. G., Private Boarding House, S. cr. St. Michael's Al. & Church St.
Willis, William, Merchant, cr. Lothrop's Wharf & E. Bay St.
Wilson & Ward, Cabinet Makers, 70 Wentworth St
Wilson, A. B., Planter, E Side St. Philip's St., near Cannon St., Neck
Wilson, Elizabeth, Widow, 96 Meeting St.
Wilson, James, Seed Store, King St., op. Beaufain St
Wilson, Samuel, M.D., 6 New St.
Wilson, William H., 100 Meeting St
Winslow, E., Factor, Crafts' N. Whf.
Winstanley, Thomas, 193 E. Bay St.
Winthrop, A., U. S. Branch Bank, 105 Tradd St.
Winthrop, C , Merchant, 105 Tradd St.
Winthrop, F. & C., Merchants, Edmondston's Whf.
Winthrop, F., Merchant, 105 Tradd St.
Winthrop, Henry, M.D., Clerk, Board of Health, Tradd St., op. Orange St.
Winthrop, Joseph, Merchant, Tradd St., op. Logan St.
Wish, Richard S , Coming St., near Bull St.
Withers, Francis, Planter, S.W. cr. John & Meeting Sts., Neck
Withers, Margaret, Widow, Reid St , Hampstead, Neck
Wood, J. P , Grocery, 210 King St.
Woods, A., Widow, N. cr. Whim Court & King St.
Woolf, S., Dry Goods Store, 362 King St., near Boundary St
Wotherspoon, R., Merchant, 3 Orange St.
Wotton, J. A., Instructor, E Side Meeting St., btw. Wolf & Reid Sts., Neck
Wragg, Middleton & Co , Factors, Crafts S. Whf.
Wragg, Samuel, Maj., Cashier, State Bank, Meeting St., near Smith's Ln.
Wragg, William T., Meeting St., near Smith's Ln.
Wrainch, John, Instructor, Market St., near King St.
Wright, Eliza, Miss, E. Side Coming St., Neck
Wright, Harriet, Grocery, 174 King St.
Wright, John Izard, Attorney, Bull St., near Pitt St
Wright, -----, Mrs., Widow, Bull St., near Pitt St.
Wright, William, Merchant, 46 E Bay St
Wulf, C., Grocer, N.E. cr. Boundary & Meeting Sts , Neck
Wulff, Jacob, 131 Church St.
Yates, D , Mrs., Widow, S. Bay St
Yates, David, Accountant, Church St., Lower End
Yates, Elizabeth Ann, Widow, Washington St., near Carew & Child's Mills, Neck
Yates, Francis S., Factor, Ladson's Court, Lower End Meeting St.
Yates, J. A., Planter, Ladson's Court, Lower End

162

Meeting St.

Yates, Jeremiah D., Attorney, Church St , Lower End

Yates, Thomas, Carpenter, 27 King St.

Yeadon, Richard, Bank of the State, 35 King St.

Yeadon, Richard, Jr., Magistrate, 27 King St

Yeadon, William, Attorney, Beaufain St.

You, John C., Instructor, 4 Archdale St.

You, John C , Jr., 4 Archdale St.

You, Thomas S , 4 Archdale St.

Young, Joseph, Jr., Accountant, E. Bay St.

Young, Joseph, Ship Chanderly, N cr. E. Bay St. & Fitzsimons' Whf.

Young, -----, Misses, Female Boarding School, 77 Broad St.

Young, -----, Mrs., Female Boarding School, 77 Broad St

Zealy, Ann C., Widow, 61 King St

Zealy, Joseph, Accountant, 61 King St.

Zealy, William E. Accountant, 61 King St

Zylstra, P. C., Accountant, op. Baptist Church

CPSIA information can be obtained at www.ICGtesting.com
Printed in the USA
BVOW03s1023150415

396159BV00019B/127/P

9 780806 346656